eli 1520-1586
Pierluigi da Palestrina c.1525-1594
e Lassus c.1532-1594
William Byrd 1543-1623
Giulio Caccini c.1546-1618
Marenzio c. 1553-1599
Giovanni Gabrieli c.1557-1612
nas Morley 1557-1602
Carlo Gesualdo, Prince of Venosa 1560-1613
Jacopo Peri 1561-1633
John Dowland 1563-1626
Claudio Monteverdi 1567-1643
Orlando Gibbons 1583-1625
Heinrich Schütz 1585-1672
Giacomo Carissimi 1605-1674
Jean-Baptiste Lully 1632-1687
Arcangelo Corelli 1653-1713
Henry Purcell 1659-1695
François Couperin 1668-1733
Antonio Vivaldi 1678-1741
Georg Phillip Telemann 1681-1767
Jean-Philippe Rameau 1683-1764
Johann Sebastian Bach 1685-1750
Domenico Scarlatti 1685-1757
George Frideric Handel 1685-1759
Francesco Geminiani 1687-1762
Giovanni Battista Sammartini 1701-1775
Baldassare Galuppi 1706-1785
Giovanni Battista Pergolesi 1710-1736
Wilhelm Friedemann Bach 1710-1784
Christoph Willibald Gluck 1714-1787
Carl Philipp Emanuel Bach 1714-1788
Joseph Haydn 1732-1809
Johann Christian Bach 1735-1782
Wolfgang Amadeus Mozart 1756-1791
Ludwig van Beethoven 1770-1827
Carl Maria von Weber 1786-1826
Giacomo Meyerbeer 1791-1864
Gioacchino Rossini 1792-1868
Franz Schubert 1797-1828
Gaetano Donizetti 1797-1848
Hector Berlioz 1803-1869
Mikhail Ivanovitch Glinka 1804-1857
Felix Mendelssohn 1809-1847
Frédéric François Chopin 1810-1849
Robert Schumann 1810-1856
Franz Liszt 1811-1886
Richard Wagner 1813-1883
Giuseppi Verdi 1813-1901
César Franck 1822-1890
Bedřich Smetana 1824-1884
Anton Bruckner 1824-1896
Stephen Foster 1826-1864
Johannes Brahms 1833-1897
Alexander Borodin 1834-1887
Camille Saint-Saëns 1835-1921
Mily Balakirev 1837-1910
Georges Bizet 1838-1875
Modest Musorgsky 1839-1881
Peter Ilyich Tchaikovsky 1840-1893
Antonín Dvořák 1841-1904
Emmanuel Chabrier 1841-1894
Jules Massenet 1842-1912
Edvard Grieg 1843-1907

The Enjoyment of Music

THIRD EDITION

The Enjoyment
of Music

AN INTRODUCTION TO PERCEPTIVE LISTENING

By JOSEPH MACHLIS

PROFESSOR OF MUSIC, QUEENS COLLEGE OF THE

CITY UNIVERSITY OF NEW YORK

THIRD EDITION

W · W · NORTON & COMPANY · INC · New York

For

EARLE FENTON PALMER

Contents

Part One

THE MATERIALS OF MUSIC

Part Two ·

NINETEENTH-CENTURY ROMANTICISM

SONG AND PIANO PIECE

Part Five ·

MEDIEVAL, RENAISSANCE, AND
BAROQUE MUSIC

Part Six

THE TWENTIETH CENTURY

Preface to the Third Edition

THE ORIGINAL EDITION of this book grew out of the introductory course in music at Queens College of the City University of New York. Those of us who inaugurated and developed the course were working at a new college untrammeled by tradition or set procedures. We were able to experiment freely, to learn from our successes and our failures. Since the project in music appreciation embraces a thousand students a year, we have had as extensive a laboratory as could be desired in which to test both our theory and our practice.

Fairly early in our work we realized that the appreciation of an art is not the same thing as its history. We therefore abandoned chronological order in favor of a psychological approach. By beginning with pieces either familiar to the student or easily accessible to him, we strove to build up his confidence in his ability to enjoy music; and by proceeding gradually from the simplest level to a more advanced, to expand his horizons and develop his taste. For this reason, once the materials of music have been explained, the book starts with nineteenth-century romanticism, the style that is apt to be most accessible to a beginner. From there we move back to late eighteenth-century classicism, again back to the older music, and finally forward to the twentieth century. Thus Tchaikovsky, Beethoven, Bach, Debussy, and Stravinsky are encountered in a sequence that bears some relationship to the ascending order of difficulty represented by their music, rather than in a sequence depending exclusively on the dates of their birth.

My primary goal throughout has been to arouse the student's interest in and enjoyment of music; beyond that, to impart to him such knowledge as will help him respond to the works that constitute our musical heritage. The knowledge covers several areas in the territory loosely known as music appreciation. I have tried to explain in terms understandable to the layman how music is put together; to present the art against its social background, as part of the history of culture and in relation to parallel developments in the sister arts; to bring alive the great composers, both as artists and men; to analyze forms and styles; and to apply this combination of knowledges to an understanding of characteristic works. The book, naturally, covers a much wider field than the course, but like the course it strives never to lose sight of the main goal—to create music lovers.

The Third Edition mirrors some of the broadening in tastes and attitudes that has taken place in the past decade. Under Song and Piano Piece, the discussion of short lyric forms has been expanded to include such works as Berlioz's *Absence*, Grieg's *Ein Traum*, Musorgsky's *Field-Marshal Death*, Wolf's *In dem Schatten meiner Locken*, Chopin's Mazurka in B-flat, Liszt's *Sonetto 104 del Petrarca* and Twelfth Hungarian Rhapsody. Several substitutions have been made, among them Strauss's *Don Juan* for *Till Eulenspiegel*, Wagner's *Die Walküre* for *Tannhäuser*, and Beethoven's *Pathétique Sonata* for the *Appassionata*. The discussion of nationalism now includes Sibelius's *Swan of Tuonela*. Also added are Mendelssohn's Italian Symphony, an example of an early romantic work in this genre, Bruckner's Fourth Symphony, and Verdi's *La Traviata*. The section on eighteenth-century classicism has been enriched by important additions: passages from Haydn's *The Creation*; Beethoven's Seventh Symphony and Piano Concerto No. 3; Mozart's Piano Concerto in C, K. 467; Haydn's "Emperor" String Quartet (instead of the early Opus 3, No. 5, now regarded as spurious), and Beethoven's String Quartet, Opus 18, No. 1.

The section on Medieval, Renaissance, and Baroque Music has been completely rewritten to reflect the recent surge of interest and scholarly research in these areas. Illustrating various aspects of this music are two Gregorian melodies; two organa of the Notre Dame School; the Agnus Dei (I) from Machuat's *Notre Dame Mass*; the Kyrie (I) from the Mass *Se la face ay pale* by Dufay; and Binchois's chanson *Adieu m'amour et ma maistresse*. In the section on sixteenth-century music, you will find such masterpieces as Giovanni Gabrieli's *In ecclesiis*, Gesualdo's madrigal *Moro lasso*, Byrd's motet *Ego sum panis vivus*, and John Dowland's lute ayre *My Thoughts Are Wing'd with Hope*. An entire chapter has been devoted to the life and music of Claudio Monteverdi, and his madrigal *Zefiro torna* is discussed, along with an excerpt from his opera *Orfeo*. The early Baroque is further represented by a scene from Carissimi's oratorio *The Judgment of Solomon* and Schütz's magnificent cantata *Saul*. The chapters on the late Baroque have been augmented to include Telemann's Suite in A Minor; Rameau's *Tambourin* and Couperin's *La Galante* as examples of the art of the French clavecinists; Domenico Scarlatti's Sonata in C minor illustrating the gallant style; the great Passacaglia in C minor and the Chaconne in D minor of Bach, together with a sizeable section from the *St. Matthew Passion*; three arias from Handel's *Giulio Cesare* and his *Music for the Royal Fireworks*. Opera in the pre-classical era is well represented by an expanded discussion of Gluck's *Orfeo ed Euridice*.

The section on twentieth-century music has been expanded with the addition of a number of historically important works: Strauss's *Salome*; Mahler's Fourth Symphony; Stravinsky's *Rite of Spring* and *Symphony of Psalms*; Schoenberg's *Five Pieces*, Opus 16 (replacing his earlier *Verklärte Nacht*); Webern's *Five Pieces for Orchestra*, Opus 10, and Cantata No. 1; Bartók's *Music for Strings, Percussion, and Celesta*; Milhaud's *La Création du monde* and Prokofiev's Piano Concerto No. 3. The American school is now represented by Ives's song *General William Booth Enters Into Heaven* as well as his *Three Places in New England*; Varèse's *Ionisation*; works by Sessions, Gershwin, Copland, and Barber; plus an entire new chapter on developments in American jazz, written especially for this book by the noted critic Martin Williams. To answer the great curiosity among our young people about what is being done today, a section has been added on the New Music, with a discussion of its principal trends and composers and an analysis of six representative works: Schuller's *Seven Studies on Themes of Paul Klee*; Babbitt's *Ensembles for Synthesizer*; Penderecki's *Threnody for the Victims of Hiroshima*; Berio's *Circles*; Carter's *Variations for Orchestra*; and Cage's *Fontana Mix*. The appendices have been expanded, especially the reading list, which emphasizes recent and easily available books. The Chronological List has been brought up to date.

I hope that these and similar changes will make the text more useful for both teacher and student. At the same time, I have taken care to leave unchanged the basic structure and character of the original book.

I am heavily indebted to David Hamilton, John Castellini, Rubin Bergreen, and Claire Brook for their devoted reading of the manuscript; to Roger Kamien and Saul Novack for stimulating discussions on the material to be included; to Frederick Fales for his translation of the text of Monteverdi's *Zefiro torna*; to Tanya E. Mairs for her translation of the text of the Musorgsky song; to Rosemary Andersen for her assistance in gathering illustrations; to Barbara Greener and Joseph Ponti, music librarians of Queens College, for innumerable kindnesses. I am especially grateful to Martin Williams for contributing his illuminating discussion of jazz. And I want very much to thank the colleagues who were sufficiently interested in the project of revision to send me their suggestions for making this a better book.

Joseph Machlis

ACKNOWLEDGMENTS

Photographs have been supplied by the owners or custodians of the works of art except for the following, whose courtesy is gratefully acknowledged:

American Airlines: p. 20.
Ampliaciones y Reproducciones Mas: p. 8.
Archiv für Kunst und Geschichte: pp. 104, 173, 183, 246, 373, 376, 377, 522.
Art Reference Bureau, Inc.: pp. 318 (bottom), 348, 349, 351.
ASCAP: p. 567.
Associated Music Publishers, Inc.: p. 624.
Bayerische Staatsoper: p. 170.
The Bettmann Archive: pp. 78, 110, 152, 245, 258, 318 (top), 325, 333, 396, 447, 515.
Bodleian Library, Oxford: p. 410
Boosey and Hawkes: p. 569 (photo by John Ardoin).
Boston Symphony Orchestra: p. 44.
Brown Brothers: p. 121.
Photographie Bulloz: pp. 11, 85, 116, 368, 429, 458, 461.
Columbia-Princeton Electronic Music Center, New York: pp. 609 (photo by Manny Warman), 619.
Conn Corporation, Elkhart, Indiana: pp. 34 (except English horn and saxophone), 36.
Culver Pictures, Inc.: pp. 125, 335, 381, 493, 590.
Czechoslovak Government Committee for Tourism: p. 133.
J. M. Dent & Sons, Ltd.: p. 71 (from *Schubert, A Documentary Biography* by Otto Erich Deutsch).
Fred Fehl: pp. 211, 415, 496, 570.
Festspielleitung Bayreuth: p. 191.
Alison Frantz: p. 236.
Gabinetto Fotografico Nazionale: p. 328.
Photographie Giraudon: pp. 4, 62.
G. D. Hackett: pp. 506, 507.
Henmar Press, Inc.: p. 627.
Historisches Museum der Stadt Wien: p. 276.
Holtkamp Organ Company: p. 42 (organ).
Jenco, Decatur, Illinois: p. 39 (celesta).
The Juilliard School: p. 622.
Dr. John G. Lexa, Secretary General of the Czechoslovak Society of Arts and Sciences in America, Inc.: p. 143.
Ludwig Drum Company: pp. 39-40 (except chimes, xylophone, glockenspiel, marimba, vibraphone and celesta).
Lyon-Healy Harps, Chicago: p. 42 (harp).
Marks Music Corporation: p. 565.
Metropolitan Opera Association: pp. 178, 181, 193, 197, 263, 435, 445, 526 (photos by Louis Melançon).
Musser, Division of Ludwig Industries: pp. 39-40 (chimes, xylophone, glockenspiel, marimba, vibraphone).
The New York Public Library at Lincoln Center, Music Division, Research Library of Performing Arts, Astor, Lenox and Tilden Foundations: p. 274.
Fred Plaut: pp. 562, 583, 586.
Embassy of the Polish People's Republic, Press Office: p. 618.
RCA Records: p. 581.
Scala, New York/Florence, facing p. 364.
William H. Scheide, Princeton, N.J.: p. 384 (owner, used by permission).
G. Schirmer, Inc.: pp. 573, 614.
Selmer Division of The Magnavox Company: p. 34 (English horn and saxophone).
Spanish National Tourist Office: p. 51.
Steinway & Sons: p. 42 (piano).
TASS from Sovfoto: p. 204.
Theodore Presser Company: p. 529.
Trans World Airlines: p. 320.
Trustees of the National Gallery, London: p. 16.
Rembert Wurlitzer, Inc.: p. 31.

PART ONE

THE MATERIALS
OF MUSIC

"There are only twelve tones. You must treat them carefully."

Paul Hindemith

1 By Way of Introduction

"Music to me is a power that justifies things."
Igor Stravinsky

The Art of Listening

We intend it as a great compliment when we say of someone that he is a good listener. We mean that he not only listens passively to what we are telling him but that he enters actively into our tale, drawing us out and making us want to continue. The very fact that we single out certain people as good listeners makes it clear that not everyone has mastered the art of listening.

The same goes for music. It is not enough to be in the same room with the sounds, or to listen intermittently while one's thoughts wander hither and yon. To listen perceptively requires that we fasten our whole attention upon the sounds as they come floating through the air; that we observe the patterns they form, and respond to the thought and feeling out of which those patterns have emerged. Responding to music is the most natural thing in the world, judging from the multitudes who sing, dance, hum, whistle, nod, and tap. But to listen perceptively to a great musical work—that is, really to hear it—is an art in itself: an art that may come more easily to some than to others, but that can be acquired through practice and application.

Our time, unfortunately, does not encourage the art of listening. Formerly it was not so easy to hear a symphony performed. You had to get to the concert hall and buy a ticket. Having invested the time and the effort, you were ready to listen when the orchestra finally struck up. Today you need only flick a knob, and the music comes pouring into the room. On Sunday morning millions of people flick that knob—and for the next ten hours are surrounded by music of one sort or another. They converse, eat, talk on the telephone, read the funnies, do crossword puzzles, and all the while that ceaseless tinkle, tinkle is sluicing past their ears, half-heeded, quarter-heeded, or unheeded. By a supreme irony,

Edgar Degas (1834–1917), MUSICIANS IN THE ORCHESTRA. (Louvre, Paris)
Music is one of the great arts of our civilization.

the very invention that brought music into every home in the land has all but
ended the art of listening to it. People think they've been listening to music just
because their ears happened to be in the path of the sounds. They do not seem
to realize that there is only one way to listen to music, and that is—to listen!

As a matter of fact, we vary greatly in our way of responding to music. During
the playing, shall we say, of the Triumphal March from *Aïda*, one listener will
summon up a vision of ancient tombs and Pharaohs. Another floats off in a
daydream equally far removed from the music and the world. A third is filled
with a strange sense of power at the ringing tone of the trumpets. His neighbor
for no apparent reason recollects the half hour he spent in the dentist's chair.

This one is pleased with himself for having noticed the reappearance of a theme. That one has decided that the conductor is a shoemaker and wonders how he ever managed to get an orchestra. The musicologist reflects upon the contribution of Verdi to grand-opera style. The critic polishes a phrase for his next review. The budding composer is oppressed by a suspicion that he was born too late.

In all these ways of listening, one factor is constant—the ability of the sounds to convey significant meaning. Music as an art bases its appeal on the sensuous beauty of musical sounds. But man is almost incapable of experiencing a physical stimulus without attaching to it a deeper meaning. A sunset, a glass of wine, a summer breeze will awaken associations that extend beyond the physical into the realm of thought and feeling. Music begins as a disturbance in the air; yet it is a disturbance that reaches to the farthermost limits of man's emotional and intellectual life.

There are people who tell you that they prefer not to know anything about the music they hear. Technical information, they claim, spoils their enjoyment. But they would never suggest that the best way to enjoy a football match is to know nothing about the rules of the game. What they really fear, one suspects, is that knowledge of any kind might interfere with the fantasies they like to interpose between themselves and the sounds. They would rather immerse themselves in a tonal bubble bath, achieving thereby a state of hazy contentment.

The mature music lover has no such fear of knowledge. He realizes that the true source of the musical experience is not in himself but in the sounds. Consequently, whatever brings him closer to the sounds heightens his musical perceptions and his enjoyment. He is curious to know how the sounds are put together and why they do one thing rather than another. His information need not be as technical as that of the professional musician, but it demands some knowledge of the rules of the game.

"To understand," said Raphael, "is to equal." When we completely understand a great work of music we grasp the "moment of truth" that gave it birth. For the nonce we become, if not the equal of the master who created it, at least worthy to sit in his company. We receive his message, we fathom his intention. In effect, we listen perceptively; and that is the one sure road to the enjoyment of music.

The Meaning of Music

Music has been called the language of emotions. This is a not unreasonable metaphor; for music, like language, aims to communicate meaning. But it is a different kind of language. Words are concrete; tone is fluid and intangible. A word taken by itself has a fixed meaning; a tone assumes meaning only from its association with other tones. Words convey specific ideas; music suggests elusive states of mind.

Because of this elusiveness music has been subject to a constant attempt to translate its message into words. Yet this is hardly possible. Suppose we say of Schubert's *Moment Musical* in F minor that it is graceful, tender, expressive. Will this convey the remotest conception of the music to one who never heard it? We are able to explain the meaning of a word through other words, but we are not able to explain the meaning of a melody. It means—itself! Beyond that it will mean something different to each listener.

Even if we reject the possibility of translating the meaning of music into words, there still remains much for us to talk about. It will heighten our perception if we know something about the elements of which music is composed, and the way that composers go about organizing tones into patterns and forms. We may inquire into the forces that have shaped musical activity at various periods, the schools and movements within the art and their relationship to the social-cultural environment. We should have some knowledge of the men whose genius enriched the lives of their fellows, of their style, and of their contribution to the art. This information by no means constitutes the meaning of a musical work, but it will help each one of us to fathom that meaning for himself.

The practical musician is apt to distrust talk about music. This, he complains, is generally so complicated that it stands in the way of the music itself. Such mistrust is based on a valid intuition. There is only one way to learn to listen to music and that is—to listen, continually and intensively. It will help to focus our listening if we read and talk about music; but this is no more than a preliminary. The true meaning, the ultimate wisdom, is to be found in one place only: the sounds themselves.

Art as Experience

Music is an art dealing with the organization of tones into patterns. It is one of the great arts of our civilization, along with literature, painting, sculpture, architecture, and the dance. Wherever men have lived together, art has sprung up among them as a language charged with feeling and significance. The desire to create such a language appears to be universal. It shows itself in primitive societies as in our own. It has become a part of man's need to impose his will upon the universe; to bring order out of chaos; to endow his moments of highest awareness with enduring form and substance.

Art, like love, is easier to experience than define. It would be not easy to find two philosophers who agree on a definition. We may say that art concerns itself with the communication of certain ideas and feelings by means of a sensuous medium—color, sound, bronze, marble, words. This medium is fashioned into works marked by beauty of design and coherence of form. They appeal to our mind, arouse our emotions, kindle our imagination, and enchant our senses.

Children are artists. The world for them is a thing of wonder. They invent stories and poems, they make up songs, they paint. But as they grow up this creativity is often dulled in them; they lose the magic touch. The artist is one who retains his wonder at the world as well as a childlike need to communicate his feelings. He possesses that natural ability to express himself in one medium or another which we call talent. He thus learns to project his creative impulse through the symbols of his art; to capture his visions within a stable form.

A work of art embodies a view of life. It brings us the artist's personal interpretation of human destiny, the essence of his experience both as artist and man. In order to comprehend the work we must enter the secret world out of which it sprang. The greater our understanding, the better we capture the joy, the illumination that went into its making. In so doing we are carried to heights of awareness, to intensities of experience of which we had hardly thought ourselves capable.

The function of literature, André Malraux has said, is to reveal to man his hidden greatness. The art work begins by opening to us the landscape of its creator's inner life. It ends by revealing us to ourselves.

2 Music and Life: The Sources of Musical Imagery

"Art is a human activity having for its purpose the transmission to others of the highest and best feelings to which man has risen."   Tolstoi

The beginnings of music are shrouded in prehistory. However, a number of theories have been advanced to explain its origin. One derives music from the inflections of speech, another from mating calls, a third from the cries of battle and signals of the hunt, a fourth from the rhythms of collective labor. Some attribute the rise of music to the imitation of nature, others connect it with the play impulse, with magic and religious rites, or with the need for emotional expression. These explanations have one factor in common: they relate music to the profoundest experiences of the individual and the group. Underlying all is the fact that man possesses in his vocal cords a means of producing song, in his body an instrument for rhythmic movement, and in his mind the capacity to imagine and perceive musical sounds.

The art of music has come a long way from its primitive stage; but it has retained its connection with the springs of human feeling, with the accents of joy and sorrow, tension and release. In this sense we may speak of music as a universal language, one that transcends the barriers men put up against each other. Its procedures have been shaped by thousands of years of human experience; its expressive content mirrors man's existence, his place in nature and in society.

Song

Song is the most natural form of music. Issuing from within the body, it is projected by means of the most personal of all instruments, the human voice. From time immemorial, singing has been the most widespread and spontaneous way of making music.

We have in folk music a treasury of song that reflects all phases of life—work songs, love songs, drinking songs, cradle songs, patriotic songs, dance songs, songs of mourning, marching songs, play songs, narrative songs. Some are centuries old, others are of recent origin. A folk song originates with an individual, perhaps on the spur of the moment. It is taken up by others, a detail is changed, a stanza added. In the course of its wanderings it assumes a number of versions. It becomes the collective expression of a group.

One has but to listen to a love song like *Greensleeves* or *Black Is the Color of My True Love's Hair* to realize how compellingly a melody may capture the accent of tenderness and longing. Songs such as *Water Boy*, which sprang up among prisoners on the chain gang, or *Lord Randall*, with its theme of betrayal, are surcharged with emotion. Treating of basic human experience, they are understood everywhere. At the same time they are rooted in the speech rhythms, the soil, and the life of a particular place—which is why they possess the raciness and vivid local color that are among the prime attributes of folk song.

The same directness of expression is found on a more sophisticated level in the art song. Here the sentiment is more special, more sharply focused. Text and music are of known authorship, and bear the imprint of a personality. Whereas folk song usually reflects the pattern of life in rural areas, the art song issues from

Jacob Jordaens (1593–1678), THREE MUSICIANS. (Prado, Madrid)
Song is the most natural form of musical expression.

the culture of cities. Like the folk song, however, its musical content is shaped by man's experience and projects deeply human emotion. Schubert's famous *Serenade* has become the archetype of the love song. Brahm's *Lullaby* of the cradle song, Schumann's *Two Grenadiers* of the martial ballad. Such songs have universal appeal and exemplify the power of music to set forth the imagery of life.

Dance

Dance springs from man's joy in his body, his love of expressive gesture, his release of tension through rhythmic movement. It heightens the pleasure of being, and at the same time mirrors the life of society. The dance of the countryside is different from the city dance; both, throughout the ages, were set off from the court dance. Folk, popular, and court dances nourished centuries of European art music.

A dance piece may be intended for actual use in the ballroom, like the dance-songs of our popular music. Such was also the case with the waltzes of Johann Strauss, who brought to its height the most popular city dance of the nineteenth century. Or a dance rhythm may serve as the basis for an abstract composition. This type of piece is not intended for dancing; it evokes images of body movement on an imaginary plane. In this category is a whole group of dance pieces such as the gavottes of Bach, the minuets of Mozart, the waltzes of Chopin. Certain dance pieces exude a peasant gusto, others idealize the spirit of the

John Singer Sargent (1856–1925), EL JALEO.
(Isabella Stewart Gardner Museum, Boston)
Dance reflects the pleasure of rhythmic movement.

dance, but all testify to the persuasive power of rhythm. For it is through rhythm that music mirrors the patterns of man's activity in the physical world.

Other Types of Musical Imagery

The march, which is related to the dance, descends from the ceremonial processions of tribal life. Its music is associated with trumpets and drums, with the pageantry of great occasions, religious, military, or patriotic. Whether it be the quick march made popular by Sousa or a grand processional such as the Triumphal March from Verdi's *Aïda,* which is played when the conquering hero Radamès is welcomed home, this type of music is imbued with the imagery of human experience.

March rhythm may serve too as the basis for an abstract piece that is not intended actually to be marched to. Characteristic is the *Marche militaire* of Schubert, which tempers the military mood with lyricism, or the polonaises of Chopin, which recreate the proud processional dance in which the nobles of Poland paid homage to their king. The march creates an atmosphere of pomp and ceremony. Like the dance, it unites appealing melody and decisive rhythm. Like the dance, too, the march captures for music something of the movement and gesture of man's activity in space and time.

The religious impulse has motivated a considerable amount of the world's great music. Most works in this category were composed expressly for use in the church service; others are concert pieces on sacred themes. In either case they hold an expressive content that music is particularly well able to achieve: the spiritual aura that surrounds the sacred music of Palestrina, Bach and Handel.

Procession of Assyrian musicians: wall relief from Nineveh, c. 700 B.C.
(British Museum, London)
Throughout history, music has been an integral part of processions and ceremonies.

Hans Memling (c. 1430–94), ANGEL MUSICIANS.
Music plays an important role in the religious experience.

The opera forms another potent link between life and music. Its theme is man, his passions, his conflicts, his actions. Through opera, composers learned to transform into musical images the most varied sentiments and situations. In this way music was encouraged to draw its substance directly from the drama of human existence. Today, in their operas and ballets as in their music for the theater and films, composers are affirming anew the relationship between music and human experience.

3   Melody: Musical Line

"It is the melody which is the charm of music, and it is that which is most difficult to produce. The invention of a fine melody is a work of genius."   Joseph Haydn

Melody is that element of music which makes the widest and most direct appeal. It has been called the soul of music. It is generally what we remember and whistle and hum. We know a good melody when we hear it and we recognize its unique power to move us, although we might be hard put to explain wherein its power lies. The melody is the musical line—or curve, if you prefer—that guides our ear through a composition. The melody is the plot, the theme of a musical work, the thread upon which hangs the tale. As Aaron Copland aptly puts it, "The melody is generally what the piece is about."

A *melody* is a succession of single tones perceived by the mind as a unity. In order to perceive a melody as a unity, we must find a significant relationship among its constituent tones. We must derive from them an impression of a conscious arrangement: the sense of a beginning, a middle, and an end. We hear the words of a sentence not singly but in relation to the thought as a whole. So too we perceive tones not separately but in relation to each other within a pattern. A melody seems to move up and down, its individual tones being higher or lower than each other. It also moves forward in time, one tone claiming our attention for a longer or shorter duration than another. From the interaction of the two dimensions emerges the total unit which is melody.

In addition, a melody may move stepwise along the scale or it may leap to a tone several degrees away. The leap may be narrow or wide, as may be the *range* of the melody (the distance from its lowest to highest tone). Compare the narrow range and stepwise movement of *America* with the bold leaps and far-flung activity of *The Star-Spangled Banner*. Clearly *The Star-Spangled Banner* is the more vigorous melody. A melody may be fast or slow, loud or soft. A loud and fast tune such as *Dixie* creates the atmosphere of jaunty activity proper to a marching song as surely as a soft, slow melody like *Silent Night* suggests a hymn-like serenity and peace. In short, the character of a melody is determined by its overall pattern of movement.

The Structure of Melody

Let us examine the pattern of a well-known tune.

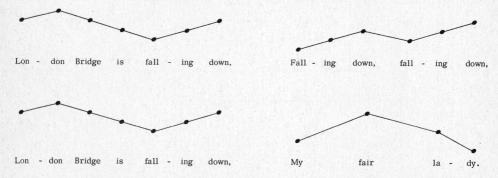

You will notice that this melody divides itself into two halves. Such symmetry is found frequently in melodies dating from the eighteenth and nineteenth centuries. Each of these halves is called a *phrase*. In music, as in language, a phrase denotes a unit of meaning within a larger structure. Two phrases together form a musical period.

Each phrase ends in a kind of resting place that punctuates the flow of the music. Such a resting place is known as a cadence. The first phrase of *London Bridge* ends in an upward inflection, like a question. This is an inconclusive type of cadence, indicating, like a comma in punctuation, that more is to come. The second phrase ends in a full cadence that creates a sense of conclusion. The vigorous downward inflection on the word "la-dy" contributes to this decisive ending. (It should be pointed out, however, that not all final cadences move downward.) Both phrases of *London Bridge* combine in a question-and-answer formation: the second phrase grows out of the first and completes its meaning. We find here the quality of organic unity that is of prime importance in art.

The composer unifies his structure by repeating some of his musical ideas. Thus both phrases of *London Bridge* begin in identical fashion. The necessary contrast is supplied by fresh material, which in our example comes on the words "my fair lady." Through repetition and contrast the composer achieves both unity and variety. This combination of traits is basic to musical architecture, for without unity there is chaos, without variety—boredom.

The melody line does not leave off haphazardly, as if it suddenly found something better to do. On the contrary, it gives the impression of having reached its goal. If you will hum the last phrase of several well-known tunes such as *The Star-Spangled Banner*, *America*, and *Auld Lang Syne*, you will notice they all end on tones that produce this effect of finality. We encounter here what for centuries has been a basic principle in our music: one tone is singled out as the center of the group and serves as a landmark for the others. This central tone is the one to which, in most cases, the melody ultimately returns.

The phrase as a whole may trace an upward or downward curve. Not infrequently, the one is balanced by the other. *The Farmer in the Dell* presents an ascending first phrase which is answered by a descending second phrase:

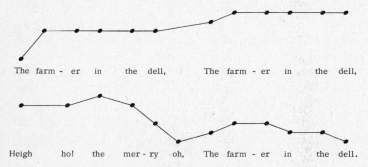

The melody moves forward in time, now faster, now slower, in a rhythmic pattern that holds our attention even as does its up-and-down movement. Without the rhythm the melody loses its aliveness. Try singing *London Bridge* or *The Farmer in the Dell* in tones of equal duration, and see how much is lost of

Pablo Picasso (b. 1881), FOUR BALLET DANCERS. (Collection, The Museum of Modern Art, New York; Gift of Mrs. John D. Rockefeller, Jr.)

The unfolding line, in a painting or a melody, sustains movement.

the quality of the pattern. Without rhythm, the melody could not be organized into clear-cut phrases and cadences.

Our gestures when we speak are purely physical movements, yet they carry emotional meaning. In the same way, the physical facts that make up a melody take on psychological implications. The melodic line may be described as angular or smooth, tense or relaxed, energetic or languid. Above all, the melody must be interesting. We say of a painter that he has a sense of line, meaning that he is able to sustain movement over the whole of his canvas. The same holds for the unfolding melody line with its rising and falling, its peaks and valleys. A melody has to have what musicians call the "long line." It must build tension as it rises from one level to the next, and must retain its drive until the final note.

What makes a striking effect on the listener is the climax, the high point in the melody line that usually represents the peak of intensity. The climax gives purpose and direction to the melody line. It creates the impression of crisis met and overcome. Our national anthem contains a fine climax in the last phrase, on the words "O'er the land of the free." There can be no doubt in anybody's mind that this song is about freedom. Clearly, too, freedom must be striven for, to judge from the effort we have to make to get up to the crucial tone.

The principles we have touched upon are to be found in the melodies of the masters. Let us take some familiar examples. Brahms's popular *Hungarian*

Dance No. 5 opens with vigorous upward leaps. The impression of energy is reinforced by the lively rhythm. As is often the case with dance tunes, the phrases are symmetrical, with a clearly marked cadence at the end of each. The activity of this melodic line contrasts with the gentle flow of the Air from Bach's Suite No. 3 for Orchestra, which moves at a much slower pace. So too the soaring line of the March from *Aïda* contrasts with the restricted activity of Chopin's Prelude in E minor, which moves mostly stepwise and within a narrow range. However, this melody ascends to a dramatic climax in the final section, whence it subsides to a serene final cadence.

Chopin's Mazurka in B-flat, Opus 7, No. 1, exemplifies a type of melody that, because of its wide range and leaps, is more suitable for an instrument than the voice. Its lively rhythm underlines the dance character of this piece. (*Opus*, abbreviated Op., the Latin for "work," is used together with a number to indicate the chronological position of a piece—or a group of pieces—in a composer's output. The opus number may refer to either the order of composition or the order of publication.) A fine example of how rhythm can make a melody memorable is offered by the Hallelujah Chorus from Handel's *Messiah*. The sharply defined rhythm on the word "Hallelujah," repeated again and again in the course of the piece, stamps itself unforgettably on the mind.

"Melody," writes the composer Paul Hindemith, "is the element in which the personal characteristics of the composer are most clearly and most obviously revealed." For melody is the essential unit of communication in music: the direct bearer of meaning from composer to listener.

4 Harmony: Musical Space

"The evolution of the harmonic idiom has resulted from the fact that musicians of all generations have sought new means of expression. Harmony is a constant stream of evolution, a constantly changing vocabulary and syntax."   Roger Sessions

We are accustomed to hearing melodies against a background of *harmony*. To the movement of the melody, harmony adds another dimension—depth. Harmony is to music what perspective is to painting. It introduces the impression of musical space. The supporting role of harmony is apparent when a singer accompanies his melody with chords on the guitar or banjo, or when the pianist plays the melody with his right hand while the left strikes the chords. We are jolted if the wrong chord is sounded, for at that point we become aware that the necessary unity of melody and harmony has been broken.

Harmony pertains to the movement and relationship of intervals and chords. An *interval* may be defined as the distance—and relationship—between two tones. In the familiar *do-re-mi-fa-sol-la-ti-do* scale, the interval *do-re* is a second,

Meindert Hobbema (1638–1709), THE AVENUE, MIDDELHARNIS.
(The National Gallery, London)
Harmony lends a sense of depth to music, as perspective does to painting.

do-mi is a third, *do-fa* a fourth, *do-sol* a fifth, *do-la* a sixth, *do-ti* a seventh, and from one *do* to the next is an octave. The tones of the interval may be sounded in sucession or simultaneously.

A *chord* may be defined as a combination of three or more tones that constitutes a single unit of harmony. Just as the vaulting arch rests upon columns, so melody unfolds above the supporting chords, the harmony. The melodic line constitutes the horizontal aspect of music; the harmony, consisting of blocks of tones (chords), constitutes the vertical:

The Function of Harmony

Chords have meaning only in relation to other chords; that is, only as each leads into the next. Harmony therefore implies movement and progression. In the larger sense, harmony denotes the over-all organization of tones in a musical work in such a way as to achieve order and unity.

The most common chord in our music is a certain combination of three tones known as a *triad*. Such a chord may be built by combining the first, third, and fifth degrees of the do-re-mi-fa-sol-la-ti-do scale: do-mi-sol. A triad may be built on the second degree (steps 2–4–6 or re-fa-la); on the third degree (steps 3–5–7 or mi-sol-ti); and similarly on each of the other degrees of the scale. The triad is a basic formation in our music. "In the world of tones," observes one authority, "the triad corresponds to the force of gravity. It serves as our constant guiding point, our unit of measure, and our goal."

Although the triad is a vertical block of sound, its three tones often appear horizontally as a melody. The first three tones of the *Blue Danube Waltz* form a triad, as do the first three of our national anthem (on the words "O-oh-say"). When the lowest tone (or root) of the chord is duplicated an octave above, we have a four-tone version of the triad. This happens at the beginning of *The Star-Spangled Banner*, on the words "say can you see." It is apparent that melody and harmony do not function independently of one another. On the contrary, the melody implies the harmony that goes with it, and each constantly influences the other.

Active and Rest Chords

Music is an art of movement. Movement to be purposeful must have a goal. In the course of centuries musicians have tried to make the progression of chords meaningful by providing such a goal.

We noticed, in the previous chapter, that a number of melodies ended— that is, came to rest—on a central tone. This is the *do* which comes both first and last in the do-re-mi-fa-sol-la-ti-do scale. The triad on *do* (do-mi-sol) is the I chord or *Tonic*, which serves as the chord of rest. But rest has meaning only in relation to activity. The chord of rest is counterposed to other chords which are active. The active chords seek to be completed, or *resolved*, in the rest chord. This striving for resolution is the dynamic force in our music. It shapes the forward movement, imparting direction and goal.

The fifth step of the do-re-mi-fa-sol-la-ti-do scale is the chief representative of the active principle. We therefore obtain two focal points: the active triad on *sol* (sol-ti-re), the V chord or *Dominant*, which seeks to be resolved in the restful triad on *do*. Dominant moving to Tonic constitutes a compact formula of activity completed, of movement come to rest.

We saw that the cadence is a point of rest in the melody. This point of rest is underlined by the harmony. For example, Dominant resolving to Tonic is the most common final cadence in our music. We hear it asserted over and over again at the end of many compositions dating from the eighteenth and nineteenth centuries. After generations of conditioning we feel a decided expectation that an active chord will resolve to the chord of rest.

Following is the harmonic structure of *London Bridge*, involving a simple progression from Tonic to Dominant and back.

London Bridge is falling down, Falling down, falling down;
I———————— I————————— V————————— I—————————

London Bridge is falling down, My fair   lady.
I———————— I————————— V————————— I—————————

The triad built on the fourth scale step *fa* (fa-la-do) is known as the IV chord or *Subdominant*. This too is an active chord, but less so than the Dominant. The progression IV–I creates a less decisive cadence than the other. It is familiar to us from the two chords associated with the Amen often sung at the end of hymns.

These three triads, the basic ones of our system, suffice to harmonize many famous melodies.

Silent night!   Holy night!   All is calm,   all is bright,
I————————   I—————————   V—————————   I—————————

Round yon Virgin Mother and Child! Holy Infant, so   tender and mild,
IV———————   I—————————   IV————————   I—————————

Sleep in heavenly   peace,   sleep in heavenly peace.
V————————   I—————————   I———V———   I—————————

Consonance and Dissonance

Harmonic movement, we saw, is generated by the tendency of active chords to be resolved in chords of rest. This movement receives its maximum impetus from the dissonance. *Dissonance* is restlessness and activity, *consonance* is relaxation and fulfillment. The dissonant chord creates tension. The consonant chord resolves it.

Dissonance introduces the necessary tension into music. Without it, a work would be intolerably dull and insipid. What suspense and conflict are to the drama, dissonance is to music. It creates the areas of tension without which the areas of relaxation would have no meaning. Each complements the other; both are a necessary part of the artistic whole.

In general, music has grown more dissonant through the ages. It is easy to understand why. A combination of tones that sounded extremely harsh when first introduced began to seem less so as the sound became increasingly familiar. As a result, a later generation of composers had to find ever more dissonant tone-combinations in order to produce the same amount of tension as their predecessors. This process has extended across the centuries, as is apparent if we listen in succession to music of different epochs. For example, the Kyrie from the Mass for Pope Marcellus by Palestrina, published in 1567, has all the seraphic calm we associate with the sacred music of that composer; yet it must have sounded considerably less consonant to Palestrina's contemporaries than it does to us. Next, listen to the first movement of Mozart's *Eine kleine Nachtmusik* or the duet *Là ci darem la mano* from his opera *Don Giovanni*; both works date from 1787. The harmony will strike you as predominantly consonant, although less so than the Palestrina piece. In the Prelude to *Tristan und Isolde* Wagner tried to express the unfulfilled yearning of the lovers in his music drama. There is a markedly higher level of dissonance tension here than in the music of Mozart. Finally, for an example of twentieth-century dissonance, listen to Arnold Schoenberg's *Vorgefühle* (Premonition), Opus 16, No. 1 (1909). This piece will suggest to you the distance that separates the music of our century, in regard to dissonance tension, from the music of earlier times.

Harmony is a much more sophisticated phenomenon than melody. Historically it appeared much later, about a thousand years ago. Its real development took place only in the West. The music of the Orient to this day is largely melodic. Indeed, we may consider the great achievement of Western music to be harmony (hearing in depth), even as in painting it is perspective (seeing in depth). Our harmonic system has advanced steadily over the past ten centuries. Today it is adjusting to new needs. These constitute the latest chapter in man's age-old attempt to impose law and order upon the raw material of sound; to organize tones in such a way that they will manifest a unifying idea, a selective imagination, a reasoning will.

5 Rhythm: Musical Time

"In the beginning was rhythm."
Hans von Bülow

Rhythm—the word means "flow" in Greek—is the term we use to refer to the controlled movement of music in time. The duration of the tones, the frequency, and the regularity or irregularity with which they are sounded determine the rhythm of a musical passage. Rhythm is the element of music most closely allied to body movement, to physical action. Its simpler patterns when repeated over and over can have a hypnotic effect on us. For this reason rhythm has been called the heartbeat of music, the pulse that betokens life. It is this aspect of rhythm that people have in mind when they say of a musician that "he's got rhythm," meaning an electrifying quality, an aliveness almost independent of the notes. Yet, since music is an art that exists solely in time, rhythm in the larger sense controls all the relationships within a composition, down to the minutest detail. Hence Roger Sessions's remark that "an adequate definition of rhythm comes close to defining music itself."

The Nature of Rhythm

It is rhythm that causes people to fall in step when the band plays, to nod or tap with the beat. Rhythm releases our motor reflexes even if

Lincoln Memorial, Washington, D.C.
In art, the regular repetition of elements is the basis of rhythm.

we do not respond with actual physical movement. We feel it in ourselves as a kind of ideal motion; we seem to dance without leaving our chairs.

Rhythm springs from the need for order inherent in the human mind. Upon the tick-tock of the clock or the clacking of train wheels we automatically impose a pattern. We hear the sounds as a regular pulsation of strong and weak beats. In brief, we organize our perception of time by means of rhythm.

The ancients discerned in rhythm the creative principle of the universe, manifested alike in the regular movement of planets, the cycle of seasons and tides, of night and day, desire and appeasement, life and death. Yet these rhythms framed an existence that all too often lacked design and meaning. Rivers overflowed for no good reason, lightning struck, enemies pillaged. Exposed to the caprice of a merciless destiny, man fashioned for himself an ideal universe where the unforeseen was excluded and divine order reigned. This universe was art; and its controlling principle was rhythm. The symmetrical proportions of architecture, the balanced groupings of painting and sculpture, the patterns of the dance, the regular meters of poetry—each in its own sphere represents man's deep-seated need for rhythmical arrangement. But it is in music, the art of ideal movement, that rhythm finds its richest expression.

Meter

If we are to grasp the flow of music through time, time must be organized. Musical time is usually organized in terms of a basic unit of length, known as a *beat*—the regular pulsation to which we may tap our feet. Some beats are stronger than others—these are known as *accented* or *strong* beats. In much of the music we hear, these strong beats occur at regular intervals—every other beat, every third beat, every fourth, and so on—and thus we perceive the beats in groups of two, three, four, or more. These groups are known as *measures,* each containing a fixed number of beats. The first beat of the measure generally receives the strongest accent.

Meter, therefore, denotes the fixed time patterns within which musical events take place. Within the underlying metrical framework, the rhythm flows freely. In a dance band, the drummer will beat a regular pattern, with an accent on the first beat of every measure, while the trumpeter or another soloist will play a melody, containing many notes of different lengths, flowing freely over the regular pattern. Together, both of them articulate the rhythm or over-all flow of the music. We may say that all waltzes have the same meter: ONE-two-three ONE-two-three. Within that meter, however, each waltz follows its own rhythmic pattern.

Although meter is one element of rhythm, it is possible to draw a subtle distinction between them. This may be noted in the domain of poetry. A metrical reading of a poem—such as these lines by Robert Frost—will bring out the regular pattern of accented and unaccented syllables:

> The wóods are lóve-ly, dárk and déep.
> But í have próm-is-és to kéep,

When we read rhythmically, on the other hand, we bring out the natural flow of the language within the basic meter and, more important, the expressive meaning of the words. It is this distinction that the English critic Fox-Strangways has in mind when he observes: "A melody—an Irish reel perhaps—is in strict time, or people could not dance to it correctly; but if it had not also rhythm, they would not dance to it passionately."

Metrical Patterns

The simpler metrical patterns, in music as in poetry, depend on the regular recurrence of accent. Simplest of all is a succession of beats in which a strong alternates with a weak: ONE-two ONE-two—or in marching, LEFT-right LEFT-right. This is known as duple meter and is often encountered as two-four time ($\frac{2}{4}$). The pattern occurs in many nursery rhymes and marching songs.

Twín - kle	twín - kle	lít - tle	stár————,
ONE - two	ONE - two	ONE - two	ONE - two

Hów I	wón - der	whát you	áre————.
ONE - two	ONE - two	ONE - two	ONE - two

The best way to perceive rhythm is through physical response. The above tune can be accompanied, while singing, with a downward movement of the hand on ONE and an upward movement on *two.*

Duple meter, then, contains two beats to the measure, with the accent generally falling on the first beat. Within this meter a tune such as *Yankee Doodle* presents a somewhat more active rhythmic pattern than the above example. That is, in *Twinkle twinkle little star* there is mostly one melody note to a beat. *Yankee Doodle* contains, for the most part, two melody notes to a beat. Here the meter is the steady ONE-two ONE-two that constitutes the underlying beat, above which flows the rhythmic pattern of the melody.

Yánkee Doodle	wént to town	Ríding on a	pó - ny
ONE - two	ONE - two	ONE - two	ONE - two

Another basic metrical pattern is that of three beats to the measure, or triple meter, with the accent normally falling on the first beat. This is the pattern of three-four time (¾) traditionally associated with the waltz and minuet.

Two celebrated examples of triple meter are *America* and *The Star-Spangled Banner*.

My coun- try	'tís————of thee,
ONE - two - three	ONE - two - three
Swéet land of	lí————ber- ty
ONE - two - three	ONE - two - three
Of thee I	síng————
ONE - two - three	ONE - two - three

Oh	sáy can you	sée————
three	ONE - two - three	ONE - two -
by the	dáwn's ear - ly	líght————
three	ONE - two - three	ONE - two

Quadruple meter, also known as common time, contains four beats to the measure. The primary accent falls on the first beat of the measure, with a secondary accent on the third: ONE-two-Thrée-four. Quadruple meter, generally encountered as four-four time (⁴⁄₄), is found in some of our most widely sung melodies: *Good Night, Ladies; Annie Laurie;* the *Battle Hymn of the Republic; Long, Long Ago; Auld Lang Syne*, and a host of others.

Góod night, lá - dies! ——	Góod night, lá - dies! ——	
ONE - two - Three - four	ONE - two - Three - four	
Góod night, lá - dies!——We're	góing to leave you now————.	
ONE - two - Three - four	ONE - two - Three - four	

Should	áuld————ac-quain - tance	bé————for - got,
four	ONE - two - Three - four	ONE - two - Three
and	né——ver brought to	mínd————,
four	ONE - two - Three - four	ONE - two - Three

Duple, triple, and quadruple meter are regarded as the simple meters. The compound meters contain five, six, seven, or more beats to the measure, with primary and secondary accents marking the metrical pattern. Most frequently encountered among the compound meters is *sextuple meter*: six-four or six-eight time. This is often marked by a gently flowing effect. Popular examples are *My Bonnie Lies over the Ocean, Sweet and Low, Silent Night, Believe Me if All Those Endearing Young Charms, Drink to Me Only with Thine Eyes.*

Drínk to me ón————ly	wíth————thine éyes————and
ONE - two - three - Four - five - six	ONE - two - three - Four - five - six

I————will plédge——with	míne————————————————
ONE - two - three - Four - five - six	ONE - two - three - Four - five - six

You may hear examples of duple meter in the Gavotte from Bach's Suite No. 3, Schubert's *Marche militaire* and the Hungarian Dance No. 5 of Brahms. Three-four time is exemplified by the Minuet from Mozart's *Eine kleine Nacht-musik*, Chopin's Mazurka in B-flat, Opus 7, No. 1, and the *Emperor Waltz* of Johann Strauss. The Triumphal March from Verdi's *Aïda* is a good example of ⁴⁄₄ time, as is the March from Prokofiev's *The Love for Three Oranges*. For examples of ⁶⁄₈ time listen to *Morning* from *Peer Gynt Suite No. 1* by Grieg or Mendelssohn's *Venetian Boat Song* in G minor. When ⁶⁄₈ time is taken at a rapid pace the ear hears the beats in two groups of three, so that the effect is akin to that of duple meter. An example is the Gigue from Bach's Suite No. 3.

The four meters just mentioned are the ones most frequently encountered in folk music and in the art music of the eighteenth and nineteenth centuries.

Syncopation

In music based on dance rhythm the meter has to be very clearly defined. This accounts for the decisive accents in a piece such as Brahms's Hungarian Dance No. 5 or Chopin's Mazurka in B-flat. Lyric pieces, on the other hand, achieve a more flowing effect by not emphasizing the accent so strongly, as in *Morning* or the *Venetian Boat Song*. In Debussy's popular piece *Clair de lune* (Moonlight) there is hardly any accent at all, so that the meter flows dreamily from one measure to the next.

Composers devised a number of ways to keep the recurrent accent from becoming monotonous. They used ever more complex rhythmic patterns within the measure, and learned how to vary the underlying beat in many subtle ways. The most common of these procedures is *syncopation*. This term denotes a deliberate upsetting of the normal accent. Instead of falling on a strong beat of the measure, the accent is shifted to a weak beat, or to an off-beat (between the beats), as in *Good Night, Ladies*, on the second syllables of *ladies*. Through this irregularity the accent is made to conflict with the pattern that has been set up in the listener's mind. The pleasure of satisfying his expectations is abandoned for the equally important pleasure of surprise. Syncopation has figured in European art music for centuries, and was used by the masters with great subtlety. It is also associated in the popular mind with the Negro dance rhythms out of which modern jazz developed.

To sum up: music is an art of movement in time. Rhythm, the artistic organization of musical movement, permeates every aspect of the musical process. It shapes the melody and harmony, and binds together the parts within the whole: the notes within the measure, the measures within the phrase, the phrases within the period. Through the power of rhythm the composer achieves a dimension in time comparable to what painter, sculptor, and architect achieve in space.

Time is the crucial dimension in music. And its first law is rhythm.

6 Tempo: Musical Pace

"The whole duty of a conductor is comprised in his ability to indicate the right tempo."
Richard Wagner

Meter tells us how many beats there are in the measure, but it does not tell us whether these beats occur slowly or rapidly. The *tempo*, by which we mean the rate of speed, the pace of the music, provides the answer to this vital matter. Consequently the flow of the music in time involves both the meter and the tempo.

Tempo carries emotional implications. We hurry our speech in moments of agitation. Our bodies press forward in eagerness, hold back in lassitude. Vigor and gayety are associated with a brisk gait as surely as despair demands a slow one. In an art of movement such as music, the rate of movement is of prime importance. We respond to musical tempo physically and psychologically. Our pulse, our breathing, our entire being adjusts to the rate of movement and to the feeling engendered thereby on the conscious and subconscious levels.

Because of the close connection between tempo and mood, tempo markings indicate the character of the music as well as the pace. The tempo terms are generally given in Italian, a survival from the time when the opera of that nation dominated the European scene. In the following table, *Andante* (literally, going; from the Italian *andare*, to go) indicates the speed of a normal walking pace. With this term as a midpoint, the table gives the most common Italian markings for the various tempos:

Solemn (very, very slow):	*Grave*
Broad (very slow):	*Largo*
Quite slow:	*Adagio*
Slow:	*Lento*
A walking pace:	*Andante*
Somewhat faster than andante:	*Andantino*
Moderate:	*Moderato*
Moderately fast:	*Allegretto*
Fast (cheerful):	*Allegro*
Lively:	*Vivace*
Very fast:	*Presto*
Very very fast:	*Prestissimo*

(For the pronunciation of these and other terms see the Index.) Frequently encountered too are modifying adverbs such as *molto* (very), *meno* (less), *poco* (a little), and *non troppo* (not too much). It should be noted that *Andante*, which in the eighteenth century indicated a "going" pace, in the nineteenth came to mean "fairly slow."

Of great importance are the terms indicating a change of tempo. The principal ones are *accelerando* (getting faster) and *ritardando* (holding back, getting slower); *a tempo* (in time) indicates a return to the original pace.

For examples of the various tempos, listen to the opening section of the following works: *Largo*: Dvořák, *New World Symphony*, second movement; Chopin, Prelude in E minor. *Adagio*: Beethoven, *Sonata pathétique*, second movement. *Lento*: Chopin, Etude in E major, Opus 10, No. 3. *Andante*: Bach, Brandenburg Concerto No. 2, second movement; Mozart, *Don Giovanni*, *Là ci darem la mano*. *Andantino*: Schubert, *Trout Quintet*, theme of fourth movement. *Allegretto*: Mozart, Symphony in G minor, Minuet (third movement); Tchaikovsky, *Nutcracker Suite, Arabian Dance. Allegro*: Mozart, *Eine kleine Nachtmusik*, first movement; Beethoven, *Sonata pathétique*, third movement. *Vivace*: Chopin, Mazurka in B-flat, Opus 7, No. 1. *Presto*: Haydn, String Quartet in C, Opus 76, No. 3, fourth movement.

Wagner's statement about tempo, quoted at the head of this chapter, is of course an exaggeration; the conductor has many other duties besides setting the tempo. It does make clear, however, that when a conductor hits on "the right tempo" he has correctly gauged the meaning and intent of the music.

7 Dynamics: Musical Volume

"The player must know how to relieve the soft with the loud and how to apply each of these in its proper place, for, following the familiar expression in painting, this is called light and shade."   Leopold Mozart

Dynamics denotes the degree of loudness or softness at which the music is played. In this area, as in that of tempo, certain responses seem to be rooted in the nature of our emotions. Mystery and fear call for a whisper, even as jubilation and vigorous activity go with full resonance. A lullaby or love song moves in another dynamic range than a triumphal march. Modern instruments place a wide gamut of dynamic effects at the composer's disposal.

The principal dynamic indications are:

Very soft:	*pianissimo* (*pp*)
Soft:	*piano* (*p*)
Moderately soft:	*mezzo piano* (*mp*)
Moderately loud:	*mezzo forte* (*mf*)
Loud:	*forte* (*f*)
Very loud:	*fortissimo* (*ff*)

A page from the score of Bach's Brandenburg Concerto No. 2 (note the lack of expression marks).

A page from the score of Tchaikovsky's *Pathétique Symphony* (observe the profusion of expression marks).

Rembrandt van Rijn (1606–69), A GIRL WITH A BROOM. (National Gallery of Art, Washington, D.C.; Andrew Mellon Collection) *Dynamic contrasts in music are analogous to light and shade in painting.*

Of special importance are the directions to change the dynamics. Such changes are indicated by words or signs. Among the commonest are:

Growing louder: *crescendo* (⬌)
Growing softer: *decrescendo* or *diminuendo* (⬌)
Sudden stress: *sforzando* (*sf*, forced)—accent on a single note or chord

As the orchestra increased in size and precision, composers extended the range of dynamic markings in both directions, so that we find *ppp* and *fff*. Ultimately four and even five p's or f's were used.

The markings for tempo and dynamics are so many clues to the expressive content of a piece of music. These so-called "expression marks" steadily increased in number during the late eighteenth century and during the nineteenth, as composers tried ever more precisely to indicate their intentions. In this regard it is instructive to compare a page of Bach (early eighteenth century) with one of Tchaikovsky (late nineteenth century; see pp. 26–27).

Tempo and Dynamics as Elements of Musical Expression

Crescendo and diminuendo are among the important expressive effects available to the composer. Through the gradual swelling and diminishing of the tone volume, the illusion of distance enters music. It is as if the source of sound were approaching us and then receding. As orchestral style developed, composers quickly learned to take advantage of this procedure. Rossini, for example, was so addicted to employing a long-drawn-out swell of tone for the sake of dramatic effect that he was caricatured in Paris as "Monsieur Crescendo." The impact of such a crescendo can be little short of electrifying, as is apparent from the closing section of his Overture to *The Barber of Seville*. A similar effect is to be observed in Ravel's *Bolero*, in which an extended melody is repeated over and over while the music grows steadily louder. The crescendo is achieved, first, by piling on instruments one after the other; second, by causing the various instruments to play progressively louder.

Wagner's Prelude to *Lohengrin* is intended to depict the descent from heaven of the Holy Grail. The image of a band of angels approaching from the distance and then receding is translated into what has become a basic pattern in music, the crescendo-and-decrescendo (◄===== =====►). A stunning example of this dynamic scheme is to be found in the second half of Debussy's nocturne for orchestra, *Fêtes* (Festivals).

Crescendo in conjunction with accelerando (louder and faster) creates excitement as surely as decrescendo together with ritardando (softer and slower) slackens it. The effect of an intensification of volume and pace is exemplified in Honegger's *Pacific 231*, in which the composer tries to suggest the sense of power conjured up by a locomotive as it gradually builds up momentum and tears through the night. Here crescendo and accelerando are translated into the imagery of motion, as is the case in the finale of Tchaikovsky's Waltz of the Flowers, which is designed to build up to a rousing curtain for the *Nutcracker* ballet. In the Tchaikovsky piece the music climbs steadily from the middle register to the bright and nervous high, so that the three elements—acceleration of pace, increase in volume, and rise in pitch—reinforce one another to create the climax.

Devices of this kind never fail in their effect upon audiences, which would seem to indicate that they are not the arbitrary procedures of a single imagination but are rooted in certain basic responses inherent in our nature.

8 Instruments of the Orchestra (I)

"With these artificial voices we sing in a manner such as our natural voices would never permit."

John Redfield: *Music—A Science and an Art*

Timbre: Musical Color

A note played on a trumpet will sound altogether different from the same note played on a violin or a flute. The difference lies in the tone color characteristic of each instrument, its *timbre*. (The word retains its French pronunciation, *tám'br*.)

The composer has at his disposal two basic media—human voices and musical instruments. He may write for either or both, according to his purpose. If he is writing for a group of instruments, he tries to make each instrument do the things for which it is best suited, taking into account its capacities and limitations. There are, to begin with, the limits of each instrument's range—the distance from its lowest to its highest tone, beyond which it cannot go. There are also the limits of dynamics—the degree of softness or loudness beyond which it cannot be played. There are technical peculiarities native to its low, middle, and high register, as a result of which a certain formation of notes will be executed more easily on one instrument than another. (By *register* we mean a specific area in the range of an instrument or voice, such as low, middle, or high.) These and a host of similar considerations determine the composer's choice as he clothes his ideas in their instrumental garb.

An *instrument* is a mechanism that is able to generate musical vibrations and launch them into the air. Each instrument, according to its capacities, enables us to control the four properties of musical sound: pitch, duration, volume, and color.

By *pitch* we mean the location of a tone in the musical scale in relation to high or low. The pitch is determined by the rate of vibration, which to a large extent depends on the length of the vibrating body. Other conditions being equal, the shorter a string or column of air, the more rapidly it vibrates and the higher the pitch. The longer a string or column of air, the fewer the vibrations per second and the lower the pitch. The width, thickness, density, and tension of the vibrating body also affect the outcome.

Duration depends on the length of time over which vibration is maintained. We hear tones as being not only high or low but also short or long.

Volume (dynamics) depends on the degree of force of the vibrations, as a result of which the tone strikes us as being loud or soft. As for the timbre or tone color, that is influenced by a number of factors, such as the size, shape, and the proportions of the instrument, the material of which it is made, and the manner in which vibration is set up.

Instruments figure in our music singly; in small groups (chamber music); and as part of that most spectacular of ensembles, the orchestra. In the orchestra they are divided into four sections (or choirs): string, woodwind, brass, and percussion.

The String Section

The string section of the orchestra includes four instruments—violin, viola, violoncello (or cello), and double bass. These have four strings, which are set vibrating by either drawing a bow across them or plucking them. The hair of the bow is rubbed with rosin so that it will "grip" the strings. The player holds the bow in his right hand. He *stops* the string by pressing down a finger of his left hand at a particular point on the fingerboard, thereby leaving a certain portion of the string free to vibrate. By stopping the string at another point he changes the length of the vibrating portion, and with it the rate of vibration and the pitch.

The *violin* was brought to its present form by the brilliant instrument makers who flourished in Italy from around 1600 to 1750. Most famous among them were the Amati and Guarnieri families—in these dynasties the secrets of the craft were transmitted from father to son—and the master builder of them all, Antonio Stradivari (c. 1644–1737).

Violin

Viola

Violin bow

Cello

Double Bass

The violin, the highest-pitched of the string choir, is universally admired for its singing tone, which brings it of all instruments closest to the human voice. Pre-eminent in lyric melody, the violin is also capable of brilliance and dramatic effect, of subtle nuances from soft to loud, of the utmost rhythmic precision and great agility in rapid passages. It has an extremely wide range. (For the compara-

31

tive range of the instruments and the tuning of the strings, see Appendix II.)

The *viola* is somewhat larger than the violin, and is lower in range. Its strings are longer, thicker, heavier. The tone is husky in the low register, somber and penetrating in the high. The viola is an effective melody instrument, and often serves as a foil for the more brilliant violin by playing a secondary melody. It usually fills in the harmony, or may *double*—that is, reinforce by duplicating, usually at an octave—another part.

The *violoncello*, popularly known as cello, is lower in range than the viola and is notable for its lyric quality, which takes on a dark resonance in the low register. Composers value highly its expressive tone. In the orchestra the cellos perform functions similar to those of the violins and violas. They often carry the melody. They enrich the sonority with their full-throated songfulness. They accentuate the rhythm. And together with the basses they supply the foundation for the harmony of the string choir.

The *double bass*, known also as contrabass or bass viol, is the lowest in range of the string section. Accordingly, it plays the bass part—that is, the foundation of the harmony. Its deep indistinct tones come into focus when they are duplicated an octave higher, usually by the cello. When this is done, the double bass assumes great carrying power and furnishes basic support for the entire orchestra. In more recent music, the dark timbre of the instrument has also been much used to achieve special color effects.

The string instruments are pre-eminent in playing *legato* (smooth and connected), though they are capable too of the opposite quality of tone, *staccato* (short and detached). A special effect, *pizzicato* (plucked), is executed by the performer's plucking the string with his finger instead of using the bow. *Vibrato* denotes a throbbing effect achieved by a rapid wrist-and-finger movement that slightly alters the pitch. In *glissando* the player moves a finger of his left hand rapidly along the string while the right hand draws the bow, thereby sounding all the pitches of the scale. *Tremolo*, the rapid repetition of a tone through a quick up-and-down movement of the bow, is associated in the popular mind with suspense and excitement. No less important is the *trill*, a rapid alternation between a tone and its neighbor. *Double-stopping* involves playing two strings simultaneously; when three or four strings are played simultaneously, it is called triple- or quadruple-stopping. Thereby the members of the violin family, essentially melodic instruments, became capable of harmony. The *mute* is a small attachment that fits over the bridge, muffling (and changing) the sound. *Harmonics* are crystalline tones in the very high register. They are produced by lightly touching the string at certain points while the bow is drawn across the string. (For an explanation of harmonics, see Appendix V.)

The string section has come to be known as "the heart of the orchestra." The title indicates the versatility and general usefulness of this choir. The strings also figure prominently as solo instruments and in chamber music: in duets, trios, quartets, quintets, and the like.

The Woodwind Section

In the woodwind instruments the tone is produced by a column of air vibrating within a pipe that has little holes in its side. When one or another of these holes is opened or closed, the length of the vibrating air column within the pipe is changed. The woodwind instruments are capable of remarkable agility by means of an intricate mechanism of keys arranged so as to suit the natural position of the fingers.

The woodwinds are a less homogeneous group than the strings. Nowadays they are not necessarily made of wood, and they represent several methods of setting up vibration: by blowing across a mouth hole (flute family); by blowing into a mouthpiece that has a single reed (clarinet and saxophone families); by blowing into a mouthpiece fitted with a double reed (oboe and bassoon families). They do, however, have one important feature in common: the holes in the side of the pipes. In addition, their timbres are such that composers think of them and write for them as a group.

The *flute* is the soprano voice of the woodwind choir. Its timbre ranges from the poetic to the brilliant. Its tone is cool and velvety in the expressive low register, and smooth in the middle. In the upper part of the range the timbre is bright, birdlike, and stands out against the orchestral mass. The present-day flute, made of a silver alloy rather than wood, is a cylindrical tube that is held horizontally. It is closed at one end. The player blows across a mouth hole (embouchure) cut in the side of the pipe at the other end. The flute is much prized as a melody instrument and offers the player complete freedom in playing rapid repeated notes, scales, and trills.

The *piccolo* (from the Italian *flauto piccolo,* "little flute") has a piercing tone that produces the highest notes in the orchestra. In its upper register it takes on a shrillness that is easily heard even when the orchestra is playing fortissimo. For this reason the instrument contributes to many an orchestral climax. On the other hand, composers are coming more and more to make use of the limpid singing quality of its lower register.

The *oboe* is made of wood. Its mouthpiece is a double reed consisting of two slips of cane bound together so as to leave between them an extremely small passage for air. Because of this compression, the tone is focused and intense in all registers. Oboe timbre is generally described as plaintive, nasal, reedy. The instrument is associated with pastoral effects and with nostalgic moods. The pitch of the oboe is not readily subject to change, for which reason it is chosen to sound the tuning pitch, A, for the other instruments of the orchestra.

The *English horn* is an alto oboe. Its wooden tube is wider and longer than that of the oboe and ends in a pear-shaped bell, which largely accounts for its soft, somewhat mournful timbre. The instrument would be well named were it not for the fact that it is neither English nor a horn. Its expressive, gently poignant tone has made it a favorite with composers.

33

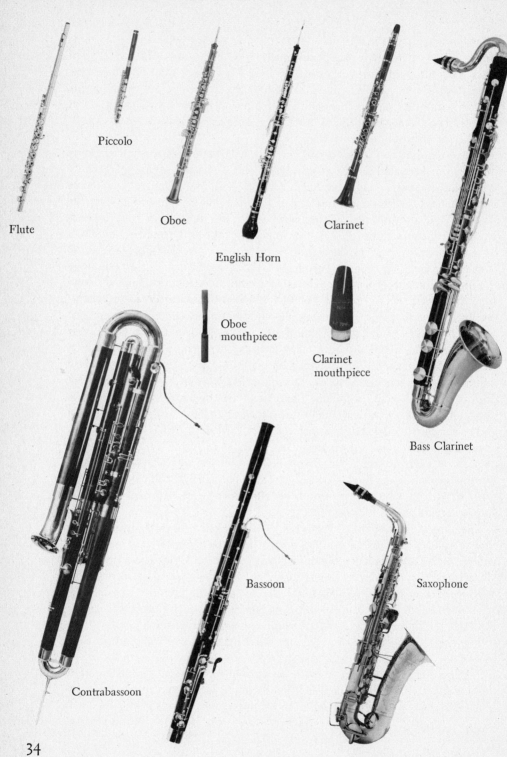

Piccolo

Flute

Oboe

English Horn

Clarinet

Oboe
mouthpiece

Clarinet
mouthpiece

Bass Clarinet

Contrabassoon

Bassoon

Saxophone

The *clarinet* has a single reed, a small flexible piece of cane fastened against its chisel-shaped mouthpiece. The instrument possesses a beautiful liquid tone, clear and powerful in the high register, relaxed in the middle, cool and almost spectral in the low. It has a remarkably wide range from low to high and from soft to loud. The clarinet is a favorite instrument when it comes to playing melody. Almost as agile as the flute, it has an easy command of rapid scales, trills, and repeated notes.

The *bass clarinet* is one octave lower in range than the clarinet. Its rich singing tone, flexibility, and wide dynamic range make it an invaluable member of the orchestral community.

The *bassoon* belongs to the double-reed family. Its tone is weighty and thick in the low register, dry and sonorous in the middle, reedy and intense in the upper. Capable of a hollow-sounding staccato and wide leaps that create a humorous effect, it is at the same time a highly expressive instrument.

The *contrabassoon*, known also as double bassoon, produces the lowest tone in the orchestra. Its tube, over sixteen feet in length, is folded four times around to make it less unwieldly. Its function in the woodwind section may be compared to that of the double bass among the strings, in that it supplies a foundation for the harmony.

The *saxophone* is of fairly recent origin, having been invented by Adolphe Sax of Brussels in 1840. It was created by combining the features of several other instruments—the single reed of the clarinet, the conical tube of the oboe, and the metal body of the brass instruments. The saxophone blends well with either woodwinds or brass. In the 1920s it became the characteristic instrument of the jazz band. Although its figures prominently in a number of important modern scores, it has not yet established itself as a permanent member of the orchestra.

9 Instruments of the Orchestra (II)

"Lucidity is the first purpose of color in music."
Arnold Schoenberg

The Brass Section

The brass section consists of the French horn, trumpet, trombone, and tuba. These instruments have cup-shaped mouthpieces (except for the horn, whose mouthpiece is shaped like a funnel). The tube flares at the end into an opening known as a *bell*. The column of air within the tube is set vibrating

Trombone

Trumpet mute

Trumpet

Tuba

Cornet

Euphonium

French Horn

by the tightly stretched lips of the player, which act as a kind of double reed. To go from one pitch to another involves not only mechanical means, such as a slide or valves, but also variation in the pressure of the lips and breath. This demands great muscular control.

Horns and trumpets were widely used in the ancient world. The primitive instruments were fashioned from the horns and tusks of animals, which at a more advanced stage of civilization were reproduced in metal. They were used chiefly in religious ceremonies and for military signals. Their tone was on the terrifying side, as is evidenced by what happened to the walls of Jericho.

The *French horn*—generally referred to simply as horn—is descended from the ancient hunting horn. Its golden resonance lends itself to a variety of uses: it can be mysteriously remote in soft passages, and nobly sonorous in loud. The timbre of the horn blends equally well with woodwinds, brass, and strings, for which reason it serves as the connecting link among them. Although capable of considerable agility, the horn is at its best in sustained utterance; for sheer majesty, nothing rivals the sound of several horns intoning a broadly flowing theme in unison. The muted horn has a poetic faraway sound; if the muted tone is forced, however, the result is an ominous rasping quality.

The *trumpet*, highest in pitch of the brass choir, possesses a firm, brilliant timbre that lends radiance to the orchestral mass. It is associated with martial pomp and vigor. Played softly, the instrument commands a lovely round tone. The muted trumpet is much used; the mute, a pear-shaped device of metal or cardboard, is inserted in the bell. When the muted tone is forced, a harsh snarling sound results that is not soon forgotten. Jazz trumpet players have experimented with various kinds of mutes, and these are gradually finding their way into the symphony orchestra.

The *trombone*—the Italian word means "large trumpet"—has a grand sonorousness that combines the brilliance of the trumpet with the majesty of the horn. In place of valves it has a movable U-shaped slide that alters the length of the vibrating air column in the tube. (There is a valve trombone that is used occasionally, but it lacks the rich tone of the slide trombone.) Composers consistently avail themselves of the trombone to achieve effects of nobility and grandeur.

The *tuba* is the bass of the brass choir. Like the string bass and contrabassoon, it furnishes the foundation for the harmonic fabric. It is surprisingly responsive for so unwieldly an instrument. To play it requires—among other things—good teeth and plenty of wind. The tuba adds body to the orchestral tone, and a dark resonance ranging from velvety softness to a growl.

Mention should be made, too, of the brass instruments used in military and outdoor bands. Most important of these is the *cornet*, which was developed early in the nineteenth century from the post-horn. The cornet has a shorter body than the trumpet and possesses greater agility. (It is basically an instrument of conical shape, whereas the body of the trumpet is cylindrical for the greater part of its length.) The tone of the cornet is rounder but less brilliant than that of the trumpet. Because of the comparative ease with which it is played, the cornet has become the mainstay of school and municipal bands. Among the brass-band instruments are the *flügelhorn*, which is similar in shape to the cornet but wider; the *baritone* and *euphonium*, which are tenor tubas; and the *helicon*, which is a double bass tuba, circular in form so that the player is able to carry the instrument over his shoulder. (An American type of helicon is the *sousaphone*, named after John Philip Sousa, who suggested its specially designed bell.) The *bugle*, originally a hunter's horn, has a powerful tone that carries in the open air. Since it is not equipped with valves, it is able to sound only certain tones of the scale, which accounts for the familiar pattern of duty calls in the army.

The Percussion Instruments

The percussion section comprises a variety of instruments that are made to sound by striking or shaking. Certain ones are made of metal or wood. In others, such as the drums, vibration is set up by striking a stretched skin.

The percussion section of the orchestra is sometimes referred to as "the battery." Its members accentuate the rhythm, generate excitement at the climaxes, and inject splashes of color into the orchestral sound. Like seasoning in food, they are most effective when used sparingly.

The percussion instruments fall into two categories, those which are capable of being tuned to definite pitches; and those which produce a single sound in the borderland between music and noise (instruments of indefinite pitch). In the former class are the kettledrums, or timpani, which are generally used in sets of two or three. The *kettledrum* is a hemispheric copper shell across which is stretched a "head" of calfskin held in place by a metal ring. Adjustable screws or a pedal mechanism enable the player to change the tension of the calfskin head, and with it the pitch. The instrument is played with two padded sticks, which may be either soft or hard. Its dynamic range extends from a mysterious rumble to a thunderous roll. The muffled drum frequently figures in passages that seek to evoke an atmosphere of mystery or mourning. The *glockenspiel* (German for a set of bells) consists of a series of horizontal tuned plates of various sizes, made of steel. The player strikes these with mallets, producing a bright metallic sound. The *celesta*, which in appearance resembles a miniature upright piano, is a kind of glockenspiel that is operated by a keyboard: the steel plates are struck by small hammers and produce an ethereal sound. The *xylophone* consists of tuned blocks of wood laid out in the shape of a keyboard. Struck with mallets with hard heads, the instrument produces a dry, crisp timbre. If mallets with soft heads are used, the tone is warmer and mellower. Expert xylophone players attain dazzling speed and accuracy. The *marimba* is a more mellow xylophone of African and South American origin, pitched an octave lower. The *vibraphone* combines the principle of the glockenspiel with resonators, each containing revolving disks operated by electric motors. Its highly unusual tone is marked by an exaggerated vibrato, which can be con-

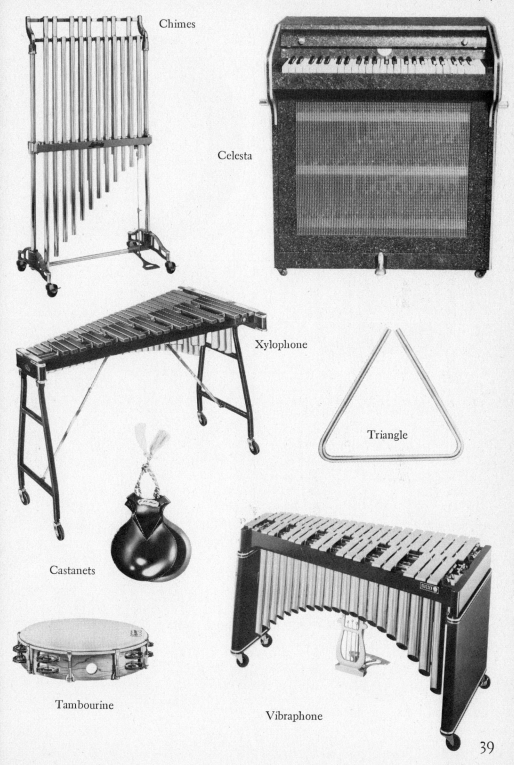

Chimes

Celesta

Xylophone

Triangle

Castanets

Tambourine

Vibraphone

Snare Drum
(showing snares)

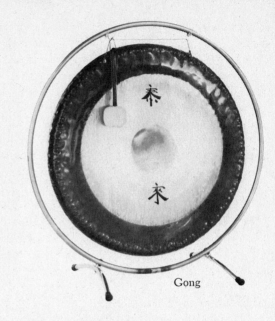

Gong

Bass Drum

Cymbals

Kettledrum

Glockenspiel

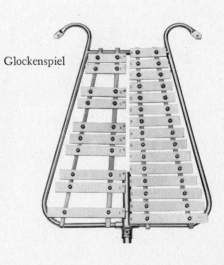

trolled by changing the speed of the motor. Also known as a *vibraharp*, this instrument plays a prominent part in jazz, and has been used by a number of contemporary composers. *Chimes* consist of a set of tuned metal tubes of various lengths suspended from a frame and struck with a hammer. They have a broad dynamic range, from a metallic tinkle to a sonorous clang, and are frequently called upon to simulate church bells.

In the other group are the percussion instruments that do not produce a definite pitch. The *side drum* or *snare drum* (also known as *military drum*) is a small cylindrical drum with two heads stretched over a shell of metal. It is played with two drumsticks, and owes its brilliant tone to the vibrations of the lower head against taut snares (strings). The *tenor drum* is larger in size, with a wooden shell, and has no snares. The *bass drum*, played with a large soft-headed stick, produces a low heavy sound. It is much used in dance bands. The *tom-tom* is a name given to American Indian or Oriental drums of indefinite pitch, imitations of which are often used in dance bands. The *tambourine* is a small round drum with "jingles"—little metal plates—inserted in its rim. It is played by striking the drum with the fingers or elbow, by shaking, or by passing the hand over the jingles. The tambourine is much used in the folk dances of Italy. *Castanets* are widely used in Spain. They consist of little wooden clappers moved by the thumb and forefinger of the player. The *triangle* is a small round bar of steel bent in the shape of a triangle. It is open at the upper end and, when struck with a steel beater, gives off a bright tinkling sound. *Cymbals* are two large circular brass plates of equal size. When struck sidewise against each other, they produce a shattering sound. A suspended cymbal, when struck lightly with a drumstick, produces a mysterious sound. The *gong*, or *tam-tam*, is a broad circular disk of metal, suspended in a frame so as to hang freely. When struck with a heavy drumstick, it produces a deep roar. If a soft stick is used the effect can be ghostly, even terrifying.

Other Instruments

Besides the instruments just discussed, several are occasionally used in the orchestra without being an integral part of it. Among these are the harp, piano, and organ.

The *harp* is one of the oldest of musical instruments. It appears in its earliest form on Babylonian inscriptions of over four thousand years ago. It was the traditional instrument of the bards of ancient Britain and Ireland, and became the national emblem of the latter country. Its strings are played by plucking and produce a crystalline tone that sounds lovely, both alone and in combination with other instruments. The pedals are used to tighten the strings, hence to raise the pitch. Chords on the harp are frequently played in broken form; that is, the tones are sounded one after another instead of simultaneously. From this circumstance comes the term *arpeggio*, which means a broken chord (*arpa* is the Italian for "harp"). Arpeggios occur in a variety of forms on many instruments.

Organ

Harp

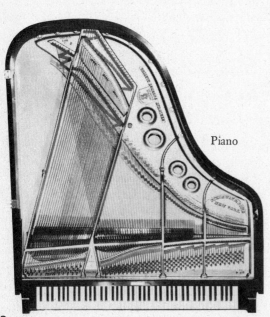

Piano

The piano was originally known as the *pianoforte*, the Italian for "soft-loud," which indicates its wide dynamic range and its capacity for nuance. Its strings are struck with little hammers controlled by a keyboard mechanism. The piano cannot sustain tone as well as the string and wind instruments, but in the hands of a fine performer it is capable nonetheless of singing melody. Each string (except in the highest register) is covered by a damper that stops the sound when the finger releases the key. There are three pedals. If the one on the right is pressed down, all the dampers are raised, so that the strings continue to vibrate, producing that luminous haze of sound which the great piano composers used to such advantage. The pedal on the left shifts the hammers to reduce the area of impact on the strings, thereby inhibiting the volume of sound; hence it is known as the "soft pedal." The middle pedal (lacking on upright pianos) is the sustaining pedal, which sustains only the tones held down at the moment the pedal is depressed. The piano is pre-eminent for brilliant scales, arpeggios and trills, rapid passages and octaves. It has a wide range from lowest to highest tone and commands great rhythmic vitality.

The *organ*, once regarded as "the king of instruments," is a wind instrument; air is fed to its pipes by mechanical means. The pipes are controlled by two or more keyboards and a set of pedals. Gradations in the volume of tone are made possible on the modern organ by means of swell boxes. The organ possesses a multicolored sonority and majestic harmonies that fill a huge space. Nowadays the electronic organ is coming into use. Here the sound is produced not by wind but by electrical oscillators.

The instruments described in this chapter form a vivid and diversified group. To composer, performer, and listener alike they offer an endless variety of colors and shades of expression.

10 The Orchestra

"Orchestration is part of the very soul of the work. A work is thought out in terms of the orchestra, certain tone-colors being inseparable from it in the mind of its creator and native to it from the hour of its birth."   Nicholas Rimsky-Korsakov

From the group of approximately twenty that Bach had at his disposal or of the forty-odd that Mozart knew, the modern orchestra has grown into an ensemble that may call for more than a hundred players. These musicians, many of artist stature, give their full time to rehearsal and performance, achieving a precision unknown in former times.

The orchestra is constituted with a view to securing the best balance of tone. The performers are divided into the four sections we have described. In large orchestras approximately two thirds are string players, one fourth are wind players. From three to five men take care of the percussion. The following distribution is typical of the orchestras of our largest cities:

Strings:	18 first violins 15 second violins 12 violas 12 violoncellos 9 double basses
Woodwinds:	3 flutes, 1 piccolo 3 oboes, 1 English horn 3 clarinets, 1 bass clarinet 3 bassoons, 1 double bassoon
Brass:	4–6 horns 4 trumpets 3 trombones 1 tuba
Percussion:	1 kettledrum player 2–4 men for bass and side drum, glockenspiel, celesta, xylophone, triangle, cymbals, tambourine, etc.

It will be noticed that the violins are divided into two groups, first and second. Each group functions as a unit and plays a separate part. In general, the size of the orchestra varies according to the demands of the music. Included in the largest ensembles are two harps and, for certain works, a piano or organ.

The instruments are arranged so as to secure the best balance of tone. Most of the strings are up front. Brass and percussion are at the back. A characteristic seating plan is shown on p. 45; this arrangement varies somewhat from one orchestra to the next.

The ensemble is directed by the conductor, who beats time and indicates the entrances of the various instruments, the shadings in the volume of tone, the principal and subordinate lines, and a host of related details that serve to make clear the structure of the work. Beyond that, like any performing artist, he presents his personal interpretation of what the composer has written. He has before him the *score* of the work. This consists of from a few to as many as

The Boston Symphony Orchestra with its conductor, William Steinberg.

twenty-five or more staves, each representing one or more instrumental parts. All the staves together comprise a single composite line. What is going on at any moment in the orchestra is indicated at any given point straight down the page. It will be observed from the illustration on p. 46 that the instruments are grouped in families, woodwinds on top, then brass, percussion, and strings.

The Art of Orchestration

The composer bent over a page of score paper envisions the colors in his imagination as he blends and contrasts the timbres. He judges accurately the kind of sound he desires, be it powerful, caressing, or delicate; and he uses color to highlight the rhythmic patterns and the architectural design, to set off the principal ideas from the subordinate, and to weld the innumerable details into a whole.

The foregoing should dispel the widespread misconception that one man writes the music while another orchestrates it. This is true of most popular music, the score of a musical comedy, and the movie industry. But in art music, as the quotation from Rimsky-Korsakov makes clear, the two functions cannot be separated. What the composer says and how he says it are part and parcel of his individual manner of conceiving sound.

Erroneous too is the notion that the composer first writes his orchestral piece for the piano and then arranges it for instruments. An orchestral work, from its inception, is conceived in terms of the orchestra. If many composers like to have

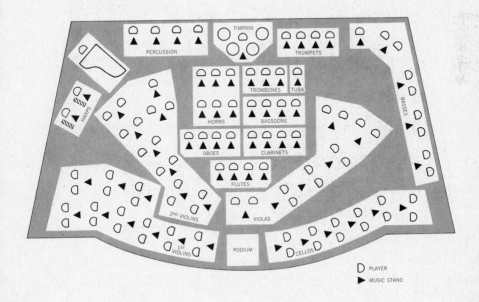

The seating plan of the Boston Symphony Orchestra.

A page from Brahms's Third Symphony, showing the arrangement of instrumental parts in an orchestral score.

a piano in the room while writing, it is primarily because this gives them contact with the living sound. But the piano is no more able to render a symphonic piece than a black-and-white reproduction can reveal the colors of a Raphael or a Titian.

Listening to the orchestra is a favorite pastime of the musical public today. Most of this listening is done via recordings, radio, and television, so that many listeners never come in contact with the living orchestral sound. A pity, for the best way to become familiar with the orchestral instruments is to be in the concert hall, where one can see as well as hear them. Recorded music plays a vital role in our musical life, but it should be regarded as a preparation for the live performance, not as a substitute.

The Orchestra in Action: Tchaikovsky's *Nutcracker Suite*

We shall in the course of this book have ample occasion to comment on how various composers wrote for the orchestra. At this point, however, the reader may find a helpful introduction to the orchestra in a work such as Tchaikovsky's *Nutcracker Suite,* which is a particularly fine example of vivid orchestral sonorities. The word *suite* indicates an instrumental work consisting of a number of short pieces (movements) related to a central idea. The suite may be either an independent work or a set of pieces drawn from a larger work. The *Nutcracker Suite* was drawn from a Christmas Eve ballet concerning a little girl who dreams that the nutcracker she received as a gift has turned into a handsome prince. Russian nutcrackers are often shaped like a human head, hence the transformation. The fairy-tale atmosphere impelled Tchaikovsky to some enchanting music.

The Miniature Overture sets the mood. It is in 2/4 time, marked Allegro giusto (a fitting Allegro), and begins pianissimo. To achieve an effect of lightness, Tchaikovsky omitted most of the bass instruments—cellos, double basses, trombones, tuba—as well as trumpets. The percussion section is represented only by the triangle. The dainty effect is enhanced by the use of staccato and the prevalence of the upper register. The sense of climax at the end is achieved through a crescendo—the music moves from pianissimo to fortissimo—as well as a rise in pitch.

There follows the March, in a lively 4/4 time. The characteristic march rhythm is set forth by clarinets, horns, and trumpets. The triplet rhythm is widely associated with military flourishes, but in this setting takes on a fanciful quality. Winds are answered by strings—a widely used orchestral device. Worthy of note is the filigree work in the accompaniment, in this case presented by the cellos and double basses pizzicato, an effect dear to Tchaikovsky's heart. In the middle section a staccato theme in high register is presented by three flutes and clarinet, mezzo forte, and vividly conveys a suggestion of ballet movement. The first part is repeated and the piece ends fortissimo.

"I have discovered a new instrument in Paris, something between a piano and a glockenspiel, with a divinely beautiful tone," wrote Tchaikovsky to his publisher in 1891. "I want to introduce this into the ballet." The instrument was the celesta, whose ethereal sound pervades the Dance of the Sugar-Plum Fairy. The piece, marked Andante non troppo (fairly slow, not too much so) is in 2/4 time. It opens with four bars of pizzicato introduction, pianissimo; soon the celesta tone is effectively contrasted with that of the bass clarinet. There is a passage for celesta alone, after which the opening theme is repeated. The piece ends with a pizzicato chord marked forte.

The Trepak or Russian Dance, marked Molto vivace (very lively), is in 2/4 time. The fast tempo, active rhythm, and heavy accents create the suggestion of vigorous movement proper to a peasant dance. The orchestral sonority is enlivened by the presence of the tambourine. Tchaikovsky, at the end, achieves a climax through a crescendo and an accelerando; the final measures are played fortissimo.

The little girl and her prince are entertained by various sweetmeats in the castle of the Sugar-Plum Fairy. The character representing Coffee dances the Arab Dance, a subdued number marked Allegretto that forms an effective contrast with the Trepak that preceded. It is in 3/8 time. Muted violas and cellos set up a *rhythmic ostinato*—that is, a rhythmic pattern repeated over and over with an almost hypnotic insistence. Against this dark curtain of sound, after introductory chords in the woodwinds, the muted violins unfold an oriental-sounding melody. Striking is the long-drawn-out Oriental wail of the oboe, in the upper register, over the quiet movement of the melody and harmony in the strings below. The music dies away at the end.

Not to be outdone, the character representing Tea presents the Chinese Dance, an Allegro moderato in 4/4 time. The piece begins mezzo forte. Bassoons, playing staccato, establish a rhythmic ostinato against which flute and piccolo trace a somewhat shrill melody. Whether this music bears any resemblance to that heard in Peking is beside the point. It is sufficiently close to what Western ears have come popularly to regard as Chinese—which means that it is pleasantly exotic and colorful. This dance closes with a crescendo and a chord played fortissimo.

The Dance of the Toy Flutes, marked Moderato assai (very moderate) and in 2/4 time, has always been a favorite with devotees of Tchaikovsky. Against a pizzicato accompaniment of violas, cellos, and double basses, three flutes outline a suave and beguiling melody. A short solo on the English horn arrests the ear, after which the opening theme returns. The middle section of the piece is devoted to a telling idea presented by the trumpets against a background of brass and percussion sounds, with a slight swell as the melodic line ascends and a decrease in volume as it moves downward. After this the gracious melody of the flutes is heard again.

The Waltz of the Flowers that closes this suite displays to the full Tchaikovsky's gift as a composer of ballet music. It is marked Tempo di Valse and is, of course, in ¾ time. Flowing melody and brilliancy of color are here associated with that sense of movement and gesture which are of the essence in the dance theater. The introduction alternates chords in the woodwinds and horns with arpeggios on the harp. The harp has a striking *cadenza* (a solo passage frequently introduced into an orchestral work in order to display the virtuosity of the performer and the capacities of the instrument). After four bars of an "oom-pah-pah" introduction, the waltz proper begins with a phrase for the horns marked piano, alternating with one for the solo clarinet. A contrasting melody emerges on the strings, punctuated by a measure on the woodwinds—always an effective orchestral procedure. Both melodies are repeated; the first is set off by ornamentation on the flutes. The middle section presents a second waltz, also consisting of two tunes. The first is sung by the flutes and oboes, piano; the second is a full-throated melody presented by the violas and cellos, forte. The first waltz is repeated and works up to a climax through a steady crescendo, accelerando, and rise to the brilliant upper register; the final measures are marked *fff*. With its suggestion of swirling ballerinas, this music conjures up everything we have come to associate with the romantic ballet.

The modern orchestra, with its amplitude of tonal resources, its range of dynamics and infinite variety of color, offers a memorable experience both to the musician and the music lover. There is good reason for the widespread conviction that it is one of the wonders of our musical culture.

11 Form: Musical Structure and Design

"The principal function of form is to advance our understanding. It is the organization of a piece which helps the listener to keep the idea in mind, to follow its development, its growth, its elaboration, its fate."   Arnold Schoenberg

Form is that quality in a work of art which presents to the mind of the beholder an impression of conscious choice and judicious arrangement. It represents clarity and order in art. It shows itself in the selection of certain details and the rejection of others. Form is manifest too in the relationship of the parts to the whole. It helps us to grasp the work of art as a unity. It can be as potent a source of beauty as the content itself.

Whether in the domestic arts—the setting of a table, the weaving of a basket —or in the loftier ones, a balance is required between unity and variety, between symmetry and asymmetry, activity and repose. Nor is this balance confined to

49

art. Nature has embodied it in the forms of plant and animal life and in what man likes to think of as her supreme handiwork—his own form.

Form in Music

Our lives are composed of sameness and differentness: certain details are repeated again and again, others are new. Music mirrors this dualism. Its basic law of structure is repetition and contrast—unity and variety. Repetition fixes the material in our minds and ministers to our need for the familiar. Contrast sustains our interest and feeds our love of change. From the interaction of the familiar and the new, the repeated elements and the contrasting ones, result the lineaments of musical form. These are to be found in every type of musical organism, from the nursery rhyme to the symphony.

The principle of form is embodied in a variety of musical forms. These utilize procedures worked out by generations of composers. No matter how diverse, they are based in one way or another on repetition and contrast. The forms, however, are not fixed molds into which the composer pours his material. What gives a piece of music its aliveness is the fact that it adapts a general plan to its own requirements. All faces have two eyes, a nose, and a mouth. In each face, though, these features are to be found in a wholly individual combination. The forms that students in composition follow are ready-made formulas set up for their guidance. The forms of the masters are living organisms in which external organization is delicately adjusted to inner content. No two symphonies of Haydn or Mozart, no two sonatas of Beethoven are exactly alike. Each is a fresh and unique solution of the problem of fashioning musical material into a logical and coherent form.

Three-Part or Ternary Form (A-B-A)

A basic pattern in music is three-part or ternary form. Here the composer presents a musical idea, next presents a contrasting idea, and then repeats the first. Hence this type of structure embodies the principle of "statement-departure-return" (A-B-A). The repetition safeguards the unity, while variety is supplied by the middle section.

This principle is manifest in its simplest form in a nursery song such as *Twinkle twinkle little star*:

a) Twinkle twinkle little star, how I wonder what you are.
b) Up above the world so high, like a diamond in the sky!
a) Twinkle twinkle little star, how I wonder what you are.

Often the first phrase is immediately repeated, so as to engrave it on the mind. This a (a)-b-a structure is to be found in many melodies such as *Believe Me if All Those Endearing Young Charms; Maryland, My Maryland;* and *Old Man River.* It is the standard formula for the tunes of Tin Pan Alley. Our need for

El Escorial (Madrid), Courtyard of the Kings.
Three-part (a-b-a) form is as effective to the eye as to the ear.

security is so great that, in a song consisting of four phrases, we are quite content to hear the opening phrase three times.

The four phrases in the a(a)-b-a structure make up a unit that corresponds roughly to a paragraph in prose. Such a unit may be built up into a larger formation. For instance, a contrasting unit may be fashioned from new material (melodies c and d), after which the composer repeats the first unit, either as before or with some variation. There results a large A-B-A structure, each section of which is itself a three-part form or some variant thereof. (Notice that we use capital letters for the over-all sections and small letters for the components within the section.) Tchaikovsky's *Waltz of the Flowers* (after the introduction) is a good example of this kind of formation:

A	B	A	Coda
a-b-a-b	c-d-c	a-b-a-b	

Coda, the Italian word for *tail*, indicates the concluding section of a composition, which is added to the form proper to round it off.

Three-part form became the standard pattern for innumerable short pieces of a simple song or dance type. This pattern is clear in several of the compositions mentioned in the preceding chapters. You will have no difficulty in recognizing the basic pattern of statement-departure-return in such pieces as the minuets from Mozart's *Eine kleine Nachtmusik* and Symphony in G minor, or Chopin's

Etude in E major and the *Dance of the Toy Flutes* from Tchaikovsky's *Nutcracker Suite*.

With its attractive symmetry and its balancing of the outer sections against the contrasting middle one, the three-part or ternary form constitutes a simple, clear-cut formation that is a favorite in painting and architecture no less than in music.

The statement-departure-return principle is presented most effectively when there is a real departure; that is to say, when the middle section offers a decided contrast to the first and third parts. This contrast may show itself in a number of ways. An agitated first section may be opposed to a lyric middle part. The first part may lie in the dark lower register, the second in the middle or upper range. The contrast may be further underlined by opposing loud to soft, fast to slow, staccato to legato, strings to woodwinds and/or brass. These and similar ways serve to emphasize the contrast between the first and second sections as well as between the second section and the return of the first. Thus, in Chopin's celebrated *Fantasie-Impromptu* for piano, the first section is based on an impetuous running melody that extends across the keyboard, while the middle part presents a serenely songlike idea in the treble register.

Two-Part or Binary Form (A-B)

Two-part or binary form is based on a statement and a departure, without a return to the opening section. This type of structure can be observed in the question-and-answer formation of a tune like *America*. A similar structure is to be observed in the Italian folksong *Santa Lucia* and in Brahms's *Lullaby*. Binary form is much in evidence in the short pieces that made up the suite of the seventeenth and eighteenth centuries, a period of lively experimentation in the realm of musical structure. Since each section generally is repeated, two-part form is not quite as apparent to the ear as is the three-part pattern. You will hear examples of A-B form in the third movement, the Allegro, from Corelli's Sonata, Opus 3, No. 7 and the Gigue from Bach's Suite No. 3.

We will examine in subsequent chapters the great forms of Western music. No matter how imposing their dimensions, they all show the principle of repetition and contrast, of unity in variety, that we have traced here. In all its manifestations our music displays the striving for organic form that binds together the individual tones within the phrase, the phrases within the musical period, the periods within the section, the sections within the movement, and the movements within the work as a whole; even as, in a novel, the individual words are bound together in phrases, sentences, paragraphs, sections, chapters, and parts.

It has been said that architecture is frozen music. By the same token, music is floating architecture. Form is the structural principle in music. It distributes the areas of activity and repose, tension and relaxation, light and shade, and integrates the multitudinous details, large and small, into the spacious structures that are the glory of Western music.

12 Musical Style

"The style is the man."
Buffon

Style may be defined as the characteristic manner of presentation in any art. The word may refer to the element of fitness that shapes each type of art work to its function. We distinguish between the style of the novel and that of the essay, between the style of the cathedral and that of the palace. The word may also indicate an artist's personal manner of expression, i.e., the distinctive flavor that sets him apart from all others. Thus we speak of the style of Dickens or Thackeray, of Raphael or Michelangelo, of Wagner or Brahms. In a larger sense we often identify style with national culture, as when we speak of French, Italian, or German style; or with an entire civilization, as when we contrast the musical style of the West with that of the Orient.

Since all the arts change from one age to the next, one very important use of the word is in connection with the various historical periods. Here the concept of style enables us to draw the proper connection between the artist and his time, so that the art work is placed in its social-historical frame. No matter how greatly the artists of a particular era may vary in personality and outlook, when seen in the perspective of time they turn out to have certain qualities in common. The age has put its stamp upon all. Because of this we can tell at once that a work of art—whether music, poetry, painting, or architecture—dates from the Middle Ages or the Renaissance, from the eighteenth century or the nineteenth. The style of a period, then, is the total art-language of all its artists as they react to the forces—artistic, political, economic, religious, philosophic—that shape their environment.

Scholars will always disagree as to precisely where one style period ends and the next begins. Each period leads by imperceptible degrees into the following one, dates and labels being merely convenient signposts. The following outline shows the main style periods in the history of Western music. Each represents a conception of form and technique, an ideal of beauty, a manner of expression and performance attuned to the cultural climate of the period; in a word—a style! (The dates, naturally, are approximate.)

350–600 A.D.	Period of the Church Fathers.
600–850	Early Middle Ages. Gregorian Chant.
850–1150	Romanesque. Development of the staff in musical notation, about 1000.
1150–1450	Gothic.
1450–1600	Renaissance.
1600–1750	Baroque.

53

1725–1775	Rococo.
1775–1825	Classical.
1820–1900	Romantic.
1890–1915	Postromantic, including impressionism.
1910–	Twentieth-Century

13 Musical Notation

"Musical notation is so familiar to us that few are aware of the difficulty of the problems which had to be solved, and the innumerable experiments undertaken for the invention and perfection of a satisfactory method of recording musical sounds."

Sylvia Townsend Warner

Our musical notation is the result of an evolution that reaches back to antiquity. It has adapted itself to successive systems of musical thought, and continues to do so. It is by no means a perfect tool, but it has proved adequate to the constantly new demands made upon it.

The Notation of Pitch

Musical notation presents a kind of graph of the sounds with regard to their duration and pitch. These are indicated by symbols called *notes*, which are written on the *staff*, a series of five parallel lines with four spaces between:

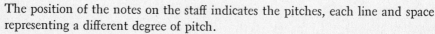

The position of the notes on the staff indicates the pitches, each line and space representing a different degree of pitch.

A symbol known as a *clef* is placed at the left end of the staff, and determines the group of pitches to which that staff refers. The *treble clef* (𝄞) is used for pitches within the range of the female singing voices, and the *bass clef* (𝄢) for a lower group of pitches, within the range of the male singing voices.

Pitches are named after the first seven letters of the alphabet, from A to G; the lines and spaces are named accordingly. (From one note named A to the next is the interval of an octave, which—as we have seen—is the distance from one *do* to the next in the do-re-mi-fa-sol-la-ti-do scale). The pitches on the treble staff are named as follows:

E   F   G   A   B   C   D   E   F

And those on the bass staff:

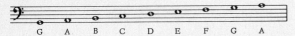

G   A   B   C   D   E   F   G   A

For pitches above and below these, short extra lines called *ledger lines* can be added:

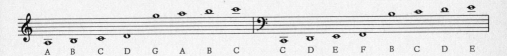

A   B   C   D   G   A   B   C   C   D   E   F   B   C   D   E

Middle C—the C that, on the piano, is situated approximately in the center of the keyboard—comes between the treble and bass staffs. It is represented by either the first ledger line above the bass staff or the first ledger line below the treble staff, as the following example makes clear. This combination of the two staffs is called the *great staff* or *grand staff*:

C   D   E   F   G   A   B   C   D   E   F   G   A   B   C

There are also signs known as *accidentals*, which are used to alter the pitch of a written note. A sharp (♯) before the note indicates the pitch a semitone above; a flat (♭) indicates the pitch a semitone below. A natural (♮) cancels a sharp or flat. Also used are the double sharp (✗) and double flat (♭♭), which respectively raise and lower the pitch by two half-tones—that is, a whole tone.

The piano keyboard exemplifies this arrangement of whole and half tones. The distance from one piano key to its nearest neighbor is a *half tone* (also

called a *semitone*, or *half step*.) This is true whether the adjacent keys are both white, or one white and the other black: thus, from E to F is a semitone, also from C to C♯.

Each of the black keys has two names, depending on whether it is considered in relation to its upper or lower neighbor. For example, the black key between C and D can be called either C♯ or D♭. Similarly, D♯ is the same as E♭, F♯ as G♭, G♯ as A♭, and A♯ as B♭.

55

In many pieces of music, where certain sharped or flatted notes are used consistently throughout the piece, the necessary sharps or flats are written at the beginning of each line of music, in order to save repetition. This may be seen in the following example of piano music. Notice that piano music is written on the great staff, with the right hand usually playing the notes written on the upper staff and the left hand usually playing the notes written on the lower:

The Notation of Rhythm

The duration of tones is indicated by the appearance of the notes placed on the staff. These use a system of relative values. For example, in the following table each note represents a duration half as long as the preceding one:

| whole note | half note | quarter note | eighth note | sixteenth note | thirty-second note | sixty-fourth note |

In any particular piece of music, these note values are related to the beat of the music. If the quarter note represents one beat, then a half note lasts for two beats, a whole note for four, with two eighth-notes on one beat, or four sixteenths. The following chart makes this clear:

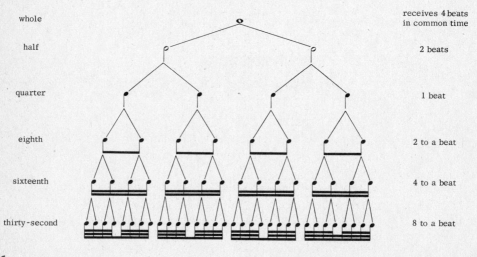

56

When a group of three notes is to be played in the time normally taken up by only two of the same kind, we have a *triplet*:

It is possible to combine successive notes of the same pitch, using a curved line known as a *tie*:

beats: 4 + 4 = 8   2 + 4 = 6   1 + ½ = 1½

A *dot* after a note extends its value by half:

beats: 4+2 = 6   2+1 = 3   1 + ½ = 1½   ½ + ¼ = ¾

Time never stops in music, even when there is no sound. Silence is indicated by symbols known as *rests*, which correspond in time value to the notes:

whole rest	half rest	quarter rest	eighth rest	sixteenth rest	thirty-second rest	sixty-fourth rest

The metrical organization of a piece of music is indicated by the *time signature*, which specifies the meter. This consists of two numbers, written one above the other. The upper numeral indicates the number of beats within the measure; the lower one shows which unit of value equals one beat. Thus, the time signature ¾ means that there are three beats to a measure, with the quarter note equal to one beat. In 6/8 time there are six beats in the measure, each eighth-note receiving one beat. Following are the most frequently encountered time signatures.

Duple meter	2/2	2/4	2/8	
Triple meter	3/2	3/4	3/8	3/16
Quadruple meter		4/4	4/8	
Sextuple meter		6/4	6/8	

Also in use are 9/8 (3 groups of 3) and 12/8 (4 groups of 3). Contemporary music shows a wide use of nonsymmetrical patterns such as 5/4 or 5/8 (3 + 2 or 2 + 3) and 7/4 or 7/8 (4 + 3, 3 + 4, 2 + 3 + 2, etc.).

Four-four (4/4) is known as *common time* and is often indicated by the sign **C**. A vertical line drawn through this sign (**¢**) indicates *alla breve* or cut time, generally quick, with the half note receiving one beat instead of the quarter; in other words, two-two (2/2).

The following examples show how the system works. It will be noticed that the measures are separated by a vertical line known as a *bar line;* hence a measure is often referred to as a bar. As a rule, the bar line is followed by the most strongly accented beat, the ONE.

PART TWO

NINETEENTH-CENTURY ROMANTICISM

"Music is the most romantic of all the arts—one might almost say, the only genuinely romantic one—for its sole subject is the infinite. Music discloses to man an unknown realm, a world in which he leaves behind him all definite feelings to surrender himself to an inexpressible longing."
E. T. A. Hoffmann (1776–1822)

14 The Romantic Movement

"Romanticism is beauty without bounds—the beautiful infinite."
Jean Paul Richter (1763–1825)

Historians observe that style in art moves between two poles, the classic and the romantic. Both the classic artist and the romantic strive to express significant emotions, and to achieve that expression within beautiful forms. Where they differ is in their point of view. The classical spirit seeks order, poise, and serenity as surely as the romantic longs for strangeness, wonder, and ecstasy. The classic artist is apt to be more objective in his approach to art and to life. He tries to view life sanely and "to see it whole." The romantic, on the other hand, is apt to be intensely subjective, and view the world in terms of his personal feelings. The German philosopher Friedrich Nietzsche, in his writings on art, dramatized the contrast between the two through the symbol of Apollo, god of light and measure, as opposed to Dionysus, god of intoxication and passion. Classic and romantic have alternated and even existed side by side from the beginning of time, for they correspond to two basic impulses in man's nature: on the one hand his need for moderation, his desire to have emotion purged and controlled; on the other his desire for uninhibited emotional expression, his longing for the unknown and the unattainable.

Specifically, the classic and romantic labels are attached to two important periods in European art. The one held the stage in the last quarter of the eighteenth century and the early decades of the nineteenth. The other, stemming out of the social and political upheavals that followed in the wake of the French Revolution, came to the fore in the second quarter of the nineteenth century.

Romanticism in the Nineteenth Century

The French Revolution was the outcome of momentous social forces. It signalized the transfer of power from a hereditary feudal-agricultural

Eugéne Delacroix (1798–1863), LIBERTY LEADING THE PEOPLE. (Louvre, Paris)
Revolutionary ardor was one of the mainsprings of 19th-century romanticism.

aristocracy to the middle class, whose position depended on commerce and industry. As in the case of the American Revolution, this upheaval heralded a social order shaped by the technological advances of the Industrial Revolution. The new society, based on free enterprise, emphasized the individual as never before. Freedom—political, economic, religious, personal—was its watchword. On the artistic front this urge for individualism found expression in the romantic movement.

The slogan of "Liberty, Equality, Fraternity" inspired hopes and visions to which few artists failed to respond. Sympathy for the oppressed, interest in simple folk and in children, faith in man and his destiny—all these, so intimately associated with the time, point to the democratic character of the romantic movement. Whereas the eighteenth century had found inspiration in the art of ancient Greece, the romantics discovered the so-called Dark Ages. King Arthur and Siegfried, fairy tale and medieval saga usurped the place formerly held by the gods and heroes of antiquity. Romantic architecture fell under the spell of the Gothic revival. So too, the formal gardens of the eighteenth century, with their spacious symmetries, were supplanted in public favor by picturesque grottoes and mysterious bowers. The romantics became intensely aware of nature, but nature as a backdrop for the inner conflicts of man. When the heroine of a romantic novel felt sad, it rained.

The romantic poets rebelled against the conventional form and matter of their classical predecessors; they leaned towards the fanciful, the picturesque, and the passionate. In Germany a group of young writers, following in the footsteps of Goethe and Schiller, created a new kind of lyric poetry that culminated in the art of Heinrich Heine; he became one of the favorite poets of the romantic composers. A similar movement in France was led by Victor Hugo, its greatest prose writer, and Alphonse Lamartine, its greatest poet. In England the revolt against the formalism of the classical age numbered among its adherents a line of lyric poets such as Gray, Cowper and Burns, Wordsworth and Coleridge, Byron, Shelley, and Keats. The new spirit of individualism expressed itself in the romantic artist's sense of his uniqueness, his heightened awareness of himself as an individual apart from all others. "I am different from all the men I have seen," proclaimed Jean Jacques Rousseau. "If I am not better, at least I am different."

Thus, one of the prime traits of romantic art was its emphasis on an intensely emotional type of expression. It has been well said that with romanticism the pronoun "I" made its appearance in poetry. Gone were the elegantly abstract couplets of the eighteenth-century classicists. The new age found expression in the passionate lyricism of such lines as Shelley's—

> Oh! lift me as a wave, a leaf, a cloud!
> I fall upon the thorns of life! I bleed!

or Keats's—

> When I have fears that I may cease to be
> Before my eager pen has gleaned my teeming brain . . .

The newly won freedom of the artist proved a not unmixed blessing. He confronted a philistine world from which he felt himself more and more cut off. A new type emerged—the artist as bohemian, the rejected dreamer who starved in an attic and through peculiarities of dress and behavior "shocked the bourgeois." This was the sensitive individual who was both too good for the moneyed world about him and not good enough. Increasingly the romantic artist found himself arrayed against the established order. He was free from the social restraints imposed by court life; but he paid dearly for his freedom in loneliness, in knowing himself apart from his fellows. Withdrawal from the world brought a preoccupation with inner problems. Eternal longing, regret for the lost happiness of childhood, an indefinable discontent that gnawed at the soul—these were the ingredients of the romantic mood. Yet the artist's pessimism was not without its basis in external reality. It became apparent that the high hopes fostered by the Revolution were not to be realized overnight. Despite the brave slogans, men were not yet equal or free. Inevitably optimism gave way to doubt and disenchantment—"the illness of the century."

63

J. M. W. Turner (1775–1851), GRAND CANAL, VENICE. (The Metropolitan Museum of
Art, New York; Bequest of Cornelius Vanderbilt, 1899)

A yearning for picturesque scenes was one of the prime traits of romantic art.

This malaise was reflected in the art of the time. Thus, Balzac's *Human
Comedy* depicted the warping of human relationships in the new society. Hugo
dedicated *Les Misérables* "to the unhappy ones of the earth." The nineteenth-
century novel found its great theme in the conflict between the individual and
society. Jean Valjean and Heathcliff, Madame Bovary and Anna Karenina,
Oliver Twist, Tess of the d'Urbervilles, and the Karamazovs—a varied company
rises from those impassioned pages to point up the frustrations and guilts of the
nineteenth-century world.

Hardly less persuasive was the art of those who sought escape. Some
glamorized the past, as did Walter Scott and Alexandre Dumas. Longing for
far-off lands inspired the exotic scenes that glow on the canvases of Turner
and Delacroix. The romantic poets and painters showed a remarkable fondness
for the picturesque, the fantastic, and the macabre. Theirs was a world of
"strangeness and wonder": the eerie landscape we encounter in the writings
of a Coleridge, a Hawthorne, or a Poe.

Romanticism, in fine, dominated the art output of the nineteenth century.
It gave its name to a movement and an era; and created a multitude of colorful
works that still hold millions in thrall.

15 Romanticism in Music

"Music is the melody whose text is the world."
Schopenhauer

Great changes in the moral, political, and social climate of an epoch seek to be expressed also in the art of that epoch. But they cannot be unless the new age places in the artist's hand the means of giving expression to new ideas. This was precisely the achievement of the romantic movement in music—that it gave composers the means of expressing what the age demanded of them.

In the first place, the Industrial Revolution brought with it not only the production of cheaper and more responsive instruments, but also introduced important improvements in the wind instruments that strongly influenced the sound of romantic music. For example, the addition of valves to the brass instruments made them much more maneuverable, so that composers like Wagner and Tchaikovsky could assign melodies to the horn that would have been unplayable in the time of Haydn and Mozart. So too, as a result of improved manufacturing techniques, the piano acquired a cast-iron frame and thicker strings that gave it a deeper and more brilliant tone. If the impassioned Sonata of Liszt sounds different from a sonata of Mozart it is not only because Liszt's time demanded of him a different kind of expression, but also because it put at his disposal a piano capable of effects that were neither available nor necessary in the earlier period.

Secondly, the gradual democratization of society brought with it a broadening of educational opportunities. Conservatories that trained more and better musicians than formerly were established in the chief cities of Europe. As a result, nineteenth-century composers could count on instrumental performers whose skill was considerably in advance of what it had been in former times. As music moved from palace and church to the public concert hall, orchestras increased in size and efficiency, and gave the composer a means of expression more varied and colorful than he had ever had before. This naturally had a direct influence upon the sound. For example, where most eighteenth-century music ranged in dynamic level from piano to forte, the dynamic range of the orchestra in the nineteenth century was far greater. Now came into fashion the heaven-storming crescendos, the violent contrasts of loud and soft that lend such drama to the music of the romantics. As orchestral music became more and more important, the technique of writing for orchestra—that is, orchestration —became almost an art in itself. At last the musician had a palette comparable to the painter's, and used it as the painter did—to conjure up sensuous beauty and enchantment, to create mood and atmosphere, to suggest nature scenes and calm or stormy seascapes.

The desire for direct communication led composers to use a large number of expressive terms intended to serve as clues to the mood of the music, with the result that a highly characteristic vocabulary sprang up. Among the directions frequently encountered in nineteenth-century scores are *espressivo* (expressively), *dolce* (sweetly,), *cantabile* (songful); *pastorale, agitato, misterioso, lamentoso, trionfale; dolente* (weeping), *mesto* (sad), *maestoso* (majestic), *gioioso* (joyous); *con amore* (with love, tenderly), *con passione, con fuoco* (with fire). These suggest not only the character of the music but the frame of mind behind it.

The interest in folklore and the rising tide of nationalism impelled the romantic musicians to make use of the folk songs and dances of their native lands. As a result, a number of national idioms—Hungarian, Polish, Russian, Bohemian, Scandinavian—came to the fore and opened up new areas to European music, greatly enriching its melody, harmony, and rhythm.

Even when written for instruments, romantic melody was easy to sing and hum. The nineteenth century above all was the period when musicians tried to make their instruments "sing." It is no accident that the themes from romantic symphonies, concertos, and other instrumental works are today transformed into popular songs; for romantic melody was marked by a lyricism that gave it an immediate emotional appeal, as is evidenced by the enduring popularity of the tunes of Schubert, Chopin, Verdi, and their fellows. Through innumerable songs and operas as well as instrumental pieces, romantic melody appealed to a wider audience than had ever existed before.

Nineteenth-century music strove for a harmony that was highly emotional and expressive. Under the impact of the romantic movement composers sought tone combinations that were more dissonant than what their forbears had been accustomed to. Richard Wagner was a leader in the trend towards what we shall come to know as *chromatic harmony* (a type of harmony in which chords based on the tones that belong to the key are made more colorful through the addition of tones that do not). The poignant dissonances through which he expressed the yearning of the lovers in *Tristan und Isolde* voiced the longing of an era. The tendency towards chromatic harmony became one of the important characteristics of musical romanticism.

The composers of the nineteenth century gradually expanded the instrumental forms they had inherited from the eighteenth. These musicians needed more time to say what they had to say. A symphony of Haydn or Mozart is apt to take about twenty minutes; one by Tchaikovsky, Brahms, or Dvořák lasts at least twice that long. As public concert life developed, the symphony became the most important form of orchestral music, comparable to the most spacious form in romantic literature—the novel. As a result, the nineteenth-century composer approached the writing of a symphony with greater deliberation— some would say trepidation—than his predecessors. Where Haydn wrote over a hundred symphonies and Mozart more than forty, Schubert, Bruckner, and Dvořák (following the example of Beethoven) wrote nine; Tchaikovsky, six;

Schumann and Brahms, four; César Franck, one. As the romantics well realized, it was not easy to write a symphony after Beethoven.

Romantic man desired to taste all experience at its maximum intensity. He was enchanted in turn by literature, music, painting. How much more intoxicating, he reasoned, would be a "union of the arts" that combined all three. Music in the nineteenth century drew steadily closer to literature and painting—that is, to elements that lay outside the realm of sound. The connection with romantic poetry and drama is most obvious, of course, in the case of music with words. However, even in their purely orchestral music the romantic composers responded to the mood of the time and captured with remarkable vividness the emotional atmosphere that surrounded nineteenth-century poetry and painting.

The result of all these tendencies was to make romanticism as potent a force in music as it was in the other arts. Nineteenth-century music was linked to dreams and passions, to profound meditations on life and death, man's destiny, God and nature, pride in one's country, desire for freedom, the political struggles of the age, and the ultimate triumph of good over evil. These intellectual and emotional associations, nurtured by the romantic movement, enabled music to achieve a commanding position in the nineteenth century as a moral force, a vision of man's greatness, and a direct link between his inner life and the world around him.

SONG AND PIANO PIECE

---

16 The Short Lyric Forms as an Expression of Romanticism

"Out of my great sorrows I make my little songs."
Heinrich Heine

Through the short lyric forms the romantic movement satisfied its need for intimate personal expression. Coming into prominence in the early decades of the century, the song and piano piece emerged as particularly attractive examples of the new lyricism.

The Song

The repertory of song—folk, popular, and art—is more extensive than that of all other types of music. For song combines two musical elements of universal appeal—melody and the human voice. A *song* is a short lyric composition for solo voice based on a poetic text. The vocal melody is presented as a rule with an instrumental accompaniment that gives it harmonic background and support.

A great poem is complete in itself and needs nothing more to enhance it. A melody, too, is a thing complete in itself. To blend the two into an artistic whole requires imagination of the highest order. The creators of the romantic art song were so successful in combining words and music that many of the lyric poems they used have survived mainly in their musical settings.

Types of Song Structure

We distinguish between two main types of song structure. In *strophic form* the same melody is repeated with every stanza, or strophe, of the poem. This formation, which occurs very frequently in folk and popular song, permits of no great closeness between words and music. Instead it sets up a general atmosphere that accommodates itself equally well to all the stanzas. The first may tell of the lover's expectancy, the second of his joy at seeing his beloved, the third of her father's harshness in separating them, and the fourth of her sad death, all these being sung to the same tune. The prevalence of strophic song throughout the ages points to one conclusion: the folk learned early that a lovely tune is a joy in itself, and that it heightens emotion no matter what the content of a particular stanza.

The other type is what the Germans call *durchkomponiert*, literally "through-composed"—that is, composed from beginning to end, without repetitions of whole sections. Here the music follows the story line, changing with each stanza according to the text. This makes it possible for the composer to mirror every shade of meaning in the words.

There is also an intermediate type that combines the repetition of the strophic song with the freedom of the song that is through-composed. The same melody may be repeated for two or three stanzas, with new material introduced when the poem seems to require it, generally at the climax. Schubert's celebrated *Ständchen* (Serenade) is a fine example of this structure.

The Art Song in the Romantic Period

Despite the prominence of song throughout the ages, the art song as we know it today was a product of the romantic era. It was created by the union of poetry and music in the early nineteenth century. This union was consummated with such artistry by Franz Schubert and his successors, notably Robert Schumann and Johannes Brahms, that the new genre came to be known all over Europe by the German word for song—*Lied* (plural, *Lieder*).

The lied depended for its flowering on the upsurge of lyric poetry that marked the rise of German romanticism. Goethe (1749–1832) and Heine (1799–1856) are the two leading figures among a group of poets who, like Wordsworth and Byron, Shelley and Keats in English literature, cultivated a subjective mode of expression through the short lyric poem. The lied brought to flower the desire of the romantic era for the union of music and poetry, ranging from tender sentiment to dramatic balladry. Its favorite themes were love and longing, the beauty of nature, the transience of human happiness.

The triumph of the romantic art song was made possible by the emergence of the piano as the universal household instrument of the nineteenth century. The piano accompaniment translated the poetic images into musical ones. Voice and piano together created a short lyric form charged with feeling, suited alike for amateurs and artists, for the home as for the concert room. Within a short time the lied achieved immense popularity and made a durable contribution to world art.

The Piano Piece

The short lyric piano piece was the instrumental equivalent of the song in its projection of lyric and dramatic moods within a compact frame. Among the titles most frequently used for it are *bagatelle* (literally, "a trifle"), *impromptu* (on the spur of the moment), *intermezzo* (interlude), *nocturne* (night song), *novelette* (short story), *moment musical, song without words, album leaf, prelude, romance, capriccio* (caprice); and, of larger dimensions, the *rhapsody* and *ballade*. In the dance category are the *waltz, mazurka, polka, écossaise* (Scottish dance), *polonaise* (Polish dance), *march*, and *country dance*. Composers also used titles of a fanciful and descriptive nature. Typical are Schumann's *In the Night, Soaring, Whims*; Liszt's *Forest Murmurs* and *Fireflies*. The nineteenth-century masters of the short piano piece—Schubert, Chopin and Liszt, Mendelssohn, Schumann and Brahms, and their fellows— showed inexhaustible ingenuity in exploiting the technical resources of the instrument and its capacities for lyric-dramatic expression.

The short lyric forms became one of the most popular types of music in the output of the romantic era. Yet even here we find the urge to achieve large-scale structure. This expressed itself in the cycle of songs or piano pieces joined together by a literary or musical idea, as in Schubert's *Die schöne Müllerin* (The Lovely Maid of the Mill) and Schumann's *Carnaval*. Such cycles may be compared to the series of short stories within a frame, such as *The Canterbury Tales* or *The Decameron*, that had been popular in European literature for centuries.

In any case, the short lyric forms sprang out of the composer's realization that size is no criterion in art, and that an exquisitely wrought miniature may contain as much beauty as a symphony. In the song and piano piece, nineteenth-century romanticism found one of its most characteristic means of expression.

17 Franz Schubert

"When I wished to sing of love it turned to sorrow. And when I wished to sing of sorrow it was transformed for me into love."

In the popular mind Franz Schubert's life has become a romantic symbol of the artist's fate. He suffered poverty and was neglected during his lifetime. He died young. And after his death he was enshrined among the immortals.

His Life

He was born in 1797 in a suburb of Vienna, the son of a school-master. The boy learned the violin from his father, piano from an elder brother;

his beautiful soprano voice gained him admittance to the imperial chapel and school where the court singers were trained. His creative gift asserted itself in boyhood, and his teachers were duly astonished at the musicality of the shy, dreamy lad. One of them remarked that Franz seemed to learn "straight from Heaven."

His schooldays over, young Schubert tried to follow in his father's footsteps, but he was not cut out for the routine of the classroom. He found escape in the solitude of his attic, immersing himself in the lyric poets who were the first voices of German romanticism. As one of his friends said, "Everything he touched turned to song." With a spontaneity comparable to Mozart's, the melodies took shape that gave to the new romantic lyricism its ideal expression. *Gretchen at the Spinning Wheel,* to Goethe's verses, was written in a single afternoon—when he was seventeen. A year later came his setting of the same poet's *Erlking.* One of his greatest songs, it was the work of a few hours.

Schubert's talent for friendship attracted to him a little band of followers. Their appreciation of his genius comforted him for the neglect and incomprehension of the world. Poets, painters, musicians, these young enthusiasts were the advance guard of the romantic movement. With their encouragement Schubert, not yet twenty, broke with the drudgery of his father's school. In the eleven years that were left him he occupied no official position (although he occasionally made half-hearted attempts to obtain one). He lived with one or another of his friends in a mixture of poverty and camaraderie, hope and despair. And steadily, with an almost self-devouring intensity, the music poured from the bespectacled young man. "How do you compose?" he was asked. "I finish one piece," was the answer, "and begin the next."

Schubert was singularly unable to stand up to the world. Songs that in time sold in the hundreds of thousands he surrendered literally for the price of a meal. It was borne in upon him that the creative gift is not enough for an

Franz Schubert.

artist. "The state should support me," he remarked sadly, "so that I may be untroubled and free to compose." As the years passed, the buoyancy of youth gave way to a sense of loneliness, the tragic loneliness of the romantic artist. "No one feels another's grief," he wrote, "no one understands another's joy. People imagine that they can reach one another. In reality they only pass each other by." Yet he comprehended—and in this he was the romantic—that his very suffering must open to his art new layers of awareness. "My music is the product of my talent and my misery. And that which I have written in my greatest distress is what the world seems to like best."

He still yielded to flurries of optimism when success appeared to lie within his grasp, but eventually there came to him an intimation that the struggle had been decided against him. "It seems to me at times that I no longer belong to this world." This was the emotional climate of the magnificent song cycle *Die Winterreise* (The Winter Journey), in which he struck a note of somber lyricism new to music. Depressed by illness and poverty, he abandoned himself to the mournful images of Wilhelm Müller's poems. The long, dark journey— was it not the symbol of his own life? Overcoming his discouragement, he embarked on his last effort. To the earlier masterpieces was added, in that final year, an amazing list that includes the Symphony in C major, the Mass in E-flat, the String Quintet in C, the three posthumous piano sonatas, and thirteen of his finest songs, among them the ever-popular *Serenade*.

With the great C-major Symphony behind him, he made arrangements to study counterpoint. "I see now how much I still have to learn." Ill with typhus, he managed to correct the proofs of the last part of *Die Winterreise*. The sense of defeat accompanied him through the final delirium; he fancied that he was being buried alive. "Do I not deserve a place above the ground?" His last wish was to be buried near the master he worshiped above all others—Beethoven.

He was thirty-one years old when he died in 1828. His possessions consisted of his clothing, his bedding, and "a pile of old music valued at ten florins": his unpublished manuscripts. In the memorable words of Sir George Grove, "There never has been one like him, and there never will be another."

His Music

Schubert stood at the confluence of the classic and romantic eras. His symphonic style bespeaks the heir of the classical tradition; but in his songs and piano pieces he was wholly the romantic, an artist whose magical lyricism impelled Liszt to call him "the most poetic musician that ever was." Like every composer of the nineteenth century, he was weighed down by the greatness of his predecessors. "Who can do anything more after Beethoven?" he complained. Yet within the orbit of that towering figure he developed a symphonic idiom of his own. His symphonies, for all their romantic ardor, are classical in their dramatic momentum and continuity. They rank with the finest since Beethoven.

Chamber music was Schubert's birthright as a Viennese. To the tradition of intimate social music he brought his own inwardness of spirit. The string quartets (1812–26), the *Trout Quintet* (1819), the two trios for piano, violin, and cello (1826–27), and the transcendent Quintet in C (1828) bear the true Schubertian stamp. They end the line of Viennese classicism.

In the Impromptus and *Moments musicaux* (Musical Moments) the piano sings the new lyricism. Caprice, spontaneity, and the charm of the unexpected take their place as elements of romantic art. Of comparable freshness is the popular tone of the dance pieces, waltzes, ländlers (an Austrian peasant dance), and écossaises. His piano sonatas were neglected for years, but have now found their rightful place in the repertory. Schubert's broadly flowing lyricism expanded the form he inherited from his predecessors.

Finally there are the songs, more than six hundred of them. Many were written down at white heat, sometimes five, six, seven in a single morning. Certain of his melodies achieve the universality of folk song, others display the highest sophistication. In either case they issue directly from the heart of the poem. Their eloquence and freshness of feeling have never been surpassed. Of special moment are the accompaniments: a measure or two, and the rustling brook is conjured up, the dilapidated hurdy-gurdy, or the lark "at heaven's gate." Of Schubert's songs may be said what Schumann remarked about the C-major Symphony: "This music transports us to a region where we cannot remember ever to have been before."

Erlkönig

This masterpiece of Schubert's youth (1815) captures the romantic "strangeness and wonder" of Goethe's celebrated ballad. *Erlkönig* (the Erlking) is based on the legend that whoever is touched by the King of the Elves must die. The poem has four characters: the narrator, the father, the child, and the seductive Elf.

NARRATOR:

Wer reitet so spät durch Nacht und Wind? | Who rides so late through night and wind?

Es ist der Vater mit seinem Kind; | It is the father with his child.
er hat den Knaben wohl in dem Arm, | He holds the boy firmly in his arm,
er fasst ihn sicher, er hält ihn warm. | He clasps him tight, he keeps him warm.

FATHER:

"Mein Sohn, was birgst du so bang dein Gesicht?" | "My son, why hide your face in fear?"

SON:

"Siehst, Vater, du den Erlkönig nicht? | "Father, do you not see the Erlking?
den Erlenkönig mit Kron' und Schweif?" | The Erlking with crown and tail?"

FATHER:

"Mein Sohn, es ist ein Nebelstreif." | "My son, it is only a streak of mist."

ERLKING:

"Du liebes Kind, komm, geh mit mir!   "You sweet child, come, go with me!
gar schöne Spiele spiel' ich mit dir;   Such pleasant games I'll play with you.
manch bunte Blumen sind an dem Strand;   Many bright flowers bloom along the shore,
meine Mutter hat manch' gülden Ge-   My mother has many a robe of gold."
wand."

SON:

"Mein Vater, mein Vater, und hörest du   "Oh father, father, do you not hear
nicht,
was Erlenkönig mir leise verspricht?"   What the Erlking gently promises me?"

FATHER:

"Sei ruhig, bleibe ruhig, mein Kind;   "Be calm, my child, stay calm;
in dürren Blättern säuselt der Wind."   It is only the wind among the dead leaves."

ERLKING:

"Willst, feiner Knabe, du mit mir gehn?   "Lovely boy, will you come with me?
meine Töchter sollen dich warten schön;   My daughters will serve you well.
meine Töchter führen den nächtlichen   My daughters keep nightly revels,
Reihn
und wiegen und tanzen und singen dich   They'll sing and dance and rock you to
ein,   sleep.
sie wiegen und tanzen und singen dich   They'll sing and dance and rock you to
ein."   sleep."

SON:

"Mein Vater, mein Vater, und siehst du   "Oh father, father, do you not see
nicht dort
Erlkönigs Töchter am düstern Ort?"   The Erlking's daughters in the darkness?"

FATHER:

"Mein Sohn, mein Sohn, ich seh' es genau,   "My son, my son, I see quite clearly
es scheinen die alten Weiden so grau."   The old willow trees gleaming gray."

ERLKING:

"Ich liebe dich, mich reizt deine schöne   "I love you, your beauty charms me,
Gestalt,
und bist du nicht willig, so brauch' ich   And if you're not willing, I'll use force!"
Gewalt."

SON:

"Mein Vater, mein Vater, jetzt fasst er   "Oh father, father, he seizes me!
mich an!
Erlkönig hat mir ein Leids gethan!"   The Erlking has done me harm!"

NARRATOR:

Dem Vater grauset's, er reitet geschwind,   The father shudders, he rides swiftly,
er hält in Armen das ächzende Kind,   Holding fast the moaning child.
erreicht den Hof mit Müh' und Noth: He reaches home with pain and dread:
in seinen Armen das Kind war todt.   In his arms the child lay dead!

The eerie atmosphere of the poem is established by the piano part. Gallop-ing triplets are heard against a rumbling figure in the bass. This motive, so romantic in tone, pervades the canvas and imparts to it an astonishing unity.

The characters are vividly differentiated through changes in the melody, harmony, rhythm, and type of accompaniment. The child's terror is suggested by clashing dissonance. The father, allaying his son's fears, is represented by a more rounded vocal line. As for the Erlking, his cajoling is given in suavely melodious phrases.

The song is through-composed; the music follows the unfolding of the narrative with a steady rise in tension—and pitch—that builds to the climax. Abruptly the obsessive triplet rhythm lets up, giving way to a ritard as horse and rider reach home. "In his arms the child"—a dramatic pause precedes the two final words—"lay dead."

The thing seems strangely simple, inevitable. The doing of it by a marvelous boy of eighteen was an event in the history of romanticism.

Heidenröslein

The strophic song is well exemplified by this gem of Schubertian melody. Set to a poem by Goethe, *Heidenröslein* (Heather Rose; 1815) displays the engaging traits of the romantic lied: simplicity of sentiment, feeling for nature, directness of communication, and spontaneous melody.

Sah ein Knab' ein Röslein stehn,	A boy saw a rosebud,
Röslein auf der Heiden,	Rosebud on the heather,
war so jung und morgenschön,	Young and fresh in morning light,
lief er schnell, es nah' zu sehn,	He ran to see her closely,
sah's mit vielen Freuden.	Gazed upon her with delight.
Röslein, Röslein, Röslein rot,	Rosebud, roscbud, rosebud red,
Röslein auf der Heiden.	Rosebud on the heather.
Knabe sprach: ich breche dich,	Said the boy: "I'll pluck you,
Röslein auf der Heiden!	Rosebud on the heather!"
Röslein sprach: ich steche dich,	Said the rose: "I'll scratch you,
dass du ewig denkst an mich,	You will long remember me
und ich will's nicht leiden.	When I show my anger!"
Röslein, Röslein, Röslein rot,	Rosebud, rosebud, rosebud red,
Röslein auf der Heiden.	Rosebud on the heather.
Und der wilde Knabe brach	And the cruel boy plucked the rose,
's Röslein auf der Heiden;	Rosebud on the heather;
Röslein wehrte sich und stach,	She defended herself and pricked him,
half ihm doch kein Weh und Ach,	In vain, alas, her pain and grief,
musst' es eben leiden.	She had to yield and suffer.
Röslein, Röslein, Röslein rot,	Rosebud, rosebud, rosebud red,
Röslein auf der Heiden.	Rosebud on the heather.

The mood is indicated by the marking *lieblich* (graceful). The accompaniment is of the simplest. The charming nonsymmetry of Goethe's seven-line

stanza is reflected in the music. The first two lines comprise one phrase, the next three another, while the last two serve as a refrain that is echoed by the piano in a little postlude after each stanza. The melody line is narrow in range, moves mostly by step or with narrow leaps, and has a lilt to it. Delightful is the ascent along the scale to the climactic high note in the line, "Röslein, Röslein, Röslein rot", followed by a graceful descent.

This type of Schubert song occupies a position in Germany similar to that of Stephen Foster's melodies with us. As one critic well put it, "Schubert does not try to imitate folk song. He creates it."

Impromptu in A-Flat

A publisher of Vienna hit on the title "Impromptu," the French word for "on the spur of the moment." The name accorded with the romantic notion that music came in a flash of inspiration. The Impromptu in A-flat, Opus 90, No. 4, one of Schubert's most widely played piano pieces, was written in 1827. It is an A-B-A form, with each section subdividing into symmetrical smaller sections. The piece is an Allegretto in ¾ time. The principal idea involves arpeggios that sweep down gently in a broad arc, beneath which an

upward-thrusting melody presently emerges in the bass. The middle part presents an effective contrast to the opening sections. A somber melody, consisting of sustained legato tones, is heard over an accompaniment of repeated chords. Tension builds in a steady line to a fortissimo climax; the emotion is direct, concentrated, inescapable. Then the first section is repeated, rounding off the form.

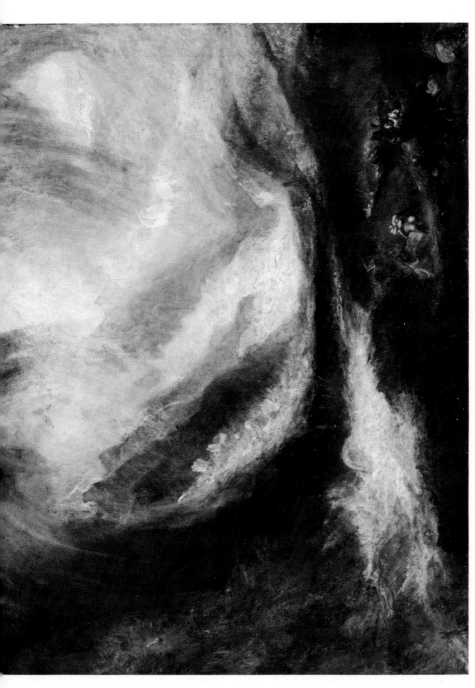

J.M.W. Turner (1775–1851), VALLEY OF AOSTA—SNOWSTORM, AVALANCHE AND THUNDERSTORM (The Art Institute of Chicago)

The romantics discovered nature, but nature as a backdrop for the inner conflicts of man.

Théodore Géricault (1791–1824), THE RAFT OF THE "MEDUSA" (The Louvre, Paris) Romanticism seized upon themes of passionate intensity.

Moment Musical in F Minor

In title, form, and substance the most famous of the "Musical Moments," Opus 94, No. 3 (c. 1825) epitomizes the short lyric piece. It is intimate and unassuming; one would almost say artless, were it not for the omnipresence of art.

The piece consists of brief symmetrical sections, each of them repeated. So small a frame does not allow for great contrasts. The mood of the opening prevails more or less throughout. Notice the grace notes that embellish the melody. (A *grace note* is a very short note having no time value of its own, which is interpolated as an ornament before a longer note. It is printed in small type.)

In this compact little work are manifest the qualities that set Schubert apart, in the eyes of his devotees, from all others: his charm of melody, his tenderness and an ineffably romantic longing that can only be described as Schubertian.

18 Robert Schumann

"Music is to me the perfect expression of the soul."

The turbulence of German romanticism, its fantasy and subjective emotion, found their voice in Robert Schumann. His music is German to the core, yet he is no local figure. A true lyric poet, he rose above the national to make his contribution to world culture.

His Life

Robert Schumann (1810–56) was born in Zwickau, a town in Saxony, son of a bookseller whose love of literature was reflected in the boy. At his mother's insistence he undertook the study of law, first at the University of Leipzig, then at Heidelberg. The youth daydreamed at the piano, steeped

Robert Schumann.

himself in Goethe and Byron, and attended an occasional lecture. His aversion to the law kept pace with his passion for music; it was his ambition to become a pianist. At last he won his mother's consent and returned to Leipzig to study with Friedrich Wieck, one of the foremost pedagogues of the day. "I am so fresh in soul and spirit," he exulted, "that life gushes and bubbles around me in a thousand springs."

The young man practiced intensively to make up for his late start. In his eagerness to perfect his technique he devised a contrivance that held the fourth finger immobile while the others exercised. The gadget was so effective that he permanently injured the fourth finger of his right hand. The end of his hopes as a pianist turned his interest to composing. In a burst of creative energy he produced, while still in his twenties, his most important works for the piano.

The spontaneity of his production astonished him. "Everything comes to me of itself," he wrote, "and indeed, it sometimes seems as if I could play on eternally and never come to an end." Such intensity—the prime quality of the lyricist—carried with it a premonition of early doom. "Oh I cannot help it, I should like to sing myself to death like a nightingale. . . ."

He was engaged concurrently in an important literary venture. With a group of like-minded enthusiasts he founded a journal named *The New Magazine for Music.* Schumann threw himself into his editorial activities as impetuously as he had into composing. Under his direction the periodical became one of the most important music journals in Europe. Schumann's critical essays revealed the composer as a gifted literary man. Cast in the form of prose poems, imaginary dialogues, or letters, they were as personal as his music. He fought the taste of the bourgeois—the Philistines, as he liked to call them—and agitated for the great works of the past as well as the new romanticism.

The hectic quality of this decade was intensified by his courtship of the gifted pianist Clara Wieck. When he first came to study with her father she was an eleven-year-old prodigy who lost her heart to the young man. She was about sixteen when Robert realized he loved her. Wieck's opposition to the marriage bordered on the psychopathic. Clara was the supreme achievement of his life and he refused to surrender her to another. For several years she was cruelly torn between the father she revered and the man she loved. At length, since she was not yet of age, the couple was forced to appeal to the courts against Wieck. The marriage took place in 1840, when Clara was twenty-one and Robert thirty. His happiness overflowed into a medium more personal even than the piano. This was his "year of song," when he produced over a hundred of the lieder that represent his lyric gift at its purest.

The two artists settled in Leipzig, pursuing their careers side by side. Clara became the first interpreter of Robert's piano works and in the ensuing decade contributed substantially to the spreading of his fame. Yet neither her love nor that of their children could ward off his increasing withdrawal from the world. Moodiness and nervous exhaustion culminated, in 1844, in a severe breakdown. The doctors counseled a change of scene. The couple moved to Dresden, where Schumann seemingly made a full recovery. But the periods of depression returned ever more frequently.

In 1850 Schumann was appointed music director at Düsseldorf. But he was ill-suited for public life; he could neither organize music festivals nor deal with masses of men, and was forced to relinquish the post. During a tour of Holland, where Clara and he were warmly received, he began to complain of "unnatural noises" in his head. His last letter to the violinist Joachim, two weeks before the final breakdown, is a farewell to his art. "The music is silent now . . . I will close. Already it grows dark."

He fell prey to auditory hallucinations. Once he rose in the middle of the night to write down a theme that he imagined had been brought him by the spirits of Schubert and Mendelssohn. It was his last melody. A week later, in a fit of melancholia, he threw himself into the Rhine. He was rescued by fishermen and placed in a private asylum near Bonn. Despite occasional flashes of lucidity, the darkness did not lift. He died two years later at the age of forty-six.

His Music

As a piano composer Schumann was one of the most original figures of the century. Whimsy and ardent expressiveness pervade his miniatures, which brim over with impassioned melody, novel harmonies, and vigorous rhythms. The titles of the collections strike the romantic note; among them we find *Fantasy Pieces, Papillons* (Butterflies), *Romances, Scenes from Childhood*. Among his large piano works are three sonatas, the Fantasy in C, the Symphonic Etudes, and the Piano Concerto in A minor.

As a composer of lieder he ranks second only to Schubert. His songs are finely wrought and rich in poetic suggestion. His favorite theme is love, particularly from the woman's point of view. His favored poet was Heine, for whom he had an affinity like that of Schubert for Goethe.

Thoroughly romantic in feeling are the four symphonies. Schumann has been taken to task for his inability to develop thematic material and for his occasional awkwardness in orchestration. Yet the best of his symphonies, the First and Fourth, communicate a lyric freshness that has kept them alive long after many more adroitly fashioned works have fallen by the way. What could be closer to the essence of German romanticism than the "nature sound" of the horns and trumpets at the opening of the *Spring Symphony*, his First? "Could you infuse into the orchestra," he wrote the conductor, "a kind of longing for spring? At the first entrance of the trumpets I should like them to sound as from on high, like a call to awakening."

Die beiden Grenadiere

Heinrich Heine's ballad, *The Two Grenadiers*, about two homecoming Napoleonic soldiers, furnished the text for Schumann's most celebrated song (1840).

Nach Frankreich zogen zwei Grenadier',
die waren in Russland gefangen,
Und als sie kamen in's deutsche Quartier,
sie liessen die Köpfe hangen.
Da hörten sie beide die traurige Mähr,
dass Frankreich verloren gegangen,
besiegt und geschlagen das tapfere Heer
und der Kaiser, der Kaiser gefangen!

Da weinten zusammen die Grenadier',
wohl ob der kläglichen Kunde.
Der Eine sprach: "Wie weh wird mir,
wie brennt meine alte Wunde!"
Der And're sprach: "Das Lied ist aus,
auch ich möcht' mit dir sterben,
doch hab' ich Weib und Kind zu Haus,
die ohne mich verderben."

"Was schert mich Weib, was schert mich
Kind,
ich trage weit bess'res Verlangen;
lass sie betteln geh'n wenn sie hungrig sind,
mein Kaiser, mein Kaiser gefangen!
Gewähr mir, Bruder, eine Bitt':
Wenn ich jetzt sterben werde,
so nimm meine Leiche nach Frankreich
mit,
begrab' mich in Frankreichs Erde.

Das Ehrenkreuz am rothen Band
sollst du auf's Herz mir legen;
die Flinte gieb mir in die Hand,

Two soldiers returned at last to France,
Set free from their prison in Russia;
When they reached the German frontier
They lowered their heads in anguish.
For there they heard the sad news
That France in disgrace had retreated,
Her army in ruins, her power destroyed,
And the Emperor, the Emperor captured!

Then tears filled the eyes of the grenadiers,
Oppressed with grief at these tidings.
The older said, "All hope is gone!
My wounds ache and burn in torment!"
The other said, "The end has come!
My life has lost its meaning.
But I've a wife and child at home
Who need me to protect them!"

"What care I for wife, what care I for
child?
My heart feels a grander emotion!
Let them go and beg if they wish to eat—
My Emperor, my Emperor's defeated!
Oh brother, grant me one request;
I feel my end approaching;
Oh promise you'll carry my body to
France,
And lay me to rest in my homeland.

The cross of honor that I won—
Lay it upon my bosom;
You'll place my musket in my hand,

und gürt mir um den Degen.	And set my sword beside me.

und gürt mir um den Degen.
So will ich liegen und horchen still,
wie eine Schildwach', im Grabe,
bis einst ich höre Kanonengebrüll
und wiehernder Rosse Getrabe.

Dann reitet mein Kaiser wohl über mein
Grab,
viel' Schwerter klirren und blitzen,
dann steig' ich gewaffnet hervor aus dem
Grab,
den Kaiser, den Kaiser zu schützen!"

And set my sword beside me.
And so I'll lie in my grave at rest,
Like a sentry waiting and watchful,
Until I wake to the clangor of guns,
The thunder of hoofbeats in battle.

Oh, see how my Emperor rides over my
grave,
While swords shine bright in the sunlight,
Then armed like a warrior I'll rise from the
grave
To protect my Emperor forever!"

The song is an example of the dramatic ballad that is through-composed. A martial figure in the piano part, in ⁴⁄₄ time, immediately sets the mood. The short introduction has the dotted rhythm that Schumann loved. The little motive of sixteenth notes at its end is heard again and again throughout the

song. There is a slackening of intensity as the soldiers learn the sorrowful news. Their mounting agitation is reflected in an acceleration of pace. The request of the first grenadier—that he be buried in his homeland—steadily builds up tension through triplet rhythm in the accompaniment, followed by syncopated chords. The climax is very grand: as the soldier pictures himself in the grave, the vocal line rises to the strains of the French national anthem, the *Marseillaise*. It is one of those exciting effects that never fail. In the final measures Schumann repeats the line about the flashing swords—the only repetition of text in the whole song—to allow for the necessary musical expansion. A postlude of sustained chords in the piano part adds a thoughtful commentary.

Ich grolle nicht

The introspective side of Schumann's lyricism predominates in what is probably his most powerful love song. Heine's lines fired the composer to a lied of brooding intensity.

Ich grolle nicht,	I'll not complain,
und wenn das Herz auch bricht,	Even though my heart will break,
Ewig verlornes Lieb! ich grolle nicht.	Love forever lost, I'll not complain.
Wie du auch strahlst in Diamantenpracht,	You gleam in jeweled splendor bright,
Es fällt kein Strahl in deines Herzens- nacht.	No ray falls into your heart's unending night,
Das weiss ich längst.	This I know well.
Ich grolle nicht,	I'll not complain,
und wenn das Herz auch bricht.	Even though my heart will break.
Ich sah dich ja im Traume,	I saw you in my dream,
und sah die Nacht in deines Herzens Raume,	And saw the night within your heart's domain
und sah die Schlang', die dir am Herzen frisst,	And saw the snake that eats at your heart,
Ich sah, mein Lieb, wie sehr du elend bist.	I saw, my love, how all alone you are.
Ich grolle nicht, ich grolle nicht.	I'll not complain, I'll not complain.

Schumann here achieves the supreme aim of the romantic lied—to give utterance to a state of soul. The soaring melody becomes a kind of graph that follows sensitively the rise and fall of emotion. Sustained dissonances in the accompaniment build harmonic and psychological tension. The song falls into two halves, both of which begin identically.

Ich grolle nicht stands between the strophic song and the through-composed type. Schumann repeats material from the first half of the song in the second, and also introduces new material that builds up relentlessly to the tragic chords of the climax: "And saw the snake that eats at your heart . . ."

This song—both words and music—is a perfect embodiment of the romantic spirit.

Aufschwung and Romance in F-Sharp

Schumann's piano pieces exhibit his mastery of the miniature. Within the pattern of statement-departure-return (A-B-A) he found an ideal frame for what he had to say.

Aufschwung (Soaring) is the second of the *Phantasiestücke*, Opus 12 (Fantasy Pieces, 1837). Bold rhythmic patterns and a flow of melodic ideas made this piece precisely what its name implies: a soaring, an upsurge of spirit. The meter is ⁶⁄₈, the tempo lively. The mood is fiery, as indicated by Schumann's marking *Sehr rasch* (very spirited).

The impetuous main idea recurs in contrast with subsidiary sections more quiet in nature, producing the structural pattern A-B-A-C-A-B-A. This arresting miniature embodies the spirit of the dance, and it also shows off Schumann's individual manner of writing for the instrument.

The Romance in F-sharp, Opus 28, No. 2 (1839), is a "lied" for piano. Schumann's lyricism takes shape in a flowing melody that moves either stepwise along the scale or with narrow leaps against a background of broken chords. The mood is tender, the harmonies expressive. Schumann directs that this piece be played *einfach* (simply).

After a somewhat agitated middle section the serene melody returns. At one point right and left hand engage in a gentle dialogue, the one imitating the other. This interweaving of independent lines enriched the texture of Schumann's piano music and influenced a number of later composers. Wholly Schumannesque is the spinning out of the melody in broad sinuous curves, and the sense of incompletion at the end, where the music trails off into silence.

The listener is left suspended in a dream, as it were—an effect much prized by the romantic composers.

"Music still devours me. I must often tear myself from it by violence." This remark indicates the passionate creativity of the decade and a half in which Schumann was at his peak. His peak was the spring tide of German romanticism, during which he nobly discharged what he conceived to be the artist's mission: "To send light into the depths of the human heart!"

19 Frédéric François Chopin

"My life . . . an episode without a beginning and with a sad end."

In the annals of his century Chopin (1810–49) is known as the "Poet of the Piano." The title is a valid one. His art, issuing from the heart of romanticism, constitutes the golden age of that instrument.

His Life

The national composer of Poland was half French. His father emigrated to Warsaw, where he married a lady-in-waiting to a countess and taught French to the sons of the nobility. Frédéric, who displayed his musical gifts in childhood, was educated at the recently founded Conservatory of Warsaw. His student years were climaxed by a mild infatuation with a young singer, Constantia Gladkowska, who inspired him with sighs and tears in the best nineteenth-century manner. "It was with thoughts of this beautiful creature that I composed the Adagio of my new concerto." The concerto was the one in F minor. Frédéric was nineteen.

After a concert at which Constantia sang and he played, the young artist set forth to make a name in the world. His comrades sang a farewell cantata in his honor. Frédéric wept, convinced he would never see his homeland again. In Vienna the news reached him that Warsaw had risen in revolt against the Tsar. Gloomy visions tormented him; he saw his family and friends massacred. He left Vienna in the summer. On reaching Stuttgart he learned that the Polish capital had been captured by the Russians. The tidings precipitated a torrent of grief, and the flaming defiance that found expression in the *Revolutionary Etude.*

In September, 1831, the young man reached Paris. He thought of continuing to London, even to America. But he was introduced by his countryman, Prince

Frédéric Chopin. Painting by Eugène Delacroix. (Louvre, Paris)

Radziwill, into the aristocratic salons and there created a sensation. His decision was made, and the rest of his career was linked to the artistic life of his adopted city. Paris in the 1830s was the center of the new romanticism. The circle in which Chopin moved included as brilliant a galaxy of artists as ever gathered anywhere. Among the musicians were Liszt and Berlioz, Rossini and Meyerbeer. The literary figures included Victor Hugo and Balzac, Lamartine, George Sand, de Musset, Alexandre Dumas. Heinrich Heine was his friend, as was the painter Delacroix. Although Chopin was a man of emotions rather than ideas, he could not but be stimulated by his contact with the leading intellectuals of France.

Through Liszt he met Mme. Aurore Dudevant, "the lady with the somber eye," known to the world as the novelist George Sand. She was thirty-four, Chopin twenty-eight when the famous friendship began. Mme. Sand was brilliant and domineering; her need to dominate found its counterpart in Chopin's need to be ruled. She left a memorable account of this fastidious artist at work: "His creative power was spontaneous, miraculous. It came to him without effort or warning . . . But then began the most heartrending labor I have ever witnessed. It was a series of attempts, of fits of irresolution and impatience to recover certain details. He would shut himself in his room for days, pacing up and down, breaking his pens, repeating and modifying one bar a hundred times . . . He would spend six weeks over a page, only to end by writing it out finally just as he had sketched it in the original draft."

For the next eight years Chopin spent his summers at Mme. Sand's chateau at Nohant, where she entertained the cream of France's intelligentsia. These were productive years for him, although his health grew progressively worse and his relationship with Mme. Sand ran its course from love to conflict, from jealousy to hostility. They parted in bitterness.

According to his friend Liszt, "Chopin felt and often repeated that in breaking this long affection, this powerful bond, he had broken his life." Chopin's creative energy, which had lost its momentum in his middle thirties, came to an end. The "illness of the century," the lonely despair of the romantic artist pervades his last letters. "What has become of my art?" he writes during a visit to Scotland. "And my heart, where have I wasted it? I scarce remember any more how they sing at home. That world slips away from me somehow. I forget. I have no strength. If I rise a little I fall again, lower than ever."

He returned to Paris suffering from tuberculosis and died some months later, at the age of thirty-nine. His funeral was his greatest triumph. Princesses and artists joined to pay him homage. Meyerbeer, Berlioz, and Delacroix were among the mourners. George Sand stayed away. His heart was returned to Poland, the rest of him remained in Paris. And on his grave a friendly hand scattered a gobletful of Polish earth.

His Music

Chopin was one of the most original artists of the romantic era. His idiom is so entirely his own there is no mistaking it for any other. He was the only master of first rank whose creative life centered about the piano. From the first, his imagination was wedded to the keyboard, to create a universe within that narrow frame. His genius transformed even the limitations of the instrument into sources of beauty. (The prime limitation, of course, is the piano's inability to sustain tone for any length of time.) Chopin overcame these with such ingenuity that to him as much as to any individual is due the modern piano style. The widely spaced chords in the bass, sustained by pedal, set up masses of tone that wreathe the melody in enchantment. "Everything must be made to sing," he told his pupils. The delicate ornaments in his music—trills, grace notes, runs of gossamer lightness—seem magically to prolong the single tones. And all this generally lies so well for the hand that the music seems almost to play itself.

It is remarkable that so many of his works have remained in the pianist's repertory. His Nocturnes—night songs, as the name implies—are tender avowals tinged with varying shades of melancholy. They are usually in three-part form. The Preludes are visionary fragments; some are only a page in length, several consist of two or three lines. The Etudes crown the literature of the study piece (a composition that concentrates on a specific technical problem such as octaves, rapid arpeggios, or trills). Here piano technique is transformed into poetry. The Impromptus are fanciful, capricious, yet they have a curious rightness about them. The Waltzes capture the brilliance and coquetry of the salon. They are veritable dances of the spirit. The Mazurkas, derived from a Polish peasant dance, evoke the idealized landscape of his youth.

Among the larger forms are the four Ballades. These are epic poems of spacious structure, like sagas related by a bard. The Polonaises revive the stately processional dance in which Poland's nobles were wont to hail their kings. Heroic in tone, they resound with the clangor of battle and brave deeds. In reminding his countrymen of their ancient glory the national poet strengthens their will to freedom. The *Berceuse* (Cradle Song), the *Barcarolle* (Boat Song), the Fantasy in F minor, and the dramatic Scherzos reveal the composer at the summit of his art. The Sonatas in B minor and B-flat minor are thoroughly romantic in spirit, as are the piano concertos in E minor and F minor.

Chopin's style stands before us fully formed when he was twenty. It was not the result of an extended intellectual development, as was the case with masters like Beethoven or Wagner. In this he was the true lyricist, along with his contemporaries Schumann and Mendelssohn. All three died young, and all three reached their peak through the spontaneous lyricism of youth. In them the first period of romanticism found its finest expression.

Mazurka in B-Flat Major

The Mazurka in B-flat major, Opus 7, No. 1 (1832) exemplifies Chopin's handling of the lively dance-rhythms of his native land. The spirited melody unfolds above a simple chord accompaniment in the left hand, propelled by its own momentum. The ascending curve of the melody in the first three measures is subtly balanced by the downward leaps in the next three:

Characteristic of Chopin are the embellishments—the trill in measure 3 and the grace notes in the following measures. The form is easy to follow: the opening statement alternates with contrasting material, with the sections repeated in the pattern A-A, B-A-B-A, C-A-C-A. Chopin uses dynamics to underline the contrasts; the second melody is piano, the third pianissimo, while the first is always forte. Notice the momentary change to a darker mood in the third section, as well as the charm and grace of the whole.

87

Etude in E Major

A specific problem in pianoforte technique, the execution of double notes (two notes simultaneously) serves as the basis for the celebrated Etude in E major, Opus 10, No. 3 (c. 1830). The third, fourth, and fifth fingers of the right hand play one of Chopin's most lyrical melodies while the first and second fingers join the left hand in the accompaniment.

The middle section culminates in a brilliant passage of double notes based on extended broken chords that are the despair of pianists with small hands. When the excitement simmers down the first section returns, but in shortened form. A subtle effect, this. The composer implies that since we already know the material it suffices to touch upon it rather than restate it in its entirety.

Prelude in E Minor

The Prelude in E minor, Opus 28, No. 4 (1839) reveals Chopin's uncanny power to achieve the utmost expressiveness with the simplest means. The melody hardly moves, unfolding in sustained tones over a succession of chords that change very subtly, usually one note at a time:

The music strikes a gently mournful mood that is of the essence of romanticism. Tension gathers slowly; there is something inevitable about the rise to the climax, where the melody, advancing in bold leaps, takes on the character of a passionate outcry that subsides to a sorrowful pianissimo ending. Rarely has so much been said in a single page. Schumann did not exaggerate when he said of the Preludes, "In each piece we find in his own hand, 'Frédéric Chopin wrote it!' He is the boldest, the proudest poet of his time."

Polonaise in A-Flat

The heroic side of Chopin's art shows itself in the most popular of his Polonaises, the one in A-flat, Opus 53 (1842). The opening theme is

proud and chivalric. The octaves for the left hand in the following section approach the limits of what the piano can do. The emotional temperature drops perceptibly after the octave episode, which is Chopin's way of building up tension against the return of the theme. In the hands of a virtuoso this Polonaise takes on surpassing brilliance; it is the epitome of the grand style.

His countrymen have enshrined Chopin as the national composer of Poland. Withal he is a spokesman of European culture. It is not without significance that despite his homesickness he spent the whole of his adult life in Paris. Thus Poland was idealized in his imagination as the symbol of that unappeasable longing which every romantic artist carries in his heart: the longing for the lost land of happiness that may never be found again. Heine, himself an expatriate, divined this when he wrote that Chopin is "neither a Pole, a Frenchman, nor a German. He reveals a higher origin. He comes from the land of Mozart, Raphael, Goethe. His true country is the land of poetry."

20 Other Song Composers

"Life wherever it shows itself, *truth* no matter how bitter—to speak out boldly to people, sincerely, point-blank—this is what excites me, this is what I want!"   Modest Musorgsky

Berlioz: *Absence*

The cult of romantic song was not limited to the German countries; it attracted composers throughout Europe. Among them was the great French composer Hector Berlioz (1803–69). His song cycle *Nuits d'été* (Summer Nights, 1834–41) consists of six settings of poems by his friend Théophile Gautier. The fourth number of the set is the celebrated *Absence*.

Reviens, reviens, ma bien aimée;
  Comme une fleur loin du soleil,
La fleur de ma vie est fermée
  Loin de ton sourire vermeil.
	Return, return, my well-beloved!
	  Like a flower far from the sun,
	The flower of my life is shut
	  Far from your bright smile, my love.

Entre nos coeurs quelle distance,
  Tant d'espace entre nos baisers!
Ô sort amer! Ô dure absence!
  Ô grands désirs inapaisés!
	Between our hearts, what distance!
	  Such space between our kisses!
	O bitter fate, O harsh absence!
	  O great desires unappeased!

Reviens, reviens, ma bien aimée;
  Comme une fleur loin du soleil,
La fleur de ma vie est fermée
  Loin de ton sourire vermeil.
	Return, return, my well-beloved!
	  Like a flower far from the sun,
	The flower of my life is shut
	  Far from your bright smile, my love.

D'ici là-bas, que de campagnes,
  Que de villes et de hameaux,
Que de vallons et de montagnes,
  A lasser le pied des chevaux!
	Between us so many lands,
	  So many cities and hamlets,
	So many valleys and mountains,
	  That would tire horses' hooves.

Reviens, reviens, ma bien aimée;
  Comme une fleur loin du soleil,
La fleur de ma vie est fermée
  Loin de ton sourire vermeil.
	Return, return, my well-beloved!
	  Like a flower far from the sun,
	The flower of my life is shut
	  Far from your bright smile, my love.

The melody unfolds in long flowing lines sensitively molded to the inflections of the French language. It passes from repeated notes and stepwise movement to effective leaps. How emotional is the upward skip in the opening phrase on the second "reviens":

The musical form follows the form of the poem. Since stanzas 1, 3, and 5 are the same, Berlioz uses the same melody for those, with contrasting material for stanzas 2 and 4.

The cycle was first written for voice and piano, but Berlioz subsequently orchestrated the accompaniment. *Absence* shows the transparancy of his orchestral palette. Equally compelling is the poetic atmosphere that pervades the song from beginning to end.

Grieg: *Ein Traum*

Edvard Grieg (1843–1907) was a widely loved composer whose art was nourished by the folk songs and dances of his native Norway. Yet he was deeply influenced by German musical culture—he received his training in Leipzig. His famous song *Ein Traum* (A Dream, 1889), stands in the tradition of the romantic lied. The text is by the German lyric poet Friedrich von Bodenstedt.

Mir träumte einst ein schöner Traum;	One day I had a lovely dream;
mich liebte eine blonde Maid.	A maiden fair in love with me.
es war am grünen Waldesraum,	It was in the verdant forest glen,
es war zur warmen Frühlingszeit:	It was in the warm springtime:

die Knospe sprang, der Waldbach schwoll,	The buds bloomed, the brook overflowed,
fern aus dem Dorfe scholl Geläut'—	The distant village bells were ringing—
wir waren ganzer Wonne voll,	We were filled with wonder,
versunken ganz in Seligkeit.	We were lost in bliss.

Und schöner noch, als einst der Traum,	And even more beautiful than the dream
begab es sich in Wirklichkeit:	Was the reality:
es war am grünen Waldesraum,	It was in the verdant forest glen,
es war zur warmen Frühlingszeit.	It was in the warm springtime.

der Waldbach schwoll, die Knospe sprang,	The brook overflowed, the buds bloomed,
Geläut' erscholl vom Dorfe her:	Bells rang from the village there:
Ich hielt dich fest, ich hielt dich lang—	I held you close, I held you long—
und lasse dich nun nimmermehr!	And I shall leave you nevermore!
nimmermehr! nimmermehr!	Nevermore! Nevermore!

O frühlingsgrüner Waldesraum,	O forest glen green with spring,
du lebst in mir durch alle Zeit!	You will live within me forever!
Dort ward die Wirklichkeit zum Traum,	There reality became a dream,
dort ward der Traum zur Wirklichkeit!	There the dream became reality!

After one bar of introduction, the melody emerges against a flowing accompaniment in triplet rhythm. Notice, in the first phrase of the vocal line, how the repeated notes prepare for an expressive upward leap in the second and fourth measures:

The music of the first stanza is repeated for the second. The middle section of the song (stanzas 3 and 4) begins pianissimo and dolce (sweetly). At the fifth stanza the piano part takes over chords in both hands in triplet rhythm; this is a tension-building device. The music grows faster, louder, higher in pitch. The repetition of "nimmermehr!" (nevermore) introduces the impassioned climax of the song; the opening melody is heard again, but forte and agitato. Its high point, fortissimo, comes on the last and most important word, "Wirklichkeit!" (reality), which is followed by a brief postlude on the piano.

Musorgsky: *Field-Marshal Death*

Modest Musorgsky (1839–81), one of the most original artists of his century—we shall discuss his opera *Boris Godunov* in a later chapter—brought to his songs a fresh and powerful imagination. He had an uncanny ability to make his vocal line reflect the meaning of a poetic text, so that the

91

melody became a heightened form of speech. The cycle *Songs and Dances of Death* (1875–77) contains four of his finest songs. In the last, Death, in the character of a Field Marshal, surveys the bloody field on which lie both victors and vanquished, and exults in the fact that no matter which side wins, he alone is the victor!

Grokhochet bitva, bleshchut broni,	The battle is raging, the armor glitters,
Orud'ya mednyye revut,	The copper guns thunder out.
Begut polki, nesutsya koni	The regiments go forth and horses gallop,
I reki krasnyye tekut.	And red streams pour forth.
Pylayet polden', lyudi b'yutsya!	In the heat of midday, people meander.
Sklonilos' solntze, boĭ sil'neĭ!	At sunset the battle expands!
Zakat bledneyet, no derutsya	The sunset makes it hard to see,
Vragi vsio yarostneĭ i zleĭ!	But the armies fight still more fiercely.
I pala noch' na pole brani.	And night falls on the field of battle.
Druzhiny v mrake razoshlis' . . .	The armies separate in the darkness.
Vsio stikhlo i v nochnom tumane	All grows quiet, and in the night fog
Stenan'ya k nebu podnyalis'.	Moans ascend toward heaven.
Togda ozarena lunoyu,	Then, illuminated by moonlight,
Na boyevom svoiom kone,	Death quietly appears
Kosteĭ sverkaya beliznoyu,	On his bellicose horse,
Yavilas' smert' i v tishine,	Flashing his white bones,
Vnimaya vopli i molitvy	And, listening to wailing and praying,
Dovol'stva gordovo polna,	Is filled with pride and satisfaction
Kak polkovodetz, mesto bitvy	Like a commander on the battlefield.
Krugom ob'yekhala ona.	He rides to the top of the hill
Na kholm podnyavshis' oglyanulas',	And looks around and smiles.
Ostanovilas', ulybnylas',	And over the battlefield
I nad ravninoĭ boyevoĭ	The voice of fate resounds:
Razdalsya golos rokovoĭ:	"The battle is over.
"Konchena bitva! Ya vsekh pobedila!	I have defeated everyone.
Vse predo mnoĭ vy smirilis' boĭtzy!	You are all humbled before me.
Zhizn' vas possorila, ya pomirila,	Life made enemies of you. I united you.
Druzhno vstavaĭte na smotr, mertvetzy!	Now, dead ones, rise for the review.
Marshem torzhestvennym mimo proĭdite,	March past solemnly
Voĭsko moye ya khochu soschitat'.	So I can count my army.
V zemlyu potom, svoi kosti slozhite,	Then place your bones into the ground
Sladko ot zhizni v zemle otdykhat'!	To take a rest from life in peace!
Gody nezrimo proĭdut za godami,	Years will pass by unnoticeably.
V lyudyakh ischeznet i pamyat' o vas.	People on earth will forget all about you.
Ya ne zabudu! I gromko nad vami	But I will not forget! I will celebrate
Pir budu pravit' v polunochnyĭ chas!	Your death during the midnight hours.
Plyaskoĭ, tyazholoyu, zemlyu syruyu	With heavy dance steps, I will stamp
Ya pritopchu, chtoby sen' grobovuyu	The damp ground so that your bones
Kosti pokinut' vo vek ne mogli,	Can never leave your graves,
Chtob nikogda vam ne vstat' iz zemli!"	So that you will never rise from the ground."

Rumbling scales deep in the bass, fortissimo, suggest the fury of the battle. The tempo is Vivo, alla guerra (lively, warlike); the music unfolds in precipitous triplets in 4/4. (The same triplet pattern was used in Schubert's *Erlkönig* to suggest agitation and suspense.)

Clashing dissonances, strongly accented, underline the mood, which persists throughout the first stanza.

Introducing the second stanza, a diminuendo and ritardando suggest the end of the battle and the silence of the night; the tempo now is moderato. The emotional temperature rises; eerie chords in the bass, in a jagged rhythm, evoke the figure of Death. The third stanza, marked Andantino, opens with a memorable passage in which the vocal melody repeats the same note while the harmonies change underneath. The scene is set for the speech of the grim conqueror.

Death's utterance is marked Tempo di marcia, grave, pomposo (in march time, solemn, pompous). The music suggests a majestic processional as Death exhorts the corpses to rise up and pass before him (stanza 4). Tension builds steadily to the emotional climax of the song—the final lines, beginning with "But I will not forget!" The processional music reappears, macabre and solemn, against the moving harmonies that propel the melody to its final cadence.

This is one of the great songs of the century.

Brahms: *Die Mainacht*

From Schubert and Schumann the leadership in the realm of the art song passed to Johannes Brahms (1833–97). He handled the short form with consummate ease and craftsmanship, bringing to his songs an inwardness of feeling and a manly, restrained fervor. The sensitiveness of the vocal line is matched by the eloquence of the accompaniment. Through his finest songs sounds the note of autumnal resignation that is so characteristic of this composer.

His setting of *Die Mainacht* (May Night, a poem by Ludwig Hölty, 1868), well exemplifies these qualities.

Wann der silberne Mond	When the silvery moon
durch die Gesträuche blinkt,	shines through the rustling leaves,
und sein schlummerndes Licht	And her pale languid light
über den Rasen streut,	pours over the meadow;
und die Nachtigall flötet,	When the nightingale warbles,
wandl' ich traurig von Busch zu Busch.	I wander sadly from glade to glade.
Überhüllet vom Laub,	Hidden in the leaves
girret ein Taubenpaar	I hear a pair of doves
sein Entzücken mir vor;	Murmur in ecstasy.
aber ich wende mich,	I turn away,
suche dunklere Schatten,	Seeking darker shadows,
und die einsame Träne rinnt.	And a lonely tear wells up.
Wann, o lächelndes Bild,	When, O smiling vision
welches wie Morgenrot	that streams through my soul
durch die Seele mir strahlt,	Like the flush of dawn,
find' ich auf Erden dich?	When on earth shall I find thee?
Und die einsame Träne	And the lonely tear
bebt mir heisser die Wang' herab.	Presses hotter upon my cheek.

The melody, marked *Sehr langsam und ausdrucksvoll* (very slow and expressive), begins by outlining the tones of the Tonic chord, a characteristic procedure with Brahms. No less characteristic is the rich texture of the harmony, the accompaniment intertwining with the vocal line yet remaining independent of it. There is a nice balance in the melody between stepwise movement and narrow leaps, resulting in a broadly flowing line:

The mood changes with the second stanza. The mention of doves sends a tenderness through the music; the accompaniment shifts to the treble register. Repeated chords in the left-hand part build up tension against the line "I turn away, seeking darker shadows. . . ." A wide and tragic downward leap marks the words "turn away." The emotional climax comes in the next phrase, with a long sustained note and a spinning out of the melody on the decisive word "tear."

At the third stanza we return to the melody of the first, with a resultant A-B-A form. The last line about the tear evokes the same music that was associated with this thought in the second stanza, and serves to round off the song.

The accompaniment is now presented in triplet rhythm, as an element of intensification. In conjunction with the melody line it produces the effect of cross rhythm (three against two) of which Brahms was so fond.

Brahms: *Vergebliches Ständchen*

Another side of Brahms's personality—extrovert, robust, and delighting in broad humor—is to be observed in the *Vergebliches Ständchen* (Futile Serenade, 1881). It is his version of a lusty folk song from the Lower Rhineland.

Er: Guten Abend, mein Schatz,
  guten Abend, mein Kind,
  guten Abend, mein Kind!
Ich komm' aus Lieb' zu dir,
ach, mach' mir auf die Tür,
mach' mir auf die Tür,
  mach' mir auf, mach' mir auf,
  mach' mir auf die Tür!

He: Good evening, my darling,
  Good evening, my sweet,
  Good evening, my sweet!
I come for love of you,
Open the door for me,
Open the door for me,
  Let me in, let me in,
  Open up the door!

Sie: Mein' Tür ist verschlossen,
  ich lass' dich nicht ein,
  ich lass' dich nicht ein;
Mutter, die rät mir klug,
wär'st du herein mit Fug,
wär's mit mir vorbei,
  wär's mit mir, wär's mit mir,
  wär's mit mir vorbei!

She: My door's firmly locked,
  I shan't let you in,
  I shan't let you in!
I heard my mother say,
That if you had your way
I would rue the day,
  Rue the day, rue the day,
  I would rue the day!

Er: So kalt ist die Nacht,
  so eisig der Wind,
  so eisig der Wind;
Dass mir das Herz erfriert,
mein' Lieb' erlöschen wird,
öffne mir, mein Kind,
  öffne mir, öffne mir,
  öffne mir, mein Kind!

He: The night is so cold,
  So icy the wind,
  So icy the wind!
My heart will be frozen through,
As will my love for you,
Let me in, my dear,
  Let me in, let me in,
  Let me in, my dear.

Sie: Löschet dein' Lieb',
  lass sie löschen nur,
  lass sie löschen nur!
Löschet sie immerzu,
geh' heim zu Bett, zur Ruh',
gute Nacht, mein Knab',
  gute Nacht, gute Nacht,
  gute Nacht, mein Knab'!

She: If your love flies away,
  Let it stray,
  Let it stray!
Let it stray, I said.
And so go home to bed.
Good night, my lad,
  Good night, good night,
  Good night, my lad!

The four stanzas call forth a modified strophic form. Following a short introduction, the melody outlines the common triads and moves in an animated ¾ time, achieving the simplicity and naturalness of the folk mood. The opening phrase contains the same little figure repeated three times, each time from a lower note. The melody is marked "lively and good-humored."

The relationship of folk song to the dance is underlined by the regularity of structure: four measures to the phrase, four phrases to the stanza. Yet Brahms introduces a charming asymmetry: the usual four-bar phrase is extended for two bars by repeating the words "mach' mir auf" (let me in). This extension is repeated in every stanza, the momentary waywardness setting off the symmetry of the rest.

Charming too is the sudden change of color at the third stanza. The melody takes on a plaintive tone as the lover beseeches: "The night is so cold, so icy the wind!" This is achieved by flatting certain tones (a change from major to minor—a procedure we will discuss in a later chapter). The light-fingered accompaniment, which grows more elaborate with each stanza, keeps the song moving and creates an admirable frame for the spirited dialogue. Here is the thoroughly German aspect of Brahms—the soil from which flowered the more cultivated blossoms of his art.

Wolf: *In dem Schatten meiner Locken*

In the generation after Brahms, the most distinguished figure in the domain of song was Hugo Wolf (1860–1903). "Poetry," he declared, "is the true source of my music." In little over two years he produced almost two hundred lieder, the bulk of his output, among them fifty-one settings of poems by Goethe.

Wolf's musical language is marked by subtle harmonies based on a free use of dissonance as the dynamic factor in musical expression. His songs are miniature dramas surcharged with feeling. *In dem Schatten meiner Locken* (In the shadow of my tresses) is one of forty-four settings (1889–90) that Wolf drew from the *Spanish Song Book*, a collection of poems translated into German by Paul Heyse and Emanuel Geibel.

In dem Schatten meiner Locken
   schlief mir mein Geliebter ein.
Weck' ich ihn nun auf?—Ach nein!
	In the shadow of my tresses
	   My beloved fell asleep.
	Shall I wake him now?—Oh, no!

Sorglich strählt ich mein krausen
   Locken täglich in der Frühe,
doch umsonst ist meine Mühe,
   weil die Winde sie zersausen.
Lockenschatten, Windessausen,
   schläferten den Liebsten ein.
Weck' ich ihn nun auf?—Ach nein!
	Carefully I comb my curly
	   Locks every morning,
	But my efforts are in vain
	   For the wind dishevels them.
	Shadowy tresses, wind-disheveled,
	   Soothed my love to sleep.
	Shall I wake him now?—Oh, no!

Hören muss ich, wie ihn gräme,
   dass er schmachtet schon so lange,
	I must hear how he grieves,
	   How his heart languishes for me,

dass ihm Leben geb' und nehme	How my glowing cheeks
diese meine braune Wange.	Give him life yet take it away.
Und er nennt mich seine Schlange,	And he calls me his serpent,
und doch schlief er bei mir ein.	Yet he sleeps by my side.
Weck' ich ihn nun auf?—Ach nein!	Shall I wake him now?—Oh, no!

Marked "light, delicate, not fast," the song opens with a graceful rhythmic figure in the piano part that gives the music a lilt:

The opening rhythm is repeated throughout. Indeed, the entire accompaniment is woven out of the material of the first measures, a circumstance that imparts to the song its extraordinary degree of unity. The music moves in a flowing manner that is admirably suited to the mood of tenderness projected by the words. Notice the downward inflection of the melody whenever the words "Ach nein" (Oh, no!) recur. Typical of Wolf is the close relationship between voice and the piano accompaniment; the two seem to be taking part in an intimate conversation. Thus the poem is lifted, by the power of a distinguished musical imagination, into the realm of the deeply felt, the inescapably romantic.

21 Other Piano Composers

"The musician who is inspired by nature exhales in tones nature's most tender secrets without copying it."   Franz Liszt

Liszt: *Sonetto 104 del Petrarca*

Franz Liszt (1811–86) stands alongside Chopin as one of the creators of modern piano technique. He exploited resources of the instrument —octaves, trills, rapid runs, arpeggios—with the utmost ingenuity; in his hands the piano became an orchestra capable of the most varied colors and sonorities.

Typical of Liszt's poetic lyricism is the piece, composed in 1848, that was inspired by the 104th Sonnet of Petrarch, in which the fourteenth-century Italian poet gave utterance to a lover's anguish:

> Warfare I cannot wage, yet know not peace;
> I fear, I hope, I burn, I freeze again;
> Mount to the skies, then bow to earth my face;
> Grasp the whole world, yet nothing can obtain . . .
>
> Death I despise, and life alike I hate:
> Such, lady, dost thou make my wayward state!

The piece opens Agitato assai with a series of sequences that leads into an Adagio marked molto espressivo (very expressively). Here is presented a heart-felt melody supported by arpeggios. In the answering phrase the melody is heard in the bass, played by the left hand while the right plays arpeggios above it. Now Liszt repeats the melody in high register against a running accompaniment in the bass; it is marked cantabile con passione (singing, with passion);

The music evokes the sighs and tears of Petrarch's sonnet. Technically the piece displays several of Liszt's favorite procedures, such as articulating a melody in the middle register while the left hand wreathes it in arpeggios both above and below (this involves "crossing the hands"). In a more elaborate version heard later on, the single notes in the melody are transformed into octaves, the arpeggios in the bass become a series of double notes, and the melody itself is embellished with rapid runs that envelop it in a magical mist. The music ends on a simple triad that is sustained until the sound dies away.

Liszt: Hungarian Rhapsody No. 12

In his Hungarian Rhapsodies Liszt combined romantic feeling and brilliant virtuoso writing for the piano with the passionate Gypsy melodies of his native land. Into these celebrated pieces he injected what he called "the fantastically epic element."

Liszt used the term *rhapsody* to indicate a composition rich in fantasy, free in form, of a heroic and national character. Liszt's rhapsodies parade a succession of song-and-dance tunes before us, in the nature of a medley. They generally begin with a slow section and work up gradually to a rapid and brilliant one. The Hungarian Rhapsody No. 12 (published first in 1854) is characteristic in this regard. Its introduction, marked Mesto (sad, mournful), reveals Liszt's orchestral approach to the piano. The opening measures might be intoned by the cellos, while the answering tremolos suggest a roll on kettledrums:

We hear a succession of typical Lisztian procedures: a melody in middle register wreathed in arpeggios below and above; vivid contrasts between low and high registers; dazzling virtuoso passages. The opening melody returns in a new garb, against full chords, and is heard a third time against rumbling scales in the bass. It is followed by an Allegro zingarese—that is, in Gypsy style. A charming little tune is repeated with more elaborate figuration, and a third time quasi campanelle (bell-like). After an expressive interlude the opening melody returns, embellished by tremolos in the right hand and octaves in the bass. The atmosphere becomes martial, heroic, until the music changes to an Allegretto giocoso (fairly fast, playful). A prolonged trill in high register introduces one of Liszt's most felicitous melodies, which is immediately presented in a new guise, dolce grazioso (sweet and graceful):

Notice here two characteristics of the Hungarian Gypsy style: the grace note, and the syncopated rhythm—an eighth note followed by an accented quarter— in measures 2 and 4.

An exciting Vivace accelerates steadily; it requires a bravura style of playing. Tension builds up relentlessly until the playful theme just quoted returns in a new form, *fff*, triumphal, against a thunderous accompaniment. An avalanche of octaves and chords brings the Rhapsody to its tumultuous end.

Brahms: Intermezzo in B-Flat Minor

In the second half of the century the piano achieved enormous popularity as a household instrument, its literature enriched by composers all over Europe. It was Brahms who did the most serious work in this area. Compositions for the piano extended through the whole of his career. His favorite form in his mature years was the short lyric in A-B-A pattern, which he called a capriccio when fast, an intermezzo when slow. He also wrote rhapsodies and ballades, these terms implying more extended flights of fancy.

The Intermezzo in B-flat minor, Opus 117, No. 2 (1892), is one of Brahms's late piano works. Couched in his characteristic vein of introspective lyricism, it has the manly tenderness, the tone of gentle contemplation that we associate with the German master. The piece is marked Andante non troppo e con molto espressione (not too slow and with much expression). Its melody traces a sinuous line—now falling, now rising only to fall again—above broken chords. Distributed between both hands, the arpeggio accompaniment maintains a steady flow of harmony above which the melody unfolds.

In evidence is the composer's fondness for middle and low register, and the subdued coloring that results therefrom; also the pungent harmonies enriched by dissonance. The serene middle part balances the expressiveness of the first and third sections. It is this quieter mood that returns at the end.

The song and piano piece have maintained their popularity to this day. These short forms filled an important need for intimate lyricism and spontaneous expression. They stand as one of the most attractive manifestations of the romantic style.

PROGRAM MUSIC

---

22 The Nature of Program Music

"... The renewal of music through its inner connection with poetry."
Franz Liszt

Program music is instrumental music endowed with literary or pictorial associations; the nature of these associations is indicated by the title of the piece or by an explanatory note—the "program"—supplied by the composer. Program music is distinguished from *absolute* or *pure* music, which consists of musical patterns devoid of literary or pictorial connotations.

Program music was of special importance in a period like the nineteenth century when musicians became sharply conscious of the connection between their art and the world about them. It helped them to bring music closer to poetry and painting, and to relate their work to the moral and political issues of their time. It also helped them to approach the forms of absolute music in a new way. All the same, the distinction between absolute and program music is not as rigid as many suppose. A work entitled Symphony No. 1 or Third String Quartet falls into the former category. Yet the composer in the course of writing it may very well have had in mind specific images and associations that he has not seen fit to divulge. Beethoven, whom we think of as the master of absolute music, confessed to a friend, "I have always a picture in my thoughts when I am composing, and work to it." Conversely, a piece called *Romeo and Juliet Overture* comes under the heading of program music. Yet if we were not told the title we would listen to it as a piece of absolute music. This is what we are apt to do in any case once we get to know the work. What concerns us ultimately is the destiny not of the lovers but of the themes.

Varieties of Program Music

THE CONCERT OVERTURE. A primary impulse toward program music derived from the opera house. The overture at that time was a rousing orchestral piece in one movement designed to serve as an introduction to an opera (or a play). Many operatic overtures achieved an independent popularity as concert pieces. This pointed the way to a new type of overture not associated with an opera: a single-movement concert piece for orchestra, based on a striking literary idea, such as Tchaikovsky's *Romeo and Juliet*. This type of composition might be descriptive, like Mendelssohn's seascape *Hebrides* (*Fingal's Cave*); or it could embody a patriotic idea, as does Tchaikovsky's *Overture 1812*.

The concert overture, despite its literary program, retained the design traditionally associated with the first movement of a symphony (what will be discussed in a later chapter as *sonata-allegro form*). This consists of three sections —the Exposition (or Statement), in which the themes are presented; the Development; and the Recapitulation (or Restatement). In other words, the concert overture retained a form associated with absolute music, but combined it with the poetic or pictorial ideas associated with program music. Thus, it offered composers a single-movement form of orchestral music which they were able to invest with the imagery of romantic story or scene.

INCIDENTAL MUSIC. An engaging species of program music is that written for plays, generally consisting of an overture and a series of numbers to be performed between the acts and during the important scenes. Nineteenth-century composers produced a number of works of this type that were notable for tone painting, characterization, and theater atmosphere.

The most successful numbers were generally arranged into suites, a number of which became vastly popular. Mendelssohn's music for A *Midsummer Night's Dream* is one of the most successful works in this category. Hardly less appealing are the two suites from Bizet's music for Alphonse Daudet's play *L'Arlésienne* (The Woman of Arles) and the two from Grieg's music for Henrik Ibsen's poetic drama *Peer Gynt*.

THE PROGRAM SYMPHONY. The impulse toward program music was so strong that it invaded even the hallowed form of absolute music—the symphony. Composers tried to retain the grand form of Beethoven and at the same time to associate it with a literary theme. Thus came into being the *program symphony*. The best known examples are three program symphonies of Berlioz—*Symphonie fantastique, Harold in Italy, Romeo and Juliet*—and two of Liszt, the *Faust* and *Dante* symphonies.

THE SYMPHONIC POEM. As the nineteenth century wore on, the need was felt more and more for a large form of orchestral music that would serve the romantic era as well as the symphony had served the classical. Toward the middle of the century the long-awaited step was taken with the creation of the symphonic poem. This was the nineteenth century's one original contribution to the large forms. It was the achievement of Franz Liszt, who first used the term in 1848. His *Les Préludes* is among the best known examples of this type of music.

A *symphonic poem* is a piece of program music for orchestra, in one movement, which in the course of contrasting sections develops a poetic idea, suggests a scene, or creates a mood. It differs from the concert overture in one important respect: whereas the concert overture generally retains one of the traditional classical designs, the symphonic poem is much freer in form. The name is used interchangeably with *tone poem*. The symphonic poem as cultivated by Liszt and his disciples was an immensely flexible form that permitted its course to be shaped by the literary idea. The programs were drawn from poets and painters dear to the romantic temperament: Shakespeare, Dante, Petrarch; Goethe and Schiller; Michelangelo and Raphael; Byron and Victor Hugo. A strong influence was the "return to nature" that had been advocated by Rousseau. The symphonic poem gave composers the canvas they needed for a big single-movement form. It became the most widely cultivated type of orchestral program music throughout the second half of the century.

The varieties of program music just described—concert overture, incidental music, program symphony, and symphonic poem—comprise one of the striking manifestations of nineteenth-century romanticism. This type of music emphasized the descriptive element; it impelled composers to try to express specific feelings; and it proclaimed the direct relationship of music to life.

23 Mendelssohn: A Midsummer Night's Dream

"People often complain that music is too ambiguous; that what they should think when they hear it is so unclear, whereas everyone understands words. With me it is exactly the opposite, and not only with regard to an entire speech but also with individual words. These too seem to me so ambiguous, so vague, so easily misunderstood in comparison to genuine music, which fills the soul with a thousand things better than words."

Felix Mendelssohn stands out in the roster of musicians for the fortunate circumstances that attended his career: he was born to wealth; he found personal happiness; and he was the idol of a vast public, not only in his German homeland, but also in England.

His Life

Felix Mendelssohn (1809–47) was the grandson of Moses Mendelssohn, the Jewish philosopher who expounded Plato to the eighteenth century. His father was an art-loving banker; his mother read Homer in the original. They joined the Protestant faith when Felix was still a child. The Mendelssohn home was a meeting place for the wit and intellect of Berlin. The garden house, seating several hundred guests, was the scene of memorable musicales where an orchestra under the boy's direction performed his numerous compositions. Here, when he was seventeen, his Overture to A *Midsummer Night's Dream* was presented to an enraptured audience.

The youth's education was thorough and well-rounded. He visited the venerable Goethe at Weimar and attended Hegel's lectures at the University of Berlin. He worshiped Bach, Mozart, and Beethoven. In 1829 the twenty-year-old enthusiast organized a performance of Bach's *St. Matthew Passion*, which had lain neglected since the death of its composer. The event proved to be a turning point in the nineteenth-century revival of that master.

Mendelssohn's misfortune was that he excelled in a number of roles—as pianist, conductor, organizer of musical events, and educator. For the last fifteen years of his life his composing was carried on amid the distractions of a public career that taxed his energies and caused his early death even as poverty and neglect might have done. At twenty-six he was conductor of the Gewandhaus Orchestra at Leipzig, which he transformed into the finest in Europe. He was summoned to Berlin by Frederick William IV to carry out that monarch's plans for an Academy of Music. Later he founded the Conservatory of Leipzig, which set higher standards for the training of musicians. He made ten visits to England, where his appearances elicited a frenzy of enthusiasm. All this in addition to directing one or another of the provincial festivals that formed the

Felix Mendelssohn.

backbone of musical life in Germany. Mendelssohn composed with a speed and facility that invite comparison with Mozart or Schubert, but he seldom allowed himself the inner repose that might have imparted to much of his music the profundity it lacks.

His last major composition, the oratorio *Elijah*, was produced in 1846 at the Birmingham Festival and "touched off the emotional spring of Victorian religious respectability as no other work had done." The following year he won fresh triumphs in England, appearing as pianist and conductor of his works. He returned to Germany in a state of nervous exhaustion. The happiness he found in the company of his wife and children was shattered by a severe blow—the death of his sister Fanny, to whom he was deeply attached. Six months later, at the age of thirty-eight, he succumbed to a stroke. Huge throngs followed his bier. Condolences came from all over Europe. A world figure had died.

His Music

Mendelssohn was dedicated to a mission: to preserve the tradition of the classical forms in an age that was turning from them. His fastidious craftsmanship links him to the great tradition. Serene and elegant expression was the characteristic trait of a mind as orderly as it was conservative. Mendelssohn represents the classicist trend within the romantic movement. But it should not be supposed that he was untouched by romanticism. In his early works he is the ardent poet of nature, a landscape painter of gossamer brush. Tenderness and manly fervor breathe from his music, and a gentle melancholy that is very much of the age.

Of his symphonies the best known are the Third, the *Scotch*, and the Fourth, the *Italian*—mementos of his youthful travels. Both works were begun in 1830, when he was twenty-one. His Fifth Symphony, the *Reformation*, also dates from his early twenties. The Concerto for Violin and Orchestra (1844) retains its position as one of the most popular ever written. The Octet for Strings, which he wrote when he was sixteen, is much admired, as are the *Songs Without Words* (1829–42), a collection of short piano pieces. Mendelssohn was a prolific writer for the voice. The oratorio *Elijah* represents the peak of his achievement in this category.

In England Mendelssohn was admired as no composer had been since Handel and Haydn. The first edition of Grove's Dictionary, the musical bible of the British, which appeared in 1880, devoted its longest article to him—sixty-eight pages. Bach received eight.

A *Midsummer Night's Dream*: Overture and Incidental Music

The Overture (1826) to Shakespeare's fairy play is in Mendelssohn's happiest vein. The mood of elfin enchantment that the seventeen-year-old composer here achieved was to return again and again in his later music, but nowhere more felicitously. Four prolonged chords in the woodwinds and horns open the portals to the realm of Oberon and Titania. The Exposition begins with the fairy music, which is introduced by the violins in high register, allegro di molto (very lively) and very softly. The dots over the notes indicate that they are to be played staccato (short and detached).

Allegro di molto

The fairy music is expanded. Presently the violins introduce, fortissimo, an energetic melody that serves as a bridge between the first and second theme:

The second theme evokes the young lovers in the play. It is a lyric idea, legato and flowing, presented expressively by the strings, and provides an effective contrast with the rhythmic theme of the opening:

The third idea is the boisterous dance of the clowns. Energetic rhythm and wide leaps set the character of this theme, which is presented by the violins against a background of wind tone. The last four notes (under the bracket) suggest the "Hee-haw" of a donkey, since in the play Puck's magic spell fastens an ass's head on Bottom the Weaver.

Now that the themes have been "exposed," there follows the middle section of the overture, the Development, which is an extended fantasy on the first theme. The composer gives free rein to his imagination in exploring a mood close to his heart; an atmosphere of mystery is sustained throughout. He changes the melody slightly; or presents it in a new light, developing it through imitation:

and through expansion:

When the development of the idea has run its course, the four mystic chords are heard again, introducing the Recapitulation, in which the material is restated more or less as we heard it before. A coda extends the donkey theme, and the piece ends on a note of gentle farewell. (A coda, you will recall, is a concluding section that rounds off a musical work and brings it to its appointed end.) This coda emphasizes the energetic theme that served as a bridge in the Exposition; finally the violins play it in a gentle pianissimo:

As the youthful composer explained, "After everything has been satisfactorily settled and the principal players have joyfully left the stage, the elves follow them, bless the house and disappear with the dawn. So ends the play, and my overture too."

In 1842 Frederick William IV of Prussia decided on a production of Shakespeare's comedy at the royal theater and suggested to Mendelssohn that he write incidental music for the play. The composer added twelve numbers for this occasion, in which he recaptured the spirit of the Overture he had written sixteen years before. Several of the pieces—the Scherzo, Nocturne, and Wedding March—have achieved worldwide popularity and are frequently performed together with the Overture as a suite.

The Scherzo serves to launch Act II. To Puck's query, "How now, spirit? Whither wander you?" the Elf makes his famous reply: "Over hill, over dale, thorough bush, thorough brier. . . ."

The *scherzo*—the Italian word meaning "jest," "joke"—as cultivated by Mendelssohn, was an instrumental piece compounded of elfin grace and humor. The Scherzo from *A Midsummer Night's Dream*, in ⅜ time, is an Allegro vivace. The first idea is a rhythmic pattern introduced by the woodwinds staccato and softly in the upper register.

A contrasting second theme is presented pianissimo, in a low register, by the strings. The two ideas alternate throughout the work. This Scherzo is remarkable for its continuity of fabric. Tension is sustained from first note to last. Characteristic is the pianissimo ending in which an agile run on the flute leads to a final statement of the first theme.

The Nocturne is played while the lovers, lost in the enchanted wood, sleep. Here Mendelssohn is the poet of nature. The beauty of the forest is evoked by the French horn in a serenely tender melody.

The play ends happily with the marriage of the Duke. A fanfare on the trumpets introduces the famous Wedding March. The movement is an Allegro vivace in 4/4 time, for the most part forte. The main theme (A) is in three-part form (a-b-a).

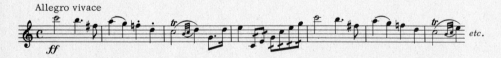

Two sections of quieter character supply the necessary contrast to the recurrent festive theme. The result is a well-rounded form—A (a:||:ba:|||)-B-A-C-A-Coda— with an abundance of melody right on to the ceremonious flourishes at the end.

Mendelssohn has always been extremely popular with the public. His elegant workmanship, melodious charm, and refinement of feeling are qualities that wear well.

108

Francisco Goya (1746–1828), EXECUTION OF THE RIOTERS, MAY 3, 1808
(The Prado, Madrid)

The greatest painter of the late eighteenth century stands outside the classical stream. His passionate realism anticipates a later age.

Eugène Delacroix (1798–1863), WOMEN OF ALGIERS IN THEIR APARTMENT
(The Louvre, Paris)

One of the most arresting offshoots of the romantic movement was the evocation of an exotic locale for the sake of picturesque effect.

Jacques Louis David (1748–1825), BONAPARTE CROSSING THE ALPS (Chateau, Malmaison)
The rise of nationalism is reflected in the heroic canvases of David.

24 Berlioz: *Symphonie fantastique*

"The prevailing characteristics of my music are passionate expression, intense ardor, rhythmic animation, and unexpected turns. To render my works properly requires a combination of extreme precision and irresistible verve, a regulated vehemence, a dreamy tenderness, and an almost morbid melancholy."

His Life

Hector Berlioz (1803–69) was born in France in a small town near Grenoble. His father, a well-to-do physician, expected him to follow in his footsteps, and at eighteen Hector was dispatched to the medical school in Paris. The Conservatory and the Opéra, however, exercised an infinitely greater attraction than the dissecting room. The following year the fiery youth made a decision that horrified his upper-middle-class family: he gave up medicine for music.

The romantic revolution was brewing in Paris. Berlioz, along with Victor Hugo and the painter Delacroix, found himself in the camp of "young France." Having been cut off by his parents, he gave lessons, sang in a theater chorus, and turned to various musical chores. He fell under the spell of Beethoven; hardly less powerful was the impact of Shakespeare, to whose art he was introduced by a visiting English troupe. For the actress whose Ophelia and Juliet excited the admiration of the Parisians, young Berlioz conceived an overwhelming passion. In his *Memoirs*, which read like a romantic novel, he describes his infatuation for Harriet Smithson: "I became obsessed by an intense, overpowering sense of sadness. I could not sleep, I could not work, and I spent my time wandering aimlessly about Paris and its environs."

In 1830 came the first official recognition of Berlioz's gifts. He was awarded the coveted Prix de Rome, which gave him a stipend and an opportunity to live and work in the Eternal City. That year also saw the composition of what has remained his most celebrated work, the *Symphonie fantastique*. Upon his return from Rome a hectic courtship of Miss Smithson ensued. There were strenuous objections on the part of both their families and violent scenes, during one of which the excitable Hector attempted suicide. He was revived. They were married.

Now that the unattainable ideal had become his wife, his ardor cooled. It was Shakespeare he had loved rather than Harriet, and in time he sought the ideal elsewhere. All the same, the first years of his marriage were the most fruitful of his life. By the time he was forty he had produced most of the works on which his fame rests.

Hector Berlioz.

To earn money he turned to music criticism, producing a stream of reviews and articles. His literary labors were a necessary part of his musical activity; he had to propagandize for his works and create an audience capable of understanding them. In the latter part of his life he conducted his music in all the capitals of Europe. But Paris resisted him to the end. Year after year he dissipated his energies in reviewing the works of nonentities while his own were neglected. Disgust and misanthropy settled upon him. His last major work was the opera *Béatrice et Bénédict*, on his own libretto after Shakespeare's *Much Ado About Nothing*. After this effort the flame was spent, and for the last seven years of his life the embittered master wrote no more. He died at sixty-six, tormented to the end. "Some day," wrote Richard Wagner, "a grateful France will raise a proud monument on his tomb." The prophecy has been fulfilled.

His Music

Berlioz was one of the boldest innovators of the nineteenth century. His approach to music was wholly original, his sense of sound unique. From the start he had an affinity—where orchestral music was concerned—for the vividly dramatic or pictorial program.

His works exemplify the favorite literary influences of the romantic period. The overtures *Waverley* (c. 1827) and *Rob Roy* (1832) were inspired by novels of Walter Scott, *The Damnation of Faust* (1846) by Goethe. *Harold in Italy*, a program symphony with viola solo (1834) and *The Corsair*, an overture (final version, 1855), are after Byron. Shakespeare is the source for the overture *King Lear* (1831) and for the dramatic symphony for orchestra, soloists, and chorus, *Romeo and Juliet* (1839).

Berlioz's most important opera, *Les Troyens* (The Trojans), on his own libretto based on Vergil, has been successfully revived in recent years. The

Requiem (Mass for the Dead, 1837) and the *Te Deum* (Hymn of Praise, 1849) are conceived on a grandiose scale. This love of huge orchestral and choral forces represents only one aspect of Berlioz's personality. No less characteristic is the tenderness that finds expression in the oratorio *L'Enfance du Christ* (Childhood of Christ, 1854); the fine-spun lyricism that wells up in his songs; the sensibility that fills his orchestra with Gallic clarity and grace.

It was in the domain of orchestration that Berlioz's genius asserted itself most fully. His daring originality in handling the instruments opened up a new world of romantic sonority. Until his time, as Aaron Copland pointed out, "composers used instruments in order to make them sound like themselves; the mixing of colors so as to produce a new result was his achievement." His scores abound in novel effects and discoveries that served as models to all who came after him. Indeed, the conductor Felix Weingartner called Berlioz "the creator of the modern orchestra."

Symphonie fantastique

Berlioz's best-known symphony was written at the height of his infatuation with Harriet Smithson, when he was twenty-seven years old. It is hardly to be believed that this remarkable "novel in tones" was conceived by a young man only three years after the death of Beethoven. Extraordinary is the fact that he not only attached a program to a symphony, but that he drew the program from his personal life. In this autobiographical approach to his art Berlioz is a true romantic. "A young musician of morbid sensibility and ardent imagination in a paroxysm of lovesick despair has poisoned himself with opium. The drug, too weak to kill, plunges him into a heavy sleep accompanied by strange visions. His sensations, feelings, and memories are translated in his sick brain into musical images and ideas. The beloved one herself becomes for him a melody, a recurrent theme [*idée fixe*] that haunts him everywhere."

The "fixed idea" that symbolizes the beloved—the basic theme of the symphony—is subjected to variation in harmony, rhythm, meter, and tempo; dynamics, register, and instrumental color. These transformations take on literary as well as musical significance. Thus the basic motive, recurring by virtue of the literary program, becomes a musical thread unifying five movements that are diverse in mood and character.

I. *Reveries, Passions.* "He remembers the weariness of soul, the indefinable yearning he knew before meeting his beloved. Then, the volcanic love with which she at once inspired him, his delirious suffering . . . his religious consolation."

A spacious introduction marked Largo establishes the atmosphere of reverie. It establishes, too, the luminous resonance of Berlioz's orchestra. The movement proper is marked Allegro agitato e appassionato assai (lively, agitated, and very impassioned). Solo flute and first violins announce a soaring melody—the "fixed idea":

Characteristic is Berlioz's frequent use of the orchestral crescendo. At the climax of the movement the "fixed idea" is recapitulated by full orchestra *ff*. The last bars, consisting of sustained chords and marked *religiosamente*, suggest what Berlioz's program refers to as "his religious consolation."

II. *A Ball.* "Amid the tumult and excitement of a brilliant ball he glimpses the loved one again." The dance movement of the symphony is marked Valse Allegro non troppo (Waltz, not too fast). The introduction presents arpeggios on the harp against a string tremolo—an enchanting sonority. The Waltz proper begins "sweet and tender."

The movement is in ternary or three-part form. In the middle section the "fixed idea" reappears in waltz time, introduced by flute and oboe. Notable is

the climax at the end, which is built up through a crescendo, an accelerando, and a rise in pitch.

III. *Scene in the Fields.* "On a summer evening in the country he hears two shepherds piping. The pastoral duet, the quiet surroundings . . . all unite to fill his heart with a long absent calm. But *she* appears again. His heart contracts. Painful forebodings fill his soul. . . . The sun sets—the distant rumble of thunder—solitude—silence . . ."

The movement, marked Adagio, is an A-B-A form in ⁶⁄₈ time. Berlioz's comment on the orchestration shows his emotional attitude toward the instruments. "The English horn repeats the phrases of the oboe in the lower octave, like the voice of a youth replying to a girl in a pastoral dialogue." His aim, he wrote, was a mood "of sorrowful loneliness." There follows a broadly spun melody for flute and violins that breathes a pastoral quiet.

The "fixed idea" appears in the middle section in a new version in 6/8 time, introduced into this idyllic setting by solo flute and oboe in octaves. The "distant rumble of thunder" is given on the kettledrums, while the English horn suggests the solitude of the unhappy lover.

IV. *March to the Scaffold.* "He dreams that he has killed his beloved, that he has been condemned to die and is being led to the scaffold. The procession moves to the sounds of a march now somber and wild, now brilliant and solemn. . . . At the very end the 'fixed idea' reappears for an instant, like a last thought of love interrupted by the fall of the axe."

Marked Allegretto non troppo in 4/4, the march movement exemplifies the nineteenth-century love of the fantastic. Not easily forgotten is the sound of the opening: muted horns, timpani, pizzicato chords on cellos and double basses. The lower strings play an energetic theme that strides down the scale:

After this idea is given to the violins, the diabolical march emerges in the woodwinds and brass:

The theme of the beloved appears at the very end, on the clarinet, and is cut off by a grim fortissimo chord. The effect ("a last thought of love interrupted by the fall of the axe") has been much criticized as being too realistic. One must remember, however, that when Berlioz wrote it he was opening up new fields of expression for his art.

V. *Dream of a Witches' Sabbath.* "He sees himself at a witches' sabbath surrounded by a host of fearsome specters who have gathered for his funeral. Unearthly sounds, groans, shrieks of laughter. . . . The melody of his beloved is heard, but it has lost its noble and reserved character. It has become a vulgar tune, trivial and grotesque. It is she who comes to the infernal orgy. A howl of joy greets her arrival. She joins the diabolical dance. Bells toll for the dead. A burlesque of the *Dies Irae.* Dance of the witches. The dance and the *Dies Irae* combined."

The movement opens with a Larghetto (not quite as slow as largo). Berlioz here exploits a vein that nourished a century of satanic operas, ballets, and

113

symphonic poems. Flickering chromatic scales, *ppp*, on muted violins and violas create the properly infernal atmosphere. In the Allegro that follows, the theme of the beloved is transformed into a "vulgar dance tune" played by a high-pitched clarinet.

The traditional religious melody *Dies irae* (Day of Wrath), from the ancient Mass for the Dead, is given out by bassoons and tubas in a section in $6/8$ time marked Lontano (distant).

It is caricatured in shorter note values. In the *Ronde du sabbat* (Witches' Dance), a driving six-eight rhythm is heard in the cellos and basses, after which it is taken up in turn by various instrumental groups.

The interweaving of the various lines makes for an intricate orchestral fabric. Berlioz points out in the score the combining of the dance theme and the *Dies irae*, not that anybody would miss it. This passage, of which he was so proud, leads to a rousingly theatrical ending for his theatrical subject.

There is a bigness of line and gesture about the music of Berlioz, an overflow of vitality and inventiveness. He is one of the major prophets in the romantic era.

25 Liszt: *Les Préludes*

"Sorrowful and great is the artist's destiny."

As composer and conductor, teacher, and organizer of musical events, Franz Liszt (1811–86) occupied a central position in the artistic life of the nineteenth century. Yet this fabulously successful artist did not escape the romantic melancholy. "To die and die young—" he once exclaimed, "—what happiness!"

His Life

Liszt was born in Hungary, son of a steward in the employ of a wealthy family. A stipend from a group of Hungarian noblemen enabled him to pursue his musical studies in Paris. There he came under the spell of French romanticism, with whose leaders—Victor Hugo, Delacroix, George Sand, Berlioz—he formed close friendships.

The appearance in Paris of the sensational violinist Paganini, in 1831, made Liszt aware of the possibilities of virtuoso playing. The new mass public required spectacular soloists. Liszt met the need. He was one of the greatest of pianists—and showmen. An actor to his fingertips, he possessed the personal magnetism of which legends are made. Instead of sitting with his back to the audience or facing it, as had been the custom hitherto, he introduced the more effective arrangement that prevails today. It showed off his chiseled profile, which reminded people of Dante's. He crouched over the keys, he thundered, he caressed. Countesses swooned. Ladies less exalted fought for his snuffbox and tore his handkerchief to shreds. Liszt encouraged these antics as a necessary part of the legend. But behind the façade was a true musician. For his friends and disciples he played the last sonatas of Beethoven; they never forgot the experience.

Inseparable from the legend of the pianist was that of the lover. Liszt never married. His path for the better part of fifty years led through a thicket of sighs, tears, and threats of suicide. Among those briefly smitten were George Sand—they toured Switzerland for a summer—Lola Montez, and Marie Duplessis, the original of Dumas's Lady of the Camellias. More important in his intellectual development was his relationship with Countess Marie d'Agoult, who wrote novels under the name of Daniel Stern. They eloped to an idyllic interlude in Switzerland that lasted for a number of years. Of their three children, Cosima subsequently became the wife of Wagner. Liszt and the Countess parted in bitterness. She satirized him in her novels.

He withdrew from the concert stage at the height of his fame in order to devote himself to composing. In 1848 he settled in Weimar, where he became court conductor to the Grand Duke. The Weimar period (1848–61) saw the production of his chief orchestral works. As director of the ducal opera house he was in a position to mold public taste. He used his influence unremittingly on behalf of the "Music of the Future," as he and Wagner named the type of program music, both dramatic and symphonic, that they, along with Berlioz, advocated. At Weimar Liszt directed the first performances of Wagner's *Lohengrin*, Berlioz's *Benvenuto Cellini*, and many other contemporary works. History records few instances of an artist so generous, so free from envy in his dealings with his fellow artists.

Franz Liszt.

The Weimar period saw his association with the woman who most decisively influenced his life. Princess Carolyne Sayn-Wittgenstein, wife of a powerful noble at the court of the Tsar, fell in love with Liszt during his last concert tour of Russia. Shortly thereafter she came to Weimar to unite her life with his. For years their home, the Altenburg, was a center of artistic activity. A woman of domineering will and intellect, the Princess assisted Liszt in his later literary efforts. These include a book on Gypsy music and a *Life of Chopin*. Both are eloquent and inaccurate.

In his last years Liszt sought peace by entering the Church. He took minor orders and was known as Abbé Liszt. This was the period of his major religious works. He divided his time between Rome, Weimar, and Budapest, the friend of princes and cardinals. The gloom of old age was dispelled by fresh triumphs. At seventy-five he was received with enthusiasm in England, which had always been reluctant to recognize him as a composer. He journeyed to Bayreuth to visit the widowed Cosima and died during the festival of Wagner's works, with his last breath naming the masterpiece of the "Music of the Future"—Wagner's *Tristan*.

His Music

Liszt's goal was pure lyric expression, the projecting of a state of soul through what he called "the mysterious language of tone." To give his lyricism free scope he created the symphonic poem. The form was held together by the continuous transformation of a few basic themes. By varying the melodic outline, harmony, or rhythm of a theme, by shifting it from soft to loud, from slow to fast, from low to high register, from strings to woodwinds or brass, he found it possible to transform its character so that it might suggest romantic love in one section, a pastoral scene in another, tension and conflict in a third, and triumph in the last.

His thirteen symphonic poems (1848–58 and 1882) exercised incalculable influence on the nineteenth century and were responsible for many a work that is still popular. His masterpiece for orchestra is the *Symphony after Goethe's Faust* (1854–57), comprising three portraits: *Faust, Gretchen, Mephistopheles.* A companion work is the *Symphony to Dante's Divine Comedy* (1855–56), also in three movements: *Inferno, Purgatory,* and *Vision of Paradise.* In these program symphonies he honored his companions in arms. The *Faust* is dedicated to Berlioz, the *Dante* to Wagner.

Liszt, we saw, was one of the creators of modern piano technique. The best of his piano pieces, like his songs, are in the vein of true romantic lyricism. Characteristic are *Sonetto 104 del Petrarca* and the *Hungarian Rhapsody* No. 12, which we discussed in Chapter 21; the vastly popular *Liebestraum* (Love Dream, c. 1850), and the first *Mephisto Waltz* (1860). In a class apart are his chief works for the piano, the Sonata in B minor and the two piano concertos that date from the 1850s. Here is the Liszt of impassioned rhetoric, the contemporary in every sense of Victor Hugo, Byron, and Delacroix.

Liszt injected the picturesque personality—embodiment of romantic individualism—into the concert hall, where it has remained ever since. A great teacher, he raised a generation of giants of the keyboard. His easily accessible music helped create the modern mass public, and he influenced composers from Wagner and César Franck to Ravel and George Gershwin.

Les Préludes

The most famous of the symphonic poems, *Les Préludes* (The Preludes), was written in 1854. It served conductors as a showpiece for several generations, and remains a basic document in any study of the romantic movement. Liszt appended to the score a program note of his own devising that had some connection in his mind with one of the *Méditations poétiques* of the mystical poet Alphonse de Lamartine. "What is our life but a series of preludes to that unknown song whose first solemn note is tolled by Death? The enchanted dawn of every life is love. But where is the destiny on whose first delicious joys some storm does not break? . . . And what soul thus cruelly bruised, when the tempest rolls away, seeks not to rest its memories in the pleasant calm of pastoral life? Yet man does not long permit himself to taste the kindly quiet that first attracted him to Nature's lap. For when the trumpet sounds he hastens to danger's post, that in the struggle he may once more regain full knowledge of himself and his strength." Such a program related the music to one of the favorite themes of the age—the image of man pitted against Fate —unfolding a series of moods, dramatic, lyric, pastoral, triumphal, that appealed immensely to the romantic mentality.

The work is fashioned from a basic motive of three notes presented by the strings. The ascending interval of a fourth imparts to the motive a questioning upward inflection. This becomes a characteristic feature of the melodic material.

There follows a passage for full orchestra, Andante maestoso (fairly slow, majestic), the "prelude to that unknown song." Notice that the characteristic upward leap of a fourth is present both in the melody and the accompaniment (under the bracket):

Two themes in Liszt's suavest manner evoke the image of love that he calls "the enchanted dawn of every life." The first, espressivo cantando (expressively, in singing style), is assigned to the second violins and cellos. The germ motive (under bracket) is embedded in the melody.

The second amorous theme is played by muted violas and a quartet of horns, espressivo ma tranquillo (expressive but tranquil). This melody contrasts with the preceding. On closer examination, however, it too turns out to be an ingenious expansion of the basic motive (notes marked ×).

Thus, behind all talk of the program and its literary associations we see the mind of the musician at work. What the piece is about, quite apart from love, nature, and destiny, is a three-note motive that contains an ascending leap. Out of these three notes is woven the musical tissue, by a process of continuous transformation.

The tempo quickens, tension mounts. The basic material is presented Allegro tempestoso. The atmosphere of struggle is associated with chromatic scales. (The *chromatic scale* takes in all twelve tones within the octave. On the piano it includes the seven white and five black keys. Chromatic scales become a favorite device of the romantics for whipping up excitement.) Naturally the tempestuous passage features the brass.

An area of relaxation ensues. There follows an Allegretto pastorale, a peaceful nature scene that features the woodwinds. The motive is now transformed into a pastoral theme scored for woodwinds and horn.

The return to the fray is marked by an Allegro marziale animato (fast, martial, animated). Through changes in pace, register, dynamics, and color, the two love themes are transformed into rousing battle calls—the second one marked "march tempo."

Finally the mood of exaltation returns, to round off the action with the grandiose ending so dear to the romantics. The basic motive has triumphed along with Man.

Today, the "Music of the Future" has become that of the past. Yet Liszt remains—man and musician—the voice of an era. "In art," he said, "one must work on a grand scale." This he did.

26 Tchaikovsky: *Romeo and Juliet*

"Truly there would be reason to go mad were it not for music."

Few composers typify the end-of-the-century mood as does Peter Ilyich Tchaikovsky (1840–93). He belonged to a generation that saw its truths crumbling and found none to replace them. He expressed as did none other the pessimism that attended the final phase of the romantic movement.

His Life

Tchaikovsky was born at Votinsk in a distant province of Russia, son of a government official. His family intended him for a career in the government. He graduated at nineteen from the aristocratic School of Jurisprudence at St. Petersburg and obtained a minor post in the Ministry of Justice. Not till he was twenty-three did he reach the decision to resign his post and enter the newly founded Conservatory of St. Petersburg. "To be a good musician and earn my daily bread"—his was a modest goal.

He completed the course in three years and was immediately recommended by Anton Rubinstein, director of the school, for a teaching post at the new Conservatory of Moscow. Despite the long hours and large classes, the young professor of harmony applied himself assiduously to composition. His twelve years at Moscow saw the production of some of his most successful works.

Extremely sensitive by nature, Tchaikovsky was subject to attacks of depression aggravated by his irregular personal life. In the hope of achieving some degree of stability, he entered into an ill-starred marriage with a student of the Conservatory, Antonina Miliukov, who was hopelessly in love with him. His sympathy for Antonina soon turned into uncontrollable aversion, and in a fit of despair he wandered into the icy waters of the Moscow River. Some days later he fled, on the verge of a serious breakdown, to his brothers in St. Petersburg.

In this desperate hour, as in one of the fairy tales he liked to turn into ballets, there appeared the kind benefactress who enabled him to go abroad until he had recovered his health, freed him from the demands of a teaching post, and launched him on the most productive period of his career. Nadezhda von Meck, widow of an industrialist, was an imperious and emotional woman. She lived the life of a recluse in her mansion in Moscow, from which she ran her railroads, her estates, and the lives of her eleven children. Her passion was music, especially Tchaikovsky's. Bound by the rigid conventions of her time and her class, she had to be certain that her enthusiasm was for the artist, not the man; hence she stipulated that she was never to meet the recipient of her bounty.

Peter Ilyich Tchaikovsky.

Thus began the famous friendship by letter which soon assumed a tone of passionate attachment. For the next thirteen years Mme. von Meck made Tchaikovsky's career the focal point of her life, providing for his needs with exquisite devotion and tact. She resisted all temptation to remove the relationship from its ideal plane. Save for an accidental glimpse of one another at the opera or during a drive, they never met.

The correspondence gives us an insight into Tchaikovsky's method of work. "You ask me how I manage the instrumentation. I never compose in the abstract. I invent the musical idea and its instrumentation simultaneously." Mme. von Meck inquires if the Fourth Symphony (which he dedicated to her) has a definite meaning. Tchaikovsky replies, "How can one express the indefinable sensations that one experiences while writing an instrumental composition that has no definite subject? It is a purely lyrical process. It is a musical confession of the soul, which unburdens itself through sounds just as a lyric poet expresses himself through poetry. The difference lies in the fact that music has far richer resources of expression and is a more subtle medium. . . . As Heine said, 'Where words leave off music begins.' "

The years covered by the correspondence saw the spread of Tchaikovsky's fame. He was the first Russian whose music caught on in the West, and in 1891 he was invited to come to America to participate in the ceremonies that marked the opening of Carnegie Hall. From New York he wrote, "These Americans strike me as very remarkable. In this country the honesty, sincerity, generosity, cordiality, and readiness to help you without a second thought are extremely pleasant. . . . The houses downtown are simply colossal. I cannot understand how anyone can live on the thirteenth floor. I went out on the roof of one such house. The view was splendid, but I felt quite giddy when I looked down on Broadway. . . . I am convinced that I am ten times more famous in America than in Europe."

The letters of his final years breathe disenchantment and the suspicion that he had nothing more to say. "Is it possible that I have completely written myself out? I have neither ideas nor inclinations!" But ahead of him lay his two finest symphonies.

Immediately after finishing his Sixth Symphony, the *Pathétique*, he went to St. Petersburg to conduct it. The work met with a lukewarm reception, due in part to the fact that Tchaikovsky, painfully shy in public, conducted his music without any semblance of conviction. Some days later, although he had been warned of the prevalence of cholera in the capital, he carelessly drank a glass of unboiled water and contracted the disease. He died within the week, at the age of fifty-three. The suddenness of his death and the tragic tone of his last work led to rumors that he had committed suicide. Almost immediately there accrued to the *Symphonie pathétique* the sensational popularity it has enjoyed ever since.

His Music

"He was the most Russian of us all!" said Stravinsky. In the eyes of his countrymen Tchaikovsky is a national artist. He himself laid great weight on the Russian element in his music. "Why is it that the simple Russian land-scape, a walk in summer through Russian fields and forest or on the steppes at evening can affect me so that I have lain on the ground numb, overcome by a wave of love for nature." At the same time, in the putting together of his music Tchaikovsky was a cosmopolite. He came under the spell of Italian opera, French ballet, German symphony and song. These he assimilated to the strain of folk melody that was his heritage as a Russian, setting upon the mixture the stamp of a sharply defined personality.

Tchaikovsky cultivated all branches of music. Of prime importance are his last symphonies, the Fourth (1877), the Fifth (1888), and the Sixth (1893). They abound in spectacular climaxes that endear them to the virtuoso con-ductor. In the domain of program music two arresting works continue to be played: the overture-fantasy *Romeo and Juliet* and the symphonic fantasy *Francesca da Rimini* (1876). Hardly less popular is the colorful *Capriccio italien* (1880). Of his eight operas, two hold the international stage: *Eugene Onegin* (1877–78) and *Pique Dame* (Queen of Spades, 1890). Based on librettos derived from the national poet Pushkin, both are essentially lyric in character. Tchaikovsky's ballets enjoy immense popularity. *Swan Lake* (1876), *The Sleeping Beauty* (1889), and *The Nutcracker* (1892) are appreciated both in the ballet theater and in the concert hall.

The Piano Concerto in B-flat minor (1875) and the Violin Concerto in D major (1878) are staple display pieces of the virtuoso. Of his more than one hundred songs a single one—*None But the Lonely Heart*, in his familiar vein of romantic melancholy—has obscured many that are more representative of him at his best.

122

We shall in a later section consider Tchaikovsky as a symphonist. In this chapter we are concerned with his most successful effort in the domain of program music.

Overture-Fantasy: *Romeo and Juliet*

Romeo and Juliet, the first work that fully revealed Tchaikovsky's gifts, was written in 1869, when the composer was twenty-nine. In 1881, he thoroughly revised the piece. The term *overture-fantasy* suggests his imaginative approach to the material. It also makes clear that this is not an overture to an opera but an independent concert piece. The form is similar to that which we encountered in Mendelssohn's Overture to *A Midsummer Night's Dream*: a large three-section structure called *sonata-allegro form*, that allows for the presentation, development, and restatement of musical ideas (Exposition-Development-Recapitulation). In this case the form is enlarged by means of a spacious introduction and epilogue. It was in no sense the composer's intent to give a detailed musical depiction of the Shakespearean drama. Rather, he selected three salient images that lent themselves to musical treatment—the gentle Friar Laurence, the feud between the two noble families of Verona, and the love of Romeo and Juliet.

Friar Laurence is evoked by a chorale which is presented in four-part harmony by two clarinets and two bassoons, Andante non tanto quasi moderato (not too slow, almost moderate; a *chorale* is a hymn or a hymnlike tune). This chorale, with its organ-like chords, creates a medieval atmosphere. It expands into a lengthy introduction, and returns at the end of the piece in a prelude-postlude formation.

The Allegro giusto (fast, in strict time) begins the Exposition with the "Feud" theme.

The brusque rhythm with its strong syncopation suggests violent action, as do the full orchestral tone and explosive accompaniment. Characteristic of Tchaikovsky are the sweeping runs, ascending and descending, on the violins.

123

The love theme is a melody long of line and tenderly lyrical, sung by English horn and muted violas. The youthful composer created here a broadly spun song whose ardor is not unworthy of Shakespeare's lovers.

The mood is rounded off by a subsidiary idea of great expressiveness, played by the muted strings. With this the exposition section comes to an end.

The agitated development section is based mainly on the Feud theme, interspersed with references to the Friar Laurence music in the horns and, ultimately, the trumpets. In the working out of his musical ideas Tchaikovsky achieves that building up of tension and momentum which is the essence of symphonic development. The Recapitulation brings back the feud theme substantially as before. The love music is now expanded and rises, wave upon wave of sumptuous orchestral sound, to one of those torrential climaxes that only an uninhibited romantic could achieve.

The epilogue is fashioned out of the love theme. Muffled drums beat a dirge for the dead lovers, and the chorale of the opening is heard again, balancing the architecture.

This is young man's music, fervid, communicative, and fashioned along broad simple lines. It captures a characteristic moment in the thought and feeling of the late romantic era. Beyond that it remains one of the more beguiling—and solidly wrought—examples of nineteenth-century program music.

27 Strauss: *Don Juan*

"I work very long on melodies. The important thing is not the beginning of the melody but its continuation, its development into a fully completed artistic form."

Among the composers who inherited the symphonic poem of Liszt, Richard Strauss (1864–1949) occupied a leading place. Although he lived well into the twentieth century, the symphonic poems he wrote during the last years of the nineteenth century came out of and belong to the romantic tradition.

His Life

Strauss was born in Munich. His father was a virtuoso horn player who belonged to the court orchestra. His mother was the daughter of

Richard Strauss.

Georg Pschorr, a successful brewer of Munich beer. In this solid middle-class environment, made familiar to American readers by the novels of Thomas Mann, a high value was placed on music and money. These remained Strauss's twin passions throughout his life.

His first works were in the classical forms. At twenty-one he found his true style in the writing of vivid program music, setting himself to develop what he called "the poetic, the expressive in music." *Macbeth* (1886–90), his first tone poem, was followed by *Don Juan* (1888), an extraordinary achievement for a young man of twenty-four. Then came the series of tone poems that blazed his name throughout the civilized world: *Tod und Verklärung* (Death and Transfiguration, 1889), *Till Eulenspiegels lustige Streiche* (Till Eulenspiegel's Merry Pranks, 1894–95), *Also sprach Zarathustra* (Thus Spake Zarathustra, 1896), *Don Quixote* (1897), *Ein Heldenleben* (A Hero's Life, 1898), and two program symphonies, the *Domestic* and the *Alpine*. These works shocked the conservatives and secured Strauss's position, around the turn of the century, as the *enfant terrible* of modern music, a role he thoroughly enjoyed.

In the early years of the twentieth century Strauss conquered the operatic stage with *Salome* (1906), *Elektra* (1909), and *Der Rosenkavalier* (The Knight of the Rose, 1911). The international triumph of the last-named on the eve of the First World War marked the summit of his career. He collected unprecedented fees and royalties for his scores. Strauss was eager to dispel the romantic notion that the artist is better off starving in a garret. On the contrary, he insisted that "worry alone is enough to kill a sensitive man, and all thoroughly artistic natures are sensitive."

Strauss's collaboration with Hugo von Hofmannsthal, the librettist of *Elektra* and *Rosenkavalier*, continued until the latter's death in 1929. By this time, new conceptions of modernism had come to the fore; the one-time bad boy of music, now entrenched as a conservative, was inevitably left behind. The coming to

125

power of the Nazis in 1933 confronted Strauss with a challenge and an opportunity. He was by no means reactionary in his political thinking; his daughter-in-law was Jewish, and the cosmopolitan circles in which he traveled were not susceptible to Hitler's ideology. Hence the challenge to speak out against the Third Reich—or to leave Germany as Thomas Mann, Hindemith, and other intellectuals were doing. On the other hand the new regime was courting men of arts and letters. Strauss saw the road open to supreme power, and took the opportunity. In 1933, on the threshold of seventy, he was elevated to the official hierarchy as president of the Reichsmusikkammer (State Chamber of Music). His reign was brief and uneasy. He declined to support the move to ban Mendelssohn's music from Teutonic ears. His opera *Die schweigsame Frau* (The Silent Woman, 1935) was withdrawn after its premiere because the librettist, Stefan Zweig, was non-Aryan; whereupon Strauss resigned.

The war's end found the eighty-one-year-old composer the victim of a curious irony. He was living in near-poverty because the huge sums owing him for performances of his works in England and America had been impounded as war reparations. He was permitted to return to his villa at Garmisch, in the Bavarian Alps. To his friends Strauss explained that he had remained in Nazi Germany because someone had to protect culture from Hitler's barbarians. Perhaps he even believed it.

There were speeches at the Bavarian Academy of Arts on the occasion of his eighty-fifth birthday. He died shortly after.

His Music

Strauss carried to its extreme limit the nineteenth-century appetite for story-and-picture music. His tone poems are a treasury of orchestral discoveries. In some he anticipates modern sound effects—the clatter of pots and pans, the bleating of sheep, the gabble of geese, hoofbeats, wind, thunder, storm. Much more important, these works are packed with movement and gesture, with the sound and fury of an imperious temperament. His scores show the most intricate interweaving of the separate instrumental parts; page after page is strewn with notes that the ear cannot possibly unravel. When chided for his complexity he would exclaim, "The devil! I cannot express it more simply."

Strauss's operas continue to be widely performed. *Salome*, to Oscar Wilde's famous play, and *Elektra*, based on Hofmannsthal's version of the Greek tragedy, are long one-act operas. Swiftly paced, moving relentlessly to their climax, they are superb theater. *Der Rosenkavalier* has a wealth of sensuous lyricism and some entrancing waltzes. The scene is Vienna in the reign of Maria Theresa. The theme is eternal: the fading of youth and beauty. The aging Marschallin, waging her losing battle with time; the disreputable Baron Ochs; Sophie and Octavian awaking to the wonder of young love—they ring true in the theater, they come alive through music. Strauss here summoned all his wizardry of orchestral color, his mastery of the stage, his knowledge of the human heart. There comes a time, alas, when *Rosenkavalier* seems a trifle long. It is a sign that one's youth is over.

Don Juan

The figure of Don Juan has attracted artists for hundreds of years, from Molière in the seventeenth century to Bernard Shaw in the twentieth. (We will discuss Mozart's handling of the legend in Chapter 53.) It is a mistake to regard the Don as a great lover. Actually he is incapable of love; what drives him is the need for conquest. Oblivious of other human beings, he cannot relate to anyone outside himself. This condemns him to the loneliness that is his real punishment, a loneliness he forever seeks to escape. Strauss, on the score of his symphonic poem, quoted excerpts from *Don Juan* by the romantic Austrian poet Nicolaus Lenau (1802–1850). Lenau's Don seeks the ideal woman, hoping through her to enjoy all women. Because he cannot find her he reels from one to another, eaten by boredom and satiety. In a duel with the son of a man he has killed he drops his sword and lets his enemy kill him, thus ending a life that has brought him only self-disgust.

Strauss's symphonic poem suggests the fiery ardor with which Don Juan pursues his ideal, the charm of the women who lure him on, and the selfish idealist's ultimate disappointment and atonement by death. This involves, in purely musical terms, the sharpest possible contrast between aggressively rhythmic themes and romantically lyrical ones—the contrast between the masculine and the eternal feminine that so strongly appealed to the romantic era. The symphonic poem, marked Allegro molto con brio (very fast, with vigor) opens with one of those upward-sweeping gestures of which Strauss knew the secret. (He once said that it was of the utmost important to capture the audience's attention at the outset. Once that was accomplished, the composer could do as he liked.) Then we hear the theme of Don Juan, a brusque impetuous melody whose tension is underlined by dotted rhythm, wide leaps, and a wide span:

Notice the syncopation in the second phrase (measures 5 and 7) where the accent falls after the first beat. This theme expands into a section of enormous vitality. There can be no question that the Don is an arresting personality.

The excitement dies down, a solo violin soars high above the orchestra. The melody representing the feminine ideal, marked tranquillo and expressivo (expressive), is a songful tune filled with romantic longing. Notice the upward leap at the beginning and the triplet rhythm in the second measure:

This section reaches a climax in a passage marked molto appassionato (very impassioned). After a calming episode, the opening theme returns fortissimo, sounding more impetuous than ever. Another lyric melody appears to evoke the eternal feminine, a full-throated song for violas and cellos, whose dark coloring gives it a somber cast.

After repetition and expansion of this theme, the scene is set for the third theme that symbolizes the feminine ideal: the love song of Don Juan. Intoned "in a sustained and expressive manner" by the oboe, this soulful melody unfolds in a broad arc and eloquently suggests the Don's unattainable ideal:

Again there is a change of mood. Horns introduce the second theme of the Don, a gallant tune that evokes the chivalric side of his nature. Notice, in the eleventh bar, the bold ascent of the melody in triplets:

One more episode furnishes the last of the thematic material. Marked giocoso (playful), this suggests a scene of merrymaking. The descending grace-note figure in the first two measures, which gives the theme a puckish character, is balanced by the ascending triplets in the following measures:

Strauss weaves a colorful fabric out of his themes, pitting one against the other, combining them, transforming them. He builds up to an *fff* marked *sempre molto agitato* (always very agitated). A diminuendo leads into a saddened version of the first "feminine ideal" theme, introduced by English horn and bassoon. The music gathers strength with the return of the opening theme (the Don's) which may be regarded as the basic idea of the piece. The final build-up expatiates on both themes of the Don, in a section notable for its sweep and passion, carrying the listener along on a current of glorious sound. An ominous silence, and the epilogue unfolds briefly in shuddering tremolos in the strings that descend from high to low register and lead to the pianissimo ending. Don Juan's hectic life is over.

A world figure, Strauss dominated his era as few artists have done. He may have suspected toward the end that the world had been too much with him. "We are all of us children of our time," he said, "and can never leap over its shadows." He was one of the major artists of our century.

28 Nationalism and the Romantic Movement

"I grew up in a quiet spot and was saturated from earliest childhood with the wonderful beauty of Russian popular song. I am therefore passionately devoted to every expression of the Russian spirit. In short, I am a Russian through and through!"

Tchaikovsky

The Rise of Musical Nationalism

In giving voice to his personal view of life the artist also expresses the hopes and dreams of the group with which he is identified. It is this identification, seeping through from the most profound layers of the unconscious, that makes Shakespeare and Dickens so English, Dostoievsky so Russian, Proust so French. Yet this national quality does not cut the artist off from other peoples. Shakespeare, Dostoievsky, and Proust belong not only to their own nations but to all mankind. In depicting the life they knew they expressed what all men feel.

Alongside the national artist stands the nationalist, who affirms his national heritage in a more conscious way. Needless to say, the two categories overlap. This was especially true in nineteenth-century Europe, where political conditions encouraged the growth of nationalism to such a degree that it became a decisive force within the romantic movement. National tensions on the Continent—the pride of the conquering nations and the struggle for freedom of the subjugated ones—gave rise to emotions that found an ideal expression in music. The romantic composers expressed their nationalism in a number of ways. Several based their music on the songs and dances of their people: Chopin in his Mazurkas, Liszt in his *Hungarian Rhapsodies*, Dvořák in the *Slavonic Dances*, Grieg in the *Norwegian Dances*. A number wrote dramatic works based on folklore or the life of the peasantry. Examples are the German folk opera *Der Freischütz* by Carl Maria von Weber, the Czech national opera *The Bartered Bride* by Bedřich Smetana, as well as the Russian fairy-tale operas and ballets of Tchaikovsky and Rimsky-Korsakov. Some wrote symphonic poems and operas celebrating the exploits of a national hero, a historic event, or the scenic beauty of their country. Tchaikovsky's *Overture 1812* and Smetana's *The Moldau* exemplify this trend; as does the glorification of the gods and heroes of German myth and legend in Richard Wagner's music dramas, especially *The Ring of the Nibelung*, a vast epic centering about the life and death of Siegfried. The nationalist composer might unite his music with the verses of a national poet or dramatist. Schubert's settings of Goethe fall into this category; also Grieg's music for Ibsen's *Peer Gynt* and Tchaikovsky's operas based on the dramas of Alexander Pushkin, the Russian national poet who also inspired Rimsky-Korsakov and Musorgsky. Of special significance was the role of music in periods of political turmoil, when the nationalist composer was able to give emotional expression to the aspirations of his people, as Verdi did when Italy was striving for unification, or Sibelius did when Finland struggled against its Russian rulers at the end of the century.

The political implications of musical nationalism were not lost upon the authorities. Verdi's operas had to be altered again and again to suit the Austrian censor. Sibelius's tone poem *Finlandia* with its rousing trumpet calls was forbidden by the tsarist police when Finland was demanding her independence at the turn of the century. During World War II the Nazis forbade the playing of *The Moldau* in Prague and of Chopin's Polonaises in Warsaw because of the powerful symbolism residing in these works.

Nationalism added to the language of European music a variety of national idioms of great charm and vivacity. By associating music with the love of homeland, nationalism enabled composers to give expression to the cherished aspirations of millions of people. In short, national consciousness pervaded every aspect of the European spirit in the nineteenth century. The romantic movement is unthinkable without it.

Exoticism

Exoticism in music, painting, and literature evokes the picturesque atmosphere and color of far-off lands. This trend, needless to say, was strongly encouraged by the romantic movement. Nineteenth-century exoticism

Eugène Delacroix, THE LION HUNT. (The Art Institute of Chicago)
The romantic imagination was captured by the exoticism of the East.

manifested itself, in the first place, as a longing of the northern nations for the
warmth and color of the South; in the second, as a longing of the West for the
fairy-tale splendors of the Orient. The former impulse found expression in the
works of German, French, and Russian composers who turned for inspiration
to Italy and Spain. The long list includes several well-known works by Russian
composers: Glinka's two Spanish Overtures, Tchaikovsky's *Capriccio italien* and
Rimsky-Korsakov's *Capriccio on Spanish Themes*. The German contribution
includes Mendelssohn's *Italian Symphony*, Hugo Wolf's *Italian Serenade*, and
Richard Strauss's *Aus Italien*. Among the French works are Chabrier's *España*
and Lalo's *Symphonie espagnole*. The masterpiece in this category is, of course,
Bizet's *Carmen*.

The glamor of the East was brought to international prominence by the
Russian national school. In an empire that stretched to the borders of Persia,
exoticism was really a form of nationalism. The fairy-tale background of Asia
pervades Russian music. Rimsky-Korsakov's orchestrally resplendent *Scheherazade* and his opera *Sadko*, Alexander Borodin's opera *Prince Igor* and symphonic
poem *In the Steppes of Central Asia*, and Ippolitov-Ivanov's *Caucasian Sketches*
are among the many orientally inspired works that for a time found favor

131

throughout the world. A number of French and Italian composers also utilized exotic themes: Saint-Saëns in *Samson and Delilah*, Delibes in *Lakmé*, Massenet in *Thaïs*, Verdi in *Aïda*, and Puccini in his operas *Madame Butterfly* and *Turandot*.

29 Nationalism in the Symphonic Poem

"I am no enemy of the old forms in the old music. But I do not hold that we now have to follow them. I have come to the conclusion that the forms of the past are finished. Absolute music is quite impossible for me."
                                                              Bedřich Smetana

Smetana: *The Moldau*

The Czech national school was founded by Bedřich Smetana (1824–84). As in the case of several nationalist composers, Smetana's career unfolded against a background of political agitation. Bohemia stirred restlessly under Austrian rule, caught up in a surge of nationalist fervor that culminated in the uprisings of 1848. Young Smetana aligned himself with the patriotic cause. After the revolution was crushed, the atmosphere in Prague was oppressive for those suspected of sympathy with the nationalists. In 1856 Smetana accepted a post as conductor in Sweden. A disciple of Berlioz and Liszt, he turned to the writing of symphonic poems during his stay abroad. On his return to Bohemia in 1861 he resumed his career as a national artist and worked for the establishment of a theater in Prague where the performances would be given in the native tongue.

Of his eight operas on patriotic themes, several still hold the boards in the theaters of his native land. One—*The Bartered Bride*—attained world-wide fame. Hardly less important in the establishing of Smetana's reputation was the cycle of six symphonic poems entitled *My Country*, which occupied him from 1874 to 1879. These works are steeped in the beauty of Bohemia's countryside, the rhythm of her folk songs and dances, the pomp and pageantry of her legends. Best known of the series is the second, *Vltava* (The Moldau), Smetana's finest achievement in the field of orchestral music.

In this tone poem the famous river becomes a poetic symbol that suffuses the musical imagery with patriotic associations. The program appended to the score explains the composer's intention. "Two springs pour forth in the shade of the Bohemian forest, one warm and gushing, the other cold and peaceful." These join in a brook that becomes the river Moldau. "Coursing through

The Moldau at Prague.

Bohemia's valleys, it grows into a mighty stream. Through thick woods it flows as the gay sounds of the hunt and the notes of the hunter's horn are heard ever closer. It flows through grass-grown pastures and lowlands where a wedding feast is being celebrated with song and dance. At night, wood and water nymphs revel in its sparkling waves. Reflected on its surface are fortresses and castles—witnesses of bygone days of knightly splendor and the vanished glory of martial times." The stream races ahead through the Rapids of St. John, "finally flowing on in majestic peace toward Prague and welcomed by historic Vysehrad"—the legendary site of the castle of the ancient Bohemian kings. "Then it vanishes far beyond the poet's gaze."

The opening is marked Allegro commodo non agitato (moderately fast, not agitated). A rippling figure is heard as a dialogue between two flutes against a pizzicato accompaniment by violins and harp. From this emerges a broadly flowing melody played by oboe and violins—the theme of the river—that describes a broad arc in its stepwise movement along the scale. Smetana adapted his melody from a Czech folk song.

This theme subsequently is heard with the G raised to G-sharp, which subtly alters the effect:

After a repetition of this idea, horns, woodwinds, and trumpets evoke a hunting scene. A fanfare such as the following not only creates an outdoor atmosphere but also underlines the descent of the modern French horn from the old hunting horn:

The section labeled *Peasant Wedding* is in the spirit of a rustic dance. Presented by clarinets and first violins against a staccato accompaniment, the melody has the stepwise movement, narrow skips within a narrow range, and repeated-note figures that we associate with folk song and dance:

Where the score is marked *Moonlight—Nymphs' Revels,* the mood changes to one of mystery. An atmosphere of woodland enchantment is evoked by the muted strings against a background of flute, clarinet, horn, and harp.

A gradual crescendo leads to the return of the principal melody. The pace quickens as the music graphically depicts the Rapids of St. John, with full use of the brass choir against the rippling of the strings. As the river approaches the ancient site of the royal castle, the principal melody returns in an exultant mood with certain tones (G and C) raised a half step to G-sharp and C-sharp. The result, as we shall learn in a later chapter, is to shift the tune from minor to major. This is taken care of by the change in key signature, which becomes four sharps:

Now the brass and woodwinds intone a triumphal chorale, as though the composer were promising his countrymen that their former glory will return.

There is a diminuendo to the end as the river "vanishes far beyond the poet's gaze."

The Czechs regard this symphonic landscape as a national tone poem that mirrors the very soul of their land. The rest of the world sees in it one of the more attractive examples of late romantic tone painting.

Sibelius: *The Swan of Tuonela*

Like Richard Strauss, Jean Sibelius (1865–1957) belonged to the postromantic generation whose historic role it was to bridge the transition from the nineteenth century to the twentieth. As in the case of Strauss, his early works, written in the 1890s, came out of and belong to the romantic tradition.

Finland at that time was swept by agitation for independence from tsarist Russia. Sibelius's art came out of this ferment and served notice that his country's music had come of age. It is in the orchestral and choral works of his first period that Sibelius is most explicitly national. The bardic *En Saga* (1892) was followed by the orchestral legends *The Swan of Tuonela* (1893) and *Lemminkäinen's Homecoming* (1895), the symphonic poem *Finlandia* (1899), and the symphonic fantasy *Pohjola's Daughter* (1906). These works, appearing during the years of tsarist oppression, caught the spirit of the liberation movement. The seven symphonies that followed established Sibelius's reputation throughout the world.

The Swan of Tuonela is based on a legend from the Finnish folk-saga *Kalevala*. The composer inscribed the following note on the score of this lyrical tone poem: "Tuonela, the Kingdom of Death, the Hades of Finnish mythology, is surrounded by a broad river of black water and rapid current in which the Swan of Tuonela glides in majestic fashion and sings." Against a dark curtain of muted string sound, an English horn intones the sad but majestic song of the swan; its poignant tone imparts a strange intensity to the broadly curved melody. Now and again a phrase is answered by an ascending solo passage on the cello or viola, and the bass drum adds its discreet roll to the ensemble.

The piece, as it unfolds, creates a brooding atmosphere; the lyricism is dream-like, subdued. There is a broadening of tempo at the climax. An arpeggio on the harp emerges from the flow of sound; the strings take over briefly in a passage marked cantabile, con gran suono (songful, with a big sound). When this upsurge subsides the strings play *ppp*, tremolo, col legno ("with the wood," that is, by moving the back of the bow across the strings); the effect is one of mystery. The swan's final song is given to the English horn, in a very soft passage marked dolcissimo (very sweetly). Divided strings add their comment, a solo cello ascends to the upper register, and the music dies away. (The strings are said to be *divided* when a group in the orchestra, such as the first violins, which ordinarily play the same notes, are divided into two or more groups for certain passages.)

In Finland Sibelius is regarded with the special reverence that a small nation lavishes on the favorite son who became a world figure. A sincere and high-minded musician, he is assured a place in the annals of his art.

ABSOLUTE MUSIC

---

30 The Symphony

> "A great symphony is a man-made Mississippi down which we irresistibly flow from the instant of our leave-taking to a long foreseen destination."
> Aaron Copland

Absolute music is music for which the composer has not indicated to us any nonmusical associations, whether of story, scene, or mood. Here the musical ideas are organized in such a way that, without any aid from external images, they give the listener a satisfying sense of order and continuity.

The Nature of the Symphony

A *symphony* is a large-scale work for orchestra, in several parts or movements. These generally are three or four in number, in the sequence fast-slow-fast or fast-slow-moderately fast-fast. (There are many exceptions to this pattern.) The movements contrast in character and mood. Taken together they form an architectural entity and establish the symphony as the most exalted type of absolute music. (By a *movement* we mean a complete and comparatively independent part of a larger musical work.)

We will postpone a detailed discussion of symphonic structure to a later part of this book. It will suffice for the present to establish the character of the first movement of the cycle as a large form based on three sections—Exposition (Statement), Development, and Recapitulation (or Restatement). Sometimes a slow introduction leads into the movement proper. The Exposition usually presents two contrasting themes—one strongly rhythmic, the other lyric—which expand into contrasting sections. There is a bridge or transitional passage that leads from the first theme group to the second. A *codetta* (little coda) completes the Exposition. The Development is marked by a tremendous increase in tension. Here the composer may break the themes into fragments, recombining them in fresh patterns and revealing them in a new light. As he does so he explores the possibilities of the material for dynamic growth and development. Conflict and drama are of the essence in the Development. In the Recapitulation we hear again the themes of the Exposition more or less in their original guise, but with the wealth of new meaning that these have taken on in the course of the movement. There follows the coda, whose function it is to round off the action and to bring the movement to its appointed conclusion.

The first movement is generally the most dramatic of the cycle. It is written in what is known as *sonata form*, *sonata-allegro form* (because the tempo of this movement is almost always allegro), or *first-movement form*. This form may also be used for an independent piece such as the overture. We encountered sonata-allegro form in the *Midsummer Night's Dream Overture* and the *Romeo and Juliet Overture*.

In contrast to the first movement, the second—in the nineteenth-century symphony—is generally a slow movement of tenderly lyric nature. It may, however, vary in mood from the whimsical, even playful, to the tragic and passionate. The tempo marking in most cases is andante, adagio, or largo. This movement may be in three-part (A-B-A) form; sometimes it is a theme and variations. (Other possibilities are indicated in later chapters.)

Third in the cycle, in the symphonies of the romantic period, is the strongly rhythmic and impetuous scherzo, with overtones of humor, surprise, whimsy, or folk dance. You may recall that *scherzo* is the Italian word for "jest"; but the mood may range from elfin lightness to demonic energy. The tempo marking indicates a lively pace—allegro, allegro molto, vivace, or the like. The form is usually a large A-B-A; the middle section, known as the *trio*, is of a somewhat quieter nature. In some symphonies the scherzo comes second.

The fourth and last member of the cycle is of a dimension and character to balance the first. It may bring the symphony to a close on a note of triumph. The movement is generally a spirited allegro. In most of the romantic symphonies to be discussed in the next chapters the final movement, like the first, is based on sonata-allegro form.

We have here given the barest outline of symphonic form, not attempting a complete picture until after we shall have heard several representative symphonies. What is important at this point is to understand that the symphony is a drama whose several movements are concerned with the presentation of abstract musical ideas. These ideas unfold in such a way as to give each movement a quality of logical continuity. The essence of symphonic style is dramatic contrast and development. It arouses emotion in the listener, but emotion not directed to any specific image.

The word *theme* figures prominently in any serious discussion of musical form. By a theme we mean a distinctive musical idea that serves as a building block, a germinating element in a large musical work. The theme may be a fully rounded melody or it may be a compact melodic-harmonic-rhythmic kernel that is capable of further growth and flowering. The theme may be broken down into its constituent fragments which are known as *motives*. For example, the melody of *London Bridge* might serve as a theme in a large work. The first four notes (on the words "London Bridge is") could constitute one motive, the next three notes (on the words "falling down"), another. In the unfolding of a work this theme and its motives might undergo continual development, in the course of which their capacity for growth would be explored. We shall have more to say on theme and motive when we discuss the classical form in detail.

The nineteenth-century symphony holds a place of honor in the output of the romantic era. It retains its hold on the public, and remains one of the striking manifestations of the spirit of musical romanticism.

31 Mendelssohn: Italian Symphony

"The *Italian Symphony* is getting on well. It is becoming the merriest piece I have yet composed."

Mendelssohn (1831)

The *Italian Symphony* dates from the "grand tour" that Mendelssohn undertook in his early twenties, in the course of which he visited England, Scotland, Italy, and France. Like most visitors from northern Europe he was enchanted by Italy, its sunny skies and exuberant people. He recorded his impressions in one of his most widely loved works, the first version of which occupied him from 1831 to 1833. Despite the success of the symphony it failed to satisfy him; he kept revising the piece for a number of years.

The first movement is a dynamic Allegro vivace (fast and lively) whose headlong pace never slackens. Its main theme is a dancelike tune of boundless energy:

The opening notes of this theme serve as an easily recognized motive that dominates the movement:

The drive and vigor of this music are not to be resisted. The strings are clearly the heart of Mendelssohn's orchestra; woodwinds and brass are set off against them with capital effect. The orchestral sound is transparent—everything is clear and bright, with much staccato in the graceful manner associated with this composer.

The second theme contrasts with the first. Less active, it is a gracious idea that begins with an ascending arpeggio scored for clarinets and bassoons:

A codetta based on the first theme rounds off the opening section of the movement, the Exposition. Mendelssohn, in accordance with classical procedure, indicates that this is to be repeated.

The Development refashions both themes into fresh patterns. It also presents a striking new motive that is bandied about by various instruments.

Some idea of how a composer develops his material may be gleaned from the following examples.

1) Expansion of the principal theme:

2) Expansion of the new motive:

3) Combination of both:

An exciting crescendo leads into the final section of the movement, the Recapitulation. The material is restated in shortened form. The coda is marked Più animato poco a poco (more animated, little by little) and provides a fitting climax to this truly sunny Allegro.

The second movement is an Andante con moto (moderately slow, with movement). The form is a modified sonata-allegro, consisting of an Exposition and Recapitulation without a Development—what is known as a *sonatina* ("little sonata"). Nineteenth-century commentators associated this movement with a religious procession. After a brief introduction the oboe, supported by "dark" instruments—two bassoons and violas—introduce a sedate melody.

Cellos and double basses supply a soft staccato background to this theme, which is then presented in octaves by the violins. Both here and in the contrasting material Mendelssohn reveals his gift for lyricism of a subdued, somewhat elegiac cast. The first section is recapitulated and a feelingful coda rounds off the movement.

Third is a lyrical movement that stands closer to the graceful minuet than to the boisterous scherzo. The first violins present a broadly designed melody, marked "with moderate movement."

The emotional temperature rises a little as this idea is expanded. The Trio features wind instruments; the prominence of horn sound imparts to this music a suggestion of the outdoors. Bassoons and horns announce a relaxed theme against which the first violins play a gracefully ascending scale that is continued by the flutes:

The opening sections is repeated, and the coda ingeniously combines a motive from the Scherzo with one from the Trio. The movement ends pianissimo.

The final movement is a Presto based on the popular Italian "jumping dance" known as the *saltarello*. Its rhythm is marked by triplets in a rapid $\frac{4}{4}$ time:

141

This Saltarello was inspired by a visit to a Roman carnival. In a letter to his family the young composer described how he was pelted with confetti. "Amid a thousand jokes and jeers and the most extravagant masks, the day ended with races." The movement evokes a scene of tumultuous merrymaking, with crowds dancing wildly in the streets. Of special note are the slowly gathering crescendos that propel the music forward. The overall effect of this hard-driving finale is one of unflagging vitality.

The *Italian Symphony* embodies the urge toward exoticism that was to occupy an important place in nineteenth-century music. Beyond that it combines the classical impulse towards clarity of form with the romantic fondness for picturesque mood and atmosphere.

32 Dvořák: *New World Symphony*

"In the Negro melodies of America I discover all that is needed for a great and noble school of music. These beautiful and varied themes are the product of the soil. They are American. They are the folk songs of America, and your composers must turn to them."

Antonín Dvořák (1841–1904) is one of several late romantic composers who based their personal style on the songs and dances of their native lands. He stands alongside Bedřich Smetana as a founder of the Czech national school.

His Life

Dvořák was born in a village near Prague where his father kept an inn and butcher shop. Poverty for a time threatened to rule out a musical career. However, the boy managed to get to Prague when he was sixteen. There he mastered his craft and wound up as viola player in the orchestra of the Czech National Theater. Success as a composer came slowly, but in time he was able to resign his orchestra post and devote himself to composing, teaching, and conducting. By the time he was forty Dvořák had left behind the material cares that plagued the first years of his career. As professor of composition at the

Antonín Dvořák.

Conservatory of Prague he was able to exert an important influence on the musical life of his time.

The spontaneity and melodious character of his music assured its popularity. When the last decade of the century arrived, Dvořák was known throughout Europe. In 1892 he was invited to become director of the National Conservatory of Music in New York City. He received fifteen thousand dollars a year at the Conservatory—a fabulous sum in those days—as compared with the·six hundred dollars that made up his annual salary as a professor in Prague. His stay in the United States was fruitful. He produced what has remained his most successful symphony, *From the New World*; a number of chamber works, including the *American Quartet*; and the Concerto for Cello and Orchestra. Dvořák spent a summer at the Czech colony in Spillville, Iowa, in an atmosphere congenial to his simple tastes. Although every effort was made to induce him to continue at the Conservatory, his homesickness overrode all other considerations. After three years he returned to his beloved Bohemia.

Dvořák spent his remaining years in Prague in the happy circle of his wife and children, students and friends. He died in his sixty-third year, revered as a national artist throughout his native land.

His Music

Dvořák was a natural musician, a type that has always been abundant in Bohemia. Songfulness was native to a temperament in which intuition predominated over the intellectual process. Having sprung from the village, he never lost touch with the soil that was the source of his strength. At the same time, he achieved a solid craftsmanship in his art that enabled him to shape his musical impulses into large forms notable for their clarity and rightness.

Dvořák's large output covered all branches of his art: operas, choral works, symphonies, concertos, chamber music, overtures, rhapsodies, symphonic poems, songs, piano pieces, Slavonic dances. The time had come for the international language of German classicism to receive an invigorating infusion of native dialects, and Dvořák—along with Edvard Grieg and the Russians—was a leader in this historic process.

Coming to the United States as one of the leading nationalists of Europe, Dvořák tried to influence his American pupils toward a national art. One of his pupils was Henry T. Burleigh, the Negro baritone and arranger of spirituals. The melodies he heard from Burleigh stirred the folk poet in Dvořák, and strengthened him in his conviction that American composers would find themselves only when they had thrown off the European past and sought inspiration in the songs—Indian, Negro, cowboy—of their own country.

The time was not ripe for his advice to be heeded. But his instinct did not mislead him concerning the future of American music. One has but to consider the rich harvest of modern American works based on folklore to realize how fruitful, in the main, was his view.

The *New World Symphony*

The subtitle *From the New World* defines the scope and intent of the Symphony No. 9, in E minor, Opus 95 (1893). Dvořák was too much the Czech to presume to write an American work. His aim was to express his emotional response to a young and growing land, even while he longingly evoked the landscape of his own Bohemia. The work consequently is a mixture of Czech and American elements.

The symphony opens with a slow introduction. Cellos introduce a serene melody:

This atmospheric introduction leads into a vigorous Allegro molto. The first theme is an energetic idea that opens with an upthrusting arpeggio figure, wide of span and syncopated in rhythm. The first phrase is presented by the horns against a curtain of string tone. The second phrase, marked by staccato, strong accents (indicated in the example by arrow-shaped signs), and dotted rhythm, is played by the woodwinds. Notice the syncopation in the second measure, where the accent falls on the off-beat (an eighth note followed by a dotted quarter), and in the fourth measure, where an eighth note is followed by a quarter:

The dotted rhythm persists throughout the bridge passage that leads into the next theme. This transition is based on a motive from the second phrase which is restated several times at lower pitches. Such a duplication of a pattern at a higher or lower pitch is known as a *sequence*.

The second theme is a plaintive tune of Bohemian folk character that is introduced by a flute and oboe. It has the narrow range and repetition of tones associated with folk song.

This theme is soon repeated on higher pitches (ascending sequence) and sounds different because of a basic change—what we shall come to recognize in a later chapter as a shift from minor to major:

Third is a songful theme announced by flute solo and taken over, in the answering phrase, by the violins. Its outlines were suggested by Dvořák's favorite Negro spiritual, *Swing Low, Sweet Chariot*. Notice again the syncopation in the second and sixth measures: an eighth note followed by a dotted quarter. Notice, too, how the upward inflection in measure 3 is subtly balanced by the downward inflection at the end of the second phrase.

A codetta, fortissimo, rounds off the Exposition.

The Development explores the possibilities of the thematic material. The following examples show how Dvořák goes about reworking his themes and motives.

1) A motive from Theme 3 answered by a motive from Theme 1:

2) The opening motive of Theme 3, with slight changes of melody and rhythm in measures 3 and 4, combined with a motive from Theme 1, slightly changed:

3) The first phrase of Theme 1 combined with new material:

4) A motive from the second phrase of Theme 1 spun out through sequence and rhythmic transformation:

5) A motive from Theme 1, with slight melodic and rhythmic changes, serving as a transition to the Recapitulation:

It is upon procedures such as these that the Development section of sonata-allegro form depends.

The Recapitulation restates the thematic material. There is a grandiose coda to which descending chromatic scales lend excitement, culminating in a fortissimo statement of the basic arpeggio figure.

The slow movement is a Largo, in $\frac{4}{4}$ time consisting of three sections (A-B-A), each of which contains subdivisions and repetitions of material. Out of the introductory chords, marked *ppp*, issues the famous melody assigned to the English horn. It shows several characteristics we associate with folk song: a narrow range, much repetition, and small skips alternating with stepwise movement:

The middle section (B) opens with a melody in the flutes and oboes, pianissimo, against a sustained tremolo in the second violins and violas. Marked "a little faster," it consists of two four-measure phrases that move by step and small skip within a narrow range:

A contrasting melody is then sung by the clarinets, *pp*, taking on a dark coloring from the pizzicato accompaniment of the double basses:

Both melodies are repeated. This section is followed by an interlude in which a staccato melody on the flute creates an outdoor atmosphere. The transition back to the first section combines simultaneously motives from Theme 1 of the first movement (trombone), the main Largo theme (trumpets), and Theme 3 of the first movement (horns and violins):

When a composition is in several movements and themes from the earlier movements recur in the later ones, the piece is said to be in *cyclical form*. Such

147

reminiscence, it goes without saying, offers a most effective way of tying the movements together. The reappearance of the first-movement themes at this point creates a dramatic moment. The first section (A) is repeated in shortened form, and the Largo ends with mysterious chords, *ppp*, which recall those at the beginning of the movement.

The Scherzo, marked Molto vivace (very lively) is a dance movement in ¾ time. Its first theme (a) is of an impetuously rhythmic character. Indeed, this theme is as much a rhythm as a melody:

This is contrasted with a suave subject (b), rich in folkloric charm, introduced by flute and oboe. Its lyric character makes it a perfect foil for the opening tune:

The opening theme returns, so that this A section of the Scherzo is really an a-b-a.

A transition leads into the Trio or middle section (B) which also alternates two themes. The first (c) is a kind of rustic waltz played by flutes and oboes:

The second (d), played by the violins, is a dancelike tune to which wide leaps and trills in descending sequence impart a lilting gayety.

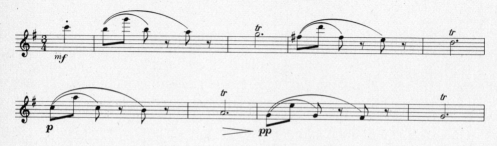

These two melodies are repeated in the pattern c-c-d-c-d-c. A brief transition leads back to the repetition of the first section, the Scherzo proper. The coda again underlines the cyclical form of the symphony by bringing back motives from earlier movements. This Scherzo demonstrates how a large-scale symphonic movement can be built up through the repetition of fairly short units:

The finale, Allegro con fuoco (fast, with fire) is an ample sonata-allegro form in 4/4 time. The stormy introduction leads into a vigorous melody in the character of a march, played by trumpets and horns.

The second theme is a flowing, lyrical idea, a reverie sung by the clarinet. The

third theme is in the nature of a popular song. Its symmetrical phrases end in three descending notes that appear to be derived from the familiar round, *Three*

Blind Mice. This little figure takes on prominence as it is bandied about by the various instrumental groups. Here, for example, is how it is spun out as a codetta to the Exposition:

The following examples from the Development well illustrate the thematic-motivic process as Dvořák and his contemporaries practised it.

1) Opening motive of the march theme in a new rhythm:

2) A motive derived from the march theme becomes an accompaniment for a motive from the Largo:

3) The Largo theme in two different rhythms:

4) The opening arpeggio of the first movement combined with the march theme in changed rhythm:

The Recapitulation presents the three themes of the Exposition in somewhat shortened form. And the coda further affirms the cyclical form of the symphony by touching upon the opening chords of the Largo, now played fortissimo by woodwinds and brass, by combining the Largo and Scherzo themes, and by bringing the symphony to an end with the triumphal proclamation of the up-and-down arpeggio with which the first Allegro began. Notice the chromatic scales that supply excitement, and the diminuendo at the very end.

The *New World Symphony* has always been a favorite in the United States. Its continuity of thought, clarity of outline, and vivacity of detail command the respect of musicians; while its appealing melodies and accessible ideas are such as make the popular classic.

33 Brahms: Symphony No. 3

"It is not hard to compose, but it is wonderfully hard to let the superfluous notes fall under the table."

Against the colorful program art of Berlioz, Liszt, and Wagner there arose an austere, high-minded musician dedicated to the purity of the classical style. His veneration for the past and his mastery of the architecture of absolute music brought him closer to the spirit of Beethoven than were any of his contemporaries.

His Life

Johannes Brahms (1833–97) was born in Hamburg, son of a double-bass player whose love of music was greater than his attainments. As a youngster of ten Johannes helped increase the family income by playing the piano in the dance halls of the slum district where he grew up. By the time he was twenty he had acquired sufficient reputation as a pianist to accompany the Hungarian violinist Eduard Reményi on a concert tour.

His first compositions made an impression on Joseph Joachim, leading violinist of the day, who made possible a visit to Robert Schumann at Düsseldorf. Schumann recognized in the shy young composer a future leader of the camp dedicated to absolute music. He published in his journal the famous essay entitled "New Paths," in which he named the twenty-year-old "young eagle" as the one who "was called forth to give us the highest ideal expression of our time." Brahms awoke to find himself famous.

Robert and Clara took the fair-haired youth into their home. Their friendship opened up new horizons for him. Five months later came the tragedy of Schumann's mental collapse. With a tenderness and strength he had not suspected in himself, Brahms tided Clara over the ordeal of Robert's illness.

The older man lingered for two years while the younger was shaken by the great love of his life. Fourteen years his senior and the mother of seven children, Clara Schumann appeared to young Brahms as the ideal of womanly and artistic perfection. What had begun as filial devotion ripened into romantic passion. She for her part found a necessary source of strength in the loyalty of the "young eagle." For Johannes this was the period of storm and stress, as his letters to her reveal. "You have taught me and every day teach me more and more to marvel at the nature of love, affection, and self-denial. I can do nothing but think of you." At the same time he was rent by feelings of guilt, for he loved and revered Schumann, his friend and benefactor, above all others. He thought of suicide and spoke of himself, as one may at twenty-two, as "a man for whom nothing is left."

This conflict was resolved the following year by Schumann's death; but another conflict took its place. Now that Clara was no longer the unattainable ideal, Brahms was faced with the choice between love and freedom. Time and again in the course of his life he was torn between the two, with the decision going always to freedom. His ardor subsided into a lifelong friendship. Two decades later he could still write her, "I love you more than myself and more than anybody and anything on earth."

His appointment as musician to the Prince of Detmold inaugurated his professional career. After four years at this post he returned to Hamburg to

Johannes Brahms.

devote himself to composition. But he failed to obtain an official appointment in his native city—the directors of the Philharmonic never forgot that Johannes came from the slums—and settled in Vienna, which remained the center of his activities for thirty-five years. In the stronghold of the classical masters he found a favorable soil for his art, his northern seriousness refined by the grace and congeniality of the South. The time was ripe for him. His fame filled the world and he became the acknowledged heir of the Viennese masters.

This exacting artist had a curiously dual nature. He could be morose and withdrawn, yet he loved rough humor. A bohemian at heart, he craved bourgeois respectability. Behind a rough exterior he hid the tenderness that found expression in his music and his love of children. He fought the softness in himself and came to be feared for his caustic wit. To a musician fishing for compliments he remarked, "Yes, you have talent. But very little!" The elderly ladies whom he was rehearsing in *The Creation* were admonished: "Why do you drag it so? Surely you took this much faster under Haydn." When a renowned quartet played his work the viola player inquired if he was satisfied with the tempo. Brahms snapped, "Yes—especially yours!" Thus the crotchety bachelor went his way through the middle-class circles of Vienna, the center of an adoring coterie. Although he complained of loneliness and on occasion fell in love, he was unable to accept the responsibility of a sustained relationship. His motto was *Free—but happy!* "It would be as difficult for me to marry," he explained, "as to write an opera. But after the first experience I should probably undertake a second!"

Just as in early manhood his mother's death had impelled him to complete *A German Requiem,* so the final illness of Clara Schumann in 1896 gave rise to the *Four Serious Songs.* Her death profoundly affected the composer, already ill with cancer. He died ten months later, at the age of sixty-four, and was buried not far from Beethoven and Schubert.

His Music

Brahms was a traditionalist. His gaze was directed back to the classical era whose splendor it was no longer possible to resurrect. This sense of being a latecomer imparts to his music its gently retrospective flavor, its autumnal resignation. Endowed with the historic sense, Brahms looked upon himself as a preserver of the great tradition. His aim was to show that new and important things could still be said in the tradition of the classical masters. In this he differed from avowed innovators such as Berlioz, Liszt, and Wagner.

Brahms's four symphonies (1876, 1877, 1883, 1885) are unsurpassed in the late romantic period for breadth of conception and design. Best known of the other orchestral works are the *Variations on a Theme by Haydn* (1873) and the concert overtures—the *Academic Festival* and the *Tragic* (1880). In the two concertos for piano and orchestra (1858, 1881) and the one for violin (1878), the solo instrument is integrated into a full-scale symphonic structure. The Double Concerto for Violin and Cello (1887) draws its inspiration from the age of Bach.

In greater degree than any of his contemporaries Brahms captured the tone of intimate communion that is the essence of chamber-music style. The duo sonatas, trios, quartets, quintets, and sextets for string and wind instruments, with and without piano, comprise a body of works marked by lyricism and a quality of introspection peculiarly his own. He is an important figure too in piano music. The three sonatas (1852–53) are works of his youth. The *Variations and Fugue on a Theme by Handel* (1861) represents his top achievement in this field. A favorite with concert performers is the set of *Variations on a Theme by Paganini* (1863), a composition that requires supreme virtuoso playing. The romantic in Brahms also found expression in short lyric pieces; the Rhapsodies, Ballades, Capriccios, and lyrical meditations known as Intermezzi are among the treasures of the literature. On the popular level are the Hungarian Dances and the set of sixteen Waltzes for piano duet.

As a song writer Brahms stands in the direct line of succession to Schubert and Schumann. His output includes about two hundred solo songs and an almost equal number for two, three, and four voices. The favorite themes are love, nature, death. His finest choral work is the *German Requiem* (1857–68), written to texts from the Bible selected by himself. A song of acceptance of death, this work more than any other spread his fame during his lifetime.

The nationalist in Brahms—he spoke of himself as *echt deutsch* (truly German)—inspired his arrangements of German folk and children's songs as well as the popular tone of many of his art songs. In his Waltzes he paid tribute to the popular dance of his beloved Vienna, but he knew he was too much the north German to capture the real Viennese flavor. When he gave his autograph to Johann Strauss's daughter—composers customarily inscribed a few bars of their music—he wrote the opening measures of the *Blue Danube Waltz* and noted beneath it, "Not, alas, by Johannes Brahms."

The Third Symphony

The Symphony No. 3 in F major, Opus 90, was completed in 1883 when Brahms was fifty years old. The rugged melodies and vigorous rhythm of this work are characteristic of his music, as is the subdued orchestral color. Woodwinds and brass are used in their lower register, blending with the strings in a silver-gray sonority that has a warmth all its own. The first movement, Allegro con brio (lively, with vigor), is in sonata-allegro form. The opening three notes in the winds constitute a motto, or recurrent motive, that pervades the first movement and returns in the last.

The motto becomes part of the accompaniment to the principal idea. This is a downward striding, vigorous theme of commanding gesture. Played by the violins, it begins by outlining the tones of the Tonic chord.

The contrasting theme, pastoral in character, is presented by the clarinet grazioso (gracefully) and mezza voce (in half voice). The same tones recur on different beats within the measure, a favorite device of Brahms that makes the melody appear to be "chasing its tail."

The two themes are subjected to a brief and intense development, the motto theme serving as a unifying element. The Recapitulation is followed by an ample coda. Characteristic throughout is the prominence of the horn, the warm but subdued orchestral sound, the wide spacing of the harmonies, and the quality of reticent emotion that is Brahms's own.

The slow movement, an Andante in 4/4 time, is a type of A-B-A structure that has assimilated certain developmental features of sonata form. The theme is announced espressivo and semplice (with simplicity) by clarinets supported

by bassoons and horns, and is spun out with echoes in the strings. A contrasting idea appears, marked by a triplet rhythm that is destined to take on significance in the final movement of the symphony. The first theme undergoes considerable development, and is restated with variation in rhythm, harmony, register, accompaniment, and orchestration. The movement ends on a serene note.

For the impetuous scherzo of Beethoven's symphony Brahms substituted a lyrical third movement in moderate tempo. The Poco allegretto is an impassioned, darkly colored orchestral song. The lyric theme in the cellos is con-

trasted with a lighter idea in the middle part. The first section is restated, with the melody originally played by the cellos now given to the French horn, then to the oboe.

The finale is a dramatic sonata-allegro marked by concise themes and abrupt changes of mood. The first idea is a searching melody, narrow in range, played in unison by bassoons and strings. The low register and the instrumentation combine to give it its somber coloration.

Contrast is provided by a festive theme played by the horn and cellos in unison. The dark coloring is characteristic of the composer. The movement proceeds

with classical logic. The principal theme is subjected to an exceedingly rich development. Here are three versions that figure prominently in the course of the movement:

A gentle allusion by the violins to the opening theme of the symphony casts a nostalgic glow over the closing measure of the work.

The art of Brahms—tender, searching, retrospective—marks the end not only of a century but of a cultural epoch. This lonely rhapsodist remains an impressive figure, one of the last representatives of nineteenth-century German idealism.

34 Tchaikovsky: *Pathétique Symphony*

"I have put my whole soul into this work."

Early in 1893, the last year of his life, Tchaikovsky wrote to his nephew that he was occupied with a new work. "This time with a program—but a program of the kind that will remain an enigma to all. Let them guess it who can. The work will be entitled *A Program Symphony*. The program is penetrated with subjective sentiment. During my journey, while composing it in my mind, I frequently shed tears." This "enigma" was the Sixth Symphony, for which his brother Modest suggested the title *Pathétique*.

He wrote down the first movement in less than four days. "There will be much in this work," he pointed out, "that is novel as regards form. The finale, for example, will not be a great allegro but an adagio of considerable dimensions." He finally shook off the fear of having outlived his creativeness. "You cannot imagine what joy I feel at the thought that my day is not yet over and that I may still accomplish much."

The introductory Adagio is somber in color and sets the tone of brooding intensity. A solo bassoon in low register moves sluggishly along the scale against the dark sound of the double basses and violas, foreshadowing the material of the Allegro proper.

Adagio

The Allegro non troppo (not too fast) is a sonata-allegro form based upon two vividly contrasted ideas. First is a tense rhythmic theme penetrated, as Tchaikovsky put it, with subjective sentiment. Staccato figures outline a nervous melodic line imbued with forward drive. Violas and cellos play the opening phrase, to be answered by flutes and clarinets.

This idea expands into a frenzied passage. The area of relaxation comes with the famous lyric theme sung by muted violins and cellos in octaves, andante. Tchaikovsky marks the passage "tenderly, very songfully, expansively." These indications well describe the flowing melody whose contours rise to a climax and gracefully subside.

This second theme expands into a spacious A-B-A formation within the Exposition. A codetta rounds off the section.

An explosive chord, fortissimo, opens the Development. Based on the first theme, this section is a vertitable catalogue of Tchaikovsky's favorite orchestral devices. Violins sweep furiously up and down the scale. Brusque accented chords spread across the orchestral gamut. The richly colored tone mass is whipped up to excitement, thrusting its way step by step to the higher register. Rhythmic figures are repeated again and again with a kind of obsessive insistence, brass tone is hurled against the busy strings and woodwinds, climax is piled upon climax in ever-ascending terraces of sound.

The Recapitulation presents the two fundamental ideas with changes in instrumental color. A new passage is introduced in which the massed brass is pitted against woodwinds and strings in spectacular fashion. The coda sounds the tragic tone. A descending scale reiterated in the strings, pizzicato, invariably suggests to commentators the footfalls of fate. The movement ends on a dramatic pianissimo.

Next is the Allegro con grazia (lively, with grace), a dance mood vivid and quite ballet-like in quality. This is an A-B-A form in what was, in the 1890s, an unprecedented meter—5/4 time. The alternation within the measure of groups of two and three beats imparts to the movement a wayward charm. The opening theme is played by the cellos.

After a departure, the melody returns in the woodwinds against a plucked-string accompaniment of ascending and descending scale passages of a kind that Tchaikovsky used again and again. The steady beat of the drum in the contrasting middle section creates an atmosphere of dramatic urgency, after which the first section returns. A quiet coda rounds off the movement.

The third movement, Allegro molto vivace (very fast and lively), is an extraordinarily exciting scherzo-march. The first theme, characterized by staccato triplets, has a dancelike impulsion that well indicates Tchaikovsky's affinity for the ballet. The second theme, based on an incisive commanding rhythm ending with a syncopated "snap," takes on the character of an imperious march.

After an extended Exposition, the two themes are restated. The march theme infiltrates the orchestral tissue and works up to an electrifying climax.

Last is the Adagio lamentoso (very slow, lamenting) in ¾ time. In form this movement is a modified sonata-allegro—that is, an Exposition and Recapitulation without a Development. The dolorous first theme, introduced by the violins, unfolds a bleak landscape of the soul.

The atmosphere of sorrow is dispelled for a space by the consoling second

theme, marked Andante. Presently the orchestral sound is lashed to a furious climax. The lament returns. An abbreviated version of the second theme serves as coda. At the end we hear a combination of bassoon and string tone similar to that with which the symphony opened. The music descends to the dark regions whence it issued.

It was through his art that Tchaikovsky conquered the forces of disunity within himself, lifted himself above despair, and won his place in history. He captured in his music the mood of a time and place, endowed it with artistic form, and by an act of will and imagination made it comprehensible to men everywhere.

35 Other Symphonists

"What Wagner did for human love, I have done for divine."
César Franck

A number of composers distinguished themselves in the symphonic field during the final decades of the nineteenth century. Among them were two major figures: César Franck and Anton Bruckner.

César Franck

César Franck (1822–90) was the most important composer of French instrumental music in the late romantic era. He forged the link between the musical traditions of France and Germany. (He was born, appropriately, in the country that lies between the two cultures—Belgium, at Liège.) Franck was for thirty years organist of the Church of St. Clotilde in Paris. His inspired improvisations on the instrument he loved constituted the summit of French achievement in this field.

Franck was a religious mystic for whom music was an act of faith. His was a nature given to contemplation and ecstasy. He saw the four movements of the sonata as a progression from conflict to triumph; a spiritual advance from inner struggle and doubt to the serenity of belief.

Franck sought to knit together the movements of the sonata structure through the use of cyclical form. He not only brought back themes from the earlier movements in the later ones, but carried the principle a step farther: he derived all his material from a few basic themes, which appear in manifold transformations throughout the different movements.

The D-minor Symphony (1886–88), Franck's most widely played work, displays the essential qualities of his style. It is an ample piece in three movements, abounding in opulent harmonies and heaven-storming proclamation. The first movement opens with a slow introduction that flowers from a motive whose intervals duplicate the three-note questioning motive at the beginning of Liszt's *Les Préludes*:

The ensuing Allegro non troppo (not too fast), in alla breve or cut time, combines dramatic and lyric elements. This is a spacious sonata-allegro form marked by much repetition and sequence. The second movement is an imaginative Allegretto that unites the principle of statement-departure-return with that of theme transformation. The principal idea is a plaintive melody sung by the English horn to the accompaniment of a harp and pizzicato strings. The impetuous finale is marked Allegro non troppo. (By a *finale* we mean the concluding movement of a multi-movement work.) This movement is an abbreviated sonata-allegro form. Its first theme, introduced by bassoons and cellos, is a melody capable of growth. This is contrasted with a second subject in the nature of a chorale introduced by the brass—one of those Franckian tunes which for many listeners is associated with spiritual aspiration. Cyclical construction is much in evidence in the Development and Recapitulation, and the work ends in a blaze of glory. The Symphony in D minor is a memorial to the late nineteenth-century style. It is the work of a musician whose dedication to lofty ideals assures him a niche in the history of his art.

Anton Bruckner

Like César Franck, Anton Bruckner (1824–96) was a religious mystic; his art was rooted in the traditions of Austrian Catholicism. He was born in a village in upper Austria and spent the first half of his life in the provinces. Bruckner did not produce his first mature work, the Mass in D minor, until he was forty. This unusually slow development may be explained partly by the fact that he worked in solitude far from the mainstream of musical activity, partly by his timid personality, which was beset by a total lack of self-confidence and a morbid sensitivity that from time to time erupted into nervous disorders. His twelve years as a church organist in the town of Linz (1856–1868) came to an end when he was forty-four. His reputation was sufficiently established by that time for him to be invited to teach theory and organ at the Vienna Conservatory. Several years later he joined the faculty of the University. Nine symphonies occupy the central position in Bruckner's list of works. The Ninth was almost finished when he died, at the age of seventy-two.

Bruckner expanded the first-movement form by substituting a group of themes for a single idea. He allowed the material to grow and develop throughout the movement. As a result, the Development frequently merged with the Recapitulation; transitional and concluding passages assumed greater importance. His adagios took on sweeping dimensions; their broadly flowing, song-like themes lent themselves ideally to extended lyricism. His orchestral language did not rely on the continual mixing of colors that was the basis of nineteenth-century orchestration; on the contrary, he was fond of contrasting complete choirs or families, brass against woodwinds or woodwinds against strings. We may recognize here the strong influence on his thinking of his favorite instrument, the organ.

The most popular of Bruckner's symphonies is the Fourth, the "Romantic" (1874–80). The first movement, marked *Ruhig bewegt* (moving quietly) unfolds serenely. How genuinely romantic is the opening; a solo horn announces a striking motive over a tremolo in the strings *ppp*:

This motive becomes the "motto" of the symphony, and in the coda of the movement grows from a whispered *ppp* to a grandiose *fff*. The lyrical Andante is followed by the lively Scherzo, in which hunting-horn figures evoke the vitality of Austrian popular song and dance. The final movement, *Mässig bewegt* (Allegro moderato), is in cyclical form: it mingles its own themes with reminiscences from the earlier movements. When the brass instruments triumphantly proclaim the rhythm of the motto theme at the end, the effect is very grand indeed.

This symphony serves as a fascinating introduction to Bruckner's world of thought and feeling. He put his mark on his time, and remains one of the major figures of the late romantic era.

36 The Concerto

The Nature of the Concerto

A *concerto* is a large-scale work in several movements for solo instrument and orchestra. (Occasionally, more than one soloist is involved.) Here the attention is focused upon the solo performer. This circumstance helps determine the style. The dramatic tension between soloist and orchestra is analogous to that between protagonist and chorus in Greek tragedy. The massive sonorities of the piano, the sweetness of the violin, or the dark resonance of the cello may be pitted against the orchestra. This opposition of forces constitutes the essential nature of the concerto.

In its dimensions the concerto is comparable to a symphony. Most concertos are in three movements: a dramatic allegro, usually in sonata form, is followed by a songful slow movement and a brilliant finale. In the opening movement, as in the first movement of a symphony, contrasting themes are stated ("exposed"), developed, and restated. In this case, however, the tension is twofold: not only between the contrasting ideas but also between the opposing forces—that is, the solo instrument against the group. Each of the basic themes may be announced by the *tutti* (literally, "all"; i.e., the orchestra as a whole) and then taken up by the solo part. Or the latter may introduce the ideas and the orchestra expatiate upon them.

A characteristic feature of the concerto is the cadenza which, you will recall, is a fanciful solo passage in the manner of an improvisation that is interpolated into the movement. The cadenza came out of a time when improvisation was an important element in art music, as it still is today in jazz. Taken over into the solo concerto, it made a dramatic effect: the orchestra fell silent and the soloist launched into a free play of fantasy on one or more themes of the movement. Before the nineteenth century the performer was usually the composer; consequently the improvisation was apt to be of the highest caliber. With the rise of a class of professional players who interpreted the music of others but did not invent their own, the art of improvisation declined. Thus the cadenza came to be composed beforehand, either by the composer or the performer.

The concerto has to be a "grateful" vehicle that will enable the performing artist to exhibit his gifts as well as the capacities of the instrument. This element of technical display, combined with appealing melodies, has helped to make the concerto one of the most widely appreciated types of concert music.

37 Grieg: Piano Concerto

"The fundamental trait of Norwegian folk song is a deep melancholy that may suddenly change to a wild unrestrained gayety.'

To the international music public Edvard Grieg (1843–1907) came to represent "the voice of Norway." The nationalist movement of which his music was an expression had a political background. Agitation for independence from Sweden came to a head during the last quarter of the nineteenth century. This cause, to which Grieg was devoted with all his heart, was crowned with success not long before his final illness. "What has happened in our country this year," he wrote, "seems like a fairy tale. The hopes and longings of my youth have been fulfilled. I am deeply grateful that I was privileged to live to see this."

Grieg was one of a rather large group of artists who start off with a lucky hit that they never quite duplicate. He was twenty-five when he wrote the Piano Concerto in A minor (1868). It remained his masterpiece.

The first movement, Allegro moderato (moderately lively), is in sonata-allegro form. It opens with a dramatic roll on the kettledrum and precipitously descending octaves in the solo part. The opening melody is introduced by the woodwinds, and with its subdued emotional coloring evokes the northern scene. We find here one of Grieg's mannerisms, a fragment of melody repeated in sequence on a higher degree of the scale:

After the orchestral statement this theme is given to the solo instrument.

The main function of the bridge is to lead from the first theme to the second. Sometimes, however, this transition is made so attractive that it takes on the character of a new idea, and that is the case here. The second theme is marked meno allegro (less fast), tranquillo e cantabile (tranquil and songful). Set forth by the cellos and taken over by the piano, this melody is in Grieg's most lyric vein.

An animated closing section concludes the Exposition. The development section, brief and intense, is marked by arpeggios on the piano that range from *pp* to *fff*. The harmonies are familiar to us now, but they sounded altogether novel to Grieg's contemporaries. The Recapitulation is climaxed by an impressive cadenza that presents the main theme embellished by ornate runs, massed chords, and octaves. There follows a coda marked Poco più allegro (a little faster).

The Adagio, an A-B-A form in ⅜ time, captures the lyric charm of a Grieg

song. The theme is presented pianissimo by muted strings. The middle section is characterized by delicate filigree work on the piano, after which the first theme is repeated *ff* in a mood of romantic pathos.

There is no break between the second and third movements. A brief transition, Allegro marcato (fast, with emphasis), leads into the finale, which is marked Poco animato (somewhat animated). This movement, in ternary (A-B-A) form, opens with a vigorously rhythmic theme of folk-dance character that is presented with bravura effect on the piano.

An effective contrast is supplied by the theme of the middle section, a dreamlike lyrical melody marked Poco più tranquillo (somewhat calmer), which is intro-

duced by a solo flute. After the restatement of the first section, a brief cadenza leads into the coda, at the climax of which the songful second theme is transformed into a sumptuous Andante maestoso. This triumphal ending, so characteristic of the romantic style, brings the work to a close.

It was given to Edvard Grieg to reveal to the world the Norwegian landscape and the soul of its people. His music, by turn dramatic and idyllic-pastoral, continues to exercise its own wistful charm.

38 Two Romantic Concertos

Mendelssohn: Violin Concerto

"I should like to write a violin concerto for you next winter. One in E minor is running through my head, and the beginning does not leave me in peace." Mendelssohn: Letter to Ferdinand David

The violin concerto in E minor (1844), a staple of the repertory, dates from the latter part of Mendelssohn's career. The work reveals his special gifts: clarity of form and grace of utterance, a subtle orchestral palette, and a vein of sentiment that is tender but reserved. The first movement, Allegro molto appassionato (very fast and impassioned), is a shapely example of sonata-allegro form. The customary orchestral introduction is omitted; the violin announces the main theme of the movement almost immediately. This is a resilient and active melody in the upper register, marked by decisive rhythm and a broad arch that unfolds in symmetrical phrases.

The expansion of this theme gives the violinist opportunity for brilliant passage work, much of it in triplets. These serve as a unifying element throughout the movement. The theme is then proclaimed by full orchestra (tutti).

As in the Grieg Concerto, the bridge between the first and second themes has so pronounced a character that it takes on the importance of a theme. It is an energetic melody of wide range:

The contrasting second theme is narrow of range and characterized by stepwise movement and narrow leaps. It is introduced by clarinets and flutes, tranquillo and pianissimo over a sustained tone on the open G string of the solo instrument. Such a sustained tone in one part while the harmonies change in the other parts is known as a *pedal point* (or organ point, from the fact that it occurs frequently in organ music as a note sustained by one of the pedal keys). The lyric theme provides an area of relaxation in the precipitous forward drive of the movement.

The development section explores motives of the principal theme and the transitional idea. It is marked by genuine symphonic momentum, culminating in the cadenza which, instead of coming at the end of the movement as is customary, serves as a link between the Development and a shortened Recapitulation. Under a curtain of widely spaced arpeggios on the violin the opening theme emerges in the orchestra. From here to the coda the movement gains steadily in power.

A brief transitional passage is in the $\frac{6}{8}$ meter of the Andante that follows. This is a large A-B-A form. The opening theme is calm and meditative:

The middle section, somber and elegiac, shows Mendelssohn in his most romantic mood; after which the serene opening melody returns.

An interlude in $\frac{4}{4}$ marked Allegretto non troppo (fairly fast, not too much so) leads into the next movement. The customary pauses between movements are omitted in this concerto, exemplifying the romantic desire to bind together the movements of a large work. The finale, an Allegro molto vivace (very fast and lively) in $\frac{4}{4}$ time, is introduced by brave flourishes scored for oboes, bassoons, horns, and trumpets, ff. It is a sonata-allegro form in the light breezy

manner that is Mendelssohn's most characteristic vein. The movement demands agile fingers and high spirits, a crisp staccato and brilliance of tone. The second theme continues in the light-hearted manner of the first, but is a much less active melody:

Mendelssohn elaborates on the chief theme and, in the Recapitulation, combines it with a singing melody in the orchestra:

Excitement builds steadily to the dazzling virtuosity of the coda.

Felicitous in melody and graceful in form, the Concerto displays the tender sentiment and classic moderation that were so typical of Mendelssohn's style.

Schumann: Piano Concerto

"In these years I have been very industrious. One must work as long as the day lasts."

The first movement of Schumann's celebrated Piano Concerto in A minor was written in 1841 as an independent Phantasie for Piano and Orchestra. The second and third movements were added four years later.

The Allegro affettuoso (lively and with feeling) opens with an imperious sequence of chords in dotted rhythms on the piano. The oboe announces the lyric theme from which the movement germinates. The piano answers. The first half of the melody for the most part moves stepwise along the scale. The leap of an octave to the topmost note (at ×) makes an arresting climax, from which the melodic curve gently subsides. Two motives (A and B) are to be distinguished, which assume importance not only in this but also in the subsequent movements.

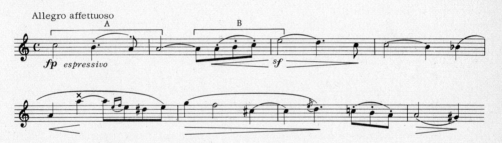

A somber melody in the violins, in the nature of a transition, ends in a third motive (C) which assumes great structural significance in the course of the movement. Notice that this motive is immediately repeated at a higher pitch (sequence):

The second theme of the movement is not a new idea at all, but an imaginative transformation of the first theme. It is played by the clarinet against impetuous

descending arpeggios on the piano. After a triumphal tutti, the principal theme is heard in a new transformation, as a tender dialogue between piano and clarinet in 6/4 time, Andante espressivo. The fantasy-like character of the movement

167

permits the composer to achieve an effect of spontaneity and caprice within the frame of sonata-allegro form, which he handles with the freedom of a poet. The thematic material is stated, developed, and restated. There is a steady drive to the rhapsodic cadenza, which is woven in whole out of the germinal theme. The latter appears in a new transformation in the coda, as a vigorous march in 2/4 time.

Schumann called the slow movement an Intermezzo (Interlude). It is marked Andantino grazioso (at a going pace, gracefully). This meditative song starts out as a gracious colloquy between piano and orchestra. Notice that the material is derived from the B motive of the first movement and is repeated in sequence:

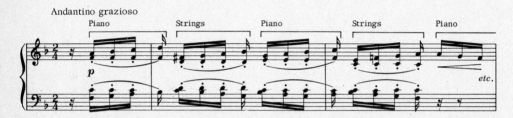

The middle section is based on a broadly flowing melody in the cellos, to which the piano responds with decorative patterns spun out in true Schumannesque manner. The opening section returns to round out the A-B-A form, and a fleeting reference to the first movement acts as a transition to the third.

The finale is an Allegro vivace in 3/4 time. A vigorous theme on the piano is seconded by the orchestra. The B motive of the germinal theme appears in a

new context. This Allegro gives the listener a sense of vigorous movement and abounds in elaborate passage work for the solo instrument. A contrasting theme appears which, through clever shifting of accent, creates a phrase of slower motion without actually changing either the meter or the tempo:

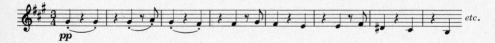

In this concerto Schumann achieved the perfect fusion of dramatic and lyric elements. The work is universally regarded as his masterpiece.

OPERA

---

39 The Nature of Opera

"It is better to invent reality than to copy it."
Giuseppe Verdi

For well over three hundred years the opera has been one of the most alluring forms of musical entertainment. A special glamor is attached to everything connected with it—its arias, singers, and roles, not to mention its opening nights. Carmen, Mimi, Aïda, Tristan—what character in fact or fiction can claim, generation after generation, so constant a public?

An *opera* is a drama that is sung. It combines the resources of vocal and instrumental music, soloists, ensembles, and chorus, orchestra and ballet, with poetry and drama, acting and pantomime, scenery and costumes. To weld the diverse elements into a unity is a problem that has exercised some of the best minds in the history of music.

At first glance opera would seem to make impossible demands on the credulity of the spectator. It presents us with human beings caught up in dramatic situations, who sing to each other instead of speaking. The reasonable question is (and it was asked most pointedly throughout the history of opera by literary men): how can an art form based on so unnatural a procedure be convincing? The question ignores what must always remain the fundamental aspiration of art: not to copy nature but to heighten our awareness of it. True enough, people in real life do not sing to each other. Neither do they converse in blank verse, as Shakespeare's characters do; nor live in rooms of which one wall is conveniently missing so that the audience may look in. All the arts employ conventions that are accepted both by the artist and his audience. The conventions of opera are more in evidence than those of poetry, painting, drama, or film, but they are not different in kind. Once we have accepted the fact that the carpet can fly, how simple to believe that it is also capable of carrying the prince's luggage.

Opera functions in the domain of poetic drama. It uses the human voice to

The interior of the Cuvilliés Theater in Munich, one of the world's most beautiful opera houses.

impinge upon the spectator the basic emotions—love, hate, jealousy, joy, grief—with an elemental force possible only to itself. The logic of reality gives way on the operatic stage to the transcendent logic of art, and to the power of music over the life of the heart.

The Components of Opera

In the classic type of opera the explanations necessary to plot and action are presented in a kind of musical declamation known as *recitative*. This vocal style imitates the natural inflections of speech; its rhythm is curved to the rhythm of the language. Instead of a purely musical line, recitative is often characterized by a rapid patter and "talky" repetition of the same note; also by rapid question-and-answer dialogue that builds dramatic tension in the theater.

Recitative gives way at the lyric moments to the *aria*, which releases the emotional tension accumulated in the course of the action. The aria is a song, generally of a highly emotional kind. It is what audiences wait for, what they cheer, and what they remember. An aria, because of its beauty, may be effective even when removed from its context. Many arias are familiar to multitudes who never heard the operas from which they are excerpts.

Grand opera is sung throughout. In opera of the more popular variety the recitative is generally replaced by spoken dialogue. This is the type known among us as operetta or musical comedy, which has its counterpart in the French *opéra-comique* and German *Singspiel*. Interestingly enough, in Italy— the home of opera—even the comic variety, the *opera buffa*, is sung throughout.

The emotional conflicts in opera are linked to universal types and projected through the contrasting voices. Soprano, mezzo-soprano, and contralto are counterposed to tenor, baritone, and bass. The coloratura- soprano has the highest range and greatest agility in the execution of trills and rapid passages. The dramatic soprano is preferred for dynamic range and striking characterization, the lyric for gentler types. If the heroine is a soprano, her rival for the hero's love will often be a contralto. The tenor may be lyric or dramatic. German opera has popularized the *Heldentenor* (heroic tenor) who, whether as Siegfried or Tristan, is required to display endurance, brilliance, and expressive power.

An opera may contain ensemble numbers—trios, quartets, quintets, sextets, septets—in which the characters pour out their respective feelings. The unique quality of an ensemble number lies in its ability to project several contrasting emotions at the same time, the music binding these together into an artistic whole.

The chorus is used in conjunction with the solo voices or it may function independently in the mass scenes. It may comment and reflect upon the action, in the manner of the chorus in Greek tragedy. Or it may be integrated into the action. In either case choral song offers the composer rich opportunities for varied musical-dramatic effects.

The orchestra provides the accompaniment. It sets the mood and creates the atmosphere for the different scenes. It also functions independently, in the overture, preludes to the acts, interludes, and postludes. Sometimes the ballet provides an eye-filling diversion in the scenes of pageantry that are an essential feature of grand opera. In the folk operas of the nineteenth century the ballet was used to present peasant and national dances.

The *libretto*, or text, of an opera must be devised so as to give the composer his opportunity for the set numbers—the arias, duets, ensembles, choruses, marches, ballets, and finales that are the traditional features of this art form. The librettist must not only create characters and plot with some semblance of dramatic insight, but he also has to fashion situations that justify the use of music and could not be fully realized without it.

Opera appeals primarily to those composers and music lovers who are given to the magic of the theater. It exerts its fascination upon those who love to hear singing. Thousands who do not feel at home with the abstract instrumental forms warm to opera, find there a graphic kind of music linked to action and dialogue, whose meaning it is impossible to mistake. Countless others are attracted for the very good reason that opera contains some of the grandest music ever written.

40 Giuseppe Verdi

"Success is impossible for me if I cannot write as my heart dictates!"

In the case of Giuseppe Verdi (1813–1901), the most widely loved of operatic composers, it happened that the time, the place, and the personality were happily met. He inherited a rich tradition, his capacity for growth was matched by masterful energy and will, and he was granted a long span of life in which his gifts attained their full flower.

His Life

Born in a hamlet in northern Italy where his father kept a little inn, the shy, taciturn lad grew up amid the poverty of village life. His talent attracted the attention of a prosperous merchant in the neighboring town of Busseto, a music lover who made it possible for the youth to pursue his studies. After two years in Milan he returned to Busseto to fill a post as organist. When he fell in love with his benefactor's daughter, the merchant in wholly untraditional fashion accepted the penniless young musician as his son-in-law. Verdi was twenty-three, Margherita sixteen.

Three years later he returned to the conquest of Milan with the manuscript of an opera. *Oberto, Count of San Bonifacio* was produced at La Scala in 1839 with fair success. The work brought him a commission to write three others. Shortly after, Verdi faced the first crisis of his career. He had lost his first child, a daughter, before coming to Milan. The second, a baby boy, was carried off by fever, a catastrophe followed several weeks later by the death of his young wife. "My family had been destroyed, and in the midst of these trials I had to fulfill my engagement and write a comic opera!" *Un Giorno di regno* (King for a Day) failed miserably. "In a sudden moment of despondency I despaired of finding any comfort in my art and resolved to give up composing."

The months passed; the distraught young composer adhered to his decision. One night he happened to meet the impresario of La Scala, who forced him to take home the libretto of *Nabucco* (Nebuchadnezzar, King of Babylon). "I came into my room and, throwing the manuscript angrily on the writing table, I stood for a moment motionless before it. The book opened as I threw it down. My eyes fell on the page and I read the line *Va pensiero sull' ali dorate* ["Go, my thought, on golden wings"—first line of the chorus of captive Jews who by the waters of Babylon mourn their ravished land]. Resolved as I was never to write again, I stifled my emotion, shut the book, went to bed, and put out the

Giuseppe Verdi.

candle. I tried to sleep, but *Nabucco* was running a mad course through my brain." In this fashion the musician was restored to his art. *Nabucco*, presented at La Scala in 1842, was a triumph for the twenty-nine-year-old composer and launched him on a spectacular career.

Italy at this time was in the process of birth as a nation. The patriotic party aimed at liberation from the Hapsburg yoke and the establishment of a united kingdom under the House of Savoy. Verdi from the beginning identified himself with the national cause. "I am first of all an Italian!" In this charged atmosphere his works took on special meaning for his countrymen. No matter in what time or place the opera was laid, they interpreted it as an allegory of their plight. The chorus of exiled Jews from *Nabucco* became a patriotic song. As the revolutionary year 1848 approached, Verdi's works—despite the precautions of the Austrian censor—continued to nourish the zeal of the nationalists. In *Attila* the line of the Roman envoy to the leader of the Huns, "Take thou the universe—but leave me Italy!" provoked frenzied demonstrations. When, in *The Battle of Legnano*, a chorus of medieval Italian knights vowed to drive the German invaders beyond the Alps, audiences were aroused to indescribable enthusiasm.

But the impact of Verdi's operas went deeper than the implications of the plot. The music itself had a dynamic force, a virility that was new in the Italian theater. This was truly, as one writer called it, "agitator's music." It happened too that the letters of Verdi's name coincided with the initials of the nationalist slogan—Vittorio Emmanuele *Re d'*Italia (Victor Emmanuel King of Italy). The cries of V*iva Verdi* that rang through Italian theaters not only hailed the composer but voiced the national dream. Rarely has a musician more ideally filled the role of a people's artist.

Although he was now a world-renowned figure, Verdi retained the simplicity that was at the core both of the artist and man. He returned to his roots, acquiring an estate at Busseto where he settled with his second wife, the singer Giuseppina Strepponi. She was a sensitive and intelligent woman who had created the leading roles in his early operas and who was his devoted companion for half a century. After Italy had won independence, he was urged to stand for election to the first parliament because of the prestige his name would bring the new state. The task conformed neither to his talents nor inclinations, but he accepted and sat in the chamber of deputies for some years.

The outer activities of this upright man framed an inner life of extraordinary richness. It was this that enabled him to move with unflagging creative tension from one masterpiece to the next. He was fifty-seven when he wrote A*ïda*. At seventy-three he completed *Otello,* his greatest lyric tragedy. In 1893, on the threshold of eighty, he astonished the world with *Falstaff*. Such sustained productivity invites comparison with the old masters, with a Monteverdi, Michelangelo, or Titian.

His death at eighty-eight was mourned throughout the world. He bequeathed the bulk of his fortune to a home for aged musicians founded by him in Milan. Italy accorded him the rites reserved for a national hero. From the thousands who followed his bier there sprang up a melody—V*a pensiero sull' ali dorate.* . . . It was the chorus from *Nabucco* that he had given his countrymen as a song of solace sixty years before.

His Music

Verdi's music struck his contemporaries as the epitome of dramatic energy and passion. Endowed with an imagination that saw all emotion in terms of action and conflict—that is, in terms of the theater—he was able to imbue a dramatic situation with shattering expressiveness. Again and again he demands of his librettists "a short drama, swift-moving and full of passion . . . Passions above all!" True Italian that he was, he based his art of melody, which to him was the most immediate expression of human feeling. "Art without spontaneity, naturalness, and simplicity," he maintained, "is no art."

Of his first fifteen operas the most important is *Macbeth* (1847), in which for the first time he derived his story material from Shakespeare, whom he called "the great searcher of the human heart." There followed in close succession the three operas that established his international fame: *Rigoletto* in 1851, based on Victor Hugo's drama *Le Roi s'amuse* (The King is Amused); *Il Trovatore* (The Troubadour) in 1853, derived from a fanciful Spanish play;

and *La Traviata* (The Lost One) also produced in 1853, which he adapted from the younger Dumas' play *La Dame aux camélias* (The Lady of the Camellias). In these works of sustained pathos the musical dramatist stands before us in full stature.

The operas of the middle period are on a more ambitious scale, showing Verdi's attempt to assimilate elements of the French grand opera. The three most important are *Un Ballo in maschera* (A Masked Ball, 1859), *La Forza del destino* (The Force of Destiny, 1862), and *Don Carlos* (1867). In these the master fights his way to a higher conception of dramatic unity. "After *La Traviata*," he declared, "I could have taken things easy and written an opera every year on the tried and true model. But I had other artistic aims."

These aims came to fruition in *Aïda*, the work that ushers in his final period (1870–93). *Aïda* was commissioned by the Khedive of Egypt to mark the opening of the Suez Canal in 1870. Delayed by the outbreak of the Franco-Prussian War, the production was mounted with great splendor in Cairo the following year. In 1874 came the Requiem Mass in memory of Alessandro Manzoni, the novelist and patriot whom Verdi revered as a national artist.

Verdi found his ideal librettist in Arrigo Boito (1842–1918), himself a composer whose opera *Mefistofele* was popular in Italy for years. For their first collaboration they turned to Shakespeare. The result was *Otello* (1887), the apex of three hundred years of Italian lyric tragedy. After its opening night the seventy-four-year-old composer declared, "I feel as if I had fired my last cartridge. Music needs youthfulness of the senses, impetuous blood, fullness of life." He disproved his words when six years later, again with Boito, he completed *Falstaff* (1893). Fitting crown to the labors of a lifetime, this luminous comic opera ranks with Mozart's *Figaro*, Rossini's *Barber of Seville*, and Wagner's *Meistersinger*.

La Traviata

Based on a libretto by Francesco Piave, *La Traviata* is a work suffused with intimate lyricism and emotion. The heroine is Violetta Valéry, one of the reigning beauties of Paris, who already is suffering from the first ravages of consumption when the drama begins. She lives for the pleasure of the moment until Alfredo Germont, a young man of good Provençal family, falls in love with her and offers to take her away from the fast life that is killing her. They go off to a country villa; but their idyllic existence is interrupted by Alfredo's father, a dignified gentleman who appeals to Violetta not to lead his son to ruin and disgrace the family name. She reveals to him that, far from taking money from Alfredo, she has been supporting them herself. The elder Germont is amazed, as the interview progresses, by the dignity of her bearing. All the same, her past is against her, and he points out to her the futility of a liaison that can never win the approval of God or man. Violetta takes the agonizing decision to leave Alfredo and returns to Baron Douphol, whose mistress she has been.

Unaware of his father's intervention, Alfredo breaks into a gay party at the home of Violetta's friend Flora. Mad with jealousy and rage, he accuses Violetta of having betrayed him, insults her in the presence of her friends, and is challenged to a duel by the Baron. The last act takes place in Violetta's bedroom. Her doctor friend comes to cheer her up but confides to her maid Annina that she is dying. Left alone, Violetta reads a letter from the elder Germont informing her that the duel has taken place. He has told his son of her great sacrifice; both are coming to ask her forgiveness. Alfredo arrives. He is followed by his father who realizes how blind he has been and, filled with admiration for Violetta, welcomes her as his daughter. It is too late. Violetta dies in Alfredo's arms.

The orchestral prelude to Act I opens with soft string music, and then launches into a broad melody that we will later recognize as the love theme. When the curtain rises, a brief introduction described in the score as "a most brilliant and very lively Allegro," sets the mood for a lively supper-party in Violetta's house. The guests ask the Baron for a song; he declines. Alfredo, at Violetta's request, obliges with the celebrated Drinking Song:

The guests go in to supper. Violetta, seized by a fit of coughing, remains behind and is joined by Alfredo. Their dialogue unfolds against the background of a lilting orchestral waltz. Violetta shrugs off his declaration of love but he persists. His aria introduces the love theme of the opera, marked "expansively":

She disclaims all hope of love in a light-hearted melody whose nimble leaps and runs show off the coloratura voice. Pleasure, she tells him, is all she expects of life. When he persists, she unpins the flower that she is wearing, hands it to him and says that he may come back when it has faded. "Tomorrow?" Alfredo asks. He takes the flower and leaves, full of hope.

Dawn has arrived; the guests take their departure in an exciting chorus. Left alone, Violetta is moved in spite of herself by the promise of love and pours out her feelings in one of the opera's favorite arias:

The music shifts to an Allegro brillante as she remembers that what she really desires is freedom:

As the act moves to a brilliant close, we see her torn between the two.

Act II, Scene 1, takes place in a country house near Paris. Alfredo, in hunting costume, sings of his new-found happiness in an appealing Andante. He learns that Violetta has gone to Paris to raise some money. He leaves; Violetta returns. The scene between her and Alfredo's father covers a wide range of emotion, from Germont's plea that she not bring disgrace on his family to Violetta's anguish at the thought of giving up Alfredo. In the end she yields. After the elder Germont has left, she sends a message to the Baron that she is returning to Paris; then she writes Alfredo a farewell letter. He returns. Without telling him the truth, she takes leave of him in an intensely moving scene. The melody at this point is a variation of the love theme:

After she leaves, Alfredo receives her letter and realizes the truth. He lets out a cry of despair as his father returns to console him. Germont, in a popular aria, advises his son to leave the wicked city and return to the simple pleasures of their life in Provence:

But Alfredo refuses to be consoled.

The second scene is set in Flora's town house. Her guests are entertained by a Gypsy ballet. Alfredo arrives and takes his place at the gaming table; Violetta

LA TRAVIATA, Act II, Scene 2: Alfredo throws his winnings at the feet of Violetta. (Metropolitan Opera production)

comes in on the arm of the Baron. The Baron and Alfredo play for huge stakes; Alfredo wins. The scene builds steadily to the climax of the act, when Alfredo calls the guests together, tells them how Violetta has betrayed him, and with furious contempt hurls his winnings at her feet. She faints in Flora's arms; Germont arrives in time to witness his son's dreadful behavior, and the act ends with a grand ensemble in which each of the characters gives expression to his feelings.

The Prelude to Act III sets the mood for the melancholy outcome of the drama. Violetta, in bed, is attended by the faithful Annina. She reads Germont's letter while the orchestra intones the love theme pianissimo. Then, looking into the mirror and seeing the ravages wrought by her disease, she laments her fate in a profoundly moving aria:

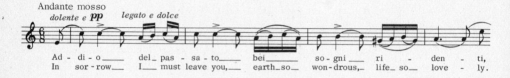

It is carnival time. The voices of the merrymakers outside accentuate the gloom within. The music, ever more animated, builds up to a climax as Alfredo arrives.

The lovers are reunited in a grand duet and dream of a happy future together:

Germont appears. Humbled by Violetta's nobility of character, he embraces her tenderly, but she sinks rapidly. Her death leaves her friends stunned.

This is romantic opera at its best. Dumas's heroine lives on in the opera house—a perennially appealing figure whose all too human frailties have been endowed with nobility and pathos by the lovely strains with which Verdi invested her love, suffering, and her death.

Aïda

Grand opera is a more formal type than lyric opera; in plot and music it strives for a style of lofty pathos, and exploits all the possibilities of the opera house for spectacular display. In Aïda Verdi produced what has been called "the perfect grand opera." The libretto by Antonio Ghislanzoni gives ample opportunity for picturesque scenery, ballets, processionals and mass scenes; the exotic setting admirably frames the inner experiences of the protagonists. Character and situation are conceived in the grand manner.

The action is laid in Egypt in the time of the Pharaohs during a war with the Ethiopians. Aïda, princess of Ethiopia, has been captured and is slave to Amneris, the Egyptian princess. The latter is in love with the conquering general Radamès but rightly suspects that he loves Aïda rather than herself. Aïda's father Amonasro, the Ethiopian king, is brought into captivity, his identity unknown to his enemies. He still hopes to break the Egyptian power. Radamès, torn between his passion for the enemy princess and devotion to his country, is induced to flee with Aïda and her father, but the plan is foiled by the jealous Amneris. Aïda and Amonasro make their escape, Radamès surrenders to the High Priest. He is sentenced to die by being entombed in a subterranean vault. Amonasro having been killed while leading the revolt, Aïda returns in time to make her way into the crypt. The lovers die together.

The Prelude is evolved from the lyrical phrase associated with Aïda through-

out the opera. Act I is in two scenes, the first of which is laid in the palace of the Pharaohs at Memphis. Radamès reveals his love in the famous aria Celeste Aïda:

Andantino con espressione

Ce - les - te A - i - da, ____ for - ma ____ di - vi - na ____
Ce - les - tial A - i - da, ____ Fair - est a - mong wo - men ____

The basic conflict is established in a dramatic trio in which Amneris voices her jealousy, Radamès fears she suspects the truth, and Aïda wavers between love and her devotion to the Ethiopian cause. The entrance of the King and court introduces the note of pomp that alternates throughout the play with the expression of personal emotion. Radamès is appointed leader of the Egyptian forces against the Ethiopians. Aïda, alone, echoes the words with which the Egyptians acclaimed Radamès, *Ritorna vincitor!* (Return a conqueror!), but realizes that his victory would spell her father's defeat and is cruelly torn between both loyalties.

The second scene takes place in the temple at Memphis. Priests pray to the

Andante con moto

Pos - - sen - te, pos - sen - te ____ Fthà ____
Hail, ____ might - y, hail, might - y ____ Ptah, ____

god Phtah. The music assumes an oriental coloring as priestesses perform a sacred dance. Radamès receives the consecrated arms and is blessed by the High Priest.

Act II opens in the royal palace. Moorish slaves perform a lively dance to distract the Princess. Aïda enters. A tense scene ensues between both women, at the climax of which Amneris in a jealous rage threatens to destroy her rival.

There follows the great scene at the gates of Thebes where the returning hero is welcomed by King, court, and populace. Trumpets sound the theme of the Triumphal March.

Ablaze with color and movement, this grand finale of Act II culminates in a stirring sextet. Amneris and the High Priest demand death for the prisoners. Amonasro, in chains, begs for mercy. The King, in a magnanimous mood, releases all the prisoners except Amonasro, and bestows the hand of his daughter upon the victorious general. Radamès and Aïda hide their consternation. This mass scene, with its interplay of personal drama and regal splendor, has come to represent everything we associate with grand opera.

Act III is packed with action of the kind that Verdi needed for the full deploying of his powers. The scene—"Night: stars and a bright moon"—is on

AïDA, Act II, Scene 2: The ensemble at the climax of the Triumphal Scene. (Metropolitan Opera production)

the bank of the Nile. We hear the voices of the priests in the temple of Isis; Amneris, accompanied by the High Priest, arrives to pray on the eve of her marriage. They disappear within; the theme of Aïda in the orchestra announces her arrival. In an extended aria, *O patria mia!*, in which an oboe interjects its sorrowful phrases, she bemoans the fact that she will never see her native land again:

Oh pa-tria mia, mai più, mai più__ ti ri-ve-drò!
Oh dear-est land, no more, no more, shall I see you.

There follows a dramatic encounter with her father. Amonasro begins the duet by recalling the beauties of their homeland. This is one of the most expansive melodies in the opera:

Ri-ve-drai le fo-re-ste jm-bal-sa-ma-te, le fre-sche val-li, i no-stri tem-pli d'or!
Once a-gain you shall see our fra-grant for-ests, our ver-dant val-leys, our tem-ples decked with gold!

181

He then orders her to find out from her lover the plan of the forthcoming campaign. He curses her when she refuses, and his rage breaks her will. Amonasro conceals himself at the approach of Radamès. In the rapturous duet of the lovers Aïda persuades him that they can never find happiness within reach of the vengeful Amneris. He consents to fly with her, and divulges the plan of attack against Ethiopia. Amonasro appears and reveals himself as the enemy king; Radamès realizes that he has betrayed his country. At this point Amneris, who has come out of the temple, grasps the situation and accuses Radamès of treason. Amonasro, drawing his knife, rushes upon her, but Radamès interposes and saves her life. He implores Aïda and her father to save themselves. Soldiers appear before the temple and give pursuit. Radamès, lost, surrenders to the implacable High Priest.

Act IV opens in a hall in the palace. Amneris orders Radamès to be brought before her. She tells him she can save him if he will renounce Aïda. He spurns her offer and is led back to his cell. Overcome with remorse, the Princess curses the jealousy that has brought ruin to her beloved and endless misery to herself. The priests are heard pronouncing the death sentence.

In the final scene we see the subterranean vault and the temple above it. As the fatal stone is lowered Radamès voices his hope that Aïda will never learn his fate. Then he discovers her in the crypt. Against the chorus of the priests in the temple above, the eerie chant of the priestesses, and the lamenting of Amneris, the lovers sing their final duet, a farewell to earth, a vision of eternal bliss to come:

The creator of this majestic drama incarnated the soul of his nation. Boito recognized this when he saluted in Verdi "the genius of our race. He revealed to the world the ardor, the dash, the affection, the force of the Italian spirit."

41 Richard Wagner

"The error in the art genre of opera consists in the fact that a means of expression—music—has been made the object, while the object of expression—the drama—has been made the means."

Richard Wagner (1813–83) looms as probably the single most important phenomenon in the artistic life of the latter half of the nineteenth century.

Historians, not without justice, divide the period into "Before" and "After" Wagner. The course of postromantic music is unthinkable without the impact of this complex and fascinating figure.

His Life

He was born in Leipzig, son of a minor police official who died when Richard was still an infant. A year later the widow married Ludwig Geyer, a talented actor, playwright, and painter, who encouraged the artistic inclinations of his little stepson. The future composer was almost entirely self-taught; he had in all about six months of instruction in music theory. At twenty he abandoned his academic studies at the University of Leipzig and obtained a post as chorus master in a small opera house. In the next six years he gained practical experience conducting in provincial theaters. He married the actress Minna Planer when he was twenty-three, and produced his first operas—*Die Feen* (The Fairies, 1834) and *Das Liebesverbot* (Love Prohibited, 1836, after Shakespeare's *Measure for Measure*). As with all his later works, he wrote the librettos himself. He was in this way able to achieve a unity of the musical-dramatic conception beyond anything that had been known before.

While conducting at the theater in Riga he began a grand opera based on Bulwer-Lytton's historical novel *Rienzi, Last of the Tribunes*. This dealt with the heroic figure who in the fourteenth century led the Roman populace against the tyrannical nobles and perished in the struggle. With the first two acts of *Rienzi* under his arm he set out with Minna to conquer the world. His destination was Paris. But the world, then as now, was not easily conquered; Wagner failed to gain a foothold at the Paris Opéra.

The two and a half years spent in Paris (1839–42) were fruitful nevertheless. He completed *Rienzi* and produced *A Faust Overture*, the first works that bear the imprint of his genius. To keep alive he did hack work such as arranging

Richard Wagner.

popular arias for the cornet, and turned out a number of articles, essays, and semifictional sketches. He also wrote the poem and music of *The Flying Dutchman* (1841). All this despite poverty and daily discouragement.

Just as the harassed young musician was beginning to lose heart a lucky turn rescued him from his plight: *Rienzi* was accepted by the Dresden Opera. Suddenly his native land was wreathed in the same rosy mist as had formerly enveloped Paris. He started for Dresden, gazed on the Rhine for the first time, and "with great tears in his eyes swore eternal fidelity to the German fatherland." *Rienzi*, which satisfied the taste of the public for historical grand opera, was extremely successful. As a result, its composer in his thirtieth year found himself appointed conductor to the King of Saxony.

With *The Flying Dutchman* Wagner had taken an important step from the drama of historical intrigue to the idealized folk legend. He continued on this path with the two dramas of the Dresden period—*Tannhäuser* (1843–45) and *Lohengrin* (1846–48)—which bring to its peak the German romantic opera as established by his revered model, Carl Maria von Weber (1786–1826). The operas use subjects derived from medieval German epics, display a profound feeling for nature, employ the supernatural as an element of the drama, and glorify the German land and people. But the Dresden public was not prepared for *Tannhäuser*. They had come to see another *Rienzi* and were disappointed.

A dedicated artist who made no concessions to popular taste, Wagner dreamed of achieving for opera something of the grandeur that had characterized the ancient Greek tragedy. To this task he addressed himself with the fanaticism of the born reformer. He was increasingly alienated from a frivolous court that regarded opera as an amusement; from the bureaucrats in control of the royal theaters, who thwarted his plans; and from Minna, his wife, who was delighted with their social position in Dresden and had no patience with what she considered his utopian schemes. He was persuaded that the theater was corrupt because the society around it was corrupt. His beliefs as an artist led him into the camp of those who, as the fateful year 1848 approached, dreamed of a revolution in Europe that would end the power of the reactionary rulers. With reckless disregard of the consequences, Wagner appeared as speaker at a club of radical workingmen, and published two articles in an anarchist journal: "Man and Existing Society" and "The Revolution." "The present order," he wrote, "is inimical to the destiny and the rights of man. The old world is crumbling to ruin. A new world will be born from it!"

The revolution broke out in Dresden in May 1849. King and court fled. Troops dispatched by the King of Prussia crushed the insurrection. Wagner escaped to his friend Liszt at Weimar, where he learned that a warrant had been issued for his arrest. With the aid of Liszt he was spirited across the border and found refuge in Switzerland.

In the eyes of the world—and of Minna—he was a ruined man; but Wagner did not in the least share this opinion. "It is impossible to describe my delight when I felt free at last—free from the world of torturing and ever unsatisfied desires, free from the distressing surroundings that had called forth such desires." He settled in Zurich and entered on the most productive period of his career. He had first to clarify his ideas to himself, and to prepare the public for the novel conceptions toward which he was finding his way. For four years he wrote no music, producing instead his most important literary works, *Art and Revolution, The Art Work of the Future*, and the two-volume *Opera and Drama* which sets forth his theories of the music drama, as he named his type of opera. He next proceeded to put theory into practice in the cycle of music dramas called *The Ring of the Nibelung*. He began with the poem on Siegfried's death that came to be known as *Götterdämmerung* (Dusk of the Gods). Realizing that the circumstances prior to this action required explaining, he added the drama on the hero's youth, *Siegfried*. The need for still further explanation led to a poetic drama concerning the hero's parents, *Die Walküre* (The Valkyrie). Finally, the trilogy was prefaced with *Das Rheingold* (The Rhinegold), a drama revolving about the curse of gold out of which the action stems.

Although he wrote the four librettos in reverse order he composed the operas in sequence. When he reached the second act of *Siegfried* he grew tired, as he said, "of heaping one silent score upon the other," and laid aside the gigantic task. There followed his two finest works—*Tristan und Isolde* (1857–59) and *Die Meistersinger von Nürnberg* (The Mastersingers of Nuremberg, 1862–67). The years following the completion of *Tristan* were the darkest of his life. The mighty scores accumulated in his drawer without hope of performance: Europe contained neither theater nor singers capable of presenting them. Wagner succumbed to Schopenhauer's philosophy of pessimism and renunciation—he who could never renounce anything. He was estranged from Minna, who failed utterly to understand his artistic aims. His involvement with a series of women who did understand him—but whose husbands objected—obtruded the *Tristan* situation into his own life and catapulted him into lonely despair. As he passed his fiftieth year, his indomitable will was broken at last. He contemplated in turn suicide, emigration to America, escape to the East.

At this juncture intervened a miraculous turn of events. An eighteen-year-old boy who was a passionate admirer of his music ascended the throne of Bavaria as Ludwig II. One of the young monarch's first acts was to summon the composer to Munich. The King commissioned him to complete the *Ring*, and Wagner took up the second act of *Siegfried* where he had left off a number of years before. A theater was planned especially for the presentation of his music dramas, which ultimately resulted in the festival playhouse at Bayreuth. And to crown his happiness he found, to share his empire, a woman equal to him in will and courage—Cosima, the daughter of his old friend Liszt. For the last time the *Tristan* pattern thrust itself upon him. Cosima was the wife of his fervent disciple, the conductor Hans von Bülow. She left her husband and children in order to join her life with Wagner's. They were married some years later, after Minna's death.

The Wagnerian gospel spread across Europe, a new art-religion. Wagner societies throughout the world gathered funds to raise the temple at Bayreuth. The radical of 1848 found himself, after the Franco-Prussian War, the national artist of Bismarck's German Empire. The *Ring* cycle was completed in 1874, twenty-six years after Wagner had begun it, and the four dramas were presented to worshipful audiences at the first Bayreuth festival in 1876.

One task remained. To make good the financial deficit of the festival the master undertook his last work, *Parsifal* (1877–82), a "consecrational festival drama" based on the legend of the Holy Grail. He finished it as he approached seventy. He died shortly after, in every sense a conqueror, and was buried at Bayreuth.

His Music

Wagner gave shape to the desire of the romantic era for the closest possible connection between music and dramatic expression; and beyond that, for the closest connection between music and life. "Every bar of dramatic music," he maintained, "is justified only by the fact that it explains something in the action or in the character of the actor."

He did away with the old "number" opera with its arias, duets, ensembles, choruses, and ballets. His aim was a continuous tissue of melody that would never allow the emotions to cool. This meant abandoning the old distinction between recitative and aria. He evolved instead an "endless melody" that was molded to the natural inflections of the German language, more melodious than traditional recitative, more flexible and free than traditional aria.

The focal point of Wagnerian music drama, however, is not the melody but the orchestra. Here is the nub of his operatic reform. He developed a type of symphonic opera as native to the German genius as vocal opera is to the Italian. The orchestra is the unifying principle of his music drama. It is both participant and ideal spectator; it remembers, prophesies, reveals, comments. The orchestra floods the action, the characters, and the audience in a torrent of sound that incarnates the sensuous ideal of the romantic era.

The orchestral tissue is fashioned out of concise themes, the *leitmotifs*, or "leading motives"—Wagner called them basic themes—that recur throughout the work, undergoing variation and development even as the themes and motives of a symphony. The leitmotifs carry specific meanings, like the "fixed idea" of Berlioz or the germ theme in a symphonic poem of Liszt. They have an uncanny power of suggesting in a few strokes a person, an emotion, or an idea; an object —the Gold, the Ring, the Sword; or a landscape—the Rhine, Valhalla, the lonely shore of Tristan's home. Through a process of continual transformation the leitmotifs trace the course of the drama, the changes in the characters, their experiences and memories, their thoughts and hidden desires. As the leitmotifs accumulate layer upon layer of meaning, they themselves become characters in the drama, symbols of the relentless process of growth and decay that rules the destinies of gods and heroes.

Wagner's musical language was based on *chromatic harmony*, which he pushed to its then farthermost limits. Chromatic dissonance imparts to Wagner's music its restless, intensely emotional quality. Never before had the unstable tone combinations been used so eloquently to portray states of soul. The active chord (Dominant) seeking resolution in the chord of rest (Tonic) became in Wagner's hands the most romantic of symbols: the lonely man—Flying Dutchman, Lohengrin, Siegmund, Tristan—seeking redemption through love, the love of the ideal woman, whether Senta or Elsa, Sieglinde or Isolde.

Die Walküre

In *The Rheingold*, the first drama of *The Ring of the Nibelung*, Alberich the dwarf (a Nibelung) tries to make love to the three Rhinemaidens who guard the river's gold. When they mock him, he steals their treasure and fashions from it the ring that will give power to him who has abjured love. In turn, Wotan, father of the gods (his name survives in our Wednesday, or Wotan's day), wrests the treasure from Alberich, who thereupon puts a curse on the ring and whoever shall possess it. Wotan uses the stolen treasure to pay the giants Fafner and Fasolt for having built the castle of Valhalla; they force him to include the ring as part of their fee. In the course of these transactions Wotan himself has become corrupt, and we see him in the ensuing dramas trying to escape the curse that Alberich has laid upon the ring.

His one hope is to breed a race of heroes who will return the ring to its rightful owners. He becomes father of the twins Siegmund and Sieglinde; their mother is of the heroic Volsung race. With Siegmund and Sieglinde the human element enters into the action, since the first drama dealt exclusively with gods, giants, and dwarfs. Siegmund and Sieglinde are reared in the forest; they are separated in their youth, and Sieglinde is married against her will to a stern warrior named Hunding.

Die Walküre (The Valkyrie) opens on a stormy night when the exhausted Siegmund, fleeing from his enemies, staggers into Hunding's dwelling and collapses on the hearth. Sieglinde revives the stranger. He wants to continue his journey, lest his habitual ill luck fall on the woman who has sheltered him; but she assures him that he cannot bring ill luck to a house where it already dwells. Hunding returns and is struck by the resemblance between the stranger and his wife. He asks Siegmund to reveal his identity. Siegmund tells how, one day while he was hunting with his father, their enemies burned their dwelling, slew his mother and carried off his sister; in a subsequent fight he was separated from his father and never saw him again. Misfortune continued to follow him.

187

While trying to defend an unfortunate maiden whose brothers were forcing her into a hateful marriage, he killed them. For this reason he is justified in calling himself Wehwalt, the woeful one.

It turns out that he had killed Hunding's kinsmen. Hunding had been summoned to help them but arrived too late, and has returned home to find his enemy on his hearth. He tells Siegmund that he will respect the laws of hospitality and let him spend the night; on the morrow they will fight. He orders Sieglinde to the inner room, repeats his challenge, and follows her. Before she leaves, Sieglinde looks yearningly at Siegmund and indicates a particular spot in the giant ash tree around which Hunding's dwelling is built.

At this point begins the scene with which we are concerned. Siegmund, left alone, broods on the unkind fate that has led him into the arms of his enemy. The orchestra reflects his mood by sounding the rhythm of Hunding's leitmotif in the horns and timpani:

His thoughts turn to the compassionate woman who has filled his heart with a strange emotion. The cellos play the Love motive:

Siegmund remembers that his father had promised him a sword in his hour of need. He calls upon Wälse—the name by which he knows Wotan—to keep his promise. The fire in the hearth flares up, illuminating the spot in the trunk of the ash tree to which Sieglinde had tried to draw his attention. A trumpet proclaims the motive of the Sword, which will take on growing importance as the scene unfolds:

Out of these three motives is woven the texture of Siegmund's soliloquy.

Sieglinde comes out of the inner chamber. She says that she has put a sleeping potion in her husband's drink; now Siegmund may flee. His reply makes it clear that he has no intention of leaving her. She then tells him that she will guide him to the weapon he needs. She describes how at her wedding, as she sat among Hunding's kinsmen with grief in her heart, an old man entered, clad in gray. The majestic motive of Valhalla in the orchestra tells us who this was:

All were filled with fear at his glance, but upon her he gazed with tenderness. He drew out a sword which he thrust into the trunk of the ash tree until only the hilt remained visible. Since that day many strove to draw it forth, but in vain: the sword still awaits the one strong enough to possess it, the hero who— she hopes—will come to free her of her unhappiness. Siegmund embraces her. With growing ardor he proclaims his new-found hope and courage. The storm outside has passed; the door opens wide, revealing a glorious spring night; the full moon shines in. Siegmund's Spring Song is a hymn to the awakening of nature and love:

Sieglinde takes up this rapturous—if incestuous—love song. "You are the spring for which I longed. . . ." She clings to him, recognising herself in the features of the long-lost brother and playmate of her happy childhood. He had called himself Wehwalt, the woeful; she now renames him Siegmund, the victorious. Transported, they approach the tree. "With a mighty effort," Wagner directs, "Siegmund pulls the sword from the tree and shows it to the astonished and enraptured Sieglinde." In the orchestra, the brass triumphantly proclaim the motive of the Sword. Siegmund names his sword Nothung—Needful!— and tells Sieglinde that it will protect her and their love.

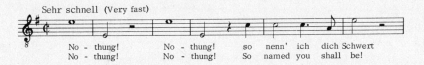

The orchestra weaves a glowing fabric out of the Sword and Love motives, to which are added two others, the motive of their clan, the Volsungs:

189

and that of Rapture:

The act reaches a frenzied climax as the lovers embrace.

This scene well illustrates Wagner's method of organizing his dramatic-musical material into great architectural units that have an organic unity. It reveals the symphonic ideal that underlies his music dramas, achieved by weaving the leitmotifs into a glowing orchestral texture that carries the action forward with irresistible force. How majestic is the conception, and how masterful its execution.

In the next act Fricka, Wotan's wife and the goddess of the hearth, demands of him that he punish Siegmund for the sinful love that violates the laws of gods and men. Sorrowfully Wotan yields to her imprecations and summons his favorite daughter, the goddess Brünnhilde, to carry out the verdict: in the ensuing battle between Hunding and Siegmund, he tells her, Siegmund must die. Brünnhilde is one of the nine daughters of Wotan known as Valkyries, warrior-maidens whose task it is to circle above the battlefield on their steeds, pick up the warriors who have fallen and carry them off to Valhalla where they will feast forevermore. When Brünnhilde comes to Siegmund to announce the dread decision, she is moved to pity, and in the battle between the two warriors she tries to help him instead of Hunding. Wotan appears, Siegmund is slain, and Hunding—at one glance from the enraged god—falls dead. Brünnhilde flees with Sieglinde, who desires only death; but Brünnhilde tells her that she must live because she carries within her a new life—Siegmund's son.

By disobeying Wotan Brünnhilde has brought upon herself the full force of her father's wrath. He decrees that she is to forfeit her position as a goddess and become a mortal, to suffer all the pain and sorrow of mortal women. Brünnhilde, horrified, asks Wotan how he can possibly leave her to the mercy of any man who will overpower her. Wotan makes one concession: he will put her into a deep sleep and cause a magic fire to surround the rock on which she lies. Only the true hero—he who knows no fear—shall be able to pass through the flames and claim her as his bride.

Die Walküre (notice that the opera is named for Brünnhilde, the Valkyrie, rather than for Sieglinde or Siegmund) ends with the Magic Fire Scene. Brünnhilde dons her armor and lies down on the rock, sinking into a deep sleep as Wotan raises his spear to summon Loge, the god of fire. Loge's motive suggests the leaping and crackling of the flames that surround the rock, gradually hiding

DIE WALKÜRE, Act III: Wotan bids farewell to Brünnhilde. (Bayreuth Festival production)

Brünnhilde from view. Chromatic scales add to the excitement. The orchestra plays the serene motive of the Magic Fire:

Wotan ends his farewell: "He who fears my spear shall never pass through the flames!" As he sings this line we hear the valorous theme of Siegfried; for he, son of the ill-fated Siegmund and Sieglinde, is the hero who in the next drama of the cycle will pass fearlessly through the flames and awaken Brünnhilde with a kiss:

191

As the curtain slowly falls upon this German version of the "Sleeping Beauty" legend, the rock is enveloped in flames, against which is outlined, in his black cloak, spear uplifted, the majestic figure of the father of the gods.

Tristan und Isolde

For unity of mood, sustained inspiration, and intensity of feeling *Tristan und Isolde* is the most perfectly realized of Wagner's lyric tragedies. Certainly no more eloquent tribute has ever been offered to consuming passion.

Isolde, proud princess of Ireland, has been promised in marriage to the elderly King Mark of Cornwall. Tristan, the King's nephew and first knight of his court, is sent to bring her to her new home. They had met before when Tristan fought against her country. What had begun as hate, wounded pride, and desire for revenge turns to overpowering love.

The Prelude to the drama depicts the passion that enmeshes them. This extraordinary tone poem evolves from a leitmotif that recurs throughout the opera. Used always to suggest the yearning, tenderness, and rapture of the lovers, the famous progression is the epitome of chromatic—that is, romantic—harmony. Notice how the voices move by half step along the chromatic scale:

Prelude, in Wagner's use of the term, indicates a freer and more flexible form than overture. It is more in the character of a fantasy, lyric rather than dramatic, contemplative rather than narrative. This prelude comes as close as any piece ever did to those twin goals of musical romanticism, intoxication and ecstasy.

Tristan and Isolde prepare to disembark in Cornwall, at the end of Act I. (Metropolitan Opera production)

The Love Duet is from Act II, which takes place outside King Mark's castle. The King leaves, ostensibly on a hunt. Tristan and Isolde meet in the garden. The scene between them is one of the high points of Wagnerian drama. The lovers hymn the night: "O sink down upon us, night of love, Allow us to forget life, Free us forever from the world." Day represents the loathed reality that stands between them, the pretense and hopelessness of their worldly existence. Night is the symbol of their inner life—the real life. In this scene is consummated the great romantic theme of the individual estranged from society. Love is the dream and the search; the longing for oblivion. Since happiness is not to be attained in life, love leads beyond its confines, becoming the ultimate escape. Thus the impulse that generates life is transformed, by a magnificently romantic gesture, into the self-destroying passion whose fulfillment is death.

At the high point of the Duet, King and retinue burst in upon the lovers. Tristan has been betrayed by his false friend Melot. He takes leave of Isolde and in the ensuing scuffle suffers himself to be mortally wounded. The doom they knew was inescapable is now upon them.

Act III is laid before Tristan's castle in Brittany, where he has been brought by his faithful servant Kurvenal. In his delirium he fancies himself back in the garden with Isolde. She arrives in time to see him die. The opera culminates in her hymn to love and death, the *Liebestod*. She envisions herself united with Tristan, the obstacles that kept them apart in life surmounted at last. Transfigured, she sinks lifeless on Tristan's body.

The Love Death follows a basic design in music. Beginning softly and from

a low pitch it builds up in a steadily mounting line to the torrential climax, whence it subsides. The aria is fashioned from a motive first heard during the love scene in Act II. There it was cruelly interrupted by the arrival of the King. Now, ascending wave upon wave, it achieves its final resolution.

Wagner satisfied the need of an era for sensuous beauty, for the heroic, the mystical, the grandiose. He takes his place in history as the most commanding figure of the romantic period: a master whose achievements have become part and parcel of our musical heritage.

42 Bizet: *Carmen*

"The composer gives the best of himself to the making of a work. He believes, doubts, enthuses, despairs, rejoices, and suffers in turn."

Blazing with color and passion, *Carmen* is one of the rare works that enjoy the admiration of musicians no less than that of a world-wide public. It exemplifies the Gallic genius at its best.

His Life

Georges Bizet (1838–75) was born and raised in Paris. A student at the Conservatory, in his twentieth year he won the highest award of the school, the Prix de Rome, which made possible a three-year stay in the Italian capital. The rest of his career was passed in his native city. The works of his youth were followed by three operas that display the composer's power of evoking exotic atmosphere. *Les Pêcheurs de perles* (The Pearl Fishers, 1863) is a drama of love and ritual in Ceylon. Four years later came *La jolie fille de Perth* (The Fair Maid of Perth, after Walter Scott's novel), which takes place in a romanticized Scotland. *Djamileh* (1872) is laid in Cairo. Although none of these was an overwhelming success, they established Bizet's reputation as a composer to be reckoned with.

The greater Bizet emerges in the incidental music to Alphonse Daudet's somber drama *L'Arlésienne* (The Woman of Arles, 1872). He revealed himself here as the master of a limpid style with a tenderness all his own. Bizet was now offered the libretto that Meilhac and Halévy had fashioned from Prosper Mérimée's celebrated story of Gypsy life and love. He was ready for his appointed task. There resulted the greatest French opera of the century.

Mérimée's tale belonged to a new type of literature dealing with elemental beings and passions, seeking to bring literature closer to the realities of life. Mérimée's Gypsies, smugglers, and brigands were depicted with an honesty that heralded the new realism. The opera softened the naked fury of the original story. But enough remained to disturb the audience that assembled for the opening night on the third of March, 1875. The Opéra-Comique was a "family theater" where the bourgeois of Paris brought their wives and marriageable daughters. Passion on the stage was acceptable if it concerned kings and duchesses long dead; Carmen and her unsavory companions were too close for comfort.

The opera was not the fiasco that popular legend makes it out to have been. It did fail, incomprehensibly, to conquer its first audience. However, the rumor that the piece was not quite respectable helped give it a run of thirty-seven performances in the next three months, an average of three a week. In addition the manager offered the composer and his librettists a contract for their next work. The failure of *Carmen* was only in Bizet's mind. He had put every ounce of his genius into the score. Its reception was a bitter disappointment. His delicate constitution, worn out by months of rehearsals and by the emotional tension that had attended the production, was ill-prepared to take the blow. Exactly three months after the premiere he succumbed to a heart attack, at the age of thirty-seven. His death came just when he had found his mature style.

The work was immediately dropped by the Opéra-Comique. Yet within three years it had made its way to Vienna and Brussels, London and New York. Five years later it returned to Paris, was received rapturously, and embarked on its fabulously successful career. Today it is one of the best-loved operas of the world.

Carmen

The power of this lyric drama stems from the impact with which it projects love, hate, desire. The story line follows one of the most compelling themes literature has to offer—the disintegration of a personality. The action is swift and unfaltering as the characters are carried step by step to their doom. The libretto is a tightly knit affair revolving around a few key words—love, fate, death, nevermore—all of them eminently singable. Carmen dominates the action, by turn tender, cruel, seductive, imperious, sensual, arch. She remains one of the great characters in opera. As for Don José, the simple soldier who is brought to ruin through his obsessive love, he is caught in a web not of his making, in which he is held by the deepest forces of his nature. Escamillo, the bullfighter who supplants José in Carmen's fickle affections, is properly vain and swaggering. Micaela, José's childhood sweetheart who seeks in vain to lead him back to the wholesome life of his village, is the incarnation of goodness and devotion. (As frequently happens, she comes off less vividly than the questionable characters.) These personages and their conflicts are realized on the highest level of operatic art. They come to life through the music; they are unthinkable without it.

The Prelude foreshadows the contrasting moods of the opera. The opening theme is the one that returns in the final scene outside the bull ring at Seville: a melody gay, external, charged with excitement and pleasure-seeking, its character accentuated by the pounding rhythm and the bright orchestration.

There follows the suave melody of the Toreador Song.

Against this is posed the motive of Fate. Beneath a tremolo on the strings is heard the ominous phrase, played by clarinet, bassoon, trumpet, and cellos, that runs like a dark thread through the score.

The curtain rises on a square in Seville. Soldiers loiter before the guard house. Micaela appears, inquiring for Don José. Abashed by the flirtatious young men, she withdraws. A trumpet in the distance announces the changing of the guard. The relieving company, led by Lieutenant Zuniga and Corporal Don José, is preceded by a crowd of urchins who enter to the strains of a captivating march. The clock strikes twelve. The girls emerge from the cigarette factory, which

Carmen sings the HABANERA:
"Love is fickle and wild and
free." (Grace Bumbry in the
Metropolitan Opera
production)

attracts the young blades of Seville. Carmen's entrance is heralded by a rhythmic transformation of the Fate motive.

Her character is established at once by the Habanera, based on a teasing tango rhythm. Bizet rewrote it thirteen times before he was satisfied. "Love is fickle and wild and free, A bird that none may ever tame. . . . If you love me not, I love you. And if I love—beware!" The refrain is enhanced by the emphasis of the chorus on the crucial word—*l'amour.*

Don José, waiting for Micaela to return, is absorbed in his thoughts. Piqued by his indifference, Carmen takes the flower from her dress and throws it to him.

197

José, bewildered, picks it up. The orchestra sounds the motive of Fate. Meanwhile, the clock having struck in the factory, the girls withdraw. Micaela enters with a letter from José's mother. The ensuing duet establishes José and Micaela as the "good people" in the play.

Micaela's exit is followed by a quarrel in the factory between Carmen and another girl. At once the stage is filled with two factions of chattering women. Carmen is led in, insolent, self-assured. She tries to strike one of the women who demands that she be sent to jail. Zuniga and his men go off to obtain an order for her arrest. Carmen, hands tied behind her back, is left in the custody of José.

She loses no time in exerting her wiles. "Near the ramparts of Seville, at the inn of my friend Lillas Pastia, I shall soon dance the gay seguidilla." What

is more, she will dance it with him. Only two steps are necessary for them to achieve this delightful prospect: that he set her free and that he join her there. José manfully resists her allurements, but the outcome is assured. By the time the lieutenant returns, the rope around Carmen's wrists has been loosened. She is marched off to jail guarded by José. At the bridge, as prearranged, she knocks him down and escapes.

The Entr'acte (Prelude to the second act) opens with a lonely melody, Moorish in coloring, played by two bassoons accompanied by strings and drum. The curtain rises on Lillas Pastia's tavern. Carmen's song celebrates the joys of Gypsy life. She is joined in the refrain by her friends Mercedes and Frasquita.

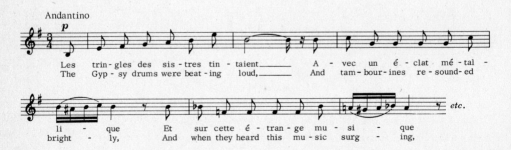

Lieutenant Zuniga presses his attentions on Carmen. She learns from him that José, who received two months in jail for helping her escape, has just been set free. Escamillo arrives, his musical portrait being given by the swaggering open-

Allegro moderato

Vo - tre toast, je peux__ vous le ren - dre, Se -
Here's a toast, a toast I drink__ glad - ly, Se -

ñors, se - ñors__ car a - vec les sol - dats__
ñors, se - ñors,__ For we are broth - ers all!__

ing of the Toreador Song. He is taken with Carmen, which does not in the slightest please Lieutenant Zuniga. Both men leave, the lieutenant promising to return.

The Quintet follows, a brilliant ensemble number in which two of the smugglers invite Carmen and her friends to join them in a little matter of contraband that evening. Mercedes and Frasquita accept with delight. Carmen declines. Her reason? She awaits Don José. His voice is heard in the distance, singing the plaintive melody of the Entr'acte. The Gypsies leave, suggesting that Carmen recruit her new lover into the smugglers' band.

The scene between her and José covers a wide range of emotions. She begins by dancing for him, accompanying herself on the castanets. José is enchanted. When the retreat sounds from the distant barracks he prepares to leave. Carmen, infuriated at a lover who puts duty above her, mocks him as a dullard and bids him go. José, sadly drawing from his pocket the flower he has treasured these many weeks, sings an aria that is a favorite: "Here is the flower that you threw me, I kept it still in my dark cell. In dead of night I saw your face. I had but one desire, one hope—to see you once again."

Andantino
p

La fleur que tu m'a-vais je - té - e, Dans ma pri-son__ m'é-tait res - té - e,
Here is the flow-er that you threw me, I kept it still__ in my dark cell.__

Carmen, realizing her power over him, decides to lure José into the smugglers' band. She holds out to him the attractions of a life of freedom. José implores her not to tempt him. He begins to realize that he must renounce her. At this point there is a knocking at the door. Lieutenant Zuniga demands admittance, breaks in, and scoffs at Carmen for taking a common soldier when she can have an officer. He orders José to leave. The latter, mad with jealousy, draws his saber. The two men fight and are separated by the Gypsies. Zuniga is hustled out by Carmen's friends. For José the die is cast: he has attacked an officer and may return no more to the life he knew. The smugglers welcome the deserter into their midst with a rousing finale that hails the freedom of their lawless life.

The Prelude to the third act affords a breathing spell in the unfolding tragedy. A flute solo over harp accompaniment evokes the quietude of a mountain fastness. The curtain rises on the hide-out of the smugglers, who enter to an eerie march. Don José gloomily reflects on his situation. His mother still thinks him an honest man. If she but knew. Carmen, already tired of him, suggests that perhaps he had better return to his village. They quarrel. The orchestra comments with the motive of Fate.

The Card Trio is one of the highlights of the opera. Frasquita and Mercedes tell their fortunes. The cards promise each what her heart desires—to Frasquita a handsome young lover, to Mercedes a rich old husband who will die and leave her his money. Carmen cuts the cards and draws the ace of spades. "Death! I've read it well. First I, then he." In a monologue of great pathos she accepts her fate. "In vain you shun the answer that you dread, in vain you cut the cards. To no avail—the cards remain sincere. . . . Though you try twenty times, the pitiless cards repeat—Death!" One must hear it in the opera house to realize the explosive power of that word *mort*.

There follows the famous aria of Micaela, who comes seeking José, hoping still to rescue him from his madness. The horn adds romantic luster to the melody.

Je dis,———— que rien ne m'é - pou - van - te Je——— dis,———— hé -
I say———— that I'll not be a - fraid———— I —— say,———— a -

Escamillo arrives, eager to join Carmen. A fight develops between him and the jealous José. The men draw knives but are separated. José learns from Micaela that his mother is dying and is persuaded to leave with her. "We will meet again!" he warns Carmen as the motive of Fate is heard.

The Prelude to the last act, with its somber melody on the oboe above an accompaniment of pizzicato strings and tambourine, has a quality of foreboding. The curtain goes up on a brilliant scene outside the arena in Seville. The crowd hails the various groups of bullfighters who march in to the blatant tune of the Overture. Finally Escamillo enters, with a radiant Carmen on his arm. There is a tender exchange between them. The crowd accompanies him into the ring. Carmen remains to face José.

The encounter is taut, volcanic. Each is driven by the basic law of his nature: José cannot give up his love, she cannot surrender her freedom. He entreats her to go with him—there is still time to begin anew. She refuses. "Then you love me no more?" "No, I love you no more." "But I, Carmen, I love you still!" He reaches the breaking point against the jubilant strains of the chorus in the arena. "For the last time, you fiend, will you come with me?" "No!" He stabs her as the Toreador Song rises from the crowd pouring out of the arena. José, dazed, kneels beside her body. The orchestra sounds the motive of Fate.

It was a German philosopher who, awakening from the intoxication of Wagnerian music drama, discovered in *Carmen* the ideal lyric tragedy. "It is necessary to Mediterraneanize music!" Nietzsche declared in one of the most eloquent tributes ever penned to a work of art. "I envy Bizet for having had the courage of this sensitiveness—this southern, tawny, sunburnt sensitiveness—which hitherto in the music of European culture had found no means of expression. I know of no case in which the tragic irony that constitutes the kernel of love is expressed with such severity or in so terrible a formula as in the last cry of Don José: 'Yes, it is I who killed her—Ah, my adored Carmen!' "

43 Musorgsky: *Boris Godunov*

"The artist believes in the future because he lives in it."

His Life

The most unmistakably Russian of composers, Modest Musorgsky (1839–81) was born in the town of Karevo in the province of Pskov. He prepared for a military career, in accordance with the family tradition, and was commissioned an officer in a fashionable regiment of Guards. At eighteen he came under the influence of a group of young musicians whose dream it was to found a Russian national school. With him as one of their number they formed "The Mighty Five," as an admiring critic named them. Their leader was Mily Balakirev (1837–1910), a self-taught composer who persuaded his four disciples —Alexander Borodin (1834–87), César Cui (1835–1918), Nicholas Rimsky-Korsakov (1844–1908), and Musorgsky—that they had no need of exercises in German counterpoint to give expression to the Russian soul.

As his talents developed, the young officer found his duties irksome and decided to withdraw from the military so that the could devote his life to music. His young friends had not yet accepted music as a full-time profession; Borodin was studying medicine, Cui was preparing for his later career as an expert on military fortification, and Rimsky-Korsakov was being trained as a naval officer. They counseled prudence. But Musorgsky, an ardent youth confident of his powers, was not to be dissuaded. At the age of twenty-two he resigned his commission.

Modest Musorgsky, Painting
by Ilya Repin.

History intervened at this point. The emancipation of the serfs in 1861 proved disastrous to the smaller landowners, Instead of being free to devote himself to art, the young aristocrat was obliged to seek employment. He established himself in St. Petersburg, where a post at the Ministry of Transport gave him a modest subsistence. Evenings were devoted to reading, musical sessions with his four comrades, and his first attempts at composition.

There asserted itself almost immediately a personality that would accept neither tradition nor guidance. He was one of those who must find their own path. His path led to an uncompromisingly realistic approach to life and art: "To trace the finest traits in man's nature and in the mass of humanity, digging resolutely through these unexplored regions and conquering them—that is the true mission of the artist!" How close in spirit to the credo of Dostoievsky, that other interpreter of "the insulted and the injured": "My function is to portray the soul of man in all its profundity."

Musorgsky at twenty-nine was ready for the great task of his life. In *Boris Godunov* he found a worthy theme out of his country's past. He fashioned the libretto himself, after Pushkin's drama and the old chronicles. The years spent in the composition of this drama were the happiest he was ever to know. He was sustained by the fellowship of the "Mighty Five" and was especially close to Rimsky-Korsakov. When *Boris* was submitted to the Imperial Opera, it was rejected on the ground that it lacked a leading woman's part. Musorgsky revised the work, adding the role of Marina. Finally all obstacles were overcome and the opera was presented in 1874. The critics damned it but the public was impressed. Nor were its political implications lost on the young intelligentsia, at that time seething with unrest under the tsarist regime. The choruses depicting the revolt against Tsar Boris were soon heard on the streets of St. Petersburg. Despite its success—or because of it—the opera was regarded with suspicion by the censor and, it was rumored, aroused the displeasure of the imperial family. In the following season it was presented with drastic cuts and ultimately dropped from the repertory.

The withdrawal of *Boris* ushered in the bitter period of Musorgsky's life. In the six years that remained to him he moved ever farther from his comrades of the "Five." He had outgrown his admiration of Balakirev. Cui, by now an influential critic, had betrayed him by attacking *Boris*. Rimsky and Borodin, he felt, had sold out for success, capitulating to the academic spirit which he regarded as the enemy of true art. He remained alone, a rebel to the end.

But the lonely struggle demanded sterner stuff than he was made of. Moods of exuberant belief in himself alternated with periods of depression. Poverty, lack of recognition, and the drudgery of his clerical post played their part. His need for escape revived a craving for stimulants that he had kept more or less under control since early manhood. Increasingly his life lost its direction and followed the erratic course of the alcoholic.

To these years of despair belong his greatest songs, the cycles *Sunless* and the *Songs and Dances of Death*. The major work of this period was the national opera *Khovanshtchina*, on his own libretto, dealing with the revolt of the imperial bodyguard against Peter the Great. But the creative force that had carried him through *Boris* was spent. He worked at this somber·drama until his death, refashioning it again and again, but left it unfinished.

As his former comrades rose higher in the social scale, Musorgsky sank lower. He who since childhood had identified himself with the humble of the earth now joined their ranks. The arc was complete, from the debonair young officer of the Guards to the slovenly tragic figure of Repin's famous portrait. Yet the spirit of the fighter remained with him to the end. In the last year of his life, when his friends had abandoned all hope of saving him, he still was able to write, "My motto remains unchanged. 'Boldly on! Forward to new shores!' . . . To seek untiringly, fearlessly, and without confusion, and to enter with firm step into the promised land—there's a great and beautiful task! One must give oneself wholly to mankind."

To give himself wholly he left his post and tried to support himself by accompanying singers. He was soon destitute. While attending a musical evening he collapsed and was placed in a hospital, suffering from delirium tremens. His comrades rallied to his side. But he died—as he had lived—alone, on his forty-second birthday, crying out, "All is ended. Ah, how wretched I am!"

Boris Godunov

In *Boris Godunov* (first version 1868–69, second version 1871–72) Musorgsky gave his country its great national drama. It has been said that the real hero of the opera is the Russian people. In the magnificent choral tableaux we encounter, instead of the conventional operatic chorus, vivid types drawn from the peasantry. The drama (in four acts with a prologue), which covers the years 1598–1605, centers about the guilt of a usurper. Boris Godunov, having contrived the murder of the young Tsarevich Dmitri, rightful heir to the throne, has himself proclaimed Tsar. As the years pass he is tormented by remorse. An adventurous young monk named Gregory resolves to pass himself off as the murdered Dmitri. He escapes to the Lithuanian frontier and proclaims himself heir to the throne. Welcomed by the Polish nobility who are opposed to Boris, he falls in love with the haughty Marina, daughter of the noble house of Mnishek. Marina knows that his claims are false, but she sees in him a means of becoming Empress and encourages him to aspire to her hand. The Pretender, back in Russia, rallies to his standard all who are discontented with Boris's rule. Boris, a prey to his guilt, is obsessed by hallucinations in which he sees the ghost of the murdered boy advancing toward him. He dies as the victorious Gregory-Dmitri marches on the Kremlin.

The Prologue, which takes place some years before the drama proper, consists of two great choral scenes. In the first the people gather before a monastery outside Moscow imploring Boris to accept the crown. They are egged on by a police officer who threatens them for not evincing sufficient enthusiasm. There follows the Coronation Scene, in which Musorgsky captures the majesty of tone and movement appropriate to a national drama. The bells of the Kremlin peal as the boyars proceed into the cathedral. The people sing a hymn of praise based on an ancient folk tune.

BORIS GODUNOV, Prologue, Scene 1: The populace entreats Boris to ascend the throne. (Bolshoi Theater production)

Like the sun when he fills___ the heav-ens with splen-dor, Glo - ry!

In the first scene of Act I the aged monk Pimen, alone in his cell, works through the night on his chronicle, "that future generations of the Faithful may know the fateful story of their land." (This line was chosen by Musorgsky's friends to be carved on his tomb.) Gregory, awaking from a troubled dream in which he saw himself raised above all the world, muses on the usurper in the Kremlin. None dares remind Boris of the murdered child, yet in this cell an unknown hermit records the terrible truth. The powerful archaic harmonies that Musorgsky loved evoke a distant, troubled time.

The second scene takes place in an inn on the Lithuanian frontier. Song is interspersed with action. The proprietress of the inn, as she darns, sings the Song of the Drake. Missail and Varlaam, two vagabonds masquerading as mendicant friars, arrive at the inn. With them is Gregory, anxious to cross the frontier. Warmed by the good woman's wine, Varlaam sings a ballad in old folk style of how Tsar Ivan smote the Tartars at Kazan. When the patrol arrives seeking the runaway monk, Gregory manages to divert their suspicion to Varlaam and makes his escape.

The second act, laid in the royal apartment in the Kremlin, sets off lyric song forms against dramatic recitative. Xenia, daughter of Boris, mourns her betrothed who has fallen in battle. To distract her the old nurse—the familiar Mamka of Russian tradition—sings the Song of the Gnat. Boris's young son Feodor responds with a "clapping song"—a worthy companion to Musorgsky's *Songs of Childhood*. Counterposed to these is the great monologue of the guilt-ridden Tsar. "I am supreme in power . . . and yet all happiness eludes my tortured soul."

I am su - preme in pow - er.   I've ruled this land five years in peace and qui - et.

The scene in which the agonized Tsar struggles with his hallucination is on the level of Shakespearean tragedy. "O conscience, thou art cruel. . . ." In his horror Boris becomes aware of the supreme irony: he, the all-powerful, is helpless against his fears.

Act III opens in the castle of the Mnisheks in Poland. Marina is characterized from the start—beautiful, proud, calculating. She dismisses the song of her maidens in praise of her beauty; for her, only songs of brave deeds. The rhythms of mazurka and polonaise are associated with the princess throughout. She has a short and violent encounter with the Jesuit Rangoni, who orders her to gain the throne through the Pretender in order to lead Russia back to the true faith.

The second scene takes place in the garden where Gregory, tormented by love, awaits her. Marina and her guests issue from the castle to the strains of a

Alla polacca, non troppo allegro

spirited polonaise. The ensuing love scene is admirable for its characterization of Gregory and Marina, the dramatic interplay between them, and the love melody—which makes a capital effect in the theater.

Andante
dolce

O Tsa-re-vitch, I__ im-plore you, o pray for-give me, yes for-give my an-ger.__

Act IV opens outside a convent near Moscow. The people await Boris and his retinue. They entreat the Tsar for bread; his boyars distribute alms. The village idiot, tormented by boys, appeals to Boris: "These boys took my only coin away. Why don't you have them murdered, as long ago you murdered our Tsarevich!" The courtiers would arrest the simpleton; but Boris, shaken, restrains them. "Go, pray for your Tsar, poor idiot. . . ." The second scene takes place in the throne room of the Kremlin. Boris, half crazed by guilt, appears before the Council of Boyars. The old monk Pimen tells of a vision in which he heard the voice of the murdered Dmitri. Boris, overcome, falls into the arms of the boyars. Feeling his end approach, he calls for his son. The boyars coldly eye the dying monarch as he takes leave of the boy. Musorgsky's recitative rises to the heights of lyric tragedy. "O bitter death! How cruel is thy clutch. Not yet, not yet—I still am Tsar! Death, be merciful. . . ."

The closing scene is set in a forest clearing. Peasants revolting against Boris's authority bind one of his noblemen and make sport of him. The Pretender appears at the head of his army and is acclaimed by the people. All leave save the village idiot who, seated on a stone, sings to himself. "Flow, silent tears, flow, bitter tears . . . Weep, Russian folk. Weep, hungry folk." It is a surpassingly eloquent ending. The curtain falls as Musorgsky—crowning audacity!—ends his work on an incomplete cadence.

The creator of this profound drama of conscience was forgotten by his countrymen for several decades after his death. It was in the Paris of the nineties that his work first came to be understood. Musicians of a new generation, among them Debussy and Ravel, discovered in him the first exponent of the modern temper, and found in his audacious harmonies an inspiration for their own.

The twentieth century has made amends for the incomprehension of the nineteenth. He who died so abjectly is recognized today as one of the towering figures of the late romantic period. As far as certain contemporary musicians are concerned, he is Russia's greatest composer.

44 Puccini: *La Bohème*

"Almighty God touched me with his little finger and said, 'Write for the theater—mind you, only for the theater!' And I have obeyed the supreme command."

The Italian operatic tradition was carried on, in the postromantic era, by a group of composers led by Giacomo Puccini (1858–1924). His generation included Ruggiero Leoncavallo, remembered for *I Pagliacci* (The Clowns, 1892), and Pietro Mascagni, whose reputation likewise rests on a single success, *Cavalleria rusticana* (Rustic Chivalry, 1890). These Italians were associated with the movement known as *verismo* (realism), which tried to bring into the lyric theater the naturalism of Zola, Ibsen, and their contemporaries. Instead of choosing historical or mythological themes, they picked subjects from everyday life and treated them in down-to-earth fashion. Puccini was strongly influenced by this trend towards operatic realism.

His Life

He was born in 1858 in Lucca, son of a church organist in whose footsteps he expected to follow. It was at Milan, where he went to complete his studies, that his true bent came to the fore. He studied at the Conservatory with Amilcare Ponchielli, composer of *La Gioconda*. The ambitious young musician did not have to wait long for success. His first opera, *Le Villi* (The Vampires, 1884), produced when he was twenty-six, was received with enthusiasm. *Manon Lescaut* (1893), based on the novel of Abbé Prévost, established him as the most promising among the rising generation of Italian composers. In Luigi Illica and Giuseppe Giacosa he found an ideal pair of librettists, and with this writing team he produced the three most successful operas of the early twentieth century: *La Bohème* in 1896; *Tosca* in 1900; and *Madame Butterfly*, after a play by David Belasco, in 1904. The dates should dispel the popular notion of Puccini as a facile melodist who tossed off one score after another. Each of his operas represented years of detailed work involving ceaseless changes until he was satisfied.

The Girl of the Golden West (1910) was based, like its predecessor, on a play by Belasco. The world premiere at the Metropolitan Opera House was a major event. A more substantial achievement was the trio of one-act operas:

Il Tabarro (The Cloak), *Suor Angelica* (Sister Angelica), and the comic opera *Gianni Schicchi* (1918). The first two are not heard frequently. The third is a masterpiece.

Handsome and magnetic, Puccini was idolized and feted wherever he went. His wife was jealous not without reason. "I am always falling in love," he confessed. "When I no longer am, make my funeral." As he entered middle age this singer of youth and love began to feel that his time was running out. "I am growing old and that disgusts me. I am burning to start work but have no libretto and am in a state of torment. I need work just as I need food." After much seeking he found a story that released the music in him and embarked on his final task—*Turandot*. He labored for four years on this fairy-tale opera about the beautiful and cruel princess of China. A work of consummate artistry, it is his most polished score. Puccini, ill with cancer, pushed ahead with increasing urgency. "If I do not succeed in finishing the opera someone will come to the front of the stage and say, 'Puccini composed as far as this, then he died.' "

He was sent to Brussels for treatment, accompanied by his son and the rough draft of the final scene. He died in 1924, following an operation, at the age of sixty-six. *Turandot* was completed from his sketches by his friend Franco Alfano. However, at the first performance at La Scala on April 25, 1926, the composer's wish was fulfilled. Arturo Toscanini, his greatest interpreter, laid down the baton during the lament over the body of Liù. Turning to the audience he said in a choking voice, "Here ends the master's work."

La Bohème

Puccini's best-loved work is based on Henri Murger's *La Vie de Bohème* (Bohemian life). The novel depicts the joys and sorrows of the young artists who flock to Paris in search of fame and fortune, congregating in the Latin Quarter on the Left Bank of the Seine. "A gay life yet a terrible one," Murger called their precarious existence woven of bold dreams and bitter realities. Puccini's music was peculiarly suited to this atmosphere of "laughter through tears." Remembering his own life as a struggling young musician in Milan, he recaptured its wistfulness and charm.

The Bohemian mood is set by the exuberantly rhythmic motive with which the opera opens.

The curtain rises at once, disclosing the attic in which live Rodolfo the poet, Marcello the painter, and their two comrades-in-arms, the young philosopher Colline and the musician Schaunard. Rodolfo's first arietta, *Nei cieli bigi*, is associated with him throughout the work. Its mixture of ardor and dreaminess well characterizes the young poet.

Nei cie-li bi-gi guar-do fu-mar dai mil-le co-mi-gno-li Pa-ri-gi,____
High o-ver Par-is, rings of smoke as-cend-ing from ev-'ry roof and chim-ney.____

Marcello and Rodolfo try to work, but can think of nothing but the cold. They are presently joined, first by Colline, then by Schaunard, who by a stroke of luck has come on some money. The landlord arrives with a nasty word—rent!—and is gotten rid of. The young men go off to the Café Momus to celebrate Christmas Eve, Rodolfo remaining behind to finish an article he is writing.

There is a knock on the door. Enter Mimi and romance. Her arrival is heralded in this act as in later ones by a poignant phrase in the orchestra. Her candle has gone out. Will Rodolfo light it? Their dialogue, bathed by the orchestra in a current of emotion, exemplifies the spell that Puccini casts over the homeliest sentiments. "A little wine? . . . Thank you . . . Here it is . . . Not so much . . . Like this? . . . Thank you."

Mimi returns, having lost her key. Their candles are extinguished by a gust of wind; they search for the key on the floor, in the dark. Rodolfo, finding it, has the presence of mind to slip it into his pocket. Their hands touch and Rodolfo sings his aria *Che gelida manina* (How cold your little hand, let me warm it here in mine). Here is the Italian *cantabile*, the melody gliding along the scale and rising in a broad golden curve to its crest. Three centuries of operatic tradition stand behind an aria such as this.

Rodolfo asks who she is. Mimi replies with the aria *Mi chiamano Mimi*:

Mi chia-ma-no Mi-mì, ma il mio no-me è Lu-ci-a____
I'm known____ as Mi-mi, I'm not sure____ just why.____

There follows a duet, based on a phrase from Rodolfo's aria, which now becomes the love theme of the opera.

Ah! tu sole co-man-di a-mor!____
Ah, this won-drous ec-sta-sy____

209

Rodolfo, smitten, invites her to the café, to phrases that have become part of the Italian folklore of flirtation. "Give me your arm, my little one. . . . I obey you, signor." The act ends, as it should, with a high C on the word *amor*.

Act II—Christmas Eve in the Latin Quarter—is a festive street scene in which Puccini's Italian sensibility blends with the Parisian setting. His feeling for atmosphere is manifest in the bright, brassy parallel chords with which the act opens. Rodolfo, having bought his new flame a rose-colored bonnet, brings her to the table where his friends are waiting. The appearance of Musetta causes a stir, proving especially agitating to her former love Marcello. This pert young lady is accompanied by an elderly dandy named Alcindoro, whom she persists in calling, in the tone of addressing a pet dog, Lulù. Marcello's agitation increases visibly as she sings her coquettish waltz song *Quando me'n vo.'*

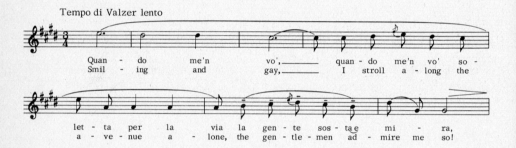

Having decided to get rid of "the old boy," she sends him on an errand. A grand reconciliation ensues between her and Marcello. The waiter brings the bill. The young men realize to their dismay that they haven't enough to pay it, whereupon the resourceful Musetta instructs the waiter to add it to Alcindoro's and present it to that gentleman upon his return. The young people disappear in the crowd as the act ends in the liveliest fashion.

In dramatic contrast, Act III opens in a pallid wintry dawn. We see a toll gate outside Paris. Peasant women enter bringing butter and eggs. From the tavern sound the voices of the last carousers, including Musetta's. Mimi appears, seeking Marcello. She confides to him her difficulties with Rodolfo, who is insanely jealous and makes their life unbearable. In this dialogue and the next the voices occasionally move in a free plastic declamation while the orchestra sings the melody. It is a favorite device with Puccini, and one that he uses with infallible effectiveness.

Rodolfo awakes within. To avoid a scene Mimi hides to one side behind some trees. Rodolfo appears and pours out his heart to Marcello; he is helpless against his jealousy and fears. Mimi is ill, she is dying; he is too poor to provide her with the care she needs. Mimi's tears and coughing

LA BOHÈME, Act II: The Bohemians react to Musetta's waltz song. (New York City Opera production)

reveal her presence. She bids farewell to Rodolfo in a touching aria, *Addio, senza rancor* (Goodbye, without bitterness).

The peak of the act is the quartet—better, double duet—at the close. Mimi and Rodolfo melodiously resign themselves to the parting they dread; while Marcello and Musetta quarrel violently, he accusing her of flirting, she retaliating with lively epithets. This Puccinian blend of pathos and comedy offers an excellent example of how an ensemble number may project the conflicting emotions of several characters. Marcello and Musetta run off in fury, leaving Mimi and Rodolfo to conclude their melancholy farewell.

Act IV is introduced by the Bohemian motive of the opening. We are back in the attic. Marcello and Rodolfo try to work, as they did in the opening scene; but their thoughts revert to their lost loves. Schaunard and Colline arrive with four rolls and a herring for their scanty meal. The young men indulge in horseplay that comes to an abrupt halt with the entrance of Musetta. In great agitation she tells them that Mimi is below, too weak to climb the stairs. They help her in.

The friends depart on various errands to lighten Mimi's last moments. Now the lovers are alone. "Ah, my lovely Mimi" . . . "You still think me pretty?" . . . "Lovely as the sunrise" . . . "You've made the wrong comparison; you

211

should have said, 'Lovely as the sunset . . .' " They recollect the night they met. The scene derives its impact from Puccini's masterful use of reminiscence. How better underline their blasted hopes than by quoting the music of that first encounter?

The others return, Marcello with medicine, Musetta with a muff to warm Mimi's hands. Rodolfo weeps. Mimi comforts him. "Why do you cry so? Here . . . love . . . always with you! My hands . . . warm . . . and . . . to sleep . . ." Musetta prays. Schaunard whispers to Marcello that Mimi is dead. Rodolfo's outcry "Mimi . . . Mimi!" is heard against the brief and terrible postlude of the orchestra. Puccini wrote the final scene with tears in his eyes. It has been listened to in like fashion.

La Bohème has retained its freshness for more than half a century. Within its genre it is a masterpiece.

PART THREE

MORE MATERIALS
OF MUSIC

"In any narrative—epic, dramatic or musical— every word or tone should be like a soldier marching towards the one, common, final goal: conquest of the material. *The way the artist makes every phrase of his story such a soldier, serving to unfold it, to support its structure and development, to build plot and counterplot, to distribute light and shade, to point incessantly and lead up gradually to the climax—in short, the way every fragment is impregnated with its mission towards the whole, makes up this delicate and so essential objective which we call* FORM."

Ernst Toch

45 The Organization of Musical Sounds: Key and Scale

"All music is nothing more than a succession of impulses that converge towards a definite point of repose."

Igor Stravinsky

At the beginning of this book we discussed various elements of music. Now that we have had occasion to hear how these are interwoven in a number of works, we are ready to consider the materials of music on a more advanced level, particularly as they relate to the organization of the large classical forms.

Tonality

A system of music must have set procedures for organizing tones into intelligible relationships. One of the first steps in this direction is to select certain tones and arrange them in a family or group. In such a group one tone assumes greater importance than the rest. This is the *do*, the Tonic or keynote around which the others revolve and to which they ultimately gravitate.

By a *key* we mean a group of related tones with a common center or Tonic. The tones of the key serve as basic material for a given composition. When we listen to a composition in the key of A we hear a piece based in large part upon the family of tones that revolve around and gravitate to the common center A.

This "loyalty to the Tonic" is inculcated in us by most of the music we hear. It is the unifying force in the do-re-mi-fa-sol-la-ti-do scale that was taught us

215

in our childhood. You can test for yourself how strong is the pull to the Tonic by singing the first seven tones of this pattern, stopping on *ti*. You will experience an almost physical compulsion to resolve the *ti* up to *do*.

The sense of relatedness to a central tone is known as *tonality*. This sense, needless to say, resides in our minds rather than in the tones themselves. Tonality underlies the whole system of relationships among tones as embodied in keys, scales, and the harmonies based on those, such relationships converging upon the "definite point of repose." Specifically, tonality refers to those relationships as they were manifest in Western music from around 1600 to 1900.

The "Miracle of the Octave"

A string of a certain length, when set in motion, vibrates at a certain rate per second and produces a certain pitch. Given the same conditions, a string half as long will vibrate twice as fast and sound an octave above. A string twice as long will vibrate half as fast and sound an octave below. When we sound together on the piano two tones other than an octave, such as C-D or C-F, the ear distinctly hears two different tones. But when we strike an octave such as C-C or D-D, the ear recognizes a very strong similarity between the two tones. Indeed, if one were not listening carefully one would almost believe that he was hearing a single tone. This "miracle of the octave" was observed at an early stage in all musical cultures, with the result that the octave became the basic interval in music. (An interval, we saw, is the distance and relationship between two tones.)

The method of dividing the octave determines the scales and the character of a musical system. It is precisely in this particular that one system differs from another. In Western music the octave is divided into twelve equal intervals. The fact is apparent from the look of the piano keyboard, where counting from any tone to its octave we find twelve keys—seven white and five black. These twelve tones are a half tone (semitone) apart. That is, from C to C-sharp is a half step, as is from C-sharp to D. The half step is the smallest unit of distance in our musical system. From C to D is a distance of two semitones, or a whole tone.

Oriental music is based on other units. In India, for example, quarter-tone scales are used. The Javanese divide the octave into five nearly equal parts. Arabic music contains a scale that divides the octave into seventeen parts. We are not able to play oriental music on the piano, which is tuned in semitones. Nor could we readily sing it, since we have been trained to think in terms of the whole- and half-tone intervals of our system.

The twelve semitones into which Western music divides the octave constitute what is known as the *chromatic scale*. They are duplicated in higher and lower octaves. No matter how vast and intricate a musical work, it is made up of the twelve basic tones and their higher and lower duplications.

216

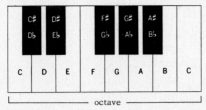

Note: The black keys are named in relation to their white neighbors. When the black key between C and D is thought of as a semitone higher than C, it is known as C-sharp. When it is regarded as a semitone lower than D, the same key is called D-flat. Thus D-sharp is the same tone as E-flat, F-sharp is the same tone as G-flat, and G-sharp is the same tone as A-flat. Which of these names is used depends upon the scale and key in which a particular sharp or flat appears.

The Major Scale

A *scale* is a series of tones arranged in consecutive order, ascending or descending. Specifically, a scale presents the tones of a key. The word is derived from the Italian *scala,* "ladder." In the widest sense a scale is a musical alphabet revealing at a glance the principle whereby tones are selected and related to one another in a given system.

The music of the classic-romantic period is based on two contrasting scales, the *major* and the *minor.* These consist of seven different tones, with the octave *do* added at the end of the series. The major scale has the familiar do-re-mi-fa-sol-la-ti-do pattern. Its seven tones are picked out of the possible twelve in order to form a centralized family or key out of which musical compositions may be fashioned. It becomes clear that compositions based on the major scale represent a "seven out of twelve" way of hearing music.

If you play the white keys on the piano from C to C you will hear the familiar do-re-mi-fa-sol-la-ti-do series; in other words, the major scale. Let us examine this series a little more closely.

We notice that there is no black key on the piano between E-F (*mi-fa*) and B-C (*ti-do*). These tones, therefore, are a semitone apart, while the others are a whole tone apart. Consequently, when we sing the do-re-mi-fa-sol-la-ti-do sequence we are measuring off a pattern of eight tones that are a whole tone apart except steps 3–4 (*mi-fa*) and 7–8 (*ti-do*). In other words, we are singing the pattern *do,* whole step, whole step, half step, whole step, whole step, whole step, half step. You will find it instructive to sing this scale trying to distinguish between the half- and whole-tone distances.

This scale implies certain relationships based upon tension and resolution. We have already indicated one of the most important of these—the thrust of the seventh step to the eighth (*ti* seeking to be resolved to *do*). There are others: if we sing *do-re* we are left with a sense of incompleteness that is resolved when *re* moves back to *do; fa* gravitates to *mi; la* descends to *sol.* These tendencies, we saw, reside not in the tones but in our minds. They are the meanings attached by our musical culture to the raw material of nature.

217

Most important of all, the major scale defines the two poles of classical harmony: the *do* or Tonic, the point of ultimate rest; and the *sol* or Dominant, representative of the active harmony. Upon the trackless sea of sound this relationship imposes direction and goal. Tonic going to Dominant and returning to Tonic becomes a basic progression of classical harmony. It will also serve, we shall find, as a basic principle of classical form.

The Key as an Area in Musical Space

The major scale, we said, is a "ladder" of whole and half tones.

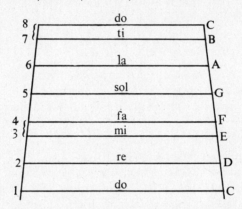

A ladder may be placed on high ground or low, but the distance between its steps remains the same. So too the major scale may be measured off from one starting point or another without affecting the sequence of whole and half steps within the pattern.

Any one of the twelve tones of our octave may serve as starting point for the scale. Whichever it is, that tone at once assumes the function of the Tonic or key center. The other tones are chosen according to the pattern of the ladder. They immediately assume the functions of activity and rest implicit in the major scale. Most important, they all take on the impulse of gravitating more or less directly to the Tonic.

With each different Tonic we get another group of seven tones out of the possible twelve. In other words, every major scale has a different number of sharps or flats. The scale of C major is the only one that has no sharps or flats. If we build the major scale from G we must include an F-sharp in order to conform to the pattern of whole and half steps. (Try building the pattern whole step, whole step, half step, whole step, whole step, whole step, half step, from G. You will find that F-natural does not fit this pattern.) If we build the major-scale pattern from D, we get a group of seven that includes two sharps. If F is our starting point the scale includes B-flat. (The twelve major scales are listed in Appendix III.) When we play a tune like *America* on the piano with C as keynote—that is, in the key of C major—we use only the white keys. Should we play it with G as a keynote—that is, in the key of G major—we should in the course of it have to sound F-sharp, not F-natural. Were we to play F-natural. we would be off key.

It becomes clear that the meaning of a tone, its direction and drive are determined not by its intrinsic nature but by its position in the scale. The tone C may be the Tonic or point of rest in one scale. In another it may be the seventh step seeking to be resolved by ascending to the eighth. In still another it may be the second step thrusting down to the first. In any case its impulse of activity or rest depends not on its character as the tone C but on its function as the *do*, the *ti*, or the *re*—the 1, 7, or 2—of that particular key and scale. The classical system is based on the eminently social doctrine that the significance of a tone depends not upon itself but upon its relationship to other tones.

The key serves as a means of identification. The title Symphony in A major refers to a work based in large measure upon the tones of the A-major scale and the harmonies fashioned from those, with the keynote A serving as the central tone to which the others gravitate. This group is the one that includes three sharps.

The Minor Scale

Whether the major scale begins on C, D, E, or any other tone, it follows the same pattern in the arrangement of the whole and half steps. Such a pattern is known as a *mode*. Thus, all the major scales exemplify the major mode of arranging whole and half steps.

There is also a minor mode, which complements and serves as a foil to the major. It differs primarily from the major in that its third degree is lowered a half step; that is, the scale of C minor has E-flat instead of E. In the pure or natural minor scale the sixth and seventh steps are also lowered: C-D-E♭-F-G-A♭-B♭-C. (For two other versions of the minor scale—harmonic and melodic—see Appendix III.) The minor is pronouncedly different from the major in mood and coloring. *Minor*, the Latin word for "smaller," refers to the fact that the distinguishing interval C-E♭ is smaller than the corresponding interval C-E in the major ("larger") scale.

Like the major, the pattern of the minor scale may begin on each of the twelve tones of the octave. In each case there will be a different group of seven tones out of twelve; that is, each scale will include a different number of sharps or flats. It becomes clear that every tone in the octave may serve as starting point or keynote for a major and a minor scale. This gives us twelve keys according to the major mode and twelve keys according to the minor mode. If the mode of a work is not specified, the major is implied; as when we speak of the Melody in F, Minuet in G, or Symphony in A. The minor is always specified, as in the case of Schubert's Symphony in B minor or Mendelssohn's Violin Concerto in E minor.

Is the minor "sadder" than the major? Such connotations exist only in reference to the music of a particular time and place. The nineteenth century seems to have regarded the minor as more somber than the major. The funeral music of Beethoven, Mendelssohn, Chopin, Wagner, and Grieg is conspicuously in the minor, while the triumphal finales of a number of symphonies and overtures of the same period are as conspicuously in the major.

The minor mode has a certain exotic ring to Western ears and is associated in the popular view with oriental and east European music. This aspect of the minor is prominent in such works as the *Turkish Rondo* of Mozart; in a number of pieces in Hungarian style by Schubert, Liszt, and Brahms; in the main theme of Rimsky-Korsakov's *Scheherazade*, César Cui's *Orientale*, and similar exotica. The folk songs of certain regions appear to incline to the major while others lean toward the minor. There are, however, so many exceptions that such a generalization must be viewed with caution.

The contrast between minor and major became an element of musical structure during the classic-romantic period. For example, in A-B-A form, the outer sections might be in one mode and the contrasting middle section in the other. Or a symphony might start out in the minor and shift to the major in an access of triumph, as in Beethoven's Fifth, Franck's D-minor, and Tchaikovsky's Fifth. Thus the distinction between major and minor lent itself to contrasts of color, mood, and emotional intensity.

The key signature at the head of a piece announces the number of sharps or flats that prevail in that particular composition. Notice that beneath each major

G major	D major	A major	E major	F major	Bb major	Eb major	Ab major
E minor	B minor	F# minor	C# minor	D minor	G minor	C minor	F minor

key in the example is listed the minor key with the same number of sharps or flats. This is known as its *relative minor*.

The twelve major and twelve minor keys make up the harmonic system of the classical period. There had to come into existence an art form that would mobilize the resources of this system, that would bring into focus its capacities for dramatic conflict and architectural expanse. It was the great achievement of the eighteenth century to evolve and perfect this form.

46 The Major-Minor System

"Form follows function."
Louis Sullivan

Transposition

Suppose a certain melody begins on G. If one felt that the song lay a little too high for his voice, he might begin on F instead of G and shift all the tones of the melody one step lower. Someone else might find that the song lay too low for his voice. He would begin on A and sing each tone of the melody one step higher than it was written. The act of shifting all the tones of a musical composition a uniform distance to a higher or lower level of pitch is called *transposition.*

When we transpose a piece we shift it to another key. We change the level of pitch, the keynote, and the number of sharps or flats. But the melody line remains the same because the pattern of its whole and half steps has been retained in the new key as in the old. That is why the same song can be published in various keys for soprano, alto, tenor, and bass.

We have all transposed melodies without being aware of it. For example, a group of children will begin a song from a certain note. If the melody moves too high or too low for comfort, their teacher will stop them and have them begin again from another tone. On an instrument, transposing is a more complicated matter. The player must adjust his fingers to another arrangement of sharps or flats. If he is a pianist or organist he must shift not only the melody but the harmonies as well. The ability to transpose a piece at sight is a skill that musicians regard with respect. It is a necessity for professional accompanists, who are constantly required to transpose songs to higher or lower keys to suit the range of singers.

Why does a composer choose one key rather than another for his piece? In former times external factors strongly influenced this choice. Up to the time of Beethoven, for example, the brass instruments were not able to change keys as readily as they are now. In writing for the string instruments composers considered the fact that certain effects, such as playing on the open strings, could be achieved in one key rather than another. Several composers of the romantic period seemed to associate a certain emotional atmosphere or color with various keys. Characteristic was Mendelssohn's fondness for E minor, Chopin's for C-sharp minor.

Modulation

If a piece of music can be played in one key as in another, why not put all music in the key of C and be done with it? Because the contrast between keys and the movement from one key to another is an essential element of musical structure. We have seen that the tones of the key form a group of "seven out of twelve," which imparts coherence and focus to the music. But this closed group may be opened up, in which case we are shifted—either gently or abruptly—to another area centering about another keynote. Such a change gives us a heightened sense of activity. It is an expressive gesture of prime importance.

The process of passing from one key to another is known as *modulation.* There is no way to describe in words something that can be experienced only in the domain of sound. Suffice it to say that the composer has at his disposal a number of ways of modulating; therewith he "lifts" the listener from one tonal area to another. As Arnold Schoenberg put it, "Modulation is like a change of scenery."

The twelve major and twelve minor keys may be compared to so many rooms in a house, with the modulations equivalent to corridors leading from one to the other. The eighteenth-century composer as a rule established the home key, shaped the passage of modulation—the "corridor"—in a clear-cut manner, and usually passed to a key area that was not too far away from his starting point. There resulted a spaciousness of structure that was the musical counterpart of the rolling sentences of the eighteenth-century novel and the balanced façades of eighteenth-century architecture.

Nineteenth-century romanticism, on the other hand, demanded a whipping-up of emotions, an intensifying of all musical processes. In the romantic era modulations were ever more frequent and abrupt. There came into being a hyperemotional music that wandered restlessly from key to key in accord with the need for excitement of the mid- and late-romantic era. By the same token, the balanced structure of the classical system, with its key areas neatly marked off one from the other, began to disintegrate.

Chromaticism

When seven tones out of twelve are selected to form a major or minor key, the other five become extraneous in relation to that particular Tonic. They enter the composition as transients, mainly to embellish the melody or harmony. If the piece is to sound firmly rooted in the key, the seven tones that belong to the key must prevail. Should the composer allow the five foreign tones to become too prominent in his melody and harmony, the relationship to the key center would be weakened and the key feeling become ambiguous. The distinction between the tones that do not belong within the key area and those that do is made explicit in the contrasting terms *chromatic* and *diatonic*. "Chromatic," as we saw, refers to the twelve-tone scale including all the semitones of the octave. Chromatic melody or harmony moves by half steps, taking in the tones extraneous to the key. The words comes from the Greek *chroma*, which means "color." "Diatonic," on the other hand, refers to musical progression based on the seven tones of a major or minor scale, and to harmonies that are firmly rooted in the key.

Diatonic harmony went hand in hand with the clear-cut key feeling that marked the late eighteenth-century style. We may say that the music of Haydn, Mozart, and Beethoven tends to be diatonic. (There are of course many passages in their music, especially in their late works, that belie this generalization.) Chromatic harmony, on the other hand, characterized the ceaseless modulation and surcharged emotional atmosphere of nineteenth-century music. The romantic composers, from Schubert to Wagner and his followers, indefatigably explored the possibilities of chromaticism. In an earlier section of this book we described the romantic movement in music. We may now establish, as one of its important characteristics, a tendency towards chromatic harmony.

The Key as a Form-Building Element

By marking off an area in musical space with a fixed center, the key provides the framework within which musical growth and development take place. The three main harmonies of the key—Tonic (I), Dominant (V), and Subdominant (IV)—become the focal points over which melodies and chord progressions unfold. In brief, the key is the neighborhood inhabited by a tune and its harmonies. Thus the key becomes a prime factor for musical unity.

At the same time the contrast between keys may further the cause of variety. The classical composer pitted one key against another, thereby achieving a dramatic opposition between them. He began by establishing the home key. Presently he modulated to a related key, generally that of the Dominant (for example, from C major with no sharps or flats to G major, one sharp; or from G major to D major, two sharps). In so doing he established a tension, since the Dominant key was unstable compared to the Tonic. This tension required resolution, which was provided by the return to the home key.

The progression from home key to contrasting key and back outlined the basic musical pattern of statement-departure-return. The home key was the anchorage, the safe harbor; the foreign key represented adventure. The home key was the symbol of unity; the foreign key ensured variety and contrast.

The tension between two keys and their ultimate reconciliation became the motive power of the music of the classical era. This conflict-and-resolution found its frame in the grand form of the latter half of the eighteenth century— the ideal tone-drama known as the sonata.

47 The Development of Themes: Musical Logic

"I alter some things, eliminate and try again until I am satisfied. Then begins the mental working out of this material in its breadth, its narrowness, its height and depth."

Ludwig van Beethoven

Thinking, whether in words or tones, demands continuity and sequence. Every thought must flow out of the one before and lead logically into the next. In this way is created a sense of steady progression toward a goal. If we were to join the beginning of one sentence to the end of another, it would not make any more sense than if we united the first phrase of one melody and the second of another. In our discussion of melody (pages 11–14) we compared the two phrases of *London Bridge* to a question-and-answer formation. A similar impression of cause and effect, of natural flow and continuity, must pervade the whole musical fabric.

When a melodic idea, we noted, is used as a building block in the construction of a musical work it is known as a theme or subject. The theme is the first in a chain of musical situations, all of which must grow out of the basic idea as naturally as does the plant from the seed. The process of spinning out a theme, of weaving and reweaving the threads of which it is composed, is the essence of musical thinking. This process of expansion has its parallel in prose writing, where an idea stated at the beginning of a paragraph is embroidered and enlarged upon until all its aspects appear in view. Each sentence leads smoothly into the one that follows. In similar fashion, every measure takes up where the one before left off and brings us inexorably to the next.

The most tightly knit kind of expansion in our music is known as *thematic development*. To develop a theme means to unfold its latent energies, to search out its capacities for growth and bring them to fruition. Thematic development represents the constructional element in music. It is one of the most important techniques in musical composition, demanding of the composer imagination, master craftsmanship, and intellectual power.

In the process of development, certain procedures have proved to be particularly effective. The simplest is repetition, which may be either exact or varied; or the idea may be restated at another pitch. For example, in *America*, the melodic idea on the words "Land where my fathers died" is restated immediately, but a tone lower, on the words "Land of the pilgrims' pride." Such a restatement at a higher or lower pitch level is known, we saw, as a sequence. The original idea may also be varied in regard to melody, harmony, rhythm, timbre, dynamics, and register. It may be attended by expansion or contraction of the note values as well as by bold and frequent changes of key.

A basic technique in thematic development is the breaking up of the theme into its constituent motives. A *motive*, we found, is the smallest fragment of a theme that forms a melodic-rhythmic unit. The motives are the cells of musical growth. Through fragmentation of themes, through repeating and varying the motives and combining them in ever fresh patterns, the composer imparts to the musical organism the quality of dynamic evolution and growth.

Thematic development is too complex a technique to appear to advantage in short lyric pieces, songs, or dances. In such compositions a simple contrast between sections and a modest expansion within each section supplies the necessary continuity. By the same token, thematic development finds its proper frame in the large forms of music. To those forms it furnishes an epic-dramatic quality, along with the clarity, coherence, and logic that are the indispensable attributes of this most advanced type of musical thinking.

48 The Sonata: The First Movement

"The history of the sonata is the history of an attempt to cope with one of the most singular problems ever presented to the mind of man, and its solution is one of the most successful achievements of his artistic instincts."

Hubert Parry

The name sonata comes from the Italian *suonare*, "to sound," indicating a piece to be sounded on instruments, as distinct from cantata, a piece to be sung. A *sonata* (as Haydn, Mozart, and their successors understood the term) is an instrumental work consisting of a series of contrasting movements, generally three or four in number. The name sonata is used when the piece is intended for one or two instruments. If more than two are involved the work is called, as the case may be, a trio, quartet, quintet, sextet, septet, octet, or nonet. A sonata for solo instrument and orchestra is called a concerto; a sonata for the whole orchestra, a symphony. The sonata, clearly, accounts for a large part of the instrumental music we hear.

Sonata-Allegro Form

The most highly organized and characteristic member of the several movements that make up the sonata cycle is the opening movement. This is in what is variously known as *first-movement form, sonata-allegro form,* or *sonata form.* Each of these names is useful but somewhat misleading. "First-movement form" is good provided we remember that this form may also be used for the other movements, and also for single-movement works. "Sonata-allegro form" is appropriate, since this type of movement is at its most characteristic in a lively or allegro movement. Unfortunately, the name fails to take into account that slow movements were sometimes cast in this form, especially in the eighteenth century. "Sonata form" is correct, and is much used by modern writers; but it is too easily confused with the term "sonata," which includes all the movements.

A movement in sonata-allegro form is based on two assumptions. The first is that a musical movement takes on direction and goal if, after establishing itself in the home key, it modulates to other areas and ultimately returns to the home key. We may therefore regard sonata form as a drama between two contrasting key areas. The "plot," the action, and the tension derive from this contrast. Sonata-allegro form, in brief, is an artistic embodiment of the principles underlying the major-minor system—the establishment, that is, of different key areas which serve as points of reference for a statement, a departure, and a return.

Second is the assumption that a theme may have its latent energies released through the development of its constituent motives. Most useful for this purpose is a brief incisive theme, one that has momentum and tension, and that promises more than at first sight it reveals. The themes will be stated or "exposed" in the first section; developed in the second; and restated or "recapitulated" in the third.

The Exposition (Statement)

The opening section, the Exposition or Statement, sets forth the two opposing keys and their respective themes. (A theme may consist of several related ideas, in which case we speak of it as a theme group.) The first theme and its expansion establish the home key. A transition or bridge leads into a contrasting key; in other words, the function of the bridge is to modulate. The second theme and its expansion establish the contrasting key. A closing section or codetta rounds off the Exposition in the contrasting key. In the classical sonata form the Exposition is repeated. The adventurous quality of the Exposition derives in no small measure from the fact that it brings us from the home key to the contrasting key.

The Development

The Development wanders farther through a series of foreign keys, building up tension against the inevitable return home. Temperature is kept at fever pitch through frequent modulation, resulting in a sense of breathless activity and excitement.

At the same time the composer proceeds to reveal the potentialities of his themes. He breaks them into their component motives; recombines them into fresh patterns; and releases their latent energies, their explosive force. Conflict and action are the essence of drama. In the development section the conflict erupts, the action reaches maximum intensity. The protagonists of the drama are hurled one against another; their worlds collide. Emotion is transformed into motion. The theme may be modified or varied, turned upside down (*inversion*), expanded to longer note values (*augmentation*), contracted into shorter note values (*diminution*), combined with other motives or even with new material. If the sonata is for orchestra—that is, a symphony—a fragment of the theme may be presented by one group of instruments and imitated by another. Now it appears in the upper register, now deep in the bass. Each measure seems to grow out of the preceding by an inescapable law of cause and effect. Each adds to the drive and the momentum. Unity and diversity, logic and passion fuse at white heat to create much out of little.

The Recapitulation (Restatement)

When the developmental surge has run its course, the tension abates. A transition passage leads back to the home key. The beginning of the third section, the Recapitulation or Restatement, is in a sense the psychological climax of sonata form, just as the peak of many a journey is the return home. The first theme appears as we first heard it, in the home key, proclaiming the victory of unity over diversity, of continuity over change.

The Recapitulation follows the general path of the Exposition, restating the first and second themes more or less in their original form, but with the wealth of additional meaning that these have taken on in the course of their wanderings. Most important of all, in the Recapitulation the opposing elements are reconciled, the home key emerges triumphant. For this reason, the third section differs in one important detail from the Exposition: the composer now remains in the home key. He generally shifts the second theme, which was originally in a contrasting key, to the home area. In other words, although the second theme and its expansion unfold in substantially the same way as before, we now hear this material transposed into the home key. There follows the final pronouncement, the coda, in the home key. This is fashioned from material previously heard in the codetta, to which new matter is sometimes added. The coda rounds off the movement and asserts the victory of the home key with a vigorous final cadence.

The procedure just described is summed up in the following outline.

SONATA-ALLEGRO FORM (SONATA FORM)

Exposition* (or Statement)	Development	Recapitulation (or Restatement)
First theme (or theme group) and its expansion in home key	Builds up tension against the return to home key by	First theme (or theme group) and its expansion in home key
Bridge—modulates	(1) Frequent modulation to foreign keys	Bridge
Second theme (or theme group) and its expansion in contrasting key	(2) Fragmentation and manipulation of themes	Second theme (or theme group) and its expansion transposed to home area
Codetta. Cadence in contrasting key	Transition back to home key	Coda. Cadence in home key.

* Note: The Exposition may be preceded by a slow introduction. Also, certain classical masters, especially Haydn, occasionally based the sonata-allegro movement on a single theme, which appeared first in the home key, then in the contrasting key. However, as time went on composers preferred a movement based on contrasting themes.

The main features of the above outline are present in one shape or another in innumerable sonata-allegro movements, yet no two are exactly alike in their disposition of the material. Each constitutes a unique solution of the problem in terms of character, mood, and relation of forces, for the true artist—and it is his work alone that endures—shapes the form according to what he desires to express; so that what looks on paper like a fixed plan becomes, when transformed into living sound, a supple framework of infinite variety.

Even as the dramatist creates opposing personalities as the chief characters of his work, so the composer achieves a vivid contrast between the musical ideas that form the basis of the movement. The opposition between two themes may be underlined in a number of ways. Through a contrast in dynamics—loud against soft; in register—low against high; timbre—strings against winds, one instrumental combination against another; rhythm and tempo—an animated pattern against one that is sustained; tone production—legato against staccato; type of melody—an active melody line with wide range and leaps against one that moves quietly along the scale; type of harmony—consonance against dissonance, diatonic harmony against chromatic; type of accompaniment—quietly moving chords against extended arpeggios. Not all of these may appear in a given work. One contrast, however, is required, being the basis of the form: the contrast of key. And the opposition may be further intensified by putting one theme in the major and the other in minor.

The reader should be cautioned, in conclusion, against a widespread misconception. The conventional description of sonata-allegro form, by its emphasis upon the few themes that serve as building blocks for an instrumental movement, seems to imply that everything between these themes is in the nature of filling-in or transitional material. Unfortunately many people listen in precisely this way to a symphonic movement, waiting for the themes—that is, the melodies they recognize—just as, in another context, they wait for the arias in an opera. But from everything we have said it is clear that the sonata-allegro movement is an organic unity in which the growth, the development, the destiny of a theme is no less important than the theme itself (just as, in assessing a human action, we consider its consequences no less than the deed proper). The music examples in the past chapters and in those to come represent what is generally regarded as "Theme 1," "Theme 2," or "Theme 3" of a sonata movement. They are actually only the kernels, the beginnings of themes. The theme, in the profoundly musical sense, must be considered to include not only the few notes in the example but also the "etc."—that is, the passage or section that constitutes the flowering of the idea. It is only when we take this larger view of the theme (or theme group) that we come to understand the symphonic movement for what it is: a continuous expansion and growth of musical ideas from first note to last, from which not a measure may be omitted without disturbing the equilibrium and the organic oneness of the whole. Only by listening to the movement in this way do we apprehend the essential qualities of sonata style, its concentration, its continuity, its unflagging dynamism. It should be added that sonata-allegro form is the representative form of the classical period.

49 The Sonata, Continued: The Other Movements

"To write a symphony means, to me, to construct a world."
Gustav Mahler

We now consider the other types of musical structure that came to be included in the sonata cycle.

Theme and Variations

We found that repetition is a basic element of musical structure. This being so, composers devised ways of varying an idea when they restated it. Variation is an important procedure that is to be found in every species of music. But there is one type of piece in which it constitutes the ruling principle —the *theme and variations*. The theme is stated at the outset, so that the audience will know the basic idea that serves as the point of departure. The melody may be of the composer's invention, as in the second movement of Haydn's *Surprise Symphony*; or one that he has borrowed from another, as in the case of Brahms's *Variations on a Theme by Paganini*. The theme is apt to be a small two- or three-part form, simple in character so as to allow room for elaboration. There follows a series of variations in which certain features of the original idea are retained while others are altered. Each variation sets forth the idea with some new modification—one might say in a new disguise—through which the listener glimpses something of the original theme.

To the process of variation the composer brings all the techniques of musical embellishment. He may, to begin with, vary the melody. To indicate the simplest way that this is done, suppose a melodic line moves C-D-E. One may ornament it by including intermediate notes, transforming the melodic progression into C-D-D♯-E or C-C♯-D-E, or C-C♯-D-D♯-E. In this way a more florid line results, although the melody is not fundamentally changed. Conversely, one may omit certain notes and thereby reduce the melody to its skeletal outline: C-E. Or one may shift the melody to another key, thereby throwing new light upon it. Melodic variation is a favorite procedure in the jazz band, where the solo player embellishes a popular tune with a series of arabesques.

In harmonic variation the chords that accompany a melody are replaced by others. Diatonic harmonies may give way to chromatic, simple triads to complex dissonances. Or the melody may be entirely omitted, the variation being based on the harmonic skeleton. The type of accompaniment may be changed; for example, from chords in block formation to decorative broken chords (arpeggios). Or the melody may be shifted to a lower register with new harmonies sounding above it.

So too the rhythm, meter, and tempo may be varied, with interesting changes in the nature of the tune. This may take on the guise of a waltz, a polka, a minuet, a march. The texture may be enriched by interweaving the melody with new themes. Or the original theme may itself become an accompaniment for a new melody. By combining these methods with changes in dynamics and tone color, the expressive content of the theme may be changed, so that it is presented now as a funeral march, now as a serenade, folk dance, caprice, or boat song. This type of character variation was much in favor in the romantic era.

The theme with variations challenges the composer's inventiveness and enables him to achieve a high degree of unity in diversity. One therefore understands why variation form has attracted composers for more than three hundred years, both as an independent piece and as one of the movements of the sonata.

Minuet and Trio

The *minuet* originated in the French court in the mid-seventeenth century; its stately ¾ time embodied the ideal of grace of an aristocratic age. In the eighteenth century the minuet was taken over into the sonata, where it served as the third movement, occasionally the second.

Since dance music lends itself to symmetrical construction, we often find in the minuet a clear-cut structure based on phrases of four and eight measures. (All the same, the minuets of Haydn and Mozart reveal an abundance of non-symmetrical phrases.) In tempo the minuet ranges from stateliness to a lively pace and whimsical character. As a matter of fact, certain of Haydn's minuets are closer in spirit to the village green than to the palace ballroom.

The custom prevailed of presenting two dances as a group, the first being repeated at the end of the second (A-B-A). The one in the middle was frequently arranged for only three instruments; hence the name *trio*, which persisted even after the customary setting for three was abandoned. The trio as a rule is lighter in texture and quieter of gait. Frequently woodwind tone figures prominently in this section, creating an out-of-doors atmosphere that lends it a special charm. At the end of the trio we find *da capo* or D.C. (from the beginning), signifying that the first section is to be played over again. Minuet-Trio-Minuet is a symmetrical three-part structure in which each part in turn is a small two-part or three-part form:

Minuet (A)	Trio (B)	Minuet (A)
a-b-a	c-d-c	a-b-a
or	or	or
a-b	c-d	a-b

This structure is elaborated through repetition of the subsections, a procedure that the composer indicates with a *repeat sign* (:||:). However, when the minuet returns after the trio the repeat signs are customarily ignored. A codetta may round off each section.

Minuet (A)	Trio (B)	Minuet (A)
|:a:||:b-a(codetta):|	|:c:||:d-c:|	a-b-a (codetta)
or	or	or
|:a:||:b(codetta):|	|:c:||:d:|	a-b (codetta)

In the nineteenth-century symphony the minuet was displaced by the scherzo. This is generally the third movement, occasionally the second. It is usually in ¾ time. Like the minuet, it is a three-part form (scherzo-trio-scherzo), the first section being repeated after the middle part. But it differs from the minuet in its faster pace and vigorous rhythm. The scherzo—the name, as you will recall, is the Italian word for "jest"—is marked by abrupt changes of mood ranging from the humorous or the whimsical to the mysterious and even demonic. In the hands of Beethoven the scherzo became a movement of great rhythmic drive.

The Rondo

The *rondo* is a lively movement suffused with the spirit of the dance. Its distinguishing characteristic is the recurrence of a central idea—the rondo theme—in alternation with contrasting elements. Its symmetrical sections create a balanced architecture that is satisfying esthetically and easy to grasp. In its simplest form, A-B-A-B-A, the rondo is an extension of three-part form. If there are two contrasting themes the sections may follow an A-B-A-C-A or similar pattern.

The true rondo as developed by the classical masters was more ambitious in scope. Characteristic was the formation A-B-A-C-A-B-A. The first A-B-A was in the nature of an exposition and the corresponding A-B-A at the end was a recapitulation. Between them was the C section, which served as a kind of development. What with contrasts of key and elaborate transitional passages, this type of rondo took on the spaciousness of sonata form and came to be known as a rondo-sonata.

Actually one may speak of rondo style as well as rondo form, for the essence of the rondo—at any rate as Haydn and Mozart cultivated it—is its vivacity and good humor. Because the theme is to be heard over and over again it must be catchy and relaxing. One should point out, however, that not every movement that follows the rondo form has the spirit of the gay classical rondo. The rondo figured in eighteenth- and nineteenth-century music both as an independent piece and as a member of the sonata cycle. In the sonata it often served as the final movement.

The Sonata Cycle as a Whole

The four-movement cycle of the classical masters, as found in their symphonies, concertos, sonatas, string quartets, and other types of chamber music, became the vehicle for their most important instrumental music. The following outline sums up the common practice of the classic-romantic era. It will be helpful to the reader, provided he remembers that it is no more than a general scheme and does not necessarily apply to all works of this kind. In Beethoven's Ninth Symphony, for example, the scherzo is the second movement while the Adagio comes third.

Movement	Character	Form	Tempo
First	Epic-dramatic	Sonata-allegro	Allegro
Second	Slow and lyrical	Theme & variations Sonata form A-B-A	Andante, Adagio, Largo
Third	Dancelike: Minuet (18th century)	Minuet and trio	Allegretto
	Scherzo (19th century)	Scherzo and trio	Allegro
Fourth	Lively, "happy ending" (18th century) Epic-dramatic, with triumphal ending (19th century)	Sonata-allegro Rondo Rondo-sonata Theme and variations	Allegro, Vivace, Presto

The classical masters of the sonata thought of the four movements of the cycle as self-contained entities connected by identity of key. First, third, and fourth movements were in the home key, with the second movement in a contrasting key. The nineteenth century sought a more obvious connection between movements—a thematic connection. This need was met by cyclical structure, in which a theme from the earlier movements appeared in the later ones as a kind of motto or unifying thread.

The sonata cycle satisfied the need of composers for an extended instrumental work of an abstract nature. It mobilized the contrasts of key and mode inherent in the major-minor system. With its fusion of sensuous, emotional, and intellectual elements, its intermingling of lyric contemplation and action, the sonata cycle may justly claim to be one of the most ingenious art forms ever devised by man.

PART FOUR

EIGHTEENTH-CENTURY CLASSICISM

"When a nation brings its innermost nature to consummate expression in arts and letters we speak of its classic period. Classicism stands for experience, for spiritual and human maturity which has deep roots in the cultural soil of the nation, for the mastery of the means of expression in technique and form, and for a definite conception of the world and of life; the final compression of the artistic values of a people."
  Paul Henry Lang: Music in Western Civilization

50 The Classical Spirit

" 'Tis more to guide, than spur the Muse's steed;
Restrain his fury, than provoke his speed;
The winged courser, like a gen'rous horse,
Shows most true mettle when you check his course."
Alexander Pope: *Essay on Criticism*

The dictionary defines classicism in two ways: in general terms, as pertaining to the highest order of excellence in literature and art; specifically, pertaining to the culture of the ancient Greeks and Romans. Implicit in the classical attitude is the notion that supreme excellence has been reached in the past and may be attained again through adherence to tradition.

Being part of a tradition implies a relationship to things outside oneself. The classical artist neither glories in nor emphasizes his apartness from other men. He regards neither his individuality nor his personal experience as the primary material of his art. For him, therefore, the work of art exists in its own right rather than as an extension of his ego. Where the romantic is inclined to regard art primarily as a means of self-expression, the classicist stresses its powers as a means of communication. His attention is directed to clarity of thought and beauty of form. In effect, he is considerably more objective in his approach than is the romantic. For the extremely personal utterance of the romantic, he substitutes symbols of more universal validity. Classicism upholds the control and the discipline of art, its potentialities for rational expression and exquisite workmanship, its vision of an ideal beauty. This wholeness of view encourages the qualities of order, stability, and harmonious proportion that we associate with the classical style.

As we pointed out in our discussion of romanticism, neither the classical nor the romantic spirit is limited to any one time. Both have alternated throughout the history of culture. However, just as conditions in the nineteenth century

The Parthenon, Athens
The art of ancient Greece embodied the ideals of order, stability, and harmonious proportion.

gave rise to an extended period of romanticism, so the social climate of the eighteenth century favored the emergence of the classical spirit.

Eighteenth-Century Classicism

The culture of the eighteenth century was under the patronage of an aristocracy for whom the arts were a necessary adornment of life. Art was part of the elaborate ritual that surrounded the existence of princes. In such a society, where the ruling caste enjoys its power through hereditary right, tradition is apt to be prized and the past revered. The center of art life is the palace and the privileged minority residing therein. In these high places the emphasis is on elegance of manner and beauty of style.

The art of the eighteenth century bears the imprint of the spacious palaces and formal gardens, with their balanced proportions and finely wrought detail, that formed the setting for enlightened despotism. In the middle of the century, Louis XV presided over the extravagant fetes in Versailles (although he foresaw the deluge). Frederick the Great ruled in Prussia, Maria Theresa in Austria, Catherine the Great in Russia. Yet disruptive forces were swiftly gathering beneath the glittering surface. The American Revolution dealt a shattering blow to the doctrine of the divine right of kings. And before the century had ended, Europe was convulsed by the French Revolution.

The second half of the eighteenth century, consequently, witnessed both the twilight of the *ancien régime* and the dawn of a new political-economic alignment in Europe; specifically, the transfer of power from the aristocracy to the middle class, whose wealth was based on a rapidly expanding capitalism, on mines and factories, steam power and railroads. This shift was made possible by the Industrial Revolution, which gathered momentum in the mid-eighteenth century with a series of important inventions, from Watt's steam engine and Hargreaves's spinning jenny in the 1760s to Cartwright's power loom in 1785 and Eli Whitney's cotton gin in 1793.

These decades saw significant advances in science. Benjamin Franklin discovered electricity in 1752, Priestley discovered oxygen in 1774, Jenner perfected vaccination in 1796, Laplace advanced his mechanistic view of the universe and Volta invented the voltaic pile in 1800. There were important events in intellectual life, such as the publication of Winckelmann's *History of Ancient Art* (1764), of the French *Encyclopédie* (1751–72), and the first edition of the *Encyclopaedia Britannica* (1771). The final quarter of the century produced such landmarks as Adam Smith's *The Wealth of Nations,* Kant's *Critique of Pure Reason,* Rousseau's *Confessions,* Gibbon's *Decline and Fall of the Roman Empire,* Boswell's *Life of Johnson,* and Malthus's *Essay on Population.*

The intellectual climate of the classical era, consequently, was nourished by two opposing streams. On the one hand classical art captured the exquisite refinement of a way of life that was drawing to a close. On the other it caught the intimations of a new way of life that was struggling to be born. This dualism is of the essence in the classical era and pervades all its attitudes. For example, the eighteenth century has been called the Age of Reason; but the two opposing camps invoked reason in diametrically opposite ways. The apologists of the status quo appealed to reason in order to justify the existing order. Early in the century Leibnitz taught that this was "the best of all possible worlds," and Pope proclaimed that "Whatever is, is right." As the century wore on, however, this spurious optimism became ever more difficult to maintain. The opponents of the established order, the *philosophes* who created the *Grande Encyclopédie* as an instrument of the Enlightenment—Voltaire, Diderot, Rousseau, Condorcet, d'Alembert and their comrades—also invoked reason, but for the purpose of attacking the existing order. Therewith these spokesmen for the rising middle class became the prophets of the approaching upheaval.

The romantics, we saw, idealized the Middle Ages. But to eighteenth-century thinkers the medieval period represented a thousand years of barbarism—the Dark Ages. The term *Gothic* represented everything that was opposed to what they regarded as rational and cultivated. Their ideal was the civilization of ancient Greece and Rome. To the Gothic cathedral, with its stained-glass

Jacques Louis David (1748–1825), THE DEATH OF SOCRATES. (The Metropolitan Museum of Art, New York; Wolfe Fund, 1931)

Modern classicism drew its inspiration from the art and culture of ancient Greece.

windows, its bizarre gargoyles, its ribbed columns soaring heavenward in passionate mysticism, they opposed the Greek temple, a thing of beauty, unity and proportion, lightness and grace.

Yet here too the revival of interest in classical antiquity meant different things to the opposing camps. The aristocrats and their spokesmen exalted Hellenism as the symbol of a rational, objective attitude that guarded one against becoming too deeply involved with the issues of life. They saw the ancient gods, kings, and heroes as a reflection of themselves—themselves ennobled, transfigured. But to the protagonists of the middle class, Greece and Rome represented city-states that had rebelled against tyrants and thrown off despotism. It was in this spirit that the foremost painter of revolutionary France, Jacques Louis David, decked his canvases with the symbols of Athenian and Roman democracy. In this spirit, too, Thomas Jefferson praised David for having "ennobled the contemporary countenance with the classical quality of ancient republican virtue." Jefferson patterned both the Capitol and the University of Virginia after Greek and Roman temples, thereby giving strength to the classic revival in this country, which made Ionic, Doric, and Corinthian columns an indispensable feature of our public buildings well into the twentieth century.

The classical point of view held sway in English letters to such an extent that the mid-eighteenth century is known as the Augustan Age (after the Roman emperor Augustus, patron of the poet Vergil). Its arbiter was Samuel Johnson, whose position of leadership in literature was as undisputed as was that of his

238

The Rotunda, University of Virginia
Jefferson's design is modelled on the temples of Greece and Rome.

friend Sir Joshua Reynolds in painting. Both men upheld a highly formal, aristocratic type of art. Yet within the formal stream of Augustan classicism we become aware of a current of tender sentiment that is an early sign of the romantic spirit. The novels of Samuel Richardson, Henry Fielding, Laurence Sterne, and Tobias Smollett were suffused with homely bourgeois sentiment, as were the poems of Thomas Gray, Oliver Goldsmith, and William Cowper. For the Age of Reason was also, curiously, the Age of Sensibility, and the sensibility steadily broadens into a trend toward the romantic.

Thus it is that the Age of Reason begins to give way to the Age of Romance considerably earlier than is commonly supposed. In the 1760s there already appeared a number of works—such as Percy's *Reliques of Ancient English Poetry*—that clearly indicate the new interest in a romantic medievalism. In the same decade Rousseau, the "father of romanticism," produced some of his most significant writings. His celebrated dictum, "Man is born free and everywhere he is in chains," epitomizes the temper of the time. So too the first outcropping of the romantic spirit in Germany, the movement known as *Sturm und Drang* ("Storm and Stress"), took shape in the 1770s, when it produced two characteristic works by its most significant young writers—the *Sorrows of Werther* by Goethe and *The Robbers* by Schiller. (Goethe, it will be remembered, became a favorite lyric poet of the romantic composers.) By the end of the century the atmosphere had completely changed. The two most important English poets of the late eighteenth century—Robert Burns and William Blake—stand entirely outside the classical stream. As does the greatest end-of-the-century painter, Goya, whose passionate realism anticipates a later age.

Late eighteenth-century culture, therefore, is neither as exclusively aristocratic nor as exclusively classical as we have been taught to believe. It assimilated and was nourished by both democratic and romantic elements. Precisely its dual nature lends it its subtle charm.

The Artist Under Patronage

The eighteenth-century artist generally functioned under the system of aristocratic patronage. He created for a public high above him in social rank; his patrons were interested in his product rather than in his personality. Inevitably he was directed toward a classical objectivity and reserve.

The artist under patronage was a master craftsman, an artisan working on direct commission from his patron. He produced works for immediate use, sustained by daily contact with his public. It is true that in point of social status the artist in livery was little better than a servant. This was not quite as depressing as it sounds, for in that society virtually everybody was a servant of the prince save other princes. The patronage system gave the artist economic security and a social framework within which he could function. It offered important advantages to the great artists who successfully adjusted to its requirements, as the career of Haydn richly shows. On the other hand, Mozart's tragic end illustrates how heavy was the penalty exacted from those unable to make that adjustment.

Eighteenth-century classicism, then, mirrored the unique moment in history when the old world was dying and the new was in process of being born. From the meeting of two historic forces emerged an art of noble simplicity whose achievement in music constitutes one of the pinnacles of Western culture.

51 Classicism in Music

"Ought not the musician, quite as much as the poet and painter, to study nature? In nature he can study man, its noblest creature."
Johann Friedrich Reichardt (1774)

The classical period in music (c. 1775–1825) centers about the achievements of the four masters of the Viennese school—Haydn, Mozart, Beethoven, and

Schubert—and their contemporaries. Their art reached its flowering in a time of great musical experimentation and discovery, when musicians were confronted by three challenging problems: first, to explore to the full the possibilities offered by the major-minor system; second, to perfect a large form of absolute instrumental music that would mobilize those possibilities to the fullest degree; and third, having found this ideal form in the sonata cycle, to differentiate between its various types—the solo and duo sonata, trio, quartet, and other kinds of chamber music, the concerto, and the symphony.

If by classicism we mean adherence to traditional forms we certainly cannot apply the term to the composers of the Viennese school. They experimented boldly and ceaselessly with the materials at their disposal. An enormous distance separates Haydn's early symphonies and string quartets from his later ones; the same is true of Mozart, Beethoven, and Schubert. Nor can we call these masters classical if we mean that they—like the poets and painters of the mid-eighteenth century—subordinated emotional expression to accepted "rules" of form. The slow movements of Haydn and Mozart are filled with emotion of the profoundest kind, and what could be more impassioned than Beethoven's music, or more suffused with lyric tenderness than Schubert's?

Even in point of time the classical label does not fit music very well. The classical era in literature and painting spread across the middle of the eighteenth century, whereas in music it appeared several decades later, in the last quarter of the eighteenth and the first quarter of the nineteenth centuries, when the forces of romanticism already were coming to the fore. It should not surprise us that romantic elements abound in the music of Haydn, Mozart, and Beethoven, especially in their late works. As for Schubert, although his symphonies and chamber music fall within the classical orbit, his songs and piano pieces—as we saw in an earlier section of this book—stamp him a romantic.

In consequence, the term classicism applies to the art of the four Viennese masters in only one—but that one perhaps the most important—of its meanings: "as pertaining to the highest order of excellence." They and their contemporaries solved the problems presented to them so brilliantly that their symphonies and concertos, piano sonatas, duo sonatas, trios, string quartets, and similar works remained as unsurpassable models for all who came after. They evolved a dynamic instrumental language that was the perfect vehicle for the processes of thematic growth and development. They perfected spacious designs born of reason and logic, whose over-all structure was flexible enough to allow for free expression of the most varied sentiments. And in doing so they created a new world of musical thought and sound.

Vocal Music in The Classical Period

The opera house was a center of experimentation in the classical era. Opera was the most important branch of musical entertainment and the one that reached the widest public. Classical opera was based on principles directly opposite to those that prevailed in the romantic music drama. The music was the point of departure and imposed its forms on the drama. Each scene was a closed musical unit. The separate numbers were conceived as parts of the whole and held together in a carefully planned framework. There was the greatest possible distinction between the rapid patter of recitative and the lyric curve of aria. The voice reigned supreme, yet the orchestra displayed all the vivacity of the classical instrumental style.

A significant development was the importance of Italian comic opera (*opera buffa*), which adopted certain features of the serious opera and in turn influenced the latter. Far from being an escapist form of entertainment, comic opera was directly related to the life of the time. Its emphasis was on the affairs of "little people," on swift action, pointed situations, spontaneous emotion, and sharpness of characterization. This popular lyric theater showed an abundance of racy melody, brilliant orchestration, and lively rhythms. Characteristic were the ensemble numbers at the end of the act, of a verve and drive that influenced all branches of music. From its cradle in Italy, classical *opera buffa* spread all over Europe, steadily expanding its scope until it culminated in the works of the greatest musical dramatist of the eighteenth century—Mozart.

As a center of music making, the Church retained its importance alongside opera house and aristocratic salon. Whereas the first half of the century had seen the high point of Protestant music in the art of Bach and his contemporaries, the Catholic countries now assumed first place, especially the Hapsburg domains. The masters of the classical Viennese school produced a great deal of Catholic church music, Masses, vespers, litanies, and the like. They did as composers have always done: they used the living idiom of their day (an idiom based on opera and symphony) to express their faith in God and man.

Instrumental Music of the Classical Period

The classical masters established the orchestra as we know it today. They based the ensemble on the blending of the four instrumental groups. The heart of this orchestra was the string choir. Woodwinds, used with great imagination, ably seconded the strings. The brass sustained the harmonies and contributed body to the tone mass, while the kettledrums supplied rhythmic life and vitality. The eighteenth-century orchestra numbered from thirty to forty players. The volume of sound was still considered in relation to the salon rather than the concert hall. (It was toward the end of the classical period that musical life began to move from the one to the other.) Foreign to classical art were the swollen sonorities of the late nineteenth century. The orchestra of Haydn and Mozart lent itself to delicate nuances in which each timbre stood out radiantly.

It follows that the classical masters conceived their works on a smaller scale than did their nineteenth-century successors. They created a dynamic style of orchestral writing in which all the instruments participated actively. The interchange and imitation of themes among the various instrumental groups assumed the excitement of a witty conversation. The classical orchestra brought to absolute music a number of effects long familiar in the opera house. The gradual crescendo and decrescendo established themselves as staples of the new symphonic style. Hardly less conspicuous were the abrupt alternations of soft and loud, sudden accents, dramatic pauses, the use of tremolo and pizzicato. These and similar devices of operatic music added drama and tension to the classical orchestral style.

The central place in classical instrumental music was taken by the "sonata for orchestra"—the symphony. This grew rapidly in dimension and significance until, with the final works of Mozart and Haydn, it became the most important type of absolute music (which it remained throughout the romantic period). Important, too, was the "sonata for solo instrument and orchestra"—the concerto, which combined a virtuoso part for the featured player with the resources of the orchestra. The piano concerto was the chief type, although other solo instruments were not neglected.

Chamber music enjoyed a great flowering in the classical era, as did a type of composition that stood midway between chamber music and symphony, known as *divertimento*. The title fixes the character of this category of music as sociable diversion or entertainment. Closely related were the serenade, the *notturno* (night piece), and the *cassation* (a term of obscure origin probably referring to something in the streets or out-of-doors). Contemporary acounts tell of groups of street musicians who performed these works—for strings, winds, or both— outside the homes of the wealthy or in a quiet square before an appreciative audience of their fellow townsmen. At this time too the piano came into favor, supplanting harpsichord and clavichord as an instrument for the home. The piano sonata became the most ambitious form of solo music, in which composers worked out new conceptions of keyboard style and sonata structure, creating a rich literature for both the amateur and the virtuoso.

Classical sonata form was based upon a clear-cut opposition of keys. This demanded a harmony well rooted in the key. What gives certain works of Haydn and Mozart their pure, even chaste quality is the fact that their harmony is firmly diatonic, as distinct from the tendency toward chromaticism that gained strength throughout the nineteenth century.

Other Aspects of Musical Classicism

The classical era created a universal style disseminated through two international art forms—Italian opera and Viennese symphony. These represented an all-European culture that transcended national boundaries. In this regard classicism reflected the international character of the two most powerful institutions in eighteenth-century society, the aristocracy and the

Church. Indeed, the eighteenth century was the last stronghold of internationalism in art (until the twentieth began). German, French, and Italian influences intermingle in the art of Haydn and Mozart. These masters were not German in the way that Wagner was, or Schumann, or Brahms. Romantic nationalism, we saw, opened up new dialects to composers. By the same token something was lost of the breadth of view that made artists like Beethoven and Goethe citizens of the world in the highest sense.

The classical composers were far less concerned with exotic atmosphere than the romantics (in spite of the *Turkish Rondo* of Mozart and the *Turkish March* of Beethoven). They already were strongly influenced by the "return to nature," especially Haydn in *The Creation* and *The Seasons* and Beethoven in the *Pastoral Symphony*; these works foreshadowed the numerous landscapes and sea-scenes that were to play such an important part in nineteenth-century music. Also, significantly, despite the aristocratic spirit of the late eighteenth century, folklore elements entered increasingly into the classical style. Popular song and dance are manifest not only in the German dances, contradances, ländler, and waltzes of the Viennese masters but also in the allegros and rondos of their larger works.

Classicism, to sum up, achieved the final synthesis of the intellectual currents of eighteenth-century life. The great theme of this pure and serene art was man, the measure of all things: a rational creature working out his destiny in an ordered universe whose outer garment was the beauty of nature and whose inner law was the clarity of reason. The classical masters struck a perfect balance between emotion and intellect, heart and mind. So delicate an equilibrium is as rare in art as in life.

We have made reference to Nietzsche's distinction between the Dionysian and the Apollonian. The classical spirit finds a fit symbol in the god of light, whose harmonious proportions so eloquently proclaim the cult of ideal beauty.

52 Joseph Haydn

"I have only just learned in my old age how to use the wind instruments, and now that I do understand them I must leave the world."

The long career of Joseph Haydn (1732–1809) spanned the decades when the classical style was being formed. He imprinted upon it the stamp of his personality, and made a contribution to music that in scope and significance was second to none.

His Life

He was born in Rohrau, a village in Lower Austria, son of a wheelwright. Folk song and dance were his natural heritage. Displaying uncommon musical aptitude as a child, he was taught the rudiments by a distant relative, a schoolmaster. The beauty of his voice secured him a place as chorister in St. Stephen's Cathedral in Vienna, where he remained till he was sixteen. With the breaking of his voice his days at the choir school came to an end. He established himself in an attic in Vienna, managed to obtain a dilapidated clavier, and set himself to master his craft. He eked out a living through teaching and accompanying, and often joined the roving bands of musicians who performed in the streets. In this way the popular Viennese idiom entered his style along with the folk idiom he had absorbed in childhood.

Haydn before long attracted the notice of the music-loving aristocracy of Vienna, and was invited to the country house of a nobleman who maintained a small group of musicians. His next patron kept a small orchestra, so that he was able to experiment with more ample resources. In 1761, when he was twenty-nine, he entered the service of the Esterházys, a family of enormously wealthy Hungarian princes famous for their patronage of the arts. He remained in their service for almost thirty years—that is, for the greater part of his creative career. The palace of the Esterházys was one of the most splendid in Europe, and music played a central part in the constant round of festivities there. The musical establishment under Haydn's direction included an orchestra, an opera company, a marionette theater, and the chapel. The agreement between prince and composer sheds light on the social status of the eighteenth-century artist. Haydn is required to abstain "from undue familiarity and from vulgarity in eating, drinking, and conversation." He is enjoined to act uprightly and to influence his subordinates "to preserve such harmony as is becoming in them,

Joseph Haydn.

The performance of THE CREATION in Haydn's honor at the Vienna University a year before his death.

remembering how displeasing any discord or dispute would be to His Serene Highness. . . . It is especially to be observed that when the orchestra shall be summoned to perform before company the said Joseph Heyden shall take care that he and all the members of his orchestra do follow the instructions given and appear in white stockings, white linen, powdered, and with a pigtail or tie-wig."

Haydn's life is the classic example of the patronage system operating at its best. Though he chafed occasionally at the restrictions imposed on him by court life, he inhabited a world that questioned neither the supremacy of princes nor the spectacle of a great artist in livery. His final estimate of his position in the Esterházy household was that the advantages outweighed the disadvantages. "My Prince was always satisfied with my works. I not only had the encouragement of constant approval but as conductor of an orchestra I could make experiments, observe what produced an effect and what weakened it, and was thus in a position to improve, alter, make additions or omissions, and be as bold as I pleased. I was cut off from the world, there was no one to confuse or torment me, and I was forced to become *original*."

Haydn had married when still a young man, but did not get on with his wife. They ultimately separated, and he found consolation elsewhere. By the time he reached middle age his music had brought him fame throughout Europe. He was asked to appear at various capitals but accepted none of these invitations as long as his patron was alive. After the Prince's death he made two visits to England (1791-92, 1794-95), where he conducted his works with phenomenal success. He returned to his native Austria laden with honors and financially well off.

When he was seventy-six a memorable performance of *The Creation* was organized in his honor by the leading musicians of Vienna and members of the aristocracy. At the words "And there was light"—who that has heard it can forget the grandeur of the C-major chord on the word "light"?—the old man was deeply stirred. Pointing upward he exclaimed, "It came from there!" His agitation increased as the performance advanced, so that it was necessary to take him home at the end of the first part of the work. As he was carried out in his armchair his admirers thronged about him. Beethoven, who had briefly been his pupil, kissed his hands and forehead. At the door he turned around and lifted his hands as if in blessing. It was his farewell to the public.

He died a year later, revered by his countrymen and acknowledged throughout Europe as the premier musician of his time.

His Music

It was Haydn's historic role to help perfect the new instrumental language of the late eighteenth century, a language based on the dynamic development of themes and motives. The mature classical idiom seemed to be fully realized for the first time in his terse, highly personal style with its angular themes and nervous rhythms, its expressive harmony, structural logic, and endlessly varied moods.

The string quartet occupied a central position in Haydn's art. The eighty-three quartets he left are an indispensable part of the repertory. The works of his middle and late years contain notable experiments in sonority and form. One understands Mozart's remark, "It was from Haydn that I first learned the true way to compose quartets."

Like the quartets, the symphonies—over a hundred in number—extend across the whole of Haydn's career. Especially popular are the twelve written in the 1790s, in two sets of six, for his appearances in England. Known as the "Salomon Symphonies," after the impresario who brought him to England and arranged the concerts, they abound in effects that the public associates with later composers: syncopation, sudden crescendos and accents, dramatic contrasts of soft and loud, daring modulation, and an imaginative color scheme in which each choir and instrument plays its allotted part. Of Haydn's symphonies it may be said, as it has been of his quartets, that they are the spiritual birthplace of Beethoven.

Haydn was a prolific composer of church music. His fourteen Masses form the chief item in this category. The prevailing cheerfulness of these works reflects a trusting faith undisturbed by inner travail or doubt. "At the thought of God," he said, "my heart leaps for joy and I cannot help my music doing the same." Among his oratorios, *The Creation*, which we will discuss, attained a popularity second only to that of Handel's *Messiah*. Haydn followed it with another work based on English literature—*The Seasons* (1801), on a text drawn from James Thomson's celebrated poem. Completed when the composer was on the threshold of seventy, it was his last major composition.

Haydn's tonal imagery was instrumental in character. Yet he recognized that a good melody must be rooted in the nature of the human voice. "If you want to know whether you have written anything worth preserving," he counseled, "sing it to yourself without any accompaniment." His attitude toward his work shows that the time was passing when pieces were written for a single occasion or season. "I never was a quick writer and always composed with care and deliberation. That alone is the way to compose works that will last." His ceaseless experimenting with form should dispel the notion that the classicist adheres to tradition. On the contrary, he chafed against the arbitrary restrictions of the theorists. "What is the good of such rules? Art is free and should be fettered by no such mechanical regulations. The educated ear is the sole authority on all these questions, and I think I have as much right to lay down the law as anyone." He upheld the expressive power of music against all rules. "Supposing an idea struck me as good and thoroughly satisfactory both to the ear and the heart, I would far rather pass over some slight grammatical error than sacrifice what seemed to me beautiful to any mere pedantic trifling." So, too, when his attention was called to an unconventional passage in a string quartet of Mozart's, he retorted, "If Mozart wrote it so he must have had good reason."

Haydn enriched the literature of the divertimento, the concerto, and the song. His piano sonatas, of late years unjustly neglected, are returning to favor. His numerous operas and marionette plays were designed specifically for the entertainment needs of the Esterházy court. "My operas are calculated exclusively for our own company and would not produce their effect elsewhere." But several, revived in recent years, have given delight.

The *Surprise Symphony*

The best known of Haydn's symphonies, the *Surprise*, in G major, is one of the set of six written for his first visit to London in 1791. The orchestra that presented these compositions to the world consisted of about forty players: a full string section; two each of flutes, oboes, bassoons, horns, trumpets; harpsichord and timpani.

The first movement opens with a brief introduction marked Adagio cantabile. This passage in Haydn's most reflective mood is notable for its limpid scoring for winds and strings. The movement proper is a forceful Vivace assai (very lively) in sonata-allegro form, imbued with all the symphonic drive and forthrightness of the classical style.

The first theme, assigned to the first violins, is in the home key of G major.

Notice that the first five notes are immediately restated a step lower, that is, in sequence. They constitute a motive that will figure prominently in the Development. This idea flowers into a vigorous section, at the close of which a bridge passage leads into the contrasting key of D major. In the course of this transition the basic motive, momentarily in D minor, takes on a new shape:

The second theme, in D, is played by the first violins.

As often happens in Haydn, the two basic ideas do not present a marked contrast to one another. The movement is built rather on the opposition between home and contrasting key. A graceful closing theme rounds off the Exposition:

The transparent orchestration and economy of means are characteristic traits of Haydn's style, as are the breadth of design and prevailing good humor.

He begins the Development by changing the first interval of his basic motive:

A segment of the basic motive leads to a new idea:

Out of these and similar threads Haydn weaves a closely-knit fabric. Frequent modulations give that sense of excitement, of releasing hidden energies, which marks the Development. The abrupt changes from *p* to *f* impart a dynamic quality to the music. They are characteristic of Haydn's orchestral writing, and look ahead to Beethoven's dramatic style.

The Recapitulation presents the material in shortened form. The second theme is transposed from the contrasting key of D to the home key of G—that is, from the Dominant key to the Tonic. The coda brings the movement to an affirmative cadence in G.

The second movement is the Andante, a theme and variations in C major. The theme is of a folksong simplicity. It is announced by the violins, staccato.

The eight-bar phrase is repeated pianissimo and ends in an abrupt fortissimo crash—the "surprise" that gives the symphony its name. "There," Haydn told a friend, "all the ladies will scream." But despite the famous anecdote, in an artist of Haydn's stature one must seek a deeper motivation for the effect. The contrast between soft and loud was one of the dynamic elements of the new orchestral language and was bound to fascinate an innovative artist like Haydn, quite apart from the ladies.

Haydn's variations are notable for their ease, taste, humor, and workmanship. Variation 1. The theme is combined with arabesques in the first violins.

Variation 2. The theme is shifted into the minor, and is played fortissimo by all the woodwinds and strings.

Variation 3 returns to the major. The theme is heard piano in a new rhythm.

In the second half of this variation the theme is heard underneath counter-melodies traced by solo flute and oboe.

Variation 4 brings changes in dynamics (fortissimo), register (high and middle), orchestration (melody in the woodwinds and brass), and a new triplet rhythm in the first violins against fortissimo chords on the off-beat in the other strings. The melody, too, is subtly changed.

The second half of this variation introduces a new version of the melody based on dotted rhythm.

This striking variation ends on a sustained chord which leads into the coda. The theme is wreathed in new harmonies. The final measures, which are in the nature of a gentle summing up, have a wonderful sound.

The third movement, a Minuet in G major, is a rollicking Allegro molto that leaves far behind it the manner of the courtly dance. Peasant humor and the high spirits of folk dance permeate this movement.

The first section (A) shows a structure typical of the classical minuet: |:a:||b-a-codetta:|. At the very outset we encounter one of Haydn's delightful irregularities in structure: two four-bar phrases are answered by one of four and another of six bars. The b section ends with an inimitably droll effect when flute and oboe are answered by bassoon and cello. The Trio (section B) is quieter in movement, combining bassoon and violins in octaves. The form of this section is |:c:||:d-c:|.

The minuet proper is repeated da capo, giving the movement a clear-cut A-B-A form.

The fourth movement is a vigorous Allegro molto (very lively) in sonata-allegro form. Like the first and third movements, it is in G major. Imbued with the spirit of popular dance, this Allegro has all the verve of the Haydn finale. The principal theme establishes the home key of G.

An energetic bridge passage leads to the second theme in the contrasting key, D major. This is a roguish little tune that is followed by a codetta in the same key. The first theme undergoes a forceful development, in the course of which the music touches upon various major and minor keys. In the Restatement, both first and second themes are in the home key of G. The coda sustains the jovial mood; and an energetic cadence in G major ends a work which captured, for Haydn's aristocratic listeners, all the charm and humor of the folk.

The Creation

In this celebrated oratorio, the creation of the world and its creatures is described with that capacity for wonder which only children and artists know. (An *oratorio* is a large-scale musical work for solo voices, chorus, and orchestra, set to a libretto of a sacred or serious character.) Due to reasons which we will examine when we discuss the life of Handel, the oratorio was extremely popular in England, with the result that during Haydn's two visits there he was made fully aware of the possibilities of this art-form. He wrote *The Creation* (1797–98) after his return to Vienna, when he was in his mid-sixties.

The libretto is based on the biblical Book of Genesis and on Milton's *Paradise Lost*. Milton's majestic poem reached Haydn in a roundabout way; he wrote his music to a German translation prepared by his librettist, a Baron von Swieten; this was retranslated into English so as to fit the music he had composed. In this process the nobility of Milton's verse inevitably was lost, its place being taken by a text that is at its best when it quotes the Book of Genesis but leaves much to be desired everywhere else. Recently, new translations have begun to supplant the original version; most recordings are sung in German.

The recitatives, solos, and ensemble numbers are assigned to three archangels —Gabriel (soprano), Uriel (tenor), and Raphael (bass), and to Adam and Eve in Part III. The archangels' voices, whether singly or together, contrast with the chorus that represents the heavenly hosts. The *recitativo secco* (literally, dry recitative), in the older opera and oratorio, was a kind of musical declamation that followed the inflections of speech and was accompanied by the harpsichord. In contrast, the more expressive *recitativo accompagnato* (accompanied recitative) was supported by the orchestra and had a more melodious character.

The Overture, marked Largo, is a "Representation of Chaos" that begins with the emptiness of the octave, a sustained C held by the full orchestra. The eighteenth century, we have seen, moved toward law and order through tonality—that is, the system of the major-minor keys. Haydn's attempt to depict the null and void of pre-Creation inevitably led him to ambiguous tonality, dissonance, and chromatic harmonies. The music starts out uncertainly from C minor, drifts into the key of D-flat and thence to E-flat major, but the feeling of a single key never lasts. Notable is Haydn's use of the motive of a descending scale-step, which to his era suggested a sigh. The Overture reaches a climax on a fortissimo C repeated decisively by the orchestra. Haydn assignes a daring glissando-like run to the clarinet that is followed by a similar one on the flute—an effect without precedent. The final passage contains chromatic harmonies that are strangely prophetic of Wagner's. Compare, for example, the look (and sound) of the following measures with that of the opening of *Tristan* on page 192. This is astonishing music to have been written in 1798!

The recitatives and the chorus that follows are based on the opening lines of Genesis:

RAPHAEL (Recitative):

In the beginning God created the heaven and the earth; and the earth was without form, and void; and darkness was upon the face of the deep.

CHORUS:

And the Spirit of God moved upon the face of the waters. And God said, Let there be light, and there was light.

URIEL (Recitative):

And God saw the light, that it was good: and God divided the light from the darkness.

Raphael's recitative sets out from C minor; touches briefly—between the void and the darkness—on E-flat major and minor; and makes a cadence in E-flat. The chorus begins pianissimo. We have already alluded to the great moment here—the change from C minor to major on the word *light*. At the end of Uriel's recitative, notice the two chords (what musicians recognize as a dominant-seventh chord and its Tonic); they give the same effect of finality as a period at the end of a sentence. This underlining of the cadence at the end of a recitative is characteristic of eighteenth-century oratorio and opera.

The aria—the English call it *air*—and chorus that follow carry the action forward. Haydn shows great originality in the way he ends each day with choral passages.

URIEL (Aria):

Now vanish before the holy beams
The gloomy dismal shades of dark;
The first of days appears.
Now chaos ends and order fair prevails.
Aghast the fiends of hell confounded fly,
Down they sink in the deep abyss to endless night.

CHORUS:

Despairing, cursing rage attends their rapid fall;
A new-created world springs up at God's command.

Uriel's aria, in A major, depicts the end of chaos in a melodious Andante. A vivid contrast is provided by the agitated Allegro moderato in C minor that deals with the affrighted spirits of hell. Rapid chromatic scales, ascending and descending, suggest their agitation. This mood prevails throughout the section for chorus. The line "Despairing, cursing rage attends their rapid fall" is accompanied by chromatic scales, tumultuous harmonies, and modulation. Presently the commotion passes, the music returns to a serene A major to describe the new-created world. Both moods are repeated: Uriel's Allegro is heard again briefly, and the first day ends with a chorus in praise of the new world.

You will notice the repetition of phrases and lines that is characteristic of choral music, especially in the eighteenth century. Composers realized that music is slower than words in establishing a mood. They therefore repeated single words, phrases, and entire lines over and over again to give the music time to create the proper atmosphere. Such repetition also made it easier for the listener to catch the words. In this particular case it is interesting to observe that when Haydn restates the phrase "A new-created world," he changes the harmony.

The first part of *The Creation* proceeds with the biblical narrative. A favorite number is Gabriel's recitative and aria describing the final event of the third day.

RECITATIVE:

And God said, let the earth bring forth grass, the herb yielding seed, and the fruit-tree
yielding fruit after his kind, whose seed is in itself, upon the earth: and it was so.

ARIA:

With verdure clad the fields appear,
Delighted to the ravished sense;
By flowers sweet and gay
Enhancèd is the charming sight.

Here perfumed herbs their fragrance shed,
Here grows the healing plant.
The heavy boughs with golden fruit abound,
The leafy arches twine in shady groves;
O'er lofty hills majestic forests wave.

This aria, an Andante, is in Haydn's most melodious style. After a four-bar introduction we hear the melody:

The form rests firmly upon a structure of key relationships. The first four lines of text are set to music that establishes the home key of B-flat major. The middle section begins with the second stanza, and contains a modulation from B-flat major, which has two flats, to F major, which has one. Notice how the word *plant* is expanded to stretch over a whole line of florid melody. Such expansion of a single word is as characteristic of the classical vocal style as is the repetition of lines and phrases.

The last three lines of text complete the middle part of this A-B-A aria. Here the music modulates frequently to build up tension for the inevitable return to the home key. When that is reached, the first section is repeated with two important modifications: first, the melody is subtly varied with an occasional embellishment; second, the vocal line changes its course to accommodate the fact that this time, instead of modulating, it must remain in the home key.

A high point of the work is the recitative and chorus that brings Part I to a close. Uriel's recitative—both *secco* and *accompagnato*—describes the creation of the sun, moon, and stars on the fourth day. It is followed by one of Haydn's most majestic choruses, *The Heavens Are Telling*, in which the choral passages are contrasted with two interjections by a trio of the archangels Gabriel, Uriel, and Raphael.

URIEL:

In shining splendor, radiant now, the sun
Climbs in the sky; a joyful happy spouse,
A giant proud and glad to run his measur'd course.

With milder pace and gentle shimmer
Steals the silver moon through silent night;
The boundless vaults of Heav'n's domain
Shine with unnumber'd magnitude of stars.

And the sons of God rejoiced in the fourth day,
In chorus divine praising God's great might, singing:

CHORUS:

The heavens are telling the glory of God,
The wonder of His work displays the firmament;

TRIO:

Revealed are his ways by day unto day,
By the night that is gone to following night.

CHORUS:

The heavens are telling the glory of God,
The wonder of His work displays the firmament.

The orchestral introduction to Uriel's accompanied recitative, an Andante, depicts the sunrise. Beginning pianissimo, the melody climbs up the scale step by step. Meanwhile fresh instruments are added in almost every measure until the fortissimo climax on a repeated D-major chord makes it clear that the world is flooded with light. A passage marked Più adagio (slower) suggests the creation of the moon and stars.

The chorus, a vigorous Allegro in C major, opens with a full sound and moves forward with all the momentum of a steady rhythm. The music is based on contrasts: between wind and string tone in the orchestral background; between chorus and orchestra, which continually answer each other; above all, between the massive combination of chorus and orchestra and the lyrical passages of the three soloists. The music unfolds in symmetrical four-measure phrases. The flowing melodic line is based on movement mostly by step, enlivened by occasional narrow leaps. In the following example, notice how the stepwise movement and repetition of notes in the first two measures is balanced by the narrow leaps in the third:

Allegro

The heav-ens are tell - ing the glo - ry of God,___

The chorus is in four parts: soprano, alto, tenor, bass. In a number of passages the voices sing the same words together; but this style alternates with another in which one section of the chorus enters alone and is imitated in turn by the other sections. The latter style, based on the interweaving of the voice parts, appears more and more in the second half of the piece. Text is repeated in order to give the music time to establish the mood. The sense of climax towards the end, achieved through crescendo and accelerando, is strengthened by vigorous movement in the orchestra. This closing section is marked Più allegro (faster). In the final phrase all the voices unite in massive chords for a majestic cadence.

The second part of the oratorio begins with the fifth day of Creation, when the animals are created. Here Haydn's love of nature holds full sway; his impish humor illumines the description of the birds and beasts. A favorite number in the second part is the chorus *Achievèd Is the Glorious Work*. In the third part the human element enters the scene with Adam (bass) and Eve (soprano). Accompanied by the chorus, they praise the Creator. There is a love-duet, and the work ends with a spacious chorus, *Sing the Lord, Ye Voices All*.

Haydn's is an optimistic music that even in its darker moments accepts life and finds it good. The nineteenth century, with its love of the grandiose, was not overly responsive to his wholesome discourse. Thus was created the stereotype of an amiable "Papa Haydn" in court dress and powdered wig who purveyed harmless pleasantries to the lords of the old regime. It has remained for the twentieth century to rescue this great musician from such incomprehension and to restore to its rightful place his deeply felt, finely wrought art—an art of moderation and humor, polished and lucid, profoundly human and unfadingly fresh.

53 Wolfgang Amadeus Mozart

"People make a mistake who think that my art has come easily to me. Nobody has devoted so much time and thought to composition as I. There is not a famous master whose music I have not studied over and over."

Something of the miraculous hovers about the music of Mozart (1756–91). One sees how it is put together, whither it is bound, and how it gets there; but its beauty of sound and perfection of style, its poignancy and grace defy analysis and beggar description. For one moment in the history of music all opposites were reconciled, all tensions resolved. That luminous moment was Mozart.

His Life

He was born in Salzburg, son of Leopold Mozart, an esteemed composer-violinist attached to the court of the Archbishop. He began his career as the most extraodinarily gifted child in the history of art. He first started to compose before he was five, and performed at the court of the Empress Maria

Wolfgang Amadeus Mozart.

Theresa at the age of six. The following year his ambitious father organized a grand tour that included Paris, London, and Munich. By the time he was thirteen the boy had written sonatas, concertos, symphonies, religious works, an *opera buffa* and the operetta *Bastien and Bastienne*.

He reached manhood having attained a mastery of all forms of his art. The speed and sureness of his creative power, unrivaled by any other composer, is best described by himself: "Though it be long, the work is complete and finished in my mind. I take out of the bag of my memory what has previously been collected into it. For this reason the committing to paper is done quickly enough. For everything is already finished, and it rarely differs on paper from what it was in my imagination. At this work I can therefore allow myself to be disturbed. Whatever may be going on about me, I write and even talk."

His relations with his patron, Hieronymus von Colloredo, Prince-Archbishop of Salzburg, were most unhappy. The high-spirited young artist rebelled against the social restrictions imposed by the patronage system. At length he could endure his position no longer. He quarreled with the Archbishop, was dismissed, and at twenty-five established himself in Vienna to pursue the career of a free artist, the while he sought an official appointment. Ten years remained to him. These were spent in a tragic struggle to achieve financial security and to find again the lost serenity of his childhood. Worldly success depended on the protection of the court. But the Emperor Joseph II—who referred to him as "a decided talent"—either passed him by in favor of lesser men or, when he finally took Mozart into his service, assigned him to tasks unworthy of his genius such as composing dances for the court balls. Of his remuneration for this work Mozart remarked with bitterness, "Too much for what I do, too little for what I could do."

In 1782 he married Constanze Weber, against his father's wishes. The step signalized Mozart's liberation from the close ties that had bound him to the well-meaning but domineering parent who strove so futilely to ensure the happiness of the son. Constanze brought her husband neither the strength of character nor the wealth that might have protected him from a struggle with the world for which he was singularly unequipped. She was an undistinguished woman to whom Mozart, despite occasional lapses, was strongly attached. It was not till many years after his death that she appears to have realized, from the adulation of the world, the stature of her husband.

With the opera *The Marriage of Figaro*, written in 1786 on a libretto by Lorenzo da Ponte, Mozart reached the peak of his career as far as success was concerned. The work made a sensation in Vienna and in Prague, and his letters from the latter city testify to his pleasure at its reception. He was commissioned to do another work for the following year. With da Ponte again as librettist he produced *Don Giovanni*. The opera baffled the Viennese. His vogue had passed. The composer whom we regard as the epitome of clarity and grace was, in the view of the frivolous public of his time, difficult to understand. His music, it was said, had to be heard several times in order to be grasped. What better proof of its inaccessibility? In truth, Mozart was entering regions beyond the aristocratic entertainment level of the day. He was straining toward an intensity of utterance that was new in the world. Of *Don Giovanni* Joseph II declared, "The opera is heavenly, perhaps even more beautiful than *Figaro*. But no food for the teeth of my Viennese." Upon which Mozart commented, "Then give them time to chew it." One publisher advised him to write in a more popular style. "In that case I can make no more by my pen," he answered. "I had better starve and die at once."

The last years of his life were spent in growing want. The frequent appeals to his friends for aid mirror his despair and helplessness. He describes himself as "always hovering between hope and anxiety." He speaks of the black thoughts that he must "repel by a tremendous effort." The love of life that had sustained him through earlier disappointments began to desert him. Again and again he embarked on a journey that seemed to promise a solution to all his difficulties, only to return empty-handed.

In the last year of his life, after a falling off in his production, he nerved himself to the final effort. For the popular Viennese theater he wrote *The Magic Flute*, on a libretto by the actor-impresario-poetaster Emanuel Schika-neder. Then a flurry of hope sent him off to Prague for the coronation of the new Emperor, Leopold II, as King of Bohemia. The festival opera he composed for this event, *The Clemency of Titus*, failed to impress a court exhausted by the protracted ceremonies of the coronation. Mozart returned to Vienna broken in body and spirit. With a kind of fevered desperation he turned to his last task, the Requiem. It had been commissioned by a music-loving count who fancied himself a composer and intended to pass off the work as his own. Mozart in his overwrought state became obsessed with the notion that this Mass for the Dead was intended for himself and that he would not live to finish it. A tragic race with time began as he whipped his faculties to this masterwork steeped in visions of death.

His last days were cheered by the growing popularity of *The Magic Flute*. The gravely ill composer, watch in hand, would follow the performance in his mind. "Now the first act is over . . . Now comes the aria of the Queen of Night . . ." His premonition concerning the Requiem came true. He failed rapidly while in the midst of the work. His favorite pupil, Süssmayr, completed the Mass from the master's sketches, with some additions of his own.

Mozart died in 1791, shortly before his thirty-sixth birthday. In view of his debts he was given "the poorest class of funeral." His friends followed to the city gates; but the weather being inclement, they turned back, leaving the hearse to proceed alone. "Thus, without a note of music, forsaken by all he held dear, the remains of this prince of harmony were committed to the earth—not even in a grave of his own but in the common paupers' grave."

His Music

Many view Mozart as one in whom the elegance of court art reached its peak. To others he represents the spirit of artless youth untouched by life. Both views are equally far from the truth. Neither the simplicity of his forms nor the crystalline clarity of his texture can dispel the intensity of feeling that pervades the works of his maturity. Because of the mastery with which everything is carried out, the most complex operations of the musical mind are made to appear effortless. This deceptive simplicity is truly the art that conceals art.

It has been said that Mozart taught the instruments to sing. Into his exquisitely wrought instrumental forms he poured the lyricism of the great vocal art of the past. The peasant touch is missing from Mozart's music, which draws its inspiration neither from folk song nor nature. It is an indoor art, sophisticated, rooted in the culture of two musical cities—Salzburg and Vienna.

The Salzburg years saw the composition of a quantity of social music, divertimentos and serenades of great variety. In chamber music he favored the string quartet. His works in this form range in expression from the buoyantly songful to the austerely tragic. The last ten quartets rank with the finest specimens in the literature, among them being the set of six dedicated to Haydn, his "most celebrated and very dear friend." Worthy companions to these are the string quintets, in which he invariably used two violas. The somber Quintet in G minor represents the peak of his achievement in this medium.

One of the outstanding pianists of his time, Mozart wrote copiously for his favorite instrument. Among his finest solo works are the Fantasia in C minor and the Sonata in the same key, K. 475 and 457. (The K followed by a number refers to the catalogue of Mozart's works by Ludwig Koechel, who enumerated them all in what he took to be the order of their composition.) Mozart was less experimental than Haydn in regard to formal structure, yet he led the way in developing one important form: the concerto for piano and orchestra. He wrote more than twenty works for this medium. They established the piano concerto as one of the important types of the classical era.

The more than forty symphonies—their exact number has not been determined—that extend across his career tend toward ever greater richness of orchestration, freedom of part writing, and depth of emotion. The most important are the six written in the final decade of his life—the "Haffner" in D (1782), the "Linz" in C (1783), the "Prague" in D (1786), and the three composed in 1788. With these works the symphony achieves its position as the most weighty form of abstract music. In an age when composers produced their works almost exclusively on commission, it is significant that Mozart's last three symphonies were never performed during his lifetime: he wrote them for no specific occasion but from inner necessity. They came into being because the composer had something in him that had to be said, no matter who heard.

But the central current in Mozart's art that nourished all the others was opera. Here were embodied his joy in life, his melancholy, all the impulses of his many-faceted personality. None has ever surpassed his power to delineate character in music and to make his puppets come alive. His lyric gift, molded to the curve of the human voice, created a wealth of melody whose sensuous loveliness sets it apart in music. His orchestra, although it never obtrudes upon the voice, becomes the magical framework within which the action unfolds.

In Lorenzo da Ponte, an Italian-Jewish adventurer and poet who was one of the picturesque figures of the age, Mozart found a librettist whose dramatic vitality was akin to his own. (Da Ponte ultimately emigrated to America, operated a grocery store and sold illicit liquor on the side, taught Italian at Columbia College, was one of the first impresarios to bring Italian opera to New York, wrote a fascinating book of memoirs, and died in 1838.) The collaboration produced three works: *The Marriage of Figaro* (1786), which da Ponte adapted from the comedy of Beaumarchais satirizing the old regime; *Don Giovanni* (1787), "the opera of all operas"; and *Così fan tutte* (1790), which has been translated in a variety of ways from "So do all women" to "Girls will be girls!" These crown the history of classical *opera buffa;* just as *The Abduction from the Seraglio* (1782) and *The Magic Flute* (1791), a gigantic fantasy steeped in the symbolism of Freemasonry, bring to its apex the German *Singspiel* (song-play). Abounding in irony and satire, these masterpieces reach beyond the world of satin and lace whence they issued. They achieve what da Ponte set forth as his and Mozart's intention: "To paint faithfully and in full color the divers passions."

Don Giovanni

Conceived in the tradition of the *opera buffa, Don Giovanni* oversteps that tradition into the realm covered by our term tragicomedy. Da Ponte called it a "jocose" or cheerful drama. The opera is unique for its range of emotions.

Da Ponte's Don heralds a new type in literature as in society: the supreme individualist who brooks no restraints and brushes aside every obstacle in the way of his self-realization. Don Juan is the eternal type of libertine for whom the pursuit of pleasure has become the final assertion of will. Mozart's music humanizes him, transforms him into one of the boldest conceptions in the entire range of the lyric theater.

Mozart put off writing the Overture until the last moment. He had to sit up the night before the dress rehearsal, Constanze telling him stories to keep him awake, in order to set it down. The parts were copied that day and read at sight by the orchestra. Mozart, who conducted, remarked that "plenty of notes fell under the table." From the statement quoted earlier in the chapter it is clear that we must amend this famous story in one detail. He did not compose the Overture that night; he committed to paper what was already finished in his mind.

The Overture begins with an Andante in cut time that establishes the key of D minor. The opening measures are of an impressive dignity that will be associated at the climax of the work with the ghost of the Commandant. There follows a sonata-allegro movement in D major that serves to introduce the opera

without being related to it by theme. The richness of sound and free interweaving of orchestral parts bespeak the high classical style.

The curtain rises on Don Giovanni's servant Leporello, who is standing outside the residence of Donna Anna bemoaning his fate: "Night and day I slave for one who's never pleased. I have to bear wind and rain, am fed badly, and sleep badly. I'd like to play the gentleman and serve no more. A fine gentleman you are, in there making sport with beauty while I stand watch outside . . ."

Don Giovanni, who had broken into Donna Anna's chamber, rushes out of the house struggling with her and concealing his face. Donna Anna, determined to discover the identity of her assailant, calls for help. Her father—the Commandant—appears, drawing his sword. Donna Anna withdraws into the house. The Don does not wish to fight the old man but is goaded into a duel in the course of which he mortally wounds the Commandant. The conversation between Don Giovanni and Leporello establishes the moral climate they inhabit. "Who is dead, you or the old man?" "Silly question. The old man." "Bravo. Nice work—attacking the daughter and murdering the father." "He asked for it." "And Donna Anna, what did she ask for?" "Shut up and come away. Unless you too are asking for something." "Oh no, master. I shan't say another word." They escape. Donna Anna comes out of the house with Don Ottavio, her betrothed. She discovers her father's body and is overcome by grief. In the ensuing duet she and Don Ottavio swear to track down the murderer and make him pay for his crime.

As in *The Creation*, the recitative veers between the unadorned *secco* accompanied by harpsichord and the more expressive *accompagnato* supported by the

DON GIOVANNI, Act I: Leporello unfolds his extensive catalogue of the Don's conquests. (Metropolitan Opera production)

orchestra. The dialogue between Don Giovanni and Leporello is given in *recitativo secco*, while the emotional interchange between Donna Anna and Don Ottavio has an orchestral background. Donna Anna is established forthwith as the great lady, noble of bearing and somewhat remote, who throughout the work represents the aristocracy; even as the middle station in life and the peasantry have their representatives. Conspicuous is the repetition of lines and phrases of the text, which allows space for the necessary expansion and repetition of musical material. This accords with Mozart's dictum that in opera the poetry must be the obedient daughter of the music. As in the symphony, large units are given shape and coherence through the unifying power of key. The opening scene ends in D minor, forming a musical entity that launches the dramatic-musical action.

Leporello's Catalogue Aria, which concludes the second scene, is sung to Donna Elvira, who has been abandoned by the Don but still loves him. To

Ma-da-mi-na! il ca-ta-lo-go è que-sto del-le bel-le che a-mò il pa-dron mi-o,
My dear la-dy! Let me draw your at-ten-tion to this list of the loves of my mas-ter,

persuade her of the futility of her passion Leporello reads her the list of his master's amours. "In Italy six hundred and forty. In Germany two hundred and thirty-one. A hundred in France, in Turkey ninety-one. But in Spain it's already one thousand and three (*'mille e tre'*). Country girls, servant girls, city girls, countesses, baronesses, princesses. All ranks, all shapes, all ages . . ." What is left unsaid in the vocal line is filled in by the saucy accompaniment. This *buffo* aria, in which the singer with a knowing wink takes the audience into his confidence, is in the great tradition of the theater of buffoons.

In the next scene, *Là ci darem la mano*—a little duet, as Mozart called it— is sung by Don Giovanni and Zerlina, the artless peasant maid who has momen-

Là   ci da-rem   la   ma - no,   là   mi di-rai di   sì,
Give me your hand, sweet maid- en,   Whis- per a gen-tle "yes,"

tarily caught his fancy. He succeeds indetaching her from her fiancé, the country bumpkin Masetto; assures her that he intends to marry her, and invites her to come with him to his villa. The voices alternate, the phrases becoming ever shorter as he grows more ardent and she more amenable. "I should feel happy. What if he's only making sport of me . . . Come, my delight . . . I'm sorry for Masetto . . . I'll change your life . . . How quickly I yield . . ." The tempo changes from andante to allegro; 2/4 time gives way to 6/8 as she throws herself into his arms. Together they sing, "Let us go, my dearest, and ease the pangs of innocent love." There is much repetition of the key word *andiam* (let us go) to allow for musical expansion. The melody is Mozart at his suavest.

In the course of the opera Donna Anna realizes that Don Giovanni is the man who broke into her room on the fatal night. She and Don Ottavio plan to deliver him to justice. Don Giovanni, meanwhile, during one of his escapades takes refuge in the dead of night in the cemetery where stands the statue of the Commandant. The stone figure chides Don Giovanni for disturbing the peace of the dead. Enjoying Leporello's terror, the Don now commits the crowning blasphemy: he invites the Statue to sup with him that evening. The stone figure nods acceptance.

The final scene is the momentous supper in Don Giovanni's mansion. He directs his musicians to play while he eats. The entrance of the Commandant's statue is one of the supreme moments in opera. The music returns to the key in which the Overture began. Three trombones join the *tutti* (the whole orchestra) to herald the entrance of the specter.

Don Gio-van - ni!   a   ce-nar te - co   m'in-vi - ta - sti,   e son ve - nu - to!
Don Gio-van - ni,   pray bid me wel-come!   Since you asked me,   I've come to sup-per.

The awesome pronouncement is heard against the harmonies that opened the Overture. The melodic line, based on the downward leap of an octave, is of a supernatural dignity.

The Statue asks the Don to repay the visit and take supper with him. Leporello, shaking with fear, implores his master to decline. "He hasn't the time—please excuse him!" But the Don will not be accused of cowardice. "I have no fear. I'll come." "Give me your hand in pledge." "Take it!" He holds out his hand and feels the Statue's icy clasp. "Repent! Change your life before it is too late." The Don struggles to free himself, yet even now his courage does not desert him; he cannot renounce his destiny. "No, I will not repent, you old fool!" "Then it is too late." Flames shoot up. The demons of hell rise to claim their prey. They drag the sinner to his doom.

The scene ends in D major, which prepares for the final sextet, in which Leporello describes Don Giovanni's fate to the interested parties—Donna Anna and Don Ottavio, Elvira, Zerlina and Masetto. This cheerful ending, implied in da Ponte's description of *Don Giovanni* as a "jocose drama," restores the *opera buffa* character of the work. It is heavenly music.

Symphony No. 40 in G Minor

It was in the summer of 1788, during the darkest period of his life, that Mozart in the space of a little over six weeks composed his last three symphonies: in E-flat (K. 543); in G minor (K. 550); and in C, the "Jupiter" (K. 551). They are popularly known as Nos. 39, 40, and 41.

The G-minor Symphony represents that mingling of classic and romantic elements which marked the final decades of the eighteenth century. Along with several important works that preceded it, the Symphony strikes a tenderly impassioned note. (In Vienna it is known as the "Romantic.") The first movement, in sonata-allegro form, plunges immediately into the Allegro molto. The Exposition opens with an intense theme for the violins that establishes the home key of G minor. Pointing to a new expressiveness in music, it flowers out of a

three-note germ motive (A) that is genuinely symphonic in its capacity for growth, and contains two other motives (B and C) that play their part in the development of the material. Notice that the second phrase is a sequence, one step lower, of the first. Great rhythmic activity gives the melody a feeling of restlessness that is heightened by the animated accompaniment of the lower strings. Stepwise movement in the first measure is balanced by the dramatic upward leap in the second and the gradual descent of the melody in the third. A vigorous bridge passage that sustains tension through a steady crescendo leads into the contrasting key, the relative major—B-flat. The second theme, shared by woodwinds and strings, provides an area of comparative relaxation in the headlong drive of the movement. This melody is in direct contrast to the restlessness of the first subject. It moves in a flowing rhythm, mostly stepwise and within a narrow range. Notice that each phrase begins by gliding downward along the chromatic scale:

The codetta, in which we hear echoings of the basic motive (A), establishes the cadence in the contrasting key. In most recordings of this work the Exposition is repeated, which is in accordance with classical usage. (The short Exposition of the classical symphony demands to be repeated, otherwise the whole design is upset. As the Exposition grew ever longer in nineteenth-century music, the practice was abandoned.)

The Development is brief and packed with action. It searches out the possibilities of the opening theme, concentrating on the three-note motive. The music wanders far afield, modulating rapidly from one foreign key to the next. Here are some examples of Mozart's developmental technique:

1. Theme 1 with change at the end:

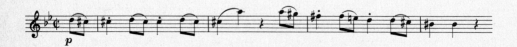

2. Theme 1 in the bass with a new melody above it:

3. Expansion through a pattern combining Motives C and B, which is repeated in a descending sequence:

266

4. Expansion through repetition of Motive A, forming a pattern that is repeated in a descending sequence:

5. Inversion of Motive A (upside-down), used together with the motive in its original position as part of the transition back to the home key:

Never slackening its course, the Development is crowned by the transition back to the home key, one of those miraculous passages that only Mozart could have written. We hear the initial theme as it sounded in the beginning.

The Recapitulation follows the course of the first section. The bridge is expanded and circles about the home key. The second theme is given in G minor rather than major, taking on a strangely tender tone. The coda energetically confirms the home key.

The second movement, an Andante in E-flat also in sonata-allegro form, is pitched on a less subjective level. The classical masters did not find it incongruous to cast a slow movement in the form so closely identified with the first (allegro) movement. Violas, second violins, then first violins enter in turn with the first theme in the home key.

The horns provide a background for the strings. There is Viennese grace in the characteristic dip of the melody in the answering phrase, which is heard in the first violins.

The theme unfolds amid an abundance of ornament. This is not the kind of sonata movement that depends on a dynamic contrast between first and second themes. The composer contents himself in the Exposition with the opposition between the home key—E-flat major—and the contrasting key—B-flat—and modulates actively in the Development. The transition back to the home key is accomplished through a dialogue for woodwinds—bassoon, clarinets, and flutes. With its graceful embellishments, this movement reflects the courtly refinement of an era that was drawing to a close.

The third movement, in G minor, recaptures the emotional tension of the first. This Minuet is remarkable for its vigor and onrush. Mozart here reaches out beyond the aristocratic dance that gave the movement its name. The opening section is marked by a type of nonsymmetrical phrase structure that appears in Mozart, as in Haydn, more frequently than is generally realized. Two phrases of three measures each are followed by a phrase of five measures and one of three.

In form this section is characteristic of the minuet of a classical symphony: |:a:||:b-a-codetta:|. The a section is varied somewhat when it is repeated.

The Trio is in G major; the change from the minor contributes to its relaxed mood. Color becomes an element of form as oboe, flute, and bassoon in turn take the phrase. Notice that the second group of five notes duplicates the first group a tone higher (sequence):

How beautifully the horn mingles its sound with the strings when the melody is restated. The subsections of the Trio are repeated in the customary manner

(∥:c:∥:d-c:∥), after which the Minuet is heard again, but without repeats. There results a rounded three-part form.

The finale, Allegro assai (very fast), is a compact sonata-allegro form, abrupt and imperious. A tragic restlessness lurks beneath its polished surface. The first subject, in G minor, is presented by the first violins. Based on an upward-bounding arpeggio, it represents a pattern dear to the classical era and known as a *rocket theme.*

The contrasting theme, sung by the first violins·in the related key of B-flat major, provides the necessary foil in point of serenity and grace. It has longer —that is, fewer—notes, moves within a narrow range, mostly stepwise or with narrow leaps, and is rhythmically quieter.

It is repeated, with subtle embellishments, by the clarinet.

The Development is highly dramatic. The rocket motive is bandied about by various instruments that crowd upon one another in hurried imitation as they spin out a complex orchestral fabric. Tension is maintained at maximum pitch by the rapid modulations through foreign keys. The Recapitulation presents the material again with certain changes, most important of which is the shifting of the second theme into the home key of G minor. From that moment of enchantment until the final cadence we witness the exciting spectacle of a great artist functioning at the summit of his powers.

Piano Concerto in C Major, K.467

Mozart, we saw, played a crucial role in the development of the piano concerto. His concertos were written primarily as display pieces for his own public performances. They abound in the brilliant flourishes and ceremonious gestures characteristic of eighteenth-century social music.

The sunny Piano Concerto in C major (K. 467, 1785) belongs to one of Mozart's most productive periods. He is nothing short of prodigal with his tunes, and proceeds to weld them—with the firm hand of a master—into an architec-

269

tural unity. The first movement is an Allegro maestoso whose opening pages show how richly Mozart's instrumental art was nourished by the opera house; the principal theme could have come straight out of a scene in an *opera buffa*. (Indeed, it bears a close resemblance to Leporello's opening aria in *Don Giovanni*.) More important, its first two measures constitute a motive wonderfully capable of growth. This motive dominates the movement.

The theme is presented by the strings in unison. (We say that instruments are playing *in unison* when they are all playing the same notes.)

In this movement we should speak of a theme group rather than a theme. The first of several subsidiary ideas is divided between brass and woodwinds:

Another subsidiary idea is no less appealing:

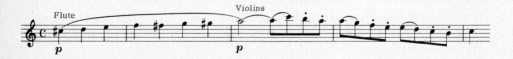

In his concertos Mozart uses the sonata-allegro form with infinite variety; no two first movements are alike. In this case, since the movement is fashioned out of flowing melodies, the result is an unusually spacious form. The orchestra gives the first theme-group in C; the piano enters with a series of flourishes and takes off from Theme 1 through a transitional passage that modulates to G. Although one expects a major tonality, Mozart surprises the hearer with a melody in G minor that bears a startling resemblance to the opening theme of the G-minor Symphony. Compare the following with the example on page 265. Moving though it is, this idea does not appear again.

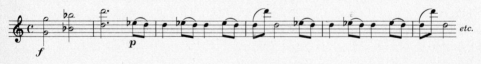

The stage is now set for the appearance of the second theme in G major. It is introduced by the piano and repeated in the orchestra:

Brilliant passage work by the piano rounds out the Exposition; the Development is ushered in by the whole orchestra. With such a wealth of material to draw upon, Mozart—astonishingly—still finds it necessary to introduce a new melody, in a passage in E minor that wreathes the music in a romantic glow:

The Development, despite its heightening of tension, never forfeits its melodious character. The virtuoso figuration in the solo instrument is heard against broadly spun phrases in the strings or woodwinds. Thus virtuosity never becomes an end in itself but remains a means of expression. The Recapitulation opens with the strings playing the main theme in the home key. This time the second theme follows immediately after the first. Where are the subsidiary themes? It turns out that Mozart is saving them for the coda, which rounds out the movement with all the courtly gestures of the eighteenth century. We unfortunately do not possess Mozart's cadenza; it is a wise artist who makes his own as short as possible. The basic motive returns in the final measures. One might have expected so bright an Allegro to have a brilliant ending. Mozart surprises us. The movement ends like one of those *opera buffa* scenes in which the characters tiptoe off stage.

The second movement is a serenely flowing Andante in F. Against a triplet rhythm in the strings, the muted first violins gravely unfold a melody that is taken over by the piano:

Its gentle poignancy explains why composers such as Chopin and Tchaikovsky worshipped Mozart above all others. The form unfolds freely, shaped by the material. Unity is provided by the ever-present triplets, diversity by the soaring melodic line. After a middle section that stresses D minor, the melody returns

271

in the remote key of A-flat major—a procedure closer to the romantic mind than the classical. Mozart does not repeat the theme literally; he varies it with fanciful embellishments. The movement finds its way back to the home key, and the coda rounds it off with a pianissimo ending.

The gay finale is a rondo in C major, marked Allegro vivace assai (very fast and lively). The secret of such a piece lies in the impression it gives of effortless motion. It opens with an *opera buffa* tune in the violins that is taken over by the piano:

The second theme in G continues the mood of the opening idea, as does the codetta; then the main theme returns. This movement, in its vivacity and good humor, typifies the classical rondo finale. But at this time the rondo was absorbing certain features of sonata-allegro form, especially the dynamic movement from key to key and—most important of all—the development of themes and motives. There resulted a form that may be considered a rondo-sonata, of which this Allegro is an example.

The filigree work on the piano demands nimble fingers. Clearly Mozart enjoyed displaying his prowess as a pianist. There is much lively interplay between piano and orchestra, both of which—after a brief cadenza that ushers in the final appearance of the theme—share in the brilliant C-major ending.

Eine kleine Nachtmusik

Mozartian elegance and delicacy of touch are embodied in this serenade for strings (K. 525, 1787), whose title means "A Little Night Music." Probably the work was intended for a double string-quartet supported by a bass. The version we know has four movements, compact, intimate, and beautifully proportioned; originally there were five.

The opening Allegro is a sonata form in $\frac{4}{4}$ time in G major. As was customary in music of this type, the first movement has a marchlike character—as if the musicians were arriving for their cheerful task.

Second is the Romanza, an eighteenth-century Andante that maintains the balance between lyricism and a pleasant reserve. The key is C, the meter ₵; symmetrical sections are arranged in an A-B-A-C-A structure. The Minuet, marked Allegretto, is in G major and regular four-bar structure. The Trio, which is marked sotto voce (in an undertone, subdued), traces a soaring curve of Mozartian melody; after which the Minuet is repeated.

The rondo finale, Allegro, is in cut time in the home key of G. It is based on a vivacious principal theme:

This alternates with a subordinate idea. (The sign over the last note in measure 2 of the example indicates a *turn,* a type of ornament or embellishment.)

The movement displays certain features of sonata form—opposition between home and contrasting key, development of the rondo theme, and modulation far afield. We have said that there is a rondo style as well as a rondo form. This is the perfect example, bright, jovial, and—a trait inseparable from this master —stamped with an aristocratic refinement.

In the music of Mozart subjective emotion is elevated to the plane of the universal. The restlessness and the longing are exorcised by the ideal loveliness of Apollonian art. Mozart is one of the supreme artists of all time; the voice of pure beauty in music, and probably the most sheerly musical composer that ever lived.

54 Ludwig van Beethoven

"Freedom above all!"

Beethoven (1770–1827) belonged to the generation that received the full impact of the French Revolution. He was nourished by its vision of the freedom and dignity of the individual. The time, the place, and the personality combined to produce an artist sensitive in the highest degree to the impulses of the new century. He created the music of a heroic age and in accents never to be forgotten proclaimed its faith in the power of man to shape his destiny.

His Life

He was born in Germany, in the city of Bonn in the Rhineland, where his father and grandfather were singers at the court of the local prince, the Elector Max Friedrich. The family situation was unhappy, the father being addicted to drink, and Ludwig at an early age was forced to take over the support of his mother and two younger brothers. At eleven and a half he was

Ludwig van
Beethoven.

assistant organist in the court chapel. A year later he became harpsichordist in the court orchestra. A visit to Vienna in his seventeenth year enabled him to play for Mozart. The youth improvised so brilliantly on a theme given him by the master that the latter remarked to his friends, "Keep an eye on him—he will make a noise in the world some day."

Arrangements were made some years later for him to study with Haydn in Vienna at the Elector's expense. He left his native town when he was twenty-two, never to return. Unfortunately, the relationship between pupil and teacher left much to be desired. The aging Haydn was ruffled by the young man's volcanic temperament and independence of spirit. Beethoven worked with other masters, the most academic of whom declared that "he has learned nothing and will never do anything in decent style."

Meanwhile his powers as a pianist took the music-loving aristocracy by storm. He was welcome in the great houses of Vienna by the powerful patrons whose names appear in the dedications of his works—Prince Lichnowsky, Prince Lobkowitz, Count Razumovsky, and the rest. Archduke Rudolph, brother of the Emperor, became his pupil and devoted friend. These connoisseurs, no less than the public, were transported by his highly personal style of improvisation, by the wealth of his ideas, the novelty of their treatment, and the surging emotion behind them.

To this "princely rabble," as he called them, the young genius came—in an era of revolution—as a passionate rebel, forcing them to receive him as an equal and friend. "It is good to move among the aristocracy," he observed, "but it is first necessary to make them respect you." Beethoven, sensitive and irascible, stood up for his rights as an artist. When Prince Lichnowsky, during the Napoleonic invasion, insisted that he play for some French officers, Beethoven stormed out of the palace in a rage, demolished a bust of Lichnowsky that was in his possession, and wrote to his exalted friend: "Prince! what you are, you are through the accident of birth. What I am, I am through my own efforts. There have been many princes and there will be thousands more. But there is only one Beethoven!" Such was the force of his personality that he was able to make the aristocrats about him accept this novel idea. Beneath the rough exterior they recognized an elemental power akin to a force of nature.

Beethoven functioned under a modified form of the patronage system. He was not attached to the court of a prince. Instead, the music-loving aristocrats of Vienna helped him in various ways—by paying him handsomely for lessons, or through gifts. He was also aided by the emergence of a middle-class public and the growth of concert life and music publishing. At the age of thirty-one he was able to write, "I have six or seven publishers for each of my works and could have more if I chose. No more bargaining. I name my terms and they pay." A youthful exuberance pervades the first decade of his career, an almost arrogant consciousness of his strength. "Power is the morality of men who stand out from the mass, and it is also mine!" Thus spoke the individualist in the new era of individualism.

Then, as the young eagle was spreading his wings, fate struck in a vulnerable spot: he began to lose his hearing. His helplessness in the face of this affliction dealt a shattering blow to his pride. "Ah, how could I possibly admit an infirmity in the one sense that should have been more perfect in me than in others. A sense I once possessed in highest perfection. Oh I cannot do it!" As his deafness closed in on him—the first symptoms appeared when he was in his late twenties—it became the symbol of his terrible sense of apartness from other men, of all the defiance and insecurity and hunger for love that had rent him for as long as he could remember. Upon the mistaken advice of his doctors he retired in 1802 to a summer resort outside Vienna called Heiligenstadt. A titanic struggle shook him, between the destructive forces in his soul and his desire to live and create. It was one of those searing experiences that either break a man or leave him stronger. "But little more and I would have put an end to my life. Only art it was that withheld me. Ah, it seemed impossible to leave the world until I had produced all that I felt called upon to produce, and so I endured this wretched existence."

It was slowly borne in on him that art must henceforth give him the happiness life withheld. Only through creation could he attain the victory of which fate had threatened to rob him. The will to struggle asserted itself; he fought his way back to health. "I am resolved to rise superior to every obstacle. With

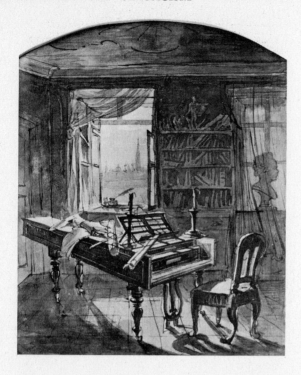

Beethoven's studio. Drawing by H. N. Hoechle

whom need I be afraid of measuring my strength? If possible I will bid defiance to my fate, although there will be moments in life when I will be the unhappiest of God's creatures . . . I will take Fate by the throat. It shall not overcome me. Oh how beautiful it is to be alive—would that I could live a thousand times!" He had stumbled on an idea that was to play a decisive part in nineteenth-century thought: the concept of art as refuge, as compensation for the shortcomings of reality; art as sublimation, atonement, faith—the idealized experience, the ultimate victory over life.

Having conquered the chaos within himself he came to believe that man could conquer chaos. This became the epic theme of his music: the progression from despair to conflict, from conflict to serenity, from serenity to triumph and joy. The revelation that had come to him through suffering was a welcome message to the world that was struggling to be born. The concept of man the master of his fate hit off the temper of the new middle-class society in its most dynamic phase. In giving expression to his personal faith Beethoven said what his generation needed to hear. He became the major prophet of the nineteenth century, the architect of its heroic vision of life. "I am the Bacchus who presses out the glorious wine for mankind. Whoever truly understands my music is freed thereby from the miseries that others carry about in them."

The remainder of his career was spent in an unremitting effort to subjugate the elements of his art to the expressive ideal he had set himself. Fellow musicians and critics might carp at the daring of his thoughts, but his victory was assured. A growing public, especially among the younger generation, responded to the powerful thrust of his music. His life was outwardly uneventful. There were the interminable quarrels with associates and friends—he grew increasingly suspicious and irritable, especially in his last years when he became totally deaf. There were the complicated dealings with his publishers, in which he displayed an impressive shrewdness; his turbulent love affairs (he never married); his high-handed interference in the affairs of his brothers; his tortured relationship with his nephew Carl, an ordinary young man upon whom he fastened a tyrannical affection. All these framed an inner life of extraordinary intensity, an unceasing spiritual development that reached down to ever profounder levels of insight and opened up new domains to tonal art.

Biographers and painters have made familiar the squat sturdy figure—he was five foot four, the same as that other conqueror of the age, Napoleon—walking hatless through the environs of Vienna, the bulging brow furrowed in thought, stopping now and again to jot down an idea in his sketchbook; an idea that, because he was forever deprived of its sonorous beauty, he envisioned all the more vividly in his mind. A ride in an open carriage in inclement weather brought on an attack of dropsy that proved fatal. He died in his fifty-seventh year, famous and revered.

His Music

Beethoven is the supreme architect in music. His genius found expression in the structural type of thinking embodied in the sonata-symphony. The sketchbooks in which he worked out his ideas show how gradually they reached their final shape and how painstakingly he molded the material into its one inevitable form. "I carry my thoughts within me long, often very long before I write them down. In doing this my memory stands me in such good stead that even years afterward I am sure not to forget a theme I have once grasped . . . As I know what I want, the fundamental idea never deserts me. It mounts, it grows in stature. I hear, I see the picture in its whole extent standing all of a piece before my spirit, and there remains for me only the task of writing it down."

Inheriting the sonata form from Haydn and Mozart, he transformed it into a spacious frame for his ideas. He expanded the dimensions of the first movement, especially the coda. Like Haydn and Mozart, he treated the development section as the dynamic center of sonata form. His short incisive themes offer limitless opportunity for expansion and development; they unfold with volcanic energy and momentum. The slow movement acquired in his hands a hymnic character, the embodiment of Beethovenian pathos. He transformed minuet into scherzo, making it a movement of rhythmic energy ranging from "cosmic laughter" to mystery and wonder. He enlarged the finale into a movement comparable in size and scope to the first, ending the symphony on a note of triumph.

The piano occupied a central position in Beethoven's art. His thirty-two sonatas are an indispensable part of its literature, whether for the amateur pianist or concert artist. They are well called the pianist's New Testament (the Old being the *Well-Tempered Clavier* of Bach). Dynamic contrasts, explosive accents, opposition of low and high register, syncopation, and powerful crescendos are essential features of his idiom. Characteristic is his fondness for the theme and variations. Here he becomes the master builder, marshaling his inexhaustible wealth of ideas to fashion out of the simplest material a towering edifice.

In the symphony Beethoven found the ideal medium wherein to address mankind. His nine symphonies are spiritual dramas of universal appeal. Their sweep and tumultuous affirmation of life mark them a pinnacle of the rising democratic art. They are conceived on a scale too grand for the aristocratic salon; they demand the amplitude of the concert hall. With his Third Symphony, the *Eroica* (1803–04), Beethoven achieved his mature style. The work was originally dedicated to Napoleon, First Consul of the Republic, in whom he saw incarnated the spirit of revolution and the freedom of man. When the news came that Napoleon had proclaimed himself Emperor, Beethoven was disenchanted. "He too is just like any other! Now he will trample on the rights of man and serve nothing but his own ambition." The embittered composer tore up the dedicatory page of the just-completed work and renamed it "Heroic Symphony to celebrate the memory of a great man."

The Fifth Symphony (1805–07) has fixed itself in the popular mind as the archetype of all that a symphony is. The Seventh (1812) rivals it in universal appeal. The Ninth, the *Choral Symphony* (1817–23), strikes the searching tone of Beethoven's last period. Its finale, in which soloists and chorus join with the orchestra, contains the famous line, "Be embraced, ye millions!" The choral movement is a setting of Schiller's *Ode to Joy*, a ringing prophecy of the time when "all men shall be brothers." In these works there sounds the rhetoric of the new century. Complementing them are the Fourth (1806) and Eighth (1812), two buoyant and serene symphonies; and the Sixth, the hymn to nature known as the *Pastorale* (1808).

The concerto offered Beethoven a congenial public form in which he combined virtuosity with symphonic architecture. Most popular of his works in this medium are the Third Piano Concerto, which we will discuss; the Fourth in G (1806); the Fifth, in E-flat (the *Emperor*, 1809); and the noble Concerto for Violin in D (1806). He wrote much chamber music, the string quartet being closest to his heart. The six quartets Opus 18 are the first in a series that extended throughout the whole of his career. They were followed by the three of Opus 59 dedicated to Count Razumovsky, works pre-eminent for profundity of feeling and technical mastery. His supreme achievements in this area are the last five quartets, which, together with the Grand Fugue, Op. 133, occupied the final years of his life. In these, as in the last five piano sonatas, Beethoven found his way to a skeletal language from which all nonessentials had been rigidly pared—a language far transcending his time. The master's gaze is focused within, encompassing depths that music never before had plumbed.

Although his most important victories were won in the instrumental field, Beethoven enriched the main types of vocal music. Of his songs the best known is the cycle of six, *An die ferne Geliebte* (To the Distant Beloved). His sole opera *Fidelio* (originally called *Leonora*, completed in 1805) centers about wifely devotion, human freedom, and the defeat of those who would destroy it. There is much memorable music in it. All the same, Beethoven's imagination was hampered by the trappings of the stage; he is at his most dramatic in the abstract forms. Although the pious Haydn considered him an atheist, he hymned "Nature's God" through the traditional form of religious music. The *Missa solemnis* (Solemn Mass in D, 1818–23) ranks in importance with the Ninth Symphony and the final quartets. The work transcends the limits of any specific creed or dogma. Above the Kyrie of the Mass he wrote a sentence that applies to the whole of his music: "From the heart . . . may it find its way to the heart."

His creative activity, extending over a span of thirty-five years, bears witness to a ceaseless striving after perfection. "I feel as if I had written scarcely more than a few notes," he remarked at the end of his career. And a year before his death: "I hope still to bring a few great works into the world." Despite his faith in his destiny he knew the humility of the truly great. "The real artist has no pride. Unfortunately he sees that his art has no limits, he feels obscurely how far he is from the goal. And while he is perhaps being admired by others he mourns the fact that he has not yet reached the point to which his better genius like a distant sun ever beckons him."

The Fifth Symphony

The most popular of all symphonies, Beethoven's Fifth, in C minor, Opus 67, is also the most concentrated expression of the frame of mind and spirit that we have come to call Beethovenian. It embodies in supreme degree the basic principle of symphonic thinking—the flowering of an extended composition from a kernel by a process of organic growth. The popular story that Beethoven, when asked for the meaning of the opening theme, replied, "Thus Fate knocks at the door," is probably not authentic. Such literalness seems unlikely in one who was so completely the tone poet. If the work continues to be associated with Fate it is rather because of the inevitable, the relentless logic of its unfolding.

The first movement, marked Allegro con brio (lively, with vigor), springs out of the rhythmic idea of "three shorts and a long" that dominates the symphony. Announced in unison by strings and clarinets (Beethoven holds his full forces in reserve), the motive establishes the home key of C minor. It is the most compact and commanding gesture in the whole symphonic literature.

Allegro con brio

Out of this motive flowers the first theme, which is a repetition, at different levels of the scale and with altered intervals, of the germinating rhythm.

a) The motive. b) Sequence, with smaller interval. c) Sequence. d) The motive with larger interval. e) Same as b. f) Sequence of motive. g) Motive with the interval filled in. h) Inversion (upside-down) of g.

The power of the movement springs from the almost terrifying singlemindedness with which the underlying idea is pursued. It is rhythm, torrential yet superbly controlled, that is the generating force behind this "storm and stress." Beethoven here achieved a vehemence that was new in music. The bridge to the related key of E-flat major is fashioned out of the basic motive. Notice how much more compact is this bridge than the leisurely transition in the first movement of Mozart's G-minor Symphony:

We reach an area of relaxation with the lyric second theme. Yet even here the headlong course of the movement does not slacken. As the violins, clarinet, and flute sound the gentle melody in turn, the basic rhythm of "three shorts and a long" persists in the cellos and double basses.

Basic rhythm

The Exposition is rounded off with a short section (codetta) reaffirming the basic rhythm.

The Development is dramatic, peremptory, compact. The following examples show how Beethoven weaves a tightly knit fabric out of the basic motive.

1. Motive with interval filled in. Expansion through a descending sequence:

2. Motive with interval filled in. Expansion through a descending sequence coupled with inversion (turning the motive upside-down):

3. Expansion through repetition. This passage leads into the Recapitulation:

No less characteristic of Beethoven's style are the powerful crescendos and the abrupt contrasts between soft and loud. The transition back to the home key culminates in a fortissimo proclamation of the underlying rhythm by full orchestra.

The Restatement is interrupted when an oboe solo introduces a note of pathos, momentarily slackening the tension. The second theme is transposed into C major. There is an extended coda in which the basic rhythm reveals a new fund of explosive energy.

Beethovenian serenity and strength imbue the second movement, Andante con moto (at a going pace, with movement). The key is A-flat; the form, a theme and variations. There are two melodic ideas. The first is a broadly spun

281

theme sung by violas and cellos. It is followed by one of those hymnic upward-thrusting subjects so characteristic of the master, which echoes the basic rhythm—the "three shorts and a long" of the opening movement.

In the course of the movement Beethoven brings all the procedures of variation—changes in melodic outline, harmony, rhythm, tempo, dynamics, register, key, mode, and type of accompaniment—to bear upon his two themes. Here is how the first theme is embellished with running sixteenth notes in Variation 1:

In Variation 2 this melody is presented in thirty-second-note rhythm:

In the next variation the melody is divided up among the various woodwind instruments:

Finally the melody is shifted into the minor:

The second theme undergoes analogous transformations, gathering strength until it is proclaimed by the full orchestra. The coda, marked Più mosso, opens with a motive on the bassoon derived from Theme 1 against syncopated chords in the strings. A dynamic crescendo rounds off the movement.

Third in the cycle of movements is the Scherzo, which returns to the somber C minor that is the home key of the work. From the depths of the bass rises a characteristic subject, a rocket theme introduced by cellos and double basses.

The basic rhythm of the first movement reappears fortissimo in the horns. Nourished by dynamic changes and a crescendo, the movement steadily accumulates force and drive. The Trio shifts to C major. It is based on a gruffly humorous motive of running eighth notes stated by cellos and double basses and imitated in turn, in ever higher register, by violas, second violins, and first violins.

The motive of the double basses was described by Berlioz in a celebrated phrase as the "gambols of a frolicsome elephant." Here the term scherzo is applicable in its original meaning of "jest." Beethoven's cosmic laughter resounds through these measures: a laughter that shakes—and builds—a world.

This motive is expanded through repetition and sequence:

The Scherzo (Section A) returns in a modified version, with changed orchestration. It is followed by a mysterious transitional passage that is spun out of the Scherzo theme and the basic rhythm, which is presented by various instruments and finally tapped out mysteriously by the kettledrums:

283

The Scherzo theme is developed through motivic expansion of its last three notes:

There is a steady accumulation of tension until the orchestra, in a blaze of light, surges into the triumphal Allegro in C major.

Beethoven achieves dramatic contrasts of color through his changes of mode. The first movement is in a somber minor. The second, with its classical serenity, is in major. The third, save for the jovial Trio, returns to minor. Then the dark C minor is dispelled for good with the upsurge of the finale. At this point three instruments make their appearance for the first time in the symphonies of the classical Viennese school—piccolo, double bassoon, and trombone, lending brilliance and body to the orchestral sound.

The fourth movement is a monumental sonata form in which Beethoven overcomes what would seem to be an insuperable difficulty: to fashion an ending that will sustain the tension of what has gone before. Rhythmic energy, bigness of conception, and orchestral sonority carry the work to its overpowering conclusion. Two themes in C major are opposed to one in G. The opening idea

is based on a chord-and-scale pattern. This is followed by a theme that serves

as a bridge from C to G major. The contrasting key of G major is represented by a vigorous theme containing triplets:

There follows a closing theme (codetta) played by clarinets and violas. It rounds off the Exposition with a decisive gesture:

The Development is marked by dynamic rhythm and free modulation. Then —an amazing stroke!—Beethoven brings back the "three shorts and a long" as they appeared in the third movement. This bringing back of material from an earlier movement gives the symphony its cyclical form. He deliberately allows the momentum to slacken so that he may build up tension against the upsurge of the Recapitulation, which is followed by an extensive coda fashioned from materials already heard. The pace accelerates steadily up to the concluding Presto. There is a final outcropping of the basic rhythm. The symphonic stream at the very end becomes an overwhelming torrent as the Tonic chord—source and goal of all activity—is hurled forth by the orchestra again and again.

The *Pathétique Sonata*

As in the case of the *Moonlight* and the *Appassionata*, the title of the Piano Sonata in C minor, Opus 13—*Pathétique*—was not Beethoven's. Such fanciful names were frequently added by music publishers in order to stimulate sales. If they caught on as they did, it was because they expressed something of what this music meant to those who heard it.

Certainly the quality of Beethovenian pathos is manifest from the first chords of the slow introduction. Marked Grave (solemn), this celebrated opening has something fantasy-like about it, as if Beethoven had captured here the passionate intensity that so affected his listeners when he improvised at the keyboard. Notice the dotted rhythm that contributes to the solemnity of these measures, and the contrary motion: when the melody ascends in the first measure, the bass line descends—and vice versa. The chord pattern is repeated at a higher level in measures 2 and 3 (ascending sequence):

Striking, too, are the contrasts between forte and piano. This type of contrast, an essential feature of Beethoven's dynamism, is used with maximum effectiveness a little farther on when it is combined with a change of register: fortissimo chords in the bass are contrasted with a softly expressive melody in the treble. All in all this introduction, written on the threshold of the nineteenth century (1799), speaks a powerful language new to piano music. It ends with a descending chromatic scale and the instruction "attacca subito il Allegro" (attack the Allegro immediately).

The movement proper, marked Allegro di molto e con brio (very fast and with vigor), opens in the home key—C minor—with an impetuous idea that climbs to its peak and descends, while the left hand maintains the rumble of a sustained tremolo in the bass.

A bridge passage modulates, leading to the second theme in E-flat minor, whose gentle lyricism offers an effective contrast to the first. This is a supplicating melody that leaps from the bass register to the treble, which involves crossing the hands.

A third theme in E-flat, the relative major key, moves steadily upward in a gradual crescendo; a codetta rounds off the Exposition. Before proceeding with the next section Beethoven brings back the dramatic theme of the introduction, like a fleeting reminiscence. In the Development he skillfully combines the first theme of the Allegro with the theme of the introduction:

For a while the two hands reverse their roles as the left hand carries the melody while the right takes over the tremolo. A transitional passage that descends from high F to a low C leads back to the home key of C minor. In the Recapitulation the material is restated. The second theme is transposed not to the home key but to F minor. This makes possible an effective return to the home key when the third theme appears in C minor. Very dramatic, just before the end of the movement, is a brief reminder of the slow introduction, followed by a precipitous cadence in the home key.

Throughout Beethoven uses the resources of the instrument most imaginatively. In addition to the contrasts we have mentioned between higher and lower register, as well as between soft and loud, he exploits the somber coloring of the bass, the rich sound of full chords, the brilliance of rapid scale passages, the excitement of a sustained tremolo, and the power of a slowly gathering crescendo allied with a gradual climb in pitch.

The second movement is the famous Adagio cantabile (slow and songful) which shows off the piano's ability to sing. A lyric melody is introduced in the middle register over a simple accompaniment. Here is the combination of inwardness and strength that impelled nineteenth-century writers to describe the slow movement of Beethoven as a "hymnic adagio":

This melody alternates with two contrasting sections, giving an A-B-A-C-A structure. Urgency is added to the third idea (C) by triplet rhythm, sudden accents, crescendos, and dramatic arpeggios deep in the bass. The principal melody is repeated with more elaborate figuration. A beautiful coda leads to the pianissimo ending.

Beethoven in this sonata abandons the usual four-movement scheme; the third is the final movement. This is a rondo, to whose principal theme the C-minor tonality imparts a darker coloring that sets it apart from the usually cheerful rondo-finales of Haydn and Mozart.

With such a point of departure Beethoven constructs a movement with more drama to it than had been customary in the rondo. The principal theme alternates with two other ideas in the pattern A-B-A-C-A-B-A, with a codetta after the B section and a coda at the end. The frame is spacious; within it, lyric episodes alternate with dramatic.

The *Pathétique* has been a favorite for generations. In the hands of a great artist it stands revealed as one of Beethoven's most personal sonatas.

The Seventh Symphony

In a letter to a friend written in July 1812 Beethoven stated, "A new symphony is now ready." In this simple fashion was announced the completion of a titanic work.

The first movement opens with an introduction of unusual breadth, marked Poco sostenuto (a little held back). The sudden accents and slowly

287

gathering crescendos are hallmarks of Beethoven's dynamic style. Majestic chords either alternate with or are accompanied by ascending scales, out of which there presently emerges an ingratiating tune:

The sense of expectancy generated by this section is amply fulfilled when the Vivace finally arrives. It turns out to be based on a dancelike melody introduced by the flute.

Characteristic is the syncopation in the fourth measure, which begins with an accented eighth note followed by a quarter. Notice that the two phrases are almost identical; they part company at the cadence. Worthy of note too are the grace notes with which Beethoven embellishes his tune, and the predominantly stepwise movement except for the bold downward leap in the second and sixth measures. The dotted rhythm that is present in all but the last two measures becomes a propelling force that dominates the entire movement.

Probably because of the long introduction, Beethoven avoids a striking second theme. Its function rather is to establish the neighboring key of E major. Note that the first two measures are immediately repeated in sequence:

Like the first movement of the Fifth Symphony, this is music born of a powerful rhythmic thrust. The constant use of the winds as melody instruments gives the movement its rugged outdoor sound, which accords with the enormous harmonic-rhythmic tension of these measures. The codetta, fashioned out of the basic motive, establishes a cadence in E major.

In the Development Beethoven reweaves his material into a fascinating tapestry. The following example shows how the first three notes of his main theme give rise to a new idea. In measure 2 the three-note motive is inverted and then repeated in sequence. Measure 3 duplicates measure 2 at a higher pitch. Measure 4 duplicates measure 3 upside down (inversion), and measure 5 finishes the idea by duplicating the three-note motive for the last time. Notice that the dotted rhythm prevails throughout.

This idea is introduced by the cellos and basses, and imitated in turn by the first violins, the second violins and violas, oboes, and flutes in a rich interweaving of lines.

When he has thoroughly explored the capacities for growth of his theme and its motives, Beethoven is ready for the Recapitulation. This restates the material substantially as we heard it in the Exposition. The second theme is now transposed into A major; Beethoven strengthens the final victory of his home key by preceding it with several exciting modulations. The coda begins with the unifying dotted rhythm; the music steadily gathers power until this rhythm is hurled forth by the orchestra in triumphal proclamation.

The celebrated Allegretto in A minor contains some of Beethoven's most moving pages. After the very first chord, beginning forte and dying away to a pianissimo, a mysterious procession of chords in the lower strings outlines a melody (A) that is dimly intimated in its first presentation but grows steadily, in the course of three variations that follow, until it is proclaimed in an exultant fortissimo by the full orchestra. The following example shows the theme in the first of these variations. It consists of three eight-bar phrases, the third being a repetition, pianissimo, of the second (a-b-b). The melody in the upper line (second violins) establishes a basic rhythm that fixes itself in the mind, while the lower (violas and cellos) presents another melody against it—that is, a *countermelody*.

Notice that the upper melody itself is quite uneventful: one note, E, is repeated throughout the first four measures, while another note, G, is repeated throughout the next three. Obviously the countermelody and the changing harmonies underneath supply the necessary tension. By presenting very little at first Beethoven leaves room for the development of his ideas: a typical classical procedure.

A new idea (B) appears in A major, which takes on an indescribable serenity after the somber minor that preceded it. Despite this change of mood, the cellos and the double basses, playing pizzicato, maintain the basic rhythm of the opening section. The first melody (A) returns in the woodwinds against a more active accompaniment in the strings. This A-B-A is followed by a Development in which a motive of the theme is imitated by the various string instruments in a kind of intimate conversation. This passage is like a round in which each voice enters in turn with the tune—what will be identified in a later chapter as a *fugato*; it builds up tension against the majestic return of the main theme (A) in a new version. The serene A-major episode (B) is repeated in part, and the final return of the main theme (A) serves as a coda in which the melody is divided among woodwinds and horns in various register. The form consequently might be described as A-B-A: Development: A-B-A (Coda). The A-major tonality serves as an area of relaxation, contrasting with the A-minor that prevails for most of the movement. Since the essence of symphonic thinking is a sense of organic growth, this is one of the most symphonic slow movements ever written.

Third is the Scherzo, a Presto in F major marked by a sense of effortless movement and powerful crescendos. The principal theme opens with two bars of introduction followed by a four-measure phrase that is immediately repeated a tone higher—that is, in sequence:

The Trio is an Assai meno presto (much less fast). Woodwinds and horns carry a rather stationary tune—it moves almost completely by step—against a sustained tone in the violins.

When this melody returns, fortissimo, the sustained tone is carried by the trumpet—a memorable effect. The Scherzo is repeated, as is the Trio; Beethoven here expands the traditional A-B-A form into an A-B-A-B-A. After the final reprise of the Scherzo he seems for a moment to be returning to the Trio. One cannot help thinking, "What, again?" But he is only teasing. The movement is brought to an end with five emphatic chords.

It is in the finale, an Allegro con brio, that Beethoven fully unleashes the overpowering force of his rhythm. In this movement rhythm becomes the form-creating principle. Here is a dance of exultation, almost of abandon; yet for all its recklessness, these onrushing masses of sound are ruled by the discipline of a relentless will.

The movement is in sonata-allegro form. The first theme, played at a furious clip, is carried by the first violins. Its power stems from repetition. Notice that the second measure restates the first a step higher (sequence), while the third duplicates the first exactly. Thus, of the eight measures given below, six present the same pattern:

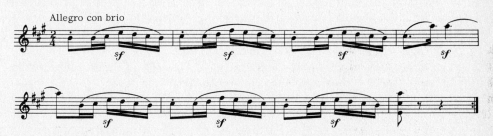

A transition based on dotted rhythm leads to the second idea in C-sharp minor, which is an effective foil for the first. Rests instead of dots maintain the angular rhythm with a kind of capricious effect.

The Development, based on a relentless affirmation of the principal theme, modulates boldly. The Recapitulation pulses forward with increased momentum; the second subject, transposed, hovers around A major-minor; and the tumultuous coda brings a final resolution of the underlying idea.

Wagner called the Seventh Symphony "the apotheosis of the dance." Certainly, in this tumultuous finale, the spirit of dance rhythm is glorified into a primeval creative force.

Piano Concerto No. 3 in C Minor

Inheriting the classical concerto from Mozart, Beethoven responded with all the force of his dramatic temperament to the opposition between soloist and orchestra. Like Mozart, too, he brought to the concerto the instincts and techniques of the symphonist.

The Piano Concerto No. 3 in C minor (1800) is as rich in the element of the "pathétique" as the piano sonata in the same key. The first movement, an Allegro con brio, opens with a theme that is tense, terse, granitic. Its first three notes outline the Tonic chord of C minor. More important from the standpoint of subsequent events, the first phrase of this theme divides into two motives with great capacities for development:

Played in unison by the strings, the opening phrase is answered by the winds. Notice that measures 1 and 2 are repeated in sequence (one step higher) in measures 5 and 6; while the rhythm of measures 3 and 4 is duplicated in measures 7 and 8.

An ample expansion allies this idea with subsidiary motives. There is a bridge to the key of E-flat, the relative major. The second theme is a lyrical idea, whose grace is counterposed to the ruggedness of the first.

Beethoven restates this theme in C major. By doing so he prepares for his return to the home key and the entrance of the solo. In short, we find here a double Exposition, one by the orchestra and one by the soloist—the usual procedure in the classical concerto.

The piano enters brusquely with ascending scales—an imperious gesture, this!—and takes over the first theme-group, which is varied to suit the idiom of the instrument. Notice how Beethoven exploits the piano's capacity for rapid scales, arpeggios, and trills. The second theme, now marked dolce (sweetly), sounds lovely in its new garb. The dialogue between. piano and orchestra exploits the contrast between the two dissimilar bodies of sound; while the rhythm of Motive B persists throughout as a unifying device. An extended codetta rounds off the second Exposition.

The Development begins with an emphatic orchestral tutti. Again the imperious gesture of ascending scales on the piano, the basic rhythm (Motive B), and a dramatic presentation of the first theme in G minor. Passages of arpeggios, broken octaves (octaves, that is, whose notes are not played simultaneously), and similar kinds of figuration carry the action forward through a series of keys until the Recapitulation is reached, and with it the home key. Beethoven's imagination is too active to permit him to restate the material in its original form; he varies it throughout. The second theme is transposed to

C major. Its elaboration gives the pianist ample opportunity to display his technique. The orchestra comes to a halt that ushers in the cadenza. We are fortunate to possess Beethoven's own, which gives us an idea of his style of improvisation. Notice particularly the passage in which one hand imitates the other in presenting the first theme:

He then uses the first two notes of the theme as a motive interspersed with arpeggios that run the gamut of the keyboard. Notice, too, his imaginative elaboration of the second theme. The cadenza ends, as was customary, with trills; the coda begins most dramatically with the basic rhythm (Motive B) tapped out mysteriously on the kettledrums against the whisper of descending arpeggios on the piano. It is an unforgettable effect. A mighty crescendo brings the movement to a close.

The Largo exemplifies the contemplative slow movement that became closely associated with Beethoven. Noteworthy is the choice of E major, a key so remote from C minor that the opening chord of this movement comes as a surprise. Like the slow movement of Mozart's G-minor Symphony, this one is in sonata form. The principal theme, presented by the piano, breathes an atmosphere of serene lyricism:

Piano and orchestra, treated as equals, engage in an intimate conversation. A transitional theme takes on all the ornateness of an eighteenth-century operatic aria. The second theme, in the key of B, is followed by a lyrical dialogue between bassoon and flute accompanied by elaborate figuration in the piano part. The music modulates, giving this episode the function of a Development that builds tension before it ultimately returns to the home key of E. The Recapitulation is abbreviated. The opening theme is heard pianissimo, with elaborate variation in the piano part. This section centers about the home key. Instead of repeating the transition and second subject, Beethoven fashions an ample coda out of material previously heard in the orchestra. A short cadenza marked sempre con gran espressione (always with great expression) leads into the final measures of this beautiful meditation.

293

The finale is a broadly molded rondo in C minor. Its main theme is a striking idea that bears repeating. The triangular sign above the notes in the example indicates the forceful articulation that goes with an accent.

This melody alternates with subsidiary themes that provide contrast; they lead us away from and at the same time prepare us for the return of the main idea. In its fleet and effortless movement this Allegro is a worthy offspring of the rondo-finales of Haydn. The great surprise comes with the coda where, after a brief cadenza, the music shifts to a Presto in C major in ⁶/₈ time. Here is how the theme is transformed:

This C-major ending, affirmative and brilliant, has the effect of a burst of light.

Overture to *Coriolan* (Coriolanus)

Sonata form has one important element in common with the drama. The classical tragedy centered about the conflict within the hero between two opposing forces such as love and honor. Classical sonata form centered about a conflict between two opposing keys and theme groups. Sooner or later composers were bound to adjust the musical drama to the literary one. It was Beethoven who consummated this adjustment. In his Overtures to *Coriolan* (1807), a play by Heinrich von Collin, and Goethe's *Egmont* (1810), as in the four Overtures to his opera *Fidelio,* the opposition between a rhythmically aggressive theme and a lyrically yielding theme was harnessed to the dramatic conflicts of the theater. In this way sonata-allegro form—the grand form of absolute music—was laid open to the influence of a literary program, a development of great significance for the nineteenth century.

The hero of Collin's tragedy, as of Shakespeare's, is the Roman patrician Coriolanus, whose opposition to the tribunes of the people results in his being exiled from Rome. He goes over to the enemy Volscians, gathers a huge army, and marches on his native city, determined to lay it waste. A deputation of his countrymen pleads with him to spare Rome, but he turns a deaf ear. As a last resort his mother, wife, and little son are dispatched to his camp. Their entreaties finally move him to desist from his purpose. In Plutarch's account as in

Shakespeare's, Coriolanus is murdered by the infuriated Volscians. In Collin's play the remorseful general commits suicide.

Beethoven, we saw, was at his most dramatic in instrumental music. The Overture to *Coriolan*, Opus 62, projects the essence of the tragedy. After a brief introduction we hear a fateful motive that establishes the home key of C minor. Its expressive content suggests the somber state of mind of the hero of the play.

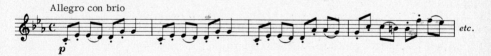

This essentially rhythmic subject, presented by the first violins and violas, is opposed to the tender, supplicating melody in the contrasting key of E-flat. Stepwise movement in the first measure is balanced by downward skips in the second and the dramatic leap of an octave that ushers in the third:

This phrase is heard three times with different instrumentation; then the entire melody is restated twice, each time a tone higher (ascending sequence) with changes of key.

The third or closing theme is based on dotted rhythm. (The place of dots is here taken by rests.)

This idea seems not too important at its first appearance, its function being to round off the Exposition. It reveals its true importance in the Development, which is based upon it and has an intensely dramatic quality.

The Recapitulation presents the material in shortened form and departs in certain details from the traditional pattern of sonata-allegro. The first theme returns not in the home key of C minor but in F minor. The second theme is transposed to C major. As in the Exposition, this is heard in ascending sequence with changes of key. The stirring coda follows the course of the codetta. It begins with the second theme, which is given in both major and minor:

Then we hear again the dotted rhythm of the third (closing) theme; the introduction is restated; and the work ends with a slowing up of the first theme that
is based not on a ritardando but on longer note values:

sempre più **p**

Chronologically Beethoven's life fell in almost equal parts in the eighteenth
and nineteenth centuries. His career bridged the transition from the old society
to the new. The sum of his message was freedom. By freedom, though, he
understood not romantic revolt but the inner discipline that alone constitutes
freedom. His music stems from a Promethean struggle for self-realization. It is
the expression of a titanic force, the affirmation of an all-conquering will.

55 Classical Chamber Music

> "No other form of music can delight our senses with such ex-
> quisite beauty of sound, or display so clearly to our intelligence
> the intricacies and adventures of its design."
>
> Henry Hadow

By *chamber music* is meant ensemble music for from two to about eight or nine
instruments with one player to the part, as distinct from orchestral music in
which a single instrumental part is presented by anywhere from two to eighteen
players. The essential trait of chamber music is its intimacy and refinement; its
natural setting is the home. In this domain we find neither the surge and
thunder of the symphony nor the grand gesture of the operatic stage. The drama
is of an inward kind. Each instrument is expected to assert itself to the full, but
the style of playing differs from that of the solo virtuoso. Where the virtuoso is
encouraged to exalt his own personality, the chamber-music player functions as
part of a team.

The classical era saw the golden age of chamber music. Haydn and Mozart,
Beethoven and Schubert established the true chamber-music style, which is in
the nature of a friendly conversation among equals. The central position in
classical chamber music was held by the string quartet. Consisting of first and
second violins, viola, and cello, this group came to represent the ideal type of
happy comradeship among instruments, lending itself to music of exquisite
detail and purity of style. Other favored combinations were the duo sonata—
piano and violin or piano and cello; the trio—piano, violin, and cello; and the

Jack Levine (b. 1915), STRING QUARTETTE. (The Metropolitan Museum of Art, New York; Arthur H. Hearn Fund, 1942)

Teamwork is the essence of chamber music.

quintet, usually consisting of a combination of string or wind instruments, or a string quartet and solo instrument such as the piano or clarinet. The age produced, too, some memorable examples of chamber music for larger groups—sextet, septet, and octet.

Haydn: String Quartet in C ("Emperor")

Haydn's eighty-three quartets testify to a half-century of artistic growth. In the early ones he was finding his way to the four-movement form and to a texture in which all four instruments would share equally. The last ones, with their profundity of expression and mastery of form, established a style of string-quartet writing that served as a model for all who came after.

Characteristic of the mature Haydn is the *Emperor Quartet* (1797), so called because the second movement consists of a series of variations on one of his own songs, *God Save the Emperor Franz,* which he gave to his countrymen as a national anthem. It is a melody marked by great dignity and simplicity, that remained—until the fall of the Hapsburg monarchy at the end of the First World War—the only national anthem written by a great composer. Marked Poco adagio cantabile (a little slow and songful), the movement—in G major —opens with the theme in the first violins against simple harmonies:

Variation 1 presents the tune in the second violins while the first play figuration above it. In Variation 2 the melody is assigned to the cello; above it the two violins weave their melodious lines, while the viola completes the harmonies. In the third variation the viola plays the melody against new material in the other parts. Finally, in Variation 4, the melody returns to the first violin and is played with great expressiveness in the upper register, accompanied by rich harmonies in the other parts.

The first movement, in the home key of C, is an Allegro in 4/4. When the Exposition modulates to the key of the Dominant, G major, instead of introducing a contrasting theme Haydn repeats the first idea in the new key. The result is that, instead of a first-movement form based on two themes, we have here a structure that is essentially monothematic. (Which shows that the important contrast in sonata-allegro form is between keys rather than themes.) Haydn was fond of this type of structure and used it in a number of his works.

The Minuet is an Allegro. Its phrase structure illustrates the charming asymmetry that lent such variety to Haydn's forms. A phrase of five measures is answered by another of five, followed by a regular phrase of four measures that is answered by one of six, so that the first strophe consists of twenty measures. In the second part of the Trio we find a passage in A minor followed by one in A major, after which the music returns to A minor. Such changes in mode are altogether characteristic of Haydn. The Minuet is repeated da capo.

The fourth movement is a Presto in 4/4 that begins in C minor. Like the first movement, this is a sonata-allegro form that is based on a single theme; the underlying contrast is between the home key, C minor, and its relative major, E-flat. The shift to C major toward the end of the movement brings this attractive quartet to a properly happy conclusion.

Mozart: Quintet for Clarinet and Strings

The spirit of Viennese house-music pervades this celebrated quintet (K. 581). The work is based on the opposition between two protagonists —the clarinet, which because of its striking tone is the center of attention, and the string quartet. Mozart brings into play all the qualities of the clarinet, its capacity for broad singing melody as well as its agility in ornate virtuoso passages.

The first movement is an Allegro in sonata form. It is in cut time, in A major. The opening theme has a sweet serenity. Introduced by the strings, it is set off by arpeggios on the clarinet. The second theme, in E, displays the exquisite songfulness of the Mozartean cantabile. It is presented by the first violin and shifted into minor when the clarinet takes it over, imparting to the movement a

romantic tone. The development section lends itself to animated rivalry between clarinet and strings, after which the thematic material is restated.

The Larghetto, in D, is a broadly spun two-part song for clarinet against a background of muted strings. The middle section features running scale passages and contains a striking dialogue between clarinet and first violin. Then the song returns.

The Menuetto, in the home key of A major, has two trios instead of one. After each, the Minuet proper is played da capo without repeats, giving an A-B-A-C-A form. The first Trio, in A minor, is for strings alone. The second Trio, in A major, is quite different from the first. It emphasizes the clarinet and is based on one of those bouncy arpeggio themes that vividly capture the buoyancy of Austrian popular dance.

The Finale, an Allegretto in A in cut time, is a theme and variations. The melody is of the utmost simplicity, allowing room for elaboration. The variations include: 1, an embellishment of the melody; 2, a change to triplet rhythm in the accompaniment; 3, a new melody in minor; 4, the original theme heard against florid arabesques in the clarinet, with a change of pace and character, first to adagio, finally to allegro. Like Haydn's variations in the *Surprise Symphony*, Mozart's keep the melody easily recognizable throughout all its transformations. This is music stamped with aristocratic refinement.

Beethoven: String Quartet in F Major, Opus 18, No. 1

Beethoven did not undertake the writing of string quartets until he was almost thirty. The six quartets of Opus 18 date from the years 1798–1800. The Quartet in F (1799) was placed first when the set was published; actually it was written after the one now known as Opus 18, No. 3. Its opening movement, like that of the Fifth Symphony, is dominated by a rhythm as much as by a theme:

The notes under the bracket become the basic motive of the movement. Notice how subtly this motive is varied in measures 3-4 and 5-6.

There is another similarity here to the first movement of the Fifth Symphony: although the second theme is lyrical in nature, thereby contrasting with the first, Beethoven does not permit it to arrest the forward drive of the movement. An effective codetta reasserts the basic motive and brings the Exposition to a cadence in the related key of C major. Tension is heightened in the Development when the music modulates frequently as the basic motive is tossed about among the four instruments. The following example well illustrates Beethoven's developmental procedure. The motive is repeated in descending sequence in the first violin against repeated notes in the second violin and viola:

Then the second violin takes over the descending sequence while the first joins the viola in the repeated notes. Staccato scale passages, ascending and descending, lead into the Recapitulation. The principal theme is stated fortissimo in octaves; the lyrical second theme is transposed to the home key; and a sturdy coda brings the movement to a close.

The remaining movements present no special problems to the listener. The slow movement, a lyric meditation in D minor in 9/8 time, is marked Adagio affettuoso ed appassionato (very slow, tender, and impassioned). Although *affettuoso* was frequently used in the eighteenth century, as was *appassionato* in the nineteenth, the combination of the two terms was most unusual at the time when this quartet was written. Sonata-allegro form gives this passionate lament its spacious architecture. The Scherzo, in F major, is marked Allegro molto and supplies the necessary contrast. The finale, an Allegro in 2/4 time, is a good-humored rondo that ends the work on a properly optimistic note.

Schubert: The *Trout Quintet*

One of the most popular of Schubert's chamber works, the *Trout Quintet* dates from 1819, when the composer was twenty-two. He had just completed a happy journey through upper Austria, whose landscape pervades this music. In the course of the trip he was asked to make his song *Die Forelle* (The Trout) available to players of chamber music. Schubert responded with the Quintet in A major for piano and strings, whose fourth movement consists of a set of variations on the melody of the song.

In a quintet for piano and strings, a natural opposition ensues between the piano sound and that of the string mass. Schubert, significantly, strengthened the string group. Instead of writing for the usual quartet he employed a violin, viola, cello, and double bass.

The most popular movement is the set of variations on *Die Forelle*. The theme is announced in D major by the first violin, against a background of the other string instruments:

Variation 1 assigns the melody to the piano against arpeggios in the strings. In Variation 2 the viola sings the tune against exciting arabesques in the upper ·register of the violin. Variation 3 shifts the melody to the double bass against elaborate running passages on the piano. In these three variations the melody remains unchanged. The next two variations present it with changes of register, dynamics, harmony, melodic outline, rhythm, and type of accompaniment. Variation 4 shifts to D minor and triplet rhythm, and is marked by some bewitching modulations, as is Variation 5, which begins in B-flat major. In the sixth and final variation Schubert returns to the mood of *Die Forelle* by using the rippling figure of the original piano accompaniment to the song.

The other movements raise no issues that we have not already touched upon. The opening Allegro vivace in A, a cheerful movement in 4/4 time, is followed by an Andante in 3/4 in F that looks back to the quietude of the eighteenth-century slow movement and shows striking changes of key. The Scherzo is a Presto in A, in 3/4 time; it makes an effective contrast with the Theme and Variations that follow. The fifth movement is an Allegro giusto (fast, in strict time) in 2/4, in the home key of A: a beautiful rondo in Hungarian style. The prevailing optimism of Schubert's early twenties is reflected throughout the work.

Chamber music holds out to the listener a very special musical experience. It offers him delights that no other branch of music can duplicate.

56 From Classic to Romantic: Schubert's *Unfinished*

"I am very greatly obliged by the diploma of honorary membership you so kindly sent me. May it be the reward of my devotion to the art of music to become wholly worthy of such a distinction one day. In order to give musical expression to my sincere gratitude as well, I shall take the liberty before long of presenting your honorable Society with one of my symphonies in full score."

We discussed the songs and piano pieces of Franz Schubert in connection with the romantic movement, whose first stirrings found in them so vivid an expression. In his symphonies, however, as in his chamber music, he was the heir of the classical Viennese tradition.

The name *Unfinished* that has attached itself to Schubert's Symphony No. 8, in B minor, is unfortunate, suggesting as its does that the composer was snatched away by death before he could complete it. Actually the work was written when Schubert was twenty-five years old, in 1822, and was sent to the Styrian Musical Society in the town of Graz in fulfillment of the promise made in the letter just quoted. He completed two movements and sketched the opening measures of a scherzo. Given his facility, a work was no sooner conceived than written down; if he abandoned the task in this instance it was probably because he had said all that he had to say.

The work displays Schubert's radiant orchestral sonority, his power of making the instruments sing, his unique handling of woodwinds and brass. The wonder is all the greater when we remember that Schubert never heard his finest symphonic scores. The B-minor Symphony, for example, was never performed during his lifetime. The manuscript lay gathering dust for more than thirty-five years after his death.

The first movement, Allegro moderato, is based on three ideas. The first, in the nature of an introductory theme, establishes the home key of B minor. It emerges out of the lower register in a mysterious pianissimo, played by cellos and double basses. This is a simple yet memorable statement, not active rhythmically but containing three motives eminently capable of development. Melodic movement is by step and narrow leap:

There follows a broadly curved melody in the home key given out by an oboe and clarinet over the restless accompaniment of the strings. Notice how the downward leap in measures 1 and 3 is balanced by stepwise movement in measures 2 and 4 as well as in the second half of the phrase:

The bridge between the home key and the contrasting key consists of a sustained tone in the bassoon and horns, followed by three chords that modulate effectively from B minor into G major. Now is heard the great lyric subject sung by cellos against syncopated chords in the clarinets and violas. Extraordinary is the broad arch traced by the forward surge of this melody, yet how simple is its pattern:

The fragmenting of this theme into its motives begins already in the Exposition. Measure 6 is extracted and is bandied about by the upper and lower strings, one group imitating the other as the motive is repeated in sequence:

A serene codetta, fashioned from the same material in a new version, brings the Exposition to a close.

The Development section is remarkable for its architectonic force, its dramatic intensity and momentum. With sure symphonic instinct Schubert picks what seems like the least promising of his themes—the first—for expansion and working out. The idea reveals its latent energies in a symphonic fabric that grows steadily in power and impetus. Now it is presented by the lower strings and imitated in the upper; now a fragment flowers into new lines of thought. Here are several examples of Schubert's procedures:

Introductory theme in another key and with a new ending:

Introductory theme expanded by presenting the first two notes of Motive C in ascending sequence:

Motive A of the introductory theme inverted and expanded, with each of its three notes falling in turn upon the accented (first) beat of the measure:

The Recapitulation restates the material of the first section. The lyric theme of the cellos is transposed to D major, the relative major of B minor. The coda brings back the introductory theme, so that the movement ends in the home key with the idea out of which it flowered.

The second movement in E major is marked Andante con moto (at a going pace, with motion). It is in abbreviated sonata form; that is, an Exposition and Recapitulation without a Development. How sheerly romantic is the sonority of the opening chords, played by bassoons and horns against a descending pizzicato on the double basses, out of which emerges the principal motive in the strings.

An orchestral crescendo leads to the second theme in the related key of C-sharp minor. This is a long-breathed song introduced by clarinet and answered

by oboe against syncopated chords in the strings. The closing section of the Exposition undergoes an animated symphonic expansion. Then the two ideas return in the Recapitulation, with subtle changes of color. This time, for example, it is the oboe that introduces the broadly curved second theme and the clarinet that answers. The coda looks back to the opening measures.

The creator of this music passed his uneventful life in the city of Beethoven; too diffident to approach the great man, he worshiped from afar. He could not know that of all the composers of his time, his name alone would be linked to that of his idol. They who far surpassed him in fame and worldly success are long forgotten. Today we speak of the four masters of the classical Viennese school: Haydn, Mozart, Beethoven—and Schubert.

PART FIVE

MEDIEVAL, RENAISSANCE, AND BAROQUE MUSIC

"Music was originally discreet, seemly, simple, masculine, and of good morals. Have not the moderns rendered it lascivious beyond measure?"
Jacob of Liège (fourteenth century)

57 Harmony and Counterpoint: Musical Texture

In writings on music we encounter frequent references to the fabric or texture. Such comparisons between music and cloth are not as unreasonable as may at first appear, since the melodic lines may be thought of as so many threads that make up the musical fabric. This fabric may be one of several types.

Monophonic Texture

The simplest is *monophonic* or single-voice texture. ("Voice" refers to an individual part or line even when we speak of instrumental music, a reminder of the fact that all music stems from vocal origins.) Here the melody is heard without either a harmonic accompaniment or other vocal lines. Attention is focused on the single line. All music up to about a thousand years ago, of which we have any knowledge, was monophonic.

To this day the music of the oriental world—of China, Japan, India, Java, Bali, and the Arab nations—is largely monophonic. The melody may be accompanied by a variety of rhythm and percussion instruments that embellish it, but there is no third dimension of depth or perspective such as harmony alone confers upon a melody. To make up for this lack the single line, being the sole bearer of musical meaning, takes on great complexity and finesse. The monophonic music of the Orient boasts subtleties of pitch and refinements of rhythm unknown in our music.

Polyphonic Texture

When two or more melodic lines are combined we have a *polyphonic* or many-voiced texture. Here the music derives its expressive power and its interest from the interplay of the several lines. Polyphonic texture is based on counterpoint. This term comes from the Latin *punctus contra punctum*, "point against point" or "note against note"—that is to say one musical line against the other. *Counterpoint* is the art and science of combining in a single texture two or more simultaneous melodic lines, each with a rhythmic life of its own.

It was a little over a thousand years ago that European musicians hit upon the device of combining two or more lines simultaneously. At this point Western art music parted company from the monophonic Orient. There ensued a magnificent flowering of polyphonic art that came to its high point in the fifteenth and sixteenth centuries. This development of counterpoint took place at a time when composers were mainly preoccupied with religious choral music, which by its very nature is many-voiced.

Homophonic Texture

In the third type of texture a single voice takes over the melodic interest while the accompanying voices surrender their individuality and become blocks of harmony, the chords that support, color, and enhance the principal part. Here we have a single-melody-with-chords or *homophonic* texture. Again the listener's interest is directed to a single line; but this line, unlike that of oriental music, is conceived in relation to a harmonic background. Homophonic texture is familiar to all; we hear it when the pianist plays the melody with his right hand while the left sounds the chords, or when the singer or violinist carries the tune against a harmonic accompaniment on the piano. Homophonic texture then, is based on harmony, just as polyphonic texture is based on counterpoint.

We have said that melody is the horizontal aspect of music while harmony is the vertical. The comparison with the warp and woof of a fabric consequently has real validity. The horizontal threads, the melodies, are held together by the vertical threads, the harmonies. Out of their interaction comes a weave that may be light or heavy, coarse, or fine.

The three types of texture are apparent from the look of the music on the page:

MONOPHONIC

Do - mi - ne De - us Rex coe - le - stis De - us Pa - ter o - mni - po - tens

POLYPHONIC

etc.

HOMOPHONIC

A composition need not use one texture or the other exclusively. For example, a symphonic movement may present a theme against a homophonic texture. In the development section, however, the texture is apt to become increasingly contrapuntal. So, too, in a homophonic piece the composer may enhance the effect of the principal melody through an interesting play of counterthemes and counterrhythms in the accompanying parts. This is the case in the best orchestral and piano music of the classic-romantic period.

The problem of texture is related, too, to the general style of an era. There was a great shifting of interest from polyphonic to homophonic music around the year 1600. Contrapuntal and harmonic texture existed side by side, the one influencing the other. After 1750 and throughout the classic-romantic period, composers emphasized the homophonic aspect of music over the contrapuntal. A reaction set in with the twentieth century, which turned back to independent part writing. We may sum up the various periods of music history, from the standpoint of texture, as follows.

Before the tenth century A.D.:	monophonic
From around 1000 to 1600:	polyphonic (contrapuntal)
1600–1750:	polyphonic-homophonic
1750–1900:	homophonic. Contrapuntal procedures absorbed into orchestral and chamber music
Since 1900:	revival of interest in polyphonic texture

We have studied the sonata-symphony and other forms that stemmed out of the homophonic-harmonic period. In subsequent chapters we will examine the great forms of polyphonic music.

Devices of Counterpoint

When several independent lines are combined, composers try to give unity and shape to the texture. A basic procedure for achieving this end is *imitation*, in which a subject or motive is presented in one voice and then restated in another. While the imitating voice restates the theme, the first voice continues with counterpoint. This continuing repetition of an idea by all the voices is musically most effective. It is of the essence in contrapuntal thinking. We have spoken of the vertical and horizontal threads in musical texture. To these imitation adds a third, the diagonal, as is apparent from the following example:

How long is the statement that is to be imitated? This varies considerably. It may be the entire length of a melodic line that runs from the beginning to end of a piece. Or the imitation may occur intermittently. When the whole length of a line is imitated, we have a strict type of composition known as a *canon*. The name comes from the Greek word for "law" or "order." Each phrase heard in the leading voice is repeated almost immediately in an imitating voice throughout the length of the work. The most popular form of canon is the round, in which each voice enters in succession with the same melody. A *round*, therefore, is a canon for voices at the unison or octave. Composers do not often cast an entire piece or movement in the shape of a canon. What they do is to use canonic devices as effects in all sorts of pieces. The example of diagonal texture just given shows canonic imitation as it occurs in the final movement of César Franck's Sonata for Violin and Piano. Since this canon is supported by harmonies in the piano part, it is obvious that Franck here combines contrapuntal and harmonic texture.

Contrapuntal writing is marked by a number of devices that have flourished for centuries. *Inversion* is a species of treatment in which the melody is turned upside down; that is, it follows the same intervals but in the opposite direction. Where the melody originally moved up by a third, the inversion moves down a third. Where it descended by a fourth, it now ascends a fourth. Thus, D-F-C (up a third, down a fourth), inverted becomes D-B-E (down a third, up a fourth). *Augmentation* consists of presenting a theme in longer time values. A quarter note may become a half, a half note a whole, and so on. In consequence, if the tempo remains the same, the theme in its new version sounds slower. *Diminution* consists of presenting a theme in shorter time values. A whole note may become a half, a half note a quarter; which, at the same tempo, makes the theme sound faster. *Retrograde*, also known as *cancrizans* or *crab motion*, means to state the melody backwards. If the original sequence of notes reads B-D-G-F, the imitation reads F-G-D-B. Retrograde-and-inversion imitates the theme by turning it upside down and backwards at the same time. It should be added that, while imitation is an important element in contrapuntal writing, not all counterpoint is imitative.

Musical Texture and the Listener

The different types of texture require different kinds of listening. Homophonic music poses no special problem to the music lover of today. He is able to differentiate between the principal melody and its attendant harmonies, and to follow their interrelation. He is helped in this by the fact that most of the music he has heard from the time of his childhood consists of melody and chords.

The case is different with polyphonic music, which is not apt to appeal to those who listen with half an ear. Here we must be aware of the independent lines as they flow alongside each other, each in its own rhythm. This requires much greater concentration on our part. Only by dint of repeated hearings do we learn to follow the individual voices and to separate each within the contrapuntal web.

As an exercise in listening contrapuntally let us take a simple example, the chorale *Wachet auf, ruft uns die Stimme* (Awake, a Voice Is Calling) as it is presented in the fourth movement of Bach's cantata of that name. The tenors are singing the chorale melody, mostly in quarter notes. Above them the violins are playing a florid counterpoint of a livelier nature. Below them the cellos and double basses are carrying the bass line, mostly in quarter and eighth notes. Thus the three lines are distinct not only in register but also in rhythm and color. It is well to listen to the piece several times, concentrating first on each voice alone, then on any two, finally on all three. One becomes aware in following the three planes of movement, of the illusion of space which it is the unique capacity of counterpoint to create; of the fascinating tensions, both musical and psychological, brought into being by the simultaneous unfolding of several lines.

Contrapuntal music does not yield its secrets as readily as do the less complex kinds. By the same token it challenges our attention and holds our interest. With each rehearing we seem to discover another of its facets.

58 The Remote Past

"Nothing is more characteristic of human nature than to be soothed by sweet modes and stirred up by their opposites. Infants, youths, and old people as well are so naturally attuned to musical modes by a kind of spontaneous feeling that no age is without delight in sweet song."

Boethius (c. 480–524)

The relics of the ancient civilizations—Sumer, Babylonia, Egypt—bear witness to a flourishing musical art. In the antique world, religious myth and tradition

Cross Page from the
LINDISFARNE GOSPELS,
c. 700 A.D. (British
Museum, London)
*The free undulating line of
Gregorian chant parallels the
arabesques of Romanesque
art.*

ascribed divine powers to music. The walls of Thebes rose and those of Jericho fell to the sound of music. David played his lyre to cure the melancholy of Saul. In the temple at Jerusalem the Levites, who were the musicians, "being arrayed in fine linen, having cymbals and psalteries and harps, stood at the east end of the altar, and with them an hundred and twenty priests sounding with trumpets."

Only a few fragments have descended to us of the music of antiquity. The centuries have forever silenced the sounds that echoed through the Athenian amphitheater and the Roman circus. Those sounds and the attitudes they reflected, in Greece and throughout the Mediterranean world, formed the subsoil out of which flowered the music of later ages. They became part of the heritage of the West.

Gregorian Chant

Music functioned in the Christian Church from its earliest days. St. Paul exhorted the Ephesians to be filled with the Spirit by "speaking to yourselves in psalms and hymns and spiritual songs, singing and making melody in your heart to the Lord." The music of the Church absorbed Greek, Hebrew, and Syrian influences. It became necessary in time to assemble the ever growing body of chants into an organized liturgy. The task extended over several gen-

The evolution of notation in Western music

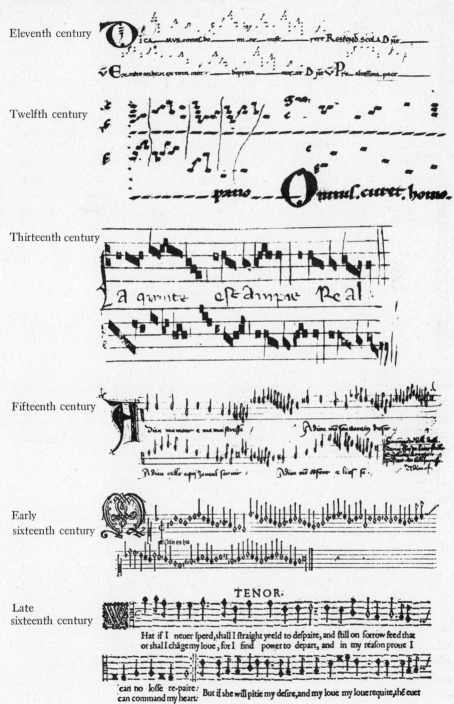

Eleventh century

Twelfth century

Thirteenth century

Fifteenth century

Early
sixteenth century

Late
sixteenth century

erations but is traditionally associated with the name of Pope Gregory the Great, who reigned from 590 to 604.

Like the music of the Greeks and Hebrews from which it descended, *Gregorian chant* (also known as *plainchant* or *plainsong*) consists of a single-line melody. In other words, it is monophonic in texture and does not know the third dimension of harmony and counterpoint. Its freely flowing vocal line is subtly attuned to the inflections of the Latin text. Gregorian melody is free from regular accent. It embodies what may be called prose rhythm in music, or free-verse rhythm, as distinguished from metrical-poetry rhythm such as we find in the regularly accented measures of duple or triple meter.

The Gregorian melodies, numbering more than three thousand, were worked over in the course of generations until they took on their traditional shape. They formed a body of anonymous melody whose roots reached deep into the spiritual life of the folk; a treasure of religious song which, as someone well said, relates to "Everyman rather than Me." Gregorian chant avoids the excitement of wide leaps and dynamic contrasts. Its gentle rise and fall constitute a kind of disembodied musical speech, "a prayer on pitch." Free from the shackles of regular phrase structure, the continuous, undulating vocal line is the counterpart in sound of the sinuous traceries of Romanesque art and architecture.

At first the Gregorian chants were handed down orally from one generation to the next. As the number of chants increased, singers needed to be reminded of the general outlines of the different melodies. Thus came into being the *neumes* (see p. 316), little ascending and descending signs that were written above the words to suggest the course of the melody.

As far as the setting of text is concerned, the melodies fall into three main classes: *syllabic*, that is, one note to each syllable; *neumatic*, generally with groups of two to four notes to a syllable, each group represented by a single neume in the original notation; and *melismatic*, with a single syllable extending over longer groups of notes, as in the setting of the word *Alleluia*. The melismatic style, descended from the rhapsodic improvisations of the Orient, became a prominent feature of Gregorian chant and exerted a strong influence on Western music.

The Medieval Modes

The melody patterns of Gregorian chant were classified according to *modes*. (A mode, it will be recalled, is a specific pattern of whole and half steps.) The medieval or church modes were groups of eight tones, each of which had its central tone. There were eight modes, four *authentic* ("original") and four *plagal* ("derived"). The central or "final" tone, indicated in the following examples by the whole notes with vertical lines on either side, was the first tone of the authentic modes, the fourth tone in the plagal. In addition, each mode had a *dominant,* a secondary tonal center, indicated in the examples by ordinary whole notes:

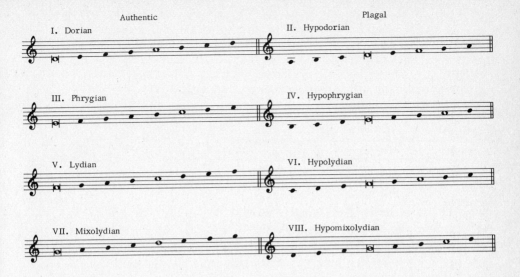

I. Dorian — Authentic
II. Hypodorian — Plagal
III. Phrygian
IV. Hypophrygian
V. Lydian
VI. Hypolydian
VII. Mixolydian
VIII. Hypomixolydian

It will be noticed that if Mode I, the Dorian, is sung with a B-flat it corresponds to the natural minor scale, while Mode V, the Lydian, with a B-flat corresponds to the major. Thus modal harmony bore within it the seeds of the major-minor harmony that ultimately supplanted it. Notice, too, that the authentic modes can be played on the white keys of the piano, whereas to build the major or minor scales from the same starting points we would have to use sharps or flats.

The church modes served as the basis for European art music for a thousand years. With the development of polyphony, or many-voiced music, a harmonic system evolved based on the modes. The adjective *modal* consequently refers to the type of melody and harmony that prevailed in the early and later Middle Ages. It is frequently used in opposition to *tonal*, which refers to the harmony based on the major-minor tonality that supplanted the modes.

Two Gregorian Melodies

The Alleluia from the Mass of the Epiphany (the Visit of the Magi) is a beautiful example of melismatic setting of text.

Alleluia.
Vidimus stellam ejus in Oriente
et venimus cum muneribus
ad orare Dominum.   Alleluia.

Alleluia.
We have seen His Star in the East,
and are come with gifts
to worship the Lord.   Alleluia.

The melody is in Mode II (Hypodorian) and is divided between solo and chorus; it lies within a narrow range and moves by step or narrow leap. Notice how the final syllable is extended in the response of the chorus:

Al - le - lu - ia_____ * Al - le - lu - ia_____

Here is how this plainchant looks in Gregorian notation:

Al - le - lú - ia.   * ij.

The melody is more highly organized than appears at first hearing. For example, the opening Alleluia is restated in slightly abbreviated fashion at the end, thus anticipating the prelude-postlude formation (or even A-B-A) that was to come into fashion hundreds of years later. So too, the music on the words *stellam ejus* is repeated on the words *cum muneribus*. In addition, motives from one section are repeated, either exactly or somewhat modified, in other sections. Thus the principle of repetition and contrast that we found to be so prominent in music of the classic-romantic period was already operating a thousand years earlier.

Victimae paschali, from the Mass for Easter, is an example of syllabic setting. The melody is in Mode I (Dorian) and, except for the first phrase, is sung by the chorus.

1. Victimae paschali laudes immolent Christiani.

To the Paschal Victim, Christians, offer praise.

2. Agnus redemit oves: Christus innocens Patri reconciliavit peccatores.

The Sheep has ransomed the lamb: innocent Christ reconciles sinners to the Father.

3. Mors et vita duello conflixere mirando: dux vitae mortuus regnat vivus.

Death and life fought a wondrous duel: the Lord of life, though dead, reigns deathless.

4. Dic nobis Maria quid vidisti in via?

Tell us, Mary, what you saw on your journey.

5. Sepulchrum Christi viventis, et gloriam vidi resurgentis:

The tomb of the living Christ I saw, and the glory of Him who rose from death:

6. Angelicos testes sudarium, et vestes.

Angels attesting the shroud and the garments.

7. Surrexit Christus spes mea: Praecedet suos in Galilaeam.

The Lord hath risen, my hope: He goes before you into Galilee.

8. Scimus Christum surrexisse a mortuis vere: tu nobis, victor Rex, miserere.

Amen. Alleluia.

We know that Christ is risen, ever living: Have mercy on us, victorious king.

Amen. Alleluia.

Attributed to the eleventh-century monk Wipo of Burgundy, the poem has symmetries of meter and rhyme that are reflected in the music. The first four phrases, for example, have a regularity of structure that we do not ordinarily associate with Gregorian chant. Note that, as in the preceding example, melodic movement is mainly by step or narrow leap:

Vi - cti - mae pa - scha - li lau - des * im - mo - lent Chri - sti - a - ni.

These symmetries are reinforced by the repetition of material. The music for Verse 2 is repeated for Verse 3, that for Verse 4 is repeated for 6, that for Verse 5 is repeated for 7. In addition, motives recur to unify the over-all structure. On the Amen and Alleluia, also in Verses 4 and 5, we hear examples of neumatic setting, in which a single syllable is extended for two or three notes.

The Gregorian melodies constitute our richest legacy from the period of pure monophonic melody. They nourished fifteen hundred years of European folk, popular, and art music. They bring us as close as we shall ever come to the lost musical art of the ancient Mediterranean culture—the art of Greece, Syria, and Palestine.

59 The Later Middle Ages

Within the Romanesque period (c. 850–1150) took place the single most important development in the history of Western music: the emergence of polyphony as a stylistic factor of prime importance. This occurred at about the same time that European painting was developing the science of perspective. Thus hearing and seeing in depth came into European culture together, and must be accounted among its most significant products.

Once several melodic lines proceeded side by side, there could no longer be the flexible prose rhythms of single-line music. Polyphony brought about the emergence of regular meters that enabled the different voices to keep together. This music had to be written down in a way that would indicate precisely the rhythm and the pitch. In this way evolved our modern staff, whose lines and spaces made it possible to indicate the exact pitch, and whose notes, by their appearance, could indicate the duration of each sound.

With the development of exact notation, music took a long step from being an art of improvisation and oral tradition to one that was carefully planned and that could be preserved accurately. Henceforth a musical work could be studied

Detail from the Bayeux Tapestry, c. 1073–83: William the Conqueror's army attacks a castle.

Giotto (c. 1267–c. 1337), MEETING OF ST. JOACHIM AND ST. ANNE. (Arena Chapel, Padua)

European painting moved from the flat surface to perspective as music passed from monophonic to polyphonic texture.

318

by many musicians; the creative experience of one could nourish all the others. The period of anonymous creation characteristic of folk art drew to a close. The individual composer appeared upon the scene.

This development took shape during the Gothic era (c. 1150–1450). The period saw a flourishing secular music in the art of the minstrels and troubadours of the feudal courts. More important, it witnessed the rise of the cathedrals with their choirs and organs. The mastery of construction that made possible the building of those mighty edifices had its counterpart in music. The new science of counterpoint was brought to heights of virtuosity. The learned musicians, for the most part monks and priests, mastered the art of constructing extended musical works through the various devices of counterpoint. Their prime interest at this point was in the structural combining of musical elements, which explains the derivation of the word "composer" from the Latin *componere*, "to put together." The creative musician of the late Gothic period thought of himself primarily as a master builder.

The Notre Dame School

The earliest kind of polyphonic music was called *organum*. This developed when the custom arose of adding to the Gregorian melody a second or organal voice that ran parallel to the plainchant at the interval of a fifth or a fourth above or below. When these lines were duplicated an octave above, there resulted a piece of four voices that moved in parallel octaves, fifths, and fourths, as in the following example of ninth-century organum:

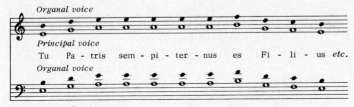

The way was now open for the development of a polyphonic art in which the individual voices moved with ever greater independence, not only in parallel but also in contrary motion. Leaders in this development were the composers whose center was the Cathedral of Notre Dame in Paris during the twelfth and thirteenth centuries. The two outstanding members of the Notre Dame school were Leonin and his disciple and successor Perotin, who was active somewhere between 1180 and 1230.

It was self-evident to the medieval mind that the new must be founded on the old. Therefore the composer of organum based his piece on a pre-existent Gregorian chant. For example, Leonin's organum for two voices, *Viderunt*

319

The Cathedral of Notre Dame, Paris.
In both architecture and music, the Gothic period saw advances in techniques of construction.

omnes, is based on the opening phrase of a Gregorian melody from the Gradual of the Mass for Christmas Day. The complete verse reads: *Viderunt omnes fines terrae salutare Dei nostri* (All the ends of the earth have seen the salvation of our Lord).

Dating from the end of the twelfth century, this is a far more advanced example of organum than the rather primitive example of the ninth century quoted earlier. The tenor sings the melody in enormously long notes while above it the organal voice moves freely in melismatic passages. Here is the extensive melisma over the opening note of the Gregorian melody:

This rhapsodic style gives way to a passage in which the notes of the bass become much shorter and both voices move in clear-cut rhythms. It begins with the fifth note of the Gregorian tune:

While Leonin limited himself to counterpoint in two voices, Perotin extended the technique by writing for three and four parts. His music shows a tendency toward shorter melodic phrases, clear-cut rhythms, and at times even a vaguely "major" feeling. In his larger compositions the music takes on a spacious resonance that evokes the echoing vaults of the Gothic cathedral. His Alleluia for the Feast of the Nativity of the Virgin Mary is based on a Gregorian Alleluia:

Each of these notes is held by the tenor, while the two upper voices unfold their melismas. Notice that the rhythm here is more regularly measured than in the piece by Leonin:

The two upper voices lie in the same register and frequently cross. The phrase lengths vary; the upper melodies occasionally outline a major triad. There is a roughness to the vocal lines that suggests the power of Perotin's writing. Notice the droning effect, in certain passages, of the sustained lower voice.

321

The Mass

The Mass is the most solemn ritual of the Roman Catholic Church. It constitutes a re-enactment of the sacrifice of Christ. The name is derived from the Latin *missa,* "dismissal" (of the congregation at the end of the service).

The aggregation of prayers that make up the Mass falls into two categories: those that vary from day to day throughout the church year, the Proper; and those that remain the same in every Mass, the Ordinary. The liturgy, which reached its present form about nine hundred years ago, provides Gregorian melodies for each item of the ceremony. With the rise of polyphony composers began to weave additional voices around the plainchant. They concentrated on the prayers that were an invariable part of the service rather than on the variable items that were heard only once during the liturgical year. Thus came into prominence the five sections that the public knows as the musical setting of the Mass: Kyrie, Gloria, Credo, Sanctus, and Agnus Dei (Today these sections of the Mass are recited or sung in the language of the country.) The opening section, the Kyrie—a prayer for mercy—dates from the early centuries of Christianity, as its original Greek text attests. It is an A-B-A form that consists of nine invocations: three *Kyrie eleison* (Lord, have mercy), three *Christe eleison* (Christ, have mercy), and again three *Kyrie eleison.* There follows the *Gloria in excelsis Deo* (Glory to God in the highest). This is a joyful hymn of praise which is omitted in the penitential seasons, Advent and Lent. The third movement is the confession of faith, *Credo in unum Deum, Patrem omnipotentem* (I believe in one God, the Father Almighty). It includes also the *Et incarnatus est* (And He became flesh), the *Crucifixus* (He was crucified), and the *Et resurrexit* (And He rose again). Fourth is *Sanctus Sanctus Sanctus* (Holy Holy Holy), which concludes with the *Hosanna in excelsis* (Hosanna in the highest) and the *Benedictus qui venit in nomine Domini* (Blessed is He who comes in the name of the Lord), after which the *Hosanna in excelsis* is repeated as a kind of refrain. The fifth and last part, *Agnus Dei, qui tollis peccata mundi* (Lamb of God, who takes away the sins of the world), is sung three times. Twice it concludes with *Miserere nobis* (Have mercy on us), and the third time with the prayer *Dona nobis pacem* (Grant us peace).

The polyphonic setting of the Mass was generally based on a fragment of Gregorian chant. This was sung in long-drawn-out notes by the tenor while the other voices wove florid designs around it, and was known as the *cantus firmus* (fixed melody). The cantus firmus served as the skeletal structure of the work and, when used in all the movements of a Mass, welded it into a unity. As we noted in our discussion of organum, the combining of a composer's original creation with a pre-existing melody appealed to the medieval mind. It provided him with the fixed element that he could embellish with all the resources of his artistry; somewhat as, centuries later, did the theme and variations. Of the Masses for special services the most important is the Mass for the Dead, which is sung at funeral and memorial services. It is known as the Requiem, from the opening verse *Requiem aeternam dona eis, Domine* (Rest eternal grant unto them, O Lord). Included are prayers in keeping with the solemnity of the occasion, among them the awesome evocation of the Last Judgment, *Dies irae* (That Day of Wrath).

The history of the Mass as an art form extends over the better part of eight hundred years. In that time it garnered for itself some of the greatest music ever written.

Machaut: Agnus Dei (I) from the *Notre Dame Mass*

The break-up of the feudal social structure brought with it new concepts of life, art, and beauty. This ferment was reflected in the musical style that made its appearance at the beginning of the fourteenth century in France and somewhat later in Italy, known as *ars nova* (new art). The music of the French *ars nova* shows greater refinement than the *ars antiqua* (old art) which it displaced. Its outstanding figure was the French composer-poet Guillaume de Machaut (c. 1300–77). He took holy orders at an early age, became secretary to John of Luxemburg, King of Bohemia, and was active at the court of Jean, Duke of Normandy, who subsequently became king of France. He spent his old age as a canon of Rheims, admired as the greatest musician of the time.

Machaut's double career as cleric and courtier impelled him to both religious and secular music. His poetic ballads reveal him as a proponent of the ideals of medieval chivalry, a romantic who exalted the moral and social code of an age that was finished. He was the first known composer to make a complete polyphonic setting of the Ordinary of the Mass: the *Notre Dame Mass*, which is said to have been written for the coronation of Charles V at Rheims in 1364.

Its Agnus Dei (I) displays the chief traits of Machaut's style. The counterpoint is freer than in the *ars antiqua* of Leonin and Perotin, the melody lines less angular, the harmonies less harsh, even if the music abounds in discords that from the standpoint of a later age might be judged arbitrary. The text is the traditional *Agnus Dei, qui tollis peccata mundi, miserere nobis* (Lamb of God, who takes away the sins of the world, have mercy on us). The piece is in four parts; the tenor sings a cantus firmus drawn from Gregorian chant. The uppermost voice is melismatic; the two upper parts lie in approximately the same register and occasionally cross, while the lowest has no text and probably was performed on an instrument (in modern performances it is generally played on a small organ whose tone resembles that of the medieval choir organ). Throughout the piece, unity is underlined through the repetition of rhythmic and melodic patterns. The four lines combine, especially at the cadences, to form triads; while the modal harmony imparts an archaic sound that falls pleasantly upon twentieth-century ears.

323

The Burgundian School

At the waning of the Middle Ages stands the Burgundian school that flourished in the fifteenth century in the duchy of Charles the Bold. The Burgundian masters abandoned the complexities of Gothic counterpoint in favor of a simpler and more appealing style. They established the practice of basing all movements of the Mass on the same melody, thereby achieving unity within a large-scale architecture. They used the voices in high register along with a mixture of contrasting instruments—double reeds, recorders, viols, trombones —to attain a bright, lustrous tone. Under their influence the intervals of a fifth and fourth—hitherto the basic consonances—were supplemented with the more euphonious third (as from *do* to *mi* or C-E) and sixth (as from *mi* up to *do* or E-C). The Burgundians spearheaded the movement to replace the meandering vocal lines of the past with well-defined melodies and clear-cut rhythms. Their harmony grew ever simpler and more direct, foreshadowing a language based on triads, Tonic-Dominant relationships, and a sense of key.

Dufay: Kyrie (I) from the Mass
Se la face ay pale

Chief figure of the Burgundian school was Guillaume Dufay (c. 1400–74). Sprung from the peasantry, he brought into art music the charm of folksong. Dufay was a master of intimate lyric forms. He bridged the gap between the late Gothic in France and the Renaissance in Italy, where he lived for nine years. He has been "discovered" by the twentieth century and is much admired by contemporary musicians.

By the time of Dufay the cantus firmus on which the Mass was based no longer had to be drawn from Gregorian chant; it could be a popular tune, which then gave its name to the Mass based on it. This mingling of the sacred and the secular might prove disturbing to believers today, but it was in keeping with the spirit of an age whose faith was so complete as to embrace all aspects of life. Dufay was one of the first to use secular melodies in his religious works. His Mass *Se la face ay pale* (If my face is pallid) is named after the popular love song on which it is based:

Se la face ay pa - - le, la cause est a - mer,
If my face is pal - - lid, know the cause is love,

The first half of this tune became the cantus firmus of the opening movement of Dufay's Mass. The borrowed melody lies in the tenor and moves in longer note values than do the other parts:

The text consists of two words, *Kyrie eleison* (Lord, have mercy), which are repeated over and over, dissolved in music. The setting for the most part extends single syllables for two, three, or four notes; there are also melismatic passages. The bass part begins with one syllable to a note. The most active and melodious part is the soprano, foreshadowing a time when melodies would generally lie in the topmost part. The three upper parts lie close together and frequently cross. As time went on each of the four parts developed its own register and function, so that there was less crossing.

Despite the widespread notion that old music was exclusively vocal (perhaps based on the fact that the musical manuscripts never specify whether a given part is vocal or instrumental), we know from pictures and documents of the period that instruments were frequently used, both in support of the voices and as contrast to them, in interludes. Most modern performances make use of instruments in both these ways.

Characteristic of Dufay are the sweet harmonies and the radiant sonority of the interweaving voices. This euphony was new to music. It was one of the signal

Guillaume Dufay and Gilles Binchois (miniature from a fifteenth-century manuscript)

achievements of Dufay's serene art, an art that lies between the twilight of the Middle Ages and the dawn of the Renaissance.

Binchois: *Adieu m'amour et ma maistresse*

Dufay's most celebrated contemporary, Gilles Binchois (c. 1400–60), was a soldier before he entered the chapel of Duke Philip the Good of Burgundy. He wrote secular as well as religious works and distinguished himself in a genre much favored by fifteenth-century composers: the *chanson* or solo song with instrumental accompaniment, which they inherited from Guillaume de Machaut. (The French word for song gave its name to a widely cultivated type of music, much as did centuries later the German lied.) Many of Binchois's chansons are settings of courtly love poems that breathe a gentle melancholy. Characteristic of Binchois's style are simple melodies marked by symmetrical phrases and clear-cut cadences, clarity of texture, and an atmosphere of intimacy. These qualities are manifest in his chanson *Adieu m'amour et ma maistresse* (Farewell my love and my dear lady):

A - dieu m'a - mour et ma mais - tres - se,_____
Fare - well my love and my dear la - dy,_____

Binchois's chanson consists of two parts. The first has four phrases, of which the first and third are sung, the second and fourth serving as instrumental interludes. The second part consists of three phrases, of which the middle one is instrumental. The two parts alternate and are repeated, as are lines of the text, in a pattern that makes for both unity and variety. As in the music of Dufay, the harmonies move smoothly and euphoniously.

Among the instruments used in the performance of these chansons are viols and recorders. The *recorder* is a kind of flute that is held vertically, like a clarinet or oboe, and is played by blowing into the end, the player's breath passing through a "whistle" mouthpiece and against the sharp edge of a side opening. It has a soft, slightly reedy tone, was extremely popular in the sixteenth and seventeenth centuries, and has been revived in the twentieth. *Viols* were a family of string instruments that later gave way to the violin; delicate and soft in timbre, they were ideally suited to intimate music-making. There were three standard sizes: treble viol, tenor viol, and bass viol or *viola da gamba* (so-called from the Italian word "gamba," which means leg; this largest viol was held like a cello). Later, the trend toward larger rooms and more brilliant tone displaced these instruments by their modern equivalents.

The Gothic age—early, middle, and late—extended over centuries, during which the heritage of the ancient Mediterranean culture was fused with the genius of the rude northern tribes. Out of this union came a new thing into the world: the European tradition.

60 The Renaissance

"I am not pleased with the Courtier if he be not also a musician, and besides his understanding and cunning [in singing] upon the book, have skill in like manner on sundry instruments."
Baldassare Castiglione: *The Courtier* (1528)

The Renaissance (c. 1450–1600) is one of the beautiful if misleading names in the history of culture: beautiful because it implies an awakening of intellectual awareness, misleading because it suggests a sudden rebirth of learning and art after the presumed stagnation of the Middle Ages. History moves continuously rather than by leaps and bounds. The Renaissance was the next phase of a cultural process that, under the leadership of the universities and princely courts, had begun long before.

What the Renaissance does mark is the passing of European society from an exclusively religious orientation to a secular; from an age of unquestioning faith and mysticism to one of belief in reason and scientific inquiry. The focus of man's destiny was seen to be his life on earth rather than in the hereafter. There was a new reliance on the evidence of the senses rather than on tradition and authority. Implied was a new confidence in man's ability to solve his problems and rationally order his world. This awakening found its symbol in the culture of Greek and Roman antiquity. The men of the Renaissance discovered the summit of human wisdom not only in the Church fathers and saints, as their ancestors had done, but also in Homer and Vergil and the ancient philosophers.

Historians used to date the Renaissance from the fall of Constantinople to the Turks in 1453 and the emigration of Greek scholars to the West. It might be better, if a date is needed, to pick that of the invention of printing and paper around the year 1440. Several momentous events set off the new era from the old. The introduction of gunpowder brought to an end the age of knighthood. The development of the compass made possible the voyages of discovery that opened up a new world and demolished old superstitions. The revival of ancient letters was associated with the humanists. This revival had its counterpart in architecture, painting, and sculpture. If the Romanesque found its grand architectural form in the monastery and the Gothic in the cathedral, the Renaissance lavished its constructive energy upon palace and château. The gloomy fortified castles of the medieval barons gave way to spacious edifices that displayed the harmonious proportions of the classical style. In effect, renaissance architecture embodied the striving for a gracious and reasoned existence that was the great gesture of the age.

Donato Bramante (1444–1514), Tempietto di San Pietro in Montorio, Rome. *Renaissance art drew inspiration from Classical antiquity.*

So, too, the elongated saints and martyrs of medieval painting and sculpture were replaced by the Venus of Botticelli and the Athenian sages of Raphael. Even where artists retained the religious atmosphere, the Mother of Sorrow and the symbols of grief gave way to smiling madonnas—often posed for by very secular ladies—and dimpled cherubs. The human form, denied for centuries, was revealed as a thing of beauty; also as an object of anatomical study. Nature entered painting along with the nude, and with it an intense preoccupation with the laws of perspective and composition. Medieval painting had presented life as an allegory; the Renaissance preferred realism. The medieval painters posed their figures frontally, impersonally; the Renaissance developed psychological characterization and the art of portraiture. Medieval painting dealt in types; the Renaissance concerned itself with individuals. Space in medieval painting was organized in a succession of planes over which the eye traveled as over a series of episodes. The Renaissance created unified space and the simultaneous seeing of the whole. It discovered the landscape, created the illusion of distance, and opened up endless vistas upon the physical loveliness of the world.

The Renaissance came to flower in the nation that stood closest to the classical Roman culture. Understandably the great names we associate with its painting and sculture are predominantly Italian: Donatello (c. 1386–1466), Masaccio (1401–28), Botticelli (1444–1510), Leonardo da Vinci (1452–1519), Michelangelo (1475–1564), Raphael (1483–1520), and Titian (1488–1576). With the masters who lived in the second half of the century, such as Tintoretto

(1518–94) and Veronese (1528–88), we approach the world of the early Baroque.

The Renaissance achieved a heightened awareness of the human personality. Its turbulence and dynamic force were in marked contrast to the static nature of medieval society. It gave impetus to the twin currents of rationalism and realism that have prevailed in European culture ever since. Granted that its love of art and beauty existed side by side with tyranny, ignorance, superstition; that its humanism took shape in a scene dominated by treachery and lust. It is the noble usage of history to judge an age by its finest. By that measure this period ranks high. From the multicolored tapestry of renaissance life emerge figures that have captured the imagination of the world: Lorenzo de' Medici and Ludovico Sforza, Benvenuto Cellini and Machiavelli, Pope Alexander VI and Sir Thomas More, Lucrezia Borgia and Beatrice d'Este. Few centuries can match the sixteenth for its galaxy of great names. The list includes Erasmus (1466–1536) and Martin Luther (1483–1546), Rabelais (1494?–1553) and Cervantes (1547–1616), Marlowe (1564–93) and Shakespeare (1564–1616).

With these men we find ourselves in a world that speaks our language. The Renaissance marks the birth of the modern European temper and of Western man as we have come to know him. In that turbulent time was shaped the moral and cultural climate we still inhabit.

61 Sixteenth-Century Music

"He who does honor and reverence to music is commonly a man of worth, sound of soul, by nature loving things lofty."
Pierre de Ronsard to Francis II (1560)

The painting and poetry of the Renaissance abound in references to music. Nothing more clearly attests to the vast importance of the art in the cultural life of the time. The pageantry of the Renaissance unfolded to a momentous musical accompaniment. Throwing off its medieval mysticism, music moved toward clarity, simplicity, and a frankly sensuous appeal.

The age achieved an exquisite appreciation of *a cappella* music. (Literally, "for the chapel." This term denotes a vocal work without instrumental accompaniment.) The sixteenth century has come to be regarded as the golden age of the a cappella style. Its polyphony was based on a principle called *continuous imitation*. The motives wandered from vocal line to vocal line within the texture, the voices imitating one another so that the same theme or motive was heard now in the soprano or alto, now in the tenor or bass. There resulted an extremely close-knit musical fabric that was capable of the most subtle and varied effects.

The composers of the Flemish school were pre-eminent in European music from around 1450 to the end of the sixteenth century. They came from the southern Lowlands, which is now Belgium, and from the adjoining provinces of northern France and Burgundy. In their number were several outstanding figures in the history of music, from among whom we may single out the two most important.

Josquin des Prez: *Ave Maria*

Josquin des Prez (c. 1450–1521) was the most representative and admired musician of his time. He inherited the canonic techniques of the earlier Flemish masters. During his stay in Italy his northern art absorbed the classical virtues of balance and moderation, the sense of harmonious proportion and lucid form that found their archetype in the radiant art of Raphael. He advanced to a free and continuous imitation of themes that left room for the imaginative development of musical ideas. His music is rich in sentiment; his serene melodiousness, clarity of structure, and humaneness of spirit bespeak the man of the Renaissance. Martin Luther, who admired him greatly, said, "He is the master of his notes. They have to do as he bids them; other composers have to do as the notes will."

The motet *Ave Maria*—one of several of Josquin's works with this title—exemplifies the technique of continuous imitation as practiced in the High Renaissance. (A *motet* is a choral work, with or without accompaniment, of either sacred or secular character, and originally intended to be performed at religious or festive occasions.)

Ave Maria, gratia plena, Dominus tecum;	Hail Mary, full of grace, the Lord is with thee;
benedicta tu in mulieribus,	blessed art thou among women,
et benedictus fructus ventris tui,	and blessed is the fruit of thy womb,
Jesus Christus Filius Dei vivi.	Jesus Christ, Son of the living God.
Et benedicta sint beata ubera tua	And blessed be thy breasts,
quae lactaverunt regem regum,	that have suckled the King of Kings,
et Dominum Deum nostrum.	and the Lord our God.

The thematic material is drawn from a Gregorian melody, *Ave Maria, gratia plena*; but this is no longer quoted literally or confined to the tenor, as in the past. On the contrary, Josquin treats it with great freedom. The following example shows the Gregorian melody:

A - ve Ma - ri - a, gra - ti - a ple - na, Do - mi - nus te - cum, *etc.*

In transforming this into a theme for his motet Josquin fills in the skips in the melodic line, ornaments it, and gives it a rhythmic profile. Here is how the first seven notes of the plainchant are transformed:

This is further varied in the process of imitation as each of the other three voices makes its entrance:

The motet is for four voices; the two middle ones lie in the same range and frequently cross. Each phrase of the text is set separately; but a continuous fabric is achieved by causing the phrases to overlap—that is, a new phrase is begun in one voice while the others are finishing the old. Although imitative counterpoint prevails, there are passages that approach a homophonic style, or that lie between the two styles. Characteristic of Josquin is the way in which one pair of voices is pitted against the other; this occurs on the words *benedicta tu* and again, later, on the words *Et benedicta sint*. When the music shifts from duple to triple meter, on the word *vivi* (living), Josquin underlines the change with a full cadence. The passage in triple meter is in a somewhat livelier style; the music returns to duple meter after the words *regem regum* (King of Kings), recapturing thereby the seraphic calm of the opening section. Despite the modal harmony, certain passages give the impression of B-flat major, others of G minor.

Josquin brought to his art a new vision of beauty. His age justly named him "the Prince of Music."

Lassus: *Tristis est anima mea*

The Flemish tradition culminates in the towering figure of Roland de Lassus (c. 1532–94). A citizen of the world (he was equally well

Pieter Brueghel (c. 1525–69), PEASANT DANCE. (Kunsthistorisches Museum, Vienna) *The earthy realism of this Flemish master is paralleled by the expressive range of the music of Lassus.*

known in Italy as Orlando di Lasso) Lassus absorbed into his art the main currents of renaissance music—the elegance and wit of the French, the profundity and rich detail of the Germans, the sensuous beauty of Italian music. His works number over two thousand, from impetuous love songs (some of whose texts are too erotic for the concert hall) to noble Masses, motets, and the profoundly felt *Penitential Psalms*. In his panoramic view of life, as in his feeling for vivid detail, Lassus elicits comparison with another great Fleming—his contemporary, Pieter Brueghel (c. 1525–69). His music is compounded of passion, tenderness, brilliance, humor, and—at the last—mysticism.

The mystical mood pervades his motet *Tristis est anima mea* (1568). This moving composition reveals the high artistic level attained by the motet and the a cappella style in the late sixteenth century.

Tristis est anima mea usque ad mortem:	My soul is exceedingly sorrowful, even unto death;
sustinete hic, et vigilate mecum:	wait here, and watch with me:
nunc videbitis turbam, quae circumdabit me;	now you will see the multitude that will surround me;
vos fugam capietis et ego vadam immolari pro vobis.	you will run away, and I will go to be sacrificed for you.

The flowing lines of the counterpoint unfold in flexible rhythms that follow the natural inflection of the words. The over-all effect remains that of a smoothly flowing duple meter. The motet is set for five voices—two sopranos, alto, tenor, and bass. By separating the topmost voice from the other four voices Lassus obtains a powerful effect at the outset; each voice enters in succession with the key word *tristis* (sad), building up to the expressive entrance of the first soprano:

In the same class is the affecting rendition of the word *mortem* (death), which is set to a bleak chord consisting of the octave and the fifth, the euphonious interval of the third having been omitted. This was rather unusual in the later sixteenth century. Certain phrases are repeated two or even three

Roland de Lassus (seated, center) with an ensemble of musicans at the Bavarian Court Chapel (from a sixteenth-century manuscript).

times, which sets them off from those that occur only once. Lassus underlines the thought *nunc videbitis turbam* (now you will see the multitude) by stopping the contrapuntal flow in favor of chords. The thought *quae circumdabit me* (that will surround me) calls forth pungent harmonies. The excitement of the crowd is suggested by the voices entering in quick succession on a theme that begins with short notes. A similar effect is achieved by close imitation on the words *vos fugam capietis* (you will run away). Again massive chords emphasize the announcement *et ego vadam immolari* (and I will go to be sacrificed), with a florid expansion of a single syllable in the last phrase.

Lassus's art brings to its final statement a century and a half of Flemish polyphony. It incarnates the verve and splendor of the Renaissance, and well merits the judgment carved on his tomb: "Here lies that Lassus who refreshes the weariness of the world, and whose harmony resolves its discord."

Palestrina and the Catholic Reform

After the revolt of Martin Luther the desire for a return to true Christian piety brought about a reform movement within the Catholic Church. This movement became part of the Counter-Reformation whereby the Church strove to recapture the minds of men. Among its manifestations were the activities of Franciscans and Dominicans among the poor; the founding of the Society of Jesus (Jesuits) by St. Ignatius Loyola (1491–1556); and the deliberations of the Council of Trent, which extended—with some interruptions—from 1545 to 1563.

In its desire to regulate every aspect of religious discipline, the Council took up the matter of church music. The cardinals were much concerned over the corruption of the traditional chant by the singers, who added all manner of embellishments to the Gregorian melodies. They objected to the use of instruments other than the organ in the religious service, to the practice of incorporating popular songs in Masses, to the secular spirit that was invading sacred music, and to the general irreverent attitude of church musicians. They pointed out that in polyphonic settings of the Mass the sacred text was made unintelligible by the overelaborate contrapuntal texture. Certain zealots advocated abolishing counterpoint altogether and returning to Gregorian chant, but there were many music lovers among the cardinals who opposed so drastic a step. The committee assigned to deal with the problem contented itself with issuing general recommendations for a more dignified service. The authorities favored a pure vocal style that would respect the integrity of the sacred texts, that would avoid virtuosity and encourage piety.

Giovanni Pierluigi, called da Palestrina after his birthplace (c. 1525–94), met the need for a reformed church music in so exemplary a fashion that for posterity he has remained *the* Catholic composer. He served as organist and choirmaster at various churches including that of St. Peter's in Rome. His patron Pope Julius III appointed him a member of the Sistine Chapel choir even

Giovanni Pierluigi da Palestrina.

though, as a married man, he was ineligible for the semi-ecclesiastical post. He was dismissed by a later Pope but ultimately returned to St. Peter's, where he spent the last twenty-three years of his life. Palestrina's music gives voice to the religiosity of the Counter-Reformation, its transports and its visions. He created a universal type of expression ideally suited to moods of mystic exaltation. The contemplative beauty of his music does not exclude intense emotion; but this is emotion directed to an act of faith.

A true Italian, Palestrina was surpassingly sensitive to the sensuous loveliness of the voice. His melodious counterpoint is eminently singable. In his most celebrated work, the Mass for Pope Marcellus II (c. 1555), he shows himself aware of the objections that had been raised against polyphonic settings of the Mass. He sets the text clearly and distinctly. He enhances the meaning of the words without flooding them with music. The musical expansion is kept within modest limits. Only the most important words are repeated.

The Pope Marcellus Mass is for six voices—soprano, alto, two tenors, and two basses. The opening Kyrie (Lord, have mercy) is predominantly contrapuntal. It unfolds a motive marked by the interval of an ascending fourth (at ✕), which appears in one form or another in all the parts.

In the next section the opening phrase, *Gloria in excelsis Deo* (Glory to God in the highest), is a Gregorian melody that is chosen by the priest, who intones it alone; the choir responds, voices joined, *Et in terra pax hominibus bonae voluntatis* (And on earth peace to men of good will). Notable is the elasticity of rhythm that results from the free intermingling of duple and triple meters, an elasticity that can only be approximated in modern notation. There is a change of intensity at the *Qui tollis peccata mundi* (You who take away the sins of the world). Chordal passages are subtly balanced against the contrapuntal ones.

In the Credo the opening phrase, *Credo in unum Deum* (I believe in one God), is again a Gregorian melody intoned by the priest, after which Palestrina's composition begins. We find here the characteristic joining of the voices in chordal style on the crucial words *Et incarnatus est* (And He became flesh) as well as on *Et homo factus est* (and was made man). At the *Crucifixus* Palestrina reduces the voices to four—soprano, alto, tenor, bass—setting the text for the most part one note to a syllables, in a harmonic style that points to the future. There is an access of joy at *Et resurrexit* (And He rose again); yet the changes in mood and emotion are in no sense as great as we shall find, say, in the B-minor Mass of Bach. With the *Et in Spiritum Sanctum* (And I believe in the Holy Spirit) Palestrina returns to the six-voice setting.

Celebration of the Mass (engraving from a sixteenth-century book). (The Metropolitan Museum of Art, New York, Whittelsey Fund, 1949)

The Sanctus opens with the soprano voice moving freely, almost like a solo, supported by the other five voices. This movement shows the luminous sense of sound that underlies Palestrina's conception. Characteristic is the way in which a theme heard in one voice furnishes the motives that are imitated in the others. The *Hosanna in excelsis* (Hosanna in the highest) begins with chords that serve as supporting pillars for the counterpoint. The calm and remote *Benedictus* (Blessed is he), in four voices—soprano, alto, first and second tenors—is marked by greater expansion of single syllables than in the earlier movements. The rest of the Mass is in the usual six voices. The first Agnus Dei flowers from the same interval of the ascending fourth that was heard at the beginning of the Mass. The second Agnus Dei is a triple canon; that is, the theme in the first voice is followed, in strict imitation, by two voices instead of one.

Palestrina's style incarnates the pure a cappella ideal of vocal polyphony, in which the individual voice fulfilled its destiny through submergence in the group. His music remains an apt symbol of the greatness art can aspire to when it subserves a profound moral conviction.

The Venetian School

Something there was about Venice that impelled its artists to a special awareness of the shapes and colors of the visible world. The play of light and shade on the canals that laced the city, the vivid tints of its palaces, the pleasure-loving disposition of its inhabitants, and the glittering ceremonies so closely bound up with the life of the Queen of the Adriatic were faithfully reflected in the canvases—drenched in color—of the Venetian school of painters. Among these were, to name only the greatest, Gentile Bellini (1429–1507) and his brother Giovanni (c. 1430–1516), Carpaccio (c. 1465–1526), Titian, Giorgione (c. 1477–1510), Tintoretto, and Veronese.

In similar manner were the composers of the Venetian school impelled towards color. Music was an integral part of the lavish celebrations that marked the victories of the Venetian fleet or the induction of the Doge. Trumpets and trombones accompanied stately processions such as Bellini painted, of senators clad in scarlet approaching the Byzantine splendor of the Cathedral of St. Mark. The Venetians were drawn to religious music in which voices mingled with instruments. St. Mark's had two choir galleries on opposite sides of the building, each with its own organ; hence its composers could experiment with works in which groups of singers and players, with the width of the church between them, performed separately or together, as if answering each other, in what is known as the *antiphonal* style. In effect, the works of the Venetian masters introduced a spatial element into music—what we today would call stereophonic; certainly the effects at which they aimed can be captured most effectively through stereo recording.

Giovanni Gabrieli: *In ecclesiis*

The two outstanding composers of the Venetian school were Andrea Gabrieli (c. 1520–86) and his nephew Giovanni (1557–1612). The latter served his apprenticeship under Lassus and succeeded his uncle as first organist of St. Mark's, a post he held for the last twenty-six years of his life. Giovanni Gabrieli continued his uncle's experiments with polychoral effects. (A *polychoral* work is one written for two or more choirs.) He took full advantage of carefully planned contrasts of soft and loud, comparable to the interplay of colors in Venetian architecture and painting. With his *Sonata pian e forte* he became the first composer in history to use dynamic indications. In an age that was still preoccupied with vocal music, Gabrieli achieved a new kind of balance in sound between voices and instruments, and consistently developed the instrumental side of the art.

His motet *In ecclesiis* is one of a series of *Sacrae symphoniae* (Sacred symphonies) published in Venice in 1615. Its text is nonliturgical; it was probably written for a ceremonial occasion at St. Mark's. The work consists of five verses, each of which concludes with the identical music on the word *Alleluia*. Such a repeated passage—a kind of musical refrain—is known as a *ritornello*, a term that suggests its outstanding feature; it returns throughout the work.

In ecclesiis benedicite Domino. Alleluia! — In the churches bless the Lord. Alleluia!

In omni loco dominationis, / benedic, anima mea, Dominum. Alleluia! — In all places of His dominion, / bless, o my soul, the Lord. Alleluia!

In Deo, salutari meo et gloria mea. / Deus, auxilium meum et spes mea / in Deo est. Alleluia! — In God is my salvation and my glory. / O God, my help and my hope / is in God. Alleluia!

Deus meus, te invocamus, / te adoramus. / Libera nos, salva nos, vivifica nos. Alleluia! — O my God, we call upon You, / we worship You. / Deliver us, save us, give us life. Alleluia!

Deus, adjutor noster, in aeternam. Alleluia! — O God, our refuge in all eternity. Alleluia!

In ecclesiis is a work in fifteen voices: eight vocal, six instrumental, with organ accompaniment. The eight vocal parts may be thought of as constituting a double chorus, even though only the final passage of the work employs the two groups of four voices each. Gabrieli is more interested in contrasting unequal masses of sound. In this way he is able to achieve a texture in which the elements are constantly shifting. The score calls for three cornetts, one viola, and two trombones—a rather strange combination for modern ears. The *cornett*, also known by its Italian name *cornetto*, combined the fingerholes of the woodwinds with the cup-shaped mouthpiece of the brass. Its tube, either straight or curved, was made of wood or ivory. Extremely popular in the fifteenth and sixteenth centuries, the instrument produced a gentle sound that blended well with strings and with the human voice. Modern performances of *In ecclesiis* generally use three trumpets and three trombones accompanied by the organ.

The first verse, in duple meter, is sung by the altos and sopranos of the first chorus against an organ accompaniment. There is a sharp contrast between the breadth and majesty of the opening phrase and the shorter notes on the words *benedicite Domino:*

The Alleluia opens with the second chorus singing in a quicker triple meter that shifts to duple. This beautiful ritornello runs through the work like a unifying thread.

Verse 2 is sung by the tenors and basses in unison accompanied by the organ. Gabrieli repeats the word *dominationis* (dominion) in an ascending sequence that is most effective. The second Alleluia is followed by a brief "Sinfonia" for the six brass instruments—their bright timbres make a marvelous sound—and organ. The festive opening of the Sinfonia is followed by chords in dotted rhythm and a running passage in imitation that ends on an A-major chord.

Verse 3 is a duet between the altos and tenors of the first chorus, accompanied by the brass instruments and organ in constantly shifting combinations. The key words *In deo* (In God) are much repeated; the idea of glory (*gloria mea*) is reflected in the instrumental accompaniment. The setting is mostly syllabic, except for a melisma on the word *meum* in the phrase *auxilium meum* (my help). The rapid changes in the harmony here contribute to the impression of vigorous movement. When the words *in Deo* return at the end of the verse, they are pointed up by imitative counterpoint of a florid kind. The third Alleluia is sung by the altos and tenors of Chorus I against the full Chorus II, accompanied by all the instruments.

Verse 4 is a duet between Soprano I and Tenor I accompanied by the organ. The soprano leads off with an ornate melisma:

Thereupon the two voices engage in an intimate dialogue in which one imitates (or echoes) the other. Like all the previous sections, this one ends on an A-major chord. In the fourth Alleluia the sopranos and tenors of Chorus I are pitted against the full Chorus II. Here the sopranos carry the principal melody line.

The final verse is for the full ensemble—double (eight-part) chorus, instruments, and organ, fortissimo. The affective harmonies unfold with something akin to grandeur; the setting is mostly syllabic. One word is singled out for melismatic treatment: *aeternam* (eternity). The final Alleluia, extended through repetition, leads to a majestic modal cadence that converges on an A-major chord. This brings to an end a work that is both a culminating point of the Renaissance and a harbinger of the Baroque.

The Renaissance Madrigal

In the *madrigal* the Renaissance found one of its chief forms of secular music. The sixteenth-century madrigal was an aristocratic form of poetry-and-music that came to flower at the small Italian courts, where it was a favorite diversion of cultivated amateurs. The text was a short poem of lyric or reflective character, rarely longer than twelve lines, marked by elegance of diction and refinement of sentiment. Conspicuous in it were the affecting words for weeping, sighing, trembling, dying that the Italian madrigalists learned to set with such a wealth of expression. Love and unsatisfied desire were by no means the only topics of the madrigal. Included, too, were humor and satire, political themes, scenes and incidents of city and country life; with the result that the Italian madrigal literature of the sixteenth century presents a vivid panorama of renaissance thought and feeling.

Instruments participated, duplicating or even substituting for the voices. Sometimes only the top part was sung while the other lines were played on instruments. During the first period of the renaissance madrigal—the second quarter of the sixteenth century—the composer's chief concern is to give pleasure to the performers, without much thought to an audience. In the middle phase (c. 1550–80), the renaissance madrigal becomes a conscious art form directed toward the listener. It takes on the elaborateness of concert music, with much contrapuntal imitation and development of musical ideas. Also, there is a closer relationship between words and music.

The final phase of the Italian madrigal (1580–1620) extends beyond the late Renaissance into the world of the Baroque. The form achieves the height of sophistication both in poetry and music. It becomes the direct expression of the composer's personality and feelings. Certain traits are carried to the point of mannerism: rich chromatic harmony, dramatic declamation, vocal virtuosity, and vivid depiction in music of emotional words.

Marenzio: *S'io parto, i' moro*

Luca Marenzio (c. 1553–99) is generally regarded as the greatest master of the Italian madrigal. His contemporaries called this imaginative artist "the divine composer" and "the sweetest swan." Legend has it that Marenzio died of a broken heart. The tale accords with the romantic character of his music.

Marenzio's choice of texts from Dante, Petrarch, Tasso, and other leading Italian poets reveals his fastidious literary taste. His extraordinary feeling for mood and atmosphere, his sensitive declamation, and his mastery of contrapuntal devices—a mastery that did not preclude his responding to the new harmonic style—amply justify his great reputation both during his lifetime and afterward.

Marenzio's madrigal *S'io parto, i' moro* (1594) illustrates his poignantly expressive writing. The piece is in five voices—soprano, alto, two tenors, and bass. The text is set phrase by phrase, in a continuous texture whose flow is defined by frequent cadences. Contrapuntal imitation plays a far less important part in the artistic scheme than was common at the time. Marenzio's piece looks to the future in its chordal style and its direct expressivity. Despite the modal atmosphere, the music foreshadows later harmonic conceptions in its fluctuations from G modal-minor to D major (the Dominant) and to B-flat (the relative major); the final cadence is in the home key. The free plastic rhythm is subtly molded to the words, twice giving rise to a measure in triple instead of duple meter. This plasticity of rhythm is characteristic of renaissance music. The last lines of the poem are repeated to allow for musical expansion.

S'io parto, i' moro, e pur partir conviene.	If I leave, I die; and yet I must leave you.
Morrò dunque, il mio bene, e questa mia partita	I shall die, my treasure, and this departure,
Che mi ti toglie mi torrà la vita.	That tears me from you, will take my life.
Dolorosa partita che m'uccidi.	O sad parting that slays me!
Quei che congiuns' Amor, perche dividi?	Whom love has joined—why must they be parted?

Notice the poignancy of the downward inflection of the soprano on the word *moro* (I die) in the first line. The affective quality of this phrase is heightened

S'io   par - to   i'   mo - ro,

by the rest that precedes it, as though the singer were choking with emotion—an effect much prized in the madrigals of that time. Key words are expanded to give them heightened expressivness: *vita* (life) in the alto part; *m'uccidi* (slays me) in the first tenor, and with a perceptible rise in tension when the word returns in the second tenor part; *perche dividi?* (why must they be parted?) in the alto, then in the second tenor, and in the final phrase again in the alto. Worthy of note is the questioning upward inflection on *perche* (why), which becomes the key word of the closing section.

In Marenzio's madrigal we encounter the intimacy and refinement of a subtle court art: a union of music and poetry as sensitive as it is moving.

Gesualdo: *Moro lasso*

Carlo Gesualdo, Prince of Venosa (c. 1560–1613), one of the most imaginative experimenters in the history of his art, enjoys another distinction that bears no relation to music. When he discovered that his wife was

341

having an affair with a certain Duke of Andria, in true Renaissance fashion he had the lovers murdered. This lamentable event took place in 1590, when Gesualdo was about thirty. His second wife was Leonora d'Este, daughter of the Duke of Ferrara. Although he did not remain faithful to the lady, she appears to have been genuinely saddened at his death.

Gesualdo's unique position among composers derives from the harmonic audacity of his music. In his later compositions he evolved a style of extreme chromaticism that was far in advance of his time. His madrigals exhibit an astonishing directness of expression and emotional power. Their harmonies sound surprisingly fresh and modern. Gesualdo favored brief poems dealing with pain, sorrow, and longing, whose lines he could sculpt into short musical phrases surcharged with feeling. His favorite method is to alternate a texture based on chords with one in which the voices imitate each other rather strictly. This procedure is evident in his celebrated madrigal *Moro lasso*, for soprano, two altos, tenor, and bass (1611).

Moro lasso al mio duolo,	I die, alas! from my pain,
e chi mi può dar vita,	And she who can give me life,
ahi, che m'ancide e non vuol darmi vita.	Alas, kills me and will not give me life.
Moro lasso al mio duolo,	I die, alas! from my pain,
e chi me può dar vita,	And she who can give me life,
ahi, che m'ancide e non vuol darmi aita.	Alas, kills me and will not give me aid.
O dolorosa forte,	O painful fate:
chi dar vita mi può,	She who can give me life,
ahi, mi dà morte.	Alas, gives me death.

The opening chords establish the charged emotional atmosphere of the piece as well as the chromatic progression of its harmonies: In these measures, con-

sisting of a progression of changing chords, the music moves from C-sharp major to A minor. The first line of text is set one note to a syllable. The second line overlaps the first, beginning in the soprano while the other voices are finishing the first. The texture is contrapuntal, the voices entering one after the other in close imitation and without chromaticism. Words are repeated to allow for musical expansion; the first syllable of *vita* (life) is extended over a series of notes.

The third line returns to chromaticism and alternates both kinds of texture. The altos sing an ascending motive while the three other voices sing a descending one, all in imitation; then the voices unite in chords on the phrase *e non vuol darmi vita*, which is repeated as an echo effect. The word *ahi* (alas) creates the sighing effect that was so prized by the madrigalists. We encounter here the intimacy of emotion that has always been associated with chamber music, whether vocal or instrumental. The second stanza of the poem repeats the first except for the last word. Gesualdo accordingly repeats the music, but varies it subtly.

The third stanza is set to new material; hence the form of the madrigal may be described as A-A-B. This section begins with the voices in imitation on *O dolorosa forte*, with its unexpected chromatic inflection on *forte* (fate). The phrase is repeated, but at a higher pitch. *Chi dar vita mi può* is set to chords. Contrapuntal texture returns with the phrase *ahi, mi dà morte*, which is repeated four times. The music maintains the mood of intensely personal lyricism through the final measures.

Gesualdo was an isolated phenomenon in his time; he had no disciples. The twentieth century rediscovered him, and has been fascinated by the originality of his art.

Byrd: *Ego sum panis vivus*

England in the sixteenth century produced a towering figure in the person of William Byrd (1543–1623), one of her greatest composers. This contemporary of Palestrina and Lassus served as organist in the Royal Chapel under Queen Elizabeth. He distinguished himself in every branch of composition known in his day, in religious music as in secular, in vocal as in instrumental.

Byrd's motet *Ego sum panis vivus* (1607) shows the freshness of melody, euphonious harmony, and vigorous rhythms characteristic of the English school.

Ego sum panis vivus	I am the living bread
qui de coelo descendi:	which came down from heaven:
si quis manducaverit ex hoc pane	if any man eat of this bread,
vivet in aeternum. Alleluia.	he shall live forever. Alleluia.
	John 6:51

The soprano enters with a distinctive theme that is imitated at the interval of a fifth below, first by the tenor, then by the bass, and at the interval of a third below—in modified form—by the alto. The following example shows the entrance of the theme in the four voices:

343

The vocal lines avoid every impression of meandering; the harmonic movement is remarkably smooth. Notice that the words of the first phrase are set syllabically up to the key word *vivus* (living), which is extended in melismatic fashion. The words *Ego sum panis vivus* are repeated by all the voices, always with the extension of the first syllable of *vivus*. Byrd follows the method of overlapping that we have observed in the music of this period: a new phrase begins in one voice while the others are finishing the old, thereby assuring a continuous texture. The rhythm in the individual voices is powerful enough to modify the rhythm of the whole, so that in an edition with modern notation we have the unequal measures typical of renaissance music. The text of the second line impels Byrd to "word painting": he consistently sets *coelo* (heaven) to the highest note in the phrase, followed by a downward-moving figure on *descendi* (came down). This is especially effective when the line is repeated.

The thought of eternal life (*vivet in aeternum*) introduces a bar of the lively triple rhythm that the Renaissance associated with joy. This mood is accentuated in the Alleluia that follows, in which smaller note values suggest an accelerated tempo. Byrd adds a fillip to the music by repeating harmonic and melodic patterns in sequence. In addition, the music remains in triple meter for six measures before the basic duple meter is re-established in the final phrase.

The masters of Tudor and Elizabethan church music were forgotten for centuries in their native land. When a national school arose in England at the end of the nineteenth century, their art was resurrected. Thus the music of Byrd and his contemporaries became a seminal influence on the modern English school.

Dowland: *My Thoughts are Wing'd with Hope*

The custom arose during the Renaissance of singing only the top part of a polyphonic vocal piece while three or four melody instruments, preferably viols, played the lower parts; or those might be arranged so that they could be played on an accompanying instrument such as the lute. (The sixteenth-century *lute*, extremely popular in Spain, Italy, France, and England, was a plucked-string instrument that had a round body, a flat neck, one single and five double strings, and a pegbox bent back at an angle. A modern descendent is the mandolin.) Collections of such song arrangements were known as lute song books. Those published in England contained both the polyphonic and solo versions of each song on facing pages, which made it possible to perform the music under various conditions.

The most important member of the English school of lutenists was John Dowland (1563–1626). He was famous throughout Europe both as a performer on the lute and as a singer, and served as court musician to several princes on the Continent, among them Christian IV of Denmark. His final years were spent in England. Dowland's several books of "Songes or Ayres" constitute a milestone in the creation of the art song. The melodic interest in these songs is no longer shared by all the voices, as in a madrigal, but centers about the top part. The accompanying harmonies can either be sung by three voices, or played on a lute; in addition, a bass viol may be used to reinforce the lowest part.

My Thoughts are Wing'd with Hope, from *The First Booke of Songes or Ayres* (1597), is a delightful example of Dowland's art (*ayre* is the old English name for a song or aria). This is a strophic song; Dowland's book included a second and third stanza for which the music was repeated.

> My thoughts are wing'd with hopes, my hopes with love,
> Mount, love, unto the moon in clearest night,
> And say as she doth in the heavens move,
> In earth so wanes and waxeth my delight.
>> And whisper this but softly in her ears,
>> Hope oft doth hang the head, and trust shed tears.

The melody, of the utmost simplicity, has a tender lyricism:

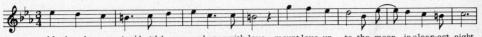

My thoughts are wing'd with hopes, my hopes with love, mount love, un - to the moon_ in clear-est night,

The song unfolds in regular four-bar phrases with a clearly marked cadence at the end of each phrase. Such regularity of structure, allied to the symmetries of folk song and dance, is prophetic of later musical developments. The rhythm established in the first phrase is retained throughout, with subtle variations. Although we do not find here the repetition of material that characterizes the melodies of a later age, the phrases of this song have a high degree of structural unity. In the example shown above, the first three notes of the second phrase duplicate the first three of the opening phrase in sequence, and the pattern returns, syncopated, in the third measure of this phrase. We found that some major-minor tonality coexisted with modal harmony in the early music we have studied thus far. Here the feeling of tonality is unusually strong, supported as it is by Dominant-Tonic cadences. How remarkable to find, on the threshhold of the sixteenth century, a work anticipating so accurately the music of a later age.

Morley: *Sing We and Chant It*

As in the case of the sonnet, England took over the madrigal from Italy and developed it into a native art form. All the brilliance of the Elizabethan age is reflected in the school of madrigalists who flourished in the late sixteenth century and on into the reign of James I. The English madrigal soon developed a character all its own.

Thomas Morley (1557–1603) was one of the chief figures among the first generation of English madrigalists. He was active in cultivating a type of madrigal known as the *ballett* which, imported from Italy, took on a characteristically

English stamp in the hands of the Elizabethans. This was a light choral piece which, as its name implies, was in the character of a dance-song. Where the madrigal was through-composed, the ballett was strophic in structure, the same music being repeated for each stanza. Where the madrigal leaned toward sophistication and subtlety, the ballett favored freshness of feeling, and all the charm and lightness of the popular style. Characteristic of the ballett was the fa-la refrain.

A delightful example of Morley's art is the perennial *Sing We and Chant It*. The first stanza establishes the mood.

> Sing we and chant it, while love doth grant it.
> Fa-la-la-la-la-la, fa-la-la-la.
> Not long youth lasteth, and old age hasteth.
> Now is best leisure to take our pleasure.
> Fa-la fa-la la-la-la.
> Fa-la fa-la la-la-la.

This is a ballett for five voices—two sopranos, alto, tenor bass—in binary form, in a mixture of duple and triple meter taken at a lively pace. This flexibility of rhythm contributes to the charm and vitality of the music, as does the rhythmic variety in the different parts. The regular structure of four-bar phrases

indicates the dance character of the piece. For variety there is a three-bar phrase in the last line—a charming asymmetry—followed by one of four bars. The harmonizing in parallel thirds (between the two sopranos) was typical of English choral song. The chordal texture shows the predominantly harmonic nature of popular music, which from this time on was to exert an increasing influence upon the "learned" contrapuntal style. With its unpretentiousness and spontaneity, its pastoral charm and lilting rhythm, this piece is in the finest vein of English lyricism.

Gibbons: *The Silver Swan*

The second generation of madrigalists included such masters as Thomas Weelkes (c. 1575–1623), John Wilbye (1574–1638), and Orlando Gibbons (1583–1625). Gibbons is one of the greatest of English church composers. He was less active as a madrigalist than most of his contemporaries. His work in this area is contained in a single volume, published in 1612 as *The First*

Set of Madrigals and Mottets of 5. Parts: apt for Viols and Voyces. The inclusion in the title of "and Mottets" was unusual, and indicates the serious character of the volume. Its first number, *The Silver Swan,* became the most celebrated madrigal of the period.

> The silver swan who living had no note,
> When death approached unlocked her silent throat:
> Leaning her breast against the reedy shore
> Thus sung her first and last, and sung no more:
> "Farewell all joys, O death come close mine eyes,
> More geese than swans now live, more fools than wise."

Although quite short and simply written, *The Silver Swan* reveals the finely-spun fabric of Gibbons's art. The madrigal unfolds with the full-throated lyricism—of a decidedly contemplative cast—that was native to this composer's

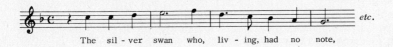

The sil - ver swan who, liv - ing, had no note,

style. Characteristic are the overlapping phrases, the plasticity of rhythm, the modal harmony, the melodious counterpoint that flows effortlessly within a chordal texture, and the compact formal frame that bespeaks a master of the miniature. Gibbons pits the five mixed voices against one another—sometimes two against three—in a highly effective manner. The distribution of the text is exceedingly artful. After the opening chords, the voices rarely sing the same word together; which enables the composer to make a capital effect when they do, as on the final word of four of the six lines: *note, shore, more,* and *wise.* The music communicates its message despite the emotional reserve with which this is stated. It speaks well for the taste of the age that so subtle a work should have achieved such enormous popularity.

England's madrigals remain a rich legacy of her golden age. Their enchanting strains still echo through the choral pieces of English composers today.

62 The Baroque

"Nothing is beautiful but the true. The true alone is to be loved."
Boileau (1636–1711)

The period of the Baroque stretched across a turbulent century and a half of European history. It opened shortly before the year 1600, a convenient signpost

Michelangelo (1475–1564), CREATION OF THE SUN AND THE MOON (Sistine Chapel, Vatican City).
The emergence of the Baroque style is seen in the swirling draperies and dramatic gestures of Michelangelo's figures.

that need not be taken too literally; and may be regarded as having come to a close with the death of Bach in 1750.

The term *baroque* was probably derived from the Portuguese *barroco*, a pearl of irregular shape much used in the jewelry of the time. The century and a half of baroque art divides itself into three fifty-year periods; early, middle, and late Baroque. Since public interest until recently concentrated on the late phase, many came to think of Bach and Handel as the first great composers. Viewed against the total panorama of their era, these masters are seen rather to have been the heirs of an old and surpassingly rich tradition.

The period 1600–1750 was a time of change and adventure. The conquest of the New World stirred the imagination and filled the coffers of the Old. The middle classes gathered wealth and power in their struggle against the aristocracy. Empires clashed for mastery of the world. Appalling poverty and wasteful luxury, magnificent idealism and savage oppression—against contradictions such as these unfolded the pomp and splendor of baroque art: an art bold of gesture and conception; vigorous, decorative, monumental.

The transition from the classically minded Renaissance to the Baroque was foreshadowed by Michelangelo (1475–1564). His turbulent figures, their torsos twisted in struggle, reflect the baroque love of the dramatic. In like fashion the Venetian school of painters—Titian, Tintoretto, Veronese—captured the dynamic spirit of the new age. Their crowded canvases are ablaze with color and movement. They glory in the tension of opposing masses. They dramatize the diagonal.

The Baroque was the era of absolute monarchy. Princes throughout Europe took as their model the splendor of Versailles. Louis XIV's famous "I am the State!" summed up a way of life in which all art and culture served the cult of

The Court of Honor of Louis XIII, Versailles.
The palace of the French kings became a model for the rest of Europe.

the ruler. Courts large and small maintained elaborate musical establishments including opera troupes, chapel choirs, and orchestras. Baroque opera, the favorite diversion of the aristocracy, aimed at a lofty pathos that left no room for the frailties of ordinary men. It centered about the gods and heroes of antiquity, in whom the occupant of the royal box and his courtiers found a flattering likeness of themselves.

The Baroque was also an age of reason. Adventurers more bold than the conquistadors set forth upon the uncharted sea of knowledge. The findings of Kepler, Galileo, and Copernicus in physics and astronomy, of Descartes in mathematics and Spinoza in philosophy were so many milestones in the intellectual history of Europe. Harvey discovered the circulation of the blood. Locke laid the foundation for a scientific study of the workings of the mind. Newton's theory of gravitation revealed a universe based upon law and order. Descartes expressed the confidence of a brave new age when he wrote, "Provided only that we abstain from receiving anything as true which is not so, there can be nothing so remote that we cannot reach it, nor so obscure that we cannot discover it."

Excluded from the salons of the aristocracy, the middle classes created a culture of their own. Their music-making centered about the home, the church, and the university group (known as *collegium musicum*). For them came into being the comic opera which, like the prose novel, was filled with keen and witty observation of life. For them painting forsook its grandiose themes and turned to intimate scenes of bourgeois life. The leaders of the Dutch school—Vermeer, Frans Hals, Ruysdael—embodied the vitality of a new burgher art that reached its high point in Rembrandt (1609–69), a master whose insights penetrated the recesses of the soul. Under the leadership of merchant princes and financiers,

349

Jan Vermeer (1632–75), LADY WITH A LUTE. (The Metropolitan Museum of Art, New York; Bequest of Collis P. Huntington, 1925)

The masters of the Dutch school turned to intimate scenes of middle-class life.

the culture of the city came to rival that of the palace. These new connoisseurs vied with the court in their love of splendor, responding to the opulence of baroque art, to the sensuous beauty of brocade and velvet, marble and jewels and precious metals. This aspect of the Baroque finds expression in the art of Peter Paul Rubens (1577–1640), whose canvases exude a driving energy, a reveling in life. His voluptuous nudes incarnate the seventeenth-century ideal of feminine beauty. He himself was a symbol of the rising order: rugged individualist, dreamer, and man of action; entrepreneur and conqueror all in one.

The Baroque was an intensely devout period. Religion was a rallying cry on some of the bloodiest battlefields in history. The Protestant camp included England, Scandinavia, Holland, and the north German cities, all citadels of the rising middle class. On the Catholic side were the two powerful dynasties, Hapsburg and Bourbon, who fought one another no less fiercely than they did their Protestant foes. After decades of struggle, the might of the Spanish-Hapsburg empire was broken. France emerged as the leading state on the Continent;

Lorenzo Bernini (1598–1680), THE ECSTASY OF ST. THERESA OF AVILA. (Church of Santa Maria della Vittoria, Rome) *The theatricality of the Baroque is brilliantly manifested in Bernini's famous altarpiece.*

Germany was in ruins; England rose to world power. Europe was ready to advance to the stage of modern industrial society.

Protestant culture was rooted in the Bible. Its emphasis upon the individual promoted a personal tone and strengthened the romantic tendency in the Baroque. Milton (1608–74) in *Paradise Lost* produced the poetic epic of the Protestant world view, even as Dante three and a half centuries earlier had produced that of the Catholic in *The Divine Comedy*. The heroic hymn tunes of the Reformation nourished the profoundly spiritual art of Bach. The oratorios of Handel harnessed baroque splendor to an ethical ideal. The two composers mark the supreme musical achievement of the Protestant spirit.

The Catholic world for its part tried to retrieve the losses inflicted by Luther's secession. The Counter-Reformation mobilized all the forces of the church militant. The Jesuits, recognizing faith to be a matter of the whole personality, strove to fire the hearts and minds and senses of the faithful. They made music, sculpture, architecture, painting, and even the theater arts tributary to their purpose. The rapturous mysticism of the Counter-Reformation found expression in the canvases of El Greco (c. 1542–1614). His elongated ash-gray figures, bathed in an unearthly light, are creatures of a visionary mind that distorts the real in its search for a reality beyond. Baroque theatricalism and pathos came to fullness in the sculptor Lorenzo Bernini (1598–1680). His famous *Ecstasy of St. Theresa* captures in marble all the restlessness and dramatic quality of the Baroque.

Between the conflicting currents of absolute monarchy and rising bourgeois power, Reformation and Counter-Reformation, the Baroque fashioned its grandiose art. Alien to its spirit were restraint and detachment. Rather it achieved its ends through violent opposition of forces, lavish creativity, and abandon. With these went the capacity to organize a thousand details into a monumental, overpowering whole.

The artist played a variety of roles in baroque society. He might be an ambassador and intimate of princes, as were Rubens and Van Dyck; or a priest, as was Vivaldi; or a political leader, like Milton. He functioned under royal or princely patronage, as did Corneille and Racine; or, like Bach, was in the employ of a church or free city. To the aristocrats whom he served he might be little more than a purveyor of elegant entertainment, Yet, beneath the obsequious manner and fawning dedications demanded by the age, there was often to be found a spirit that dared to probe all existing knowledge and shape new worlds; a voice addressing itself to those who truly listened—a voice that was indeed "the trumpet of a prophecy."

63 Main Currents in Baroque Music

"The end of all good music is to affect the soul."
Claudio Monteverdi

The Emergence of Opera

With the transition from Renaissance to Baroque came a momentous change: the shifting of interest from a texture of several independent parts of equal importance to music in which a single melody predominated; that is, from polyphonic to homophonic texture. The new style, which originated in vocal music, was named *monody*—literally, "one song," music for one singer with instrumental accompaniment. (Monody is not to be confused with monophony, see p. 307.) The year 1600 is associated with the emergence of the monodic style. Like many such milestones, the date merely indicates the coming to light of a process that was long preparing.

The victory of the monodic style was achieved by a group of Florentine writers, artists, and musicians known as the Camerata, a name derived from the Italian word for "salon." Among their numbers were Vincenzo Galilei, father of the astronomer Galileo, and the composers Jacopo Peri and Giulio Caccini. The men of the Camerata were aristocratic humanists. Their aim was to resurrect the musical-dramatic art of ancient Greece. Since almost nothing was known of the music of the Athenian tragedy, they imagined it in terms of their own needs and desires. Instead of resurrecting something dead the Camerata came forth with an idea that was very much alive.

This idea was that music must heighten the emotional power of the text. The Florentine humanists dreamed of bringing their music into close relationship with poetry, and through poetry with life itself. "I endeavored," wrote Caccini in 1602, "the imitation of the conceit of the words, seeking out the chords more or less passionate according to the meaning." Thus came into being what its inventors regarded as the *stile rappresentativo* (representational style), consisting of a recitative that moved freely over a foundation of simple chords.

The Camerata soon realized that the representational style could be applied not only to a poem but to an entire drama. In this way they were led to the invention of opera, considered by many to be the single most important achievement of baroque music. The first complete opera that has come down to us, *Euridice*, was presented in 1600 at the marriage of Henry IV of France to Maria de' Medici. The libretto was by Ottavio Rinuccini, the music by Peri (with the addition of some passages by Caccini).

The Camerata appeared at a time when it became necessary for music to free itself from the complexities of counterpoint. The year 1600, like the year 1900, bristled with discussions about *le nuove musiche*—"the new music" and what its adherents proudly named the *expressive style*. As sometimes happens with inventors, the noble amateurs of the Florentine salon touched off more than they realized.

The Figured Bass

The melody-and-chords of the New Music was far removed from the intricate interweaving of voices in the old. Since musicians were soon familiar with the basic harmony, it became unnecessary to write the chords out in full. Instead the composer put a numeral, indicating the harmony required, above or below the bass note. For example, the figure 6 under a bass note indicated a chord whose root lay a sixth above the note. Thus, a 6 below the note A called for the F major or minor triad. The application of this principle on a large scale resulted in "the most successful system of musical shorthand ever devised"—the *figured bass* or *thorough-bass*. (From *basso continuo*, a continuous bass, "thorough" being the old form of "through.") The actual filling in and elaboration of the harmony was left to the performer. A similar practice obtains in jazz music today, where the player elaborates on the harmonies from the skeletal version on the page.

So important was this practice for a century and a half that the Baroque is often referred to as the period of thorough-bass. The figured bass required at least two players: one to perform the bass line on a bass instrument: cello, double bass, or bassoon, and the other to fill in or "realize" the chords on a harmonic instrument such as harpsichord, organ, lute, or guitar.

The shorthand of figured-bass writing was particularly valuable at a time when printing was an involved and costly process. Since most works were intended for a single occasion or season they were left in manuscript, the parts being copied out by hand. It was a boon to composers to be able to present their music in abbreviated fashion, knowing that the performers would fill in the necessary details. When we read of an old master producing hundreds of cantatas and dozens of operas, we may be sure that "there were giants in the earth in those days." But the thorough-bass helped.

The Major-Minor System

The Baroque witnessed one of the most significant changes in all music history: the transition from the medieval church modes to major-minor tonality. As music turned from vocal counterpoint to instrumental harmony, it demanded a simplification of the harmonic system. The various church modes gave way to two standard scales: major and minor. With the establishment of major-minor tonality, the thrust to the keynote or *do* became the most powerful force in music.

Now each chord could assume its function in relation to the key center. Composers of the Baroque soon learned to exploit the opposition between the chord of rest, the I (Tonic), and the active chord, the V (Dominant). So, too, the movement from home key to contrasting key and back became an important element in the shaping of musical structure. Composers developed larger forms of instrumental music than had ever been known before.

Important in this transition was a major technical advance. Due to a curious quirk of nature, keyboard instruments tuned according to the scientific laws of acoustics (first discovered by the ancient Greek philosopher Pythagoras) give a pure sound for keys with signatures of up to three flats or sharps, but the intervals become increasingly out-of-tune as more sharps or flats are added. As instrumental music acquired greater prominence, it became more and more important to be able to play in all the keys. In the seventeenth century, a discovery was made: by slightly mis-tuning the intervals within the octave—and thereby spreading the discrepancy evenly among all keys—it became possible to play in every major and minor key without unpleasant results. This adjustment is known as *equal temperament*. It increased the range of harmonic possibilities available to the composer, as Johann Sebastian Bach demonstrated in *The Well-Tempered Clavier*, whose two volumes each contain a Prelude and Fugue in every one of the twelve major and twelve minor keys. Equal temperament made the major-minor system at last a completely flexible medium of expression.

The growing harmonic sense brought about a freer handling of dissonance. Baroque musicians used dissonant chords for emotional intensity and color. In the setting of poetry the composer heightened the impact of an expressive word through dissonance. Such harmonic freedom could not fail to shock the conservatives. The Italian theorist Artusi, writing in 1600 *On the Imperfections of Modern Music*—an attack on Monteverdi and his fellow innovators—rails against those musicians who "are harsh to the ear, offending rather than delighting it," and who "think it within their power to corrupt, spoil, and ruin the good old rules."

The major-minor system emphasized the distinction between the tones included in the key, that is, the diatonic tones, and the five foreign or chromatic tones. Baroque composers associated moods of well-being with diatonic harmony, anguish with chromatic.

The major-minor system was the collective achievement of several generations of musicians. It expressed a new dynamic culture. By dividing the world of sound into definite areas and regulating the movement from one to the other, it enabled the composer to mirror the exciting interplay of forces in the world about him.

64 Further Aspects of Baroque Music

"Musick hath 2 ends, first to pleas the sence, & that is done by the pure Dulcor of Harmony, & secondly to move ye affections or excite passion."

Roger North: *The Musicall Grammarian* (1728)

The Doctrine of the Affections

Now that man was become the measure of all things, there was much speculation concerning the passions and affections, by which were meant the deep-lying forces that determine our emotional life. It was realized that these are peculiarly responsive to music. The *doctrine of the affections* related primarily to the union of music and poetry, where the mental state was made explicit by the text. The Baroque developed an impressive technique of what is known as tone painting, in which the music vividly mirrored the words. Ideas of movement and direction—stepping, running, leaping, ascending, descending—were represented graphically through the movement of the melody and rhythm. Bach exhorted his pupils to "play the chorale according to the meaning of the words." He associates the idea of resurrection with a rising line. The sorrow of the Crucifixion is symbolized by a bass line that may descend stepwise along the chromatic scale. Temptation is allied to a sinuous theme that suggests the serpent. Once the musical figure is brought into being, it abandons its picture quality and becomes abstract musical material to be developed according to purely musical procedures. In short, the imagination of the pure musician takes over.

This supremacy of music shows itself in two traits that strike the listener when he hears the vocal literature of the Baroque. In the first place, lines, phrases, and individual words are repeated over and over again in order to allow room for the necessary musical expansion. This practice springs from the realization that music communicates more slowly than words and needs more time in which to establish its meaning. In the second place, a single syllable will be extended to accommodate all the notes of an expressive melodic line, so that the word is stretched beyond recognition (the style of setting known as melismatic). Thus, the music born of words ends by swallowing up the element that gave it birth.

In instrumental music the practice took root of building a piece on a single mood—the basic "affection." This was established at the outset by a striking musical subject out of which grew the entire composition. In this way composers discovered the imperious gesture that opens a piece of baroque music, of a tension and pathos that pervade the whole movement.

Rhythm in Baroque Music

The Baroque, with its fondness for energetic movement, demanded a dynamic rhythm based on the regular recurrence of accent. The bass part became the carrier of the new rhythm. Its relentless beat is an arresting trait in many compositions of the Baroque. This steady pulsation, once under way, never slackens or deviates until the goal is reached. It imparts to baroque music its unflagging drive, producing the same effect of turbulent yet controlled motion as animates baroque painting, sculpture, and architecture.

Composers became ever more aware of the capacity of the instruments for rhythm. They found that a striking dance rhythm could serve as the basis for an extended piece, vocal or instrumental. Popular and court dances furnished an invigorating element to musical art. Nor, in that stately age, were the rhythms necessarily lively. Idealized dance rhythms served as the basis for tragic arias and great polyphonic works. In a time when courtiers listened to music primarily for entertainment, composers dressed up a good part of their material in dance rhythms. Many a dance piece served to make palatable a profounder discourse. In effect, rhythm pervaded the musical conception of the Baroque and helped it capture the movement and drive of a vibrant era.

Continuous Melody

The elaborate scrollwork of baroque architecture bears witness to an abundance of energy that would not leave an inch of space unornamented. Its musical counterpart is to be found in one of the main elements of baroque style—the principle of continuous expansion. A movement based on a single affection will start off with a striking musical figure that unfolds through a process of ceaseless spinning out. In this regard the music of the Baroque differs from that of the classical era, with its balanced phrases and cadences. It is constantly in motion, in the act of becoming. When its energy is spent, the work comes to an end.

In vocal music the melody of the Baroque was imbued with the desire always to heighten the impact of the words. Wide leaps and the use of chromatic tones served to emphasize the affections. There resulted a noble melody whose spacious curves outlined a style of grand expressiveness and pathos.

Terraced Dynamics

Baroque music does not know the constant fluctuation of volume that marks the classic-romantic style. The music moves at a fairly constant level of sonority. A passage uniformly loud will be followed by one uniformly soft, creating the effect of light and shade. The shift from one level to the other has come to be known as *terraced dynamics* and is a characteristic feature of the baroque style.

The composer of the classic-romantic era who desired greater volume of tone directed each instrument to play louder. The baroque composer wrote instead for a larger number of players. The classic-romantic musician used the crescendo as a means of expression within a passage. The baroque composer found his main source of expression in the contrast between a soft passage and a loud—that is, between the two terraces of sound. Each passage became an area of solid color set off against the next. This conception shapes the structure of the music, endowing it with a monumental simplicity. (Probably, in performance, singers and players used the crescendo and decrescendo more than we think.)

It follows that baroque composers were much more sparing of expression marks than those who came after. The music of the period carries little else than an occasional forte or piano, leaving it to the player to supply whatever else may be necessary.

Two-Part Form

Two-part or binary (A-B) form played an important role in baroque music. This is the question-and-answer type of structure found, in its simplest form, in a tune such as *London Bridge*. The principle gave rise to a tightly knit structure in which the A part moved from home to contrasting key while the B part made the corresponding move back. Both parts used closely related or even identical material. The form was made apparent to the ear by the modulation and a full stop at the end of the first part. As a rule each part was repeated, giving an A-A: B-B structure.

In three-part form contrast is injected by the middle section. Binary form, on the other hand, is all of a piece of texture and mood. It embodies a single affection, for which reason it was favored by a musical style based on continuous expansion. Binary form prevailed in the short harpsichord pieces of dance character that were produced in quantities during the seventeenth and early eighteenth centuries. It was a standard type in the suite, one of the favorite instrumental forms of the Baroque.

The Ground Bass

The principle of unity in variety expressed itself in an important procedure of baroque music, the *ground bass* or *basso ostinato* ("obstinate bass"). This consisted of a short phrase that was repeated over and over in the bass while the upper voices pursued their independent courses. With each repetition of the bass, some aspect of melody, harmony, and/or rhythm would be changed. The upper voices were frequently improvised. Thus the ostinato supplied a fixed framework within which the composer's imagination disported itself. Baroque musicians developed a masterful technique of variation and embellishment over the ground bass.

The ostinato is extremely effective both as a unifying device and as a means of building tension. Later we shall find it playing an important part in twentieth-century music.

Instrumental Color

The Baroque was the first period in history in which instrumental music was comparable in importance to vocal. The interest in this branch of the art stimulated the development of new instruments and the perfecting of old. The spirit of the age demanded increased brilliancy of tone. The gentle lute was ousted by the less subtle guitar. The reserved viol with its "still music," as Shakespeare called it, was supplanted by the more resonant violin. Baroque music made generous use of trumpet, trombone, flute, oboe, and bassoon. On the whole, composers thought in terms of line, so that a string instrument, a woodwind, and a brass might be assigned to play the same line in the counterpoint. Besides, since a movement was based on a single affection, the same instrumental color might be allowed to prevail throughout, as opposed to the practice of the classical and romantic periods when color was constantly changed. Much music was still performed by whatever instruments happened to be available at a particular time and place. At the same time composers—especially in the late Baroque—chose instruments more and more for their color. They specified ever more clearly what instruments were to play a particular work, with the result that music moved steadily toward an art of orchestration.

Virtuosity and Improvisation

The interest in instruments went hand in hand with a desire to master their technique. Virtuosity on the organ and harpsichord, violin and trumpet had its counterpart in the opera house in a phenomenal vocal technique that has never been surpassed.

Technical mastery brought a growing awareness of what each instrument could do best, and with it a heightened sense of style. Composers differentiated ever more clearly among the various styles: vocal and instrumental; church, theater, chamber; keyboard, string, woodwind, brass. At the same time they were given to mixing the styles. It was part of the baroque straining for effect to cause one medium to take over the qualities of another: to make Dresden china imitate the daintiness of lace, wrought iron the curl of leaves and flowers. In like fashion instrumental music copied the brilliant coloratura of the voice, while vocal music emulated the arabesques of the instruments. Church music used to advantage the dramatic style of opera and the rhythms of the dance. The delicate ornamentation of harpsichord music influenced the writing for strings. Organ sonority affected the style of the orchestra. Each nourished the other, to the enrichment of all.

Improvisation played a prominent part in the musical practice of the Baroque. The realizing of the thorough-bass would have been impossible if musicians of the period had not been ready to "think with their fingers." A church organist was expected as a matter of course to be able to improvise an intricate contrapuntal piece. The ability in this regard of great organists such as Bach and Handel was legendary. This abandonment to the inspiration of the moment suited the rhapsodic temper of the Baroque, and even influenced the art of composition. Many passages in the fantasias and toccatas of the time, with their abrupt changes of mood, bear the mark of extemporaneous speech.

Improvisation functioned in baroque music also in another way. The singer or player was expected to add his own embellishments to what was written down (as is the custom today in jazz). This was his creative contribution to the work. The practice was so widespread that baroque music sounded altogether different in performance from what it looked like on paper.

Keyboard Instruments

The three important keyboard instruments of the Baroque were the organ, the harpsichord, and the clavichord. The baroque organ had a pure, transparent tone. Its stops did not blend the colors into a symphonic cloudburst, as is the case with the twentieth-century organ, but let the voices stand out clearly so that the ear could follow the counterpoint. The colors of the various stops contrasted sharply; but, although the tone was penetrating, it was not harsh because the wind pressure was low. Through the use of two keyboards it was possible to achieve even levels of soft and loud.

A harpsichord (by Johann Adolph Hass, Hamburg, ca. 1770; Yale University Collection of Musical Instruments)

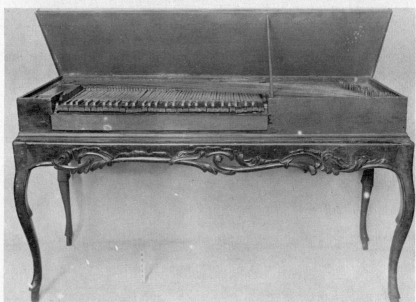

A clavichord (The Metropolitan Museum of Art, New York; The Crosby Brown Collection of Musical Instruments, 1889)

The harpsichord too was capable of terraced dynamics because of its two keyboards. The instrument differed from the piano in two important respects. First, its strings were plucked by quills instead of being struck with hammers. The resultant tone was bright and silvery, but it could not be sustained like the tone of the piano. There had to be continual movement in the sound: trills, embellishments of all kinds, chords broken up into arpeggio patterns, and the like. Second, the pressure of the fingers on the keys varied the tone only slightly on the harpsichord, whereas the piano has a wide range of dynamics. The harpsichord was therefore incapable of the crescendo and decrescendo that became so essential a feature of classic-romantic music. But it was an ideal medium for contrapuntal music, for it brought out the inner voices with luminous clarity. It lent itself to a grand manner of playing that on the one hand was elevated and dramatic, on the other, rhythmically precise, refined, and playful. It was immensely popular during the Baroque as a solo instrument. In addition, the harpsichord was indispensable in the realization of the thorough-bass, and was the mainstay of the ensemble in chamber music and at the opera house.

The clavichord consisted of a wooden oblong box, from two to five feet long, that rested on legs or on a table. The strings were set vibrating by small brass wedges known as tangents. Dynamic gradations were possible, within a limited range, through pressure on the keys. Clavichord tone was tender, subtle, intimate. It was, however, a small tone. By the end of the eighteenth century both clavichord and harpsichord had been supplanted in public favor by the piano.

The word "clavier" (or "klavier") was used in Germany as the general term for keyboard instruments, including harpsichord, clavichord, and organ. Whether a certain piece was intended for one rather than the other must often be gathered from the style rather than the title. In any event, the rendering of Bach's *Wohltemperiertes Clavier* as "Well-Tempered Clavichord" is misleading. Closer to the mark is "Well-Tempered Clavier."

65 Claudio Monteverdi

"The modern composer builds upon the foundation of truth."

The innovations of the Florentine Camerata awaited the composer who would infuse life into them and enrich them with the resources of the past. That composer was Claudio Monteverdi (1567–1643), in whom the dramatic spirit of the Baroque found its first spokesman.

His Life and Music

Monteverdi spent twelve fruitful years at the court of the Duke of Mantua. In 1613 he was appointed choirmaster of St. Mark's in Venice, and retained the post until his death thirty years later. Into his operas and ballets, madrigals and religious works he injected an emotional intensity that was new to music. The new-born lyric drama of the Florentines he welded into a coherent musical form and tightened their shapeless recitative into an expressive line imbued with drama. He originated what he called the *stile concitato* (agitated style) to express the hidden tremors of the soul, introducing such novel sound-effects as tremolo and pizzicato as symbols of passion. Monteverdi aspired above all to make his music express the emotional content of poetry. "The text," he declared, "should be the master of the music, not the servant."

Monteverdi used dissonance and instrumental color for dramatic expressiveness, atmosphere, and suspense. He emphasized the contrast between characters by abrupt changes of key. He held that rhythm is bound up with emotion. A master of polyphonic writing, he retained in his choruses the great contrapuntal tradition of the past. There resulted a nobly pathetic art rooted in the verities of human nature. The characters in his music dramas were neither puppets nor abstractions, but men and women who gave vent to their joys and sorrows through song. When his patron the Duke of Mantua suggested a libretto on a

Claudio Monteverdi.
(Collection André Meyer)

mythological subject of the kind fashionable at the time—a dialogue of the winds—the composer of *Orfeo* (1607) and of *Arianna* (1608) protested: "How shall I be able to imitate the speaking of winds that do not speak; and how shall I be able to move the affections by such means? Arianna was moving because she was a woman, and likewise Orfeo was moving because he was a man and not a wind. The harmonies imitate human beings, not the noise of winds, the bleating of sheep, the neighing of horses."

Tu se' morta from *Orfeo*

The qualities of Monteverdi's art are well exemplified in the recitative from *Orfeo* (Orpheus), *Tu se' morta*. Orfeo, having learned of Eurydice's death, decides to follow her to the nether regions:

Tu se' morta, se' morta, mia vita,	You are dead, dead, my darling,
ed io respiro; tu se' da me partita,	And I live; you have left me,
se' da me partita per mai più,	Left me forevermore,
mai più non tornare, ed io rimango—	Never to return, yet I remain—
nò, nò, che se i versi alcuna cosa ponno,	No, no, if verses have any power,
n'andrò sicuro al più profondi abissi,	I shall go boldly to the deepest abysses,
e intenerito il cor del rè dell'ombre,	And having softened the heart of the king of shadows,
meco trarotti a riverder le stelle,	Will take you with me to see again the stars,
o se ciò negherammi empio destino,	Or if cruel fate will deny me this,
rimarrò teco in compagnia di morte!	I will remain with you in the presence of death!
addio terra, addio cielo, e sole, addio.	Farewell earth, farewell sky, and sun, farewell.

The recitative is accompanied by a small organ and a bass lute that realizes the harmonies. With what economy of means Monteverdi transforms the text into a grandly pathetic declamation! The vocal line is the epitome of simplicity,

yet it floods the words with emotion. Notice how the repetition of key words and phrases heightens the pathos; how the voice descends on the words *profondi abissi* (deepest abysses), and rises again on the phrase *meco trarotti a riverder le stelle* (will take you with me to see again the stars). The harmony is for the most part composed of simple triads, with dissonances used sparingly to generate tension. Chromatic intervals and an occasional wide leap project the tragic mood. Wholly Italian is the sensitivity to the beauty and affective power of the voice. Wholly Monteverdian is the poignancy of the emotion conveyed, a poignancy that music henceforth was never to forget.

When an art form genuinely reflects the soul of a nation, its history manifests a striking unity of outlook and achievement. From Monteverdi the heritage descends through two hundred and fifty years of Italian opera to Giuseppe Verdi. In the plaint of Orfeo we hear the throb of passion, the profoundly human quality that echoes in more familiar guise through the measures of *Aïda* and *Otello*.

Zefiro torna

Monteverdi's madrigals span the transition from Renaissance to Baroque. They assimilated the techniques of the new style, such as an instrumental accompaniment with basso continuo, recitative, and the expressive melody of the newly created opera.

The poem of *Zefiro torna* (1632) is by Ottavio Rinuccini, the librettist of *Arianna*. This madrigal is not to be confused with another of the same title that Monteverdi wrote to a sonnet by Petrarch.

Zefiro torna e di soavi accenti	The West Wind returns and with gentle accents
L'aer fa grato e'l piè discioglie a l'onde,	Makes the air pleasant and quickens one's step,
E mormorando tra le verdi fronde,	And, murmuring among the green branches,
Fa danzar al bel suon su'l prato i fiori;	Makes the meadow flowers dance to its lovely sound.
Inghirlandato il crin Fillide e Clori,	With garlands in their hair Phyllis and Clorinda
Note temprando amor care e gioconde;	Are sweet and joyous while Love makes music,
E da monti e da valli ime e profonde,	And from the mountains and valleys hidden deep,
Raddoppian l'armonia gli antri canori.	The echoing caves redouble the harmony.
Sorge più vaga in ciel l'aurora el Sole,	At dawn the sun rises in the sky more gracefully,
Sparge più luci d'or, più puro argento,	Spreads abroad more golden rays, a purer silver,
Fregia di Teti più il bel ceruleo manto.	Adorns the sea with an even lovelier blue mantle.
Sol io per selve abbandonate e sole,	Only I am abandoned and alone in the forest,
L'ardor di due begli occhi el mio tormento,	The ardor of two beautiful eyes is my torment:
Come vuol mia ventura hor piango, hor canto.	As my fate may decree, now I weep, now I sing.

Among the works of Monteverdi's mature years, *Zefiro torna* stands out for its lightness of mood and a lyric charm inspired by the nature images in the poem. It is a duet for two tenors (or sopranos), accompanied by a viola da gamba that

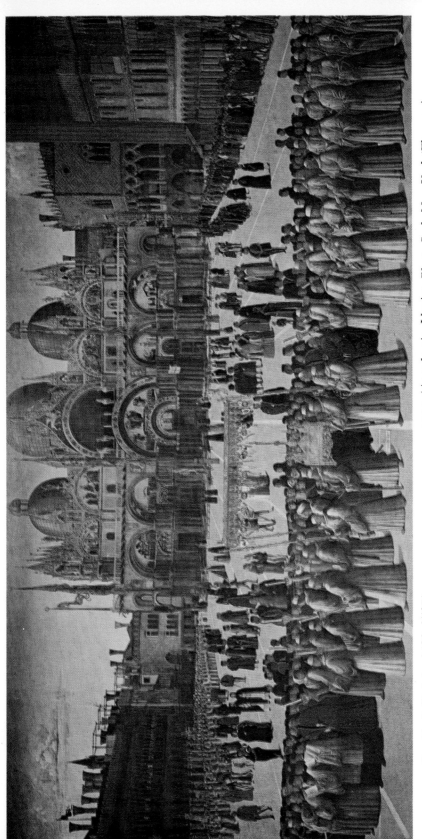

Gentile Bellini (c. 1429–1507), PROCESSION IN PIAZZA SAN MARCO (Accademia, Venice; Photo Scala New York/Florence)

Venetian painters captured in their canvases the splendid pageantry of their city.

Leonardo da Vinci (1452–1519), THE VIRGIN AND CHILD WITH SAINT ANNE (The Louvre, Paris)

The Renaissance created unified space and the simultaneous seeing of the whole. It discovered the landscape, created the illusion of distance, and opened up endless vistas upon the physical loveliness of the world.

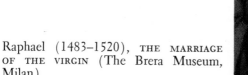

Raphael (1483–1520), THE MARRIAGE OF THE VIRGIN (The Brera Museum, Milan)

plays the bass line, and a harpsichord that realizes the harmonies. The bass part consists of a two-bar motive that is repeated fifty-six times in succession, and then recurs five more times toward the end. Over this basso ostinato Monteverdi releases a flow of melody that moves forward in a continuous evolution, each phrase growing inevitably out of the one before.

Since only two voices are involved, each takes on greater profile than would be the case in a madrigal for three, four, or more voices. In certain passages Monteverdi distributes the melody between the two voices, so that they seem to be sharing a single melodic line. This occurs in the opening measures:

At times the two voices imitate one another; or they harmonize, sometimes in the mellifluous thirds and sixths that were to become a staple of Italian opera. Characteristic is the repetition of important words and phrases, such as the first two words of the poem. Also the expansion of basic words across a succession of notes (melismatic setting), especially if the meaning justifies this: for example, *l'aer* (the air) in line 2, and *mormorando* (murmuring) in line 3. *Fa danzar al bel suon su'l prato* (makes the meadow flowers dance...) inspires the dance-like rhythm in triple meter that pervades the piece.

Striking is the gradual ascent on the repeated word *note* (notes—that is, music) in line 2 of the second stanza, as if Love were slow in striking up his lyre. The next line impels the master to tone painting: on *monti* (mountains), the first tenor part leaps upward, on *valli* (valleys), the second as precipitously descends. The image of echoing caves in line 4 is reflected in the alternation of loud and soft. Rather than depend on the performers for this echo effect, Monteverdi wrote the words forte and piano into the score. *Ciel* (sky) and *aurora* (dawn), in the opening line of the third stanza, are set on the highest notes of the phrase. Notice how the melodic line ascends on *Sole*, to suggest the rising of the sun.

With the final stanza the personal pronoun enters the picture: *Sol io per selve abbandonate e sole* (Only I am abandoned and alone in the forest). Here the mood changes abruptly; the flowing madrigal style gives way to operatic recitative and a considerably slower tempo. The music passes from G major, which has predominated until this point, to E modal-major, whence it moves through a series of changing harmonies back to the home key. It is amazing how much dramatic power Monteverdi is able to achieve through a simple recitative supported by chords.

365

The recitative continues through the first phrase of the last line: *come vuol mia ventura hor piango* (as my fate may decree, now I weep), sung in succession by the two voices in ascending sequence; the rise in pitch intensifies the emotion, as does the dissonance at the end of each phrase. On *hor canto* (now I sing) the music returns to the home key of G major and to the original meter, tempo, and mood, while the basso ostinato starts up again. This is interrupted once more, by four measures of recitative. The last reference to *piango* (I weep) impels Monteverdi to the kind of affective dissonance he customarily reserved for ideas of passion, sorrow, and death. The final passage is a brilliant fantasy on the last two words of the poem, *hor canto*, which are expanded in both voices in a melisma that is altogether operatic in character. The madrigal ends with a quiet cadence in G major.

Claudio Monteverdi was one of the great pioneers in the communication of feeling through tone. He was indeed—as his contemporaries called him—a "Prophet of Music."

66 Baroque Opera

"I was aware that it is contraries which greatly move our mind. Where I have been able to find no variety in the affections I have at least sought to bring variety into my music."

Claudio Monteverdi

The formal or serious opera of the Baroque, the *opera seria*, was attuned to the social order that ended with the French Revolution. This was an opera for princely courts, the favorite diversion of Hapsburgs, Bourbons, Medici, and the rest, embodying the world-view of a feudal caste whose gaze was directed to the past, to an imaginary realm where heroes torn between love and honor declaimed to noble music while time stood still in an enchanted grotto out of antiquity or the medieval age.

This art form was much too stylized and formal to appeal to the nineteenth century. However, in the twentieth a reaction has occurred. The upsurge of interest in the Baroque brought about a revival of some of its operas; and it has become apparent that if these noble works are approached with imagination and adapted to the modern taste, they have much to say to us.

One of the characteristic conventions of baroque opera was the assignment of heroic roles to the *castrato*, the artificial male soprano or alto who dominated the operatic scene of the early eighteenth century. Such singers submitted—or were subjected by their elders—to an operation during their boyhood that preserved the soprano or alto range of their voices for the rest of their lives.

Stage design by the Galli-Bibiena family (early eighteenth-century).
Baroque opera embodied the splendor and monumentality of baroque art.

What resulted, after years of training, was an incredibly agile voice that combined the power of the male with the brilliance of the high register and that, strange as it may seem to us, was associated by baroque audiences with heroic male roles. The great castrati were famous throughout Europe, even though the French philosophers, in the spirit of the Enlightenment, made fun of the Italians for "having Alexander, Caesar, and Pompey settle the destiny of the world with women's voices." The era of the French Revolution saw the decline and eventual abolition of a custom so incompatible with the dignity of man. When castrato roles are revived today they are usually sung in lower register by a tenor or baritone.

Baroque opera was a vital force whose influence extended far beyond the theater. It created the great forms of the lyric drama—recitative and aria, ensemble and chorus—that served as models to every branch of the art. The *da capo aria*, in which the first part is repeated after the middle section, established the ternary form (A-B-A) as a basic formula of musical structure. Within its own conventions, baroque opera taught composers to depict the passions and the affections, the lyric contemplation of nature, the quintessence of love,

367

Jean-Baptiste Lully.

hate, fear, jealousy, exaltation. In sum, the opera house of the Baroque was the center for new trends and experiments, through which music attained a dramatic-expressive power such as it had never possessed before.

Lully: Overture to *Armide*

"The assurance of pleasing you has lifted me above myself and filled me with those divine transports which I could feel only in the service of Your Majesty. Indeed, Sire, there is no end I could not reach if it were necessary to obey you."

Lully to Louis XIV

Jean-Baptiste Lully (1632–87) was one of those dominating personalities who have the good fortune to appear precisely when the time is ripe for their gifts. He captured in his music the impulses of the era of French absolutism. In so doing he stamped his image upon a century.

Born in Florence of humble parentage, he displayed in boyhood a gift for singing and dancing. His talent attracted the notice of a French nobleman who offered to take him to France. At the age of fourteen the miller's son Gianbattista Lulli set forth on the eventful journey that was to transform him into Jean-Baptiste Lully, supreme arbiter of musical entertainment at the most sumptuous court in Europe.

Lully's art must be viewed against the resplendent milieu for which it was created. His ballets and operas were performed at the famous festivities of Versailles in the open-air marble court lined with silver candelabras and rows of orange trees in silver tubs. Here was an enchanted pleasure dome created out of the misery of a nation for a monarch whose whim it was to transform his life into a work of art. In this setting music was meant to soothe the ear and delight the senses; to be elegant, clear, and well-ordered. Lully's goals remained valid for French music for the next two hundred years. We shall meet them again in the pronouncements of Claude Debussy.

But Versailles subserved also another ideal: the aggrandizement of the king as the symbol of absolute power. It testifies to Lully's capacity for growth that he was able to pass from the comedy-ballets of his early years at court to the *tragédie lyrique* in which was incarnated the lofty formalism of the age of Louis XIV. Just as Monteverdi created a style of pathetic expressivity for the Italians, Lully established for the French an art of restraint and decorum.

Lully is particularly associated with the development of the French overture, a type that consists of three sections in the sequence slow-fast-slow. An example is the overture to his lyric tragedy *Armide* (1685). It opens with a majestic slow section in duple meter. The stately dotted rhythms, the forthright harmonies, easy melodiousness, and full sonority of the strings are Lullian characteristics. This is music commanding of gesture; its theme is pomp and power. The opening motive, announced by the first violins, is imitated and expanded

by the lower strings. This section is repeated softly. The lively middle section, in sextuple meter, opens in fugal fashion; but Lully does not pursue this in any methodical way. His melodious counterpoint is not meant to burden the mind. He puts most of the imitation in the outer parts, where the ear will hear it most easily. The opening motive of the section is made much of, and is occasionally inverted. The third and final section, in slow duple meter, resembles the first in its stately pace and massive sound. The texture is rather chordal. The second and third sections are repeated, rounding out the form in a clear and concise manner.

Lully ruled the French stage for decades and affected the development of instrumental music all over Europe. The boy who left Florence as a penniless tumbler gave his adopted country the grand manner of her golden age. For her he remained, as Molière called him, "the incomparable M. de Lully."

Purcell: *Dido and Aeneas*

"As Poetry is the harmony of Words, so Musick is that of Notes; and as Poetry is a Rise above Prose and Oratory, so is Musick the exaltation of Poetry."

Henry Purcell (1659–95) occupies a special niche in the annals of his country. He was last in the illustrious line that, stretching back to pre-Tudor times, won for England a foremost position among the musically creative

Henry Purcell.

nations. With his death the ascendancy came to an end. Until the rise of a native school of composers almost two hundred years later, he remained for his countrymen the symbol of an eminence they had lost.

Purcell's brief career unfolded at the court of Charles II, extending through the turbulent reign of James II into the period of William and Mary. He held various posts as singer, organist, and composer. Purcell's works cover a wide range, from the massive contrapuntal choruses of the religious anthems and the odes in honor of his royal masters, to patriotic songs like *Britons, Strike Home*, which stir his countrymen even as do the patriotic speeches that ring through the histories of Shakespeare.

Yet this national artist realized that England's music must be part of the European tradition. It was his historic role to assimilate the achievements of the Continent—the dynamic instrumental style, the movement toward major-minor tonality, the recitative and aria of Italian opera and the pointed rhythms of the French—and to acclimate these to his native land.

Purcell's odes and anthems hit off the tone of solemn ceremonial in an open-air music of great breadth and power. His instrumental music ranks with the finest achievements of the middle Baroque. His songs display the charm of his lyricism no less than his gift for setting our language. In the domain of the theater he produced, besides a quantity of music for plays, what many of his countrymen still regard as the peak of English opera—*Dido and Aeneas*. The work, presented in 1689 "at Mr. Josias Priest's boarding-school at Chelsey by young Gentlewomen . . . to a select audience of their parents and friends," achieved a level of pathos for which there was no precedent in England.

From the Overture, whose stately dotted rhythms point to the influence of Lully, the score abounds in felicitous strokes. Dido's first aria, "Ah! Belinda, I am prest with torment," wreathes the lovelorn queen in the atmosphere of noble grief that surrounds her throughout the work. A favorite with Purcell devotees is the chorus "To the hills and vales"; as is the Laughing Chorus of the Witches. In Vergil's epic the departure of Aeneas is motivated by the hero's manifest destiny. The libretto by Nahum Tate, one of the drearier poets laureate of England, simplifies this into a malicious plot of the Witches against Dido, a twist presumably more easily understood by the young ladies of Chelsea. In any case, one of the witches brings Aeneas a faked command from Jove to be on his way. The sailors of the final scene are as English a lot as ever sailed from Troy. Their chorus contains one of Tate's happiest lines: "Take a boozey short leave of your nymphs on the shore." Hardly less memorable is the Witches' comment: "Our plot has took, the Queen's forsook."

The culminating point of the opera is Dido's lament after Aeneas's departure: "When I am laid in earth." This majestic threnody, scored for soprano and

strings, unfolds over a ground bass that descends along the chromatic scale. The aria builds in a continuous line to the searing high G on "Remember me"— one of those strokes of genius that, once heard, is never forgotten.

Purcell in this work struck the true tone of lyric drama. He might have established opera in England, even as Lully did in France, had he lived twenty years longer. As it was, his masterpiece had no progeny. It remained as unique a phenomenon in history as the wonderful musician whom his contemporaries named "the British Orpheus."

67 Vocal Music of the Baroque

"Staying in Venice as the guest of old friends, I learned that the
long unchanged theory of composing melodies had set aside the
ancient rhythms to tickle the ears of today with fresh devices."
Heinrich Schütz

Oratorio and Cantata

The Baroque inherited the great vocal polyphony of the sixteenth
century. At the same time composers pursued the new interest in solo song
accompanied by instruments and in dramatic musical declamation. Out of the
fusion of all these came two important forms—oratorio and cantata.

The *oratorio* descended from the religious play-with-music of the Counter-
Reformation. It took its name from the Italian word for a place of prayer. The
first oratorios were sacred operas, and were produced as operas. However, toward
the middle of the seventeenth century the oratorio shed the trappings of the
stage and developed its own characteristics as a large-scale musical work for the
solo voices, chorus, and orchestra, based as a rule on a biblical story and imbued
with religious feeling. It was performed in a church or hall without scenery,
costumes, or acting. The action unfolded with the help of a Narrator, in a series
of recitatives and arias, ensemble numbers such as duets, trios, and the like, and
choruses. The role of the chorus was emphasized.

The *cantata* (from the Italian *cantare*, "to sing"—that is, a piece to be sung)
was a work for vocalists, chorus, and instrumentalists based on a poetic narrative
of a lyric or dramatic nature but shorter and more intimate in scope than an
oratorio. Consisting of several movements such as recitatives, arias, and ensemble
numbers, it bore the same relation to the oratorio as a one-act opera would to
a full-length one. Two types emerged: the sacred cantata and the secular.

Carissimi: Scene from *The Judgment of Solomon*

Giacomo Carissimi (1605–74), a Roman church musician,
played a leading role in the development of both the oratorio and cantata.
The Judgment of Solomon, one of his best-known oratorios, illustrates his
method of building a full-scale work out of the simplest materials. The piece
belongs to the shorter type of oratorio that was known as *cantata da chiesa*
(church cantata)—which shows how musical terms overlapped during this
formative period. After an instrumental introduction the Narrator assembles
the people; there follows the scene in which two mothers appear before King

Solomon to gain possession of a child that each claims is hers. "Go take thou the sword," the king orders, "and sever the child, and give a half to the one and likewise to the other." Carissimi sets the Latin text one note to a syllable. The movement from one tonal center to another gives shape and contour to the declamation; for example, Solomon's opening recitative moves from F major to a cadence in G.

The woman who pretends to be the child's mother agrees with Solomon. "Righteous and wise is thy judgment, O king. Let the child be neither for me nor for her, but divided." Leaps in the melody line underline her self-assurance. The key word *dividatur* (let it be divided) is repeated and extended in a florid manner. The supporting harmony modulates from G major to B-flat.

The speech of the true mother strikes a more emotional note and establishes the difference between the two women. "Ah, my son! My heart doth yearn for thee. Give her the living infant and in no wise harm it." Her opening notes, separated by rests, suggest sighs; the sorrowful mood is underlined by the harmony. Solomon repeats his suggestion, and each of the women reaffirms her stand, which gives Carissimi an opportunity to restate part of his material.

Solomon's final speech—the text is stated twice—awards the child to the true mother, and ends with a flourish on the decisive phrase, "for she is indeed his mother." It is clear from this scene that the oratorio was still at a rather primitive stage. But already it contained the elements that were to bring it to its future greatness.

Schütz: *Saul*

The life of Heinrich Schütz (1585–1672) spanned the transition from Renaissance to Baroque. More important, his art united two great musical cultures, those of Germany and Italy. As a young man he was sent by his patron,

Heinrich Schütz.

Prince Maurice of Hesse-Cassel, to study with Giovanni Gabrieli in Venice. There he came in contact with the polychoral splendor of the Venetian school and the new concerted style of vocal and instrumental music. Years later he returned to Italy to study the dramatic innovations of Monteverdi. It was Schütz's great achievement to introduce these epoch-making developments into his native land. Mastery of polyphony, profundity of thought and intensity of feeling were part of his heritage as a German. To these he was able to add the ardor, dash, and brilliance of the Italians.

The cantata *Saul* (1650)—Schütz called it a "Sacred Symphony"—reveals the power and intensity of his music. The work is written for a double chorus, two violins, and continuo. The vocalists are divided into a group of six solo voices—two sopranos, two tenors, and two basses—and two supporting groups, each consisting of soprano, alto, tenor, and bass. The cantata is based on two sentences from Acts (Chapter 9, verses 4–5). Saul of Tarsus, later Paul, is active in persecuting Christ's disciples when, on the road to Damascus, Christ appears to him in a vision:

Saul, Saul, was verfolgst du mich?	Saul, Saul, why do you persecute me?
Es wird dir schwer werden,	It will be hard for you
wider den Stachel zu löcken.	to kick against the traces.

The solo voices enter at once with startling urgency; the cry *Saul, Saul,* uttered at first by the two basses, is repeated insistently until it becomes a shattering call hurled forth by the entire ensemble. The music passes rapidly from forte to mezzo piano to pianissimo; Schütz, a true pupil of Gabrieli, specified the dynamic gradations. In his hands the echo effect becomes part of the drama. It is as if the question "Why do you persecute me?," coming now from near, now from afar, gives the one to whom it is addressed a moment to reflect upon his acts.

This opening section is in chordal texture. By contrast, the second sentence of the text is introduced by the first tenor and imitated by the second, in a calmer mood and with slight expansion of the important word *löcken* (kick). The agitation of the opening section returns when the first sentence is restated in smaller note values. Schütz then develops the second sentence in a contrapuntal passage, with imitation between the voices and an ornate melisma on the word *löcken*. He pairs off the voices, at one point pitting tenor, bass, and soprano against each other, at another all six voices against the two violins. The violins are treated as another pair of voices rather than in a strictly instrumental way. In this respect Schütz foreshadows the tendency of Baroque composers, so pronounced in Bach, of writing interchangeable lines for voices and instruments.

Having established a dramatic contrast between the chordal texture of the first sentence of his text and the imitative counterpoint of the second, Schütz combines the two at the climax of the cantata. Soprano, alto, and bass intone a phrase of the second sentence while the other solo voices repeat *Saul, Saul* like an incantation, joined by the accompanying choirs. In the final section the tenors repeat *Saul, Saul* in sustained notes, like a cantus firmus, while the other voices chant *was verfolgst du mich?*, each time a step higher. This use of an ascending sequence not only builds tension but gives shape to the music. At the very end the diminuendo of the opening passage is repeated, with a dramaticism that is nothing short of overwhelming.

The impulses that Schütz set in motion culminated, a century later, in the art of Johann Sebastian Bach. For us Schütz stands as a profoundly creative spirit whose achievements vitally influenced the course of music history.

68 Baroque Instrumental Music

"For by exactly observing this opposition or rivalry of the slow and the fast, the loud and the soft, the fullness of the great choir and the delicacy of the little trio, the ear is ravished by a singular astonishment, as is the eye by the opposition of light and shade."
Georg Muffat (1701)

The Sonata

The sonata was widely cultivated throughout the Baroque. It consisted of either a movement in several sections, or several movements that contrasted in tempo and texture. A distinction was drawn between the *sonata da camera* or *chamber sonata*, which was usually a suite of stylized dances intended for performance in the home, and the *sonata da chiesa* or *church sonata*. This was more serious in tone and more contrapuntal in texture. Its four movements, arranged in the sequence slow-fast-slow-fast, were supposed to make little use of dance rhythms. In practice the two types somewhat overlapped. Many church sonatas ended with one or more dancelike movements, while many chamber sonatas opened with an impressive introductory movement in the church-sonata style. (It should be noted that "sonata," to the Baroque, did not mean the highly structured, three-sectional movement it became in the Classical period.)

Sonatas were written for from one to six or eight instruments. The favorite combination for such works was two violins and continuo. Because of the three printed staves in the music, such compositions came to be known as *trio sonatas.* Yet the title is misleading, because it refers to the number of parts rather than to the number of players. As we saw, the basso continuo needed two perform-ers—a cellist (or bass viol player or bassoonist) to play the bass line, and a harpsichordist or organist to realize the harmonies indicated by the figures.

375

Corelli: *Sonata da chiesa* in E Minor

Arcangelo Corelli (1653–1713) was one of the leaders of the Italian violin school. He was educated at Bologna and spent the major part of his career at Rome, where he was vastly admired both as a violinist and composer. His compositions were printed throughout Europe, and students flocked to Rome to study with him. Toward the end of his life Corelli found himself superseded in public favor and took this eclipse so much to heart that his health began to fail. He died at the age of sixty and was buried in a magnificent tomb in the Pantheon, not far from Raphael.

Himself a great violinist, Corelli developed a pure style of violin playing that exploited to the full the technical and lyrical capacities of the instrument. His sonatas and concerti grossi are marked by clarity of thought and nobility of style. Of special merit are the slow movements, conceived with a dignity and pathos that eloquently reveal the violin's capacity for songful expression.

Corelli's *Sonata da chiesa* in E minor, Opus 3, No. 7 (1689), is a fine specimen of the church sonata of the middle Baroque. The basso continuo is played by cello and organ. The opening Grave, in common time, takes wings from the affecting tone of the violin. The lofty pathos of this slow movement is characteristic of the Italian master. The texture is based on imitation, as is apparent from the opening line, where first violin, second violin, and cello enter in succession with the same motive. Both violins play in the same register, their parts

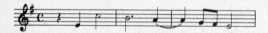

frequently crossing, so that the effect is that of a continuous dialogue between them.

The second movement, an Allegro in duple meter, is based on imitation. Each violin enters successively with the theme, followed by the cello, after which the

Arcangelo Corelli.

movement proceeds in free style. Here too the violins play in the same register, their parts intertwining, the result being a flowing melodiousness in which both share equally. The cello participates in the thematic work, and the organ lends both support and dimension to the proceedings. Third is an Adagio in triple time. Again the two violins unfold a loosely imitative texture in which the cello takes part now thematically, now as supporting instrument. The finale is a melodious Allegro with a dancelike lilt. This movement is a binary or two-part form, each part being repeated. The first section, in the Tonic key of E minor, reaches a cadence on the Dominant, a B major chord. The second part modulates to the related key of G major, whence it returns to E minor.

With unerring instinct Corelli built his art on what conformed to the true nature of the violin. He was thus able to lay a foundation on which his pupils and successors built an Italian school of instrumental music that remains one of the glories of the Baroque.

The Concerto Grosso

No less important than the principle of unity in baroque music was that of contrast. This found expression in the *concerto grosso*, a form based on the opposition between two dissimilar masses of sound. (The Latin verb

Francesco Guardi (1712–93), THE GALA CONCERT (Alte Pinakothek, Munich)
A scene from Venetian musical life, by the famous contemporary of Vivaldi.

377

concertare means "to contend with," "to vie with." The *concertante* style is based on this principle.) A small group of instruments known as the *concertino* was pitted against the large group, the concerto grosso or *tutti* (all). The contrast was one of color and dynamics, a uniform level of soft sound being set off against loud. In other words, the orchestra here took over the terraced dynamics of organ and harpsichord.

The concertino, or solo group, might consist of a string trio such as two violins and a cello, or any combination that caught the composer's fancy. The large group as a rule was based on the string choir, but might be supplemented by winds. The harpsichord furnished harmonic support for both groups. The composer was able to write more difficult music for the solo group than for the full ensemble. This was a signal advantage in an age when expert players were none too plentiful.

The concerto grosso embodied what one writer of the time called "the fire and fury of the Italian style." Two Italian masters were outstanding in this field, Arcangelo Corelli and Antonio Vivaldi.

Vivaldi: Concerto Grosso in D Minor

For many years interest in the Baroque centered about Bach and Handel to such an extent that the earlier masters were neglected. None suffered more in this regard than Antonio Vivaldi (1678–1741), who has been rediscovered by the twentieth century. Amazingly prolific even for that prolific age, he produced quantities of concertos and sonatas, operas and choral pieces, many of them still unknown. Only with the publication of his complete works —a number of volumes have already appeared—will it be possible fully to evaluate the achievement of this strikingly original musician.

Vivaldi was born in Venice, the son of a violinist. He was ordained in the Church in his twenties and came to be known as "the red priest," an epithet

Antonio Vivaldi.

which in that distant age referred to nothing more than the color of his hair. Some years thereafter he took up a musical career, during the greater part of which he was connected with the educational institutions of his native city.

In his love of brilliant color Vivaldi was a true son of Venice. His instrumental music marks one of the high points of the Italian violin school. His novel use of rapid scale passages, extended arpeggios, and contrasting registers contributed decisively to the development of violin style. He also played a leading part in the history of the concerto grosso, exploiting with vast effectiveness the contrast in sonority between large and small groups of players.

Characteristic of Vivaldi's style is the Concerto Grosso in D minor, Opus 3, No. 11, for two violins and cello with string orchestra. This is the eleventh of a set of twelve that the composer fancifully named *L'Estro armonico* (The Harmonic Whim). Six of these works were transcribed—or better, adapted—by Bach, who assiduously studied Vivaldi's music: three for organ and three for harpsichord. So completely was the Venetian master forgotten after his death that for generations these adaptations were regarded as original works by Bach.

The Concerto Grosso in D minor open with an Allegro introduction based on an arpeggio figure for the three soloists and continuo. An Adagio of three bars for the entire ensemble leads into the movement proper, an Allegro. The theme, announced by the cellos, has a sharp rhythmic profile and is in Vivaldi's happiest vein.

The first section is presented by the solo group (concertino) and the accompanying body of strings (tutti). Then the concertino plays alone. Since both the solo group and the accompanying body consist of string instruments, the composer cannot rely on tone color for his contrasts. He obtains these through variety of dynamics and rhythm, echo effects, and by skillfully pitting high register against low. (The movement is a fugue, a type that we shall discuss in the next chapter.)

The Largo e spiccato (very slow and detached) is a singing movement in the grand tradition of the classical Italian school. The 12/8 meter with its dotted rhythms is characteristic of the *siciliano*, a dance of Sicilian origin much favored by the Baroque, in moderate tempo, usually with a lyrical melody and flowing accompaniment of broken chords. The siciliano was much used to suggest a gentle, pastoral mood. In this instance the melody is introduced by the solo violin, with the first violins playing in unison.

It unfolds in a vaulting arch over an accompaniment of affective harmonies. In a number of passages in this movement we find the concerto grosso drawing closer to the solo concerto.

The finale, which begins with the concertino, corresponds in weight to the first movement, and completes the arch of the work. It is one of those busy allegros that vividly conjure up the world of the eighteenth century. Worthy of

note are the passages for two solo violins in thirds, in the mellifluous manner of Italian opera; the terraced dynamics that rapidly alternate areas of light and shade; the lucid counterpoint; the continuous motion and forward thrust of the music. This is a tissue woven without effort and without seams. Vivaldi gets the movement under way, keeps it going, and brings it to a close without wasting a note. Such economy bespeaks a surpassing sense of style.

Vivaldi's music flowered from a noble tradition. His dynamic conceptions pointed to the future. How strange that he had to wait until the mid-twentieth century to come into his own.

The Suite

The *suite* consisted mainly of a series of dance movements, all in the same key. It presented an international galaxy of dance types: the German allemande, in duple meter at a moderate tempo; the French courante, in triple meter at a moderate tempo; the Spanish sarabande, a stately dance in triple meter; and the English jig (gigue), in a lively 6/8 or 6/4. These had begun as popular dances, but by the time of the late Baroque they had left the ballroom far behind and become abstract types of art music. Between the slow sarabande and fast gigue might be inserted a variety of optional numbers of a graceful song or dance type such as the minuet, the gavotte, the lively bourrée or passepied. These dances of peasant origin introduced a refreshing earthiness into their more formal surroundings. The suite sometimes also incorporated the operatic overture, as well as a variety of short pieces with attractive titles. In short, once a composer passed the formal prelude or overture he had wide choice in the organization of the suite, whether it was for solo instrument or orchestra.

The standard form of the pieces in the suite was the binary structure (A-B) consisting of two sections of approximately equal length, each being rounded off by a cadence. The first part, you will recall, usually moved from the home key (Tonic) to a contrasting key (Dominant), while the B part made the corresponding move back. Composers might have demurred, a century later, at writing a group of five, six, or seven pieces all in the same key; but at a time when major-minor tonality was still a novelty, the assertion of the home key over and over again had a reassuring effect.

The essential element of the suite was dance rhythm, with its imagery of physical movement. The form met the needs of the age for elegant entertainment music. At the same time it offered composers a wealth of popular rhythms that could be transmuted into art.

Telemann: Suite in A Minor

Georg Philipp Telemann (1681–1767) was a famous composer in the first half of the eighteenth century. He was active in Hamburg and, being both facile and industrious, left behind him a prodigious amount of music. The list includes forty operas, forty-four Passions, twelve complete Lutheran services for the year, and a mass of vocal and instrumental music of all kinds, including no less than six hundred overtures in the French style. He was almost completely forgotten in the nineteenth century, but was swept back into favor by the revival of interest in baroque music that gained momentum during the 1950s.

Georg Philipp Telemann.

His Suite in A minor has become a favorite with present-day audiences. It is generally known as the Suite for Flute and Strings, but this is misleading. The term *flauto* in Telemann's day referred to the recorder, while the cross-blown flute was called *flauto traverso*. (The *recorder* is a type of wooden flute blown from the end rather than the side.) In any case Telemann's Suite has become an exhibition piece for flutists as well as recorder players. The suite is scored for alto recorder (known also as *flauto dolce* or "sweet flute"), strings, and basso continuo, and is in seven movements.

The opening movement adheres to the tradition of the French overture as it had been established by Lully, consisting of three sections: slow-fast-slow. It opens with a Lento in A minor that has the stateliness of gesture and dotted rhythms associated with this form:

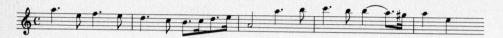

The first section of the Overture is played by strings and harpsichord, leading to a cadence on the Dominant, E major. Then the section is repeated, with ornamentation, by the solo instrument. In evidence are the terraced dynamics and echo effects so prized by the Baroque, although these are less apparent on the recorder, because of its limited dynamic range, than on the flute. Notice the baroque style of orchestration, which permits the flute or recorder to carry the melody line througout an entire section.

There follows one of those busy little Allegros that starts out in fugal style but goes on to lighter things. The soloist is given every opportunity to exhibit his fleet fingers and sureness of breath. The Overture concludes with a second slow section that, without being a literal repetition of the first, recaptures its mood.

Les Plaisirs (Pleasures) is a Presto in cut time (alla breve). This opens with a two-part form, each of whose sections is heard twice, first loud, then soft. The spirit is French as well as the title. The recorder or flute enters in the Trio, accompanied only by harpsichord; the solo part moves at a breathtaking clip, featuring terraced dynamics and echo effects. At the end of the Trio the first section is heard again, without repeats, resulting in an A-B-A form.

The *Air à l'Italien* (song in the Italian style) is a Largo that emulates the noble pathos of the slow operatic aria of the Baroque. The melody is introduced by the strings. Notice the ascending sequences in measures 3-4, and the irregular phrase length of five measures:

After this brief introduction the solo instrument takes over the ornate "aria" much as a singer would. The middle section of the movement is an agile Allegro whose intricate figuration shows off both the instrument and its player. Then the first section is repeated, da capo, with ornamentation, giving an A-B-A form.

The next movement consists of two minuets. Minuet I is regular in structure. Each of its two sections is repeated with baroque ornamentation. The solo instrument does not enter until Minuet II (which corresponds to the section later known as Trio). Telemann's pattern building is of charming simplicity. The first part is then heard again, without repeats, in a clear-cut A-B-A structure.

Réjouissance (Rejoicing) is a Presto in common time. Here again a French title emphasizes the origins of the suite. In one brief passage solo and strings imitate each other; then the solo embarks on figuration that, whether on recorder or flute, takes the deftest kind of playing. There follows the Passepied, which was originally a gay dance in vogue at the French court under Louis XIV and Louis XV. The first part is in A minor, the middle section in A major after which the opening section is repeated da capo. The Polonaise that ends the suite is a far cry from the heroic piano piece that Chopin gave the world. This one is rather like a stately minuet, but differs from the latter in its triplet rhythms and its subtle accent on the second beat.

The three types of composition discussed in this chapter—trio sonata, concerto grosso, and suite—account for a considerable body of music that speaks to us persuasively today.

69 Johann Sebastian Bach (Instrumental Music)

"The aim and final reason of all music should be nothing else but the Glory of God and the refreshment of the spirit."

Johann Sebastian Bach (1685–1750) was heir to the polyphonic art of the past. This he vitalized with the passion and humanity of his own spirit. He is the culminating figure of baroque music and one of the titans in the history of art.

His Life

He was born at Eisenach in Germany, of a family that had supplied musicians to the churches and town bands of the region for upwards of a century and a half. Left an orphan at the age of ten, he was raised in the town of Ohrdruf by an older brother, an organist who prepared him for the family vocation. From the first he displayed inexhaustible curiosity concerning every aspect of his art. "I had to work hard," he reported in later years, adding with considerably less accuracy, "Anyone who works as hard will get just as far."

His professional career began when he was eighteen with his appointment as organist at a church in Arnstadt. The certificate of appointment admonishes the young man to be true, faithful, and obedient to "our Noble and Most Gracious Count and Master . . . to conduct yourself in all things toward God, High Authority, and your superiors as befits an honorable servant and organist." High Authority soon had cause to reprove the new organist "for having made many curious *variationes* in the chorale and mingled many strange tones in it, and for the fact that the Congregation has been confused by it." The church elders were inquiring shortly after "by what right he recently caused a strange maiden to be invited into the choir loft and let her make music there." The maiden seems to have been his cousin Maria Barbara, whom he married in 1707.

Johann Sebastian Bach

After a year at a church in Mühlhausen, Bach—at twenty-three—received his first important post: court organist and chamber musician to the Duke of Weimar. His nine years at the ducal court (1708–17) were spent in the service of a ruler whose leaning toward religious music accorded with his own. The Weimar period saw the rise of his fame as an organ virtuoso and the production of many of his most important works for that instrument.

Disappointed because the Duke had failed to advance him, Bach decided to accept an offer from the Prince of Anhalt-Cöthen. He needed his master's permission to take another post. This the irascible Duke refused to give. The musician stood up for his rights; whereupon, as the court chronicle relates, "on November 6, the former Concertmeister and court organist Bach was placed under arrest in the County Judge's place of detention for too stubbornly forcing the issue of his dismissal and finally on December 2 was freed from arrest with notice of his unfavorable discharge."

At Cöthen, Bach served a prince partial to chamber music. In his five years there (1717–23) he produced suites, concertos, sonatas for various instruments, and a wealth of clavier music; also the six concerti grossi dedicated to the Margrave of Brandenburg. The Cöthen period was saddened by the death of Maria Barbara in 1720. The composer subsequently married Anna Magdalena, a young singer in whom he found a loyal and understanding mate. Of his twenty children—seven of the first marriage and thirteen of the second—half did not survive infancy. One son died in his twenties, another was mentally deficient. Four others became leading composers of the next generation: Wilhelm Friedemann and Carl Philipp Emanuel, sons of Maria Barbara; and Anna Magdalena's sons Johann Christoph and Johann Christian.

Bach was thirty-eight when he was appointed to one of the most important posts in Germany, that of Cantor of St. Thomas's in Leipzig. The cantor taught at the choir school of that name, which trained the choristers of the city's principal churches (he was responsible for nonmusical subjects too); and served as music director, composer, choirmaster and organist of St. Thomas's Church. Several candidates were considered before him, among them the then much more famous composer Telemann, who declined the offer. As one member of the town council reported, "Since the best man could not be obtained, lesser ones would have to be accepted." It was in this spirit that Leipzig received the greatest of her cantors.

Bach's twenty-seven years in Leipzig (1723–50) saw the production of stupendous works. The clue to his inner life must be sought in his music. It had no counterpart in an outwardly uneventful existence divided between the cares of a large family, the pleasures of a sober circle of friends, the chores of a busy professional life, and the endless squabbles with a host of officials of town, school, and church who never conceded that they were dealing with anything more than a competent choirmaster. The city fathers were impressed but also disquieted by the dramaticism of his religious music. Besides, like all officials they were out to save money and not averse to lopping off certain rights and fees that Bach felt belonged to him. He fought each issue doggedly, with an expenditure of time and emotion that might have gone to better things. Despite his complaints he remained in Leipzig. With the years the Council learned to put up with their obstinate cantor. After all, he was the greatest organist in Germany.

The routine of his life was enlivened by frequent professional journeys, when he was asked to test and inaugurate new organs. His last and most interesting expedition, in 1747, was to the court of Frederick the Great at Potsdam, where his son Carl Philipp Emanuel served as accompanist to the flute-playing monarch. Frederick on the memorable evening announced to his courtiers with some excitement, "Gentlemen, old Bach has arrived." He led the composer through the palace showing him the new pianos that were beginning to replace the harpsichord. Upon Bach's invitation the King gave him a theme on which he improvised one of his astonishing fugues. After his return to Leipzig he further elaborated on the royal theme, added a trio sonata, and dispatched *The Musical Offering* to "a Monarch whose greatness and power, as in all the sciences of war and peace, so especially in music everyone must admire and revere."

The prodigious labors of a lifetime took their toll; his eyesight failed. After an apoplectic stroke he was stricken with blindness. He persisted in his final task, the revising of eighteen chorale preludes for the organ. The dying master dictated to a son-in-law the last of these, *Before Thy Throne, My God, I Stand.*

His Music

The artist in Bach was driven to conquer all realms of musical thought. His position in history is that of one who consummated existing forms rather than one who originated new ones. Whatever form he touched he brought to its ultimate development. He cut across boundaries, fusing the three great national traditions of his time—German, Italian, French—into a convincing unity. His sheer mastery of the techniques of composition has never been equaled. With this went incomparable profundity of thought and feeling and the capacity to realize to the full all the possibilities inherent in a given musical situation.

Bach was the last of the great religious artists. He considered music to be "a harmonious euphony to the Glory of God." And the glory of God was the central issue of man's existence. His music issued in the first instance from the Lutheran hymn tunes known as chorales. Through these, the most learned composer of the age was united to the living current of popular melody, to become the spokesman of a faith.

The prime medium for Bach's poetry was the organ. His imagery was rooted in its keyboard and pedals, his inspiration molded to its majestic sonorities. He created for the instrument what is still the high point of its literature. In his own lifetime he was known primarily as a virtuoso organist, only Handel being placed in his class. When complimented on his playing he would answer disarmingly, "There is nothing remarkable about it. All you have to do is hit the right notes at the right time and the instrument plays itself."

In the field of keyboard music his most important work is the *Well-Tempered Clavier*. The forty-eight preludes and fugues in these two volumes (1722, 1744) have been called the pianist's Old Testament (The New, it will be recalled, being Beethoven's sonatas). In the suites for clavier the Leipzig cantor dons the grace and elegance of the French style. Two sets of six each, dating from the 1720s, came to be known as the *French* and *English Suites*. Another six from the Leipzig period were named Partitas (1731). The keyboard music includes a wide variety of pieces. Among the most popular are the *Chromatic Fantasy and Fugue* (c. 1720), the *Italian Concerto* (1735), and the *Goldberg Variations* (1742; so called after a virtuoso of the time).

Of the sonatas for various instruments, a special interest attaches to the six for unaccompanied violin (c. 1720). The master creates for the four strings an intricate polyphonic structure and wrests from the instrument forms and textures of which one would never have suspected it capable. *The Brandenburg Concertos* (1721) present various instrumental combinations pitted against one another. The four Suites for Orchestra contain dance forms of appealing lyricism. We will discuss in detail the Suite No. 3 and the *Brandenburg Concerto* No. 2.

The two-hundred-odd cantatas that have come down to us form the centerpiece of Bach's religious music. They constitute a personal document of transcendent spirituality; they project his vision of life and death. The drama of the

Crucifixion inspired Bach to plenary eloquence. His Passions are epics of the Protestant faith. That according to St. John (1723) depicts the final events in the life of Christ with almost violent intensity. *The Passion According to St. Matthew* (1729), which we shall discuss, is more contemplative in tone.

The Mass in B minor occupied Bach for a good part of the Leipzig period. The first two movements, the Kyrie and Gloria were written in 1733, and were dedicated to Friedrich Augustus, Elector of Saxony. The greatest of Protestant composers turned to a Catholic monarch in the hope of being named composer to the Saxon court, a title that would strengthen him in his squabbles with the Leipzig authorities. The honorary title was eventually granted. To the Kyrie and Gloria originally sent to the Elector "as an insignificant example of that knowledge which I have achieved in musique" he later added the other three movements required by Catholic usage, the Credo, Sanctus, and Agnus Dei. The dimensions of this mightiest of Masses make it unfit for liturgical use. In its mingling of Catholic and Protestant elements the work symbolically unites the two factions of Christendom. It has found a home in the concert hall, a place of worship to whose creed all that come may subscribe.

In his final years the master, increasingly withdrawn from the world, fastened his gaze upon the innermost secrets of his art. *The Musical Offering* (1747), in which he elaborated the theme of Frederick the Great, runs the gamut of contrapuntal thinking. The work culminates in an astounding six-voice fugue. Bach's last opus, *The Art of the Fugue* (1748–50), constitutes his final summation of the processes of musical thought. There is symbolism in the fact that he did not live to finish this encyclopedic work; the ultimate question had still to remain unanswered.

The Fugue

From the art and science of counterpoint issued one of the most exciting types of baroque music, the fugue. The name is derived from *fuga*, the Latin for "flight," implying a flight of fancy, possibly the flight of the theme from one voice to the other. A *fugue* is a contrapuntal composition in which a theme or subject of strongly marked character pervades the entire fabric, entering now in one voice, now in another. The fugue consequently is based on the principle of imitation. The subject constitutes the unifying idea, the focal point of interest in the contrapuntal web.

A fugue may be written for a group of instruments; for a solo instrument such as organ, harpsichord, or even violin; for several solo voices or for full chorus. Whether the fugue is vocal or instrumental, the several lines are called voices, which indicates the origin of the type. In vocal and orchestral fugues each line is articulated by another performer or group of performers. In fugues for keyboard instruments the ten fingers—on the organ, the feet as well—manage the complex interweaving of the voices.

The *subject* or theme is stated alone at the outset in one of the voices—

soprano, alto, tenor, or bass. It is then imitated in another voice—this is the *answer*—while the first continues with a *countersubject* or countertheme. Depending on the number of voices in the fugue, the subject will then appear in a third voice and be answered in the fourth, with the other voices usually weaving a free contrapuntal texture against these. (If a fugue is in three voices there is, naturally, no second answer, since there is no fourth voice.) When the theme has been presented in each voice once, the first section of the fugue, the Exposition, is at an end. The Exposition may be restated, in which case the voices will enter in a different order. From there on the fugue alternates between exposition sections that feature the entrance of the subject and less weighty interludes known as *episodes*, which serve as areas of relaxation.

The subject of the fugue is stated in the home key, the Tonic. The answer is given in a related key, that of the Dominant, which lies five tones above the Tonic. There may be modulation to foreign keys in the course of the fugue, which builds up tension against the return home. The baroque fugue thus embodied the contrast between home and contrasting keys that was one of the basic principles of the new major-minor system.

As the fugue unfolds there must be not only a sustaining of interest but the sense of mounting urgency that is proper to an extended art work. The composer throughout strives for continuity and a sense of organic growth. Each recurrence of the theme reveals new facets of its nature. The composer manipulates the subject as pure musical material in the same way that the sculptor molds his clay. Especially effective is the *stretto* (from the Italian *stringere*, "to tighten"), in which the theme is imitated in close succession, with the subject entering in one voice before it has been completed in another. The effect is one of voices crowding upon each other, creating a heightening of tension that brings the fugue to its climax. A frequent feature of the fugue— generally toward the end—is the *pedal point*, by which we mean one tone, usually the Dominant or Tonic, that is sustained in the bass while the harmonies change in the other parts. (The pedal point sometimes occurs in the treble register.) The final statement of the subject, generally in a decisive manner, brings the fugue to an end.

The fugue is based on a single affection, or mood—the subject that dominates the piece. Episodes and transitional passages are usually woven from its motives or from those of the countersubject. There results a remarkable unity of texture and atmosphere. Another factor for unity is the unfaltering rhythmic beat (against which, however, the composer may weave a diversity of counter-rhythms). The only section of the fugue that follows a set order is the Exposition. Once that is done with, the further course of the fugue is bound only by the composer's fancy. Caprice, exuberance, surprise—all receive free play within the supple framework of this form.

Fugal technique reached unsurpassable heights at the hands of Bach and Handel. In the classic-romantic period the fugue was somewhat neglected, although fugal writing became an integral part of the composer's technique.

Passages in fugal style occur in many a symphony, quartet, and sonata, often in the development section. Such an imitative passage inserted in a nonfugal piece is known as a *fugato*. It affords the composer the excitement of fugal writing without the responsibilities.

The fugue, then, is a rather free form based on imitative counterpoint, that combined the composer's technical skill with imagination, feeling, and exuberant ornamentation. There resulted a type of musical art that may well be accounted one of the supreme achievements of the Baroque.

Organ Fugue in G Minor

The G-minor Fugue known as "the Little," to distinguish it from a longer fugue in the same key called "the Great," is one of the most popular of Bach's works in this form. This organ fugue is in four voices. The subject is announced in the soprano and is answered in the alto. Next it enters in the tenor and is answered in the bass. In accordance with fugal procedure these entries alternate between the home key (G minor) and the contrasting key (D minor). The subject is a sturdy melody that begins by outlining the Tonic chord and flowers into fanciful arabesques.

The Exposition completed, an episode appears in which a striking motive is heard in imitation between alto and soprano. This motive takes on increasing significance as the fugue proceeds.

The piece is marked by compactness of structure and directness of speech. The subject, as is customary in fugues in the minor mode, is presently shifted to the major. After a climactic expansion of the material the theme makes its final appearance on the pedals, in the home key. The work ends brilliantly with a major chord.

Suite No. 3 in D Major

Bach wrote four orchestral suites. The first two are supposed to have been written during the Cöthen period (1717–23), the last two at Leipzig. The Suite No. 3 is scored for two oboes, three trumpets, drums, first and second violins, violas, and basso continuo.

1. *Overture.* The stately opening, in common time, with its dotted rhythms and sweeping gesture, is a French overture in the tradition of Lully. The oboes play along with the first violins. Trumpets, in the upper part of their range, and timpani introduce a note of grandeur that is surprising when one considers the economy of means wherewith it is produced. Bach does not attempt to blend the various instrumental colors. Quite the contrary, the different timbres are individualized throughout, the contrast serving to bring out the lines of the texture.

The massive introduction is followed by a lively fugal section that unfolds in the effortless, self-generating contrapuntal lines of which the old masters had the secret. Bach indicated the tempo with V*ite*, the French word for fast. The

subject is compact and full of animation. Bach occasionally repeats its motives in sequence, either higher or lower. Based as it is on a "single affection," the movement displays the highest degree of organic unity. The unflagging rhythm, the forward drive of the counterpoint, and the steady building of tension show the baroque style at its most characteristic.

There follows a return to the slower pace of the opening. Bach places a repeat sign at the end of the first section, another at the end of the movement. These are not always observed in performances of the work.

2. *Air.* Modeled on the operatic aria, this lyric type of movement was introduced into the suite for greater contrast. The Air from Bach's Suite No. 3, for strings only, won universal popularity in an arrangement for the violin by the nineteenth-century virtuoso August Wilhelmj, under the title *Air for the G String.* The seamless melody unfolds in a continuous flow, presented by the

etc.

first violins over the steady beat of the cellos. The Air is a two-part form. The first part, which is repeated, modulates from the Tonic, D major, to the Dominant, A major. The second part, twice as long as the first, leads back to D major, ending with a strong cadence. This part too is repeated.

3. *Gavotte.* A sprightly dance piece in quick duple time, the Gavotte displays the terraced dynamics of the baroque style. A phrase for the full ensemble alternates with one scored solely for oboes and strings. This movement really consists of two gavottes. Gavotte I is a two-part structure, each part being repeated; the first modulates from D major to A, the second back to D. The second part opens with an inversion of the basic motive. Gavotte II serves as the Trio or middle section. It too consists of two sections, each of which is repeated. The terraced dynamics of the orchestration continue to present contrasting areas of light and shade. The key scheme of the Trio parallels that of the Gavotte proper: from D to A in the first part, while the second returns to the home key. Gavotte I is repeated da capo.

4. *Bourrée.* A light-hearted dance form in duple meter and two-part structure. The same motive serves as point of departure for both sections. The first section modulates from D to A, the second returns to the home key, D.

5. *Gigue.* A sprightly dance piece to which the 6/8 time imparts a most attractive lilt. (The French gigue, it will be recalled, developed from the Irish and English jig.) The formal scheme is similar to that of the other dance numbers: a two-part structure in which each part is repeated. As has been pointed out, not all the repeat signs are likely to be observed in performance. Once again, the first part modulates from D to A major; the second part returns to D. The piece is noteworthy for Bach's use of melodic patterns in sequence.

This Suite in D, like its companions, shows the lighter side of Bach's genius. Its courtly gestures and ornate charm evoke a vanished world.

Brandenburg Concerto No. 2 in F Major

In 1719 Bach had occasion to play before the Margrave Christian Ludwig of Brandenburg, son of the Great Elector. The prince was so impressed that he asked the composer to write some works for his orchestra. Two years later Bach sent him the six pieces that have become known as the *Brandenburg Concertos*, with a dedication in flowery French that beseeched His Royal Highness "not to judge their imperfection by the strictness of that fine and delicate taste which all the world knows You have for musical works; but rather to take into consideration the profound respect and the most humble obedience to which they are meant to bear witness." It is not known how the Margrave responded to the works that have immortalized his name.

In these pieces Bach captured the spirit of the concerto grosso, in which two groups vie with each other, one stimulating the other to sonorous flights of fancy. The second of the set, in F major, has long been a favorite, probably because of the brilliant trumpet part. The solo group—the concertino—consists of trumpet, flute, oboe, and violin, all of them instruments in the high register. The accompanying group—the tutti—includes first and second violins, violas, and double basses. The basso continuo is played by cello and harpsichord.

The opening movement is a sturdy Allegro, bright and assertive. The broad simple outlines of its architecture depend on well-defined areas of light and shade—the alternation of the tutti and the solo group. The virile tone of the opening derives from the disposition of the parts. Flute, oboe, and violin play

the theme in unison with the first violin of the accompanying group, while the trumpet outlines the tonic triad. The contrapuntal lines unfold in a continuous, seamless texture, powered by a rhythmic drive that never flags from beginning to end. The movement modulates freely from the home key of F major to the neighboring major and minor keys. When its energies have been fully expended it returns to F for a vigorous cadence.

The slow movement is an Andante in D minor, a soulful colloquy among solo violin, oboe, and flute. Each in turn enters with the theme:

The continuo instruments articulate the affective harmonies of the accompaniment, while the solo instruments trace serenely melodious lines. This moving Andante is informed with all the noble pathos of the Baroque.

Third and last is an Allegro assai (very fast). Trumpet, oboe, violin, and flute enter in turn with the jaunty subject of a four-voiced fugue. The contra-

puntal lines are tightly drawn, with much crisscrossing of parts. The lively interchange is in the nature of a gay conversation among four equals, abetted in frothiest fashion by the members of the tutti. The movement reaches its destination with the final pronouncement of the subject by the trumpet.

Passacaglia and Chaconne

One of the most majestic forms of baroque music is the *passacaglia,* which utilizes the principle of the ground bass. A melody is introduced alone in the bass, usually four or eight bars long, in a stately triple meter. The theme is repeated again and again, serving as the foundation for a set of continuous variations that exploit all the resources of polyphonic art. A related type is the *chaconne,* in which the variations are based not on a melody but on a succession of harmonies repeated over and over. Passacaglia and chaconne exemplify the baroque urge toward abundant variation and embellishment of a musical idea, and that desire to make much out of a little which is the essence of the creative act.

The passacaglia lent itself particularly well to organ playing, for the basic theme could be articulated by the pedals while the upper parts were played on the manuals. Bach's Passacaglia in C minor is a magnificent example of the form. The solemn melody heard at the outset engraves itself immediately on the mind:

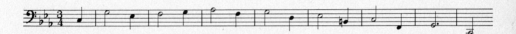

With this as his point of departure Bach built a work that is overwhelming in its cumulative power. The theme is repeated twenty times. The first two variations move mostly in dotted eighth and quarter notes, the third in a continuous eighth-note rhythm, the fourth and fifth alternate eighth notes and sixteenths. Variations 6 to 10 move in continuous sixteenth-note rhythm, with increasing complexity of texture. In Variation 11 the bass melody moves to the soprano:

The melody remains in the topmost part for Variation 12, moves to an inner voice in Variation 13, and is disguised in running arpeggios in Variations 14 and 15. The sixteenth variation returns the melody to the pedals beneath a powerful figure that ends each measure with a massive chord; the seventeenth has both hands rushing forward in rapid triplets; the eighteenth, more lyrical in character, unfolds over the ostinato in a somewhat altered rhythm; Variations 19 and 20 build tension against the fortissimo cadence in C minor.

Having explored the possibilities of his theme in this manner, Bach combines its first four measures with a countermelody to form the subject of an exciting double fugue in four voices.

The two themes always appear together against flowing counterpoint in the other voices. The themes in C minor are answered in the key of the Dominant, G minor. When they have appeared in all four voices the Exposition is complete. From then on the entrances of the themes alternate with episodes that are lighter in character; these grow ever more fanciful as the fugue unfolds. The music modulates through the keys that lie close to C minor. The final section of the fugue accumulates tremendous tension, which finds its release in the grandiose coda and cadence in C major.

The *Chaconne in D minor* is the final movement of the Sonata No. 4 for Unaccompanied Violin. By writing for the violin without harpsichord accompaniment Bach forced it to transcend its nature as a melody instrument and to carry harmony and counterpoint as well. His six sonatas for solo violin even contain fugues. These works reveal an extraordinarily imaginative approach to the violin and are among the masterpieces of its literature.

As in the case of the Passacaglia, Bach in the Chaconne builds a stupendous edifice out of the simplest materials. The theme is a chord sequence in stately triple meter. The second phrase parallels the first, or may be regarded as a variation of it.

This succession of harmonies serves as the background for a set of variations in which Bach explores all the technical resources of the violin. Like the Passacaglia, the Chaconne moves steadily from longer note values to shorter ones. The first two variations feature dotted rhythm; the next two begin with eighth notes and pass over to sixteenths. Variation 5 and 6 are based on continuous sixteenth notes; the seventh presents an enrichment of texture that suggests counterpoint. Variations 8 and 9 are based on rapid scales, ascending and descending, in thirty-second notes. In Variation 10, an arpeggio figure in the first phrase gives way to rapid figuration in the second. Thirty-second notes predominate in the next three variations. The musical fabric becomes increasingly elaborate, introducing arpeggios that require spectacular bowing. Variation 14 brings a triplet rhythm, with six thirty-second notes to the beat instead of four. Here is the elaboration of the first measure and a half, corresponding to the first four chords in the previous example:

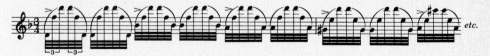

The next variation is four bars long instead of eight. Single notes in the lower register are contrasted with soft scale passages in the upper. Variation 16 concludes the first section in minor.

The following ten variations are in D major, which sounds suave and caressing after the minor. With inexhaustible invention and continual change of mood, Bach explores the capacities of the violin for singing melody, chords, scales, running figures, staccato, accents, various types of bowing, and contrast between the upper and lower registers. Yet this marshaling of technical resources is never an end in itself, but always serves the expression of profound thought and stirring emotion. The final variation in major is in the nature of a climax; the return to D minor is emphasized in a variation based on the contrast between chords and arpeggio figures. The final variations in the home key present a building up of tension which is resolved when the chord sequence out of which the structure grew returns as a coda.

Both passacaglia and chaconne began as popular dance rhythms that were taken over by the composers of the Baroque and stylized into impressive works of art. Within the limits imposed by both art forms, Bach's imagination disports itself with a fecundity that is little short of dazzling.

70 Johann Sebastian Bach (Vocal Music)

"To God alone be the praise."
Bach's inscription at the end of his religious works.

Bach's lyricism found its purest expression in the arias distributed throughout his vocal works. These are elaborate movements with ornate vocal lines and expressive instrumental accompaniments. Many are in the da capo aria form of

Italian opera, in which the contrasting middle section is followed by an exact repetition of the first part (A-B-A). Others follow less clear-cut patterns. The orchestral accompaniments abound in striking motives that combine contrapuntally with the vocal line to create the proper mood for the text and illustrate its meaning. In many cases the aria is conceived as a kind of duet between the voice and a solo instrument—violin, flute, oboe, or the like—so that a single instrumental color is apt to prevail throughout the piece. The aria is introduced by the recitative, which may be either secco (accompanied by organ or harpsichord) or accompagnato (supported by the orchestra.)

The Lutheran Chorale

A *chorale*, we saw, is a hymn tune, specifically one associated with German Protestantism. The chorales served as the battle hymns of the Reformation. Their sturdy contours bear the stamp of an heroic age.

As one of his reforms, Martin Luther (1483–1546) established that the congregation participate in the service. To this end, he inaugurated services in German rather than Latin, and allotted an important role to congregational singing. "I wish," he wrote, "to make German psalms for the people, that is to say sacred hymns, so that the word of God may dwell among the people also by means of song."

St. Thomas's Church in Leipzig.

Sandro Botticelli (c. 1444–1510), SPRING (The Uffizi Gallery, Florence)

The Renaissance marks the passing of European society from an exclusively religious orientation to a secular.

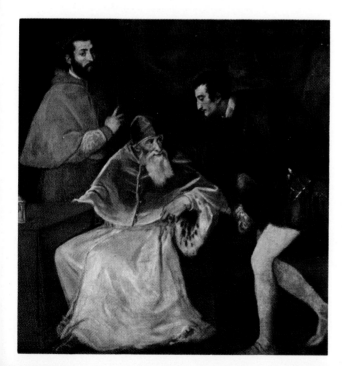

Titian (c. 1477–1576), POPE PAUL III AND HIS NEPHEWS (The National Museum, Naples)

Medieval painting dealt in types; the Renaissance concerned itself with individuals.

Rembrandt (1606–69), THE NIGHT WATCH (The Rijksmuseum, Amsterdam)

The leaders of the Dutch school embodied the vitality of a new burgher art that reached its high point in Rembrandt.

Peter Paul Rubens (1577–1640), THE GARDEN OF LOVE (The Prado, Madrid)

Baroque art reveled in the sensuous beauty of brocade and velvet, marble, jewels, and precious metals.

Luther and his aides created the first chorales. They adapted a number of tunes from Gregorian chant, others from popular sources and from secular art music. Appropriate texts and melodies were drawn, too, from Latin hymns and psalms. In the course of generations there grew up a body of religious folk song that was in the highest sense a national heritage. Originally sung in unison, these hymns soon were written in four-part harmony to be sung by the choir. The melody was put in the soprano, where all could hear it and join in singing it. In this way, the chorales greatly strengthened the trend to clear-cut melody supported by chords (homophonic texture).

In the elaborate vocal works that appeared in the Protestant church service, the chorale served as a unifying thread. When at the close of an extended work the chorale unfolded in simple four-part harmony, its granitic strength reflected the faith of a nation. One may imagine the impact upon a congregation attuned to its message. The chorale nourished centuries of German music and came to full flower in the art of Bach.

Cantata No. 140: *Wachet auf, ruft uns die Stimme*

Wachet auf, which dates from the Leipzig period (1731), is one of the finest examples of the chorale cantata as Bach perfected it. By that time the cantata in Germany had absorbed the recitative, aria, and duet of the opera; the pomp of the French operatic overture; and the dynamic instrumental style of the Italians. These elements were cemented into a unity by the all-embracing presence of the Lutheran chorale.

The sacred cantata was an integral part of the service. It was related, along with the sermon and prayers that followed it, to the Gospel for the day. Every Sunday of the church year required another. What with some extra works for holidays and special occasions, an annual cycle came to about sixty cantatas. Cantors of Lutheran churches were expected to furnish such cycles. Bach composed four or five cycles—approximately two hundred and forty to three hundred cantatas, of which only about two hundred have come down to us.

Wachet auf was composed for the twenty-seventh Sunday after Trinity. The Gospel for the day (Matthew 25:1–13) tells the parable of the five wise and the five foolish virgins, who went forth at midnight to meet the Bridegroom. Bach appropriately based the cantata on the chorale *Wachet auf, ruft uns die Stimme* (Awake, a Voice Is Calling) by the mystic poet-composer Philipp Nicolai (1556–1608), who wrote both the words and music of the famous hymn. The three verses of the chorale form the supporting pillars of Bach's structure. They occur at the beginning, middle, and end of the cantata. Between these are two recitatives and two duets. It is not known who wrote the text for these. The image of Christ as Heavenly Bridegroom stirred Bach's imagination to a work of poetic mysticism.

397

1. Chorale Fantasia. E-flat major, ¾ time.

Wachet auf, ruft uns die Stimme,	Awake, a voice is calling—
der Wächter sehr hoch auf der Zinne,	The watchman high on the tower,
wach auf, du Stadt Jerusalem!	Awake, city of Jerusalem!
Mitternacht heisst diese Stunde;	This is the hour of midnight;
sie rufen uns mit hellem Munde:	They call us with bright voices:
wo seid ihr klugen Jungfrauen?	Where are you, wise Virgins?
Wohl auf, der Bräut'gam kommt,	Cheer up, the Bridegroom cometh.
steht auf, die Lampen nehmt! Alleluja!	Arise, take your lamps! Alleluia!
Macht euch bereit zu der Hochzeit,	Make yourselves ready for the wedding,
ihr müsset ihm entgegen gehn.	You must go forth to greet him.

A majestic dotted rhythm, established at the outset, derives from the French overture and evokes the image of a stately procession. This is counterposed to the syncopated figure introduced in the fifth measure by the violins and imitated in the oboes:

Some commentators see in these two motives the approach of the Bridegroom's procession and the impatience of the Virgins. Be that as it may, the instrumental introduction establishes the proper mood of expectancy. The music is scored for two oboes and a tenor oboe; *violino piccolo* (a small violin tuned a minor third higher than the ordinary violin); first and second violins, violas, and the figured bass, whose harmonies—in sacred music—are generally realized on the organ.

The chorus is in the usual four parts, with a horn playing along with the sopranos. The chorale is sung by the sopranos in notes of equal value, with a few intermediate notes omitted. Heard in this skeletal version, the melody stands

apart from the other voices, which sing the same text in livelier rhythms. This distinction between the soprano and the three other voices is maintained throughout the movement.

A similar distinction is drawn between the material entrusted to the instruments and that presented by the voices. Besides maintaining the basic dotted rhythm, the instruments present a more florid counterpoint. The two streams of sound, vocal and instrumental, advance side by side, the instrumental coming to the fore during the interludes that separate the lines of the chorale. There are fine examples of the tone painting dear to the Baroque. The word *hoch* (high) in line 2, for example, occurs on the highest note of the phrase. So too the lower voices generate excitement by leaping upward on such words as *wach' auf* (awake); *wo, wo, wo seid ihr* (where, where are you?); *wohl auf* (cheer up) and *steht auf* (arise). The word *Alleluja!* is treated melismatically, with the voices executing exuberant roulades on a single syllable. The altos enter first, the tenors in imitation, then the basses, in a fugal passage that serves as interlude between two lines of the chorale. Now the sopranos enter with the *Alleluja*, still maintaining their steady, unvarying rhythm.

The music for the first three lines of the poem is repeated for the next three. From then on the movement proceeds by the process of continuous expansion that is so characteristic of the Baroque. The key scheme underlines the architecture: the music modulates from the home key of E-flat to the Dominant, B-flat; from E-flat to the relative minor, C minor, and finally back to E-flat. The instrumental introduction is repeated da capo at the end, enclosing the spacious design within a frame. This fantasia is unrivaled for richness of detail within a highly coordinated scheme.

2. Recitative for Tenor.

Er kommt, er kommt, der Bräut'gam kommt!	He comes, he comes, the Bridegroom comes!
Ihr Töchter Zions, kommt heraus,	O daughters of Zion, come out,
sein Ausgang eilet aus der Höhe	He hastens to come from on high
in euer Mutter Haus.	To your dwelling place.
Der Bräut'gam kommt,	The Bridegroom comes,
der einem Rehe und jungem Hirsche	Like a roe, a young deer
gleich auf denen Hügeln springt	Who leaps among the hills,
und euch das Mahl der Hochzeit bringt.	And brings you the wedding feast.
Wacht auf, ermuntert euch!	Wake up, be of good cheer
den Bräut'gam zu empfangen;	To receive the Bridegroom.
dort, sehet, kommt er hergegangen.	There, see how he comes along.

This is *secco* ("dry") recitative, supported by double bass and organ. The vocal line makes wide leaps on such words of action as *er kommt*. Again the highest note in the vocal line is associated with the idea of height—*Höhe*. The recitative begins and ends in C minor.

3. Aria (Duet, Soprano and Bass). C minor, 6/8 time.

SOPRANO	
Wann kommst du, mein Heil?	When will you come, my salvation?
BASS	
Ich komme, dein Teil.	I am coming, your appointed one.
SOPRANO	
Ich warte mit brennendem Öle.	I wait, with the lamp lit.
Eröffne den Saal zum himmlischen Mahl,	Open the hall to the heavenly banquet.
komm, Jesu!	Come, Jesus!
BASS	
Ich öffne den Saal zum himmlischen Mahl.	I open the hall to the heavenly banquet.
ich komme; komm', liebliche Seele!	I come. O come, lovely Soul!

The instrumental introduction is a solo for *violino piccolo*, which presents not only the principal melodic idea but also the fanciful arabesques that it will subsequently execute as contrapuntal figuration behind the voices. The interchange between soprano and bass—first a phrase for each, then the two voices overlapping—creates the effect of a sweet, intimate dialogue, while the violin plays a florid line in the nature of a rhapsodic improvisation. The instrumental introduction is repeated at the end as a coda.

4. Chorale. E-flat major, ¼ time.

Zion hört die Wächter singen,	Zion hears the watchmen singing,
das Herz tut ihr vor Freuden springen,	Her heart leaps for joy,
sie wacht und steht eilend auf.	She awakes and quickly rises.
Ihr Freund kommt von Himmel prächtig,	Her friend comes from heaven, resplendent,
von Gnaden stark, von Wahrheit mächtig,	Strong in grace, powerful in truth;
ihr Licht wird hell, ihr Stern geht auf.	Her light shines bright, her star rises.
Nun komm, du werte Kron,	Now come, thou precious crown,
Herr Jesu, Gottes Sohn. Hosianna!	Lord Jesus, Son of God, Hosanna!
Wir folgen all' zum Freudensaal	We follow to the hall of joy
und halten mit das Abendmahl.	To partake of the Lord's Supper.

The second verse of the chorale is sung by the tenors in a more melodious version than was heard before; it is based on shorter note values; and the intermediate notes are included, giving the full outline of the tune. The chorale is presented in combination with a most arresting counter melody, which is

played by violins and violas.

This movement, essentially, is a trio for tenor voices, strings, and basso continuo. It is the best-known movement of the cantata.

5. Recitative for Bass.

So geh' herein zu mir, du mir erwählte Braut!	So come to me, my chosen bride!
Ich habe mich mit dir in Ewigkeit vertraut.	I have pledged my troth to you in eternity.
Dich will ich auf mein Herz, auf meinen Arm	On my heart, on my arm,
gleich wie ein Siegel setzen,	I will set you as a seal,
und dein betrübtes Aug' ergötzen.	And will delight your sorrowful eyes.
Vergiss, o Seele, nun die Angst,	Forget, dear Soul, your anguish,
den Schmerz den du erdulden müssen;	The pain you had to bear;
auf meiner Linken sollst du ruh'n,	May you rest at my left,
und meine Rechte soll dich küssen.	And be kissed on my right.

This recitative for bass is supported by strings and continuo. The music moves from E-flat to B-flat.

6. Aria (Duet for Soprano and Bass). B-flat major, 4/4 time.

SOPRANO	
Mein Freund ist mein!	My friend is mine!
BASS	
Und ich bin dein!	And I am thine!
BOTH	
Die Liebe soll nichts scheiden.	Let nothing part true love.
SOPRANO	
Ich will mit dir, du sollst mit mir,	I with you, you with me,
BOTH	
In Himmels Rosen weiden,	We'll delight in the roses of heaven,
da Freude die Fülle, da Wonne wird sein.	In the fullness of joy, of rapture.

This aria-duet is colored by the tone of the oboe, whose florid counterpoint accompanies the feelingful interchange between soprano and bass. The mood is one of quiet joy and fulfillment. The two voices not only alternate in brief phrases but also join in extended passages, now imitating, now contrasting with each other. Bach cast this number in the form of the traditional da capo aria of the opera house; the first part of the duet is repeated. Notice the repetition of text to allow for musical expansion.

7. Chorale. E-flat major, 4/4 time.

Gloria sei dir gesungen	May Gloria be sung to Thee
mit Menschen- und englischen Zungen,	With the tongues of men and angels,
mit Harfen und mit Cymbeln schon.	With lovely harps and cymbals.
Von zwölf Perlen sind die Pforten	Of twelve pearls are wrought the gates
an deiner Stadt; wir sind Konsorten	Of Thy city; we are companions
der Engel hoch um deinen Thron.	Of the angel high above Thy throne.
Kein Aug' hat je gespürt,	No eye has ever beheld,
kein Ohr hat je gehört solche Freude.	No ear has ever heard such joy
Des sind wir froh, io, io!	As we feel, ee-o, ee-o,
ewig in dulci jubilo.	Forever *in dulci jubilo* (in sweet jubilation).

The chorale is now sung in the four-part harmonization of Bach. Each voice is supported by instruments of the full ensemble. Thus, at the climax of the cantata, the melody stands revealed in all its simplicity and grandeur.

The Passion According to St. Matthew

A *Passion* is a musical setting of that portion of the Gospels which deals with the suffering and death of Christ. By the time of Bach, the Passion had developed into an extended music drama performed in the Lutheran Church during Holy Week. His two Passions, according to St. Matthew and St. John, bring this art form to its highest level.

The Passion According to St. Matthew is in two parts. The first centers about the Last Supper and the Agony in the Garden, the taking of Jesus and the flight of His apostles; the second deals with His trial, death, and burial. By this division the first part becomes predominantly lyric and contemplative, the second turbulent and dramatic. Bach completed the *St. Matthew Passion* in 1729, when he was forty-four years old; he directed its first performance in St. Thomas's Church in Leipzig on Good Friday of that year. Dividing his modest forces into two choirs and two orchestras, he utilized the vast spaces of his church for the kind of listening that we today would label stereophonic (as had been done at St. Mark's by Giovanni Gabrieli and other masters of the Venetian school). The instrumental groups included flutes, oboes, and strings, with basso continuo.

The verses of the Gospel are sung by the Evangelist, that is, the narrator, in "dry" or *secco* recitative, accompanied by organ or harpsichord. Yet this narration is dramatized. When the Evangelist tells us what Jesus, Peter, or any other character said, the voice of that character takes over. Just as medieval painters represented Christ with a halo, so Bach wreathes the words of the Savior in a "halo" of string tone. This procedure, which he adopted from earlier composers, underlines the somber sweetness of Christ's words.

Into the action narrated by the Evangelist are interpolated a series of lyric meditations. They were intended to give the congregation an opportunity to reflect on the significance of what was taking place before them. These lyric numbers are in the form of arias and duets, some with chorus; accompanied recitatives; and choruses. When the accompanied recitative takes on a lyric expressiveness, it is called *arioso*—that is, in the manner of an aria. The chorus plays a twofold role. At times it takes part in the action by representing the crowd that mocks Jesus or demands his death; at other times it represents the faithful who comment or reflect upon the action. The chorales, originally sung by the congregation, gave the listeners a chance to participate in the drama. These sturdy tunes contrast with the florid vocalism of the arias and duets; they are the pillars upon which rests Bach's vast architecture.

We will begin with the scene on the Mount of Olives, in which Jesus begins to foretell His end.

No. 20. Recitative for the Evangelist (tenor) and Jesus (bass).

And when they had sung an hymn of praise together, they went out unto the Mount of Olives. Then said Jesus unto them: "This very night ye shall be offended because of me. For it hath been written: I will smite the Shepherd, and the sheep of the flock shall be scattered abroad. But after I am risen again, I will go before you into Galilee."

The ascending scale in the bass after the Evangelist's first line is an example of Bach's musical symbolism, representing the ascent of the Mount. With the speech of Jesus, the "dry" recitative is replaced by the halo of string sound we have referred to. The idea of scattering the sheep inspires an agitated passage that contrasts with the measured tone of the rest; it is marked by decisive leaps in the melody line. At the words *Wann ich aber auferstehe* (But after I am risen again), the violins play an ascending figure, another example of Bach's symbolism. The recitative, which begins in B minor and passes through several keys, ends with a cadence in E, the key of the next section.

No. 21. Chorale. *Erkenne mich, mein Hüter* (Acknowledge me, my keeper). Here the faithful reflect on the word *Hirten* (shepherd) that has just been uttered by Jesus. This melody is the Passion chorale, which is heard five times in the course of the work.

Er - ken - ne mich, mein Hü - ter, mein Hir - te, nimm mich an,
Von dir, Quell al - ler Gü - ter, ist mir viel Gut's ge - tan.

Since the text speaks of the sweet nourishment offered by Christ, Bach gives the melody a diatonic harmonization in E major.

No. 22. Recitative for the Evangelist, Jesus, and Peter (bass).

Then Peter answered, and said to Him: "Although all men shall be offended because of Thee, yet I will never be offended." Jesus said to him: "Verily, I say to thee that in this night, before the cock crows even thou shalt thrice deny me." Peter said to Him: "Though I should die with Thee, yet will I not deny Thee." And likewise said also all the disciples.

The idea contained in Peter's word *ärgerten* (offended) calls forth an emotional chromatic harmony known to musicians as a diminished-seventh chord. (It can be sounded on the piano by striking the notes D♯, F♯, A, C.) The speech of Jesus, as before, is accompanied by strings. The diminished-seventh chord returns on the words *der Hahn krähet* (the cock crows), and again on *dreimal* (thrice), thus giving dramatic color to the idea of Peter's coming denial. His declaration of loyalty is made boldly, as is that of the disciples.

No. 23. Chorale. *Ich will hier bei dir Stehen* (I would stand here beside Thee). The Passion chorale is repeated a half-tone lower than before, in the key of E-flat. Since all the listeners knew that Peter would end by denying Christ, this contemplation of human frailty could not but strengthen their desire to conquer it through faith. There follows the scene in the Garden of Gethsemane.

No. 24. Recitative for Evangelist and Jesus.

Then cometh Jesus with them unto a place called Gethsemane, and said to the disciples: "Sit ye here, while I go yonder and pray." And He took with Him Peter, and the two sons of Zebedee, and began to be sorrowful and very heavy. Then said Jesus to them: "My soul is sorrowful, even unto death; tarry here and watch with me."

The key word *betet* (pray) is emphasized by being extended for three beats. Jesus' second utterance is given in mournful tones at a very slow tempo. His anguish calls forth a diminished-seventh chord; the word *Tod* (death) descends to the lowest note of this passage. The string sound is particularly affecting here; repeated chords in eighth-note rhythm suggest the trembling in His soul.

No. 25. Arioso and chorus. *O Schmerz! hier zittert das gequälte Herz!* (O grief, here trembles the tormented heart). At this point, when Jesus is alone in the garden of Gethsemane, Bach halts the action to introduce a lyric meditation on His plight. This is in the form of an accompanied recitative in F minor for tenor and chorus. The tenor's anguished phrases alternate with the chorus singing a rich harmonization of a chorale introduced earlier in the work (No. 3). In this manner the response of the individual to the Agony in the Garden is allied with the sorrow of the group.

> TENOR:
> O grief, here trembles the tormented Heart!
> How it sinks, how His face becomes pale!
> CHORUS:
> What is the cause of all such woes?
> TENOR:
> The judge leads Him to judgment,
> There is no comfort, no helper.
> CHORUS:
> Ah, my sins have struck Thee down.
> TENOR:
> He suffers all Hell's pains,
> He shall pay for others' sins.
> CHORUS:
> Ah, Lord Jesus, I have deserved
> What Thou art suffering.
> TENOR:
> Ah, if my love, My Savior,
> Could diminish or help Thee bear
> Thy anguish and Thy trembling,
> How gladly would I remain here with Thee.

This deeply felt lament exemplifies the baroque love of contrasts blended into a unity. The solo voice, in high register, contrasts with the flowing melodic line of the chorale. There is a contrast as well in the orchestration: flutes and oboes wreathe the solo melody in a melancholy sound, while the chorus is accompanied by the organ. Bach calls for an oboe da caccia ("hunting oboe"), a gentle-voiced alto member of the oboe family that was ultimately replaced by the English horn. The solo line moves at a moderate gait, in contrast to the slow, even pace of the chorale. Repeated sixteenth notes in the bass suggest the Savior's agitation. Although Bach's score is extremely sparing of dynamic indications, this is one spot where he specifically directs the choir to sing softly, thereby emphasizing the solemn character of the chorale.

Chromatic inflection in the melody evokes the sorrow of Christ, as does the use of diminished-seventh harmonies (for example, in the second half of the second measure at the word *gequälte*—"tormented"). The tenor melody is heard against countermelodies in the woodwinds. The first three notes of the flute recur in various guises as the basic motive of the piece. Throughout this section, chromatic harmonies and diminished-seventh chords reinforce the atmosphere of grief. The F-minor tonality gives way to an incomplete cadence that leads directly into the C minor of the following aria. Notice that the last line of the text harks back to Jesus' injunction *wachet bei mir* (watch with me).

No. 26. *Ich will bei meinem Jesu wachen* (I will watch beside my Jesus). This aria for tenor and chorus, in C minor, expands the mood of lyric contemplation into a well-rounded number that unfolds in a modified A-B-A form. Here, too, the point of departure is Jesus' injunction to "watch with me."

> TENOR:
> I will watch beside my Jesus.
> CHORUS:
> Thus all our sins are put to sleep.
> TENOR:
> For my death, His soul's anguish atones.
> His sorrowing makes me full of joys.
> CHORUS:
> So for us His passion must be
> Both truly bitter and yet sweet.

The instrumental prelude features a solo oboe, whose poignant tone is pitted against the tenor voice throughout the number. Two motives are presented, symbolizing the ideas of wakefulness and sleep contained in the first two lines of text. The first (bracket A), with its rhythmic vivacity and bold upward thrust, suggests the watchman's call; it is to be carried by the tenor. The second (B), with its more restrained movement, is in the manner of a cradle song, and will be assigned to the chorus:

When motive A is presented by the solo voice, the key word *Jesu* is expanded:

It is clear that Bach at this point does not differentiate between vocal and instrumental style. The motives presented by the orchestra are lyrical enough to be sung, while the voice is treated as another instrument, with the result that motives can be assigned interchangeably to both.

405

The contrast between solo and chorus is underlined by the instrumentation. The tenor is accompanied by oboe, the chorus by flutes and strings. The first section of the aria is taken up with a dialogue between solo and chorus on the first two lines of the text, which are repeated over and over. The florid tenor line proceeds with rhythmic animation and with frequent sixteenth notes, as in the example quoted. Following is an ornate expansion (melisma) of the key word *wachen* (watch):

wa - - - - chen,

The chorus, on the other hand, moves in even eighth notes. The first section comes to an end with a cadence in the related key of E-flat major.

The middle section expands the next four lines of text. The solo part takes on a more sustained rhythm, moving mostly in quarter notes and halves, but the accompaniment persists with the florid motives of the first part. Here again is that diversity within a unity of which the Baroque was so fond. The middle section modulates freely, with a florid melisma on the basic word *Freuden* (joys). This section maintains the distinction between the ornate character of the solo and the subdued choral part. The music returns to the home key of C minor; the A section is repeated in abridged form, this time remaining in the home key. The orchestral prelude, repeated as a postlude, rounds off the movement.

The two scenes we have discussed here will serve as an introduction to the *St. Matthew Passion*. Only a hearing of the complete work can reveal the manifold beauties of this masterpiece of religious art.

Mass in B Minor

The quality of sublimity that is the outstanding characteristic of the B-minor Mass informs the conception as a whole. In this instance too, while excerpts may serve as an introduction to the work, only a hearing of it in its entirety will reveal the vast terrain that has here been subjugated to the creative will.

The first chorus of the Gloria is a setting of the text *Gloria in excelsis Deo, et in terra pax hominibus bonae voluntatis* (Glory to God in the highest and on earth peace to men of good will). The movement, in D major, calls for three high trumpet parts that wreathe the chorus in luminous sound. Also used in this section of the Mass are two flutes, two oboes, bassoons, timpani, strings, and organ.

The movement opens with a striking motive that derives its vigor from the brisk triple meter and wide leaps. The chorus is in five parts: first and second sopranos, altos, tenors, and basses. Luxuriant counterpoint unfolds in flowing lines; words like *gloria* and *excelsis* (highest) are repeated and expanded until

they dissolve in music. There is much repetition of text. The words establish the basic affection of the movement, and are then repeated over and over again. The steady beat of the triple meter creates a framework for enormous rhythmic vitality. The voices enter in rapid succession and build steadily to the abrupt change of mood and pace at the second idea, "and on earth peace to men of good will." A new motive establishes a mood of supplication. Then the movement gathers momentum and broadens into a majestic stream.

Characteristic of Bach's writing in the Mass is the aria for alto on the text *Qui sedes ad dexteram Patris, miserere nobis* (You, who sit at the right hand of the Father, have mercy on us). This is the ninth number and is part of the

Gloria. The solo voice is contrasted with the oboe d'amore, the mezzo-soprano oboe whose sweet tone was much prized during the Baroque. The key word *miserere* (have mercy) establishes the basic affection of the music, a mood of entreaty that is admirably underlined by the dark resonance of the alto voice and the plaintive timbre of the oboe. The aria is in B minor, in a gentle 6/8 that sounds all the better for not being dragged. The vocal line is florid yet impregnated with feeling. The opening section is followed by two others, in F-sharp minor and D major, with a coda that recalls the opening phrase.

Crucifixus etiam pro nobis sub Pontio Pilato, passus et sepultus est (He was also crucified for us, suffered under Pontius Pilate, and was buried). For the most dramatic chorus of the Mass Bach ventured into the territory that lies between church and opera house. This stupendous outpouring of grief, which is part of the Credo, traces its lineage to the operatic laments of the seventeenth century, such as that of Dido. The movement unfolds above a chromatic ground bass with a striking resemblance to that used by Purcell in the culminating aria of *Dido and Aeneas*.

Two symbols of grief—chromatic harmony and descending movement—dominate this choral fresco. The ground bass is stated thirteen times. Minor mode and the use of dissonance reinforce the atmosphere of sorrow, as does the depersonalized sound of two flutes that engage in a dialogue with the violins and violas. When the nethermost point has been reached there is an extraordinary modulation to G major. Despair gives way to the jubilant chorus of the Resurrection, in D major: *Et resurrexit tertia die secundum scripturas; et ascendit in coelum, sedet ad dexteram Patris. Et iterum venturus est cum gloria judicare vivos et mortuos cujus regni non erit finis* (And on the third day He rose again according to the Scriptures; He ascended into heaven and sits at the right hand of the Father. He will come again in glory to judge the living and the dead. And of His kingdom there will be no end). Three trumpets and kettledrums help announce the joyful tidings. The basic affection is established by brisk triple meter, vigorous triplets, and the bold upthrust of the theme.

The highest trumpet part requires virtuoso playing. The voices pile one upon the other in intricate imitation as the central word *resurrexit* expands into florid arabesque. Orchestral interludes set off the ample architecture. This is music to resound over hills and valleys: the pronouncement of one who saw God enthroned in heaven and translated the vision into an enduring memorial to the divinity in man.

The notion may be dismissed that Bach was unappreciated in his lifetime. He could not have continued to write cantatas for thirty-five years if he had not reached his public. He was known and admired by his generation even if his greatness was not realized in full. It was the following generations that neglected him. The Lutheran world out of which he stemmed ceased to be a living force even while he was immortalizing its spirit. Great changes were impending, in life and art alike. In this new climate his polyphony seemed pedantic, his baroque monumentality heavy and oppressive. Rejected by fashionable taste, his music disappeared from the scene. Manuscripts of his were suffered to be lost. The plates of *The Art of the Fugue* were sold for the price of the metal when the work failed to attract purchasers. To the musical public of the 1760s the name Bach meant his four sons, whose success as composers far exceeded his. Even they considered his music old-fashioned. One of them, with an engaging lack of filial piety, referred to him as "the old Wig."

Yet the memory of him did not wholly die. It was kept alive in the decades after his death by his sons, his pupils, and by those who had heard him play. Then the revival began, tentatively at first but with increasing force until it had become a veritable renascence. The romantic age felt akin to his fervor, his chromatic harmonies, his vaulting architecture, the surge and splendor of his polyphony. The *St. Matthew Passion,* forgotten for more than three-quarters of a century, was resurrected by the twenty-year-old Mendelssohn in an epochal performance in 1829. Chopin practiced Bach before his concerts. Liszt transcribed some of the organ works for the piano. Schumann was one of the founders of the Bach Society, an organization that undertook the monumental task of publishing a complete edition of the master's works.

Bach's spirit animated not only the nineteenth century but, in even more fruitful manner, the twentieth. We see him today not only as a consummate artist who brought new meanings to music, but as one of the gigantic figures of Western culture.

71 George Frideric Handel

"Milord, I should be sorry if I only entertained them. I wished to make them better."

If Bach represents the subjective mysticism of the late Baroque, Handel incarnates its worldly pomp. Born in the same year, the two giants of the age never met. The Cantor of Leipzig had little point of contact with a composer who from the first was cut out for an international career. Handel's natural habitat was the opera house. He was at home amid the intrigues of court life. A magnificent adventurer, he gambled for fame and fortune in a feverish struggle to impose his will upon the world; and dominated the musical life of a nation for a century after his death.

His Life

He was born in 1685 at Halle in Germany, in what was then the kingdom of Saxony, the son of a prosperous barber-surgeon who did not regard music as a suitable profession for a young man of the middle class. His father's death left him free to follow his bent. After a year at the University of Halle the ambitious youth went to Hamburg, where he gravitated to the opera house and entered the orchestra as second violinist. He soon absorbed the Italian operatic style that reigned in Hamburg. His first opera, *Almira,* was written when he was twenty and created a furor.

Handel's thoughts turned to Italy. Only there, he felt, would he master the operatic art. He reached Rome shortly before his twenty-second birthday; the three years he spent in Italy unfolded against a splendid background peopled by music-loving princes and cardinals. His opera *Rodrigo* was produced in Florence under the patronage of Prince Ferdinand de' Medici. The libretto of his opera

George Frideric Handel

Agrippina was written by the Viceroy of Naples, Cardinal Grimani. Presented at Venice in 1709, the work sent the Italians into transports of delight. The theater resounded with cries of "Long live the dear Saxon!"

At the age of twenty-five Handel was appointed conductor to the Elector of Hanover. He received the equivalent of fifteen hundred dollars a year at a time when Bach at Weimar was paid eighty. A visit to London in the autumn of 1710 brought him for the first time to the city that was to be his home for well-nigh fifty turbulent years. *Rinaldo*, written in a fortnight, conquered the English public with its fresh tender melodies. A year later Handel obtained another leave and returned to London, this time for good. With the *Birthday Ode for Queen Anne* and the *Te Deum* (hymn of thanksgiving) for the Peace of Utrecht he entered upon the writing of large-scale works for great public occasions, following in the footsteps of Purcell. Anne rewarded him with a pension; whereupon nothing would make him go back to his Hanoverian master. By an unforeseen turn of events his master came to him. Anne died and the Elector ascended the throne of England as George I. The monarch was vexed with his truant composer; but he loved music more than protocol, and soon restored him to favor.

Handel's opportunity came with the founding in 1720 of the Royal Academy of Music. The enterprise, launched for the purpose of presenting Italian opera, was backed by a group of wealthy peers headed by the King. Handel was appointed one of the musical directors and at thirty-five found himself occupying a key position in the artistic life of England. For the next eight years he was active in producing and directing his operas as well as writing them. His crowded life passed at a far remove from the solitude we have come to associate with the creative process. He produced his works in bursts of inspiration that kept him chained to his desk for days at a time. He would turn out an opera in from two to three weeks.

Hardly less feverish was the struggle for power inseparable from a position such as his. Overbearing, obstinate when crossed, the Saxon was no mean master of the art of making enemies. His fiery temper found much to exercise it. He was at the mercy of the cliques at court, and was viewed with suspicion by the leaders of English thought, who saw in his operas a threat to native music and theater. Addison and Steele, in the pages of the *Spectator* and *Tatler*, missed no opportunity to attack his ventures. It must be said that other men of letters more justly estimated his stature. Pope in the *Dunciad* (1742) thus describes his monumental style:

> Strong in new Arms, lo! Giant HANDEL stands,
> Like bold Briareus, with a hundred hands;
> To stir, to rouze, to shake the Soul he comes,
> And Jove's own Thunders follow Mars's Drums.

Handel functioned in a theater riddled with the worst features of the star system. When the celebrated soprano Cuzzoni refused to sing an aria as he directed, Handel, a giant of a man, seized her around the waist and threatened to drop her out of a window if she would not obey. The rivalry between Cuzzoni and the great singer Faustina Bordoni culminated in a hair-pulling match on the stage, accompanied by the smashing of scenery and fist fights throughout the house. A rivalry no less fierce developed between Handel and his associate in directing the Academy, the composer Giovanni Bononcini. The supposition that genius resided in one or the other, which brought to the arena of art the psychology of the prize-ring, appealed strongly to the fashionable hangers-on of the Royal Academy. Bononcini was the protégé of the Tory Duchess of Marlborough; whereupon Handel, whose interest in British politics was—to say the least—limited, became *the* Whig composer. The feud was immortalized in a jingle that made the rounds of the coffee houses.

> Some say that Signor Bononcini
> Compared to Handel is a ninny;
> Whilst others say that to him Handel
> Is hardly fit to hold a candle.
> Strange that such difference should be
> 'Twixt Tweedledum and Tweedledee.

It was amid such distractions that Handel's operas—he produced forty in a period of thirty years—came into being. Some were written too hastily, in others he obviously accommodated himself to the needs of the box office; yet all bear the imprint of a genius. Despite his productivity the Royal Academy tottered to

411

Canaletto (1697–1768), VIEW OF LONDON, c. 1750. (Crown Collections, Copyright reserved to Her Majesty the Queen)

its ruin, its treasury depleted by the extravagance of the peers, its morale sapped by mismanagement and dissension. The final blow was administered in 1728 by the sensational success of John Gay's *The Beggar's Opera*. Sung in English, its tunes related to the experience of the audience, this humorous ballad opera was the answer of middle-class England to the gods and heroes of the aristocratic *opera seria*. Ironically, even a bit of Handel's *Rinaldo* found its way into the score.

It should have been apparent to the composer-impresario that a new era had dawned; but, refusing to read the omens, he invested thousands in the New Royal Academy of Music. Again a succession of operas rolled from his pen, among them *Orlando Furioso* (1733), "the boldest of his works." But not even Handel's colossal powers could indefinitely sustain the pace. He was fifty-two when he crashed. "This infernal flesh," as he called it, succumbed to a paralytic stroke. Desperate and grievously ill, he acknowledged defeat and went abroad to recover his health. His enemies gloated: the giant was finished.

They underestimated his powers of recovery. He came back to resume the battle. It needed five more expensive failures to make him realize that *opera seria* in London was finished. At this lowest point in his fortunes there opened, by chance, the road that was to lead him from opera in Italian to oratorio in English, from ruin to immortality. Many years before, in 1720, he had written a masque entitled *Haman and Mordecai*, on a text by Pope adapted from Racine's *Esther*. He subsequently decided to bring this "sacred opera" before the public. When the Bishop of London forbade the representation of biblical characters in a theater, Handel hit upon a way out. "There will be no acting upon the Stage," he announced in the advertisement, "but the house will be fitted up in a decent manner, for the audience." In this way London heard its first Handelian oratorio.

He could not remain indifferent to the advantages of a type of entertainment that dispensed with costly foreign singers and lavish scenery. *Deborah* and *Athalia* had been composed in 1733. The next six years witnessed his final struggle on behalf of *opera seria*. Then, in 1739, there followed two of his greatest oratorios, *Saul* and *Israel in Egypt*, both composed within the space of a little over three months. Many dark moments still lay ahead. He had to find his way to a new middle-class public. That indomitable will never faltered. *Messiah, Samson, Semele, Joseph and His Brethren, Hercules, Belshazzar* (1742–45), although they did not conquer at once, were received sufficiently well to encourage him to continue on his course. Finally, with *Judas Macca-baeus* (1746), the tide turned. The British public responded to the imagery of the Old Testament. The suppression of the last Stuart rebellion created the proper atmosphere for Handel's heroic tone. He kept largely to biblical subjects in the final group of oratorios (1748–52)—*Alexander Balus, Joshua, Susanna, Solomon, Jephtha*—an astonishing list for a man in his sixties. With these the master brought his work to a close.

There remained to face the final enemy—blindness. But even this blow did not reduce him to inactivity. Like Milton and Bach, he dictated his last works, which were mainly revisions of earlier ones. He continued to appear in public, conducting the oratorios and displaying his legendary powers on the organ.

In 1759, shortly after his seventy-fourth birthday, Handel began his usual oratorio season, conducting ten major works in little over a month to packed houses. *Messiah* closed the series. He collapsed in the theater at the end of the performance and died some days later. The nation he had served for half a century accorded him its highest honor. "Last night about Eight O'clock the remains of the late great Mr Handel were deposited at the foot of the Duke of Argyll's Monument in Westminster Abbey. . . . There was almost the greatest Concourse of People of all Ranks ever seen upon such, or indeed upon any other Occasion."

His Music

Himself sprung from the middle class, Handel made his career in the land where the middle class first came to power. A vast social change is symbolized by his turning from court opera to oratorio. In so doing he became one of the architects of the new bourgeois culture and a creator of the modern mass public.

The oratorios of Handel are choral dramas of overpowering vitality and grandeur. Vast murals, they are conceived in epic style. Their soaring arias and dramatic recitatives, stupendous fugues and double choruses consummate the splendor of the Baroque. With the instinct of the born leader he gauged the need of his adopted country, and created in the oratorio an art form steeped in the atmosphere of the Old Testament, ideally suited to the taste of England's middle class. In the command of Jehovah to the Chosen People to go forth and conquer the land of Canaan they recognized a clear mandate to go forth and secure the British Empire.

Handel made the chorus—the people—the center of the drama. Freed from the rapid pace imposed by stage action, he expanded to vast dimensions each scene and emotion. The chorus now touches off the action, now reflects upon it. As in Greek tragedy it serves both as protagonist and ideal spectator. The characters are drawn larger than life-size. Saul, Joshua, Deborah, Judas Maccabaeus, Samson are archetypes of human nature; creatures of destiny, majestic in defeat as in victory.

The Handelian oratorio emerged as England's national art form soon after the master's death. The hundredth anniversary of his birth was marked by a celebration in Westminster Abbey in which over five hundred singers and players participated. This number was enlarged in subsequent Handel festivals until a chorus of three and a half thousand drowned out an orchestra of five hundred, occasioning Horace Walpole's lovely remark: "The Oratorios thrive abundantly; for my part they give me an idea of Heaven, where everybody is to sing whether they have voices or not." Handel, be it remembered, produced his oratorios with a chorus of about thirty singers and a like number of instrumentalists. To increase the size of this group more than fiftyfold meant sacrificing many subtleties of his writing. Yet his art, with its grand outlines and sweeping effects, was able to take such treatment. It was indeed "the music for a great active people," inviting mass participation even as it demanded mass listening.

Handel's rhythm has the powerful drive of the Baroque. One must hear one of his choruses to realize what momentum can be achieved with a simple 4/4 time. He leaned to diatonic harmony even as Bach's more searching idiom favored the chromatic. His melody, rich in mood and feeling, unfolds in great majestic arches. His thinking is based on massive pillars of sound—the chords—within which the voices interweave. Rooted in the world of the theater, Handel made use of tone color for atmosphere and dramatic expression. His wonderful sense of sound comes out in the pieces intended for outdoor performance, the *Water Music* and *Royal Fireworks Music.*

The operas contain some of the composer's finest measures. In recent years several of these stage works have been revived with success. Handel's big choral pieces were written to celebrate occasions of national rejoicing. Most famous are the *Coronation Anthems* for the accession of George II, one of which—*Zadok the Priest*—helped crown every subsequent ruler of England. Among the master's vocal pieces are a variety of odes, cantatas, passion music, church music, chamber works, and songs. He also produced an impressive amount of instrumental music. Best known in this category are the twelve concerti grossi, Opus 6, which with Bach's *Brandenburg Concertos* represent the peak of baroque orchestral music.

Giulio Cesare

Handel's opera about Julius Caesar is one of his finest. The action hinges about Cleopatra's struggle against Ptolemy, her brother and rival for the throne of Egypt, and her love affair with Caesar—a subject that was subsequently treated, in somewhat more intellectual fashion, by George Bernard Shaw. The libretto freely departs from historical fact. This does not seem to have disturbed either Handel or his listeners, but it did give him the opportunities he needed for the arias, duets, and ensemble numbers that were his prime concern. Within the conventions of the baroque lyric theater—the role of Julius Caesar, for example, was written for an alto castrato—he created characters who came alive through the music.

A scene from GIULIO CESARE (New York City Opera production)

We will discuss three arias that show the scope of the work. The first is Caesar's *Presti omai* (No. 2), in which he exults as the proud conqueror of Egypt.

Presti omai l'Egizia	Let Egypt at last
le sue palme al vincitor!	Offer her palms to the victor!

This aria, today usually sung by a bass, is an Allegro in D in common time. The "basic affection" of vigor and assertiveness is established in the introduction, which is played by strings and continuo. The opening measures set up an unflagging rhythm that gives this number its momentum. The mood is reinforced by the energetic vocal solo, which begins with wide leaps:

415

Pre - sti o - ma - i   l'E - gi - zia ter - ra,   l'E - gi - zia ter - ra   etc.

The two lines of text are split into phrases that are repeated over and over. Structurally the aria divides into three sections. The first modulates to the key of the Dominant, A major, with a florid expansion on the word *palme*, which at this brisk gait demands real virtuosity of the singer. This melisma shows Handel's fondness for the ascending sequence; he presents a motive four times in succession, each a step higher:

(pa - - - - - - - - - -)

The second section returns to the home key, D. It begins like the first but branches off in another direction. Again there is florid expansion of *palme*. The third section begins in G major but soon returns to D, again with a melisma on *palme*, in the course of which the voice holds a long-sustained A while the harmonies change (pedal point). This time the word *vincitor* (victor) comes in for expansion as well. The forward drive of the music is interrupted, just before the end of the solo, by a *fermata* (a held note or silence of indeterminate length). This gives the singer an opportunity to improvise a cadenza. The introduction is repeated as a postlude and brings the number to an assertive close.

Cleopatra, intent upon conquering Caesar with her beauty, arranges in Act II to have him come to her palace. He is enchanted by her love song (No. 17).

V'adoro, pupille, saette d'amore,	I adore you, O eyes, arrows of love,
le vostre faville son grate nel sen.	Your sparks are pleasing to my heart.
Pietose vi brama il mesto mio core,	My sad heart begs for your mercy,
ch'ogn'ora vi chiama l'amato suo ben.	Never ceasing to call you its beloved.

In the hands of the masters the da capo aria was not a set form but was varied to accommodate the most diverse situations. In this case the orchestral introduction that would normally open the aria has been heard earlier as part of the "symphony" that greeted Caesar upon his arrival at the palace. Handel's orchestration creates the atmosphere for a passage of love. It includes, besides the usual oboes, bassoons, and strings, a harp, a viola da gamba, and a bass lute. Cleopatra's aria is a long-breathed Largo in F in ¾ time Notice how Handel uses the first four notes as a recurrent motive, continually varying the first interval:

416

He follows this by presenting the motive in an ascending sequence; it is heard five times in a row. Such insistence on a single pattern is unusual. There is the usual repetition of text. The first two lines are presented in the opening section, which ends with a cadence in F. Cleopatra's mention of her sad heart calls for a change of mood; the middle section begins in D minor (the relative minor of F) and is taken at a somewhat faster pace, reflecting the more intense feeling of the third and fourth lines. At the end of the middle section Handel, instead of proceeding immediately with the repetition of the first part, interjects a line of recitative on the part of the enraptured Caesar: "Not even the Thunderer in heaven has a melody to rival so sweet a song!" The repetition of the A section gives the soprano an opportunity for embellishing the melody with trills, runs, grace notes, and similar ornaments. These were not written down by Handel but were added by the singer in accordance with the performance practice of the Baroque.

In Act III Cleopatra is taken prisoner by Ptolemy, her brother and rival for the throne. He puts her in chains. She laments her fate in a moving da capo aria, *Piangerò la sorte mia* (No. 32; in the New York City Opera recording of *Giulio Cesare*, this aria is shifted to Act I).

Piangerò la sorte mia,	I shall weep for my fate,
si crudele e tanto ria,	So cruel and so evil,
finchè vita in petto avrò.	As long as I have life in my breast.
Ma poi morta d'ogn'intorno	But then in death, from every side,
il tiranno e notte e giorno	My ghost shall haunt the tyrant
fatta spettro agiterò.	Both night and day.

The text falls into two sentences, each of three lines, that give rise to the two contrasting sections of this A-B-A form. The first is a grandly pathetic slow movement in E with a melody of extraordinary breadth. Notice how the gently descending line in the last two measures balances the upward leaps that precede:

Flutes double the first-violin part, imparting a subtle poignance to the orchestral color. Wide leaps in the second phrase—an octave, a seventh, a ninth—add tension to the melody line. Individual words and phrases are repeated, so that the setting of the first three lines grows into a sizable section that ends with a cadence in E major.

The middle section is an Allegro in $\frac{4}{4}$, in the relative minor of E, C-sharp minor. The abrupt change of tempo, meter, key, and mode creates an intensification of emotion. There is florid expansion on the crucial word *agiterò* (shall haunt). The section ends with a cadence in the key of the Dominant, G-sharp minor. The first section is then repeated da capo, with embellishments.

Music for the Royal Fireworks

The *Music for the Royal Fireworks* underlines Handel's position as a kind of composer laureate who was expected to furnish the music for great public occasions. This particular occasion was the celebration ordered by George II to mark the Peace of Aix-la-Chapelle that ended the War of the Austrian Succession. Although the political gains to England were negligible, the plans for the celebration were on the grandest scale, including a display of fireworks and the din of a hundred and one brass cannon. As for the music, the Duke of Montague wrote that George "hoped there would be no fidles. If the thing war to be in such a manner as certainly to please the King, it ought to consist of no kind of instrument but martial instruments. Any other I am sure will put him out of humour."

Handel wanted to include strings; but, always prudent in his dealings with monarchs, he gave in. He scored his suite for a festive combination of over fifty wind instruments: nine trumpets, nine horns, twenty-four oboes, twelve bassoons and one contrabassoon, three pairs of kettledrums, and one or more side drums. He later rescored the work, adding strings, but the piece has been recorded with the original orchestration and well exemplifies the baroque fondness for grand effects.

Everything went wrong on the great day (April 26, 1749). The fireworks refused to light up, rockets went astray and fell on the crowd, a pavilion caught fire and burned down. "Very little mischief was done," wrote Horace Walpole, "and but two persons killed." An allegorical statue of "George giving Peace to Britannia dropped, with his head aflame, into a cauldron of fire." To top it all, the designer of the fireworks "machine" went out of his mind, drew his sword on one of his colleagues, and had to be hustled away. What survived was Handel's music.

The suite—in D major, save for two dances in D minor—is written in the concertante style that pits dissimilar masses of sound against each other—woodwinds against brass, trumpets against horns, trumpets and oboes against the tutti, with all sorts of opportunities for delightful echo effects and terraced dynamics. The Overture opens with a slow section in dotted rhythm that reveals all the pomp and dignity of the French style. Truly Handelian is the breadth of the opening phrase:

The Allegro that follows is in ¾ time. A fanfare-like summons on the trumpets elicits a tuneful reply from the oboes. The dotted rhythms continue:

In this Allegro Handel takes full advantage of the possibilities for contrast between trumpets, horns, and oboes, as well as between each of these and the entire group. The music modulates from D major to A, unfolding with the continuous flow and unflagging energy typical of baroque movements. Presently sixteenth notes appear, bustling up and down in rapid figuration. Following a fermata, the opening fanfare is repeated as is the melody in dotted rhythm. A section in B minor (the relative minor of D) leads into a brief adagio interlude, played softly by oboes and bassoon; then the first half of the Allegro is repeated da capo, ending with an assertive cadence in D.

The second movement is a bourrée played by oboes and bassoons. (A *bourrée* is a gay French dance in duple meter.) This number is in the shapely two-part form (A-B) favored by the dance movements of the suite. The first part modulates from D minor to the relative major, F; the second part moves back to D minor. Each part is played twice. While Handel did not mark the dynamic gradations in the score, it is the accepted practice to play the repetitions softly; then both parts are played without repeats, somewhat louder. In the first part, the opening phrase of four measures is answered by one of six. (We found similar nonsymmetrical patterns in the minuets of Haydn and Mozart.) The second part consists of four four-measure phrases. When Handel re-scored the piece with the addition of strings, he directed that only the strings play in the repetition.

Third is *La Paix* (Peace), marked Largo alla Siciliana (Broadly, in the manner of a siciliano). The pastoral character of the siciliano, which we encountered in the slow movement of Vivaldi's Concerto in D minor, is underlined by the flowing 12/8 meter, the gentle accompaniment of broken chords, and the lyrical melody in dotted rhythm:

Trumpets, horns, and oboes wreathe the movement in an open-air sound, while bassoons and contrabassoon carry the bass line. As usual, the piece is in A-B form; both parts are repeated.

The fourth movement is an Allegro entitled *La Réjouissance* (Rejoicing), whose vigor and sonority contrast vividly with the preceding movement. The bold melody makes a capital effect. The leaps in measure 4 balance the repeated notes and stepwise movement in the first three measures. Notice the use of sequence (bracketed):

The piece is in binary form (A-B). The first part modulates from D major to A; the second part begins in D and stays there. The various repetitions are scored to produce different dynamic levels, so that the orchestration brings out the terraced dynamics, in turn highlighting the form. Laid out along bold, simple lines, *La Réjouissance* with its colorful use of "martial instruments" embodies all the pomp and vigor of the Baroque.

The suite ends with two minuets, the first in D minor, the second in D major. The custom has established itself of treating the two as one number by beginning with the second minuet, using the first as a Trio or middle section, and repeating the first da capo. Here, too, orchestration and terraced dynamics serve to underline the form, which is based throughout on symmetrical four-bar phrases. The Minuet in D minor is scored for oboes and bassoons, so that it can be played softly. Handel directs that the D-major Minuet be played three times, with varying orchestrations as in *La Réjouissance*. In the end all the instruments play together; Handel's instruction is written in a curious mingling of Italian and English: "tutti insieme and the Side Drums." The effect is very grand indeed.

Messiah

"For the Relief of the Prisoners in the several Gaols, and for the Support of Mercer's Hospital in Stephen's-street and of the Charitable Infirmary on the Inn's Quay, on Monday the 12th of April, will be performed at the Musick Hall in Fishamble-Street, *Mr Handel's new Grand Oratorio, called the Messiah*, in which the Gentlemen of the Choirs of both Cathedrals will assist, with some Concertos on the Organ, by Mr Handel." In this fashion Dublin was apprised in the spring of 1742 of the launching of one of the world's most widely loved works.

The music was written down in twenty-four days, Handel working as one possessed. His servant found him, after the completion of the Hallelujah Chorus, with tears streaming from his eyes. "I did think I did see all Heaven before me, and the great God Himself!" Upon finishing *Messiah*, the master went on without a pause to *Samson*, the first part of which was ready two weeks later. Truly it was an age of giants.

With its massive choruses, tuneful recitatives, and broadly flowing arias *Messiah* has come to represent the Handelian oratorio in the public mind. Actually it is not typical of the oratorios as a whole. Those are imbued with dramatic conflict, while *Messiah* is cast in a mood of lyric contemplation.

The libretto is a compilation of verses from the Bible. The first part treats of the prophecy of the coming of Christ and His birth; the second of His suffering, death, and the spread of His doctrine; and the third of the redemption of the world through faith. The verses are drawn from various prophets of the Old Testament, especially Isaiah; from the Psalms, the Evangelists, and Paul. Upon this assorted material the music imposes a magnificent unity. The great choruses become the pillars of an architectonic structure in which the recitatives and arias serve as areas of lesser tension.

Handel's original orchestration was extraordinarily modest and clear in texture. He wrote mainly for strings and continuo; oboes and bassoons were employed to strengthen the choral parts. Trumpets and drums were reserved for special numbers. The work was conceived, in terms of baroque practice, for a small group of players supplemented at the climactic moments by a larger group. Some performances today still use the augmented orchestrations made by various musicians (including Mozart) to keep pace with the ever-growing size of the chorus, but the use of Handel's original scoring has become increasingly common.

The Overture, in the French style, opens with a *grave* (slow, solemn) in dotted rhythms, in a somber E minor; this is repeated, and leads to the Allegro, a sturdy three-voiced fugue. The recitative *Comfort ye, my people* is a tenor arioso in E major, larghetto e piano, over one of those broadly flowing accompaniments of which Handel knew the secret (*larghetto* is not as slow as largo). Characteristic is the majestic span of the melody. There follows the aria *Every valley shall be exalted*, with baroque expansion of the word "exalted." In this and later arias the architecture is broadened by orchestral introductions, interludes, and postludes. The music unfolds continuously from the opening figure, embodying that single affection which imparts to each number its sovereign unity of thought and expression.

The first chorus, *And the glory of the Lord shall be revealed,* is a vigorous Allegro in A major. The vision of divine glory fires Handel's imagination to a spacious choral fresco in which an exciting contrapuntal texture alternates with

And the glo - ry, the glo - ry of the Lord,

towering chords. From the opening motive and those that follow is fashioned a fabric of continuous imitation and expansion, with much repetition of text. The forward stride of the bass never slackens. Highly dramatic is the grand pause before the end.

The bright A-major sound gives way to a somber D minor in the accompanied recitative for bass, *Thus saith the Lord of Hosts: Yet once a little while, and I will shake the heav'ns and the earth.* The florid expansion on the word "shake" is worthy of note. Handel's operatic background is revealed by the expressive accompaniment with its urgent dotted rhythm and repeated chords. This leads into a bass aria, *But who may abide the day of His coming?* with a dramatic change from larghetto to prestissimo at the words *For He is like a refiner's fire.* The fugal chorus in G minor, *And He shall purify the sons of Levi,* is one of four choral numbers in *Messiah* whose themes Handel drew from an earlier work. There follows a gracious group in D major. The recitative for alto, *Behold! a virgin shall conceive,* leads into the aria *O thou that tellest good tidings to Zion.* The expressive melody in flowing ⁶⁄₈ meter is one of Handel's happiest inspirations. It is taken over, in subtly altered guise, by the chorus: the emotion projected at first through the individual is now experienced by mankind as a whole.

An affecting change from major to minor comes with the arioso for bass, *For behold, darkness shall cover the earth.* The idea of darkness is projected through a sinuously chromatic figure in the following aria, *The people that walked in darkness have seen a great light.* We encounter at this point a memorable example of Handel's sensitivity to key. The movement from darkness to light is marked repeatedly by a modulation from minor to major.

There follows one of the highlights of the score, the chorus *For unto us a Child is born.* The theme, taken from one of the master's Italian duets, is of Handelian sturdiness.

For un-to us a Child is born,—   *etc.*

The piece displays the unflagging rhythmic energy of the Baroque. Harmonic and contrapuntal elements are fused into a stalwart unity. There is joyously florid expansion on the word "born." Unforgettable is the pomp and glory at "Wonderful, Counselor . . ." The words peal forth in earth-shaking jubilation; yet with what economy of means the effect is achieved.

The Pastoral Symphony is the only orchestral number in *Messiah* outside the Overture. It is cast in the gently flowing, dotted ¹²⁄₈ rhythm that recurs throughout the work as a unifying thread. Generally associated with pastoral moods, this is derived from an Italian folk dance (the siciliano that we noted in the slow movement of Vivaldi's Concerto Grosso and the *Royal Fireworks Music*) and sets the scene for the following recitatives, of which the first is *There were shepherds abiding in the field, keeping watch over their flocks by night.* Wonder and tenderness pervade this music. There follows the chorus *Glory to God* in the key of D major, where for the first time in the work Handel calls for trumpets. This number is often begun in a bright fortissimo, as befits good tidings; yet Handel intended rather a quiet beginning, for he marked the trumpets Da lontano e un poco piano (as from afar and somewhat softly). The soprano aria *Rejoice greatly, O daughter of Zion!* is a brilliant allegro. The basic affection, an exalted joy, is established at the outset by the leaping figure in the vocal line.

A brief recitative for alto is followed by one of the most beautiful arias of the oratorio, *He shall feed His flock like a shepherd* (shared by alto and soprano), in the pastoral siciliano rhythm. An infinite quietude of spirit informs this promise of rest to the heavy-laden. The chorus *His yoke is easy* is a finely wrought fugal piece marked by lively interplay of the voices. Handel derived the subject from one of his Italian duets. A dramatic pause in the coda interrupts the expansive mood, after which the voices unite in the grandiose chords that bring the first part of *Messiah* to an end.

The tone of the second part is established by the sorrowful chorus *Behold the Lamb of God,* with its slow dotted rhythm and drooping inflection. The tragic mood continues with the da capo aria for alto, *He was despised and rejected of men.* The affective words "acquainted with grief" inspire chromatic harmony. The vocal declamation takes on dramatic intensity in the middle section, *He gave His back to the smiters,* as does the agitated orchestral accompaniment. Personal grief broadens into collective expression in a grandly pathetic chorus in F minor, *Surely He hath borne our griefs and carried our sorrows*—the first of three consecutive choruses. Plangent discords underline the thought *He was bruised for our iniquities.* The tone of anguish is carried into the second chorus, *And with His stripes we are healed.* The subject of this spacious fugue is marked by the downward leap of a diminished seventh—an emotionally charged interval—on the word "stripes."

And with His stripes we are heal - ed

This compact theme was common property in the eighteenth century. Among the masters who used it were Bach, in his *Well-Tempered Clavier* (Book II, No. 20); Haydn, in the String Quartet Opus 20, No. 5; and Mozart, in the Kyrie of the Requiem. The third chorus, *All we like sheep have gone astray,* completes the majestic fresco. It is marked by driving rhythm, relentless contrapuntal energy, and briskly moving harmonic masses.

Concerts today are considerably shorter than they were in the leisure-class society of Handel's time. It is customary to reduce *Messiah* in length by omitting some numbers, especially from the second and third parts. A favorite in Part II is the chorus *Lift up your heads, O ye gates!* The question "Who is the King of Glory?" elicits a reply of Handelian grandeur. Another popular number is the deeply felt soprano aria in G minor, *How beautiful are the feet of them that preach the gospel of peace*, in which we find again the $12/8$ siciliano rhythm. Hardly less popular is the bass aria *Why do the nations so furiously rage together?* in which the florid expansion of the word "rage" demands some virtuoso singing.

The climax of the second part is of course the Hallelujah Chorus. The musical investiture of the key word is one of those strokes of genius that resound through the ages. The triumphal outburst has been compared to the finale of

Beethoven's Fifth Symphony. The drums beat, the trumpets resound. This music sings of a victorious Lord, and His host is an army with banners.

The third part opens with *I know that my Redeemer liveth*, a serene expression of faith that is one of the great Handel arias. When on the crucial state-

ment "For now is Christ risen from the dead" the soprano voice ascends stepwise to the climactic G-sharp on "risen," there is established unassailably the idea of redemption that is the ultimate message of the work. The thought triumphs with the three final choral sections, *Worthy is the Lamb that was slain, Blessing and honor . . .*, and the Amen Chorus. Of the last, one need only say that it meets the supreme challenge of following the Hallelujah Chorus without a sense of anticlimax. With this is consummated a work as titanic in conception as in execution.

Messiah today is regarded as a religious work. It was, however, in no way intended for a church service, but was meant to be an Entertainment, as its librettist described it. That is, it was intended for the commercial concert hall by a bankrupt impresario-composer eager to recoup his losses. That so exalted a conception could take shape in such circumstances testifies to the nature of the age whence it issued—and to the stature of the master of whom Beethoven said, "He was the greatest of us all."

72

The Baroque, Concluded

"The state of music is quite different from what it was . . . Taste has changed astonishingly, and accordingly the former style of music no longer seems to please our ears."

Johann Sebastian Bach (writing in 1730)

Other Instrumental Forms

Baroque music developed a number of instrumental forms that we have not discussed. It may be helpful to describe briefly the most important of these.

A *prelude* is a fairly short piece based on the continuous expansion of a melodic or rhythmic figure. The prelude originated in improvisation on the lute and keyboard instruments. In the late Baroque it served to introduce a group of dance pieces or a fugue. Bach's *Well-Tempered Clavier*, we saw, consists of forty-eight Preludes and Fugues.

The prelude achieved great variety and expressiveness during the Baroque. It assimilated the verve of dance rhythm, the lyricism of the aria, and the full resources of instrumental style. Since its texture was for the most part homophonic, it made an effective contrast with the contrapuntal texture of the fugue that followed it.

The baroque *toccata* (from the Italian *toccare*, "to touch," referring to the keys) was a composition for organ or harpsichord that exploited the resources of the keyboard in a glittering display of chords, arpeggios, and scale passages. It was free and rhapsodic in form, marked by passages in a harmonic style alternating with fugual sections. In the hands of the north German organists the toccata became a virtuoso piece of monumental proportions, either as an independent work or as companion piece to a fugue.

By *fantasia* we understand a type of composition in which the play of fancy takes precedence over regularity of structure. The term includes a variety of pieces imbued with the spirit of improvisation. In the great fantasias of Bach, massive sonorities, abrupt changes of mood, poetic expression, and luxuriant ornamentation are contained within an architecture at once grandiose and supple. Like the toccata, the fantasia may be either an independent piece or coupled with a fugue.

Church organists, in announcing the chorale to be sung by the congregation, fell into the practice of embellishing the traditional melodies. In so doing they drew upon the wealth of baroque ornamentation, harmony, and counterpoint. There grew up a magnificent body of instrumental art—*chorale prelude* and

425

chorale variations—in which organ virtuosity of the highest level was imbued with the spirit of inspired improvisation.

The operatic overture was an important type of large-scale orchestral music. The *French overture* (of which we have discussed several examples) generally followed the pattern slow-fast-slow. Its middle section was in the loosely fugal style known as fugato. The *Italian overture*, associated with Alessandro Scarlatti, consisted of three sections too: fast-slow-fast. The opening section was not in fugal style; the middle section was lyrical; there followed a vivacious, dancelike finale. This pattern, expanded into three separate movements, was later adopted by the concerto grosso and the solo concerto. In addition, the operatic overture of the Baroque was one of the ancestors of the symphony.

An *invention*—the word signifies an ingenious idea—is a short piece for the keyboard in contrapuntal style. The title is known to pianists from Bach's collection of fifteen Inventions in two voices and a like number in three. Bach called the latter group *Sinfonias*, which shows how flexible was musical terminology in those days. His purpose in the Inventions, he wrote, was "upright instruction wherein the lovers of the clavier, and especially those desirous of learning, are shown a clear way not alone to have good *inventiones* but to develop the same well."

The instrumental forms of the Baroque manifest great diversity and venturesomeness. In this they epitomize the spirit of the era that shaped their being.

Types of Patronage

The Baroque was a period of international culture. National styles existed—without nationalism. Lully, an Italian, created the French lyric tragedy. Handel, a German, gave England the oratorio. There was free interchange among national cultures. The sensuous beauty of Italian melody, the pointed precision of French dance rhythm, the luxuriance of German counterpoint, the freshness of English choral song—these nourished an all-European art that absorbed the best of each.

The baroque composer was employed by a court, a church, a municipal council, or an opera house. He was in direct contact with his public. As like as not he was his own interpreter, which made the contact even closer. He created his music for a specific occasion—it might be a royal wedding or a religious service—and for immediate use: in a word, for communication. He was an artisan in a handicraft society. He functioned as a religious man fired by the word of God, or as a loyal subject exalting his king. He was not troubled overmuch by concern for self-expression, but because he spoke out of passionate conviction he expressed both himself and his era. He did not discuss esthetics or the nature of inspiration; but, impelled by a lofty moral vision, he united superb mastery of his craft with profound insights into the nature of experience. He began by writing for a particular time and place; he ended by creating for the ages.

Baroque and Classical: A Comparison of Styles

In comparing the baroque and classical styles, it becomes apparent that the Baroque favored a highly emotional type of expression. Its turbulence is at the opposite end from classical poise. It had a far greater interest in religious music than did the classical era. The Baroque gave equal importance to instrumental and vocal forms. During the classical era the emphasis shifted steadily to the instrumental branch of the art.

The great instrumental types of the classical era—solo and duo sonata, trio and quartet, symphony and concerto—traced their ancestry to the baroque sonata, concerto and concerto grosso, suite and overture. But between the baroque and classical eras there interposed a momentous shift of interest from polyphonic to homophonic texture. Baroque music exploited the contrapuntal—that is, the linear-horizontal aspect of music, even as the classical era developed the harmonic or chordal-vertical aspect. This basic difference affected every aspect of musical style.

In baroque music, a movement was usually shaped by a single affection or mood. Thus, the chief instrumental form of the Baroque, the fugue, was based on a single theme presented within a contrapuntal texture. The classical sonata-allegro, on the other hand, centered about two contrasting themes presented in a homophonic texture. The fugue depended on theme imitation, the sonata form on theme development. The fugue theme basically retains its identity throughout; the sonata themes undergo substantial changes as the material is developed. The fugue presents a continuous texture, while the sonata form consists of three contrasting sections—Exposition, Development, and Recapitulation. As someone has well said, the sonata is sewn together, the fugue is woven together.

The baroque concept of the "single affection" influenced instrumental color. An oboe will accompany the voice throughout an entire movement of a cantata or Mass. The classical style, on the other hand, demanded continual changes of tone color. So too, the relentless single rhythm that dominates an entire movement of baroque music gives way in the classical era to more flexible patterns. Composers of the Baroque did not mix timbres as the classical composers did. They used the different instruments to trace the lines of the counterpoint; for this reason they chose single colors that would stand out against the mass.

Improvisation was of the essence in Baroque style; the performer who realized the figured bass participated in creating the music. The classical era, on the other hand, influenced by the spirit of rationalism, tried to give the composer total control over his material. The classical composers wrote out all the parts, limiting improvisation to the cadenza in the concerto. They specified what instruments were to be used in the performance of their scores, as well as the dynamic markings, whereas composers of the Baroque were inclined to leave such matters to the taste and discretion of the performer. Hence it was only in the classical era that the orchestra was stabilized in the four sections that we

427

know today. Music founded on the thorough-bass emphasized soprano and bass; the classical composers aimed for a more equable distribution of the parts. Once the figured bass was eliminated, the harpsichord disappeared from the orchestra. Now the other instruments shared in the responsibility of filling in the harmonies, a circumstance that spurred the development of an orchestral style. The terraced dynamics of the Baroque resulted in even levels of soft and loud alternating in areas of light and shade. The classical era exploited the crescendo and decrescendo, as well as the dramatic surprise inherent in explosive accents, sudden fortissimos and sudden rests.

The Baroque was a period of rhapsodic improvisation. Hence its music, in its massiveness and wealth of ornamentation, its tumultuous piling-up of sonorities and its rapturous outpouring, was far closer to the romantic spirit than to the classical. For this reason we are able to trace a certain parallelism in the history of art: from the visionary mysticism of the Middle Ages to the classicism of the Renaissance; from the pathos and passion of the Baroque to the ordered beauty of late eighteenth-century classicism; and from the romanticism of the nineteenth century to the neoclassicism of the twentieth.

73 Aftermath of the Baroque: the Rococo

"There are harmonies that are sad, languishing, tender, agreeable, gay, and striking. There are also certain successions of harmonies for the expression of these passions."

Jean-Philippe Rameau (1722)

As famous as Louis XIV's "I am the State" is his successor's "After me, the deluge." In the reigns of the two Louis, which lasted for more than a hundred years, the old regime passed from high noon to twilight. The gilded minority at the top of the social pyramid exchanged the goal of power for that of pleasure. Art moved from the monumentality of the Baroque to the playfulness of the Rococo.

The word derives from the French *rocaille*, a shell, suggesting the decorative scroll- and shell-work characteristic of the style. The Rococo took shape as a reaction from the grandiose gesture of the Baroque. Its elegant prettiness is familiar to us from the Dresden china shepherdesses, the gilt mirrors and graceful curves of the Louis XV style. Out of the disintegrating world of the Baroque came an art of feminine allure centered about the salon and the boudoir—a miniature, ornate art aimed at the enchantment of the senses and predicated upon the attractive doctrine that the first law of life is to enjoy oneself.

It found its musical expression in what is known as the *style galant,* which flourished in the first half of the seventeenth century, and several decades beyond.

Couperin: *La Galante*

The greatest painter of the French rococo was Jean Antoine Watteau (1684-1721). To the dream-world of love and gallantry that furnished the themes for his art, Watteau brought the insights and the techniques of his Flemish heritage. His counterpart in music was François Couperin (1668–1733), who—although he spoke the language of the Rococo—was rooted in the illustrious past. He was one of a family of distinguished musicians and the greatest of the French school of clavecinists. (The harpsichord is known in France as *clavecin.*) His art crystallizes the miniature world of the Rococo and the attributes of Gallic genius—wit, refinement, pointed rhythm and scintillating ornament, clarity and precision. Its goal is the goal of his nation's music from Lully to Debussy and on down to Milhaud and Poulenc: to charm, to delight, to entertain.

A French trait is Couperin's love of literary titles: *The Prude, The Harvesters, Tender Nanette, The Seductress*—these are finely drawn portraits in tone, eighteenth-century miniatures that depict the world Couperin knew. Like Debussy,

Jean Antoine Watteau (1684–1721), THE EMBARKATION FOR CYTHERA (Isle of Love). (Louvre, Paris)
The elegant prettiness of Rococo art was a reaction from the monumentality of the Baroque.

429

who admired him intensely, he sought inspiration outside himself. Of his harpsichord pieces he remarked, "I always had in view different incidents that guided me in their composition. Hence the titles correspond to the ideas I had." All the same, some of his fanciful titles bear little relationship to the music itself. These delicious sketches are lovely of proportion, limpid of texture, exquisitely adapted to the crystalline sonority of the harpsichord. Many are in binary form, the first part modulating from the home key to a contrasting key, the second effecting the return. In this regard, and also in the fact that most of his pieces are cast in dance rhythms, they resemble the movements of the early eighteenth-century suite. They are built up of two- and four-bar fragments in a kind of mosaic style that avoids bigness of line. Everything is said intimately—and twice.

Characteristic of Couperin's style is *La Galante*, which amply displays the trills and other ornaments—what the French call *agréments* or graces—of the keyboard music of the gallant style. These graces not only epitomized the dainty elegance of *galanterie* but served also to emphasize and prolong the melody notes. (The harpsichord tone, it will be recalled, does not have much sustaining power.) *La Galante* is in the ⁶⁄₈ meter of a gigue. (We heard a gigue in the finale of Bach's Suite No. 3.) The piece starts out with the right-hand part being imitated by the left;

Although this pattern recurs at the beginning of each period, the contrapuntal manner is not maintained in any real sense. Couperin's pseudo-polyphony requires neither consistency of texture nor inner tension among the voices, for its principal aim is to delight the ear.

As usual, the two parts of the A-B form are repeated. The first modulates from E major to B minor; the second begins in B minor, with the same melody as the first part, and makes its way back to the home key. The structure is based on regular four-measure phrases until the end, when Couperin introduces the charming asymmetry of a six-bar phrase.

Rameau: *Tambourin*

The desire to systematize all knowledge that characterized the Enlightenment made itself felt also on the musical scene. Jean-Philippe

Rameau (1683–1764), the foremost French composer of the eighteenth century, tried to establish a rational foundation for the harmonic practice of his time. His theoretical works, such as the *Treatise on Harmony Reduced to Its Natural Principles* (1722), set forth concepts that furnished the point of departure for modern musical theory.

Rameau's operas have not maintained themselves on the stage. He is remembered today for his instrumental compositions. In his music for the harpsichord he achieved that union of lucid thinking and refined feeling which is the essence of French sensibility. Typical is *Tambourin*; the title denotes an eighteenth-century dance of rustic origin. In this piece an attractive little tune is heard several times, alternating with other melodies; *Tambourin* therefore is in the form of a rondo (A-B-A-C-A-D-A). The tempo indication is *Vif* (lively). Notice the symmetrical phrases:

The droning bass suggests a folk instrument such as a bagpipe. In evidence are the trills, embellishments, and miniature construction typical of the Rococo. The mood is sustained by the three little tunes that alternate with the rondo theme. Listening to these charming measures one understands why the greatest composer of modern France, Claude Debussy, remarked: "French music aims first of all to give pleasure. Couperin, Rameau—these are true Frenchmen!"

The Gallant Style in Germany and Italy

The Rococo witnessed as profound a change in taste as has ever occurred in the history of music. In turning to a polished entertainment music, composers embraced a new ideal of beauty. The learned counterpoint of the past seemed to them heavy and overly serious. Elaborate polyphonic texture yielded to a single melody line with a simple chord accompaniment. This age desired its music above all to be simple and natural.

The change was already apparent in the lifetime of Bach. It manifests itself in the graces and "gallantries," as he called them, of his harpsichord suites. The gallant style reached its apex in Germany in the mid-eighteenth century, a period that saw the activity of Bach's four composer sons—Wilhelm Friedemann, Carl Philipp Emanuel, Johann Christoph, and Johann Christian. They and their contemporaries consummated that revolution in taste which caused Bach's music to be neglected after his death.

431

Italy in the eighteenth century produced an important group of composers. Among them were Giovanni Battista Sammartini (1701–75), Baldassare Galuppi (1706–85), and Giovanni Battista Pergolesi (1710–36). Certain of their works combine elements of both the Baroque and the Rococo. The towering figure among them was Domenico Scarlatti.

Domenico Scarlatti

Born in the same year as Bach and Handel, Domenico Scarlatti (1685–1757) was one of the most original spirits in the history of music. He left Italy in his middle thirties to take a post at the court of Portugal. When his pupil, the Infanta of Portugal, married the heir to the Spanish throne, the composer followed her to Madrid, where he spent the last twenty-eight years of his life.

Scarlatti's genius was as subtly attuned to the harpsichord as was that of Chopin, a century later, to the piano. His art was rooted in baroque tradition. At the same time it looked forward to the classical style. Scarlatti's fame rests upon his over five hundred sonatas, of which only thirty were published by the composer himself under the unassuming title of *Esercizi per gravicembalo*— exercises or diversions for harpsichord. The individual pieces in the collection were labeled sonatas. The Scarlattian sonata is a one-movement binary form. The first part modulates from home to related key, the second marks the return. In many of these movements Scarlatti underlines the two key areas by contrasting themes. At the end of the second part, he presents the final section of the first part transposed from the Dominant to the Tonic. His sonatas thus bear the seed of the sonata-allegro form that was about to come into being.

Scarlatti's sonatas are written in an epigrammatic style of great vivacity. They abound in beguiling melody, piquant harmonies, and daring modulations. Characteristic are the abrupt contrasts of polyphonic and homophonic texture, and the equally arresting changes from rococo playfulness to baroque drama and intensity. The brilliant runs and scale passages, crossing of hands, contrasts of low and high register, double notes, repeated notes, trills and arpeggio figures, managed with inimitable grace and ingenuity, established the composer as one of the creators of the true keyboard idiom.

A typical work is the Sonata in C minor (No. 12 in Ralph Kirkpatrick's catalogue of the more than 500 Scarlatti sonatas). The music is built up from pointed ideas generally arranged in symmetrical two- or four-bar structure. As with Couperin, each thought is apt to be repeated, either at the same pitch or another, which gives the miniature effect so characteristic of rococo architecture. The movement proceeds meticulously from one thought to the next, avoiding extended development. You will notice that the key signature is two flats where we would use three for C minor. This is because of the ambiguous role of the A, which vacillates between A-natural and A-flat. (Compare the two versions of the C-minor scale given in Appendix III.)

Notice that the melody of the second measure is repeated an octave lower in the third measure and in its original position in the fourth. It moves gracefully, mostly stepwise or by narrow leaps. The first part of this A-B form modulates from C minor to G minor. The new key is represented by a second theme, whose trills and graces evoke the dainty scrollwork of the Rococo:

The cadence formula in G concludes the first part, which is repeated. The second part starts out from C minor with an adaptation of the opening theme. The ambiguous A is now firmly established as A-flat. Material from the first section is subtly varied. The second theme is transposed to C minor, the cadence formula reaffirms the home key; and the second part, like the first, is repeated.

In the past few decades Domenico Scarlatti has come into his own. He stands revealed as one of the great musicians of his time: an artist of boundless imagination whose fastidious taste led him to a superb sense of style.

74 Opera and Symphony in the Pre-Classical Era

> "Simplicity, truth, and naturalness are the great principles of beauty in all forms of art."
>
> Gluck (1769)

The Changing Opera

The vast social changes taking shape in the eighteenth century were bound to be reflected in the lyric theater. Baroque opera, geared to an era of absolute monarchy, had no place in the changing scene. Increasingly its

433

pretensions were satirized by men of letters all over Europe. The defeat of *opera seria* in London by *The Beggar's Opera* in 1728 had its counterpart in Paris a quarter century later. In 1752 a troupe of Italian singers presented in the French capital Pergolesi's famous comic opera *La Serva padrona* (The Servant as Mistress). Immediately there ensued the "War of the Buffoons" between those who favored the traditional French court opera and those who saw in the Italian *opera buffa* a new realistic art. The former camp was headed by the King, Mme. de Pompadour, and the aristocracy; the latter by the Queen and the Encyclopedists—Rousseau, d'Alembert, Diderot—who hailed the comic form for its expressive melody and natural sentiment, and because it had thrown off what they regarded as the outmoded "fetters of counterpoint." In the larger sense, the "War of the Buffoons" was a contest between the rising bourgeois art and a dying aristocratic art (even if Louis XV's Queen, for personal reasons, sided against him and with the Encyclopedists).

Rousseau's celebrated *Letter on French Music* was an outcome of the controversy. More important, he put theory into practice and composed an *opéra-comique*, *Le Devin du village* (The Village Soothsayer, 1752), to exemplify his doctrines. The versatile philosopher-humanist was a limited composer. But his little operetta with its fresh melodies, its pastoral background, and its fund of feeling gave impetus to the trend toward simplicity and naturalness, qualities that were to take a central place in the new middle-class art.

Gluck: *Orfeo ed Euridice*

It was a German-born composer trained in Italy and writing for the imperial court in Vienna who brought lyric tragedy into harmony with the thought and feeling of a new era. Christoph Willibald Gluck (1714–87) began his work within the tradition of the Italian opera based on florid vocal virtuosity. From there he found his way to a style that met the new need for dramatic truth and expressiveness. This does not mean that, as it is commonly put—and as Gluck himself expressed it—he made the music subservient to the poetry. A great composer, no matter what he says about his aims, is the last person on earth to make music subservient to anything. What it does mean is that Gluck severely curtailed the purely musical elements that had attached themselves to opera and were thwarting its dramatic purpose. "I have striven to restrict music to its true office of serving poetry by means of expression and by following the situations of the story, without interrupting the action or stifling it with a useless superfluity of ornaments."

Gluck's principles were embodied in three works written for the imperial theater at Vienna: *Orfeo ed Euridice* (Orpheus and Eurydice, 1762), *Alceste* (1767), *Paride ed Elena* (Paris and Helen, 1770). There followed the lyric dramas with which he conquered the Paris Opéra, the most important being the two based on Homeric legend—*Iphigénie en Aulide* (Iphigenia in Aulos, 1774)

ORFEO ED EURIDICE, Opening Scene: Orpheus mourning the loss of Eurydice. (Risë Stevens in the Metropolitan Opera production)

and *Iphigénie en Tauride* (Iphigenia in Tauros, 1778). In these works he successfully fused a number of elements: the monumental choral scenes and dances that had always been a feature of French lyric tragedy, the animated ensembles of comic opera, the verve and dynamism of the new instrumental style in Italy and Germany, and the broadly arching vocal line that was part of Europe's operatic heritage. There resulted a music drama whose dramatic truth and expressiveness profoundly affected the course of operatic history.

There can be no better introduction to Gluck's art than to listen, with libretto, to the complete recording of *Orfeo*. In the original version of the opera the male role was sung by a castrato. When Gluck revised the work for the Paris production he altered the role of Orpheus from contralto to tenor (a change much more in line with modern conceptions of music drama). A half century later his great admirer Hector Berlioz prepared a third version. Eager that his friend, the famous Pauline Viardot, sing Orpheus, Berlioz restored the role to the contralto register, but retained other innovations of Gluck's Paris version. It is in this version that the opera is often performed today, although it makes much more sense to have the role of Orpheus sung by a tenor.

Generations of composers had been fascinated by the legend of the poet-singer of antiquity whose music charmed rocks, trees, and savage beasts. Overwhelmed with grief at the death of his beloved Eurydice, Orpheus arouses the pity of the god Amore, who permits him to descend to Hades to find his beloved and lead her back to the land of the living. The god of love imposes only one condition; Orpheus must not turn to look at her until he has recrossed the river Styx.

The opening scene of Act II is one of the high points of the score. Orpheus braves the Furies in his descent to the underworld. Their stately dance begins in E-flat major. Orpheus enters, the strains of his lyre suggested by gentle arpeggios on the harp in C minor (the relative minor of E-flat). The Furies menace him to the accompaniment of a Presto in C minor characterized by rapid ascending and descending scales. Orpheus implores them to pity him, in an aria in E-flat, but they thunder a terrifying "No!" Gradually, the charm of his lyre begins to work. The Furies, won over in spite of themselves, finally succumb to his magic and allow him to descend into Hades; their music modulates through a series of minor keys. While Orpheus enters Hades they resume their dance to an Allegretto in D minor in triple meter.

The action shifts to the Elysian Fields where the Blessed Spirits disport themselves; Gluck added this ballet for the Paris version (1774). The serene aria of a Blessed Shade is followed by that of Orpheus, in which he expresses his wonder at the beauty of the Elysian Fields. The act ends with the Blessed Spirits leading Eurydice toward her adoring spouse.

In Act III Orpheus leads his wife out of the nether regions. He urges her on, eager to recross the Styx; but she, increasingly agitated by the fact that he has not looked at her, becomes convinced that he no longer loves her. Orpheus naturally cannot disclose the reason for his strange behavior. Finally, unable to bear her reproaches, he impetuously turns around, whereupon the god's decree comes to pass: she dies, and Orpheus sings *Che farò senza Euridice* (I have lost my Eurydice), a lament that became one of the famous arias of the eighteenth century. It displays the serene and mellifluous lyricism that was Gluck's finest vein:

This melody, in C major, is heard three times, alternating with two episodes, the first in G, the second in C minor. It is rounded off by a brief postlude. Orpheus' outpouring of grief moves not only the audience but also the god Amore, who restores Eurydice to life and a happy ending. The opera concludes with a trio (Orpheus, Eurydice, and Amore) in praise of the power of love, and a series of dances; the final number is a stately chaconne.

Gluck issued from the miniature world of the Rococo. He rose above its shortness of breath in the most ingenious way, by combining several units into one well-rounded section. What sustains his work, besides its fund of melody, is his sense of dramatic characterization and that sure intuition for what will go in the theater which makes the true opera composer.

Pre-Classical Sonata and Symphony

The decades that comprised the aftermath of the Baroque were among the most momentous in music history. They witnessed the birth of that whole new manner of thinking which came to fruition in the classical symphony.

At stake was nothing less than a revolution in musical syntax and structure. In the course of it composers traveled all the way from an idiom rooted in the vocal polphony of the past to the modern language of the orchestra. They gave up the elaborate contrapuntal imitation that was at the heart of the fugue. They enriched the new symphonic style with elements drawn from the operatic aria and overture, from the tunes and rhythms of *opera buffa*. To the charm of the gallant style they added the emotional urgency of a world in ferment. From all this was born a new thing—the idiom of the classical sonata-symphony. The new art form was the collective achievement of several generations of musicians who were active in Italy, France, and Germany throughout the pre-classical period (c. 1740–75).

One of the outstanding figures of the late Rococo was Carl Philipp Emanuel Bach (1714–88), the second son of Johann Sebastian. He deepened the emotional content of the abstract instrumental forms and played a decisive part in the creation of the modern piano idiom. His dramatic sonata style exerted a powerful influence upon Haydn, Mozart, and Beethoven. Besides more than two hundred clavier works and fifty-two clavier concertos he produced eighteen symphonies, a quantity of chamber and church music, and about two hundred and fifty songs; also a theoretical work, the *Essay on the True Art of Playing Keyboard Instruments*, which throws much light on the musical practice of the mid-eighteenth century.

A number of Carl Philipp Emanuel's works—symphonies, concertos, chamber and piano compositions—have been made available on records. They reveal his singing fluency, the freshness of his thematic material, and the poetic slow movements that endeared him to the masters of the classical era. In ideas, in expression, and in execution this pre-classical master rose above the limitations of gallant entertainment music. He could truthfully say, "It seems to me that it is the special province of music to move the heart."

Of major importance too was Carl Philipp Emanuel's half-brother Johann Christian Bach (1735–82), the youngest son of the great Cantor. Johann Christian at nineteen went to Italy, where he was converted to Catholicism and to the Italian ideal of suavely beautiful melody. Known as the "London Bach"—

437

a good part of his artistic career unfolded in that city—he was a prolific composer of operas in the Italian manner and of instrumental music, symphonies, overtures, clavier pieces, and chamber music. His tender songfulness and meticulous forms are the essence of Rococo. Johann Christian's influence upon Mozart was as marked as was Carl Philipp Emanuel's upon Beethoven.

It was the historic task of the composers of the mid-eighteenth century to pilot their art through a period of vast change in all branches of life as well as in musical taste. When they had completed their work the stage was set for the emergence of the classical school, and for the magnificent flowering of the large instrumental forms that we associate with Haydn, Mozart, and Beethoven.

PART SIX

———

THE
TWENTIETH
CENTURY

———

"The century of aeroplanes has a right to its own music. As there are no precedents, I must create anew."
                                        Claude Debussy

75 Transition to a New Age

"I came into a very young world in a very old time."

Erik Satie

It became apparent toward the end of the nineteenth century that the romantic impulse had exhausted itself. The grand style had run its course, to end in the overblown gestures that mark the decline of a tradition. The composers born in the 1860s and '70s, who reached artistic maturity in the final years of the

Arnold Böcklin (1827–1901), THE ISLE OF THE DEAD. (The Metropolitan Museum of Art, New York; Reisinger Fund, 1926)
The romantic tradition persisted in the work of many artists at the turn of the century.

century, could not but feel, as did Satie, that they had come into the world in a "very old time." It was their historic task to bridge the gap between a dying romanticism and the twentieth century.

The postromantic era, overlapping the romantic period, extended from around 1890 to 1910. This generation of composers included radicals, conservatives, and those in between. Some continued in the traditional path; others struck out in new directions; still others tried to steer a middle course between the old and the new. During these years there continued to flourish the national schools— French, Russian, Bohemian—that had ended the supremacy of German musical culture. This development came to a head with the First World War, when Germany and Austria were cut off from the rest of Europe. In the postromantic period several newcomers appeared on the musical horizon. Besides Finland these included England, Spain, and the United States. And there emerged the movement that more than any other ushered in the twentieth century— impressionism.

We discussed three members of this generation—Puccini, Sibelius, and Strauss—in the section on romanticism, because their careers started out from the nineteenth-century tradition. Yet their later works, such as Strauss's *Salome*, Sibelius's Fourth Symphony, and Puccini's *Turandot*, unquestionably belong to the new age. In any case, the decades that framed the turn of the nineteenth century are of paramount interest to music lovers. They not only brought the art from the twilight of one epoch to the dawn of another, but also contained the seeds of much that is important to us today.

76 Strauss: *Salome*

"I have always paid the greatest possible attention to natural diction and speed of dialogue, with increasing success from opera to opera."

Salome (1905) displays to the full Strauss's powers as an operatic composer: his capacity for generating excitement, his vivid delineation of character, his sensuous vocal line, his powerful evocation of mood and atmosphere. Oscar Wilde's play makes a stunning libretto; the characters are sharply drawn, the issues clear, the climax overwhelming. The beautiful and perverse Princess of Judaea, inflamed to madness by her passion for the Prophet; her stepfather Herod, cruel and crafty, pursued by fears and hallucinations; her mother Herodias, lascivious and vengeful; the handsome young captain of the guard, Narraboth, who is hopelessly enamored of her; and Jokanaan (John the Baptist), unshakable in his faith—all are enveloped in a musical ambience whose spell is not easily forgotten.

The one-act drama unfolds on a terrace in the palace of Herod, Tetrarch of Judaea. There is no overture. The opera opens with a swift upward run on the clarinet and the cry of Narraboth as he gazes adoringly towards the banqueting hall. "How beautiful is the Princess Salome tonight!" The voice of Jokanaan is heard from the cistern, where he has been imprisoned for speaking out against the abominations of the Tetrarch's court. "After me shall come another who is greater than I. I am not worthy to unloose the latchet of his shoe. . . ." The elevated tone associated throughout the work with the Prophet is set forth by the serene C-major tonality, and by the sonority of sustained horns and trombones. Salome enters. She is characterized by a chromatic theme in three-four time, capricious, sinuous, played by celesta and violins.

It is an idea capable of symphonic development, and returns in various guises throughout the action.

Jokanaan prophesies again, announcing the coming of the Son of Man. Salome, fascinated, demands to see him. The soldiers explain that Herod has strictly forbidden them to raise the cover of the well. Salome appeals to Narraboth, who is helpless against her blandishments. In deep anguish he orders that the Prophet be brought from the cistern.

Two characteristic motives are associated with Jokanaan. The first, solemn and exalted, is given out by the horns.

The second, suggesting the Prophet's denunciations, consists of a series of descending fourths intoned by trombones and cellos:

"Where is she who hath given herself to the young men of the Egyptians?" Salome knows whom he means. "It is of my mother that he speaks." Clarinets sound an eerie motive that returns throughout the opera to suggest her mad infatuation with the Prophet.

"I am amorous of thy body, Jokanaan! Thy body is white, like the lilies of the field that the mower hath never mowed." The vocal line takes on those wide leaps of well over an octave that were to figure ever more prominently in the melody structure of the Austro-German school.

"I will kiss thy mouth, Jokanaan," sings Salome, transported with desire. The Prophet shudders. "Never! daughter of Babylon! Daughter of Sodom—never!" The lovelorn Narraboth can bear his agony no longer. He plunges his sword into his heart and falls between Salome and the Prophet. Jokanaan bids Salome seek Him who is on a boat in the sea of Galilee, to bow at His feet and beg remission of her sins. But Salome is enamored of his lips. He curses her and returns to the cistern.

A change of atmosphere is needed to prepare for the entrance of the grotesque ruler and his evil queen. This is accomplished by an orchestral interlude. An E-flat clarinet introduces a shrill note. Herod is obsessed by his fancies. "The moon has a strange look tonight. She is like a mad woman. . . ." His vocal line—staccato, abrupt, querulous—at once establishes the character of the Tetrarch. He orders that the torches be lit, then steps in Narraboth's blood; persuaded that it is an evil omen, he commands the soldiers to remove the body.

The voice of Jokanaan is heard, prophesying the day of the coming of the Lord. Herodias demands that the Prophet be handed over to the Jews, who have been clamoring for him. Herod is reluctant, for he feels that Jokanaan is a man who has seen God. There follows an ensemble of five Jews, in which the music graphically mimics the acrimony of a theological disputation. Herod, inflamed with wine, gazes lustfully at his stepdaughter and asks her to dance for him. Salome, who has been brooding over Jokanaan's rejection of her, at first refuses. When Herod promises her anything that she will request of him, the thought comes to her for which she has been remembered through the ages. "Whatsoever thou shalt ask of me, even to the half of my kingdom," Herod asserts. "You swear it, Tetrarch?" He swears by his life, his crown, his gods. "You have sworn an oath, Tetrarch!" Ominous trills are heard on the clarinets. Salome attires

SALOME: The Dance of the Seven Veils (Birgit Nilsson in the Metropolitan Opera production)

herself in seven veils and makes ready to execute the most famous dance in history.

The music of the dance is in turn savage and sensual, building to an impassioned climax based on Salome's motive. Herod is enchanted and asks Salome to name her reward. The weird trill on the clarinet is heard again. Salome, "rising, laughing," demands the head of Jokanaan on a silver platter. In vain the terrified Herod seeks to deflect her, offering her the choicest treasures of his kingdom. Salome is inflexible. "Give me the head of Jokanaan!" When all his offers are refused the Tetrarch, defeated, yields.

The Princess leans over the cistern. There is a terrible stillness as Jokanaan is beheaded, punctuated by dry haunting accents on the double basses. Herod hides his face in his cloak. Herodias smiles with delight and fans herself. The opera reaches its climax as Salome addresses the head on the silver charger, in as strange and affecting an apostrophe as was ever heard. "Ah! thou wouldst not suffer me to kiss thy mouth, Jokanaan. Well, I will kiss it now. I will bite it with my teeth as one bites a ripe fruit."

The sky grows dark, the moon disappears. The Tetrarch is overwhelmed with fear. Salome, oblivious of all, gratifies her obsession. "Ah! I have kissed thy mouth, Jokanaan. I have kissed thy mouth." The motive of Salome, luminous in its orchestral garb, rises to passionate exultation.

Herod can endure no more. "Kill that woman!" he cries. The soldiers rush forward and crush Salome beneath their shields. The curtain falls.

This is theater in the grand style. The opera has a boldness of conception and a sustaining of tension that bespeak a master. Salome, Herod, Herodias, Narraboth—each is driven by a magnificent obsession. And since it is in the nature of man to be driven, they rise from the shadows of their phantasmagoric world into the realm of what is humanly comprehensible and moving.

77 Mahler: Symphony No. 4

"To write a symphony is, for me, to construct a world."

One of the striking phenomena of the mid-century musical scene has been the upsurge of Gustav Mahler's popularity. For whatever reason, his troubled spirit seems to reach our musical public in a most persuasive way. "My time will come," he used to say. It has.

His Life

Gustav Mahler (1860–1911) was born and raised in Bohemia. His father, owner of a small distillery, was not slow in recognizing the boy's talent. Piano lessons began when Gustav was six. He was sent to Vienna and entered the Conservatory at fifteen, the University three years later. His professional career began modestly enough: at the age of twenty, he was engaged to conduct operettas at a third-rate summer theatre. A dynamic conductor who found his natural habitat in the opera house, Mahler soon achieved a reputation that brought him ever more important posts, until at twenty-eight he was director of the Royal Opera at Budapest. From Budapest Mahler went to Hamburg. Then, at thirty-seven, he was offered the most important musical position in the Austrian Empire—the directorship, with absolute powers, of the Vienna opera. His ten years there (1897–1907) made history. He brought to his duties a fiery temperament, unwavering devotion to ideals, and the inflexible will of the zealot. When he took over, Massenet was the chief drawing card. By the

Gustav Mahler.

time his rule ended he had taught a frivolous public to revere Mozart, Beethoven, and Gluck, and made them listen to uncut versions of Wagner's operas.

Shortly before he was appointed to Vienna, Mahler became a convert to Catholicism. This step was motivated in the first instance by the desire to smooth his way in a city where anti-Semitism was rampant. Beyond that, Mahler belonged to a generation of Jewish intellectuals who had lost identification with their religious heritage and who sought roots in the Austro-German culture of which they felt themselves to be a part. His was the inquiring intellect of the perpetual doubter; yet he yearned for the ecstasy of faith and the wholeness of soul that came with certainty. "I am thrice homeless," he remarked. "As a Bohemian born in Austria. As an Austrian among Germans. And as a Jew throughout the world."

"Humanly I make every concession, artistically—none!" Such intransigence was bound to create powerful enemies. Mahler's final years in Vienna were embittered by the intrigues against him, which flourished despite the fact that he had transformed the Imperial Opera into the premier lyric theatre of Europe. The death of a little daughter left him grief-stricken. A second disaster followed soon after: he was found to have a heart ailment. When he finally was forced to resign his post, the blow was not unexpected. Mahler, now almost forty-eight (he had only three more years to live), accepted an engagement at New York's Metropolitan Opera. He hoped to earn enough to be able to retire at fifty, so that he finally might compose with the peace of mind that had never been granted him. His three years in New York were not free of the storms that his tempestuous personality inevitably provoked. In 1909 he assumed direction of the New York Philharmonic Orchestra. When the ladies of the Board made it plain to Alma Mahler that her husband had flouted their wishes, she expostulated, "But in Vienna the Emperor himself did not dare to interfere!"

447

In the middle of a taxing concert season with the Philharmonic he fell ill with a streptococcus infection. It was decided to bring him to Paris, where a new serum treatment had been developed. Arrived in Paris, he took a turn for the worse. Thus he set forth on his last journey, back to the scene of his greatest triumphs—the enchanting, exasperating Vienna he both loved and detested. On his deathbed he conducted with one finger on the quilt, uttering a single word: "Mozart. . . ."

He was buried, as he had requested, beside his daughter in a cemetery outside Vienna. At last that unquiet heart was at rest.

His Music

"The act of creation in me is so closely bound up with all my experience that when my mind and spirit are at rest I can compose nothing." In this identification of art with personal emotion Mahler was entirely the romantic. Music for him was vision, intoxication, fulfillment: "a mysterious language from beyond." The sounds were symbols of states of mind and soul. "What is best in music," he observed, "is not to be found in the notes." In his notes resound the great themes of an age that was drawing to its close: nature, poetry, and folklore, love of man and faith in God, the sorrow of human destiny and the loneliness of death. Mahler engaged in a gigantic effort to breathe vitality into the romantic world of thought and feeling that was in process of disintegration. This circumstance imparts to his music its fevered unrest, its nostalgia.

The spirit of song permeates Mahler's art. He followed Schubert and Schumann in cultivating the song cycle. *Lieder eines fahrenden Gesellen* (Songs of a Wayfarer), composed in 1883, is a set of four songs suffused with Schubertian longing. Mahler wrote the texts himself, roused by an image that appealed strongly to his imagination: the rejected lover wandering alone over the face of the earth. His next cycle was inspired by a famous collection of German folk poetry, *Des Knaben Wunderhorn* (The Youth's Magic Horn, 1888). The moving *Kindertotenlieder* (Songs on the Death of Children, 1902) is a cycle for voice and orchestra to the grief-laden poems of Rückert. The peak of his achievement in this direction is, of course, the cycle of six songs with orchestra that make up *Das Lied von der Erde* (Song of the Earth, 1908).

Mahler was the last in the illustrious line of Viennese symphonists that extended from Haydn, Mozart, Beethoven, and Schubert to Bruckner and Brahms. His tone imagery was permeated by the jovial spirit of Austrian popular song and dance. His nine symphonies abound in lyricism, with melodies long of line and richly expressive harmonies. (The Tenth Symphony was left unfinished at his death, but recently has been edited and made available for performance.) In his sense of color Mahler ranks with the great masters of the art of orchestration. He contrasts solo instruments in the manner of chamber music, achieving his color effects through clarity of line rather than massed sonorities It was in the matter of texture that Mahler made his most important contribution to contemporary technique. Basing his orchestral style on counterpoint, he caused two or more melodies to unfold simultaneously, each setting off the other. Mahler never abandoned the principle of tonality; he needed the key as a framework for his vast design.

Symphony No. 4 in G Major

The Fourth Symphony, completed in 1900, is one of Mahler's least problematical works. The mood of the first movement is one of heartwarming lyricism; its melodies have about them a folklike simplicity. An introduction of three measures is marked *Bedächtig, Nicht eilen* (Moderato, unhurried). It presents a jingling theme adorned with grace notes, as of sleighbells, which recurs as a unifying element both in this and the last movement:

The movement proper is marked *Recht gemächlich* (comfortable, easy-going). Its principle theme, marked grazioso (graceful), is a songful idea of great charm, presented by the first violins against a pizzicato background, and contains several motives (under the brackets) that will figure actively in the development of the movement:

The lower strings—violas, cellos, double basses—answer with a related idea that is continued by the horns. Notice that the dotted rhythm in the preceding example (measure 3) is now expanded:

Notice also the sixteenth-note triplets followed by three eighths in measure 3, a rhythm that will recur throughout the movement.

This theme group establishes the home key of G major. A vigorous transition leads into the key of the Dominant, D major, which is represented by two melodies in Mahler's most expansive mood. The first, presented by the cellos, must—as Mahler put it—be sung broadly:

The second, too, is introduced by the cellos:

This tune is rounded off by a gesture of Mahlerian impishness:

Before closing his exposition, Mahler returns to the sleighbells of the opening, and restates the principal theme in the home key—thus, an element of rondo procedure in a sonata-allegro form. The Exposition ends with a beautiful codetta.

The Development opens with another return of the sleighbells, and an imaginative use of the triplet rhythm to which we have alluded. The richness of Mahler's developmental process may be gauged from the variety of forms assumed by his principal theme:

1) Expansion through repetition and sequence:

2) Melody altered through change of intervals, and with dotted figure descending instead of ascending. Notice the change of key:

3) Intensification by use of ascending sequence at climax of phrase:

Also worthy of note, in this intricately textured Development, is the intro-duction of new elements, such as the following childlike melody in the high register of the flutes, which will take on importance in the final movement:

The Recapitulation is introduced very subtly, without the sleighbells. The two lyric themes are transposed to the Tonic, and Mahler invests the coda with a quality of leave-taking that is highly characteristic of his expressive vocabulary.

Second is the Scherzo, which Mahler described as "mystical, bewildering, and weird." Here, he wrote in a sketchbook, "Death plays the music." The figure of Death as a fiddler has haunted the imagination of Europe's artists since the Middle Ages. Mahler in this movement heightens the fantastic element by writing a solo for a violin tuned a full step higher than usual, giving it a shriller, tauter sound, and directs that the instrument be played "like a street fiddle" (as opposed to the more elegant violin). The movement, in C minor, is marked to be played "At a comfortable pace; unhurried." Its main theme is a kind of bizarre waltz whose spectral quality is not without an element of parody:

The idea returns again and again, in alternation with contrasting themes in the major of a lighter, more relaxed quality. This is a long movement that follows the pattern Scherzo-Trio-Scherzo-Trio-Scherzo-Coda. It ends in C major.

Third is the slow movement, a lyric meditation descended from the serene Andantes of Schubert. Marked Poco adagio and *Ruhevoll* (tranquil), it unfolds in broadly spun arcs of melody. Like the slow movement of Beethoven's Fifth, it is cast in the form of a set of variations on two themes. The first, marked espressivo molto cantabile, is played by the cellos: a melody in G major that rises gently above the pizzicato tread of the basses. Its simplicity leaves room for the variations to come.

The second, in E minor, is darker and more intense; Mahler thought of it as *klagend* (mournful, weeping). It is introduced by the oboe:

The continuation of this theme in the first violins becomes a structural element of great importance in the course of the movement, for it contains within itself the tension of which climaxes are made:

In form this movement is an A-B-A-B-A-Coda, but instead of repetition we have continual variation, by means of which Mahler alters the character and emotional content of his two themes, building always on the major-minor contrast between them. The main theme runs the gamut from gentle lyricism to impassioned proclamation. The coda contains a fleeting reference to a theme in the first movement and floats into the upper register, serving to prepare the listener for the celestial visions of the fourth movement.

Like many sophisticated, complex natures, Mahler longed for the innocence and trust of childhood. Something of this he found in the folk poems of *Des Knaben Wunderhorn*, which furnished texts for his songs throughout his career. From this *Youth's Magic Horn* came the poem that inspired the final movement of the Fourth Symphony, a child's view of Heaven that he transformed into an enchanting song for soprano and orchestra. The anonymous poet depicts the joys of the celestial abode in artless terms. There is much dancing and singing, encouraged by an endless supply of fresh fruit, vegetables, free wine, and bread baked by the angels. St. John furnishes the lamb, St. Luke slaughters the ox, St. Peter catches fish, St. Martha does the cooking, while St. Cecilia and her band make music to which none on earth can compare. The opening clarinet melody recalls the flute theme from the first movement's development, and the sleighbell motive recurs as a refrain between the stanzas. The opening phrase of the vocal part sets the tone of childlike innocence:

The mood is sustained until the end, when the English horn plays in longer notes the jingling grace-note figure, now becalmed, with which the work began.

78 Impressionism

For we desire above all—nuance,
Not color but half-shades!
Ah! nuance alone unites
Dream with dream and flute with horn.
　　　　　　　　　　　　Paul Verlaine

The Impressionist Painters

In 1867 Claude Monet, rebuffed by the academic salons, exhibited under less conventional auspices a painting called *Impression: Sun Rising*. Before long "impressionism" had become a term of derision to describe the hazy, luminous paintings of this artist (1840–1926) and his school. A distinctly Parisian style, impressionism counted among its exponents Camille Pissarro (1830–1903), Édouard Manet (1832–83), Edgar Degas (1834–1917), and Auguste Renoir (1841–1919). Discarding those elements of the romantic tradition that had hardened into academic formulas, they strove to retain on canvas the freshness of their first impressions. They took painting out of the studio into the open air. What fascinated them was the continuous change in the appearance of things. They painted water lilies, a haystack, or clouds again and again at different hours of the day. Instead of mixing their pigments on the palette they juxtaposed brush-strokes of pure color on the canvas, leaving it to the eye of the beholder to do the mixing. An iridescent sheen bathes their painting. Outlines shimmer and melt in a luminous haze.

The impressionists abandoned the grandiose subjects of romanticism. The hero of their painting is not man but light. Not for them the pathos, the drama-packed themes that had inspired centuries of European art. They preferred "unimportant" material: still life, dancing girls, nudes; everyday scenes of middle-class life, picnics, boating and café scenes; nature in all her aspects, Paris in all her moods. Ridiculed at first—"Whoever saw grass that's pink and yellow and blue?"—they ended by imposing their vision upon the age.

The Symbolist Poets

A parallel revolt against traditional modes of expression took place in poetry under the leadership of the symbolists, who strove for direct poetic

Édouard Manet (1832–83), BOATING. (The Metropolitan Museum of Art, New York; Bequest of Mrs. H. O. Havemeyer, 1929. The H. O. Havemeyer Collection)

Outdoor scenes reveal the impressionist painters' preoccupation with light.

experience unspoiled by intellectual elements. They sought to suggest rather than describe, to present the symbol rather than state the thing. Symbolism as a literary movement came to the fore in the work of Charles Baudelaire (1821–67), Stéphane Mallarmé (1842–98), Paul Verlaine (1844–96), and Arthur Rimbaud (1854-91). These poets were strongly influenced by Edgar Allan Poe (1809-49), whose writings were introduced into France by his admirer Baudelaire. They used a word for its color and its music rather than its proper meaning, evoking poetic images "that sooner or later would be accessible to all the senses."

The symbolists experimented in free verse forms that opened new territories to their art. They achieved in language an indefiniteness that had hitherto been the privilege of music alone. Characteristic was Verlaine's pronouncement: "Music above all!" Like the impressionist painters, the symbolists discarded the grand pathos of romanticism; they glorified the tenuous, the intimate, the subtle. They expressed the moral lassitude of their time, its longing for enchantment of the senses, its need for escape.

The essentially musical approach of the symbolists was not lost upon the musicians. According to the composer Paul Dukas, it was the writers, not the musicians, who exerted the strongest influence on Debussy.

Impressionism in Music

When young Debussy submitted to the authorities of the Conservatory his cantata *The Blessed Damozel* they stated in their report: "It is much to be desired that he beware of this vague impressionism which is one of the most dangerous enemies of artistic truth." Therewith was transferred to the domain of music a term that was already firmly established in art criticism. Debussy himself never liked the word and expressed himself acidly concerning "what some idiots call impressionism, a term that is altogether misused, especially by the critics." But the label stuck, for it seemed to describe what most people felt about his music.

Impressionism came to the fore at a crucial moment in the history of European music. The major-minor system had served the art since the seventeenth century. Composers were beginning to feel that its possibilities had been exhausted. Debussy's highly individual tone sense was attracted to other scales, such as the medieval modes that impart an archaic flavor to his music. (The reader will recall the church modes given on p. 315.) Debussy emphasized the primary intervals—octaves, fourths, and fifths—which he used in parallel motion. Notice the strong resemblance between the opening measures of *La Cathédrale engloutie* (The Sunken Cathedral)—

—and the following example of ninth-century organum:

Here Debussy evokes an image of powerful austerity, old and remote things. He was also sympathetic to the novel scales introduced by the Russian and Scandinavian nationalists, and lent a willing ear to the harmonies of Borodin, Musorgsky, Grieg. He responded to the Moorish strain in Spanish music. Especially he was impressed by the Javanese and Chinese orchestras that were heard in Paris during the Exposition of 1889. In their music he found a new world of sonority: rhythms, scales, and colors that offered a bewitching contrast to the stereotyped forms of Western music.

The major-minor system, as we saw, is based on the pull of the active tones to the Tonic or rest tone. Debussy regarded this as a formula that killed spontaneity. We do not hear in his music the triumphal final cadence of the classic-romantic period, in which the Dominant chord is resolved to the Tonic with the greatest possible emphasis. His fastidious ear explored subtle harmonic relationships; he demanded new and delicate perceptions on the part of the listener. Classical harmony looked upon dissonance as a momentary disturbance that found its resolution in the consonance. But Debussy used dissonance as a value in itself, freeing it from the need to resolve. In the following example— the closing measures of his piano prelude *Ce qu'a vu le vent d'Ouest* (What the West Wind Saw)—he creates a type of cadence in which the final chord takes on the function of a rest chord not because it is consonant, but

because it is less dissonant than what preceded. Through these and kindred procedures Debussy strengthened the drive toward the "emancipation of the dissonance." He thus taught his contemporaries to accept tone combinations that had hitherto been regarded as inadmissible, even as the impressionist painters taught them to see colors in sky, grass, and water that had never been seen there before.

Debussy is popularly associated with the whole-tone scale. This is a pattern built entirely of whole-tone intervals, as in the sequence C-D-E-F♯-G♯-A♯-C. The whole-tone scale avoids the semitone distances 3–4 and 7–8 (*mi-fa* and *ti-do*) of the major scale. Thereby it sidesteps the thrust of *ti* to *do* that gives the traditional scale its drive and direction. There results a fluid scale pattern whose charm can be gauged only from hearing it played. Debussy did not invent the whole-tone scale nor did he use it as frequently as many suppose. It lent itself admirably, however, to the nuances of mood and feeling that haunt his music, as in the following magical passage from the third act of *Pelléas et Mélisande*:

Several other procedures have come to be associated with musical impressionism. One of the most important is the use of parallel or "gliding" chords, in which a chord built on one tone is duplicated immediately on a higher or lower tone. Here all the voices move in parallel motion, the effect being one of blocks of sound gliding up or down. In the following measures from *Soirée dans Grenade* (Evening in Granada), the entire passage consists of a single chord

structure which is duplicated on successive tones. Such parallel motion was prohibited in the classical system of harmony; but it was precisely these forbidden progressions that fascinated Debussy. Also, he liked to sustain a chord in the bass that suggests a definite key while the chords above it give the impression of having escaped to another key. Such "escaped" chords point the way to twentieth-century harmony. In the following example—the opening of *General Lavine—Eccentric* from the second book of Preludes—C-major tonality is established in the first measure, against which is heard a series of triads alien to the tonality:

The harmonic innovations inseparable from impressionism led to the formation of daring new tone combinations. Characteristic was the use of the five-tone combination known as *ninth chords* (from the interval of a ninth between the lowest and highest tones of the chord). These played so prominent a part in *Pelléas* that the work came to be known as "the land of ninths." Here is a characteristic sequence of parallel ninth chords from *Pelléas*.

As a result of the procedures just outlined, impressionist music wavered between major and minor without adhering to either. In this way was abandoned one of the basic contrasts of classical harmony. Impressionism advanced the disintegration of the major-minor system. It floated in a borderland between keys, creating elusive effects that might be compared to the misty outlines of impressionist painting.

These evanescent harmonies demanded colors no less subtle. No room here for the thunderous climaxes of the romantic orchestra. Instead there was a veiled blending of hues, an impalpable shimmer of pictorial quality: flutes and clarinets in their dark lower register, violins in their lustrous upper range, trumpets and horns discreetly muted; and over the whole a silvery gossamer of harp,

Pierre Auguste Renoir (1843–1919), LE MOULIN DE LA GALETTE. (Jeu de Paume, Paris) *In turning from the grandiose subjects of romanticism, the impressionists derived their themes from the everyday life of Paris.*

Edgar Degas, THE DANCING CLASS. (The Metropolitan Museum of Art, New York; Bequest of Mrs. H. O. Havemeyer, 1929. The H. O. Havemeyer Collection)
Ballet dancers furnished Degas with one of his favorite themes.

celesta, and triangle, glockenspiel, muffled drum, and cymbal brushed with a drumstick.

So too the metrical patterns of the classic-romantic era, marked by an accent on the first beat of the measure, were hardly appropriate for this new dreamlike style. In many a work of the impressionist school the music glides from one measure to the next in a gentle flow that discreetly veils the pulse of the rhythm.

Impressionism inclined toward the miniature. Debussy's turning away from the big forms led him to short lyric pieces: preludes, nocturnes, arabesques—the titles indicate his leaning toward intimate lyricism. The question arises: Was impressionism a revolt against the romantic tradition or simply its final manifestation? Beyond question Debussy rebelled against certain aspects of romanticism, notably the Wagnerian gesture. Yet in a number of ways impressionism continued the fundamental tendencies of the romantic movement: in its love of beautiful sound, its emphasis on program music, its tone painting and nature worship, its addiction to lyricism; its striving to unite music, painting, and poetry; and its emphasis on mood and atmosphere. In effect, the impressionists substituted a thoroughly French brand of romanticism for the German variety.

Impressionist music enjoyed an enormous vogue during the first three decades of the twentieth century. It attained the proportions of an international school.

459

Yet from our vantage point impressionism turns out to have been largely a one-man movement. No one else of Debussy's stature found in it the complete expression that he did. In this respect it differed from the romantic style that allowed room for so many diverse personalities. The procedures of impressionism worked in a limited area; they became stereotyped and soon lost their novelty. It grew to be practically impossible to write impressionist music without sounding like Debussy. Composers were consequently forced to seek other idioms. Also, by excluding pathos and the heroic element, impressionism narrowed its human appeal.

But on its own premises it created a finely wrought, surpassingly decorative art. It opened up to music a world of dream and enchantment. And it captured a vision of fragile beauty in a twilight moment of European culture.

79 Claude Debussy

"I love music passionately. And because I love it I try to free it from barren traditions that stifle it. It is a free art gushing forth, an open-air art boundless as the elements, the wind, the sky, the sea. It must never be shut in and become an academic art."

His Life

The most important French composer of the early twentieth century, Claude Debussy (1862–1918) was born near Paris in the town of St. Germain-en-Laye, where his parents kept a china shop. He entered the Paris Conservatory when he was eleven. Within a few years he shocked his professors with bizarre harmonies that defied the sacred rules. "What rules then do you observe?" inquired one of his teachers. "None—only my own pleasure!" "That's all very well," retorted the professor, "provided you're a genius." It became increasingly apparent that the daring young man was.

He was twenty-two when his cantata *L'Enfant prodigue* (The Prodigal Son) won the Prix de Rome. Like Berlioz before him, he looked upon his stay in the Italian capital as a dreary exile from the boulevards and cafés that made up his world. Already he discerned his future bent. "The music I desire," he wrote a friend, "must be supple enough to adapt itself to the lyrical effusions of the soul and the fantasy of dreams."

The 1890s, the most productive decade of Debussy's career, culminated in the writing of *Pelléas et Mélisande*. Based on the symbolist drama by the Belgian poet Maurice Maeterlinck, this opera occupied him for the better part of ten

Claude Monet (1840–1926), IRIS BESIDE A POND (The Art Institute of Chicago)

An iridescent sheen bathes impressionist painting; outlines shimmer and melt in a luminous haze.

Edgar Degas (1834–1917), THE MILLINERY SHOP (The Art Institute of Chicago)

Derided at first, the impressionists soon emerged as the most important school of European painting.

Claude Debussy.

years. He continued to revise the score up to the opening night, which took place on April 30, 1902, at the Opéra-Comique. *Pelléas* was attacked as being decadent, precious, lacking in melody, form, and substance. Nevertheless, its quiet intensity and subtlety of nuance made a profound impression upon the musical intelligentsia. It caught on and embarked on an international career.

After *Pelléas* Debussy was famous. He was the acknowledged leader of a new movement in art, the hero of a cult. "The Debussyists," he complained, "are killing me." He appeared in the capitals of Europe as conductor of his works and wrote the articles that established his reputation as one of the most trenchant critics of his time. In the first years of the century he exhausted the impressionist vein and found his way to a new and tightly controlled idiom, a kind of distillation of impressionism.

His energies sapped by the ravages of cancer, he worked on with remarkable fortitude. The outbreak of war in 1914 rendered him for a time incapable of all interest in music. France, he felt, "can neither laugh nor weep while so many of our men heroically face death." After a year of silence he realized that he must contribute to the struggle in the only way he could, "by creating to the best of my ability a little of that beauty which the enemy is attacking with such fury." He was soon able to report to his publisher that he was "writing like a madman, or like one who has to die next morning." To his perturbation over the fate of France were added physical torment and, finally, the realization that he was too ill to compose any longer. His last letters speak of his "life of waiting—my waiting-room existence, I might call it—for I am a poor traveler waiting for a train that will never come any more."

He died in March 1918 during the bombardment of Paris. The funeral procession took its way through deserted streets as the shells of the German guns ripped into his beloved city. It was just eight months before the victory of the nation whose culture found in him one of its most distinguished representatives.

461

His Music

For Debussy, as for Monet and Verlaine, art was primarily a sensuous experience. The epic themes of romanticism were distasteful to his temperament both as man and artist. "French music," he declared, "is clearness, elegance, simple and natural declamation. French music aims first of all to give pleasure."

Upholding the genius of his race, he turned against the grand form that was the supreme achievement of the Germans. Exposition-Development-Restatement he regarded as an outmoded formula. At a concert he whispered to a friend, "Let's go—he's beginning to develop!" But the Viennese sonata-symphony was not the only form alien to the Gallic spirit. A greater threat was posed by the Wagnerian music drama, which at that time attracted the intellectuals of France. The French, he points out, are too easily influenced by the "tedious and ponderous Teuton." Wagner's grandiose *Ring* he found especially tedious. "The idea of spreading one drama over four evenings! Is this admissible, especially when in these four evenings you always hear the same thing? . . . My God! how unbearable these people in skins and helmets become by the fourth night." In the end, however, he paid moving tribute to the master whose fascination he had had to shake off before he could find his own way. Wagner "can never quite die," he writes, and calls him "a beautiful sunset that was mistaken for a dawn."

From the romantic exuberance that left nothing unsaid Debussy sought refuge in an art of indirection, subtle and discreet. He substituted for the sonata structure those short flexible forms that he handled with such distinction. Mood pieces, they evoked the favorite images of impressionist painting: gardens in the rain, sunlight through the leaves, clouds, moonlight, sea, mist.

Debussy worked slowly, and his fame rests on a comparatively small output. Among the orchestral compositions the *Prélude à l'après-midi d'un faune* (Prelude to the Afternoon of a Faun) is firmly established in public favor, as are the three Nocturnes (1893–99)—*Nuages* (Clouds), *Fêtes* (Festivals), *Sirènes* (Sirens); *La Mer* (The Sea, 1905); and *Ibéria* (1908). His handling of the orchestra has the French sensibility. He causes individual instruments to stand out against the mass. In his scores the lines are widely spaced, the texture light and airy.

One of the important piano composers, he created a distinctive new style of writing for the instrument. The widely spaced chords with their parallel successions of seconds, fourths, and fifths create a sonorous halo. He exploits the resources of the instrument with infinite finesse—the contrast of low and high registers, the blending of sonorities through the use of pedal, the clash of overtones. His piano pieces form an essential part of the modern repertory. Among the best-known are *Clair de lune* (Moonlight, 1890), the most popular piece he ever wrote; *Soirée dans Grenade* (Evening in Granada, 1903); *Reflets dans l'eau* (Reflections in the Water, 1905), and *La Cathédrale engloutie* (The Sunken Cathedral, 1910).

Debussy was one of the most important among the group of composers who established the French song as a national art form independent of the lied. His settings of Baudelaire, Verlaine, and Mallarmé—to mention three poets for whom he had a particular fondness—are marked by exquisite refinement. In chamber music he achieved an unqualified success with his String Quartet in G minor (1893). The three sonatas of his last years—for cello and piano; flute, viola, and harp; violin and piano—reveal him as moving toward a more abstract, more concentrated style.

Finally there is *Pelléas et Mélisande*. This "old and sad tale of the woods" captures the ebb and flow of the interior life. The characters move in a trance-like world where a whisper is eloquence: Mélisande of the golden hair and the habit of saying everything twice; Pelléas, caught in the wonder of a love he does not understand; Golaud, who marries Mélisande but never fathoms her secret, driven by jealousy to the murder of his younger half-brother; and Arkel, the blind king of this shadowy land. Maeterlinck's drama gave Debussy his ideal libretto. The result was a unique lyric drama that justifies Romain Rolland's description of him as "this great painter of dreams."

Prélude à l'après-midi d'un faune

Debussy's best-known orchestral work was inspired by a pastoral of Stéphane Mallarmé that evokes the landscape of pagan antiquity. The poem centers about the mythological creature of the forest, half man, half goat. The faun, "a simple sensuous passionate being," in Edmund Gosse's phrase, awakes in the woods and tries to remember. Was he visited by three lovely nymphs or was this but a dream? He will never know. The sun is warm, the earth fragrant. He curls himself up and falls into a wine-drugged sleep.

Debussy completed the tone poem in 1894 when he was thirty-two. His imagination was attuned to the pagan setting, and his music invokes emotions as voluptuous as they are elusive. It unfolds what he well called his "harmonious harmony."

The piece opens with a flute solo in the velvety lower register. The melody glides along the chromatic scale, narrow in the range, languorous; the tempo is "very moderate":

Glissandos on the harp usher in a brief dialogue of the horns. Of these sounds it may be said, as of the opening chords of *Tristan*, that their like had never been heard before. The dynamic scheme is discreet; pianissimo and mezzo-piano predominate. There is only one fortissimo. The whole-tone scale is heard. Notable is the limpid coloring. The strings are muted and divided. Flute and oboe, clarinet and horns are used soloistically, standing out against the orchestral texture.

The work is in sections that follow the pattern of statement-departure-return. Yet the movement is fluid, rhapsodic. Debussy here achieves his goal of a music "free from motives and themes, founded in reality on a single continuous theme which nothing would interrupt and which would never return upon itself." This continuity of theme imparts to the piece an extraordinary unity of mood and texture.

Almost every fragment of melody is repeated forthwith, a trait that the composer carries to the length of mannerism. Characteristic is the relaxed rhythm which flows across the bar line in a continuous stream. By weakening and even wiping out the accent Debussy achieved that dreamlike fluidity which is a prime trait of impressionist music.

A more decisive motive emerges, marked *En animant* (growing lively). It is played by a solo oboe "softly and expressively," and leads into a slight crescendo. Its wider range and more active rhythm contrasts with the opening melody:

The third theme is marked *Même mouvement et très soutenu* (same tempo and very sustained). Played in unison first by woodwinds, then by the strings, it is an ardent melody that carries the composition to its emotional crest.

The first melody returns in altered guise. At the close, antique cymbals are heard, *ppp*. (Antique cymbals are small discs of brass, held by the player one in each hand; the rims are struck together gently and allowed to vibrate.) "Blue" chords sound on the muted horns and violins, infinitely remote. The work dissolves in silence. It takes nine minutes to play. Rarely has so much been said so briefly.

Ibéria

With *Ibéria* (1908), the second of three *Images* for orchestra, Debussy joined the line of French composers—Saint-Saëns, Bizet, Lalo, and

Chabrier before him, Ravel after—who drew inspiration from Spain. Save for an afternoon spent in San Sebastian, near the border, Debussy never visited the country. For him, therefore, as for Bizet, Spain represented that unknown land of dreams which every artist carries in his heart.

I. *Par les rues et par les chemins* (In the Streets and Byways). The movement is marked *assez animé, dans un rythme alerte mais précis* (quite lively, in a rhythm that is tense but precise). The piece opens with a triplet rhythm in the woodwinds and horns, alternating with pizzicato strings. Debussy is influenced here, as was Domenico Scarlatti in the eighteenth century, by the guitar sound that is indigenous to Spain. A plaintive melody emerges on the clarinet, marked "elegant and strongly rhythmic." Its subtle syncopations and sinuous contours point to the Moorish element in the popular music of Spain.

The mood is festive, the atmosphere Mediterranean. The steady triple meter is alive with the gestures of the dance. A transitional passage leads to a contrasting idea, "sustained and very expressive." Presented by oboe and solo viola, this is a somber, long-breathed melody that moves lanquidly within a narrow range, with the frequent repetition of fragments characteristic of the folk style.

Exciting fanfares on the horns and trumpets introduce a slower section imbued with the spirit of the Spanish dance. The original idea returns in an abbreviated version. The movement dies away.

II. *Les parfums de la nuit* (Perfumes of the Night). The tempo indication is *Lent et rêveur* (slow and dreamy). Delicate pencillings of color in the opening measures make an impressionistic sonority: flutes and oboes against muted strings in high register, a touch of xylophone, clarinet and bassoon silvered by celesta, against the subdued beat of a tambourine. A seductive melody emerges on the oboe, marked "expressive and penetrating."

In the evocative power of its half-lights, this slow movement is undisputably one of Debussy's finest.

465

III. *Le matin d'un jour de fête* (The Morning of a Feast Day). The finale follows without a break. It is marked "In the rhythm of a distant march, lively and joyous," and is ushered in by a striking rhythm. Presently a light-hearted dance tune emerges in the high register of the clarinet.

The music is vividly pictorial—even balletic—in its suggestion of movement. Those who know Debussy only in his twilight moods will be surprised at the percussive dissonance, incisive rhythm, and astringent sonorities that pervade this dance finale.

We today are so familiar with his language that it is difficult for us to realize how startlingly original it was in its own time. Like Berlioz and Wagner before him, like Stravinsky and Schoenberg after, Claude Debussy stands among the great innovators in the history of his art.

80 Maurice Ravel

"Any music created by technique and brains alone is not worth the paper it is written on. A composer should feel intensely what he is composing."

Maurice Ravel (1875–1937) may be accounted a postimpressionist. As in the case of Cézanne, a classical streak in his make-up led him to impose form and order on what, he feared, might otherwise degenerate into amorphous fantasy.

His Life

Ravel was born in Ciboure, near Saint-Jean-de-Luz, in the Basses-Pyrénées region at the southwestern tip of France. The family moved to Paris shortly after Maurice was born. His father, a mining engineer who had aspired to be a musician, was sympathetic to the son's artistic proclivities. Maurice entered the Conservatory when he was fourteen, and remained there for sixteen years—an unusually long apprenticeship.

Ravel's artistic development was greatly stimulated by his friendship with a group of avant-garde poets, painters, and musicians who believed in his gifts long

Maurice Ravel. Painting
by Ouvré. (Collection
André Meyer)

before those were recognized by the world at large. Youthful enthusiasts, they
called themselves the "Apaches." In this rarefied atmosphere the young composer found the necessary intellectual companionship. Ravel's career followed
the same course, more or less, as that of almost all the leaders of the modern
movement in art. At first his music was hissed by the multitude and cried down
by the critics. Only a few discerned the special quality of his work, but their
number steadily grew. Ultimately the tide turned, and he found himself
famous.

In the years after the First World War Ravel came into his own. He was
acknowledged to be the foremost composer of France and was much in demand
to conduct his works throughout Europe. In 1928 he was invited to tour the
United States. Before he would consider the offer he had to be assured of a
steady supply of his favorite French wines and cigarettes. Ravel and America
took to one another, although he tired first. "I am seeing magnificent cities,
enchanting country," he wrote home, "but the triumphs are fatiguing. Besides,
I was dying of hunger."

Toward the end of his life Ravel was tormented by restlessness and insomnia.
He sought surcease in the hectic atmosphere of the Parisian night clubs, where
he would listen for hours to American jazz. As he approached sixty he fell
victim to a rare brain disease that left his faculties unimpaired but attacked the
centers of speech and motor coordination. It gradually became impossible for
him to read notes, to remember tunes, or to write. Once, after a performance of
Daphnis et Chloé, he began to weep, exclaiming: "I have still so much music in

my head!" His companion tried to comfort him by pointing out that he had finished his work. "I have said nothing," he replied in anguish. "I have still everything to say."

So as not to watch himself "go piece by piece," as he put it, he decided to submit to a dangerous operation. This was performed toward the end of 1937. He never regained consciousness.

His Music

Ravel shared with Debussy an affinity for the scales of medieval and exotic music. Both men were attracted by the same aspects of nature—daybreak, the play of water and light. Both exploited exotic dance rhythms, especially those of Spain. Both loved the fantastic and the antique, and the old French harpsichordists. Both were repelled by the passion of nineteenth-century music, and believed the primary purpose of art to be sensuous delight. Ravel, too, was inspired by the symbolist poets and had a gift for setting the French language to music. Both men in surpassing degree exemplified Gallic sensibility. And both considered themselves rebels against the ninetenth-century spirit, although it is apparent to us now that romanticism was the soil out of which their music flowered.

The differences between the pair are as pronounced as the similarities. Much of Ravel's music has an enameled brightness that contrasts with the twilight softness of Debussy's. He is less visionary. His rhythms are more incisive and have a verve, a drive that Debussy rarely strives for. He goes beyond Debussy's conception of dissonance. Ravel's sense of key is firmer, the harmonic movement more clearly outlined; he is far less partial to the whole-tone scale than Debussy. He is more conventional in respect to form, and his melodies are broader in span, more direct. His texture is contrapuntal, often being based on the interplay of lines rather than on the vertical blocks of sound that fascinated Debussy. Ravel's orchestration derives in greater degree from the nineteenth-century masters; he stands in the line of descent from Berlioz, Rimsky-Korsakov, and Richard Strauss. Whereas Debussy aimed to "decongest" sound, Ravel handled the huge postromantic orchestra with brilliant virtuosity.

Ravel ranks as one of the outstanding piano composers of the twentieth century. He extended the heritage of Liszt, even as Debussy was the spiritual heir of Chopin. Among his most widely played works for the piano are *Pavane pour une infante défunte* (Pavane for a Dead Infanta, 1899), *Jeux d'eau* (Fountains, 1901), and the *Sonatine* (1905). The French art song found in Ravel one of its masters. Characteristic of his style is *Shéhérazade*, a song cycle for voice and orchestra (1903). *Trois Poèmes de Stéphane Mallarmé* (1913) exemplifies the twentieth-century interest in chamber music with voice, as do the sensuous *Chansons madécasses* (Songs of Madagascar, 1926) for voice, flute, cello, and piano.

But it was through his orchestral works that Ravel won the international public. The best known of these are *Rapsodie espagnole* (Spanish Rhapsody, 1907); *Ma Mère l'Oye* (Mother Goose, 1912); the ballet *Daphnis et Chloé*, one of his strongest works (1912); *La Valse*, which we will discuss; the ever popular *Boléro* (1928), which exploits the hypnotic power of relentless repetition, unflagging rhythm, steady crescendo, and brilliant orchestration; the classically oriented Piano Concerto in G (1931); and the dramatic Concerto for the Left Hand (1931), a masterpiece.

Ravel, like Debussy, has always been immensely popular in the United States. His harmonies and orchestration exercised a particular attraction for jazz arrangers and Hollywood composers. As a result his idiom (somewhat watered down, to be sure) become a part of the daily listening experience of millions of Americans.

La Valse

The idea of writing a piece to glorify the Viennese waltz came to Ravel as early as 1906. Thirteen years—and a world war—later, Ravel returned to the project. The dance that originally was to have given utterance to his joy in life now returned to his mind in the guise of a *danse macabre*. The external stimulus came from Serge Diaghilev, the famed impresario of the Russian Ballet, who wanted Ravel to do a piece for his company. The work was completed in 1920.

Ravel's conception of this ballet—a scene at the imperial palace, around 1855—is explained in a note that he appended to the score: "Through whirling clouds we catch a glimpse of couples waltzing. The clouds gradually lift, revealing an immense hall filled with dancers. The scene is gradually lit up. There is a burst of light from the chandeliers." It is worthy of note, in view of the pictorial character of Ravel's orchestration, that he closely associated an upsurge in sound with an upsurge of light.

In *La Valse* a number of disparate elements are deftly intertwined. The spirit of Vienna (as evoked by a sensibility that is wholly French) is combined at the beginning with the mistiness of impressionism, at the end with the dazzling sonorities of the postromantic orchestra. The radiant waltz of Johann Strauss becomes a symbol here of a dying world indulging in its last dance. Hence the duality of the emotion, that strange bittersweet quality so characteristic of Ravel. Like *Boléro*, *La Valse* is a study in orchestral crescendo—but a crescendo more capricious, more subtle.

The piece opens pianissimo with tremolos in the muted strings. Wisps of melody float out of an impressionist haze; we seem to be on the verge of hearing a waltz tune which, tantalizingly, never emerges. The only thing the ear can make out is Ravel's tempo, *Mouvement de Valse viennoise*. Finally a melody takes shape in the bassoons and violas:

Then another, a caressing tune on the violins and violas:

At this point the mutes are removed one at a time. From then on the music unfolds one seductive waltz tune after another, now gathering momentum, now returning to the pianissimo sonorities of the opening. Ravel artfully husbands his resources until the frenzied climax, when he unleashes all the clashing dissonances of which the orchestra of his time was capable. It is in these frenetic final measures that his alluring "apotheosis of the waltz" becomes a dance of terror and destruction. The harsh dissonances, *fff*, almost pass beyond what a recording is able to convey. This steep rise in dissonance content, abetted by a crescendo and accelerando, brings the work to an electrifying close.

Between them Debussy and Ravel held up an ideal of sonorous beauty that incarnated the sensibility and *esprit* of their nation. And they opened wide the door to the twentieth century.

81 Other Postromantic Composers

The French

The postromantic generation in France continued the efforts of César Franck to create a well-rounded musical culture that would not be tied to the opera house. A leading figure was Gabriel Fauré (1845–1924), who is best known for his Requiem (1887), a lovely work whose inner quietude of spirit reveals Fauré's characteristic trait of "intimate limpidity." Important, too, was the pupil and chief disciple of Franck, Vincent d'Indy (1851–1931), who is remembered for his *Symphony on a French Mountain Air* (1886). Paul

Dukas (1865–1935) achieved an international success with the brilliantly colored orchestral scherzo *The Sorcerer's Apprentice* (1897).

Albert Roussel (1869–1937) has emerged as one of the most significant figures of the transition period. Best known among his works are the Second and Third Symphonies, and the ballet *Le Festin de l'araignée* (The Spider's Feast).

Two gifted pupils of César Franck won recognition beyond the borders of their native land. Henri Duparc (1848–1933) ranks as one of the creators of the modern French art song. *Extase* and *L'Invitation au voyage* are superb examples of intimate lyric art. Ernest Chausson (1855–99) is remembered for several appealing works that show a strong Wagnerian influence, such as the Symphony in B-flat (1890) and the *Poème* for violin and orchestra (1896).

The Russians

The mantle of Tchaikovsky and Rimsky-Korsakov descended to a numerous progeny, the majority of whom were known mainly in their own land. However, two among this group became international figures: Scriabin and Rachmaninov.

Alexander Scriabin (1872–1915) experimented with the construction of chords in intervals of a fourth instead of, as was the rule in traditional harmony, a third. He was one of those who ushered in new conceptions of dissonance and tonality. His fame rests on several grandiose symphonic poems of a post-Wagnerian cast, such as the *Poem of Ecstasy*, as well as ten piano sonatas and a variety of short piano pieces—preludes, etudes, mazurkas, and the like.

Sergei Rachmaninov (1873–1943) became the accredited voice of Slavic pessimism in the post-Tchaikovsky generation. His compositions display broadly spun voluptuous melodies, somber marching rhythms, a flair for the piano and its massive chord sonorities, and a sense of theatrical effect. The most popular are the Piano Concertos Nos. 2 and 3, and the *Rhapsody on a Theme by Paganini*.

The English

For almost two hundred years after the death of Purcell, England produced no major composer of her own. With the rise of a native school in the postromantic period the nation's confidence in its ability to create music was restored. The renascence expressed itself in a nationalist movement that cultivated folk song and dance as an expression of rural England. A strengthening factor was the revival of the great church music of the time of the Tudor monarchs, of the Elizabethan madrigal and the art of Purcell.

Sir Edward Elgar (1857–1934) was the first of his generation to achieve international fame. He loved England, her past, her countryside; and became the unofficial musician-laureate of the late Victorian and Edwardian eras. The

Enigma Variations and Violin Concerto offer a good introduction to his music.

Frederick Delius (1862–1934) represents another aspect of the British character—its quietude and inwardness of spirit. His is a gentle lyricism compounded of dreams and longing. An eloquent example of his art is *Sea Drift*, a work for baritone solo, chorus, and orchestra based on the poem by Walt Whitman.

It has been said about Ralph Vaughan Williams (1872–1958) that he was an Englishman first and a musician afterward. His is the speech of a natural man, blunt, rugged, honest. At his best, as in the Symphony No. 4 in F minor, the *London Symphony*, and the Mass in G minor, he reaches beyond his island. The British regard him as one of their foremost musicians.

Others

It will suffice to mention a few other figures of the time. Ottorino Respighi (1879–1936) was one of a group of Italian composers who tried to establish a symphonic art in the land above all dedicated to operatic music. Two of his works, *Fountains of Rome* and *Pines of Rome*, show his flair for colorful orchestral effects.

Ferruccio Busoni (1866–1924), a man of brilliant intellect and versatile gifts, was active as pianist, conductor, teacher, and writer on music as well as composer. Busoni disliked nineteenth-century music but adored Bach, Mozart, and the closed forms of classical opera. His operas *Arlecchino* (1916), *Turandot* (1917), and *Doktor Faust* (1924) exemplify the neoclassic esthetic that was to play so important a part in the new age.

Leoš Janáček (1854–1928) is the representative figure of the modern Czech school. He has been compared to Musorgsky for his unconventionality of thought, his rough-hewn and original harmonies, the compassion and love of humble folk that inform his art. Now that various works of Janáček have been made available on records—notably the opera *Jenufa* (1894–1903), the *Slavonic Mass* (1926), and the Sinfonietta (1926)—the reader is in a position to acquaint himself with the art of a composer who commands extraordinary admiration throughout central Europe.

Spain produced two musicians of charm in Isaac Albéniz (1860–1909) and Enrique Granados (1867–1916). Albéniz' *Iberia*, a set of twelve piano pieces (1906–09), like Granados' *Spanish Dances* and *Goyescas* (1911), a set of piano pieces on which he later based an opera, show how effectively these two nationalists used the song and dance forms of their native land.

It testifies to the vitality of the postromantic generation that so much of their music continues to delight the public. For it was the unique mission of this group of composers not only to write the coda to the achievements of nineteenth-century musical culture, but also to set the scene for a new period in music.

82

Main Currents in Twentieth-Century Music

"The entire history of modern music may be said to be a history of the gradual pull-away from the German musical tradition of the past century."

Aaron Copland

The Reaction Against Romanticism

"Epochs which immediately precede our own," writes Stravinsky, "are temporarily farther away from us than others more remote in time." The first quarter of the twentieth century was impelled before all else to throw off the oppressive heritage of the nineteenth. Composers of the new generation were fighting not only the romantic past but the romanticism within themselves.

The turning away from the nineteenth-century spirit was manifest everywhere. Away from the subjective and the grandiose; from pathos and heaven-storming passion; from the romantic landscape and its picture-book loveliness; from the profound musings on man and fate; from the quest for sensuous beauty of tone—"that accursed euphony," as Richard Strauss called it. The rising generation viewed the romantic agony as Wagnerian histrionics. It considered itself to be made of sterner stuff. Its goal was a sweeping reversal of values. It aimed for nothing less than "to root out private feelings from art."

Non-Western Influences

The new attitudes took shape just before the First World War. The spiritual exhaustion of Western culture showed itself in an indefinable restlessness. European art sought to escape its overrefinement, to renew itself in a fresh and unspoiled stream of feeling. There was a desire to capture the spontaneity, the freedom from inhibition that was supposed to characterize primitive life. People idealized brute strength and the basic impulses that seemed to have been tamed by an effete civilization. Even as the fine arts discovered the splendid abstraction of African sculpture, music turned to the dynamism of non-Western rhythm. Composers ranged from Africa to Asia and eastern Europe in their search for fresh rhythmic concepts. Out of the unspoiled, vigorous folk music in these areas came powerful rhythms of an elemental fury that tapped fresh sources of feeling and imagination, as in Bartók's *Allegro barbaro* (1911), Stravinsky's *The Rite of Spring* (1913), and Prokofiev's *Scythian Suite* (1914).

473

Sculpture from the Mali Republic, Africa. (Museum of Primitive Art, New York) *The abstraction of African sculpture provided a new impulse for European art.*

Machine Music

With the mechanization of Western society came a widespread feeling that man had surrendered his soul to forces he neither understood nor controlled. The machine became a symbol of power, motion, energy; a symbol, too, of what one writer well called "the dehumanization of art."

The period after World War I saw the production of musical works glorifying locomotive and iron foundry, dynamo and turbine. Examples of this trend are Honegger's *Pacific 231*, John Alden Carpenter's *Skyscrapers*, Antheil's *Ballet mécanique*, Mossolov's *Iron Foundry*, and Chávez's *HP* (Horsepower), all dating from the 1920s. Composers regarded such works as the necessary antidote to the birds, waterfalls, and twilights of the romantics. They did not realize that they had merely exchanged one set of picturesque symbols for another.

Europe after the First World War found surcease for its shattered nerves in athletics and sports. The body itself came to be viewed as a rhythmic machine.

Fernand Léger, (1881–1955), THE CITY (1919). (Philadelphia Museum of Art:
A. C. Gallatin Collection)
To twentieth-century artists, the machine became a symbol of energy and movement.

It is no accident that the ballet came to provide an important platform for the
new music, and that some of the foremost musicians of the twentieth century
won success in this field.

Under the influence of non-Western music, machine music, sports, and ballet,
romantic introspection gave way to twentieth-century physicality. The emphasis
was shifted from emotion to motion. Melody, the stronghold of sentiment,
yielded to the irresistible power of rhythm. The new attitude was expressed
in Stravinsky's dictum that "rhythm and motion, not the element of feeling,
are the foundation of musical art."

The New Classicism

One way of rejecting the nineteenth century was to return to the
eighteenth. The movement "back to Bach" assumed impressive proportions in
the early Twenties. There was no question here of duplicating the accents of the
Leipzig master; the slogan implied rather a reviving of certain principles that
appeared to have been best understood in his time. Instead of worshiping at the
shrine of Beethoven and Wagner, as the romantics had done, composers began

475

Giorgio de Chirico (b. 1888), THE DELIGHTS OF THE POET. (Collection, The Museum of Modern Art, New York, Acquired through the Lillie P. Bliss Bequest)
The New Classicism exalted the classical virtues of order, balance, and proportion.

to emulate the great musicians of the eighteenth century—Handel, Scarlatti, Couperin, Vivaldi—and the detached, objective style that was supposed to characterize their music.

There was a misconception here. Only the social music of the eighteenth century, the concerti grossi, harpsichord pieces, serenades, and divertimenti, may be said to embody sweet reasonableness and detachment. In their great works Bach and Handel marshaled all the expressive power of which music in their time was capable. But each age re-creates the past in its own image. To the nineteenth century, Bach was a visionary and mystic. For the twentieth he became the model for an amiable counterpoint that jogged along as crisply as ever did a piece of dinner music for a German prince. All this implied a rejection of the intensely personal quality of romantic art. Where the nineteenth-century artist was as subjective as possible, his twentieth-century counterpart tried to see the world objectively.

Basic to the new esthetic was the notion that the composer's function is not to express emotions but to manipulate abstract combinations of sound. This view found its spokesman in Stravinsky. "I evoke neither human joy nor human sadness," he declared. "I move toward a greater abstraction." A classicist by temperament and conviction, he upheld the rule of law and order in art. Music, he maintained, "is given to us with the sole purpose of establishing an order among things." This order, to be realized, requires a construction. "Once the construction is made and the order achieved, everything is said."

The neoclassicists sought to rid the art of the story-and-picture meanings with which the nineteenth century had endowed it. "People will always insist," Stravinsky points out, "upon looking in music for something that is not there. They never seem to understand that music has an entity of its own apart from anything it may suggest to them." Neoclassicism spelled the end of the symphonic poem and of the romantic attempt to bring music closer to the other arts. It led composers from programmatic to absolute music.

Neoclassicism focused attention on craftsmanship, elegance, taste. It concentrated on technique rather than content and elevated the *how* over the *what*, as generally happens in periods of experimentation. It strove for the ideal balance between form and emotion. It went even further, proclaiming that form *is* emotion, and it pointed up the intellectual rather than emotional elements in art. Future generations will find it significant that in a period of social, political, and artistic upheaval there should have been affirmed so positively the classical virtues of objectivity, serenity, and balance.

The New Nationalism

In the twentieth century nationalism pursued different aims than in the nineteenth. The romantic composers had idealized the life of the people. They fastened on those elements of local color and atmosphere that were picturesque and exportable. The new nationalism went deeper. It approached folk song in the spirit of scientific research, separating genuine peasant music from the watered-down versions of the café musicans. It sought the primeval soul of the nation and encouraged the trend toward authenticity. We find this point of view very much to the fore in the works of such men as Béla Bartók, Manuel de Falla, and Ralph Vaughan Williams. In addition, a new type of nationalism came into being that emanated from the culture of cities rather than the countryside and sought to capture the pulse of modern urban life.

Twentieth-century nationalism uncovered the harsh dissonances, percussive rhythms, and archaic modes that became elements of a new tonal language. Its discoveries enriched the resources of music and encouraged the breaking away from nineteenth-century ideals.

Expressionism

If Paris was the center of the new classicism, Vienna remained the stronghold of dying romanticism. From the city of Freud emanated the attempt to capture for art the shadowy terrain of the subconscious.

Expressionism was the German answer to French impressionism. Whereas the Latin genius rejoiced in luminous impressions of the outer world, the Germanic temperament preferred digging down to the subterranean regions of the soul. Expressionism set up inner experience as the only reality. It enthroned the irrational. Through the symbolism of dreams it released the primitive impulses suppressed by the intellect. "There is only one greatest goal toward which the artist strives," declared Arnold Schoenberg: "*To express himself*." But expression, for the expressionists, had to take place at the deepest levels of awareness.

As with impressionism, the impulse for the movement came from painting. Wassily Kandinsky (1866–1944), Paul Klee (1879–1940), Oskar Kokoschka (1886–), and Franz Marc (1880–1916) influenced Schoenberg and his disciples even as the impressionist painters influenced Debussy. The distorted images of their canvases issued from the realm of the unconscious—hallucinated visions that defied conventional notions of beauty in order to achieve the most powerful expression of the artist's inner self. Yet, within a twentieth-century framework, expressionism retained certain nineteenth-century attitudes. It inherited the romantic love of overwhelming effect and intensity, of the strange, the macabre, the grotesque. It took over the romantic interest in the demonic forces hidden deep within the human personality. Like the romantic movement itself, expressionism in music triumphed first in the central European area that lies within the orbit of Germanic culture. The movement reached its peak in the period of the Weimar Republic. It is familiar to Americans through the paintings of Kandinsky and Klee, the writings of Franz Kafka (1883–1924), the dancing of Mary Wigman (made familiar in the United States through the art of Martha Graham), the acting of Conrad Veidt, and through such films as *The Cabinet of Dr. Caligari*. Expressionist tendencies entered European opera through Richard Strauss's *Salome* and *Elektra*, and reached their full tide in the dramatic works of Schoenberg and his disciple Alban Berg. Within the orbit of

Paul Klee (1879–1940), THE MOCKER MOCKED (1930). (Collection, The Museum of Modern Art, New York. Gift of J. B. Neumann) *The distorted images of the expressionists defied conventional ideas of beauty to achieve more powerful expressiveness.*

our own culture, expressionistic elements are to be discerned in the work of such dissimilar artists as James Joyce, William Faulkner, and Tennessee Williams.

The musical language of expressionism took its point of departure from the ultrachromatic idiom of *Tristan und Isolde.* It favored a hyperexpressive harmonic language linked to inordinately wide leaps in the melody and to the use of instruments in their extreme registers. Composers hitherto had always set texts in accordance with the natural inflections of the language; expressionist composers deliberately distorted the normal accentuation of words, just as expressionist actors distorted the normal pattern of gesture, in order to secure a heightening of tension, a reality transcending the real. Aaron Copland well describes the ambience of expressionist music when, in discussing Schoenberg's *Pierrot Lunaire,* he speaks of its "curious vocal line, half spoken and half sung, the total lack of any recognizable tonal bearings, the thinly stretched and strained sonorities, the complexities of texture, the almost neurotic atmosphere engendered by the music itself."

In its preoccupation with states of soul, expressionist music sought ever more powerful means of communicating emotion, and soon reached the boundaries of what was possible within the tonal system. Inevitably, it had to push beyond.

83 New Elements of Style

"Music is now so foolish that I am amazed. Everything that is wrong is permitted, and no attention is paid to what the old generation wrote as composition."

Samuel Scheidt (1651)

The Revitalization of Rhythm

Primitivism, machine music, ballet, the influence of sports and gymnastics, the hectic pace of city life—all these called into being increasingly complex rhythms. Twentieth-century music turned away from the standard patterns of duple, triple, or quadruple meter. Composers explored the possibilities of nonsymmetrical patterns based on odd numbers: five, seven, eleven, thirteen beats to the measure.

In nineteenth-century music a single meter customarily prevailed through an entire movement or section. Now the metrical flow shifted constantly, sometimes with each bar, as in Stravinsky's *The Rite of Spring* (1913; see the example on p. 499). Formerly music presented to the ear one rhythmic pattern at a time, sometimes two. Now composers turned to *polyrhythm*—the use of several rhythmic patterns simultaneously. As a result of these innovations,

479

Western music achieved something of the complexity and suppleness of Asiatic and African rhythms. The music of Stravinsky and Bartók revealed to their contemporaries an explosive, elemental rhythm of enormous force and tension. Both men were partial to the rhythmic *ostinato*—the use of a striking rhythmic pattern which, by being repeated over and over again, takes on an almost hypnotic power.

The twentieth century turned away from metrical rhythms based on the regular recurrence of accent, just as it turned away from metrical poetry to free verse. The new generation of composers preferred freer rhythms. The listener will not respond to these new rhythms as he would to a Strauss waltz or a Sousa march, by tapping his foot or waving his hand with the beat. As compensation, he will find rhythms that are flexible in the highest degree, of an almost physical power and drive. Indeed, the revitalization of rhythm is one of the major achievements of early twentieth-century music.

Melody

Rhythm was not the only element in which symmetrical structure was abandoned. Melody was affected too. In the nineteenth century, melody was often based on regular phrases of four or eight measures set off by evenly spaced cadences. This expansive structure is not congenial to the modern temper.

Composers today do not develop the neatly balanced repetitions that prevailed formerly. Their ideal is a direct forward-driving melody from which all nonessentials have been cut away. They assume a quicker perception on the part of the hearer than did composers in the past. A thing is said once rather than in multiples of four. The result is a taut angular melody of telegraphic conciseness. A splendid example is the resilient theme from the finale of Bartók's Concerto for Orchestra (1943; see the example on p. 511).

Nineteenth-century melody was fundamentally vocal in character; composers tried to make the instruments "sing." Twentieth-century melody is based primarily on an instrumental conception. It is neither unvocal nor antivocal; it is simply not conceived in relation to the voice. It abounds in wide leaps and dissonant intervals. The second theme in the opening movement of Shostakovich's First Symphony (1925) illustrates the instrumental character of twentieth-century melody.

Twentieth-century composers have enormously expanded our notion of what is a melody. As a result, many a pattern is accepted as a melody today that would hardly have been considered one a century ago.

Harmony

The triads of traditional harmony, we saw, were formed by combining three tones on every other degree of the scale: 1–3–5 (for example, C-E-G), 2–4–6 (D-F-A), 3–5–7 (E-G-B), and so on. Such chords are composed of a third and a fifth. (The interval from step 1 to step 3, as from C to E, is known as a third—that is, a distance of three tones counting the lower, middle, and upper tone. The interval from step 1 to step 5, as from C to G, is known as a fifth: C-D-E-F-G). Traditional harmony also employed four-tone combinations known as *seventh chords* (steps 1–3–5–7), so-called because from the lowest to the highest tone is an interval of seven steps; and five-tone combinations known as *ninth chords* (steps 1–3–5–7–9).

Twentieth-century composers added another "story" or two, forming highly dissonant combinations of six and seven tones—for instance, chords based on steps 1–3–5–7–9–11 and 1–3–5–7–9–11–13 of the scale. The emergence of these complex "skyscraper" chords imparted a greater degree of tension to music than had ever existed before.

chord
of the 11th

chord
of the 13th

A chord of seven tones, such as the second one shown above, hardly possesses the unity of the classical triad. It is composed of no less than three separate triads: the I chord (steps 1–3–5), the V chord (steps 5–7–9), and the II chord (steps 2–4–6 or 9–11–13). In this formation the Dominant chord is directly superimposed on the Tonic, so that the two poles of classical harmony, Tonic and Dominant, are brought together in a kind of montage. What our forebears were in the habit of hearing in succession is thus sounded simultaneously. Such a chord, which contains all seven steps of the major scale, not only adds spice to the traditional triad, but also increases the volume of sound, an effect much prized by composers. Here is an example:

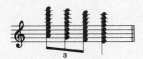

A seven-tone "skyscraper" is, in effect, a *polychord*. A succession of such chords creates several planes of harmony. One of the outstanding achievements of the new age is a kind of *polyharmony* in which the composer plays two or more streams of harmony against each other, exactly as in former times single strands of melody were combined. The interplay of the several independent

481

streams adds a new dimension to the harmonic space. The following is a famous example of polyharmony from Stravinsky's *Petrushka* (1911). The clash of the two harmonic currents produces a bright, virile sonority that typifies the twentieth-century revolt against the sweet sound of the romantic era:

The interval of a third was associated with the music of the past. To free themselves from the sound of the eighteenth and nineteenth centuries, composers cast about for other methods of chord construction; they began to base chords on the interval of the fourth. This turning from *tertial* to *quartal* harmony constitutes one of the important differences between nineteenth- and twentieth-century music. Chords based on fourths have a pungency that is very much of our century, as the following examples demonstrate.

Composers also based their harmonies on other intervals. Here is a chord of piled-up fifths from Stravinsky's *Rite of Spring* (1913), and cluster chords based on seconds from Bartók's *Mikrokosmos* (1926–37).

The Emancipation of the Dissonance

The history of music, we have seen, has been the history of a steadily increasing tolerance on the part of the listener. Throughout this long evolution one factor remained constant. A clear distinction was drawn between dissonance, the element of tension, and consonance, the element of rest. Consonance was the norm, dissonance the temporary disturbance. Twentieth-century harmony has rejected this distinction. In many contemporary works tension tends to become the norm—a clear case of art imitating life. The difference between consonance and dissonance is considered nowadays to be only a difference in degree. "Dissonant tones," Schoenberg taught, "appear later among the overtones, for which reason the ear is less acquainted with them. Dissonances are only the remote consonances." In other words, the distinction is relative rather than absolute, which means that a chord is judged not on its intrinsic character but in relation to the chords that precede or follow it. As a result, a dissonance can serve as a final cadence, as in the example from Debussy on p. 456, because it is less dissonant than the chord that came before. In relation to the greater dissonance, it is judged to be consonant.

Twentieth-century composers emancipated the dissonance, first, by making it more familiar to the ear; second, by freeing it from the obligation to resolve to consonance. Their percussive harmonies taught our ears to accept tone combinations whose like had never been heard.

Texture: Dissonant Counterpoint

The nineteenth century was occupied with harmony; the early twentieth emphasized counterpoint. The romantic composer thought in terms of vertical mass; the twentieth-century composer thought largely in terms of horizontal line. Where the romantics exalted the magic sonority of the chord, their successors stressed a neat fabric of tightly woven lines. This was part of the movement "back to Bach" and to the earlier masters of polyphony.

By adopting the contrapuntal ideal, composers substituted line for mass, thereby lightening the swollen sound of the postromantic period. The new style swept away both the romantic cloudburst and the impressionist haze. In their stead was installed a texture of widely spaced lines from whose interplay the music derived its tensions: an airy texture that fit the neoclassic ideal of craftsmanship, order, and detachment.

Consonance unites the constituent tones of harmony or counterpoint; dissonance separates them and makes them stand out against each other. Composers began to use dissonance to set off one line against another. Instead of basing their counterpoint on the euphonious intervals of the third and sixth, they turned to the astringent seconds and sevenths, as in the following example from Hindemith's *Ludus Tonalis* (1943):

Or the independence of the voices might be heightened by putting them in different keys. Thus came into being a linear texture based on dissonant counterpoint, objective, logical, powered by driving rhythms, and marked by solid workmanship as by sober sentiment.

Orchestration

Orchestral writing followed the same antiromantic direction as prevailed in other departments of the art. The rich sonorities of nineteenth-century orchestration were alien to the temper of the 1920s and '30s. The trend was toward a smaller orchestra and a leaner sound, one that was hard, bright, sober. "One is tired," wrote Stravinsky, "of being saturated with timbres."

The decisive factor in the handling of the orchestra was the change to a linear texture—the texture, for example, of Stravinsky's *Symphony of Psalms* or Schoenberg's *Variations for Orchestra*. Color came to be used in the new music not so much for atmosphere or enchantment as for bringing out the lines of counterpoint and of form. Whereas the nineteenth-century orchestrator made his colors swim together, the neoclassicist desired each to stand out against the mass. Instruments were used in their unusual registers. The emotional crescendo and diminuendo of romantic music gave way to even levels of soft or loud. This less expressive scheme revived the solid areas of light and shade of the age of Bach. The string section lost its traditional role as the heart of the orchestra. Its tone was felt to be too personal. Attention was focused on the more objective winds. There was a movement away from brilliancy of sound. The darker instruments came to the fore—viola, bassoon, trombone. The emphasis on rhythm brought the percussion group into greater prominence than ever before. The piano, which in the romantic era was pre-eminently a solo instrument, found a place for itself in the orchestral ensemble. Composers explored the piano's capacity for percussive rhythm, frequently treating it as a kind of xylophone in a mahogany box and in this way opening up new possibilities for the favored instrument of Chopin and Liszt.

Music in the second quarter of our century revived the baroque practice of pitting one instrument against another; that is, the *concertante style*. In many pieces the sound of the orchestra drew closer to the chamber-music ideal. In general, neoclassicism rejected the romantic use of timbre as an end in itself. Composers restored color to its classical function, as the obedient handmaiden of idea, structure, and design.

The Popularity of Absolute Forms

The neoclassicists took over from their romantic predecessors the large forms of absolute music—symphony and concerto, solo sonata, string quartet and other types of chamber music—which they adapted to their own esthetic. Their attitude was summed up in Prokofiev's observation, "I want nothing better than sonata form, which contains everything necessary for my needs." In addition, they revived a number of older forms: toccata, fugue, passacaglia and chaconne, concerto grosso, theme and variations, suite, and the social forms of the Viennese period—divertimento and serenade.

The tendency to elevate formal above expressive values is known as *formalism*. The second quarter of our century, it goes without saying, was a formalist age. The new classicism, like the old, strove for purity of line and proportion. Characteristic of this goal was Stravinsky's emphasis on formal beauty rather than emotional expression: "One could not better define the sensation produced by music than by saying that it is identical with that evoked by contemplating the interplay of architectural forms. Goethe thoroughly understood this when he called architecture frozen music."

The Influence of Jazz

Composers through the ages have vitalized their music by the use of forms and materials drawn from popular music. In the twentieth century, a primary source for new inspiration from outside the realm of art music was American jazz, which we will consider in detail in Chapter 96.

Among the aspects of jazz that particularly interested European composers were its rhythmic excitement, full of syncopations and polyrhythms, and its chamber-music sonority, resulting from an ensemble of soloists (woodwind and brass) playing against the rhythmic-harmonic background supplied by piano, string bass, banjo, and drums. The new level of virtuosity on such instruments as the trumpet and trombone, and the sonorities obtained with mutes and special playing techniques also found their way into art music.

Although the improvisational nature of jazz remained foreign to the music written by European composers of this period, there arose a literature that clearly attempted to evoke the unconventional sound, the contrapuntal texture, and the rhythmic freedom of ragtime and blues. Among the works reflecting various aspects of jazz influence were *Golliwog's Cakewalk* by Debussy, Erik Satie's ballet *Parade*, Stravinsky's *Ragtime* for eleven instruments and *Piano-Rag-Music*, Darius Milhaud's ballets *Le Boeuf sur le toit* and *La Création du monde*, and Ernst Krenek's opera *Jonny spielt auf*, as well as the operas of Kurt Weill (*The Three-Penny Opera* and *Mahagonny*).

Jazz assumed some strange shapes as soon as it left American hands. Nevertheless, the new classicism for a time advanced under the twin banners of Bach and jazz—a formidable combination.

485

84 New Conceptions of Tonality

"Every tone relationship that has been used too often must finally be regarded as exhausted. It ceases to have power to convey a thought worthy of it. Therefore every composer is obliged to invent anew, to present new tone relations."

Arnold Schoenberg

No single factor set off the music of our time more decisively from that of the past than the new conceptions of tonality that emerged in the twentieth century. These, in general, followed one of three paths: 1) expanded tonality; 2) the simultaneous employment of two or more keys, or polytonality; 3) the rejection of tonality, or atonality.

Expanded Tonality

In the major-minor system, seven tones were chosen out of the twelve to form a key. This "seven out of twelve" way of hearing music was expanded in the twentieth century to a "twelve out of twelve"—that is, the free use of twelve tones around a center. This approach, espoused by composers like Hindemith and Bartók, retained the basic principle of traditional tonality, loyalty to the Tonic; but, by considering the five chromatic tones to be as much a part of the key as the seven diatonic ones, it immeasurably expanded the borders of tonality. In other words, the chromatic scale of seven basic tones plus five visitors gave way to a twelve-tone scale in which eleven tones gravitated to the Tonic.

This use of twelve tones around a center not only did away with the distinction between diatonic and chromatic, but also wiped out the distinction between major and minor that was so important to the classic-romantic era. For example, traditional harmony presented two groups of seven tones with C as a center: C major and C minor. A twentieth-century piece, on the other hand, could be in the tonality of C—that is, in C major-minor, using all the twelve tones around the center C instead of dividing them into two separate groups of seven. There resulted an ambiguous tonality that suited the modern temper.

In general, the key was no longer so clearly defined an area in musical space as it used to be, and the shift from one key center to another was made with a dispatch that put to shame the most exuberant modulations of the Wagner era. Transitional passages were dispensed with. One tonality was simply displaced by another, in a way that kept both the music and the listener on the move. An excellent example is the popular theme from *Peter and the Wolf* (1936).

Prokofiev was extremely fond of this kind of displacement. (The asterisk indicates change of tonality.)

In similar fashion chords utterly foreign to the tonality were included, not even as modulations but simply as an extension of the key to a new tonal plane. As a result a passage sounded A-majorish, shall we say, rather than in A major.

Expansion of tonality was encouraged by a number of factors: interest in the exotic scales of Bali, Java, and other Far Eastern cultures; use of scales derived from the folk music of areas more or less outside the major-minor orbit, such as those of Russia, Scandinavia, Spain, Hungary and other Balkan countries; revival of interest in the medieval church modes and in composers who wrote long before the major-minor system evolved, such as the masters of fifteenth- and sixteenth-century counterpoint. The twentieth-century composer went far afield both in time and space in order to find new means of expression.

Polytonality

Tonality implied the supremacy of a single key and a single tone center. Composers in the past made the most out of the contrast between two keys heard in succession. The next step was to heighten the contrast by presenting them simultaneously.

To confront the ear with two keys at the same time meant to depart radically from the basic principle of traditional harmony. *Polytonality*—the use of two or more keys together—came to the fore in the music of Stravinsky and Milhaud, whence it entered the vocabulary of the age. Toward the end of a piece one key was generally permitted to assert itself over the others. In this way the impression was restored of orderly progression toward a central point.

Polytonality was used to bring out the different levels or planes of the harmony. By putting two or more streams of music in different keys the friction between them was immeasurably heightened. A famous example is the chord from Stravinsky's *Petrushka* that is associated with the luckless hero of this ballet: a C-major arpeggio superimposed upon one in F-sharp major.

In polytonal music the tension came from the clash of keys. Therefore each key had to be firmly established, as in the following example from Prokofiev's *Sarcasms* for piano (1912), in which right and left hand play in different keys:

So too, *Petrushka,* despite its daring harmonic combinations, has a surprisingly C-major look—that is, comparatively few sharps or flats: what used to be referred to as "white" music. The tendency toward "whiteness" was one of the characteristics of Parisian neoclassicism.

By the same token Vienna, the center of expressionism, inherited the fondness for chromatic harmony that was at the heart of German romanticism.

Atonality

Although the principle of key was flexible enough in adjusting to the needs of the new music, there was bound to appear a musician who questioned whether such adjustment was at all possible. This was Arnold Schoenberg, who proclaimed that the concept of key had outlived its usefulness.

Schoenberg rebelled against the "tyranny" of the Tonic. He maintained that as long as the tones of the key, whether seven or twelve, were kept subordinate to a central tone, it was impossible to utilize all the resources of the chromatic scale. He advocated doing away with the Tonic—in other words, treating the twelve tones as of equal importance. In this way music would be freed, he maintained, from a number of procedures that had ceased to be fruitful.

To do away with the Tonic means abandoning a principle as fundamental in the musical universe as gravitation is in the physical. Schoenberg pointed out that since the major-minor system had not existed longer than three centuries, there was no reason to suppose that it could not be superseded. "Tonality is not an eternal law of music," he asserted, "but simply a means toward the achievement of musical form." The time had come, according to him, to seek new means.

To the music of Schoenberg and his school there attached itself the label *atonality*. He disliked the term as strongly as Debussy did impressionism. "I regard the expression atonal as meaningless. Atonal can only signify something that does not correspond to the nature of tone." However, the name persisted.

Atonal music was much more of an innovation than polytonal music, for it rejected the framework of key. It excluded consonance which, according to Schoenberg, was no longer capable of making an impression. Its starting point was dissonance; it moved from one level of dissonance to another. There resulted a music that functioned always at maximum tension, without areas of relaxation. Dissonance resolving to consonance had been, symbolically, an optimistic act, affirming the triumph of rest over tension, of order over chaos. Atonal music, significantly, appeared at a time in European culture when belief in that triumph was sorely shaken.

Having accepted the necessity of moving beyond the existing tonal system, Schoenberg sought a unifying principle that would take the place of the key. He found this in a strict technique that he had worked out by the early 1920s. He named it "the method of composing with twelve tones."

The Twelve-Tone Method

"I was always occupied," Schoenberg declared, "with the desire to base the structure of my music *consciously* on a unifying idea." The twelve-tone technique made it possible for him to achieve coherence and unity in a musical composition without recourse to traditional procedures such as tonal organization, harmonic relationships, and expansion and development of themes. Each composition that uses Schoenberg's method is based on an arbitrary arrangement of the twelve chromatic tones that is called a *tone row*—or, as he terms it, a *basic set*. This row or set is the unifying idea that is the basis of that particular composition, and serves as the source of all the musical events that take place in it. The term *serial technique* is often used in this connection, an allusion to the series of twelve tones. European writers prefer the expression *dodecaphonic*, which is the Greek equivalent of *twelve-tone*.

The twelve-tone row differs from a scale in one important respect. A scale is a traditional pattern that serves as the basic series for hundreds of composers and thousands of compositions. It soon becomes familiar to the listener; any departure from the pattern is at once perceptible to the ear. The tone row, on the other hand, is the basic series of a particular composition, constituting a unique configuration of the twelve tones not to be found in any other piece. Since the twelve tones of the row are regarded as equally important, no one of them is allowed to appear more than once in the series lest it take on the prominence of a Tonic. (A tone may be repeated immediately, but this is regarded as an extension, not a new appearance.) When the basic set has unfolded it is repeated throughout the work, with the twelve tones always in the same order. Consequently the row determines the choice and succession of the intervals, shaping the over-all sound of the piece. The row may be turned upside down (inversion); it may be presented backward (retrograde); or upside down and backward (retrograde of the inversion). Each of these four versions— the original row and its three variants—may begin on any one of the twelve tones of the scale, giving forty-eight possibilities. The movement from one row form to another is loosely analogous to the passing from one key to another (modulation) in the old tonal architecture. The tone row, in fine, pervades the entire fabric of the composition, engendering not only the melody but the contrapuntal lines that unfold against it; also the harmony, since segments of the row may appear in vertical formation as chords. Thus, the unifying idea—the row—creates all the other ideas within the piece.

The basic set, of course, establishes not only a series of pitches but—even more important—a series of interval relationships. The persistence of this series of intervals in the melodies, harmonies, and counterpoints of an extended composition cannot but result in the closest possible relationship among these three dimensions of the musical tissue. The old distinction between melody and accompaniment is thereby done away with, the result being a texture of unparalleled homogeneity. Twelve-tone music, in short, seeks the utmost variety within the most stringent unity.

The following example shows the four versions of the basic set of Schoenberg's Piano Concerto, Opus 42. O stands for the original form, R for retrograde, I for inversion, and RI for the retrograde of the inversion.

All this, you will object, is quite arbitrary. To which your Schoenbergian will retort that all art is arbitrary. Precisely its artifice makes it art. Musical composition has always had its "rules of the game." If they seem to be more in evidence here, it is only because the system is new and its procedures are unfamiliar. The only valid criterion is: are Schoenberg's rules such as to enable a creative musician to express his thoughts, his feelings, and his time? Schoenberg's followers answer with an emphatic yes.

Dodecaphonic melody differs from the traditional kind in one important respect. Melody as we have come to know it generally lies in one register. However, in their desire for maximum intensity of expression, twelve-tone composers developed a jagged type of melody marked by enormous leaps from one octave to another. This poses severe problems for the performer, especially in vocal music, as in the following excerpt from Anton Webern's Cantata No. 1, Opus 29 (1939):

Hel - le   stei - gen,   bald   im   Him - mel

This angularity of line disappears if we rewrite Webern's melody so that the tones fall within the same octave:

In addition, the gravitational pull attaching to tones in the traditional harmonic system is weakened or wholly destroyed. For example, the strongest drive in tonal music is that of the seventh tone of the scale to the Tonic (*ti* to *do*; for example, B ascending to C). This drive is circumvented in twelve-tone music if the B ascends a ninth to the C of the octave above, or descends a seventh to the C below. (As a matter of fact, intervals of the seventh and ninth are extremely prominent in twelve-tone music.)

Twelve-tone thinking is essentially contrapuntal thinking. It represents a horizontal-linear conception of music, with emphasis on melodic line rather than on the harmonic mass. This conception is implemented by the devices of counterpoint: canonic and fugal imitation; augmentation and diminution (the duplication of a motive in longer or shorter note values); inversion and retrograde. The twelve-tone method eliminates the repetitions and sequences, the balanced phrases and cadences of the older style. It embodies Schoenberg's doctine of "perpetual variation." The dynamic of this music requires that no thought ever be repeated or duplicated save in some new form. As Schoenberg advised his students: "Never do what a copyist can do instead."

The tone row is not to be regarded as the theme of the piece. By the time a dodecaphonic composer has presented it in inverted and retrograde forms, and derived from it all his melodies, harmonies, and contrapuntal lines, in constantly varied rhythms, the row will have lost its identity as far as the ordinary ear is concerned. You will hardly be able to follow its wanderings as you can follow the course of a theme in a symphony. However, since the row determines the choice and succession of the intervals, its all-embracing presence governs every aspect of the music. More important, it pervades the thinking of the composer, providing him with the framework for his piece, even if that framework is no more visible to the beholder than is the steel skeleton that holds up a building.

The first masters of the dodecaphonic style display all the logic of this rigidly organized system; yet over their music brood the troubled visions that agonized the consciousness of Europe in the aftermath of the First World War. However, the twelve-tone method is not equivalent to any particular style of composition. In recent years, as Schoenberg's method has been adopted and developed by many composers of different esthetic persuasions, it has become clear that twelve-tone music can be written in many styles.

The adherents of the twelve-tone method gained world-wide influence in the years following the Second World War. In the 1950s and '60s, dodecaphonic thinking emerged as the most advanced line of thought in musical esthetics and profoundly influenced the course of contemporary music.

85 Igor Stravinsky

"I hold that it was a mistake to consider me a revolutionary. If one only need break habit in order to be labeled a revolutionary, then every artist who has something to say and who in order to say it steps outside the bounds of established convention could be considered revolutionary."

It is granted to certain artists to embody the most significant impulses of their time and to affect its artistic line in the most powerful fashion. Such an artist was Igor Stravinsky (1882-1971), the Russian composer who for half a century gave impetus to the main currents in twentieth-century music.

His Life

Stravinsky was born in Oranienbaum, a summer resort not far from St. Petersburg (Leningrad), where his parents lived. He grew up in a musical environment; his father was the leading bass at the Imperial Opera. Although he was taught to play the piano, his musical education was kept on the amateur level; his parents wanted him to study law. He matriculated at the University of St. Petersburg and embarked on a legal career, meanwhile continuing his musical studies. At twenty he submitted his work to Rimsky-Korsakov, with whom he subsequently worked for three years.

Success came early to Stravinsky. His music attracted the notice of Serge Diaghilev, the legendary impresario of the Russian Ballet, who commissioned Stravinsky to write the music for *L'Oiseau de feu* (The Firebird), which was produced in 1910. Stravinsky was twenty-eight when he arrived in Paris to attend the rehearsals. Diaghilev pointed him out to the ballerina Tamara Karsavina with the words, "Mark him well—he is a man on the eve of fame."

The Firebird was followed, a year later, by *Petrushka*. Presented with Nijinsky and Karsavina in the leading roles, this production secured Stravinsky's position in the forefront of the modern movement in art. In the spring of 1913 was presented the third and most spectacular of the ballets Stravinsky wrote for Diaghilev, *Le Sacre du printemps* (The Rite of Spring). The opening night was one of the most scandalous in modern musical history; the revolutionary score touched off a near-riot. People hooted, screamed, slapped each other, and were persuaded that what they were hearing "constituted a blasphemous attempt to

Paul Cézanne (1839–1906), MONT SAINTE-VICTOIRE (The Metropolitan Museum of Art, New York; Bequest of Mrs. H.O. Havemeyer, 1929. The H.O. Havemeyer Collection)

Ravel stands to Debussy somewhat as Cézanne does to Monet. He was a postimpressionist.

Pablo Picasso (1881–), THREE MUSICIANS (Collection, The Museum of Modern Art, New York. Mrs. Simon Guggenheim Fund)

This painting, regarded by many as the masterpiece of cubism, sums up the final stage of the movement.

Piet Mondrian (1872–1944), COMPOSITION, 1935–42 (Collection, Mr. and Mrs. Burton Tremaine, Meriden, Connecticut)

The desire for condensation of style and purity of expression, for athletic movement, economy, and architectonic unity, is embodied in the paintings of Mondrian.

Igor Stravinsky

destroy music as an art." A year later the composer was vindicated when the *Sacre,* presented at a symphony concert under Pierre Monteux, was received with enthusiasm, and established itself as a masterpiece of new music.

The outbreak of war in 1914 brought to an end the whole way of life on which Diaghilev's sumptuous dance spectacles depended. Stravinsky, with his wife and children, took refuge in Switzerland, their home for the next six years. The difficulty of assembling large bodies of performers during the war worked hand in hand with his inner evolution as an artist: he moved away from the grand scale of the first three ballets to works more intimate in spirit and modest in dimension.

The Russian Revolution had severed Stravinsky's ties with his homeland. In 1920 he settled in France, where he remained until 1939. During these years Stravinsky concertized extensively throughout Europe, performing his own music as pianist and conductor. He also paid two visits to the United States. In 1939 he was invited to deliver the Charles Eliot Norton lectures at Harvard University. He was there when the Second World War broke out, and decided to live in this country. He settled in California, outside Los Angeles, and in 1945 became an American citizen. In his later years, Stravinsky's worldwide concert tours made him the most celebrated figure in twentieth-century music, and his caustically witty books of "conversations" with his disciple Robert Craft are full of musical wisdom and footnotes to history. He died in New York on April 6, 1971.

His Music

Stravinsky has shown a continuous development throughout his career. With inexhaustible avidity he has tackled new problems and pressed for new solutions. This evolution led from the postimpressionism of *The Firebird* and the audacities of *The Rite of Spring* to the austerely controlled classicism of his maturity. In the course of it he has laid ever greater emphasis upon tradition and discipline. "The more art is controlled, limited, worked over, the more it is free." He consistently extols the element of construction as a safeguard against excess of feeling. "Composing for me is putting into an order a certain number of sounds according to certain interval relationships." A piece of music is for him first and foremost a problem. "I cannot compose until I have decided what problem I must solve." The problem is esthetic, not personal. As one of his biographers points out, "We find his musical personality in his works but not his personal joys or sorrows."

Stravinsky, we noted, was a leader in the revitalization of European rhythm. His first success was won as a composer of ballet, where rhythm is allied with body movement and expressive gesture. His is a rhythm of unparalleled dynamic power, furious yet controlled. In harmony Stravinsky reacted against the restless chromaticism of the romantic period but no matter how daring his harmony, he retained a robust sense of key. Stravinsky's subtle sense of sound makes him one of the great orchestrators. Unmistakably his is that enameled brightness of sonority, and a texture so clear that, as Diaghilev remarked, "One could see through it with one's ears."

The national element predominates in his early works; as in *The Firebird* and *Petrushka*, in which he found his personal style. The *Sacre du printemps* re-creates the rites of pagan Russia. The decade of the First World War saw the turn toward simplification of means. *L'Histoire du soldat* (The Soldier's Tale, 1918), a dance drama for four characters, is an intimate theater work accompanied by a seven-piece band. The most important work of the years that followed is *Les Noces* (The Wedding, final version 1923), a stylization of a Russian peasant wedding. Four singers and a chorus support the dancers, accompanied by four pianos and a diversified percussion group.

The neoclassical period was ushered in by the *Symphonies of Wind Instruments* (1920), dedicated to the memory of Debussy. The instrumental works that followed incarnate the principle of the old concerto grosso—the pitting against each other of contrasting tone masses. This "return to Bach" crystallized in the Concerto for Piano and Wind Orchestra (1924). Stravinsky's classical period culminated in several major compositions. *Oedipus Rex* (1927) is an "opera-oratorio"; the text is a translation into Latin of Cocteau's adaptation of the Greek tragedy. From the shattering impact of the opening chords, *Oedipus Rex* is an unforgettable experience in the theater. The archaic Greek influence is manifest too in several ballets, of which the most important is *Apollon Musa-*

gète (Apollo, Leader of the Muses, 1928), which marked the beginning of his collaboration with the choreographer George Balanchine.

The *Symphony of Psalms* (1930) is regarded by many as the chief work of Stravinsky's maturity. The Symphony in C (1940), a sunny piece of modest dimensions, pays tribute to the spirit of Haydn and Mozart. With the Symphony in Three Movements (1945), Stravinsky returns to bigness of form and gesture. In 1950 there followed *The Rake's Progress*, an opera on a libretto by W. H. Auden and Chester Kallman, after Hogarth's celebrated series of engravings. Written as the composer was approaching seventy, this radiantly melodious score, which uses the set forms of the Mozartean opera, is the quintessence of neoclassicism.

Stravinsky, imperturbably pursuing his own growth as an artist, had still another surprise in store for his public. In the works written after he was seventy, he showed himself increasingly receptive to the serial procedures of the twelve-tone style, which in earlier years he had opposed. This preoccupation came to the fore in a number of works dating from the middle Fifties, of which the most important is the *Canticum sacrum ad honorem Sancti Marci nominis* (Sacred Song to Honor the Name of St. Mark, 1956) for tenor, baritone, chorus, and orchestra. There followed the ballet *Agon* (1957) and *Threni—id est Lamentationes Jeremiae Prophetae* (Threnodies: Lamentations of the Prophet Jeremiah, completed 1958). In these works, as in the *Movements* for piano and orchestra (1958–59), *A Sermon, a Narrative and a Prayer* (1960–61), *The Flood* (1961), and the *Requiem Canticles* (1966), Stravinsky assimilated the twelve-tone technique to his personal style and turned it with utter freedom to his own use.

Stravinsky's aphorisms display his gift for trenchant expression. "We have a duty to music, namely, to invent it. . . . Instinct is infallible. If it leads us astray it is no longer instinct. . . . It is not simply inspiration that counts. It is the result of inspiration—that is, the composition. . . ." Speaking of his Mass: "The Credo is the longest movement. There is much to believe." When asked to define the difference between *The Rite of Spring* and *Symphony of Psalms:* "The difference is twenty years." Of the innumerable anecdotes to which his ready tongue has given rise it will suffice to quote one. After the out-of-town opening of *Seven Lively Arts*, which included a ballet by Stravinsky, the managers of the show, apprehensive as to how the music would be received on Broadway, wired him: "Great success. Could be sensational if you authorize arranger Mr. X to add some details to orchestration. Mr. X arranges even the works of Cole Porter." To which Stravinsky wired back: "Am satisfied with great success."

Petrushka

One of the best-known of all ballet scores, *Petrushka* presents the hapless adventures of a puppet suddenly endowed with life. The setting— a street fair during carnival week in St. Petersburg in the 1830s—enabled the

PETRUSHKA: The Moor, the Ballerina, and Petrushka (Royal Ballet, Covent Garden, production)

composer lovingly to evoke the colorful atmosphere of his native city. The score is a legitimate offspring of the Russian national school, and has found as important a place in the concert hall as in the theater.

The opening scene shows the crowds milling about the booths and stalls of the fair ground. A troop of drunken men pass by. An Italian organ grinder accompanies a dancer while nearby a rival dancer performs to the strains of a music box. The crowd is summoned by a drum roll to the marionette theater and the Showman plays his flute. The curtain of his diminutive theater rises, disclosing three puppets—Petrushka, the Ballerina, and the Moor. The Showman touches the dolls with his flute; whereupon, to the delight of the crowd, they spring to life and perform a Russian dance.

The second tableau takes place inside the marionette theater, in Petrushka's room. Petrushka is kicked unceremoniously into the room. On the wall hangs a portrait of his heartless master; he curses it. Only too aware of his unprepossessing appearance, he resents his dependence on his master. At thought of the Ballerina he is filled with tenderness; a love song takes shape in his heart. When she appears Petrushka, overwhelmed by emotion, declares his love. The Ballerina flees, leaving Petrushka in despair.

Third is the scene in the Moor's room. Stretched on the divan, the sumptuously attired Moor toys with a coconut. "Although he is brutal and stupid, his magnificent appearance charms the Ballerina." She enters; they dance together.

Petrushka appears, mad with jealousy. The Moor throws him out; the Ballerina faints.

The fourth tableau returns us to the fair grounds at evening. Nursemaids dance. A peasant plays his pipe and leads a dancing bear. A merchant in jovial mood, accompanied by two Gypsy girls, throws bank notes to the crowd. Coachmen and grooms dance and are joined by the nursemaids. A group of masked figures appear. Their antics amuse the crowd, which joins in a frenzied dance led by a masked devil. Suddenly there is a commotion in the puppet theater. Petrushka rushes out from behind the curtain, followed by the Moor, whom the Ballerina vainly tries to hold back. The Moor overtakes the luckless Petrushka and strikes him with his sword. Petrushka falls, mortally hurt. To the consternation of the crowd, he dies.

A policeman fetches the Showman who, to reassure the bystanders, picks up and shakes the little body, showing them that it is only a doll stuffed with sawdust. The crowd disperses. The Showman begins to drag the puppet to his room. Above the little theater, however, he catches sight of Petrushka's ghost, grimacing and menacing. He had not foreseen that his creation, through suffering, would achieve a soul. Stricken with fear the Showman drops the doll and steals away. . . .

The opening measures evoke the "big accordion" sound of the folk music that surrounded Stravinsky in his childhood. The orchestra teems with movement and animation. A solo flute, supported by the second flute, presents a theme that is etched precisely against a background of clarinet and horn tremolos. This melody recurs as a unifying element throughout the score.

At the rise of the curtain we encounter Stravinsky's rhythmic suppleness. The meter alternates between ¾ and ²⁄₄. Suddenly we hear the percussive harmonies, imbued with rhythmic power, that are the hallmark of this composer. The motive of the drunkards is typical of the melodies in *Petrushka*: it is compact, strong, rooted in the key. It moves stepwise along the scale, with an occasional narrow leap, and remains within a narrow range, outlining the basic interval of

a fifth and repeating fragments of itself. It bears the imprint of the folk yet is thoroughly assimilated to Stravinsky's personal style.

The hurdy-gurdy sound is well simulated by flute and piccolo, clarinet and bass clarinet. A triangle marks the beat for the dancer and casts a tinsel charm over her wistful little melody, which Stravinsky derived from a French street song. The Showman's flute solo sets the scene for miraculous doings. After he animates the dolls the orchestra breaks into the Russian Dance, another compact, scalewise tune of primitive strength whose repeated fragments outline the interval of a fifth. The C-major sound of this music announced to the world

that the turning away from post-Wagnerian chromaticism had begun, while the closely bunched dissonant chords on the piano point up the new percussive style of writing for that instrument.

The second scene presents the famous Petrushka chord, the harmonic kernel out of which the work grew: a C-major arpeggio superposed upon one in F-sharp major that serves it as a kind of "double" (see the example on p. 487). It is a strikingly original sonority, and pointed the way to the polyharmony and polytonality that were to play so important a part in the new music. Petrushka's love song, whimsical and tender, makes a fine contrast to the music that suggests his despair after the Ballerina's departure.

The third tableau, in the Moor's room, contains a series of charming numbers. The percussive harmonies that introduce this vain and brutal character are followed by the Moor's languid dance, an exotic theme presented by clarinet and bass clarinet against tricky syncopated rhythms on the bass drum and cymbal. The entrance of the Ballerina makes for a gay bit on the trumpet and snare drum. Her dance with the Moor is marked Lento cantabile: a staid duet for flute and trumpet that veers into a Viennese waltz, allegretto. The familiar trumpet fanfare announces the appearance of Petrushka. The quarrel between him and the Moor turns on agitated harmonies and colors that stem out of the romantic heritage—but with a difference!

The final tableau brings back the "big accordion" sound of the opening scene. Out of the swarming orchestral voices emerges the Dance of the Nursemaids, a memorable tune out of the heart of the Russian national school. The melody line fills in the two basic intervals, octave and fifth, which gives it simplicity and strength.

The peasant and his bear are characterized by clarinet and tuba against heavy chords in the lower strings. The dance of the coachmen and grooms affords the composer opportunity for those dark percussive harmonies that he was to exploit so brilliantly in *The Rite of Spring*. When the nursemaids join the dance, their theme is given a sumptuous orchestral garb. The carnival reaches its height with the dance of the masked figures. The appearance of Petrushka pursued by the Moor is accompanied by provocative sonorities, including chromatic scales on trumpet, xylophone, and strings. Petrushka's death is depicted with wonderful economy of means: harmonics on the violas, a flicker of piccolo sound, tremolo on muted violins, with the melody line traced in turn by clarinet, violin solo, and bassoon. The C-major chord appears against its F-sharp major "double"; and the work ends with a suggestion of the polytonal harmony from which it sprang.

Le Sacre du printemps

Le Sacre du printemps (The Rite of Spring, 1913)—"Scenes of Pagan Russia"—not only embodies the cult of primitivism that so startled its first-night audience; it also sets forth the lineaments of a new tonal language— the percussive use of dissonance, polyrhythms, and polytonality. The work is scored for a large orchestra, including an exceptionally varied percussion group.

Part I. *Adoration of the Earth.* The Introduction is intended to evoke the birth of Spring. A long-limbed melody is introduced by the bassoon, taking on a curious remoteness from the circumstance that it lies in the instrument's upper-most register. The narrow range and repetition of fragments gives this theme a primitive character:

The awakening of the earth is suggested in the orchestra. On stage, a group of young girls is discovered before the sacred mound, holding a long garland. The Sage appears and leads them toward the mound. The orchestra erupts into a climax, after which the bassoon melody returns.

Dance of the Adolescents. Dissonant chords in the lower register of the strings exemplify Stravinsky's "elemental pounding"; their percussive quality is height-ened by the use of polytonal harmonies. A physical excitement attends the dis-location of the accent, which is underlined by syncopated chords hurled out by eight horns. The ostinato—a favorite rhythmic device of Stravinsky—is repeated with hypnotic insistence. A theme emerges on the bassoons, moving within a narrow range around a central tone, with a suggestion of elemental power.

The main theme of the movement, a more endearing melody in folk style, is introduced by the horns. Stravinsky expands this idea by means of the repetition technique so characteristic of the Russian school.

Game of Abduction. The youths and maidens on the stage form into two phalanxes which in turn approach and withdraw from one another. Fanfares on the woodwinds and brass add a luminous quality to the sound.

Spring Dance. A pastoral melody is played by the high clarinet in E-flat and the bass clarinet, two octaves apart, against sustained trills on the flutes. Modal

harmonies create an archaic atmosphere. Four couples are left on stage. Each man lifts a girl on his back and with measured tread executes the Rounds of Spring. The movement is sostenuto e pesante (sustained and heavy) with block-like harmonies propelled by ostinato rhythms.

Games of the Rival Cities—Entrance of the Sage—Dance of the Earth. The peremptory beating of drums, against the sound of trombones and tubas, summons the braves of the rival tribes to a display of prowess. The main idea is presented by two muted trumpets. Notice that the third measure repeats the melodic curve of the two preceding ones, but with a rhythmic dislocation which causes the notes to fall on different beats within the measure:

The orchestration evokes a neolithic landscape. The score abounds in orchestral "finds," such as the braying sound produced by a simultaneous trill in piccolo and flutes, oboes and English horn, clarinets, horns, trumpets, and trombones over an ostinato in the basses. The Entrance of the Sage touches off a powerful crescendo that rises over a persistent figure in the brass. An abrupt silence—a pianissimo chord in the bassoons as the dancers prostrate themselves in mystic adoration of the earth. Then they leap to their feet, and to music of the sheerest physicality perform the Dance of the Earth.

Part II. *The Sacrifice.* The Introduction is a "night piece" that creates a brooding atmosphere. The Sage and the maidens sit motionless, staring into the fire in front of the sacred mound. He must choose the Elect One who will be sacrificed to ensure the fertility of the earth. A poignant melodic idea in Russian folk style, first presented by the muted violins in harmonics, pervades the movement.

The music is desolate, but there is nothing subjective about it. This desolation is of the soil, not the soul.

Mystic Circle of Young Girls. The theme of the preceding movement alternates with a melody presented by the alto flute, which stands out against a

dissonant background. The two themes are repeated in various registers with continual changes of color. The major-minor ambiguity goes hand in hand with the soft colors of the orchestration.

The Dance in Adoration of the Chosen Virgin has the Stravinskyan muscularity of rhythm. The eighth note is the metric unit, upon which are projected a series of uneven meters that change continually, sometimes with each bar. The piece develops into a frenzied dance.

Evocation of the Ancestors—Ritual Act of the Old Men. After a violent opening, the movement settles down to a kind of languorous "blues." An English horn solo presents a sinuously chromatic figure against a background of drums and pizzicato chords in the strings. The music carries a suggestion of swaying bodies and shuffling feet.

Sacrificial Dance of the Chosen Virgin. In this, the climactic number of the ballet, the sacrifice is fulfilled. The music mounts in fury while the chosen maiden dances until she falls dead. The men in wild excitement bear her body

to the foot of the mound. There is the scraping sound of the guiro (a Latin-American instrument consisting of a serrated gourd scraped with a wooden stick); an ascending run on the flutes and piccolos; and with a fortissimo growl in the orchestra this luminous score comes to an end.

More than half a century has passed since *Le Sacre* was written. It is still an amazing work.

Symphony of Psalms

The *Symphony of Psalms* (1930) was among the works commissioned by the Boston Symphony Orchestra to celebrate its fiftieth anniversary. There resulted one of Stravinsky's grandest works, "composed for the glory of God" and "dedicated to the Boston Symphony Orchestra."

The choice of instruments is unusual. The score omits clarinets, violins, and violas, and calls for two pianos and a mixed chorus. The three movements are performed without a break. The first movement is the shortest. The slow movement is about twice, and the jubilant finale about three times, as long.

Psalm XXXVIII (Vulgate)
Verses 13–14

Exaudi orationem meam, Domine,
     et deprecationem meam:
     auribus percipe lacrimas meas.
 Ne sileas, quoniam advena ego sum apud
     te,
     et peregrinus, sicut omnes patres mei.
 Remitte mihi,
     ut refrigerer prius quam abeam,
     et amplius non ero.
	Hear my prayer, O Lord,
	     and my supplication;
	     give ear to my tears.
	 Be not silent; for I am a stranger with
	     Thee,
	     and a sojourner, as all my fathers were.
	 O forgive me,
	     that I may be refreshed,
	     before I go hence, and be no more.

The symphony opens with a prelude-like section in which flowing arabesques are traced by oboe and bassoon. These are punctuated by an urgent E-minor chord which, spread out across the orchestral gamut, asserts the principal tonality. The altos enter with a chantlike theme consisting of two adjacent notes—the interval of a minor second (semitone) that plays an important role throughout the work.

This idea alternates with the fuller sound of choral passages as the movement builds to its climactic point on the words *Remitte mihi* (O forgive me) over a strong pedal point on E. The modal harmony creates an archaic atmosphere and leans towards the Phrygian (the mode that matches the pattern of the white keys on the piano from E to E). Tension is created by the fact that, although the music seems again and again to be climbing toward the key of C, that tonality will not be reached until the second movement. The sonorous cadence on a G-major triad serves to launch the slow movement.

Psalm XXXIX (Vulgate)
Verses 2, 3, and 4

Expectans expectavi Dominum,

   et intendit mihi.
Et exaudivit preces meas;
   et eduxit me de lacu miseriae,
   et de luto faecis.
Et statuit super petram pedes meos;
   et direxit gressus meos.
Et immisit in os meum canticum
     novum,
   carmen Deo nostro.
Videbunt multi et timebunt:
   et sperabunt in Domino.

With expectation I have waited for the
   Lord:
   and He was attentive to me,
And He heard my prayers,
   and brought me out of the pit of misery
   and the mire of dregs.
And He set my feet upon a rock,
   and directed my steps.
And He put a new canticle into my
     mouth,
   a song to our God.
Many shall see and shall fear:
   and they shall hope in the Lord.

The slow movement is a double fugue for chorus and orchestra whose flowing counterpoint underlines Stravinsky's affinity with Bach. Each fugue is in four voices. The orchestral subject is announced by the oboe. Wide leaps impart to the melody its assertive character:

After the exposition in the orchestra, the sopranos enter with the theme of the choral fugue. The interval of a falling fourth lends expressivity to the words *Expectans expectavi*:

This theme is taken over by altos, tenors, and basses in turn, to be treated in strict fugal fashion, while the orchestra expatiates upon the opening theme. Both the choral fugue and the orchestra build tension through a stretto—a passage, that is, in which the fugue subject enters in one voice before it has been completed in another. The choral stretto comes on the words *Et statuit super petram pedes meos*, sung without accompaniment—that is, a cappella. This is followed by a stretto in the orchestral fugue, the impression of mounting tension being underlined by dotted rhythms. In the final measures elements of the two fugal themes are combined in chorus and orchestra. The climax comes through understatement. In a sudden piano the chorus in unison sings *et sperabunt in Domino*, while a high trumpet in quarter notes, together with cellos and basses in eighths, reminds us of the subject of the first fugue.

503

Psalm CL (Vulgate)

Alleluia.	Alleluia.
Laudate Dominum in sanctis ejus:	Praise ye the Lord in His holy places:
laudate eum in firmamento virtutis ejus.	praise ye Him in the firmament of His power.
Laudate eum in virtutibus ejus:	Praise ye Him for his mighty acts:
laudate eum secundum multitudinem magnitudinis ejus.	praise ye Him according to the multitude of His greatness.
Laudate eum in sono tubae:	Praise Him with sound of trumpet:
laudate eum in psalterio et cithara.	praise Him with psaltery and harp.
Laudate eum in timpano et choro:	Praise Him with timbrel and choir:
laudate eum in chordis et organo.	praise Him with strings and organs.
Laudate eum in cimbalis benesonantibus:	Praise Him with high sounding cymbals:
laudate eum in cimbalis jubilationis:	praise Him with cymbals of joy:
omnis spiritus laudet Dominum.	let every spirit praise the Lord.
Alleluia.	Alleluia.

The solemn Alleluia serves as introduction. The C-minor harmony in the chorus is pitted against a C-major arpeggio figure in the orchestra. The Allegro proper opens with Stravinskyan rhythms that project the spirit of the *Psalm* in dancelike measures. The music starts out in a bright C major, with the tonic chord repeated against a driving rhythmic ostinato in the bass, the whole set off by staccato interjections in the orchestra. As so often in Stravinsky's music, the syncopation is underlined by melodic-rhythmic patterns that are shifted from one beat of the measure to another.

The sopranos enter on the *Laudate* with the two-note theme of the opening movement. But these notes are now a major instead of a minor second apart. The music gains steadily in power, its forward momentum reinforced by striking modulations. A sudden interruption brings a return of the opening Alleluia and a resumption of the forward drive. Presently there is a broadening into the slower tempo of the introduction, with a new dotted figure in the vocal parts. Then, subito piano e ben cantabile (suddenly soft and very songful), the peroration gets under way, on the words *Laudate eum in cimbalis benesonantibus*, in the key of E-flat. This serene coda, which takes up about one-third of the movement, unfolds over a four-note ostinato in the bass in three-four time, so that the bass pattern begins a beat later with each recurrence. The noble melody

of the sopranos reaffirms the semitone interval that has played a fertilizing role throughout the symphony; and the powerful E-flat major tonality rises at the very last to a major cadence in C major that evokes the Alleluia with which the movement opened.

For sheer grandeur of conception there is little in the output of the first half of our century to rival the closing pages of the *Symphony of Psalms*.

86 Béla Bartók

"What is the best way for a composer to reap the full benefits of his studies in peasant music? It is to assimilate the idiom of peasant music so completely that he is able to forget all about it and use it as his musical mother tongue."

It was the mission of Béla Bartók (1881–1945) to reconcile the folk melody of his native Hungary with the main currents of European music. In the process he created an entirely personal language and revealed himself as one of the major prophets of our century.

His Life

Bartók was born in a small Hungarian town where his father was director of an agricultural school. He studied at the Royal Academy in Budapest, where he came in contact with the nationalist movement that aimed to shake off the domination of German musical culture. His interest in folklore led him to realize that what passed for Hungarian in the eyes of the world—the idiom romanticized by Liszt and Brahms and kept alive by café musicians—was really the music of the Gypsies. The true Hungarian folk idiom, he decided, was to be found only among the peasants. In company with his fellow composer Zoltán Kodály he toured the remote villages of the country, determined to collect the native songs before they died out forever. He became an authority on the songs of the Danubian basin—Slovakian, Rumanian, and Bulgarian—and subsequently extended his investigations to include Turkish and Arab folk song.

Personal contact with peasant life brought to the surface the profound humanity that is the essential element of Bartók's art. "Those days I spent in the villages among the peasants were the happiest of my life. In order really to feel the vitality of this music one must, so to speak, have lived it. And this is possible only when one comes to know it by direct contact with the peasants."

In 1907 Bartók was appointed Professor of Piano at the Royal Academy in Budapest. Together with Kodály he founded a society for the presentation of contemporary music. The project was defeated by the apathy of a public that refused to be weaned from the traditional German repertory. Bartók was sufficiently embittered to give up composing for a time. He resumed his folklore studies and during the First World War devoted himself to a collection of soldier songs.

With the performance at the Budapest Opera of his ballet *The Wooden Prince*, Bartók came into his own. The fall of the Hapsburg monarchy in 1918

Béla Bartók.

released a surge of national fervor that created a favorable climate for his music. In the ensuing decade Bartók became a leading figure in the musical life of his country.

The alliance between Admiral Horthy's regime and Nazi Germany on the eve of the Second World War confronted the composer with issues that he faced squarely. He protested the performances of his music on the Berlin radio and at every opportunity took an anti-Fascist stand. To go into exile meant surrendering the position he enjoyed in Hungary. But he would not compromise. "He who stays on when he could leave may be said to acquiesce tacitly in everything that is happening here." Bartók's friends, fearing for his safety, prevailed upon him to leave the country while there was still time. He came to the United States in 1940 and settled in New York City.

The last five years of his life yielded little in the way of happiness. Sensitive and retiring, he felt uprooted, isolated in his new surroundings. He made some public appearances, playing his music for two pianos with his wife and onetime pupil Ditta Pásztory-Bartók. These did not suffice to relieve his financial straits. To his son he wrote in the fall of 1941, "Concerts are few and far between. If we had to live on those we would really be at the end of our tether."

In his last years he suffered from leukemia and was no longer able to appear in public. Friends appealed for aid to ASCAP (American Society of Composers, Authors, and Publishers). Funds were made available that provided the composer with proper care in nursing homes and enabled him to continue writing to the end. A series of commissions from various sources spurred him to the composition of his last works. They rank among his finest. He worked feverishly to complete the Third Piano Concerto and a concerto for viola and orchestra that had been commissioned by William Primrose. When he realized that he was dying he concentrated on the piano concerto in order to leave his wife "the only inheritance within his power." In his race against time he wishfully wrote vége —The End—on his working sketch a few days before he actually finished the piece. The Viola Concerto, left unfinished, was brought to completion from his sketches by his friend and disciple Tibor Serly. "The trouble is," he remarked

Bartók recording folk songs in Transylvania.

to his doctor shortly before the end, "that I have to go with so much still to say." He died in the West Side Hospital in New York City.

The tale of the composer who spends his last days in poverty and embitterment only to be acclaimed after his death would seem to belong to the romantic past, to the legend of Mozart, Schubert, Musorgsky. Yet it happened in our time. Bartók had to die in order to make his success in the United States. Almost immediately there was an upsurge of interest in his music that soon assumed the proportions of a boom. As though impelled by a sense of guilt for their previous neglect of his works, conductors, performers, record companies, broadcasting stations, and even his publishers rushed to pay him the homage that might have brought him comfort had it come in time.

His Music

Like Stravinsky, Bartók was careful to disclaim the role of revolutionary. "In art there are only fast or slow developments. Essentially it is a matter of evolution, not revolution." Despite the newness of his language he was rooted in the classical heritage. "In my youth my ideal was not so much the art of Bach or Mozart as that of Beethoven." He adhered to the logic and beauty of classical form, and to Beethoven's vision of music as an embodiment of human emotion.

Bartók found authentic Hungarian folk music to be based on ancient modes, unfamiliar scales, and nonsymmetrical rhythms. These freed him from what he

507

called "the tyrannical rule of the major and minor keys," and brought him to new concepts of melody, harmony, and rhythm. "What we had to do," he wrote, "was to divine the spirit of this unknown music and to make this spirit, so difficult to describe in words, the basis of our works."

Classic and romantic elements intermingle in Bartók's art. His classicism shows itself in his emphasis on construction. Characteristic is a type of melody that, like Stravinsky's, moves in a narrow range and creates an effect of primitive force. His harmony can be bitingly dissonant. Polytonality abounds in his work; but, despite an occasional leaning towards atonality, he never wholly abandoned the principle of key. In the popular *Allegro barbaro*, written in 1911, we find the percussive treatment of dissonant chords that was to come into vogue with Stravinsky's *The Rite of Spring*. Bartók's is one of the great rhythmic imaginations of modern times. His pounding, stabbing rhythms constitute the primitive aspect of his art. Passages in his scores have a Stravinskyan look, the meter changing almost at every bar. Like the Russian master, he is fond of syncopation and repeated patterns (ostinatos). Bartók played a major role in the revitalization of European rhythm, infusing it with earthy vitality, with kinetic force and tension.

He was more traditional in respect to form. His model was the sonata of Beethoven. In his middle years he came under the influence of pre-Bach music and turned increasingly from harmony to linear thinking. His complex texture is a masterly example of modern dissonant counterpoint. It sets forth his development toward greater abstraction, tightness of structure, and purity of style.

From the orchestra of Richard Strauss and Debussy Bartók found his way to a palette all his own. His orchestration ranges from brilliant mixtures to threads of pure color that bring out the intertwining melody lines; from a hard, bright glitter to a luminous haze. A virtuoso pianist himself, Bartók is one of the masters of modern piano writing. He typifies the twentieth-century use of the piano as an instrument of percussion and rhythm. The most important work for piano of his later years is *Mikrokosmos* (1926–37), a collection of one hundred and fifty-three pieces ranging from the simplest grade to virtuoso playing.

The six string quartets may very well rank among the finest achievements of our century. These are uncompromising and extraordinarily expressive works, certain of them impregnated with the brooding pessimism that was the aftermath of the First World War. Bartók is best known to the public by the three major works of his last period. The *Music for Strings, Percussion, and Celesta*, written in 1936, is regarded by many as his masterpiece. Tonal opulence and warmth characterize the Concerto for Orchestra (1943), a favorite with American audiences. The master's final statement, the Third Piano Concerto (1945), is an impassioned and broadly conceived work, its three movements by turn dramatic, contemplative, satanic. The last-named quality connects him with the Hungarian master of the romantic period, Franz Liszt.

Bartók's music encompasses the diverse trends of his time, the polytonal and atonal, expressionism and neoclassicism, folk dance and machine music, lyricism and the dynamic. It reaches from primitivism to the intellectual, from program music to the abstract, from nationalism to the universal. Into all these he infused the high aim of a former age: to touch the heart.

Concerto for Orchestra

In the summer of 1943 Bartók was confined in Doctors Hospital in New York City. One day he received a visit from Serge Koussevitzky, who came offering a thousand-dollar commission and a first performance by the Boston Symphony Orchestra for any piece he would write. The knowledge that his music was wanted and that a major orchestra was waiting to perform the as yet unwritten score had a beneficent effect on the incurably ill composer. He was able to quit the hospital, and set to work on the Concerto for Orchestra, which was completed in October of that year. "The general mood of the work," he wrote, "represents, apart from the jesting second movement, a gradual transition from the sternness of the first movement and the lugubrious death-song of the third to the life-assertion of the last."

Of symphonic dimension, the work is called a concerto because of its tendency, as Bartók explained, "to treat the single instruments in a *concertante* or soloistic manner." In other words, he used the term as the eighteenth century did. The element of virtuosity prevails, but the virtuoso is the entire orchestra.

1. *Introduzione. Andante non troppo—Allegro vivace.* The Introduction is spacious of gesture. It prepares the listener for a large work. In the composer's best vein are the sonorities of the opening passage, a solemn statement by cellos and basses set off by tremolos on upper strings and flute. The theme is based on the interval of the fourth (indicated by brackets), which occupies a prominent position in the melodic formations of this composer.

The first subject of the Allegro vivace consists of a vigorously syncopated figure that ascends to a climax and as briskly subsides:

Here too the fourth is prominent. A contrasting idea in folklore style consists mainly of two notes. The Development builds up tension through contrapuntal

509

imitation. The Restatement is abbreviated, as is customary in twentieth-century works. The movement has the quality of inevitable progression that is the essence of symphonic style.

II. *Giuoco delle coppie* (Game of Pairs). So called because the wind instruments are paired at specific intervals, bassoons in sixths, oboes in thirds, clarinets in sevenths, flutes in fifths, muted trumpets in seconds. This "jesting second movement," as Bartók called it, is marked Allegretto scherzando. The side drum, without snares, ushers in music of a processional nature that is

filled with teasing ideas. In evidence is the element of the bizarre that appealed to Berlioz and Mahler no less than to Bartók. The form is a "chain" of five little sections, each featuring another pair of instruments. There is a chorale for brass. The five sections are then restated with more elaborate instrumentation.

III. *Elegia. Andante non troppo.* This movement is the "lugubrious death song." An oboe traces a long line of lamentation against Bartókian flickerings of clarinet, flute, and harp tone. The music is rhapsodic, visionary; it rises to a tragic climax. This is an heroic canvas in the great line of the hymnic adagios of Beethoven.

IV. *Intermezzo interrotto* (Interrupted Intermezzo). A plaintive tune in folk-song style is introduced by the oboe and continued by the flute.

The nonsymmetrical rhythm, an alternation of ¾ and ⅝, imparts to the movement a wayward charm. There follows a broadly songful theme on the strings, one of the great melodies of the twentieth century. The mood is interrupted

as the music turns from folk lyricism to the sophisticated tone of the cafés. The return of the lyric theme on muted strings makes a grandly poetic effect. The movement is replete with capriciousness and tender sentiment.

V. *Finale. Pesante—Presto.* There is an introduction of seven bars marked pesante (heavily), in which the horns outline the germinal theme. The movement of "life-assertion" gets off to a whirlwind perpetuum mobile (perpetual motion) in the strings. The fugue that follows parades intricate devices of counterpoint; yet so lightly does Bartók wear his learning that there is nothing here to tax the untutored ear. The fugue subject is presented by the second trumpet. Notice again the decisive role played by the interval of a fourth.

The answer, played by the first trumpet, is an inversion of the theme. The folk tune as Bartók uses it here has nothing in common with the prettified peasant dances of the nineteenth century. Its harmonies are acrid, its rhythms imbued with primitive strength. The movement rises to a mood of heroic affirmation.

Music for Strings, Percussion, and Celesta

This work (1936) was a landmark in the twentieth-century cultivation of chamber-music textures. Bartók's conception called for two string groups to frame the percussion and celesta. He carefully specified the arrangement of the players on the stage:

	Double Bass I	Double Bass II	
Cello I	Timpani	Bass Drum	Cello II
Viola I	Side Drums	Cymbals	Viola II
Violin II	Celesta	Xylophone	Violin IV
Violin I	Piano	Harp	Violin III

I. Andante tranquillo. The movement is based on a single crescendo that grows inexorably from *pp* to a fortissimo climax and then works back to a *ppp*.

511

We hear a fugue based on an undulating chromatic theme that moves within the range of a fifth, from A to E, and includes all the semitones between. This subject is introduced by the muted violas. Each time the subject enters it ap-

pears alternately a fifth higher and lower, fanning out from the central tone A— first on E (a fifth above A), then on D (a fifth below A); on B (a fifth above E), G (a fifth below D), F-sharp (a fifth above B), and so on—growing steadily in power until the climactic point is reached on E-flat. Thereupon the theme is inverted and the movement returns to the central A. Thus, the crescendo-decrescendo pattern is combined with a sequence of tonal centers that are a fifth apart in an ascending-descending motion. Since the entire movements is woven out of the generating theme, this Andante achieves an extraordinary concentration of thought and consistency of texture.

II. Allegro. The main idea is a taut, imperious subject whose chromatic character relates it to the germinal theme of the preceding movement. This

Allegro is a closely knit sonata form that draws its impetus from the gestures of the dance. The key areas are loosely defined through free use of the twelve chromatic tones around a Tonic. This goes for the home-key area, C, as well as for the contrasting-key area of G, in which the first violins introduce a playful theme marked leggiero (lightly). The development section contains an exciting fugato. In the Recapitulation, the main idea returns in a typically Bartókian rhythm—an alternation of groups of two, three, and five beats—before it settles into $\frac{3}{8}$. The two groups of strings are used antiphonally, in question-and-answer formation.

III. Adagio. This "night piece" reveals Bartók's gift for evoking a magical landscape through instrumental color. The movement proceeds to a high point and then retraces its path back to the beginning. This structure is made manifest in five sections: A, in the style of an improvisation; B, lyric section; C, based on a bell-like motive; B, lyric section; A, abbreviated. The eerie repetition of the high F on the xylophone ushers in a rhapsodic cantillation on the viola (section A). The lyric section (B) is presented by celesta and violin. Bartókian flickerings of sound—runs on the celesta mingled with glissandos on harp and piano— provide a background for the free development of a chromatic idea born of the germinal theme. The climax of the movement (section C) is based on a tense five-tone motive that is bandied about among the instruments. This constitutes

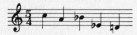

the central point of the movement. The material heard earlier then returns, but in reverse order.

IV. Allegro molto. The finale combines the passionate abandon of Magyar folk dance with contrapuntal processes that are tossed off with sheer virtuosity. The movement opens with plucked chords that conjure up the sound of folk instruments.

The central idea of this expanded rondo form outlines the Lydian mode (see p. 315). The rhythm is a Bulgarian dance pattern of eight eighth-notes (written as $\frac{2}{2}$) grouped in a pattern of 2–3–3:

The middle part of the rondo theme goes back to the sinuous contours of the germinal theme in the first movement. In the contrasting sections Bartók deploys his propulsive rhythms, which at times take on a jazzlike animation, and his powerful cluster chords on the piano. Each recurrence of the rondo theme brings fresh variation. The movement builds up to a climax that leads to the triumphal return of the germinal theme, now purged of its chromaticism. This

diatonic version is presented with expanded intervals. The coda leads to a clangorous, affirmative cadence.

Bartók's prime characteristic both as musician and man was the uncompromising integrity that informed his every act—what a compatriot of his has called "the proud morality of the mind." He was one of the great spirits of our time.

87 Arnold Schoenberg

"I personally hate to be called a revolutionist, which I am not. What I did was neither revolution nor anarchy."

It is worthy of note that, like Stravinsky and Bartók, the other great innovator of our time disclaims revolutionary intent. Quite the contrary, his disciples regard him as having brought to its culmination the thousand-year-old tradition of European polyphony.

His Life

Arnold Schoenberg (1874–1951) was born in Vienna. He began to study the violin at the age of eight, and soon afterward made his initial attempts at composing. Having decided to devote his life to music, he left school while in his teens. For a time he earned his living working in a bank, and meanwhile continued to compose, working entirely by himself. Presently he became acquainted with a young musician, Alexander von Zemlinsky, who for a few months gave him lessons in counterpoint. This was the only musical instruction he ever had.

Through Zemlinsky young Schoenberg was introduced to the advanced musical circles of Vienna, which at that time were under the spell of *Tristan* and *Parsifal*. In 1899, when he was twenty-five, Schoenberg wrote the string sextet *Verklärte Nacht* (Transfigured Night). The following year several of Schoenberg's songs were performed in Vienna and precipitated a scene. "And ever since that day," he once remarked with a smile, "the scandal has never ceased."

It was at this time that Schoenberg began a large-scale work for voices and orchestra, the *Gurre-Lieder* (Songs of Gurre). For the huge forces, choral and instrumental, required for this cantata he needed music paper double the ordinary size. Work on the *Gurre-Lieder* was interrupted by material worries. In 1901, after his marriage to Zemlinsky's sister, he moved to Berlin and obtained a post in a theater, conducting operettas and music-hall songs. Schoenberg's early music already displayed certain traits of his later style. A publisher to whom he brought a quartet observed, "You must think that if the second theme is a retrograde inverision of the first theme, that automatically makes it good!"

Upon his return to Vienna Schoenberg became active as a teacher and soon gathered about him a band of disciples, of whom the most gifted were Alban Berg and Anton Webern. The devotion of these advanced young musicians sustained him in the fierce battle for recognition that still lay ahead. With each new work Schoenberg moved closer to as bold a step as any artist has ever taken—the rejection of tonality.

The First World War interrupted Schoenberg's creative activity. Although he was past forty, he was called up for military service in the Vienna garrison. He had reached a critical point in his development. There followed a silence of seven years, between 1915 and 1923, during which he clarified his position in his own mind, and evolved a set of structural procedures to replace tonality. The goal once set, Schoenberg pursued it with that tenacity of purpose without which no prophet can prevail. His "method of composing with twelve tones"

Arnold Schoenberg in the classroom at UCLA.

caused great bewilderment in the musical world. All the same, he was now firmly established as a leader of contemporary musical thought. His fiftieth birthday was marked by a performance of his *Friede auf Erden* (Peace on Earth, 1907) by the chorus of the Vienna Opera. The next year he was appointed to succeed Ferruccio Busoni as professor of composition at the Berlin Academy of Arts. The uniquely favorable attitude of the Weimar Republic toward experimental art had made it possible for one of the most iconoclastic musicians in history to carry on his work from the vantage point of an official post.

This period in Schoenberg's life ended with the coming to power of Hitler in 1933. Like many Austrian-Jewish intellectuals of his generation, Schoenberg had been converted to Catholicism. After leaving Germany he found it spiritually necessary to return to the Hebrew faith. He arrived in the United States in the fall of 1933. After a short period of teaching in Boston, he joined the faculty of the University of Southern California, and shortly afterward was appointed professor of composition at the University of California in Los Angeles. In 1940 he became an American citizen. He taught until his retirement at the age of seventy, and continued his musical activities till his death in 1951. A seeker after truth until the end, to no one more than to himself could be applied the injunction he had written in the text of his cantata *Die Jakobsleiter* (Jacob's Ladder, 1913): "One must go on without asking what lies before or behind."

His Music

Schoenberg stemmed out of the Viennese past. He took his point of departure from the final quartets of Beethoven, the lyricism of Hugo Wolf, the richly wrought piano writing of Brahms, and the orchestral sonority of Bruckner and Mahler—behind whom, of course, loomed the un-Viennese figure of Wagner.

Schoenberg's first period may be described as one of post-Wagnerian romanticism; he still used key signatures and remained within the boundaries of tonality. The best-known work of this period is *Verklärte Nacht*, Opus 4, which poses no problems to anyone who has listened to *Tristan*. Indeed, the work became something of a popular hit after it was used by Antony Tudor as the accompaniment for his expressionist ballet *Pillar of Fire*. Schoenberg's second period, the atonal-expressionist, got under ·vay with the *Three Piano Pieces*, Opus 11 (1909), in which he abolished the distinction between consonance and dissonance as well as the sense of a home key. Concentrated and intense, these short pieces point the way to his later development. The high points of this period are the *Five Pieces for Orchestra*, Opus 16, which we will discuss, and *Pierrot Lunaire* (Moonstruck Pierrot, Opus 21, 1912), for female reciter and five instruments—flute, clarinet, violin, cello, and piano (with three alternating instruments—piccolo, bass clarinet, viola). This work, the first that carried Schoenberg's name beyond his immediate circle, introduced an eerily expressive kind of declamation midway between song and speech, known as *Sprechstimme* (speaking voice).

The best introduction to the compositions of Schoenberg's third period, that of the twelve-tone method, is through the Variations for Orchestra, Opus 31 (1927–28). This is the first twelve-tone composition for orchestra and one of Schoenberg's most powerful works. In the fourth and last period of his career—the American phase—he carried the twelve-tone technique to further stages of refinement. He also modified his doctrine sufficiently to allow tonal elements to coexist with the twelve-tone style, and on occasion wrote "old-fashioned" music with key signatures. In the category of tonal works we find the Suite for String Orchestra in G major (1934), intended for the use of students; also the *Kol Nidre* for speaker, chorus, and orchestra, Opus 39 (1939), an impressive setting of the ancient Hebrew prayer. Several among the late works present the twelve-tone style in a manner markedly more accessible than earlier pieces, often with tonal implications. Among those are the brilliant Piano Concerto (1942), which we will discuss, and the cantata *A Survivor from Warsaw* (1948), for narrator, men's chorus, and orchestra, with a text in English by Schoenberg himself—the composer's tribute to the Jews who perished in the Nazi death camps. The strict use of twelve-tone technique is represented by such compositions as the lyrical String Quartet No. 4, Opus 37 (1936), his last work in this medium, and the Violin Concerto, Opus 36 (1936), which is in Schoenberg's most uncompromising manner. Mention should be made too of·the Biblical opera *Moses and Aaron*, a major work. The first two acts were finished by 1932, but the third act was interrupted by his emigration to the United States; he never completed it.

Schoenberg was a tireless propagandist for his ideas, a role for which his verbal gifts and his passion for polemics eminently fitted him. Essays and articles flowed from his pen, conveying his views in a trenchant, aphoristic style which, late in life, he transferred from German to English. The following observations are characteristic: "Genius learns only from itself, talent chiefly from others. . . . One must believe in the infallibility of one's fantasy and the truth of one's inspiration. . . . Creation to an artist should be as natural and inescapable as the growth of apples to an apple tree. . . . The twelve tones will not invent for you. . . . It is said of many an author that he has indeed technique, but no invention. That is wrong: either he also lacks technique or he also has invention. . . . An apostle who does not glow preaches heresy. . . . The laws of nature manifested in a man of genius are but the laws of the future."

Five Pieces for Orchestra, Opus 16

The *Five Pieces for Orchestra* (1909) constitute one of the key works of Schoenberg's second period, when his language became atonal. In order to solve the problems of the new idiom, he concentrated on the short lyric forms. In line with the expressionist point of view, he connected the Five Orchestral Pieces with specific emotions and moods and gave them descriptive titles. Forty years later—in 1949—he revised the *Five Pieces,* rescoring them for an orchestra of the usual size instead of the huge ensemble required in the original version.

I. *Vorgefühle* (Premonitions). The first piece, marked "very fast," shows how well the atonal idiom lends itself to the expression of fear and anxiety. This music evokes a hallucinatory world where agony of soul reigns unrelieved. The basic theme is an ascending motive that is announced at the outset by muted cellos, against descending parallel fifths on clarinets:

This theme reappears throughout the piece in manifold guises, with changes of rhythm (augmentation and diminution) and variation in the size of its intervals. The climb to the final note underlines the continuous sense of climax. Schoenberg exploits striking instrumental effects, such as the frightening rasp of muted horn and trombone, and *fluttertonguing* (a rolling of the tongue, as if pronouncing d-r-r-r, used in playing wind instruments) on the muted trumpet. He intrigues the ear with unwonted contrasts of high and low registers, achieves a remarkable luminosity of texture, and keeps the sound mass in a state of dynamic impulsion.

II. *Vergangenes* (Yesteryears). Andante. A lyrical meditation, intensely romantic in character. The opening harmonies are composites of colors as well as tones: each note of the chord is played by a different instrument.

The bare look of the notes on the page shows the line of descent from the fervidly chromatic idiom of *Tristan* (see p. 192). The introductory motive on the cello sets the mood for a music that seems to be suspended in time.

A new section is ushered in by an expressive idea on the muted viola, which emerges as the principal theme of the piece. There enters a hopping figure on the bassoon, against a flowing ostinato on the celesta, which becomes a counter-subject for the principal idea. The climax is a whisper: sixteenth-note figures derived from the bassoon motive build up—to a *ppp!* The chief motive dominates the closing pages. The final sounds are extremely rarefied: a splash of color on the celesta, harmonics on strings and harp, against sustained harmonies in woodwinds and muted brass.

III. *Sommermorgen an einem See: Farben* (Summer Morning by a Lake: Colors). Moderato. Schoenberg originally called this study in sonority *Der wechselnde Akkord* (The Changing Chord). The piece sprang out of a conversation he had with Mahler, in which he argued that it should be possible to create a melody by sounding a single tone on the different instruments: in other words, the Schoenbergian concept of *Klangfarbenmelodie* (tone-color melody). Mahler disagreed. In the writing, Schoenberg expanded his original notion. The harmonies in the piece do change, but so imperceptibly that the ear is led to concentrate on the continual shifting of color.

When he wrote the piece Schoenberg was much interested in painting. Hence the musical conception connected itself in his mind with a visual image —the shimmer of the morning sun on the calm surface of a lake. The harmonic current flows so slowly that it seems hardly to move, gleaming gently as the various colors play upon it. The opening measure illustrates Schoenberg's method in this essay in pure orchestration. The first chord is played *ppp* by two flutes, clarinet, bassoon, and viola. It is then repeated, with a subtle change of color, by English horn, bassoon, muted horn, muted trumpet, and double bass.

IV. *Peripetie.* Molto Allegro. The Greek word *peripetia* signifies a sudden crisis or reversal in the events of a drama. We are back in the brooding atmosphere of the first piece. Woodwinds and brass by turns trace impetuous figures.

The music shows the rhythmic flexibility, fragmentation of texture, and wide leaps in the melody so characteristic of Schoenberg. He makes dramatic use of the muted brass playing fortissimo. Tension mounts to the end.

V. *Das obligate Rezitativ* (The Obligatory Recitative). Allegretto. The last of the set is in a vein of impassioned lyricism. The short breathless phrases communicate intense emotion. Schoenberg here achieves his desire to create a melody that perpetually renews itself, never weakening its tension through repetition. He was increasingly aware of the problem that his intricate polyphonic textures posed to conductor, performer, and student. In *Das obligate Rezitativ* he used for the first time a system of signs to distinguish the principal voice from the other contrapuntal lines—a practice he retained in all his later scores.

Piano Concerto, Opus 42

The Piano Concerto (1942) belongs to Schoenberg's final period. The relaxation of strict dodecaphonic procedure that manifested itself during his American sojourn is reflected in this work. Although the writing is twelve-tone, we find a vaguely tonal atmosphere.

Schoenberg retains some of the traditional features of the piano concerto in his Opus 42. There are three movements—really four, since the last is subdivided into two sections. The instrument's technical resources are fully exploited. The work boasts two cadenzas. Yet pyrotechnical display for its own sake is sedulously avoided. Piano and orchestra are integrated in a symphonic whole, with a constant interchange of ideas between them. As so often with Schoenberg, the writing for the piano, in its rich texture and sweeping use of the keyboard, bears some resemblance to the piano style of Brahms. Indeed, the look of the notes on the page—the spread of the left-hand part, the double notes and full chords in the right—would remind one of that master, were it not for the accidentals and for the fact that this, really, is another language.

The piece has a high emotional content. The continual shifting from quiet lyricism to impassioned utterance suggests its romantic ancestry. The orchestral writing is marked by a transparency of texture that justifies Virgil Thomson's description of the Concerto as "chamber music for a hundred players." There is no attempt at the grand gesture in this rather intimate work, written when the master was approaching seventy.

I. Andante, ⅜. The tone row with which the Concerto opens pervades all

three movements. The piano announces the row in the treble in a quietly lyrical mood. Notice that in this presentation Schoenberg departs from strict twelve-tone procedure, since he repeats notes 9-10-11 (C♯-A-B) before reaching the final note G (C♯ is of course equivalent to D♭).

519

This form of the row, and the following inverted and retrograde versions, make up a thirty-nine-measure statement of the theme. The meditative mood is continued as the violins take over the row and carry it to the high register against the figuration of the piano.

The first five tones of the row (under the bracket) serve as a motive that pervades the piece. Schoenberg called it the *Kopfmotif* or "head-motive" and used it as a structural element in the Concerto. The customary fragmentation of texture associated with the dodecaphonic style gives way, in this work, to a continuity of line and movement closer to traditional norms. The orchestral writing musters his favorite devices, such as harmonics on the strings, trills in the extreme registers, and fluttertonguing on the muted brass.

II. Molto Allegro. The second movement is in 2/2 time, with excursions to 3/2, 3/4, and 6/4. The opening measures present an animated dialogue that involves the whole orchestra. The frequent changes of meter and tempo impart rhythmic flexibility to the movement. A stringendo passage builds up to the climax. Tension briefly subsides and builds again in an agitato passage. A transition leads into the third movement.

III. Adagio, 3/2. One of the most lyrical movements that Schoenberg ever wrote, this Adagio opens with a passage for orchestra alone; an expressive duet between oboe and bassoon is a transposition of the basic row, accompanied by its inversion in the trombones and violas. An eleven-bar cadenza for the piano requires agile fingers. Another passage for the orchestra introduces delicate figuration on the piano against a subtle background of winds and strings. A brief cadenza for the piano ushers in the last movement.

IV. Giocoso, (playful), 2/2. The finale is a lively movement in rondo style. The opening phrase is a transposed inversion of the first six notes of the piano theme, while the next six notes present the second half of the row arranged backward.

Triplet rhythm introduces a vigorous orchestral passage that is followed by an animated exchange with the piano. The movement mounts in tension until the coda, which is marked *Stretto* and taken at an increased speed. The first four notes of the "head-motive" appear in a new guise:

In the furious final measures the full "head-motive" is combined, in the piano part, with its inversion, bringing to a close this mellow work of the master's maturity.

Schoenberg's belief in the necessity and rightness of his method sustained him and gave him the strength to carry through his revolution. His doctrines focused attention on basic compositional problems, and profoundly affected the course of musical thought in the twentieth century.

88 Alban Berg

"When I decided to write an opera, my only intention was to give to the theater what belongs to the theater. The music was to be so formed that at each moment it would fulfill its duty of serving the action."

It was the unique achievement of Alban Berg (1885–1935) to humanize the abstract procedures of the Schoenbergian technique, and to reconcile them with the expression of feeling. Upon a new and difficult idiom he imprinted the stamp of a lyric imagination of the first order.

His Life

Berg was born in Vienna. He came of a well-to-do family and grew up in an environment that fostered his artistic proclivities. At nineteen he made the acquaintance of Arnold Schoenberg, who was sufficiently impressed

Alban Berg.

with the youth's manuscripts to accept him as a pupil. During his six years with Schoenberg (1904–10) he acquired the consummate mastery of technique that characterizes his later work. Schoenberg was not only an exacting master, but also a devoted friend and mentor who shaped Berg's whole outlook on art.

The outbreak of war in 1914 hurled Berg into a period of depression. "The urge 'to be in it,' " he wrote to Schoenberg, "the feeling of helplessness at being unable to serve my country, prevented any concentration on work." A few months later he was called up for military service, despite his uncertain health (he suffered from asthma and attacks of nervous debility). He was presently transferred to the War Ministry in Vienna. Already *Wozzeck* occupied his thoughts; but he could not begin writing the music until the war was over. In December 1925 *Wozzeck* was presented at the Berlin State Opera. At one stroke Berg was lifted from comparative obscurity to international fame.

In the decade that remained to him he produced only a handful of works; but each was a significant contribution to his total output. During these years he was active as a teacher. He also wrote about music, propagandizing tirelessly on behalf of Schoenberg and his school. With the coming to power of Hitler, the works of the twelve-tone composers were banned in Germany as alien to the spirit of the Third Reich. The resulting loss of income was a source of worry to Berg, as was, to a far greater degree, the rapid Nazification of Austria. Schoenberg's enforced emigration to the United States was a bitter blow.

Exhausted and ailing after the completion of the Violin Concerto, Berg went to the country for a short rest before resuming work on his opera *Lulu*. An insect bite brought on an abscess that caused infection. Upon his return to Vienna he was striken with blood poisoning. He died on Christmas Eve 1935, seven weeks before his fifty-first birthday.

His Music

Berg's art issued from the world of German romanticism—the world of Schumann, Brahms, Wagner, Richard Strauss, and Mahler. The romantic streak in his temperament bound him to this heritage even after he had embraced the dodecaphonic style. Berg's was the imagination of the musical dramatist. For him the musical gesture was bound up with character and action, mood and atmosphere. Yet, like his teacher, he leaned toward the formal patterns of the past—fugue and invention, passacaglia, variations, sonata, and suite.

The list of his published works begins with the Piano Sonata Opus 1 (1908), a highly charged work in a post-Wagnerian idiom. The four songs of Opus 2 (1909) reveal the composer in a period of transition from Mahlerian romanticism to the expressionist tendencies of his later years. In the last of the four, the young composer abandons key signatures. The *Three Orchestral Pieces*, Opus 6 (1913–14), consist of a *Prelude, Round,* and *March.* With the third piece of this set we find ourselves in the atmosphere of *Wozzeck.* Berg's most widely known composition, after *Wozzeck,* is the *Lyric Suite,* written in 1925–26. The work is in six movements. The first and last follow strictly "the method of composing with twelve tones." Originally written for string quartet, the *Lyric Suite* achieved such popularity that in 1928 the composer arranged the three middle movements for string orchestra.

Berg spent the last seven years of his life on the opera *Lulu.* The work is based on a single twelve-tone row. The composer fashioned the libretto himself from two dramas by Frank Wedekind—*Earth Spirit* (1893) and *Pandora's Box* (1901). Lulu is the eternal type of *femme fatale* "who destroys everyone because she is destroyed by everyone." Berg was in the midst of orchestrating *Lulu* when he interrupted the task to write the Violin Concerto (1935). The opera remained unfinished at his death. However, the sketches he left behind would make it possible to complete the work according to his intentions, and it is to be hoped that this will be done. The two completed acts have been recorded and performed (usually with a makeshift third act), and *Lulu* is taking its place alongside *Wozzeck* as one of the challenging works of the modern lyric theater.

Alban Berg is probably the most widely admired master of the twelve-tone school. His premature death robbed contemporary music of a major figure.

Wozzeck

In 1914 Berg saw the play that impelled him to the composition of *Wozzeck.* He finished the draft of the libretto by the summer of 1917. Most of the music was written from 1918 to 1920 and orchestrated the following year. The vocal score was published in 1923 with the financial help of Alma Mahler, to whom *Wozzeck* was dedicated.

The author of the play, Georg Büchner (1813–37), belonged to the generation of intellectuals who were stifled by the political repressions of Metternich's Europe. His socialist leanings brought him into conflict with the authorities. After his death at twenty-four, the manuscripts of *Danton's Tod* (The Death of Danton) and the unfinished *Woyzeck* (this was the original spelling) were found among his papers. In the stolid infantryman Wozzeck he created an archetype of "the insulted and injured" of the earth.

Berg's libretto tightened the original play. He shaped the material into three acts, each containing five scenes. These are linked by brief orchestral interludes whose motivic facture serves to round off what has preceded as well as to introduce what follows. As a result, Berg's "opera of protest and compassion" has astonishing unity of texture and mood.

The action centers around Wozzeck's unhappy love for Marie, by whom he has had an illegitimate child. Wozzeck is the victim of the sadistic Captain and of the Doctor, a coldly scientific gentleman who uses Wozzeck for his experiments—to which the soldier submits because he needs the money. (Wozzeck is given to hallucinations. The Doctor is bent on proving his theory that mental disorder is related to diet.) Marie cannot resist her infatuation with the handsome Drum Major. Wozzeck slowly realizes that she has been unfaithful to him. Ultimately he kills her. Driven back to the death-scene by guilt and remorse, he drowns himself. The tragedy unfolds in three acts. The first is the Exposition of the theme: "Wozzeck in relation to his environment." The second is the Development of the theme: "Wozzeck becomes more and more convinced of Marie's infidelity." The third act is the Catastrophe: "Wozzeck murders Marie and atones by suicide."

The vocal line sensitively portrays characters and situations. Harmonically, the greater part of the opera is cast in an atonal-expressionist idiom. Berg anticipates certain twelve-tone procedures; he also looks back to the tonal tradition, puts a number of passages in major and minor keys, and uses leitmotifs in the Wagnerian manner. The snatches of popular song in the score create an effective contrast to their atonal surroundings. Appearing in so special a context, they take on a strange wistfulness.

In the opening scene, Wozzeck is shaving the Captain. From the hysterical Captain's opening remark—*Langsam, Wozzeck, langsam* (Slow, Wozzeck, go slow!)—the jagged vocal line, with its wide leaps and brusque inflections, projects the atmosphere of German expressionism. Wozzeck's music is more sustained in manner. His reply introduces the chief motive associated with him, on the words *Wir arme Leut! Sehn Sie, Herr Hauptmann, Geld, Geld! Wer kein Geld hat!* (Poor folk like us! You see, Captain, money! Without money . . .).

This motive in various guises underlines the key statement of the scene, beginning with *Ja, wenn ich ein Herr wär*: "Yes indeed, if I were a fine gentleman and had a silk hat and watch and an eyeglass, and could talk fancy, I would be virtuous too. But I'm a poor nobody."

Scene 2, in which Wozzeck and his friend Andres are seen cutting branches in a field, is one of several in which Berg conjures up an atmosphere of fear through his handling of the orchestra. Flickerings of sound on piccolos, oboes, and clarinets admirably prepare Wozzeck's *Du, der Platz ist verflucht!* (Hey, this place is cursed). In this scene, we have the first of the songs, that of Andres: *Das ist die schöne Jägerei* (Hunting is a good sport.) This is in ⁶⁄₈, a meter traditionally associated with hunting scenes; the song illustrates Berg's way of evoking popular elements, although in a somewhat distorted form. The following scene, which takes place in Marie's room, shows her growing interest in the Drum Major. Berg here uses military music in a most poignant way. Marie's enthusiastic *Soldaten sind schöne Burschen* (Soldiers are handsome fellows!) brings with it a suggestion of A-flat major despite the shifting chromatic harmonies. The lullaby that follows, in ⁶⁄₈ time—*Mädel was fängst Du jetzt an?* (Girl, what song shall you sing? You've a little child but no husband!)—is a hauntingly lovely bit. When the child falls asleep, Marie remains lost in thought. The scene ends with the strings intoning a motive of fifths closely associated with her:

"Their harmonic immobility," Berg wrote, "expresses, as it were, her aimless waiting, which is only terminated with her death."

Scene 4, between Wozzeck and the Doctor, takes places in the latter's study; we return to the atmosphere of obsession. The music takes the shape of a passacaglia. How better to express the Doctor's *idée fixe*—the connection between nutrition and insanity—than by twenty-one variations on a theme? The theme of the passacaglia is a twelve-tone row that is first played by the clarinet at the end of the orchestral interlude. As the theme of the passacaglia it is presented by the cellos and basses, extends over eight bars, and is followed by

the variations. The final scene of Act I, a street in front of Marie's door, brings the climax of the action thus far: Marie yields to the Drum Major.

525

The first scene of Act II, again in Marie's room, involves another motive of fear, this time felt by the child, when Marie bursts out impatiently *Schlaf, Bub!* ("Go to sleep, boy!"): a minor second on the xylophone, which returns in various forms throughout the scene.

When Wozzeck enters, suspicious, this motive (x) reappears in a sudden slow tempo as a canon on the muted trombones:

The second scene takes places on a street where the Captain and the Doctor meet. The Doctor feeds the Captain's neurotic fears about his health. A passage "in slow waltz time" adds an ironic touch to this obsessive dialogue. When Wozzeck appears they torment him with veiled references to Marie's infidelity. The music for this scene is based on two forms of the Baroque: an invention (which, it will be remembered, was associated with Bach's keyboard music);

WOZZECK, Act II, Scene 1: Marie and Wozzeck (Metropolitan Opera production)

526

and a fugue based on three themes, each associated earlier in the opera with one of the three men.

The scene culminates in Wozzeck's agonized outcry, *Gott in Himmel! Man könnte Lust bekommen sich aufzuhängen!* ("God in Heaven! A man might want to hang himself!"). The orchestral interlude that follows is a brooding Largo scored for chamber orchestra. In the third scene, in front of Marie's dwelling, Wozzeck threatens her. When he raises his hand against her, Marie's words point to the tragic outcome: *Rühr mich nicht an*—"Don't touch me. Better a knife in my flesh than a hand on me. My father didn't dare when I was ten." Scene 4, which takes place at the inn, is introduced by a slow *ländler* (an Austrian popular dance in the style of a rustic waltz). Various elements— a song of two young workingmen, a waltz, a chorus, a song by Andres, Wozzeck's rage at seeing Marie dance with the Drum Major, and a mock sermon by a drunken young fellow—are welded into a vivid scene in which Berg skillfully exploits the clash between the band onstage and the orchestra. Noteworthy is the guitar sound that accompanies the waltz of Marie and the Drum Major. Scene 5, which takes place in the guard house, opens with the snores of the sleeping soldiers. The Drum Major boasts of his new conquest. Wozzeck throws himself at the Major, but is beaten down by his burly opponent.

Act III opens with Marie's reading of the Bible, a profoundly moving scene. She tells her child about a poor orphan who had no one in the world, who was hungry and wept. . . . The passage stands out against its atonal surroundings because it is in F minor. A fugue unfolds as she reads about Mary Magdalen and pleads that the Lord forgive her frailty. The scene of the murder, which takes place along a forest path by a pool, abounds in ominous sonorities, as at Marie's words *Wie der Mond rot aufgeht!* ("How red the moon is!"), where the strings hold a B-natural spread out over five octaves against muted trombones and fluttertonguing on muted trumpets. Unforgettable is the repeated stroke on two timpani, going from a whisper to a spine-chilling *fff* as Wozzeck cries *Ich nicht, Marie! Und kein Andrer auch nicht!* ("If not me, Marie, then no other!") just before he kills her. The drum strokes become softer and return to a pianissimo. In the interlude that follows, the note B is sustained by the orchestra for thirteen bars in a dramatic crescendo, punctuated by the brutal rhythm that symbolizes the catastrophe.

In Scene 3 Wozzeck returns to the tavern and dances with Marie's friend Margaret, who notices blood on his hands. The scene opens with a wild polka accompanied by an out-of-tune piano.

The haunted atmosphere returns as Wozzeck, in Scene 4, goes back to the pond. How poignant is his *Marie! Was hast Du für eine rote Schnur um den*

Hals? ("Marie, what is that red string around your neck?")! His last words as he drowns, *Ich wasche mich mit Blut* . . . ("I wash myself in blood—the water is blood . . . blood . . ."), usher in a series of ascending chromatic scales that pass in a ghostly pianissimo from the strings to the woodwinds and brass.

There follows a symphonic meditation in D minor, a passionate lament for the life and death of Wozzeck. This inspired fantasy indicates how richly Berg's art was nourished by the romanticism of Mahler. The final scene takes place in the morning in front of Marie's house. Children are playing. Marie's little boy rides a hobbyhorse. Other children rush in with news of the murder, but Marie's son does not understand. The children run off. The little boy continues to ride and sing. Then, noticing that he has been left alone, he calls *Hopp, hopp* and rides off on his hobbyhorse, to the sound of clarinet, drum, xylophone, and strings *ppp*. For sheer heartbreak the final curtain has few to equal it in the contemporary lyric theater.

Wozzeck envelops the listener in a hallucinated world in which the hunters are as driven as the hunted. It could have come only out of central Europe in the Twenties. But its characters reach out beyond time and place to become eternal symbols of the human condition.

89 Anton Webern

"With me, things never turn out as I wish, but only as is ordained for me—as I must."

Anton Webern (1883–1945) is still not very well known to the public at large. All the same his works have shaped the musical thinking of our time in a most decisive fashion.

His Life

Anton von Webern (he dropped the prefix of nobility in later life) was born in Vienna. His musical gifts asserted themselves at an early age. He was twenty-one when he met Schoenberg and, with Alban Berg, formed the nucleus of the band of disciples who gathered around the master. He also studied musicology, and received his doctorate in this field.

After leaving the University, Webern conducted at various German provincial theaters and in Prague. But Vienna was the hub of his world. He directed the Vienna Workers' Symphony Concerts organized by the authorities of the then socialist city, but as the years passed he found public activity less and less

Anton Webern.

congenial to his retiring disposition. After the First World War he settled in Mödling, a suburb of Vienna, where he lived quietly, devoting himself to composition and teaching.

Webern suffered great hardship after Austria became part of the Third Reich. The Nazis regarded his music as *Kulturbolshevismus* (cultural bolshevism), forbade its performance, and burned his writings. He was permitted to teach only a few pupils, and had to give his lectures—in which he expounded the Schoenbergian point of view—in secret. In order to avoid forced labor during the war, he worked as proofreader for a Viennese publisher. To escape the Allied bombings of Vienna, Webern and his wife sought refuge at the home of their son-in-law in Mittersill, a small town near Salzburg. But fate awaited him there. On September 15, 1945, as he stepped out of his house in the evening to smoke a cigarette (the war had ended five months before, but Mittersill was still under a curfew), he failed to understand an order to halt and was shot by a trigger-happy sentry of the American occupying forces. "The day of Anton Webern's death," wrote his most celebrated admirer, Igor Stravinsky, "should be a day of mourning for any receptive musician. We must hail not only this great composer but also a real hero. Doomed to total failure in a deaf world of ignorance and indifference, he inexorably kept on cutting out his diamonds, his dazzling diamonds, of whose mines he had such a perfect knowledge."

His Music

Webern responded to the radical portion of Schoenbergian doctrine, just as Berg exploited its more conservative elements. Of the three masters of the modern Viennese school, he was the one who cut himself off most completely from the tonal past. The Schoenbergians, we saw, favored the short forms. Webern carried this urge for brevity much farther than either of his comrades, as is clear from his *Five Orchestral Pieces*. Such conciseness seems to nullify the very notion of time as we have come to understand it in music.

Hardly less novel is the musical fabric in which he clothed his ideas. His scores call for the most unusual combinations of instruments. Each tone is assigned its specific function in the over-all scheme. The instruments are often used in their extreme registers; they not infreqently play one at a time, and very little. This technique confers upon the individual sound an importance it never had before.

The Passacaglia for Orchestra, Opus 1 (1908), was followed by a number of significant works: *Five Movements for String Quartet*, Opus 5 (1909); *Six Orchestral Pieces*, Opus 6 (1910); *Six Bagatelles for String Quartet*, Opus 9 (1913); and *Five Orchestral Pieces*, Opus 10 (1913). These were flanked by the poetic songs—some with piano, others with instrumental accompaniment—in which Webern's essentially lyric gift found a congenial outlet.

With his Symphony, Opus 21 (1928) Webern came into his fully matured style. In this and the works that followed, the twelve-tone technique is used with unprecedented strictness. Schoenberg had contented himself with an organization based upon fixed series of pitches. Webern extended this concept to include timbres and rhythms. Therewith he moved toward complete control of the sonorous material—in other words, total serialization. His disciples carried the implications of Webern's music still farther. As a result, Webern emerged as the dominant influence in the dodecaphonic thinking of the mid-twentieth century.

Five Pieces for Orchestra, Opus 10

The *Five Pieces for Orchestra* (1911–13) show, early in Webern's career, his striving for that rigorous control of the musical material which became so compelling a preoccupation of his later years. These pieces bring to the fore what Webern called "the almost exclusively lyrical nature" of his music. The concentrated lyricism here makes for unprecedented brevity: the set of five numbers lasts about five minutes. The fourth is the shortest piece in the entire orchestral literature; six and one-third bars that take less than half a minute to play.

The work is scored for an orchestral group in which each player is a soloist. Webern includes mandoline and guitar, instruments that have been favored by the Viennese composers because of their bright pointed sound. The pieces belong to the composer's atonal—that is to say, pre-twelve-tone—period, and come out of the expressionist atmosphere that prevailed in central Europe at that time. However, as in the case of *Wozzeck,* the score shows an occasional foreshadowing of the twelve-tone technique.

I. *Sehr ruhig und zart* (very calm and soft). For flute, clarinet; muted trumpet and muted trombone; celesta, harp, glockenspiel; muted violin, viola, and muted cello. In 2/4 time, the piece opens with single tones on muted trumpet and harp followed by a tone on the celesta, harmonics on the viola and harp, and a single tone fluttertongued on the flute. A sparse motivic texture is woven for twelve and a quarter bars, the dynamic level ranging from *ppp* to *pp*.

II. *Lebhaft und zart bewegt* (lively, moving softly). The second piece, the only rapid one of the set, is in triple meter, save for two brief reversions to ²⁄₄ time. It is scored for piccolo, oboe, two clarinets; muted horn, trumpet, and trombone; harmonium, celesta, harp, glockenspiel, cymbals, triangle; muted violin, viola, cello, and double bass. (The *harmonium* is a small type of organ that was developed in the nineteenth century.) Clarinet and violin state their respective motives in the opening measure. A delicate fabric of sound extends for fourteen bars, woven out of motivic cells and single-note sonorities moving from *p* to a *fff* of menacing urgency. (See example below.)

III. *Sehr langsam und äusserst ruhig* (very slow and extremely calm). A true son of Austria, Webern loved the mountains of his native land and their bell sounds. The third piece is almost a study in bell sonorities, evoking as it does the clear open spaces of a mountain scene. It is eleven and a half measures in length, in ⁶⁄₄ time (except for a measure of ³⁄₄ and ²⁄₄). Harmonium, mandoline, guitar, celesta, harp, glockenspiel, and cowbells play trills and repeated notes against

gentle trills on the drums; while clarinet, muted horn and trombone, violin, muted viola and cello trace their brief, tenuous motives.

IV. *Fliessend, äusserst zart* (flowing, extremely soft) in ¾ time. Clarinet, muted trumpet and trombone, mandoline, celesta, harp, snare drum, muted violin, and viola unfold their traceries for precisely six and one-third measures. The first twelve tones are all different ones—in other words, a tone row. Nothing is scored below middle C. A figure on the mandoline, with a chord on the harp, is answered by one on the muted trumpet. The violin finishes with five notes played *ppp, wie ein Hauch* (like a whisper).

V. *Sehr fliessend* (flowing), in ¾ time, with nine measures in ²⁄₄. This movement, consisting of thirty-two bars, is the most elaborately scored, calling for flute, oboe, clarinet, bass clarinet; muted horn and trumpet; harmonium, mandoline, guitar, celesta, harp, glockenspiel, xylophone, bass and snare drum, cymbals; and the four solo strings, muted. The flickering motives work up to a climax with a fortissimo chord on the harmonium in the ninth bar. There is a sudden subsiding; a second dynamic peak is reached with several percussive chords that run the gamut of the orchestra. The last fifteen measures are sparsely scored, with the softest of dynamics. The music trails off into silence.

Cantata No. 1, Opus 29

Webern's lyricism found its fullest expression in his vocal music. The First Cantata, Opus 29 (1939), a setting of a poem by Hildegarde Jone for soprano, mixed chorus, and orchestra, is one of his most accessible works. It lasts just under seven minutes. The piece is based on a tone row whose inner symmetries are of the kind dear to Webern's heart. For example, the retrograde (backward) inversion of the row is identical with its version transposed a fifth higher:

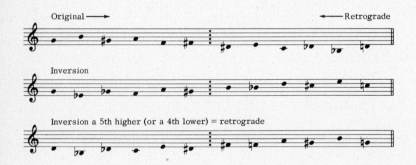

I. *Getragen—lebhaft* (solemn—lively). The first movement, for chorus and orchestra, alternates between these two tempos. In some instances each prevails for only a single measure.

Zündender Lichtblitz des Lebens schlug
ein aus der Wolke des Wortes.
Donner, der Herzschlag, folgt nach,
bis er in Frieden verebbt.

Lightning, that kindles life, hurled
Out of the cloud the Word.
Thunder, the heartbeat, follows after
Until in peace it dissolves.

The brief orchestral introduction opens with three pianissimo chords. Four forms of the row unfold simultaneously: the original version on G (muted trumpet), the inverted form on C-sharp (muted violas), the inverted form on G-sharp (muted trombone), and the original form on D (muted cellos). Each form is fragmented and distributed among various instruments. The introduction builds a sense of expectancy. The sonority changes constantly, as does the meter: $\frac{7}{2}$, $\frac{5}{4}$, $\frac{3}{4}$, $\frac{4}{4}$, $\frac{3}{4}$, and so on, resulting in a continual shifting of rhythmic patterns. A fortissimo blow in the percussion, reinforced by trombone, prepares for the "lightning" on which the chorus enters, a cappella. Sopranos, altos, tenors, and basses simultaneously unfold four forms of the row. When that is completed, the altos move in contrary motion to the sopranos, while tenors and basses duplicate the same pattern a major second below. All four voices sing the same text.

The constant alternation between the two tempos ("solemn" and "lively") makes for maximum dramatic contrast. At the same time it enables the music to mirror the words with the utmost fidelity. In the first two lines of the poem, for example, the slackening of tension on the word *Lebens* (life) contrasts with the incisive rendering of the action words—*Lichtblitz* (lightning), *schlug* (hurled), *des Wortes* (the Word). A roll on the kettledrums and two fortissimo dissonances usher in the thunder. In the last two lines the relaxation on the word *Herzschlag* (heartbeat) similarly contrasts with the tension on the words *Donner* (thunder) and *folgt nach* (follows after). As a result of these and kindred subtleties, the music illumines the text in a most imaginative way.

II. *Leicht bewegt* (slightly agitated). The second movement, for soprano solo and orchestra, alternates between $\frac{3}{16}$ and $\frac{2}{8}$, with an occasional excursion to $\frac{5}{16}$.

Kleiner Flügel, Ahornsamen, schwebst im Winde!	Little maple leaf, soaring in the wind!
Musst doch in der Erde Dunkel sinken.	You must sink to earth in darkness.
Aber du wirst auferstehn dem Tage,	But you will rise again with the day,
all den Düften und der Frühlingszeit;	With the fragrance of springtime.
wirst aus Wurzeln in das Helle steigen,	From your roots you will ascend to the light,
bald im Himmel auch verwurzelt sein.	Soon to strike roots in heaven.
Wieder wirst aus dir du kleine Flügel senden,	Once again you will put forth little leaves,
die in sich schon tragen deine ganze	That already bear your whole
schweigend Leben sagende Gestalt.	Silent, life-affirming image.

The row is presented in a single color—clarinet, starting on D—in a symmetrical rhythmic pattern that reads the same forward and backward. This extension of the serial concept to include rhythm as well as pitch is a step on the road to total serialization.

Rhythmic pattern identical forward and backward:

Webern for the most part sets the text with one syllable to a note. In this way he is able to highlight the key words by suddenly extending a single syllable for two or more notes. He also brings words into prominence through wide leaps in the melody line. For example, the two downward leaps on the words *in der Erde Dunkel sinken* (sink to earth in darkness), or the wide upward leap on *auferstehn* (rise). For this kind of word-painting Webern of course has ample precedent in the vocal music of the Baroque. The jagged melodic line never relaxes its tension. As a result, the poetic image of the little maple leaf sinking to earth only to rise again is presented with intense expressiveness.

III. *Ruhig* (quietly).

Tönen die seligen Saiten Apolls,	Resound the blessed strings of Apollo,
wer nennt sie Chariten?	Who calls them Graces?
Spielt er sein Lied durch den wachsenden Abend,	When he plays his song through the gathering evening,
wer denket Apollon?	Who thinks of Apollo?
Sind doch im Klange die früheren Namen	For in this sound the earlier names
alle verklungen;	Have all faded away;
Sind doch im Worte die schwächeren Worte	For in this word the feebler words
lange gestorben;	Have long since died;
und auch die blasseren Bilder	And even the fainter images
zum Siegel des Spektrums geschmolzen.	Have melted in the seal of the spectrum.
Charis, die Gabe des Höchsten:	O Gracious One, gift of the gods:
die Anmut der Gnade erglänzet!	The charm of her kindness shines bright!
Schenkt sich im Dunkel dem werdenden Herzen	She offers in darkness her maturing heart
als Tau der Vollendung.	As dew of perfection.

The third movement, for soprano solo, chorus and orchestra, opens with an orchestral introduction of sixteen measures. A two-voice canon is distributed among the four parts of the chorus, with the imitating voice following the leader at a distance of five quarter notes, at the interval of an augmented fourth. (An *augmented fourth*, such as the distance from C to F-sharp, contains six semitones; therefore it divides the octave exactly in half.)

The first four lines of the poem are followed by an orchestral interlude that shows the rarefied texture typical of Webern: it consists of eight measures, of which one is silent while three contain one note apiece. The emphasis on the low register prepares effectively for the entrance of the high voices of the chorus. Canonic devices abound in the ensuing passage, leading—with a broadening of the tempo—to the high point of the movement and of the Cantata as a whole—the entrance of the solo soprano voice on a high B-flat, fortissimo, descending in a wide leap on the word *Charis* (O Gracious One). This makes a brilliantly

Cha - ris, die Ga - be des Höch - sten:
Cha - ris, the gift of the high - est:

effective climax. From this point until the end there is continual interchange between soprano and chorus. The music matches the transcendental mood of the poem; clearly the composer was no less a mystic than the poet. Notice the diminuendo on the final word *Vollendung* (perfection), followed by a dying away of the orchestral sound.

The creator of this intensely lyrical work was content to go his way, an obscure figure in the musical circles of his time, overshadowed by those who made a bigger noise in the world. He had no way of knowing that little over a decade after his death, avant-garde musicians in Europe and America would think of themselves as belonging to "the age of Webern."

90 Other Modern Europeans

The French School

Darius Milhaud, born in Aix-en-Provence in 1892, was the leading figure in contemporary French music after the death of Ravel. He is one of the most prolific composers alive. His opus numbers run well past the three-hundred mark. Milhaud is essentially a lyricist. He is associated specifically with poly-tonality, having explored in greater detail than almost any of his confreres the possibilities of several keys sounding at once. Among his better-known works may be mentioned the ballet *Le Boeuf sur le toit* (named after a famous Parisian cabaret, "The Bull on the Roof," 1919); *Saudades do Brasil* (Brazilian Moods, 1921), a suite of piano pieces which the composer also arranged for orchestra; *La Création du monde* (The Creation of the World, 1923), which we will discuss; and the popular two-piano suite *Scaramouche* (1937).

Arthur Honegger (1892–1955), born in Le Havre of Swiss parents, spent the greater part of his professional life in Paris and was justly regarded as one of the French school. At the same time he was the least Gallic among them. The spacious lines of the classical sonata and the rhetoric of Wagnerian drama, neither of which flourishes in the Parisian atmosphere, appealed to his imagi-nation. Honegger had a natural affinity for the choral idiom. *King David* (1921), a "symphonic psalm" for chorus and orchestra, and the biblical opera *Judith* (1926) manifest a Handelian bigness of gesture. *Jeanne d'Arc au bûcher* (Joan of Arc at the Stake, 1938) is a kind of oratorio with a speaking part for the heroine amid vivid frescoes for chorus and orchestra. Much publicity accrued to Honegger because of his symphonic movement *Pacific 231* (1923), an orchestral depiction of a locomotive that was the last word in modernism in the Twenties. His Symphony No. 5 (1951), a profoundly felt and powerful work, may be regarded as his finest achievement.

The music of Francis Poulenc (1899–1963) is urbane, Parisian. His piano pieces form a twentieth-century brand of salon music. The *Mouvements per-petuels* for piano, written in 1918 when he was nineteen, are precisely right for what Anatole France called "the intimate conversations of five o'clock." Poulenc's chamber music shows the sympathetic handling of the woodwinds for which French composers are noted. He was one of the outstanding song com-posers of our time; his choral works too reveal a rich vein of lyricism. His operas —*Dialogues des Carmélites* (Dialogues of the Carmelites, on a libretto by Georges Bernanos, 1953–55) and *La Voix humaine* (The Human Voice, based on a one-act play by Jean Cocteau, 1958)—established him as one of the most important representatives of the trend toward a new romanticism.

Milhaud: *La Création du monde*

In 1922 Milhaud visited the United States, appearing as pianist in his own works and giving lectures on modern music. The high point of his stay in this country was a visit to Harlem. "The music I heard," he recalls in his *Autobiography*, "was absolutely different from anything I had ever heard before. . . . Its effect on me was so overwhelming that I could not tear myself away. More than ever I was resolved to use jazz for a chamber work." The resultant piece was *La Création du monde* (The Creation of the World, 1923), a ballet depicting the creation of the world from the point of view of Negro folk legends.

Milhaud's evocation of the nostalgic blues, his simultaneous use of major and minor, and his intricate counterpoint—so close in spirit to the free dissonant counterpoint of Dixieland—are all wonderfully characteristic of the 1920s. At times he captures the uninhibited improvisational quality of the jam session. Yet the jazz elements are infused with the elegance and wit of a sensibility that is wholly French.

Scene 1. The curtain rises to show the chaos before creation; a shapeless mass of bodies fills the stage as three African deities—Nazme, Membere, and Nkwa —hold council and cast their spells. Scene 2. The mass slowly begins to move; the darkness lifts. A tree appears; plants and animals come to life. Scene 3. The animals join in a lively, heavily accented dance. Presently Man and Woman emerge from the tangled mass of bodies in the center of the stage, and gaze upon one another. Scene 4. While the pair perform the Dance of Desire, other figures disengage themselves from the mass and join in a dance that grows wilder and wilder. The frenzy passes, the dancers disappear. Man and Woman remain alone in an embrace. It is springtime. . . .

The score consists of an Overture and five sections played without pause. The Overture, marked *Modéré*, establishes the mood of quiet lyricism so character-istic of Milhaud. A serene melody is sung by the saxophone, accompanied by piano and strings. The movement is punctuated by a syncopated figure in the trumpets. Glissandos on the trombone and "blue" harmonies create a jazz atmo-sphere. (For an explanation of *blues* and blue notes, see p. 579.) 1) Against arpeggios on the piano, the double bass introduces the theme of a jazz fugue, which is then presented in turn by trombone, saxophone, and trumpet, and

developed in the orchestra. 2) The melody of the Overture is heard in the flute accompanied by muted strings; the cello recalls the theme of the fugue in augmentation. In a slightly faster section, the oboe sings a blues marked *très tendre*, which is related to the fugue theme. 3) The dance of the plants and animals, marked *vif* (lively), is executed to a saucy tune in the violins, which is worked up into a fortissimo, with changes in instrumentation. The tempo

slackens, the fortissimo subsides. The theme of the blues returns as a counter-point to the dance: Man and Woman face one another. 4) Their Dance of Desire opens with a clarinet melody in improvisational style. A new melody appears containing triplet rhythms. The tranquil melody of the Overture returns in the oboe. The material undergoes free contrapuntal elaboration as the music builds to a *fff* climax. 5) The concluding section is in the nature of an epilogue. The blues theme is played by the oboe, whence it passes to other instruments. There is a fleeting reminiscence of the opening theme. Fluttertonguing on flute, clarinet, and trumpet leads to a tranquil "blue" cadence.

La Création du monde was a work of startling originality in its time. Replete with charm and humor, the score remains, to borrow Aaron Copland's description, "an authentic small masterpiece."

The Russians

The modern Russian school produced a world figure in Serge Prokofiev (1891–1953). His clean muscular music, bubbling over with wit and whimsy, struck a fresh note. Characteristic of his style are the athletic march rhythms, the harmonies pungently dissonant but rooted in the key, the sudden modulations, the unexpected turns of phrase, and the orchestral color that manifests all the brilliance we associate with the Russian school.

A greater number of Prokofiev's works have established themselves as "classics" with the international public than those of any of his contemporaries save Stravinsky. Among these are the *Scythian Suite* for orchestra (1914), with its deliberate primitivism; the *Classical Symphony* (1916–17); the Third Piano Concerto, which we will discuss; *Lieutenant Kije* (1934), a suite arranged from his music for the film; *Peter and the Wolf* (1936); *Alexander Nevsky* (1938), a cantata arranged from the music for the celebrated Eisenstein film; the ballets *Romeo and Juliet* (1935) and *Cinderella* (1944); the two Violin Concertos (1914, 1935); the Seventh Piano Sonata (1939–42); and the Fifth Symphony (1944). Several of Prokofiev's operas have found favor outside his homeland— *Love for Three Oranges* (1919); *The Flaming Angel* (1922–25); and *War and Peace* (final revision, 1952), after Tolstoi's novel. Prokofiev was one of those fortunate artists who achieve popularity with the masses and at the same time win the admiration of their fellow musicians.

Dmitri Shostakovich (b. 1906) is the first Russian composer of international repute who is wholly a product of Soviet musical culture. He was trained at the Leningrad Conservatory. His First Symphony (1925), written as a graduation piece when he was nineteen, won instant success both at home and abroad. There followed a stream of works in all branches of music, the most important being the Fifth Symphony (1937) and the Seventh, the *Leningrad Symphony* (1941); the ballet *The Golden Age* (1929–30); the opera *Lady Macbeth of Mzensk* (1930–32); eleven string quartets and the Quintet for Piano and Strings (1940); the Concerto for Piano, Trumpet, and Strings (1933) and the Violin Concerto (1955). His facility makes for unevenness of quality, but behind his output stands a vigorous creative personality in command of a big style that has caught the attention of the world.

The Armenian composer Aram Khatchaturian (b. 1903) bases his art on the folklore of his native republic. Khatchaturian's Piano Concerto (1936) combines Armenian folk elements with the grand virtuoso tradition of Liszt. Similarly his Violin Concerto (1940) displays lavishness of melody, sumptuous color, and the bravura style.

Prokofiev: Piano Concerto No. 3

The Third Piano Concerto, completed in 1921, is one of the most widely played works in the current repertory.

I. Andante—Allegro. "The first movement," Prokofiev wrote, "opens with a short introduction. The theme is announced by an unaccompanied clarinet and is continued by the violins for a few bars.

Soon the tempo changes to Allegro, the strings having a short passage in sixteenths, which leads to the statement of the principal subject by the piano." This driving theme exemplifies—as does the entire work—Prokofiev's skill in achieving rhythmic diversity within the traditional meters. Notice the abrupt change of key, so typical of this composer, at the beginning of the third measure:

"Discussion of this theme is carried on in a lively manner, both the piano and the orchestra having a good deal to say on the matter." Prokofiev exploits the contrast between piano and orchestral sonority with great vigor. "A passage in chords for the piano alone leads to the more expressive second subject, heard in the oboe with a pizzicato accompaniment."

"This is taken up by the piano and developed at some length, eventually giving way to a bravura passage in triplets. At the climax of this section the tempo reverts to Andante and the orchestra gives out the first theme, fortissimo.

The piano joins in, and the theme is subjected to an impressively broad treatment." The Allegro returns, the two main ideas are treated with great brilliance, and the movement ends with an exciting crescendo.

II. Andantino. The second movement consists of a theme with five variations. The theme, strongly Russian in character, is announced by the orchestra.

"In the first variation," the composer explained, "the piano treats the opening of the theme in quasi-sentimental fashion, and resolves into a chain of trills as the orchestra repeats the closing phrase. The tempo change to Allegro for the second and third variations, and the piano has brilliant figures, while snatches of the theme are introduced here and there in the orchestra. In Variation 4 the tempo is once again Andante, and the piano and orchestra discourse on the theme in a quiet and meditative fashion. Variation 5 is energetic (Allegro giusto) and leads without pause into a restatement of the theme by the orchestra, with delicate chordal embroidery in the piano."

III. Allegro ma non troppo. The Finale displays the gradations that Prokofiev assigned to "scherzo-ness"—jest, laughter, mockery. The mood is established at the outset by a staccato theme for bassoons and pizzicato strings:

This is interrupted by what Prokofiev called the blustering entry of the piano, playing chordal textures of great propulsive force. "The orchestra holds its own with the opening theme and there is a good deal of argument, with frequent differences of opinion as regards key." The solo part carries the first theme to a climax.

The melodist in Prokofiev is represented by the second theme, in his finest vein of lyricism, introduced by the oboes and clarinets. "The piano replies with a theme that is more in keeping with the caustic humor of the work." Then the lyric theme is developed. An exciting coda brings the Concerto to a close on a decisive C-major cadence.

Prokofiev's popularity with the public is due, in part, to his belief that the artist must communicate with his audience. "When I was in the United States and England," he wrote a year before his death, "I often heard discussions on the subject of whom music ought to serve, for whom a composer ought to write, and to whom his music should be addressed. In my view the composer, just as the poet, the sculptor or the painter, is in duty bound to serve man, the people. He must be a citizen first and foremost, so that his art may consciously extol human life and lead man to a radiant future."

Germany and Central Europe

Paul Hindemith (1895–1963) was the most substantial figure among the composers who came into prominence in Germany in the years after the First World War. Hindemith's harmony, based on the free use of twelve tones around a center, never abandoned tonality, which he regarded as an immutable law of music; hence his opposition to the Schoenbergians. Hindemith wrote an enormous quantity of music. His best-known works include the opera *Mathis der Maler* (1934), from which he developed the symphony of the same name; two ballets—*Nobilissima Visione* (1938) and *The Four Temperaments* (1940); *Das Marienleben* (The Life of Mary, 1923, revised 1948), a song cycle for soprano and piano to poems of Rainer Maria Rilke; and a choral setting of Walt Whitman's *When Lilacs Last in the Dooryard Bloom'd* (1946). Hindemith left Germany when Hitler came to power—his music was banned from the Third Reich as "cultural bolshevism"—and he spent two decades in the United States, during which he taught at Yale University and at the summer school in Tanglewood, Massachusetts, where many young Americans came under his influence.

Zoltán Kodály (1882–1967) was associated with Béla Bartók in the collection and study of peasant songs. The folklore element is paramount in his music. Two works of Kodály's have won international success: the *Psalmus Hungaricus* (Fifty-fifth Psalm, 1923) for tenor solo, mixed chorus, children's voices, and orchestra; and *Háry János* (1926), a folk play with music centering about a retired soldier of exuberant imagination.

Carl Orff was born in Munich in 1895. He took his point of departure from the clear-cut melody, simple harmonic structure, and vigorous rhythm of Bavarian folk song. Orff's best-known work is the "dramatic cantata" *Carmina burana* (Songs of Beuren, 1936), based on the famous thirteenth-century collection of student songs and poems that were discovered in an ancient Bavarian monastery. These inspired a work whose lilting melodies and appealing rhythms have made it one of the most popular of twentieth-century compositions.

Ernst Krenek was born in Vienna in 1900. In the 1920s he fell under the spell of jazz. He subsequently found his way to the twelve-tone method. When the Nazis took over Austria, Krenek came to the United States, where he has since taught at several colleges. His book *Music Here and Now* reveals an intellect that probes the complexities of contemporary musical thought. Krenek is one of the most prolific composers of our time. Among his works are eleven operas, three ballets, six piano sonatas, five symphonies, four piano concertos, and eight string quartets.

Kurt Weill (1900–1950) was one of the most arresting figures to emerge in Germany in the Twenties. To the international public his name is indissolubly linked with *Die Dreigroschenoper* (The Three-Penny Opera) that he and the poet Bertolt Brecht adapted from John Gay's celebrated *Beggar's Opera*. Upon

541

the lusty antics of Gay's work, Weill and Brecht superimposed the despair, the agonized outcry of a Germany in the aftermath of the First World War. Launched in 1928, the work was a fabulous success. Repeated revivals have made it one of the century's best-known theater pieces.

Hindemith: *Symphony, Mathis der Maler*

The hero of Hindemith's opera *Mathis der Maler* (Mathis the Painter, 1934) is the German Matthias Grünewald, who flourished around 1500. Grünewald's art encompassed both the mysticism of the dying Middle Ages and the realism of the oncoming Renaissance. His masterpiece is the series of paintings for the altar at Isenheim executed for the Brothers of St. Anthony. These display an intensity of vision that places him in the company of Albrecht Dürer, Lucas Cranach, and Hieronymus Bosch.

The peasant revolts that marked the end of medieval serfdom and the beginnings of the Reformation confronted Mathis with a moral issue: How could the artist serenely pursue his work amid the suffering of his fellow men? Should he not rather abandon his art and join the struggle against oppression? This lofty theme, raising issues as pertinent to our time as to Grünewald's, offered Hindemith a congenial subject. The opera is pervaded by a contemplative lyricism bordering on the mystical. For his symphony (1934) Hindemith extracted three orchestral movements from the score, each named after another of Mathis's paintings.

I. *Concert of Angels. Ruhig bewegt* (moving quietly). The Introduction is based on modal harmonies. A religious folk song of the Middle Ages, *Es sungen drei Engel* (Three Angels Sang) is intoned by three trombones, creating an archaic atmosphere:

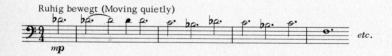

Characteristic of Hindemith are the serene chords which establish points of repose within the forward movement.

The Allegro proper, in ²⁄₂ time, has enormous breadth and energy. The main theme is played by flutes and violins. Stepwise movement along the scales is enlivened by decisive intervals at the points of stress. The upward leap of a fifth (at x) is typical of Hindemith, as is the modal harmony.

The second theme is more placid. A true contrapuntist, Hindemith fashions this idea with a view ultimately to combine it with the first. Here, too, we find an upward leap of a fifth and a modal atmosphere.

The Development derives its excitement from the devices of imitative counterpoint. It culminates in the return of the chorale on the trombones. Against it we hear an elaborate orchestral tissue woven out of the two main themes.

II. *The Entombment. Sehr langsam* (very slowly), in $\frac{4}{4}$. Muted strings answered by flutes and clarinets set the elegiac tone. A broadly arching lament on the oboe unfolds against pizzacato chords on the strings. This is imitated by the flute in a mournful dialogue between both instruments. Tension is sustained through the persistent dotted rhythms, which serve as a unifying element. At the climax wind sonority is pitted against the strings, with superb use of trumpet tone. The music is withdrawn, introspective. The movement ends with a serene major chord.

III. *The Temptation of St. Anthony.* In Grünewald's painting the Saint is tormented by noisome beasts. These become, in the scene that constitutes the emotional peak of the opera, the symbol of the painter's own doubts and desires. The score bears the motto: "Where wert Thou, good Jesus, where wert Thou, wherefore didst Thou not give aid and heal my wounds?"

The movement opens with a rhapsodic declamation of the strings in unison. This introduction is imbued with dramatic gesture. The movement proper, a frenetic Allegro in $\frac{9}{8}$, opens with a broad arch of melody. Tension mounts steadily.

There is brutal strength in the brass sound. A sustained high trill on the violins, with a suggestion of the diabolical, ushers in a languorous episode marked *Langsam* (slow), in which the orchestra takes on a Straussian sensuousness. Clearly the holy man is sorely tried. The movement resumes with a furiously syncopated section in $\frac{2}{4}$ that culminates in a fugato, out of which emerges the chorale *Lauda Sion Salvatorem* (Praise, O Zion, the Savior). The massed brasses sing a hallelujah as Anthony-Mathis (and presumably Hindemith) achieve the faith that conquers anguish and banishes doubt.

Others

Toward the end of the nineteenth century there arose in Spain a movement to create a national art based on authentic folklore. Its culminating figure was Manuel de Falla (1876–1946), whose individuality was strong enough to lift the native idiom into the mainstream of twentieth-century music. He is remembered chiefly for the ballet *El Amor brujo*, generally translated "Love the Magician"—although "Love Bewitched" might be closer to the mark (1915); *Nights in the Gardens of Spain*, three impressionist nocturnes for piano and orchestra (1909–15); the ballet *The Three-Cornered Hat* (1919); and the Concerto for Harpsichord (or Piano) and Five Instruments—flute, oboe, clarinet, violin, and cello (1923–26).

Ernest Bloch (1880-1959) differs from other composers of Jewish extraction such as Mendelssohn, Meyerbeer, Saint-Saëns, or Mahler, who were assimilated into the musical culture of the country in which they lived. He found his personal style though mystic identification with what he conceived to be the Hebraic spirit. In works such as the Hebrew Rhapsody *Schelomo* for cello and orchestra (1915)—the title is the Hebrew name of the poet-king Solomon—he evokes a biblical landscape with all the force of a temperament given to sensuous abandon and exaltation. Bloch was born in Geneva. In 1916 he settled in the United States. His pupils include several of our prominent composers, among them Roger Sessions, Randall Thompson, and Douglas Moore.

William Walton (b. 1902) assimilated the ample choral style that is England's inheritance, and drew inspiration from the Tudor church composers and the Elizabethan madrigal. Walton is best known in this country for his oratorio *Belshazzar's Feast* (1931). He is also appreciated here as a film composer. Among his most successful scores were those for Sir Laurence Olivier's *Henry V* (1944) and *Hamlet* (1947).

Benjamin Britten (b. 1913), a musician of great invention, technical mastery, and charm, is the most important English composer of his generation. Besides a quantity of orchestral, choral, and chamber music, Britten has written several operas, of which the most important is *Peter Grimes* (1945). *Billy Budd* (1951), from the story by Melville, received its American premiere on television in 1952 and made a strong impression. *The Turn of the Screw* (1954) captures the eerie atmosphere of Henry James's famous story. A *Midsummer Night's Dream* (1960), after Shakespeare, affirms Britten's position as one of the foremost operatic composers of our time. In 1962, Britten was commissioned to compose a work for the opening of the rebuilt Coventry Cathedral in England, which had been destroyed by German bombs; the resulting *War Requiem*, which intermingled the text of the Latin Requiem Mass with the war poems of Wilfred Owen, won instant recognition as a masterpiece.

PART SEVEN

THE
AMERICAN
SCENE

"What we must arrive at is the youthful opti-mistic vitality and the undaunted tenacity of spirit that characterize the American man. That is what I hope to see echoed in American music."
                                        Edward MacDowell

91 The Past

"Music . . . the favorite passion of my soul."
Thomas Jefferson

The Beginnings

The first publication to appear in British North America was the Bay Psalm Book, which was published in Cambridge in 1640. Its appearance underlines what was the chief function of music in early New England: the singing of psalms and hymns.

In Virginia, on the other hand, there evolved a society of planters who adhered to the social amenities of Cavalier England. As in the aristocratic circles of Europe, music served for polite and elegant entertainment. Jefferson was an amateur violinist, played string quartets at the weekly musicales of Governor Fauquier, and invented an ingenious violin stand which when folded did duty as an end table. Years later, in planning Monticello, he inquired of a friend in France whether there might not be found a gardener, weaver, cabinetmaker, and stone cutter who could double on French horn, clarinet, oboe, and bassoon. "The bounds of an American fortune," he writes, "will not admit the indulgence of a domestic band of musicians, yet I have thought that a passion for music might be reconciled with that economy which we are obliged to observe."

In the absence of an aristocracy to act as patrons, music in colonial America found an outlet in public concerts, which were first given in such cities as Boston and Charleston in the 1730s. Ballad opera, too, found favor with the public. The ordinance against theater in Boston stated that such entertainments discouraged industry, frugality, and piety (in that order). To get around the law, stage shows masqueraded as "moral lectures" and "readings." By the end of the century the Bostonians had succumbed to several dozen ballad operas.

The best-known of our early composers was an aristocratic amateur. Francis Hopkinson (1737–91) came from the same stratum of society in Philadelphia as did his friend Jefferson in Virginia. Composing was but one of the many interests of this jurist, writer, statesman, signer of the Declaration of Independence and framer of the Constitution.

Hopkinson's best-known song is *My Days Have Been so Wondrous Free*. In 1788 he published a collection of songs "in an easy, familiar style, intended for young practitioners on the harpsichord or fortepiano"; he was responsible also for the texts. The work was dedicated to Washington, to whom he wrote, "However small the Reputation may be that I shall derive from this work, I cannot, I believe, be refused the Credit of being the first Native of the United States who has produced a Musical Composition." To which Washington replied, "I can neither sing one of the songs, nor raise a single note on any instrument to convince the unbelieving. But I have, however, one argument which will prevail with persons of true estate (at least in America)—I can tell them that *it is the production of Mr. Hopkinson*."

A more substantial composer was William Billings (1746–1800). A tanner by trade, this exuberant figure was the product of a pioneer culture. The little knowledge he had was gleaned from the rudimentary treatises contained in the hymn books of the time. Billings is specifically associated with the lively "fuguing pieces" in which he treated psalm and hymn tunes contrapuntally. The fugal treatment—actually, merely a kind of simple imitation—produced a music that was, he claimed, "twenty times as powerful as the old slow tunes. Each part striving for mastery and victory. The audience entertained and delighted. Now the solemn bass demands their attention; next the manly tenor. Now here, now there, now here again! O ecstatic! Rush on, you sons of harmony." Such ebullience was not to be resisted. Billings's psalms, anthems, humorous pieces, and patriotic songs were widely performed in the late eighteenth century. He was rewarded for his efforts with a pauper's grave on Boston Common. His memory lived on, however, to inspire some twentieth-century Americans. Otto Luening's *Prelude on a Hymn Tune by William Billings*, William Schuman's A *Billings Overture*, and Henry Cowell's *Hymns and Fuguing Tunes* pay homage to this extraordinary American primitive.

The Nineteenth Century

The young republic attracted an influx of musicians from England, France, and Germany, who brought with them a tradition and a level of technique beyond any that existed here. In consequence, the new generation of American musicians was better equipped than their predecessors. A typical figure was Lowell Mason (1792–1872), who wrote *Nearer, My God to Thee* and other standard hymns. It was Mason's great achievement to establish music in the public-school curriculum. His son William Mason (1829–1908) studied with Liszt at Weimar and became one of the foremost pianists and teachers of his day. The circle was now complete—Europeans had come to the New World to live, Americans were returning to Europe to study.

Edward Hicks (1780–1849), THE PEACEABLE KINGDOM. (Abby Aldrich Rockefeller Folk Art Collection, Williamsburg, Virginia)
The Quaker artist is one of America's important "primitives."

The vogue of the visiting virtuoso began. The Norwegian violinist Ole Bull was followed, in 1850, by Jenny Lind. What with her gift for song and P. T. Barnum's genius for publicity, Jenny was a sensation. Toward the middle of the century, America produced its own virtuoso in Louis Moreau Gottschalk (1829–69). Born in New Orleans, the son of an English Jew and a Creole, Gottschalk was one of the adored pianists of the romantic period. Handsome and magnetic, he was a Lisztian figure who left his white gloves on the piano to be torn to shreds by overwrought ladies in need of a little something to press between the pages of a book. Gottschalk left behind some salon pieces such as *The Last Hope* and *The Dying Poet* that nourished several generations of pupils and parents. More important were the exotic miniatures he wrote during the 1840s—*Bamboula, Le Bananier, The Banjo*—which, by exploiting the New Orleans locale, pointed the way to an awakening nationalism.

The revolutions of 1848 caused thousands of liberals to emigrate from central Europe. German musicians came over in large numbers. They formed the backbone of the symphony orchestras, singing societies, and chamber-music groups. In this way the traditions of Weimar and Leipzig, Munich and Vienna were established in our midst and became a decisive factor in shaping our musical taste.

But the great American composer of the pre-Civil War period did not issue from the tradition of Haydn and Mozart. He came out of the humbler realm of the minstrel show. Stephen Foster (1826–64) was born in Lawrenceville, Pennsylvania. His was a substantial middle-class environment in which music was not even remotely considered to be a suitable career for a man. His parents took note of his talent but did nothing to encourage or train it. Foster's lyric gift, unassimilated to any musical culture, found its natural outlet in the sphere of popular song.

Foster's was a temperament unable to accommodate itself to the bourgeois ideal of success. He was, as his biographer John Tasker Howard has written, "a dreamer, thoroughly impractical and . . . never businessman enough to realize the commercial value of his best songs." His course led with tragic inevitability from the initial flurries of good fortune, through the failure of his marriage, to the hall bedroom on the Bowery and the alcoholic's lonely death at the age of thirty-eight. In that time he managed to write some two hundred songs, a half dozen of which have imprinted themselves on the American soul.

Seen in the perspective of history this lovable weakling, the despair of his parents, his wife, and his brothers, emerges as one of our great artists. He stands among the very few musicians whose personal vision created the songs of a nation.

The Postromantic Period

The decades following the Civil War witnessed an impressive expansion of musical life throughout the country. Most important, there appeared a native school of trained composers. First to achieve more than ephemeral fame was John Knowles Paine (1839–1906), who for thirty years was professor of music at Harvard, and mentor of the so-called Boston or New England group that included leading American composers at the turn of the century. Among these were George W. Chadwick (1854–1931) and Horatio Parker (1863–1919).

A more striking personality was Edward MacDowell (1861–1908), the first American composer to achieve a reputation abroad. He studied composition in Germany and came to the notice of Liszt, who secured performances of his works. MacDowell settled in Germany and taught there for several years. In 1888 he returned to the United States.

The four piano sonatas and two concertos for piano and orchestra reveal MacDowell to have been at home in the large forms. He was at his best, however, in the small lyric pieces that are still favorites with young pianists. The *Woodland Sketches* (including *To a Wild Rose*), the *Fireside Tales*, and *New England Idyls* are the work of a miniaturist of great charm and sensibility.

The composers just mentioned were really belated romanticists. The postromantic label is more properly applied to the Alsatian-born Charles Martin Loeffler (1861-1935), who came to this country when he was twenty. He is remembered chiefly for *A Pagan Poem* (1901), a chamber work he later rewrote

Winslow Homer (1836–1910), THE GULF STREAM. (The Metropolitan Museum of Art, New York; Wolfe Fund, 1906)

Like MacDowell, Homer was a postromantic.

for piano and orchestra. Loeffler was a recluse and a mystic. who anticipated what was to become an important development in American music of the twentieth century: the turning from German to French influence.

The American composers of the late nineteenth century were pioneers dedicated to a noble vision. We have every reason to remember them with pride.

92 Emergence of the Modern American School

"The way to write American music is simple. All you have to do is to be an American and then write any kind of music you wish."
Virgil Thomson

The Early Twentieth Century

During the first quarter of our century the serious American composer was something of a stepchild in his own country. His music faced a twofold handicap: it was modern, and it lacked the made-in-Europe label that

551

carries such weight with our public. He had no powerful publishers to champion his cause, no system of grants and fellowships to give him the leisure to compose, no famous conductors to bring him the performances he needed.

The composers born between 1890 and 1910 had an easier time. The gradual victory of musical modernism in Europe could not but have repercussions here. Besides, the emergence of a strong native school became a matter of national pride and found support in various quarters. The era of prosperity in the Twenties encouraged private patronage in the form of grants and fellowships. Of great help was the forward-looking policy of conductors like Serge Koussevitzky, Leopold Stokowski, and Dimitri Mitropoulos, who made a point of giving the American composer a hearing. The conservatories too, which had hitherto concentrated on the training of instrumentalists and singers, began to turn their attention to the needs of young composers. The music departments of our colleges and universities also took on new importance as centers of progressive musical activity.

During this time our composers were actively experimenting with the techniques of modern musical speech. In craftsmanship, their scores began to bear comparison with the best of Europe's. The decade before the Second World War saw this country emerge as the musical center of the world. The presence here of Stravinsky, Schoenberg, Bartók, Hindemith, Milhaud, Krenek, and their confreres had a tremendous impact on our musical life. Many of our younger musicians studied with these masters and came directly under their influence.

Toward an American Music

As American composers became more sure of themselves, they aspired in ever greater measure to give expression to the life about them. At first they concentrated on those features of the home scene that were not to be found in Europe: the lore of the Indian, the Negro, and the cowboy. They became increasingly aware of a wealth of native material that was waiting to be used: the songs of the southern mountaineers, which preserved intact the melodies brought over from England three hundred years ago; the hymns and religious tunes that had such vivid associations for Americans everywhere; the patriotic songs of the Revolutionary period and the Civil War, many of which had become folk songs; the tunes of the minstrel shows which had reached their high point in the songs of Foster. There were, in addition, the work songs from various parts of the country—songs of sharecroppers, lumberjacks, miners, river men; songs of prairie and railroad, chain gang and frontier. Then there was the folklore of the city dwellers—commercialized ballads, musical-comedy songs, and jazz: a world of melody, rhythm, and mood.

Certain composers, on the other hand, resisted this kind of local color. They preferred the international idioms of twentieth-century music that had been stripped of folk elements: impressionism, neoclassicism, atonality, and twelve-

Grant Wood (1892–1942), AMERICAN GOTHIC. (The Art Institute of Chicago, Friends of American Art Collection)

Our artists began to draw their inspiration from the American scene.

tone music. Others managed to reconcile the two attitudes. They revealed themselves as internationally minded in certain of their works, but employed folklore elements in others. It was gradually realized that Americanism in music was a much broader concept than had at first been supposed: American music could not but be as many-faceted as America itself. A work did not have to quote a Negro spiritual, an Indian harvest song, or a dirge of the prairie in order to qualify for citizenship.

The music of the modern American school follows no single formula. Rather, it reflects the contradictory tendencies in our national character: our jaunty humor, and our sentimentality; our idealism, and our worship of material success; our rugged individualism, and our wish to look and think like everybody else; our visionary daring, and our practicality; our ready emotionalism, and our capacity for intellectual pursuits. All of these and more are abundantly present in a music that has bigness of gesture, vitality, and all the exurberance of youth.

553

93 Charles Ives

"Beauty in music is too often confused with something that lets the ears lie back in an easy chair. Many sounds that we are used to do not bother us, and for that reason we are inclined to call them beautiful. Frequently, when a new or unfamiliar work is accepted as beautiful on its first hearing, its fundamental quality is one that tends to put the mind to sleep."

Charles Edward Ives (1874–1954) waited many years for recognition. Today he stands revealed as the first truly American composer of the twentieth century, and one of the most original spirits of his time.

His Life

Ives was born in Danbury, Connecticut. His father had been a bandmaster in the Civil War, and continued his calling in civilian life. Charles at thirteen held a job as church organist and already was arranging music for the various ensembles conducted by his father. At twenty he entered Yale, where he studied composition with Horatio Parker. Ives's talent for music asserted itself throughout his four years at Yale; yet when he had to choose a career he decided against a professional life in music. He suspected that society would not pay him for the kind of music he wanted to compose. He was right.

He therefore entered the business world. Two decades later he was head of the largest insurance agency in the country. The years it took him to achieve this success—roughly from the time he was twenty-two to forty-two—were the years when he wrote his music. He composed at night, on weekends, and during vacations, working in isolation, concerned only to set down the sounds he heard in his head.

The few conductors and performers whom he tried to interest in his works pronounced them unplayable. After a number of these rebuffs Ives gave up showing his manuscripts. When he felt the need to hear how his music sounded, he hired a few musicians to run through a work. Save for these rare and quite inadequate performances, Ives heard his music only in his imagination. He pursued his way undeflected and alone, piling up one score after another in his barn in Connecticut. When well-meaning friends suggested that he try to write music that people would like, he could only retort, "I can't do it—I hear something else!"

Ives's double life as a business executive by day and composer by night finally took its toll. In 1918, when he was forty-four, he suffered a physical breakdown that left his heart damaged. The years of unrewarded effort had taken more out

Charles Ives.

of him emotionally than he had suspected. Although he lived almost forty years longer, he produced nothing further of importance.

When he recovered he faced the realization that the world of professional musicians was irrevocably closed to his ideas. He felt that he owed it to his music to make it available to those who might be less hidebound. He therefore had the *Concord Sonata* for piano privately printed, also the *Essays Before a Sonata*—a kind of elaborate program note that presented the essence of his views on life and art. These were followed by the *114 Songs*. The three volumes, which were distributed free of charge to libraries, music critics, and whoever else asked for them, caused not a ripple as far as the public was concerned. But they gained Ives the support of other experimental composers who were struggling to make their way in an unheeding world. The tide finally turned in this country when the American pianist John Kirkpatrick, at a recital in Town Hall in January, 1939, played the *Concord Sonata*. Ives was then sixty-five. The piece was repeated several weeks later by Kirkpatrick and scored a triumph. The next morning Lawrence Gilman hailed the *Concord Sonata* as "the greatest music composed by an American."

Ives had already begun to exert a salutary influence upon the younger generation of composers, who found in his art a realization of their own ideals. Now he was "discovered" by the general public and hailed as the grand old man of American music. In 1947 his Third Symphony achieved performance, and won a Pulitzer Prize. This story of belated recognition was an item to capture the imagination, and was carried by newspapers throughout the country. Ives awoke at seventy-three to find himself famous. Four years later the Second Symphony was presented to the public by the New York Philharmonic, exactly half a century after it had been composed. The prospect of finally hearing the work agitated the old man; he attended neither the rehearsals nor the performances. He was, however, one of millions who listened to the radio broadcast.

He died in New York City three years later, at the age of eighty.

His Music

Charles Ives, both as man and artist, was rooted in the New England heritage, in the tradition of plain living and high thinking that came to flower in the idealism of Hawthorne and the Alcotts, Emerson and Thoreau. The sources of his tone imagery are to be found in the living music of his childhood: hymn tunes and popular songs, the town band at holiday parades, the fiddlers at Saturday night dances, patriotic songs and sentimental parlor ballads, the melodies of Stephen Foster, and the medleys heard at country fairs and in small theaters.

This wealth of American music had attracted other musicians besides Ives. But they, subservient to European canons of taste, had proceeded to smooth out and "correct" these popular tunes according to the rules they had absorbed in Leipzig or Munich. Ives was as free from subservience to the European tradition as Walt Whitman. His keen ear caught the sound of untutored voices singing a hymn together, some in their eagerness straining and sharpening the pitch, others just missing it and flatting; so that in place of the single tone there was a cluster of tones that made a deliciously dissonant chord. Some were a trifle ahead of the beat, others lagged behind; consequently the rhythm sagged and turned into a welter of polyrhythms. He heard the pungent clash of dissonance when two bands in a parade, each playing a different tune in a different key, came close enough together to overlap; he heard the effect of quarter tones when fiddlers at a country dance brought excitement into their playing by going a mite off pitch. He remembered the wheezy harmonium at church accompanying the hymns a trifle out of tune. All these, he realized, were not departures from the norm. They *were* the norm of popular American musical speech. Thus he found his way to such conceptions as polytonality, atonality, polyharmony, cluster chords based on intervals of a second, and polyrhythms. All this in the last years of the nineteenth century, when Schoenberg was still writing in a post-Wagner idiom, when neither Stravinsky nor Bartók had yet begun their careers, when Hindemith had just been born. All the more honor, then, to this singular musician who, isolated alike from the public and his fellow composers, was so advanced in his conceptions and so accurate in his forecast of the paths that twentieth-century music would follow.

The central position in his orchestral music is held by the four symphonies (1896–1916). Among his other orchestral works are *Three Places in New England*, which we will discuss; *Three Outdoor Scenes* (1898–1911), consisting of *Hallowe'en, The Pond,* and *Central Park in the Dark,* the last-named for chamber orchestra; and *The Unanswered Question* (1908). The Sonata No. 2

Wassily Kandinsky (1866–1944), PANEL (3) (Collection, The Museum
of Modern Art, New York. Mrs. Simon Guggenheim Fund)

*The images on the canvases of expressionist painters issued from the realm
of the unconscious: hallucinated visions that defied the traditional notion
of beauty in order to express more powerfully the artist's inner self.*

Jackson Pollock (1912–56), NUMBER 1, 1948 (Collection, The Museum of Modern Art, New York)

The "drip painting" of Pollock paralleled the interest in chance as an element of musical composition.

for piano—"Concord, Mass., 1840–1860"—which occupied him from 1909 to 1915, reflects various aspects of the flowering of New England; its four movements are entitled *Emerson, Hawthorne, The Alcotts,* and *Thoreau.* Ives also wrote a variety of songs, as well as chamber, choral, and piano compositions.

Three Places in New England

In this work (1903–14) Ives evokes three place-names rich in associations for a New Englander.

I. *The "St. Gaudens" in Boston Common: Col. Shaw and his Colored Regiment. Very slowly.* (The reference in the title is to the famous statue by Augustus St. Gaudens.) It will suffice to quote the opening lines of the poem that Ives wrote into the score:

> Moving,—Marching—Faces of Souls!
> Marked with generations of pain,
> Part-freers of a Destiny,
> Slowly, restlessly—swaying us on with you
> Towards other Freedom! . . .

An atmosphere of solemn dedication envelops the opening measures. No familiar tunes are actually quoted in this movement, yet the melodic line unmistakably suggests the world of the Stephen Foster songs and the range of emotions attached to the Civil War. The ostinato patterns in the bass, the urgency of the brass, the complex chord structures on the piano used for their color value, the fluid polyrhythms, and the polytonal effects are all characteristic of the composer; as are the wide-apart instrumental lines and the effect of distance that Ives achieves at the emotional climax by pitting high woodwinds against low brass. The texture is predominantly homophonic. The form is free, in the manner of a prelude or fantasy. The piece ends, as it begins, *ppp.*

II. *Putnam's Camp, Redding, Connecticut. Allegro* (Quick-Step Time). "Near Redding Center," Ives wrote, "is a small park preserved as a Revolutionary Memorial; for here General Israel Putnam's soldiers had their winter quarters in 1778–9. Long rows of stone camp fireplaces still remain to stir a child's imagination." The scene is a "4th of July" picnic held under the auspices of the First Church and the Village Cornet Band. The child wanders into the woods and dreams of the old soldiers, of the hardships they endured, their desire to break camp and abandon their cause, and of how they returned when Putnam came over the hills to lead them. "The little boy awakes, he hears the children's songs and runs down past the monument to 'listen to the band' and join in the games and dances."

In this vivid tone-painting Ives conjures up the frenetic business of having a good time on a holiday picnic in a small American town: the hubbub, the sweating faces, the parade with its two bands that overlap, their harmonies clashing. This section abounds in polytonal, atonal, and polyrhythmic effects. Its main theme is a marching song:

Characteristic is Ives's way of quoting a popular tune and then "dissolving" it in another idea. For example, a fragment of *Yankee Doodle* is "dissolved" into something else, but the four notes of the famous tune have sufficed to release a flood of associations in the listener:

This is followed by a melody, presented as a violin solo, that has all the characteristics of a folk song without being one:

Following is the marching song from the middle section (the dream sequence):

Another marchlike melody in this section illustrates Ives's singular ability to create themes that capture the accents of American popular song:

A deep love of all things American lies at the heart of this movement. There is an exciting passage where two march rhythms clash, four measures of the one equalling three of the other. The intricate polyrhythms in the final measures lead to a daringly dissonant ending, *ffff*. This is one of those works that spring from the soil and soul of a particular place, and could have been conceived nowhere else.

III. *The Housatonic at Stockbridge. Adagio molto* (Very slowly). Ives quotes the poem of that name by Robert Underwood Johnson:

Contented river! in thy dreamy realm—
The cloudy willow and the plumy elm . . .
Thou hast grown human laboring with men
At wheel and spindle; sorrow thou dost ken; . . .

. . . . Wouldst thou away!
I also of much resting have a fear;
Let me thy companion be
By fall and shallow to the adventurous sea!

The muted strings set up a rippling current of sound, *pppp*, as background for the melody that presently emerges, divided between the French horn and

English horn. It is a serene, hymnic tune that evokes the prayer meetings of Ives's boyhood. This contemplative nature piece flows calmly and steadily to the *fff* climax, then subsides to a pianissimo ending.

General William Booth Enters into Heaven

Early in 1914 Ives came across Vachel Lindsay's poem. (Booth was the London evangelist who founded the Salvation Army in the late 1870s.) Lindsay's stirring verse inspired one of Ives's most dramatic songs; it exists in two versions, one for voice and piano, the other for bass, chorus, and orchestra. The orchestration was made by Ives's close friend and associate, John J. Becker.

"Booth led boldly with his big bass drum—(Are you washed in the Blood of the Lamb? Hallelujah!) Saints smiled gravely and they said: 'He's come.' (Are you washed in the Blood of the Lamb?)" The tempo is Allegro moderato (March time). In the solo-voice version, the piano begins by imitating Booth's drum; dissonant cluster chords are heard against syncopated octaves in the low bass. The recurrent question "Are you washed in the Blood of the Lamb?" introduces the gospel-hymn material that dominates the melodic line. The poet's description of Booth's motley army—"Walking lepers followed rank on rank . . ."—arouses Ives to harsh expressiveness. Biting dissonances and shifting rhythms unfold against a series of organ points. "Vermin-eaten saints with mouldy breaths, Unwashed legions with the ways of Death . . ." The first climax of the song comes, understandably, with a slashing discord on the word "Death."

A polytonal passage in the middle register ushers in the next section, "Ev'ry slum had sent its half-a-score . . ." The mention of banjos in a following line impels Ives to a characteristic passage in which he distorts popular-song material. He expands the traditional borders of the art song by directing that the word "Hallelujah!" be shouted, and follows a four-beat measure with one of three-and-a-half beats. Soon, reflecting the text, the piano suggests the blaring of

559

trumpets. These instrumental imitations in the piano accompaniment explain why the song is so effective in its orchestral version.

The basic question "Are you washed in the Blood of the Lamb?" is heard against a passage in which the individual notes are lost in a dark blur of sound. "Jesus came from the courthouse door . . ." introduces a section marked *Adagio and with dignity.* Interesting is Ives's setting of the words "round and round and round"; three descending notes repeated over and over in varying rhythms. "Yet in an instant all that blear review marched on spotless, clad in raiment new." The drum-beat rhythm of the opening returns, building to a mighty climax on the repetition of the words "marched on." "The lame were straightened, withered limbs uncurled, and blind eyes opened on a new sweet world." The complexity of Ives's harmony is well-illustrated by his setting of the closing phrase. The final chord, on "world," combines Tonic and Dominant:

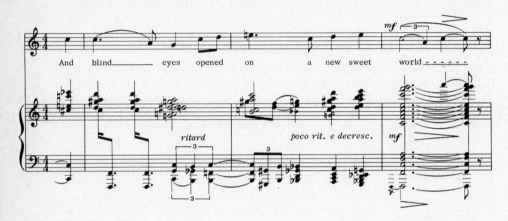

The basic question is repeated in an Adagio, and the music fades to a *pppp* ending.

Charles Ives is our first great composer. Like the writers he admired most, he has become an American classic.

Other Composers of the First Generation

Charles Tomlinson Griffes was born in Elmira, New York, in 1884. He studied abroad, where he came in contact with a rich European culture. Upon his return, he accepted a teaching post at a boys' school in Tarrytown, New York. His health, never robust, was undermined by years of protracted work at night after the hours of teaching. His death in 1920, at the age of thirty-six, robbed our music of a major talent.

Griffes's best-known piano piece, *The White Peacock* (1915), was widely played in the composer's orchestral version. The work stems from the years when the Debussyan influence was strongest. It bears the promise of important things to come, a promise cheated of fulfillment by a turn of fate.

Wallingford Riegger (Albany, Georgia, 1885–1961, New York City) was a dedicated atonalist whose symphonies and string quartets made a strong impact upon our music. Riegger found his style through the Schoenbergian technique; he used the twelve-tone language in a most personal way. Among his important works are *Study in Sonority* for ten violins or any multiple of ten (1927); *Dichotomy*, for chamber orchestra (1932), based on two opposing tone rows; *New Dance* (1944), which won popularity not only as an orchestral piece but also in a two-piano version; and the *Third Symphony* (1946–47, revised in 1957).

The rise of a national school in the United States had its parallel in Latin America. This movement united twentieth-century trends with folk elements drawn from Indian, Negro, and Spanish-Portuguese sources. The first composer of South America to command the attention of the world was the Brazilian nationalist Heitor Villa-Lobos (1887–1959), an exuberant musician who turned out music in tropical abundance. He left behind him over fifteen hundred compositions. His collected works, whenever that project is put through by a grateful nation, will cover a wall in the library at Rio de Janeiro. Out of that mass of notes enough will survive to keep his memory green.

94 American Composers (I)

Edgard Varèse

"I refuse to submit myself only to sounds that have already been heard."

Edgard Varèse was one of the truly original spirits in the music of our time. The innovations of Stravinsky, Schoenberg, and Bartók unfolded within the frame of the traditional elements of their art, but Varèse went a step farther: he rejected certain of those elements altogether.

His Life

Varèse was born in Paris in 1883, of Italian-French parentage. He studied mathematics and science at school, since his father intended him for an engineering career. But at eighteen he entered the Schola Cantorum, and subsequently studied at the Paris Conservatoire. With the outbreak of war in 1914 Varèse was mobilized into the French army, but was discharged the following year after a serious illness. He came to the United States in December, 1915,

Edgard Varèse.

when he was thirty-two, and lost no time in making a place for himself in the musical life of his adopted land.

The greater part of Varèse's music was written during the Twenties and early Thirties. He found a champion in Leopold Stokowski, who performed his scores despite the violent opposition they aroused in conventionally minded concert goers. Then, like his colleague Ives, Varèse fell silent when he should have been at the height of his powers. During the next twenty years he followed the new scientific developments in the field of electronic instruments, and resumed composing in 1949, when he began to work on *Deserts*.

By that time the scene had changed; there existed a public receptive to experimental music. When an enterprising record company made available four of his works, Varèse was enabled to reach an audience that had never before heard his music. He was invited by the State Department to conduct master classes in composition in Darmstadt, Germany. The younger generation of European composers who were experimenting with tape-recorded music suddenly discovered him as one whose work had been prophetic of theirs. The long-neglected master finally came into his own. He died in New York City in 1965.

His Music

The abstract images that brood over Varèse's music are derived from the life of the big city: the rumble of motors the clang of hammers, the shriek and hiss and shrilling of factory whistles, turbines, steam drills. His stabbing, pounding rhythms conjure up the throb and hum of the metropolis. It follows that his attention is focused on the percussion, which he handles with inexhaustible invention. His music unfolds in geometrical patterns based on the opposition of sonorous planes and volumes—patterns which, in their abstraction, are the counterpart in sound of the designs of cubist painting. Varèse's music was utterly revolutionary in its day. It sounded like nothing that had ever been heard before.

The fanciful names Varèse gave his works indicated the connection in the composer's mind between his music and scientific processes. *Hyperprism* (1923) is for a chamber orchestra of two woodwinds, seven brass, and sixteen percussion instruments. *Arcana* (1927–28), for orchestra, develops a basic idea through melodic, rhythmic, and instrumental variation, somewhat in the manner of a passacaglia. Of Varèse's other compositions for conventional instruments we should mention *Octandre*, a chamber work for eight instruments (1923), and *Intégrales*, for winds and percussion (1925).

"Speed and synthesis are characteristic of our epoch. We need twentieth-century instruments to help us realize those in music." With *Deserts* (1954) Varèse entered the world of electronic sound. The piece is written for orchestra; but at three points in the score there are interpolations of what Varèse called

Charles Sheeler (1883–1965), AMERICAN LANDSCAPE. (The Museum of Modern Art, New York; Gift of Mrs. John D. Rockefeller, Jr.)
The imagery of modern industry plays an important part in American art of the twentieth century.

"organized sound"—music on tape. There followed, in 1958, *Poème élec-tronique*, commissioned by the Philips Radio Corporation to be played in a pavilion designed by Le Corbusier at the Brussels Fair that would be "a poem of the electronic age." Thus, at the age of seventy-three, the intrepid explorer was still pursuing new paths, bringing back to his less venturesome fellows the shapes and sounds of the music of the future.

Ionisation

Varèse's most celebrated composition is scored for thirty-five different instruments of percussion and friction, played by thirteen performers. *Ionisation* (1931) is an imaginative study in pure sonority and rhythm, in which Varèse frees percussion and bell sounds from their traditional subservience to melody and harmony.

The instruments used fall into three groups. Those of definite pitch include tubular chimes, celesta, and piano. Among those of indefinite pitch are drums of various kinds, cymbals, tam-tam (gong), triangle, slapstick, Chinese blocks, sleighbells, castanets, tambourine, and two anvils. Also a number of exotic instruments, such as bongos (West Indian twin drums with parchment heads, played either with small wooden sticks or with the fingers); a guiro (a Cuban dried gourd, serrated on the surface and scratched with a wooden stick); maracas (Cuban rattles); claves (Cuban sticks of hardwood); and a cencerro (a cowbell without a clapper, struck with a drumstick). The instruments of continuous pitch include two sirens and a string drum known as a lion's-roar, consisting of a medium-size wooden barrel with a parchment head through which a rosined string is drawn, the sound being produced by rubbing the string with a piece of cloth or leather. Varèse directed that a theremin—one of the first electronic instruments—might be substituted for the sirens.

The score displays the characteristic traits of Varèse's style, especially his uncanny ability to project masses of tensile sound that generate a sense of space. The ear is teased by complex rhythmic patterns whose subtle texture recalls the rhythms of African and Asian music. Varèse deploys his array of noisemakers on interlocking planes, analogous to the soprano, alto, tenor, and bass levels of the orchestra and choir. Used in this fashion, the percussion instruments create a harmony and counterpoint all their own. The sirens set up a continuous pitch. Their protracted wail, with its mounting sense of urgency, takes shape as a vast shadowy image of our Age of Anxiety. Most adroitly managed is the relaxation that comes toward the end of the piece with the entrance of the chimes and the tone clusters in the low register of the piano. The energy stored up in these sonorous "ions" has been released; the machine comes gently to rest.

Varèse's emphasis on sheer sonority presaged one of the most important trends of our era. In the light of what is happening today *Ionisation* stands revealed as one of the prophetic scores of the twentieth century.

Roger Sessions

"I am not trying to write 'modern,' 'American,' or 'neoclassic' music; I am seeking always and only the coherent and living expression of my musical ideas."

Roger Sessions (Brooklyn, New York, 1896–) spent much of his career at Princeton University, where he exerted a strong influence on several generations of American musicians. As a composer he has been responsive to the most significant currents of his time. The shimmering outlines of some of his early music bear witness to his brief involvement with impressionist procedures. There followed a period in which he adhered to the new classicism. His music during those years was marked by the sharply defined themes, vigorous rhythms, clear-cut tonality, and motoric drive associated with the neoclassic esthetic. These elements commingled, in the mature Sessions, with expressionist and twelve-tone influences.

The central place in Sessions's output is held by his eight symphonies, which bear the imprint of profound thought and concentrated emotion so characteristic of the composer. The Third (1957) belongs to a group of works marked by a more personal lyricism and a more accessible style than his earlier compositions. This group includes the Second String Quartet (1951), the *Idyll of Theocritus* for soprano and orchestra (1954), and the Mass of 1958. Also *The*

Roger Sessions.

Trial of Lucullus (1947), based on a play by Bertolt Brecht in which the celebrated Roman general stands trial after his death, his jury consisting of the little people whose lives were shattered by his triumphs. *Montezuma,* a full-scale opera on Cortez's conquest of the Aztecs, had its premiere in Berlin in 1964.

Symphony No. 1

The First Symphony (1927) is a sunny, unproblematic piece that sums up the characteristics of Sessions's neoclassic period. It is scored for a large orchestra, including piano.

I. *Giusto* (strict time), 2/4, E minor. The imperious trumpet flourish with which the movement opens leads into a closely woven texture of imitative counterpoint. The main theme is a compact idea that lends itself admirably to motivic treatment.

The emphasis on winds rather than strings makes for the bright "objective" sonority that was in vogue in the Twenties. The frequent dislocation of accent engenders a foreshortening of the measure which adds to the rhythmic tension. A contrasting motive emerges in the trumpets and clarinets. But a movement such as this depends upon the principle of continuous expansion as practiced by the Baroque rather than on the sectional contrasts of the Haydn-Mozart period. In the Recapitulation Sessions adroitly varies the musical fabric and distributes the thematic material among the voices in a different way.

II. *Largo,* 2/4, C major. This slow movement in A-B-A form is steeped in lyricism. The florid singing line draws inspiration from the arabesque of Bach. The emphasis is on the vibrant expressiveness of the strings. The soloistic treat-

ment of the instruments results in a chamber-music texture. In the middle part, clarinet and piano set up a diaphanous background of triplets for the melodic lines lightly traced by oboe and flute. The A section is repeated in curtailed form.

III. *Allegro vivace,* 2/4, E major. The finale captures the dancelike impulsion of the classical rondo. The rondo theme is properly vivacious, the texture is limpid, the color bright. A rhythmic intensification leads to a forthright coda and vigorous cadence in E.

Sessions's is a music surcharged with nobility of thought and feeling. It presents distinguished ideas in a distinguished way.

George Gershwin

"Jazz I regard as an American folk music; not the only one, but a very powerful one which is probably in the blood and feeling of the American people more than any other style of folk music. I believe that it can be made the basis of serious symphonic works of lasting value."

In terms of native endowment George Gershwin (1898–1937) was unquestionably one of the most gifted musicians this country has produced. The Brooklyn-born composer came out of the musical world of Broadway. Whereas serious composers used the jazz idiom with some degree of self-consciousness, it was his natural speech. His success in musical comedy made him all the more determined to bridge the distance between "popular" and "classical." He achieved this aim in the *Rhapsody in Blue* (1924), which carried his name around the globe. The following year he crossed the hitherto impassable barrier between Tin Pan Alley and Carnegie Hall when he played his Concerto in F with Walter Damrosch and the New York Symphony Orchestra.

Gershwin next tackled the Lisztian tone poem and produced *An American in Paris* (1928). He was not equipped to handle the large forms, but he had the gift of song; and this, like the talisman in fairy tales, guided him safely through

George Gershwin before his painting of Arnold Schoenberg.

dangers that might have felled another. His ambition to make jazz, as he said, "the basis of serious symphonic works" was rather naïve, considering that jazz and symphony issue from two unrelated worlds. What he did was to fill his orchestral works with melody, falling back on the dependable technique of repetition-and-sequence to round out the frame. Within the limits set for him by his goal, the method worked.

The case is different with *Porgy and Bess* (1935). As time goes on, Gershwin's masterpiece more and more takes on the character of a unique work. He had tenderness and compassion, and the instinct of the musical dramatist; he had the lyrics of his brother Ira, and the wonderful tunes to go with them. And so he captured, as Lawrence Gilman put it, "the wilderness and the pathos and tragic fervor that can so strangely agitate the souls of men."

George Gershwin, dead at thirty-nine—when he was on the threshold of important advances in his art—has remained something of a legend among us. Because he was so close to us we are inclined to view him within the Broadway frame. It is well to remember that so severe a judge as Arnold Schoenberg said of him, "I grieve over the deplorable loss to music, for there is no doubt that he was a great composer."

95 American Composers (II)

Aaron Copland

"I no longer feel the need of seeking out conscious Americanisms. Because we live here and work here, we can be certain that when our music is mature it will also be American in quality."

Aaron Copland (1900–) is generally recognized as the representative figure among present-day American composers. He manifests the serenity, clarity, and sense of balance that we regard as the essence of the classical temper.

Copland was born of Russian-Jewish parentage "on a street in Brooklyn that can only be described as drab. . . . Music was the last thing anyone would have connected with it." During his early twenties he studied in Paris with Nadia Boulanger, whose first full-time American pupil he was. When Boulanger was invited to give concerts in America, she asked Copland to write a work for her. This was the Symphony for Organ and Orchestra. Contemporary American music was still an exotic dish to New York audiences. After the first performance (1925) Walter Damrosch found it necessary to assuage the feelings of his subscribers. "If a young man at the age of twenty-three," he announced from the stage of Carnegie Hall, "can write a symphony like that, in five years he will

Aaron Copland.

be ready to commit murder." Damrosch's prophecy, as far as is known, has not been fulfilled.

In his growth as a composer Copland has mirrored the dominant trends of his time. After his return from Paris he turned to the jazz idiom, a phase that culminated in his brilliant Piano Concerto (1927). There followed a period during which the neoclassicist experimented with the abstract materials of his art; he produced his *Piano Variations* (1930), *Short Symphony* (1933), and *Statements for Orchestra* (1933–35). "During these years I began to feel an increasing dissatisfaction with the relations of the music-loving public and the living composer. It seemed to me that we composers were in danger of working in a vacuum." He realized that a new public for contemporary music was being created by the radio, phonograph, and film scores. "It made no sense to ignore them and to continue writing as if they did not exist. I felt that it was worth the effort to see if I couldn't say what I had to say in the simplest possible terms." In this fashion Copland was led to what became a most significant development after the Thirties: the attempt to simplify the new music so that it would communicate to a large public.

The decade that followed saw the production of the scores that established Copland's popularity. *El Salón México* (1936) is an orchestral piece based on Mexican melodies and rhythms. The three ballets are *Billy the Kid* (1938), *Rodeo* (1942), and *Appalachian Spring* (1944). Copland wrote two works for high-school students—the "play-opera" *Second Hurricane* (1937) and *Outdoor Overture* (1938). Among his film scores are *Quiet City* (1939), *Of Mice and Men* (1939), *Our Town* (1940), *The Red Pony* (1948), and *The Heiress*

(1949), which brought him an Academy Award. Two important works written in time of war are A *Lincoln Portrait* (1942), for speaker and chorus, on a text drawn from the Great Emancipator's speeches; and the Third Symphony (1944–46). In *Connotations for Orchestra* (1962), Copland showed himself receptive to the serial techniques of the twelve-tone school.

Billy the Kid

For the ballet based on the saga of Billy the Kid, Copland produced one of his freshest scores. In it are embedded either in whole or in part such cowboy classics as *I Ride an Old Paint, Great Grand-Dad,* and *The Dying Cowboy.* They are not quoted literally. What Copland does is to use these melodies as a point of departure for his own; they flavor the music but are assimilated to his personal style.

Billy the Kid—the Brooklyn-born William Bonney—had a brief but intense career as desperado and lover, in the course of which he became one of the legends of the Southwest. The ballet touches on the chief episodes of his life. We see him first as a boy of twelve when, his mother having been killed by a stray bullet in a street brawl, he stabs the man responsible for her death. Later, during a card game with his cronies, he is accused of cheating and kills the accuser. Captured after a running gun-battle, he is put in jail. He murders his

A scene from BILLY THE KID. (American Ballet Theatre production)

jailer and gets away. A romantic interlude ensues when he rejoins his Mexican sweetheart in the desert. But the menacing shadows close in on him. This time there is no escaping. At the close we hear a lament for the death of the dashing outlaw.

The concert suite contains about two-thirds of the music of the ballet. *The Open Prairie*, which serves as a Prologue, evokes a spacious landscape. The theme, announced by oboe, then clarinet, creates an outdoor atmosphere, while modal harmonies in parallel motion give a sense of space and remoteness:

This prelude unfolds in free form, woven out of the opening theme through a process of repetition and expansion. It reaches a fortissimo climax, and is followed by a scene that conjures up "a street in a frontier town." A theme, derived from the cowboy song *Great Grand-Dad*, is presented by piccolo "nonchalantly." Copland slightly changes the melody and gives it a sophisticated harmonic background:

The A-flat major tonality of this melody persists while a contrasting tune, in the key of F, is thrust against its last note. There results a striking polytonal effect:

The contrasting melody takes over. The following example shows how Copland sets it off through the use of dissonant harmony:

Polyrhythm results when the melody, in 4/4 time, is presented against an accompaniment in 3/4. A dance performed by Mexican women is based on *I Ride an Old Paint*. Copland changes the familiar tune, giving it a more distinctive profile:

This episode builds from a quiet beginning to a *fff* climax. The next, *Card Game* (Molto moderato) has the quality of wistful lyricism so characteristic of Copland. The setting is a starry night in the desert. The music projects a mood of gentle contemplation. In violent contrast is *Fight* (Allegro)—the pursuit of Billy and the gun battle—with its overtones of brutality. The *Celebration* that follows Billy's capture is properly brassy and gay. Copland presents a jaunty tune in a striking polytonal passage: the melody, in C major, is heard against a pedal point on C-sharp and G-sharp that suggests C-sharp major. The clash between the two keys points up the tune and makes it stand out against its background. Notice how the dotted rhythm points up the melody; notice also the asymmetrical structure: a phrase of four measures is answered by one of three.

Altogether lovely is the Epilogue (Lento moderato) in which the prairie music of the opening returns. The physical landscape is transformed into a poetic symbol of all that is vast and immutable. It is in passages such as these that Aaron Copland shows himself to be, as he has often been described, the most American of our composers.

Samuel Barber.

Samuel Barber

"I began composing at seven and have never stopped."

Samuel Barber, who was born in West Chester, Pennsylvania in 1910, is one of the best-known among his generation of American composers. Barber is an avowed romantic; his music is poetic and suffused with feeling. Nor is it averse to the grand gestures of the nineteenth-century tradition.

Best known of Barber's early works are the light-hearted Overture to *The School for Scandal* (1932); *Music for a Scene from Shelley* (1933); *Adagio for Strings* (1936); and the first *Essay for Orchestra*, which we will discuss. In the decade that followed Barber showed a deepening awareness of contemporary procedures. This development is manifest in such compositions as the Symphony No. 2 (1944, revised 1947); the *Second Essay for Orchestra* (1942); and the *Capricorn Concerto* (1944). The later works include *Knoxville: Summer of 1915*, a setting of a prose poem by James Agee (1947); *Medea's Meditation and Dance of Vengeance* (1955); the opera *Vanessa*, on a libretto by Gian-Carlo Menotti (1958); the Piano Concerto (1962), and the Shakespearean opera *Antony and Cleopatra* (1966).

Essay for Orchestra, No. 1

The *Essay for Orchestra* was written in 1937, when Barber was twenty-seven. The use of the word *essay* as a title conjures up the literary form in which ideas are developed concisely within an intimate framework.

The introductory section, Andante sostenuto, opens with the main theme on the violas and cellos. This contains a three-note motive that becomes a germi-

etc.

p espr.

573

nating force within the work. For example, it appears repeatedly in the melody, in the original pattern, in inversion, and in sequence.

The music mounts in urgency through an effective passage for the brass that culminates in a flourish. There follows the charming Allegro molto in ¾ time that constitutes the main body of the piece. This section captures the elfin lightness of the Mendelssohnian scherzo, but infused with the satanism that descended through the romantic era from Liszt and Berlioz to Mahler, whence it passed into the mainstream of twentieth-century music. The germinal motive appears in the horn in longer note values (augmentation) beneath the warblings of woodwinds and strings. A brilliant climax leads into the Largamente sostenuto (broad and sustained), in which the full orchestra presents the initial theme, fortissimo, in a mood of affirmation. The music subsides. At the very end the violins present the basic motive in inverted form.

Barber avoids the knotty problems of contemporary musical thought. He stems out of the romantic past, and uses his heritage with taste, imagination, and elegance.

Other Composers of the American School

Douglas Moore (Cutchogue, Long Island, 1893–1969) taught at Columbia University, where he was Edward MacDowell Professor of Music. He was a romantic at heart and regarded romanticism as a characteristic American trait. He had his greatest success in his sixties, with the production of his opera *The Ballad of Baby Doe* (1956), on a dramatically compelling libretto by John LaTouche. An earlier opera, *The Devil and Daniel Webster* (1938), with a libretto by Stephen Vincent Benét, also achieved wide popularity.

Walter Piston (Rockland, Maine, 1894–) is a leading representative of the international outlook among American composers. He believes that art limits itself through exclusive preoccupation with native themes. Piston is a neoclassicist; his music is urbane, polished, witty. He taught at Harvard University from 1926 until his retirement in 1960. Characteristic of his style are the Concerto for Orchestra (1934); the Concertino for piano and chamber orchestra (1937); and the Fourth Symphony (1950).

The art of Virgil Thomson (Kansas City, Missouri, 1896–) is rooted in the homespun hymns and songs, many of Civil War vintage, that were the natural inheritance of a boy growing up in the middle West. On this was superimposed the cultural tradition of Harvard; and upon that, during a fifteen years' residence in Paris, the Gallic approach to art and life whose foremost American spokesman he became. He came into prominence with the production in 1934 of *Four Saints in Three Acts* on a libretto by Gertrude Stein. Among Thomson's varied list of works are the *Symphony on a Hymn Tune* (1928); a symphonic sketch, *The Seine at Night* (1947); and several notable film scores, of which the best-known is *Louisiana Story* (1948).

Roy Harris (Lincoln County, Oklahoma, 1898–) was hailed in the early

Thomas Hart Benton (b. 1889), THE COTTON PICKERS. (The Metropolitan Museum of Art, New York; George A. Hearn Fund, 1933)
As American artists became more sure of themselves, they expressed in ever greater degree the life around them.

Thirties as the great hope of American music. For a decade he was the most played and most publicized composer in the country. Harris's music is American in its buoyancy and momentum. His neoclassic bent leads him to the large instrumental forms. Ten symphonies form the core of his output; the Third (1938) has remained his finest achievement, and is a notable contribution to the repertory of American symphonies.

Howard Hanson (Wahoo, Nebraska, 1896–) played a crucial role during the Twenties when the battle for American music had still to be won. As director of the Eastman School of Music and conductor of the Rochester Symphony Orchestra, he organized annual festivals of American music at which some of the most important works of the past quarter century received their first performance. In his own music Hanson is traditional and eclectic. Of his five symphonies the most important is the Second, the *Romantic* (1930).

William Schuman (New York City, 1910–) has shown an affinity for the large forms of instrumental music. This classicist esthetic combines with the robust Americanism of a typically urban mentality. His eight symphonies form the central item in his output; the Third (1941) is the best-known. The *American Festival Overture* (1939) and *New England Triptych* (1956) have also been widely played.

Gian Carlo Menotti was born in Cadegliano, Italy, in 1911. His inclusion in the American school stretches a point, as he has never renounced his Italian citizenship. But he has spent the greater part of his life in the United States— he came here when he was seventeen—and has won his greatest successes in this country. Besides, his librettos, which he writes himself, are generally in English. Menotti is the most successful opera composer of our day. He has created a series of lyric pieces that have spread his name throughout the musical world. The list includes *The Medium* (1946); *The Consul* (1950); *Amahl and the Night Visitors* (1951); *The Saint of Bleecker Street* (1954); *The Last Savage* (1963); and *Help! Help! The Globolinks!* (1968).

David Diamond (Rochester, New York, 1915–) projects a vivid personality in music that encompasses violence and tenderness, poetry and a core of strength. Diamond is a prolific composer; eight symphonies occupy the central position on his list. *Rounds for String Orchestra* (1944) has been widely played, as has his suite *Romeo and Juliet* (1947). Diamond's songs and choral music bear witness to an exacting literary taste and an evocative handling of text. The stage works include incidental music for *The Tempest* and for Tennessee Williams's *Rose Tattoo*.

Leonard Bernstein (Boston, 1918–) was the first American-born musical director of the New York Philharmonic, and the youngest ever appointed to the post. His serious works include the *Jeremiah Symphony* (1942); *The Age of Anxiety*, for piano and orchestra (1949), based on W. H. Auden's poem of that name; and the Serenade for violin, strings and percussion (1954), after Plato's *Symposium*. In his scores for Broadway musicals Bernstein achieves a sophisticated kind of musical theater that explodes with energy. The list includes *On the Town*, a full-length version of his ballet *Fancy Free* (1944); *Wonderful Town* (1953); *Candide* (1956); and the spectacularly successful *West Side Story* (1957).

Peter Mennin (Erie, Pennsylvania, 1923–) is head of the Juilliard School of Music in New York City. His music is marked by an easy handling of the large forms, melodious counterpoint, forward-driving rhythms, and an over-all sense of bustling energy. His seven symphonies show his steady growth in the manipulation of ideas. The weightiest items in his list, beside the symphonies, are the Concertato for Orchestra (1954); *Sonata Concertante* for violin (1958), which shows him moving toward a simplification of style; and the Piano Concerto of 1958.

The United States differs from European countries in one important respect: our people do not come from a single stock. On the contrary, ours is a melting-pot culture in which many national and racial groups are represented. This diversity is reflected in the backgrounds of our composers. For example, Walter

Piston, Gian Carlo Menotti, and Peter Mennin are of Italian origin. A number of composers are Jewish, among them George Gershwin, Aaron Copland, William Schuman, David Diamond, and Leonard Bernstein. Varèse came of French-Italian, Howard Hanson of Swedish stock. The Negro's strong musical gift showed itself at first mainly in the field of spirituals and jazz, which is the Negro's specific contribution to the music of America (see Chapter 96); but in the last half century he also mastered the techniques of serious music, both as composer and performer. Among the Negro composers of the modern American school may be mentioned William Grant Still (Woodville, Mississippi, 1895–); Ulysses Kay (Tucson, Arizona, 1917–); Howard Swanson (Atlanta, Georgia, 1909–); and Julia Perry (Lexington, Kentucky, 1924–).

We have mentioned only a handful among several generations of composers whose works reflect important currents of twentieth-century musical thought. To give anywhere near a full account of their work would carry us beyond the limits of this book. Enough has been said, however, to indicate the diversity of these composers and of the tendencies they represent.

96 American Jazz

"Jazz is the most astounding spontaneous musical event to take place anywhere since the Reformation."

Virgil Thomson

Jazz, by a rough definition-of-thumb, is an improvisational, Afro-American musical idiom. It makes use of elements of rhythm, melody, and harmony from Africa, and of melody and harmony from the European musical tradition. The influence of jazz, and of closely associated Afro-American idioms, has been so pervasive that by now most of our popular music is in an Afro-American idiom, and elements of jazz have permeated a good deal of our concert music as well. (It is only in this latter sense that a composer such as George Gershwin can be called a "jazz composer.")

If we know anything at all about jazz music, we are likely to know that it is, first of all, a player's art and that, at least in part, the player may make it up for us as he goes along. (An important consequence of this fact is that recordings are the only meaningful way to preserve jazz; unlike Western concert music, it is not reproduced from a written score, but freshly invented for every performance.) Improvisation, we saw was not unknown in some periods of European music—indeed, the ability to extemporize was once a fundamental part of the equipment of every accomplished musician. (For example, Bach, Handel, Mozart, and Beethoven were all famous for their keyboard improvisations.) But in practice, European music generally confined improvisation to one performer at a time. In jazz, certain things being agreed upon (a harmonic sequence, a tempo, and the roles of the instruments), as many as eight players may improvise at once—and this occurred even at the earliest stages of its history.

Jazz was, first of all, a secular music of black men in this country. The word was first applied, in about 1917, to a style that evolved in New Orleans around the turn of the century. Jazz has changed continuously since then; it has not remained static like some European popular idioms (that of Spanish flamenco music, for example). But changes in jazz are not matters of caprice or fashion, as they often are in other popular American idioms. Jazz music has developed and refined itself, learning from its own past and building on it, rather in the manner of an art music. And it has gained, in the process, the high respect of musicians of all persuasions throughout the world.

The Origins: New Orleans

In the immediate background of New Orleans jazz were two idioms: ragtime and the blues. *Ragtime*, a sprightly, optimistic music, was basically a keyboard style, and a kind of Afro-American version of the polka or the march. The most famous of rags, Scott Joplin's *Maple Leaf Rag* (1899), is made up of four little melodies in the form, ABACD. Ragtime continued to develop parallel to jazz, but by the time the earliest jazz recordings were made, it had clearly influenced the New Orleans idiom. Rag music itself has often been hopelessly vulgarized almost from its beginnings, played with stiff, inflexible rhythm on pianos deliberately made to jangle.

The *blues* is a native American musical and verse form, with no direct European and African antecedents that we know of. It probably began as an irregular, lamentatory chant, but by the time it was written down, it had a three-line stanza in which the first two lines were identical—for example:

> The moon looks lonesome when it's shining through the trees;
> The moon looks lonesome when it's shining through the trees.
> The way a man looks lonesome when his woman packs up to leave.

Musically, the blues form is twelve measures, four measures for each line of text, harmonized simply:

line 1		line 2		line 3	
harmony:	1	IV	I	V	I
measures:	4	2	2	2	2

In practice, various intermediate chords, and even some substitute chord patterns, have been used, at least since the second decade of this century.

The blues was not sung according to European ideas of "correct" pitch, but with a free use of "bent," "quavered," "glided," and otherwise emotionally inflected vocal sounds of various kinds. When the music was written down, these effects were imitated by the so-called "blues scale," in which the third, the seventh, and sometimes the fifth scale-degrees were lowered a semitone, producing a scale resembling the minor scale. But the blue notes are not really

● = a blue note, which may be as much as a half tone above or below the written pitch.

minor notes in a major context. In practice they may come almost anywhere. One can say, however, that in instrumental music the blue notes tend to gravitate to the third, fifth, and seventh steps. By the mid-1920s, instrumental blues in a variety of tempos and moods were common, and "playing the blues" for the instrumentalist could mean extemporizing a melody within a blues harmonic sequence; brass, reed, and string players, particularly, were able to reproduce the interpretive vocal sounds of the blues singers on their instruments. (It should be pointed out that many pieces with the word "blues" in their titles are not really in blues form. Indeed, the word "blues" is sometimes used as loosely and carelessly as the word "jazz." There are, however, eight-bar blues, a sort of shortened version of the twelve-measure form, and there are sixteen-measure blues which borrow European folk forms for their outlines.)

We should not leave the subject of the blues without mentioning the great woman blues-singer of the 1920s, Bessie Smith, whose classic performances include extemporized twelve-measure blues (*Lost Your Head Blues*) and combined forms (*Young Woman's Blues*). In such performances, the emotional depth and technical perfection of her singing, the simple poetry of her lyrics, and the antiphonal interplay of her accompanying instrumentalists were of a high order.

The blues is a fundamental form in jazz, accounting for perhaps forty per cent of the music. And blues practices are applied to other forms. The blues tradition itself has continued, meanwhile, to become the so-called "rhythm and blues" of more recent times, and it is, of course, the direct progenitor of "rock and roll" as well.

Another common form that we will encounter in jazz performances is of European origin—the thirty-two-bar song form, which is usually made up of four eight-bar phrases in the pattern AABA. (The B section is often called the *bridge*, or *release*.) Typical examples of this form are *I Got Rhythm, Body and Soul*, and *Lady Be Good*. In another type of thirty-two-bar song form sometimes found, the pattern AA′ is used, as in *Embraceable You, Pennies from Heaven*, or *Indiana*. (Most popular songs have an introductory verse as well as the thirty-two-bar refrain, but this verse is usually not used in jazz performances.)

In a typical jazz performance, each repetition of the sixteen-bar blues form or the thirty-two-bar song form is known as a *chorus*; the succession of choruses —some for full ensemble, some assigned as solos, duets, and the like, to the individual members of the group, amounts to a series of variations on a theme, using the blues or song as theme.

579

Jelly Roll Morton

The music of Ferdinand "Jelly Roll" Morton might be called a pianist's, composer's, and band leader's summary of Afro-American music and New Orleans jazz up to the mid-1920s. In his best recordings, Morton beautifully balances several things: what is composed and what can be improvised, what is up to the individual and what is up to the ensemble, the effectiveness of the parts and the demands of the whole.

Dead Man Blues (RCA Victor LPM–1649; recorded in 1926) is by a seven-piece ensemble; trumpet, clarinet, trombone, piano (Morton), banjo, string bass, and drums, supplemented at one point by two additional clarinets. It is a piece built on the twelve-measure blues form, but uses, in the manner of ragtime, three themes. After a bit of comic banter, it opens with the trombonist playing a breathy version of Chopin's *Funeral March*, with just a hint of humor. What follows may be schematically represented as:

Section	twelve-measure chorus	
A	1	ensemble in improvised polyphony
A′	2	clarinet solo (Omer Simeon)
B	3	trumpet solo (George Mitchell)
B′	4	trumpet solo continues
C	5	three clarinets in harmony
C′	6	clarinets repeat, with trombone countermelody (Edward "Kid" Ory)
A″	7	ensemble in improvised polyphony

The first chorus is in the improvised polyphony that was a feature of the New Orleans or "Dixieland" style, which, in Morton's version, dances and interweaves with an exceptional lightness and lack of stridency. The trumpeter has the lead melody, which he is free to modify and embellish, the clarinetist plays a kind of continuous counterpoint, the trombonist a simpler basslike part, and the rhythm instruments provide a harmonic and percussive accompaniment. In the second chorus, the clarinetist breaks away for a one-chorus variation.

The B theme is stated in the trumpeter's version, conceived as a continuous two-chorus variation and not simply one chorus followed by another. The tight, contrasting "trio" melody (C) is stated by the three clarinets in simple, close harmony. As they repeat, the trombone re-enters with a simple, mournful improvisation beneath them. This two-part polyphony also makes a transition to the final chorus, a new three-part polyphonic variation on the A theme that is thus both a partial recapitulation and a climax.

A three-minute miniature, then, made of simple materials, with a musical intelligence guiding its patterns of likeness and contrast, partly created on the spur of the moment.

There is a hint, in the C theme of *Dead Man Blues*, of what Morton called

Jelly Roll Morton.

the "Spanish tinge," the habañera or tango rhythm, which, with further syncopation, came to be known as the "Charleston" rhythm. A variant of the Charleston dance, the "Black Bottom," is an intermittently recurring effect in Morton's
Black Bottom Stomp (RCA Victor LPM–1649; recorded in 1926). Here the
piece is in two parts, one built on sixteen-measure choruses and one on twenty,
but through variation there are in effect four (or perhaps five) themes evolved
in the performance; the basic tempo is much faster than the previous example.

Introduction	(8 bars)	ensemble, four bars repeated exactly
A	(16)	ensemble, with clarinet (Simeon) in evidence
	(16)	trumpet (Mitchell) and ensemble exchange four-bar phrases
A[1]	(16)	clarinet (Simeon) accompanied by banjo (Johnny St. Cyr) only (close to theme)
Interlude	(4)	modulation
B	(20)	ensemble, now in polyphony, with a "break" (the rhythm section ceases to accompany for two bars) shared by trumpet (Mitchell) and trombone (Ory), and a very effective use of the string bass (John Lindsay)
B[1]	(20)	clarinet solo (Simeon) nonthematic; the last two bars by the ensemble with "Black Bottom" accents
B[2]	(20)	piano solo (Morton), unaccompanied, with final two bars as in B[1]

B[3]	(20)	trumpet (Mitchell) over a stop-time rhythm (a series of two-bar breaks) suggested by the "Black Bottom" accents
B[4]	(20)	banjo solo (St. Cyr), four-beat accents, occasionally broken
B[5]	(20)	ensemble, very light, with a two bar cymbal break at bar 7
B[6]	(20)	full ensemble, forte, with pronounced tom-tom and string bass accents, and a surprise trombone break
Coda	(2)	

Such an outline can only hint at the echoed antiphonal patterns, the echoed breaks and rhythms that are surprises in themselves but which through their recurrence give order to the performance. And it can only suggest the variety of textures, timbres, and instrumental combinations Morton has used in this brief piece. Yet for all its variety, *Black Bottom Stomp* is as uncluttered as one could imagine, flowing from beginning to end with an inevitability that the novice may enjoy, and with a natural, unpretentious skill that the most sophisticated listener may miss.

One could add to the list of pieces that are among Morton's best such slower ones as *Smoke House Blues* (not a twelve-measure blues) and the quartet *Mournful Serenade*, and such faster "Stomps" as *The Chant* and *Grandpa's Spells*.

The virtues of Morton's best records are those of a jazz composer working with skillful, carefully rehearsed players. Those of the other celebrated New Orleans ensemble, that of Joseph "King" Oliver, are those of a group of improvising, blues-oriented musicians who understood each other's work so well that they could complement and even anticipate each other almost by reflex. But by 1923, when Oliver's group made its first recordings, the ensemble featured a young second cornetist whose innovative work would soon change the musical vocabulary of jazz. His name was Louis Armstrong.

Louis Armstrong

It may be difficult for some of us to realize—particularly those who may have seen only his television appearances—what a great instrumentalist and important American musician Louis Armstrong has been. His influence is everywhere. Anyone, anywhere in the world, in any musical idiom, who writes for trumpet is inevitably influenced by what Louis Armstrong and his progeny have shown can be done with the instrument. Our symphonic brass players use an unconscious vibrato in performing Bach simply because Armstrong has one. All of our jazz, real and popularized, is different because of him, and our popular singers of all kinds are deeply in his debt.

Louis Armstrong.

Although Armstrong was a superb, inventive melodist, and, for his time, imaginative (and wholly appropriate) in harmony as well, the essence of his contribution was rhythmic. Indeed the word "swing" was originally coined by musicians as a way of describing Louis Armstrong's unique melodic rhythm, and the term has become a part of the technical vocabulary of jazz. It has never been defined but has to do with the rhythmic momentum of the music. The so-called "swing style" of the 1930s is actually a Louis Armstrong style, in which soloists and composer-arrangers for the "big bands" (of about fourteen pieces) undertook to adopt and explore his ideas. But the term "swing" has been applied to subsequent styles, and even made retroactive to earlier styles as a kind of shorthand method of indicating the rhythmic character proper to the music. As in all musics, some otherwise quite capable musicians in jazz have rhythmic problems, i.e., they don't swing.

A description can account for very little in discussing the work of a performer such as Armstrong, and even a music example is limited: in musical notation, a jazz solo is the merest sketch, lacking the nuances of attack, tone, and inflection that are all-important. One way of isolating Armstrong's contribution is to compare him with what was going on around him in his early days—for example, the King Oliver ensemble's *Weather Bird Rag* contrasted to Armstrong's duet of the piece with pianist Earl Hines—or to hear him in the context of the New York ensembles with which he recorded in 1924, when he was a member of Fletcher Henderson's orchestra—as in *I Ain't Gonna Play No Second Fiddle*, with a Perry Bradford group, where he picks up the entire performance and makes it soar during his brilliant solo. Two blues performances from the mid-20s should be cited: Armstrong's series of five, passionate descending phrases from a high B-flat on *S. O. L. Blues*, and the startling stop-time chorus on the innocently titled *Potato Head Blues*.

There are examples in Armstrong's recorded repertory of solos that are in highly individual embellishment styles, of solos that are entirely improvised— that is, that are harmonically-oriented inventions with little or no melodic reference to a theme (and we hear these on both blues and nonblues structures). But perhaps Armstrong's greatest talent is his spontaneous ability to recompose a popular melody. He alters a note here, momentarily hurries this phrase, delays that one; he spots a cliché turn of melody and avoids it, often substituting a much superior phrase of his own invention. He can undertake a good popular melody like *I Gotta Right to Sing the Blues* and transform it, by an orderly simplification, into eloquence. He can take *I've Got the World on a String* and transform it by rhythmic ingenuity into something personal. Or he can take a most banal tune like *That's My Home*, and come up with true eloquence. (Incidentally, one must simply overlook the work of certain of Armstrong's accompanists at this period. It is partly because few players functioned on his level, of course, but it is also because Armstrong concerned himself primarily with his own improvising.)

It has been said that a great artist always suggests more things than either he or his immediate following can explore. And there are certain of Armstrong's solos with implications, particularly rhythmic implications, that jazzmen did not begin to deal with for over a decade. These include *West End Blues* (1928), *Sweethearts on Parade* (1930), *Between the Devil and the Deep Blue Sea* (the faster "3" take, 1931), and his second version of *Basin Street Blues* (1933).

Armstrong's portions of *West End Blues* (Columbia CL–853) represent a balance of striking virtuosity and eloquent simplicity—the opening, downward-then-upward phrase with its unusual change of tempo in measure 3, and the longer, descending phrase, extended by sequence and repetition to reach a resting place:

The first chorus begins calmly and simply, and then builds in a series of rising triplet arpeggios to a high B-flat:

After a trombone chorus, Armstrong takes part as singer in a duet with the clarinet, the two alternating phrases back and forth. The fourth chorus is taken by Earl Hines (piano), and then Armstrong launches the final strain with a passionately held high B-flat, which leads him to a series of rapid, complex ascending and descending fragments:

There is no exact precedent in Western music for such a unique combination of distillation, embellishment, and invention as one hears in Armstrong's improvising, and for it one jazz critic (André Hodeir) has borrowed the grammarian's term "paraphrase."

Duke Ellington

We mentioned above that in 1924 Louis Armstrong played with the New York orchestra of Fletcher Henderson, and from that combination emerged the beginnings of the so-called "big-band" jazz that dominated popular music in the 1930s. But the highest achievements in that idiom belong to the composer-pianist-bandleader Edward Kennedy "Duke" Ellington.

Ellington composed many well-known popular melodies, and is also the ambitious author of several long concert works of various kinds. But the great Ellington is the Ellington of the instrumental miniatures.

Duke Ellington.

There are excellences from every period of Ellington's career, from the 1920s onward, and the study of this great musician's development is a subject in itself. But the works that began to appear about 1938 announced his real maturity. The orchestra at that period included two trumpets and one cornet; three trombones (one a valve trombone—i.e., with valves like a trumpet instead of the more usual slide); two tenor saxophones, two alto saxophones, and a baritone saxophone, whose players doubled on clarinets; Ellington's piano; guitar; string bass; and drums.

Ellington's music retains the earthy, fundamental eloquence of the folk idiom, played by a relatively large ensemble in sometimes quite sophisticated scorings. His works are true collaborations between himself and his musicians, and he does not write, let us say, for just the baritone saxophone—he writes for Harry Carney's particular baritone saxophone sound or for Johnny Hodges' alto saxophone sound. With a use of various brass mutes and the imaginative employment of instrumental combinations, scored in imaginative ways, Ellington has achieved a wide range of personal colors and effects. And he was able to balance composition and improvisation in performances that are wholes, greater than the sum of their parts.

Ko-ko (RCA Victor LPM–1715; recorded in 1940) is a melodically simple, harmonically sophisticated minor blues consisting of an introduction, eight choruses, and a coda. The theme-statement is carried by Juan Tizol's valve trombone and the ensemble, in a kind of antiphonal, call-and-response sharing of the melody. The next two choruses feature Joe Nanton's trombone, played with a type of mute called a plunger, which the player can manipulate in the bell of his horn to vary the tone color as he improvises. The muted brass figure that accompanies Nanton continues in a simplified variant into the following chorus. In that chorus, Ellington on the piano introduces new thematic material, but the brass figure ties the two sections together. His music is full of that sort of orderly patterning of likeness and contrast.

The *Concerto for Cootie* (RCA Victor LPM-1715; recorded in 1940), written for Ellington's resourceful trumpeter Charles "Cootie" Williams, is a harmonically simple, but structurally and sonorously varied work. It is dedicated to the wide and flexible variety of sounds that Williams achieves on open horn and with a variety of straight, cup, and manipulated plunger mutes. The performance may be outlined briefly as A, A', B, A'', transition, C, A''', coda. Thus, the first and main section of the piece uses the standard song form, AABA. The A phrase is, however, ten measures instead of the usual eight, and in each of its appearances Ellington offers a variation on A for both the soloist and his accompaniment. (As with several of Ellington's instrumentals works, this one was simplified when it was made into a popular song, called *Do Nothin' Till You Hear From Me.*) After a transition for a key change, Williams states the sixteen-bar C theme on open horn, an excellent, expansive melodic contrast to the previous themes. He then returns to a plaintive, short (six-measure) variation of A, followed by an ingenious extended coda of ten measures.

Probably the test of a composer of Ellington's relative sophistication lies in how he handles the simplest of materials. He did brilliantly with the twelve-measure blues on *Ko-ko*, as we have seen. In *Harlem Air Shaft*, Ellington built one of his best pieces out of the imaginative use of a simple, repetitive figure of the kind jazz musicians call a *riff*. And in *Blue Serge* (RCA Victor LPM–1364; recorded in 1941) he undertook the eight-bar blues. This performance might be sketched as follows:

Introduction	four measures (in which Barney Bigard's clarinet leads and in which the theme is sketched) plus two measures of trombone vamp ("filler" material)
Chorus 1	theme, interpreted by Ray Nance's trumpet; trombones continue behind him (eight measures)
Chorus 2	a thematic variation using brass and reeds, trombones variously audible (eight measures plus two)
Chorus 3	Joe Nanton's trombone (eight measures, without a cadence, leading to next chorus)
Chorus 4	brass with plunger mutes dominate (six measures), piano (two measures)
Chorus 5	piano continues, restoring the theme (eight measures)
Chorus 6	brass plus an improvisation by Ben Webster's tenor saxophone (twelve = eight + four measures)
Chorus 7	an ensemble variation that is barely thematic. (eight measures)

Notice the imaginative ways Ellington has varied the implicit monotony of his brief form. He sets up a kind of "floating" two bars in his introduction; he uses it to extend his second chorus, uses it to break up his fourth chorus; and by doubling it to four measures, he gives himself a twelve-bar phrase at the sixth chorus. Choruses 3, 4, and 5 are tied together by leaving Chorus 3 unresolved and by introducing the piano solo at bar 7 in the fourth chorus and continuing it throughout the eighth. Finally, to have ended *Blue Serge* with only a somber, moody variation and no further recapitulation of the theme is the sort of brilliant, intuitive stroke for which one can only invoke a word like "genius."

Count Basie

Using his work as their guide, Louis Armstrong's most capable followers were able to work out personal styles, styles that showed the individuality of instrumental sound and interpretation of melody that are required of a jazz musician. Tenor saxophonist Coleman Hawkins, for example, built solos, like his celebrated *Body and Soul* (1937), on an adroit use of arpeggios. Trumpeter Roy Eldridge's best improvisations, like *Rockin' Chair* or *I Surrender Dear*, make only spare or even indirect use of Armstrong's ideas. The singer Billie Holiday brought to her songs the powers of an exceptional actress, and showed an ability at melodic paraphrase comparable to Armstrong's, as can be seen from her version of *These Foolish Things* (1952) (Verve V-8338-2):

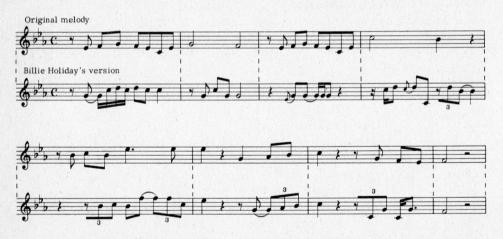

Reprinted by permission of the Estate of Eleanora McKay a/k/a Billie Holiday. *These Foolish Things* © Copyright 1935 by Boosey & Co. Ltd., London, England. Rights for the U.S.A. and Canada assigned to Bourne Co., 136 W. 52nd St., New York, N.Y. Used by permission of Bourne Co. Copyright renewed.

Pianist Art Tatum absorbed ideas of swing, and developed a largely ornamental style that showed a superb pianistic technique and an outstanding harmonic imagination—one might cite recordings like *Willow, Weep for Me* or *Too Marvelous for Words*.

By 1932, the big bands had begun to absorb Armstrong's basic rhythmic ideas and developed an ensemble swing in his manner. And in 1937, there appeared a

Willem de Kooning (1904–), WOMAN, I (Collection, The Museum of Modern Art, New York)

In the paintings of de Kooning, the demands of abstract form and color are beginning to overcome representational elements.

Robert Rauschenberg (1925–), BED (Collection of Mr. and Mrs. Leo Castelli)

A characteristic of pop art is the combination of paint and everyday objects such as cloth.

jazz orchestra which was able to build on those ideas, that of pianist William "Count" Basie. The scores were relatively simple, the ensemble was spirited, the rhythm section played with a new lightness, and the emphasis was on the soloists.

The leader's piano is a thing of deceptive simplicity. His ideas seem few, yet he never uses them monotonously; his touch is delicate, buoyant, and the bane of his imitators; and his ability to improvise orderly, sequential melodies is outstanding. The Basie orchestra's most important soloist was the tenor saxophonist Lester Young, whose swing was impeccable and whose sound was light, airy, and almost vibrato-less. Young was rhythmically imaginative—there were no "strong" or "weak" beats for him. His phrasing was asymmetrical, not confined to the traditional four- and eight-bar units. And Young was often highhanded with the harmonic structure of a piece. Thus his solos have a constant element of suspense and surprise, which his abilities as a melodist ultimately resolve.

Doggin' Around (Decca DXS–7170; recorded in 1938) gives a good introduction to both Basie and Young. The former's piano solo (which follows a long tenor sax solo and shorter ones on trumpet and baritone sax) is built almost entirely around his opening idea—a little fragment which he phrases and rephrases, expands, modifies, simplifies, for thirty-two measures. Young begins with a kind of warm-up or warning beneath Basie's final two bars. His opening phrase is only one note in the first measure. His next phrase begins at bar 2 and dances with a graceful complexity through bar 7. His eighth bar is silent, perhaps balancing that single note in the first bar. Bar 9 begins with a melodic link to bar 7. And so on.

Charlie Parker

In the Basie orchestra, then, we see the beginnings of change. That change culminates in the genius of alto saxophonist Charlie Parker, and was expressed, in 1945, in an innovative series of recordings done in collaboration with trumpeter John "Dizzy" Gillespie.

Parker was as harmonically exact as Coleman Hawkins, but as harmonically imaginative as Art Tatum. Rhythmically he was even more imaginative than Lester Young, and his accents might fall on any of the beats or variously in between the beats. He was a virtuoso saxophonist and an outstanding, inventive melodist. And he took up some of Louis Armstrong's most advanced ideas where the trumpeter had left them over a decade earlier.

His 1947 improvisation on *Embraceable You* (Roost 2210) opens with a sixnote motive that is repeated five times, although it is variously pronounced and moved around to fit the piece's chord changes. On its fifth appearance, it is the opening to an intricate burst of melody which ultimately comes to rest with a variant of the five-note motive. The little phrase subsequently appears and reappears in various guises (reaccented, condensed, expanded) in the solo, acting

Charlie Parker.

as a kind of organized reference point. Furthermore, in its general contours, the *Embraceable You* improvisation begins simply, builds to a complexity of longer phrases and shorter note values, then gradually returns to simple lyricism at its end. In jazz improvisation such as this, we hear a kind of instrumental melody considerably removed from popular song writing:

Embraceable You (G. & I. Gershwin) © 1930 by New World Music Corp. Used by permission of Warner Bros. Music. All rights reserved.

Lady be Good (Verve V–68002; 1946), recorded during a concert, is virtually an exposition of Parker's style and its relationship to the past. Parker's first five notes belong to Gershwin's tune, but he uses them to introduce a phrase of his own of quite different import. He follows this with a simple riff out of the blues tradition. His next phrase grows out of that riff and is also a kind of reverse echo of his opening phrase. A dancing descent of short notes next predicts the direction of the rest of his solo, as Parker gradually moves more directly into the rhythmic and melodic innovations he brought to the music.

Parker's innovations in jazz center around his innovations in rhythm, as did those of Louis Armstrong. Indeed, one might almost tell the story of Afro-American music and its evolution in rhythmic terms. The earliest music of which we have any record that shows an African influence, the so-called "Minstrel songs," have a rhythm based on a half note: for example, "RUfus, RAStus, JOHNson, BROWN." Ragtime broke up that half-note rhythm with syncopation, and in later ragtime style, the same song might go something like "RUfus a-RAS-tus a-JOHNson BROWN."

New Orleans jazz is fascinating in its rhythmic evolution, for we have phonograph records that carry it from a somewhat clipped, jerky rhythmic style, barely out of ragtime, to a style like that of clarinetist and soprano saxophonist Sidney Bechet, who came close to Louis Armstrong's rhythmic discoveries, and that of Armstrong himself. One may say, very roughly indeed, that Armstrong's rhythmic ideas are based on a quarter note, and Parker's on an eighth note.

An important aspect of the rhythmic evolution of jazz is the response of the rhythm sections to the innovations of the soloists. In the Basie orchestra, for example, the rhythm section played four evenly-accented quarter notes—the full expression, perhaps, of the kind of accompaniment that Armstrong's melodic rhythm had implied. But there were further refinements. The rhythmic lead passed to the string bass, playing quarter notes pizzicato, and to the drummer's cymbals. Basie himself frequently dropped the time-keeping, "oom-pah," left-hand figures of earlier pianists. Later, "rhythm guitar" (chords struck four to the bar) was eliminated from the jazz ensemble, and drummers, carrying the basic pulse on a "ride" (suspended) cymbal with (usually) the right hand, were free to make interplaying, polyrhythmic accents on snare drum and on other cymbals with the left hand, and on the bass drum with the right foot.

An excellent expression of a jazz drummer's response to Charlie Parker can be heard in Max Roach's work on a piece with the percussive, onomatopoetic title *Klacktoveedsedstene* (Roost 2210). The main theme is rather weak, but Roach's responses throughout the performance amount to a spontaneous, interplaying percussion part. Parker's solo in the second chorus is a wonder. For his first sixteen measures (the piece is in AABA song form), he seems to be tossing out intriguing but random phases, almost like a bass part, but when he plunges into the second sixteen, Parker lets us know that the piecemeal approach was more apparent than real, and very much a part of his plan.

Thelonious Monk

In what has preceded, it may seem that jazz has had two kinds of leadership: that of innovative, improvising soloists who periodically renew its basic vocabulary; and that of composers who give it a compositional synthesis and ensemble form. Further, the music seems to move in a kind of pendulum swing from great composer to great player—that is, from Morton to Armstrong to Ellington to Parker.

If that is a true version of the way jazz has evolved, one would expect a composer to emerge after Parker. And in the mid-1950s, jazz musicians began to turn to pianist-composer Thelonious Monk for guidance. Monk had been around earlier, making some of his best recordings, but his approach was somewhat unorthodox and had been overlooked by musicians and the public alike.

Monk is truly a hand-made artist, and his techniques are all jazz techniques. He has written several major pieces, and performed them in small ensembles, in which over-all form is as important as content—and in which form itself is almost as improvisational as the solos themselves.

Misterioso (Blue Note 81510; 1948) is a Monk blues, performed by a quartet featuring the leader's piano and the vibraphone of Milt Jackson. The performance opens without an introduction as Jackson and Monk state the theme, with the bass and drums phrasing along with them. The melody is an original version of what is essentially a traditional idea, based on what a jazz musician would call "walking" sixths—a melody made up of sixth degrees of different scales.

In the second chorus, the bass and drums begin a more conventional accompaniment and Jackson begins to improvise the blues. Monk, however, does not play standard blues-chord changes behind Jackson; he plays something that seems both related and not related to his theme. Monk plays "blue" sevenths, the next "implied" note of his theme, if you will. It is as if Monk were saying, "This is not just the blues in this key, this is my blues called *Misterioso*, and however much we make this up as we go along, something needs to make it *Misterioso* all the way through." In his own solo, Monk echos the upward, walking movement of the theme. And in the final chorus Monk lets Jackson carry the theme, while he counterpoints a kind of "spread-out" version of his previous accompaniment, in a recapitulation not only of the theme but, in effect, of the whole performance. (There is, incidentally, another version of *Misterioso* on Blue Note 81509, recorded at the same time as this one—more "regular," much less successful, but offering an interesting and instructive comparison nevertheless.)

Other notable Monk recordings include *Evidence, Criss Cross, Eronel, Four in One,* and his apparently simple but quite perceptive version of such standard pieces as *Smoke Gets in Your Eyes* and *I Should Care.* There is also an outstanding quartet recording of Monk's *Trinkle Tinkle*, with saxophonist John Coltrane, on which Monk resourcefully evokes a variety of textures from his four instruments. And there is a fascinating blues improvisation by Monk on *Bags' Groove* in which he spins chorus after chorus out of his brief opening idea, and uses space, rest, and silence as expressively as notes themselves.

One aspect of order in Monk's music is his return to a very personal use of thematic or melodic variation and paraphrase, rather than using harmonic variation alone. And an outstanding "pupil" of Monk's in this regard is tenor saxophonist Sonny Rollins, whose *Blue 7* is a sustained eight minutes of thematic improvisation (based on the hint in Monk's *Misterioso*), and whose *Blues for Philly Joe* turns out to be a kind of improvisational blues rondo that might be outlined as A, A, A' A", A''', B, C, A'''', D, D', E, A, A. (Between E and the final two As come piano and bass solos and exchanges of four-bar phrases between Rollins and drummer "Philly Joe" Jones.)

The vibraphonist Milt Jackson was a participant in several of Thelonious Monk's best recordings. However, he is regularly a member of the Modern Jazz Quartet; and that ensemble, in its somewhat more conservative way, has arrived at an improvisational, over-all form comparable to Monk's on pieces such as *Django, Bluesology*, and the like.

Ornette Coleman

By the late 1950s, jazz musicians had become so adroit at inventing their melodies within harmonic guidelines that it seemed time to try another approach. Trumpeter Miles Davis recorded a recital he called *Kind of Blue* that used several different approaches. On *So What?*, for example, he used AABA song form and assigned only the Dorian mode (see p. 315), to the A phrases, and the same mode a half tone higher for the B phrases, as a basis for the solos. The performance, particularly for Davis and saxophonist John Coltrane, is a classic.

Coincidentally a young alto saxophonist named Ornette Coleman was working on a similar approach to improvisation. The best introduction to Coleman's work is to go directly to a recording. *Lonely Woman* (Atlantic S–1317; 1959) begins with bass and drums, each stating a different rhythm and different tempo. The trumpet (Don Cherry) and alto sax enter at an unexpected point and begin stating the theme in a third, dirge-like tempo. One thing immediately noticeable is that, even when they are playing together, the melody instruments are free to interpret a theme individually.

At certain points in Coleman's theme, the trumpet rests and the alto continues on its own. The piece is in an AABA form, with Coleman taking the B release as a solo. The main improvisation also goes to Coleman, and something that was evident from the beginning becomes even more so. Intonation ("playing in tune") in this music is rather free and a matter of emotion and interpretation. (Coleman's own words on the matter are, "You can play sharp in tune or flat in tune"; thus a D in a context of sadness shouldn't sound the same as a D representing joy.) A writer on art music would say that Coleman uses "microtones." In jazz terms, Coleman has extended the idea of the vocally inflected blue notes to include whole phrases and episodes.

In improvising, Coleman generally stays within the key of a performance. But at certain points he does burst out of key into a momentary atonality. Since Coleman does not follow a chord pattern that would be implied by his themes, or necessarily the outline of phrases his theme sets up, he and his bass player often present a kind of freely improvised, mutually inspiring counterpoint which may momentarily clash dissonantly. This further contributes to the atmoshpere of atonality in his music.

Such things are particularly evident in *Congeniality* (Atlantic S–1317; 1959), which has a celebrated Coleman solo. One might assume that such free music, played with such raw emotion as his, invites a kind of melodic and harmonic chaos. But Coleman is the most orderly of players: a little idea appears, is turned and rephrased in every conceivable way until it yields a new idea which, in turn, is treated sequentially. And, above all, Coleman's melodic rhythm is fresh, traditional, and personal all at once, and freer and more varied than what had preceeded him.

Coleman's music shows that since improvised variation is, after all, the main attraction in small ensemble jazz, a solo need not be obeisant in structure or harmony to an opening theme. In performances like *The Riddle* and *Garden of Souls*, Coleman showed also that spontaneous or evolving changes of tempo, executed by the soloist and his accompaniment, can be functional aspects of a jazz musician's development of his musical ideas.

The music of Ornette Coleman is innovative, but its innovations are based on sound insight into the nature of jazz and the high accomplishments of its past. It provides a solid body of achievement on its own, and at the same time reaffirms the continuing growth of this indigenous and important American art.

PART EIGHT

———

THE
NEW MUSIC

———

"Composers are now able as never before to satisfy the dictates of that inner ear of the imagination."
                                                    Edgard Varèse

97 New Directions

"From Schoenberg I learned that tradition is a home we must love and forgo."

Lukas Foss

We have seen that the term "new music" has been used throughout history. Has not every generation of creative musicians produced sounds and styles that had never been heard before? All the same, the years since World War II have seen such far-reaching innovations in the art that we are perhaps more justified than any previous generation in applying the label to the music of the present. In effect, we have witnessed nothing less than the birth of a new world of sound.

Mid-Century Trends in the Arts

Only rarely does an important movement in art come into being without precursors. It should therefore not surprise us that several elements of avant-garde art can be traced back to earlier developments. For example, in the years immediately before the First World War, the Italian movement known as *futurism* attracted musicians who aspired to an "art of noises" that foreshadowed the achievements of Varèse and of electronic music. Another precursor was the *dada* movement, which grew up in Zurich during the War and after 1918 spread to other major art centers. The dadaists, in reaction to the horrors of the bloodbath that engulfed Europe, rejected the concept of Art with a capital A—that is, something to be put on a pedestal and reverently admired; to make their point, they produced works of manifest absurdity. This nose-thumbing spirit of dadaism was reflected in the music of many composers, especially in France, during the twenties; several decades later it was to influence the American composer John Cage. The dada group, which included artists like Hans Arp, Marcel Duchamp, and Kurt Schwitters, subsequently merged

Franz Kline (b. 1910), MAHONING. (Whitney Museum of American Art, New York; Gift of the Friends of the Whitney Museum)
In abstract expressionist painting, space and mass become independent values, liberated from the need to represent the physical world.

into the school of *surrealists,* who exploited the symbolism of dreams. The best-known surrealists, such as the writers Guillaume Apollinaire and André Breton, the painters Giorgio de Chirico, Max Ernst, and Salvador Dali, organized the indiscipline of dada into a visionary art based on the disassociated and distorted images of the world of dreams. Other elements entering into the family tree of contemporary art were *cubism,* the Paris-based style of painting embodied in the work of Pablo Picasso, Georges Braque, and Juan Gris, which encouraged the painter to construct a visual world in terms of geometric patterns; and expressionism, which we discussed in Chapter 82.

Art since the Second World War has unfolded against a background of unceasing social turmoil. In this regard, of course, the 1950s and '60s have been no different from many decades that preceded them. However, there can be no question that, as the second half of the century wore on, the problems confronting civilization became steadily more severe. The knowledge that man has finally achieved the capacity to wipe himself off the face of the earth broods over our time and feeds its unease. The fixed laws and certainties of Newtonian

Henry Moore (b.1898), LINCOLN CENTER RECLINING FIGURE. (©Lincoln Center for the
Performing Arts, Inc., 1965; photograph by Ezra Stoller Associates)

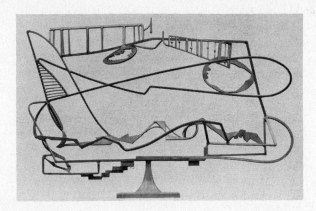

David Smith (1906-65), HUDSON RIVER LANDSCAPE. (Whitney Museum of American Art,
New York; photograph by Geoffrey Clements)

Contemporary sculpture concentrates on pure line and form.

601

physics have given way to a relativistic view of the universe in which chance and accident, the probable and unpredictable, are seen to have an increasingly important place. The moral imperatives that we inherited from our forebears are being questioned as never before. This restlessness of spirit is inevitably reflected in the arts, which are passing through a period of violent experimentation with new media, new materials, new techniques. Artists are freeing themselves from every vestige of the past in order to explore new areas of thought and feeling. Some even prefer to reject thought and feeling altogether.

Since the human eye responds more readily to fresh impressions than does the ear, contemporary painting and sculpture have reached a wider public than has contemporary music. The trend away from objective painting guaranteed the supremacy of *abstract expressionism* in this country during the 1950s and '60s. In the canvases of such men as Robert Motherwell, Jackson Pollock, Willem de Kooning, Franz Kline, and Philip Guston, space, mass, and color are freed from the need to imitate objects in the real world; they become values in the autonomous realm of painting. In other words, the abstract expressionists strengthened the tradition of "pure" painting—pure, that is, in its independence of external reality. The urge toward abstraction has been felt equally in contemporary sculpture, as is evident in the work of such artists as Henry Moore, Isamu Noguchi, and David Smith.

At the same time, a new kind of realism has come into being in the art of Jasper Johns, Robert Rauschenberg, and their fellows, who owe some of their inspiration to the dadaists of four decades earlier. Rauschenberg's aim, as he put it, was to work "in the gap between life and art." This trend culminated in *pop art*, which draws its themes and techniques from modern urban life: machines, advertisements, comic strips, movies, commercial photography, and familiar objects connected with everyday living. The desire to function "in the gap between life and art" motivates Andy Warhol's *Four Campbell Soup Cans* and *Brillo Boxes*, Jim Dine's *Shovel* and *A Nice Pair of Boots*, Claes Oldenburg's monumental *Bacon, Lettuce and Tomato* and *Dual Hamburgers*. Pop art has absorbed the literal vision of photography and the silk-screen techniques of reproducing photographs on canvas; also the dadalike inclusion of incongruous objects into art works. For example, Rauschenberg has incorporated into his abstract oils a quilt and pillow, a radio, Coke bottles, electric clocks, and fans. These impart to his paintings the three-dimensional quality of sculpture. In this respect he is one of an influential group that is determined to expand the resources of the painter's art.

In a related vein, new styles of art have grown up because of the availability of new materials. The sculptor no longer works simply with traditional marble and bronze, but reaches out to employ wood, new types of concrete, and a variety of plastics—clear or colored, solid, foamlike, or pliable. The flexibility of new materials has suggested new forms, and there is a new genre of *environmental art* that uses all the resources of art and technology to create a world

Claes Oldenburg (b. 1929), TWO CHEESEBURGERS, WITH EVERYTHING (DUAL HAM-
BURGERS). (The Museum of Modern Art, New York; Philip Johnson Fund)
Pop art monumentalizes the trivial obects of modern life.

of shapes, sounds, lights, and colors into which the spectator actually steps, to
be completely surrounded by the artist's vision.

Developments in music have paralleled these trends. A number of composers
have been strongly influenced by their painter friends. Morton Feldman, to
name one, has written: "The new painting made me desirous of a sound world
more direct, more immediate, more physical than anything that existed before.
To me my score is my canvas, my space. What I do is try to sensitize this area—
this time space." The long association between Varèse and the painter Marcel
Duchamp engendered a strikingly similar point of view in both artists. A like
parallelism exists between Jackson Pollock's attempt to achieve an "indeterminate" kind of painting by allowing the colors to drip freely onto the canvas,
and the attempt of John Cage and his followers to achieve an indeterminate
music by using procedures based on chance. Like the proponents of pop art,
Cage has tried to expand resources; he accepts "all audible phenomena as
material proper to music." When we examine the new music we find a desire
for free forms in which elements of chance and randomness are permitted to
operate. Many artists have chosen to loosen their control of the art work by
moving away from pre-established forms. A similar desire for freedom inspired
the mobiles of Alexander Calder, the component parts of which shift with each
current of air to create new relationships. Artists tend more and more to look
upon form as the all-pervading element in art that flows directly out of the
material, so that each individual work, instead of following a set pattern, must be

Alexander Calder (b. 1898), SNOW FLURRY I. (The Museum of Modern Art, New York)
The mobiles of Calder achieve an ideal of ever-changing dynamic form.

allowed to create its own form. Significant in this respect is Cage's remark that "Form is what interests everyone and fortunately it is wherever you are and there is no place where it is not."

Other arts, too, have been subject to wide experimentation. The dance, traditionally chained to specific anecdote and gesture, found itself liberated from storytelling (in the work of George Balanchine) and from traditional patterns of movement (in the work of Martha Graham), and since the Second World War the trend toward abstraction has grown apace. The most important choreographer of the avant-garde, Merce Cunningham, has worked closely throughout his career with John Cage, introducing elements of chance and indeterminacy into his dance compositions. His objective, he states, is "to make a space in which anything can happen."

In the field of literature, poetry has, understandably, been the most experimental genre. Many of our poets face the world of today with a profound sense of alienation. They reflect their disjointed epoch in the fragmentation of their syntax and the violence of their imagery. The utmost freedom of verse forms and a sardonic wit tinged with bitterness characterize many of the younger poets, such as the two best-known members of the so-called "New York group": Kenneth Koch and John Ashbery. Contemporary American poetry ranges from the elegant intellectualism of a John Hollander or a Richard Wilbur to the Whitmanesque exuberance of the two leading poets of the "Beat Generation," Allen Ginsberg and Gregory Corso. These poets and their colleagues reveal—as poets have always done—the most profound impulses of their time, but with an energy and passion that are in the great tradition. Even the word-oriented art of poetry, however, has given rise to strong abstract tendencies, most clearly embodied in the idea of "shaped" poems, in which words are arranged in abstract patterns on the page, the visual form taking precedence over the meaning.

Although the forms of drama and novel are by their very nature based on an imitation of life, they have not remained indifferent to the new trends. The theater has moved away from the social and psychological concerns that permeated the work of Arthur Miller and Tennessee Williams in the 1950s. It turned instead to the "theater of the absurd," whose leading European proponents—Samuel Beckett, Eugene Ionesco, and Jean Genet—view the world with a vast disillusionment, placing metaphysical absurdity at the core of human existence. No less pervasive has been the influence of the Englishman Harold Pinter, whose plays transform the realities of human relationship into unpredictable patterns. The spirit of the absurd has also penetrated the novel—witness such works as Joseph Heller's *Catch 22* and John Barth's *Giles Goat-Boy*, to name only two of a considerable number of novels that have captured the pulse of our time.

Finally, the cinema—of all the arts the one most securely chained to storytelling of a popular kind—has also responded to the twin impulses of experimentation and abstraction. A number of "new wave" directors have opened their films directly onto contemporary experience, mirroring with great eloquence the disjointed patterns of life about them. Among these may be mentioned Michelangelo Antonioni, Jean-Luc Godard, Federico Fellini, and Alain Resnais, in whose *Last Year at Marienbad* the abstract-expressionist urge found perhaps its most successful cinematic realization to date.

If the picture of artistic developments in recent decades often seems confused and contradictory, this is inevitable because of our very close vantage point. We have picked out only a few landmarks on the contemporary scene, but these are enough to indicate that art today has become increasingly intellectual, experimental, and abstract.

Toward Greater Organization

When Schoenberg based his twelve-tone method on the use of tone rows, he was obviously moving toward a much stricter organization of the sound material. This desire was even more clearly manifest in the music of

Webern. However, it remained for their disciples to extend the implications of the tone-row principle to the elements of music other than pitch. The arrangement of the twelve tones in a series might be paralleled by similar groupings of twelve durations (time values), twelve dynamic values (degrees of loudness), or twelve timbres. Other factors, too, might be brought under serial organization: the disposition of registers and densities, of types of attack, or sizes of intervals. By extending the serial principle in all possible directions, a composer could achieve a totally organized fabric every dimension of which was derived from and controlled by one basic premise: the generating power of the series.

This move toward *total serialism* resulted in an extremely complex, ultra-rational music, marked by the utmost unity among the ideas to be expressed, the means of expressing them, and the structures through which that expression was achieved. In such a conception the series defines all the relationships that operate within a given structure; the act of composition becomes the process whereby those relationships are realized to the fullest degree. Total serialism pushed to the farthermost limits, with the thoroughness of a scientific experiment, some of the new ways of hearing and experiencing music.

Toward Greater Freedom

The urge toward a totally controlled music had its counterpart in the desire for greater—even total—freedom from all predetermined forms and procedures. Music of this type emphasizes the antirational element in artistic experience: intuition, chance, the spur of the moment. The composer who wishes to avoid the rational ordering of musical sound may rely on the element of chance and allow, let us say, a throw of dice to determine the selection of his material, or may perhaps build his piece around a series of random numbers generated by a computer. He may construct a piece from sounds selected at random; he may arrange it in sections but allow the performer to choose the order in which these are to be played; or he may indicate the general course of events in regard to pitches, duration, registers, but leave it up to the performer to fill in the details. The performer may shuffle the pages in any sequence he desires; he may play one fragment rather than another; he may react to his fellow players in one of several ways (or not at all). In any case, the performance becomes a musical "happening" in the course of which the piece is recreated afresh each time it is played.

When chance, choice, and the operation of random elements are given a free hand, the things that happen in a piece are dissociated from any pre-existing scheme. Such indeterminate music is known as *aleatory* (from *alea*, the Latin word for dice, which from ancient times have symbolized the whims of chance). In aleatory music the overall form may be clearly indicated but the details are left to choice or chance. On the other hand, some composers will indicate the details of a composition clearly enough, but leave its over-all shape to choice or chance; this type of flexible structure is known as *open form*.

The composer John Cage has been the leader in this movement. "I try to arrange my composing means," he states, "so that I won't have any knowledge of what might happen." There are, naturally, limits beyond which the aleatory ideal cannot be pursued. At a certain point total freedom in music becomes either total chaos or total silence. All the same, contemporary composers have sought to create musical organisms that would take on a fresh form with each performance, just as Calder's mobiles constantly assume fresh forms. This desire for greater freedom complements the equally strong desire for the tightly organized, ultrarational structures of total serialism.

Related to these tendencies is the increased reliance on improvisation—a technique common enough in music of the Baroque and earlier eras, but so long dormant that it has had to be reintroduced, in the 1950s and '60s, from the domain of jazz. Traditionally improvisation consists of spontaneous invention within a framework and a style that have been clearly established, so that player and listener have fairly well-defined ideas of what is "good" and what is "bad." In the more extreme types of aleatory music no such criteria are envisaged, no value judgments called for: anything that happens is acceptable to the composer.

In the past, art has generally striven toward rational, highly organized forms functioning within an ideal universe in which cause gave rise to effect, in which the artist carefully selected what was essential and rigidly excluded what was not. To this ordered view of art, aleatory music and open form oppose an ideal of maximum freedom that mirrors an unpredictable, even irrational world continually in flux. Here art ceases to reflect life; it becomes a part of life, and as uncertain.

Electronic Music

"I have been waiting a long time for electronics to free music from the tempered scale and the limitations of musical instruments. Electronic instruments are the portentous first step toward the liberation of music."
Edgard Varèse

Perhaps the single most important musical development of the 1950s and '60s was the emergence of electronic music. This was foreshadowed, during the earlier part of the century, by the invention of a variety of electronic instruments of limited scope. The most familiar of these is the electronic organ, which was developed primarily as a cheaper substitute for the traditional pipe organ. Others, such as the Ondes Martenot—an instrument producing sounds by means of an electronic oscillator and operated by a keyboard—found occasional use in concert music. Although these instruments were not sufficiently flexible to compete successfully with the traditional ones, they did point the way to future developments.

The post-war emergence of electronic music falls into three stages. The first stage came with the use of magnetic tape recording, which was much more flexible as a medium for storing sounds than the flat disc recording that had been used previously. A group of technicians at the Paris radio station had already begun to experiment with what they called *musique concrète,* a music made up of natural sounds and sound effects recorded on discs and altered by changing the speed of the records. Their activities took on a new impetus when they began to use tape, which gave them a vastly wider range of possibilities in altering the sounds they used as source material, and also enabled them to cut and splice the sounds into new combinations. It was the great achievement of *musique concrète* to establish firmly the principle that all conceivable sounds and noises could serve as raw material for the creative musician.

There soon presented itself the possibility of using not only natural but also artificially generated sounds. A wide variety of equipment for generating and altering sounds came into use. Significant in this regard were the experiments carried on by Otto Luening and Vladimir Ussachevsky at Columbia University, and by Herbert Eimert and Karlheinz Stockhausen in Cologne. These men began their work in 1951. Within a few years there were studios for the production of tape music in many of the chief musical centers of Europe and America. With the raw sound (either naturally or electronically produced) as a starting point, the composer could isolate its components, alter its pitch, volume, or other dimensions, play it backward, add reverberation (echo), filter out some of the overtones, or add additional components by splicing and overdubbing. Even though all these operations were laborious and time-consuming—it might take many hours to process only a minute of finished music—composers hastened to avail themselves of the new medium.

The second step in the technical revolution came with the evolution of *synthesizers,* which are essentially devices combining sound generators and sound modifiers in one package with a unified control system. The first and most elaborate of these devices was the RCA Electronic Music Synthesizer, first unveiled in 1955; a more sophisticated model was installed four years later at the Columbia-Princeton studio in New York City. This immense and elaborate machine, which today would cost a quarter of a million dollars to build, is capable of generating any imaginable sound or combination of sounds, with an infinite variety of pitches, durations, timbres, dynamics, and rhythmic patterns far beyond the capabilities of conventional instruments. The synthesizer represented an enormous step forward, since the composer was now able to specify all the characteristics of the sound beforehand (by means of a punched paper tape), and thus could bypass most of the time-consuming "hand" techniques associated with tape-recorder music.

Because of its size and cost the RCA machine at Columbia has remained unique; but various smaller synthesizers have been devised that bring most of the resources of electronic music within the reach of a small studio. The best-known

The RCA Electronic Music Synthesizer at Columbia University.

of these are the Moog and the Buchla; there is even a portable synthesizer known as the Syn-Ket, designed for the composer John Eaton. The smaller instruments can be played directly (although usually only one note at a time), thus making live performance a possibility.

The third stage of electronic development, which is still in progress, involves the use of the electronic computer as a sound generator. The basic principle here is the fact that the shape of any sound wave can be represented by a graph, and this graph can in turn be described by a series of numbers, each of which will represent a point on the graph. Such a series of numbers can be translated, by a device known as a digital-to-analog converter, into a sound tape that can be played on a tape recorder. In theory then, all that a composer has to do is to write down a series of numbers representing the sound wave he wants, feed it into the converter, and play the tape. But composers do not traditionally think in terms of the shape of sound waves, so it was necessary to devise a computer program that would translate musical specifications—pitches, durations, timbres, dynamics, and the like—into numbers. Several such programs have been prepared and are now in use. Potentially, computer sound-generation is the most flexible of all electronic media, and is likely to dominate the field in years to come.

Electronic music has two aspects of novelty. The most immediately obvious one is the creation of "new sounds," and this has impelled many musicians to use the new medium. Ultimately more important, perhaps, is the fact that the composer of electronic music is able to work directly with the sounds, and can produce a finished work without the help of an intermediary—the performer.

609

We have seen that the serial approach demanded a totally controlled, totally specified music. This requirement found an invaluable ally in electronic music, which freed the composer from the limitations of conventional instruments and performers, leaving only the limitations of the human ear as restrictions upon his thought. An electronic work, once synthesized, was fixed forever in the form that the composer had intended; instead of "music to be performed," it was "music to be reproduced," and no longer needed the concert framework.

However, the combination of electronic sounds with live music has also proved to be a fertile field, especially since many younger composers have been working in both media. Works for soloist and recorded tape have become common, even "concertos" for tape recorder (or live-performance synthesizer) and orchestra. Electronic music has also influenced live music, challenging performers to extend themselves to produce new types of sound, and suggesting to composers new ways of thinking about conventional instruments.

We have used the term *electronic music* in the same way as we would speak of piano music or vocal music—to describe a medium, not a style. Just as piano music or vocal music may be in the baroque, classical, or romantic style, so a piece using electronic sounds may be in one style or another. Naturally, when a composer writes for a particular medium he tries to take advantage of the things that it alone can do. From this point of view it does not make much sense to compose a piece of electronic music in the style of Bach or Beethoven (except, perhaps, as a stunt for the popular market). Electronic music is at its best when it says things that cannot be said in any other medium. All the same, the composer of electronic music is free, just as he would be if he were writing for conventional instruments, to compose in any style that suits his fancy.

Other Aspects of the New Music

Whether it is serial or aleatory, live or electronic, most new music reflects the conviction that each composition is based upon a set of premises that are unique to it. The function of the piece is to realize fully what is implicit in these premises. Each work is regarded as a self-contained structure independent of all other structures, whose form springs from and is determined by conditions peculiar to itself. Ours obviously is no longer a time when thousands of pieces can be written in sonata, rondo, or A-B-A form. These forms ultimately had to degenerate into formulas, in spite of the infinite ingenuity with which the great masters handled them, because their rationale was based on the harmonic system of the classic-romantic era. The concept of predetermined form is completely alien to the spirit of the new music. The force that holds a piece together is not superimposed from without but flows directly out of the material. Since the material is unique to the piece, so is the form. It follows that today's composers have introduced infinite variety and flexibility into this aspect of music.

Throughout the eighteenth and nineteenth centuries it was pitch—embodied in melody, harmony, and tonality—that was the dominant structural element of music. In the first half of the twentieth century rhythm in the abstract (as opposed to rhythm embodied in a theme) emerged as a form-generating principle. The new music has elevated dynamics and timbre to equal importance with pitch and rhythm, and these four dimensions may now play an equal role in determining the character of the musical discourse.

Contemporary attitudes, it need hardly be said, have liberated all the elements of music from the restrictions of the past. The concept of a music based on the twelve pitches of the chromatic (tempered) scale has obviously been left far behind. Electronic instruments make possible the use of sounds "in the cracks of the piano keys"—the microtonal intervals, such as quarter or third tones, that are smaller than the traditional semitone—and very skilled string and wind players have begun to master these novel scales. In addition, the notion of what is acceptable sonorous material has been broadened to include the domain that lies between musical tone and noise.

Rhythm, too, has been liberated from the shackles of tradition. In the past, musical time was measured according to a system of values that existed only in relation to each other: a whole note was equal to two halves, a half note equalled two quarters, and so on. These values bore no relation to absolute or physical time; they depended on the speed at which the piece was played. But electronic tape brings the composer face to face with the requirements of physical time. An inch of tape is equivalent to so many minutes and seconds. For him, therefore, musical time can no longer exist apart from physical time.

Stravinsky, Bartók, Schoenberg, and their disciples developed a musical rhythm no longer based on equal measures and the regular recurrence of accent. Their concepts have been immensely refined in the past quarter century. Music in the past gave the impression of flowing through time in an orderly fashion toward a preordained goal. Many composers today, on the other hand, try to focus the listener's attention on a texture in which each sonority or density stands almost by itself, detached from its surroundings. Their music may unfold as a series of sonorous points, each of which is momentarily suspended in time, surrounded by plenty of "air pockets" of organized silence: great static blocks of sound juxtaposed in musical space, fashioned out of tiny cell-like clusters that spin, whirl, combine and recombine with a kind of cumulative force.

Musical styles so different from all that went before need a new breed of instrumentalists and vocalists to cope with their technical difficulties. One has only to attend a concert of avant-garde music to realize how far the art of piano playing or singing has moved from the world of Chopin and Verdi. The piano keyboard may be brushed or slammed with fingers, palm, or fist; or the player may reach inside to hit, scratch, or pluck the strings directly. A violinist may tap, stroke, and even slap his instrument. Vocal music runs the gamut from whispering to shouting, including all manner of groaning, moaning, or hissing on the way. Wind players have learned to produce a variety of double-stops, subtle changes of color, and microtonal progressions; and the percussion section has been enriched by an astonishing variety of noisemakers and special effects. True, the new performance skills have not yet filtered down to the members of our symphony orchestras. Performances of difficult new works are necessarily limited and, more often than not, unsatisfactory. When, after much effort, a contemporary composer does manage to obtain a hearing, it may be a traumatic experience for him to have his work mauled by players who are unable to cope with its technical problems. Fortunately, in each of the important musical centers groups of young players and singers are springing up who have a genuine affinity with the new music. Singers like Bethany Beardslee and Cathy Berberian, pianists like Robert Helps, Paul Jacobs, Robert Miller, and Charles Rosen, violinists like Matthew Raimondi and Paul Zukofsky, to mention only a few, are masters of a new kind of virtuosity that cannot fail to amaze those who were brought up on the old. They are performing an invaluable service for the new music, and it is an encouraging sign that their numbers are growing.

We mentioned the impact of jazz on serious music during the second quarter of the century. The two genres have grown even closer together. Serious composers today feel an affinity for the improvisational freedoms of jazz, as well as its cultivation of highly specialized, virtuoso styles of performance. Jazz composers, for their part, are strongly interested in certain avant-garde trends, such as electronics and serialism. The most successful example of this cross-fertilization is Gunther Schuller, whose music we will discuss. He is but one of a number of gifted musicians on either side of the fence who are increasingly influenced by what is happening on the other side.

The Internationalism of the New Music

The advent of tape made it easy to take down a live performance without having to wait until it was recorded, and to send it to any part of the world. This, plus the development of the other media of communication—radio, television, recordings, and the jet plane—brought about an enormous speeding-up in the dissemination of musical ideas. Composers in New York, Chicago, or Los Angeles are able to keep abreast of the latest developments in Cologne, Rome, or Paris. Many of the new composers are active on both sides of the Atlantic as performers, conductors, teachers, organizers of musical events, or participants in festivals of the new music. This inevitably has led to an internationalization of the musical scene. The new music is a language shared by European and American composers alike. In this sense music in the mid-twentieth century has recaptured something of the universality it held in the eighteenth century (and lost in the nineteenth as a result of the emphasis upon national schools).

The links between Europe and America were forged before World War II, when such leaders of European music as Stravinsky, Schoenberg, Bartók, Hindemith, and Krenek came to the United States. The war and the events leading up to it disrupted musical life on the Continent much more than in this country, with the result that the United States forged ahead in certain areas. For example, the first composer to apply serial organization to dimensions other than pitch was the American composer Milton Babbitt. The experiments of John Cage anticipated and influenced similar attempts abroad. Earle Brown was the first to use open form, Morton Feldman the first to write works that gave the performer a choice. Once the war was over the Europeans quickly made up for lost time. Intense experimentation went on in Italy, Germany, France, England, Holland, and Scandinavia. This has gradually spread eastward into the Communist world; serial and electronic music have also taken root in Japan.

In the following chapter we will discuss a group of composers—American and European—whose music is representative of the new trends. These men are pushing back boundaries and exploring frontiers; they are actively enlarging the domain of what the rest of us can perceive, experience, and understand. Their music will bring you the excitement of discovering a new world of sound.

98 Composers of Our Time

"There is no avant-garde. There are only people who are a little late."

Edgard Varèse

Schuller: *Seven Studies on Themes of Paul Klee*

"There is no question that the 'classical' world can learn much about timing, rhythmic accuracy and subtlety from jazz musicians, and jazz can learn dynamics, structure, and contrast from classical music."

Gunther Schuller (New York, 1925–) is one of the best-known composers of his generation. He has taught at Yale University and at Tanglewood, and has appeared as guest conductor with leading orchestras. In 1968 he was appointed head of the New England Conservatory of Music.

Schuller is self-taught as a composer. His music shows many of the influences to which his generation has been responsive. On the one hand he has been affected by the rhythmic freedom and instrumental innovations of experimental jazz. He has been associated with the Modern Jazz Quartet, and is a leading representative of the "third stream" movement, which combines the techniques of contemporary music with those of jazz; his *Early Jazz* (1968) is one of the best books on the subject. On the other hand he has absorbed the serial tech-

Gunther Schuller.

niques of the twelve-tone method, which he handles in an unorthodox and altogether personal manner. Schuller leans toward an expressively chromatic atonal idiom, which he uses with poetic imagination and a flair for orchestral sonorities. Much of his output is devoted to abstract instrumental works, such as the Cello Concerto and Suite for Woodwind Quintet of 1945, and the Symphony for Brass and Percussion of 1950. Among his "third stream" pieces are *12 by 11*, for chamber orchestra and jazz improvisation (1955); Concertino for Jazz Quartet and Orchestra (1959); *Densities I* and *Night Music* (1962). Jazz elements figure also in *The Visitation* (1966), an opera on Schuller's own libretto after Franz Kafka's *The Trial*.

"Ever since I learned many years ago," he writes, "that Paul Klee was a fine amateur violinist and his pictures frequently used musical forms and terms, I resolved to write a composition one day that would be based in some way on his work." The opportunity came in 1959 when Schuller was commissioned by the Minneapolis Symphony Orchestra, and conceived his *Seven Studies on Themes of Paul Klee*. He chose seven pictures by Klee, three of which, because of their musical titles—*Antique Harmonies, Abstract Trio,* and *Pastorale*—"permitted a direct translation of their visual-structural elements into musical terms." The others, he points out, provided "a natural inspiration for a freely invented parallel musical conception."

1. *Antique Harmonies*. Schuller explains that this is one of many Klee pictures constructed in irregular-size blocks. These are translated, in Schuller's piece, into intervals of a fifth, "irregularly placed in a slow-moving pattern." So too the color progression in Klee's picture, "from near black through ochre and green-tinged brown to bright yellow (and back again) finds its parallel in a timbre progression from the low dark strings and woodwinds to the bright

'yellow' of high trumpets and strings." Associated with this color scheme is the gradual crescendo-decrescendo pattern which has long been a favorite dynamic scheme in music. The piece is a Lento in ½. The use of open fifths and triads in low register, *ppp* and *pp*, suggests the "antique harmony" of the title, as does a harmonic cadence associated with fourteenth-century music that is intoned by the brass.

2. *Abstract Trio*. Klee's trio is a group of three musicians. This serves Schuller as a point of departure for his instrumentation. The first trio (flute, oboe, clarinet) is succeeded by a second (bassoon, trumpet, trombone), the dark colors and lower registers of which provide a striking contrast with the first. So too the third trio (bass clarinet, contrabassoon, tuba) contrasts with the fourth (English horn, clarinet, and horn). In the last few seconds of the piece all the groups combine.

Although *Abstract Trio* does not follow strict tone-row procedure, it displays several characteristics of the twelve-tone style: wide leaps in the melodic lines, attenuated texture, irregular "prose" rhythms, and the use of special effects such as fluttertonguing on the flute and widely spaced runs. What Schuller does is to unfold all twelve tones of the chromatic scale, each appearing once (or immediately repeated, which doesn't count), before he unfolds the next series of twelve. In the following example, the first four chords (ending on the first beat of measure 2) contain all the twelve tones. The next series of twelve brings us to the repeated G-natural in measure 3, whereupon the third series of twelve begins:

3. *Little Blue Devil*. "The comic-seriousness of Klee's famous cubist demon evolved into a jazz ('third stream') piece with a perky, fragmented tune and 'blue' instrumental colorings." After a brief introduction the solo double bass falls into a rhythmic ostinato based on even quarter notes, above which woodwinds, brass, and strings trace their tenuous lines. The percussion group, which plays an especially important part in this piece, includes a suspended cymbal of medium size in addition to two larger cymbals; also triangle, tambourine, snare

Paul Klee, THE TWITTERING
MACHINE (ZWITSCHER-
MASCHINE). (The Museum of
Modern Art, New York)

drum, glockenspiel, and—that mainstay of the contemporary jazz group—
"vibes" (vibraphone). The pervasive jazzy rhythm is characteristic of Schuller,
as are the subtle coloristic effects in which this piece abounds.

4. *The Twittering Machine.* Since music can be made to twitter, Schuller
had no problem in fashioning a little tone poem that would be vividly suggestive
of his fourth picture. Against a running background set up by oboes and English
horn, horns and violas, he unfolds delicate pencillings of sound. The use of
woodwinds and strings in their highest register gives him the effect he needs.
A woodblock and large gourd are used soloistically, as are the more conventional
instruments. Characteristic of the serial procedures of the post-Webern school is
the fragmentation of line among a number of instruments, each of which plays
only one or two notes; and the sparseness of the sound, accentuated in this case
by the fact that most of the music lies well above middle C. Schuller applies
certain serial techniques, such as the use of pre-established patterns to govern the
order in which certain instruments enter, in what he calls a strict "mechanical"
way—a humorously appropriate tribute to the machine.

5. *Arab Village.* "The listener is invited to imagine himself suspended, as in
Klee's painting, above a village baking in the North African sun. Near the edge
of the village a solitary flute plays its melancholy tune." Played backstage, the
flute evokes the monophonic texture and rhapsodic arabesques of the folk music
of the Near East. "Somewhere else an Arab oboe wails its involved melisma.

Later, a trio of musicians (oboe, viola, harp) plays its microtonal improvisations over a nasal drone." Microtones—intervals smaller than the half tone—figure prominently in oriental song. The droning bass, as on bagpipes, is a feature of folk music in many lands. A narrow range and much repetition of fragments impart to the melodic lines of this sketch a certain primitive quality.

6. *An Eerie Moment* conjures up a mood not unrelated to the first piece of Schoenberg's Opus 16, *Premonition*. "An eerie quiet and suppressed tension suddenly explode, only to collapse again quickly into silence." This kind of emotional suggestion is one to which atonal music lends itself with particular effectiveness.

7. *Pastorale*. "Subtitled *Rhythms* by Klee, this is indeed a study in the 'rhythmic' variation of abstract geometric pastoral shapes. To fully appreciate Klee's variational procedures," Schuller states, "one must read the picture's several 'lines' like a page of writing. Similarly, in my music several rhythmic lines, constantly and subtly varied, provide the basic accompaniment over which the pastoral horn and clarinet weave their 'romantic' melodies." The accompanimental lines are based on the interval of a semitone. The clarinet melody is marked by widely spaced patterns, both ascending and descending.

Imaginative in concept and expert in execution, Schuller's *Seven Studies on Themes of Paul Klee* provides a fine introduction to the new music.

Penderecki: *Threnody for the Victims of Hiroshima*

"We are at the time of the end of forms. The forms and methods of listening to music will undergo great change in the near future."

The doctrine of "social realism" that prevails in the Communist world has militated against experimentation. This doctrine requires the artist to make his work accessible to the masses, to use folk material and patriotic themes, and to place his creative talent at the disposal of the social-educational apparatus of the state. Composers, however, no matter how socially conscious, are concerned primarily with ways and means of manipulating sound. Thus the careers of the leading Soviet composers such as Prokofiev, Shostakovich, and Khatchaturian have been studded with stormy episodes in which they were denounced by the authorities for "bourgeois decadence"—the Soviet euphemism for the influence of the West.

The musical isolation of eastern Europe came to an end in the later 1950s. With ever greater momentum contemporary ideas began to infiltrate the Communist world, at first in the satellite countries but ultimately even in the Soviet Union. The leader in this development was Poland, whose musical life now stands in the mainstream of the European avant-garde.

Best-known among the younger Polish composers is Krzysztof Penderecki (1933–). Endowed with a vivid imagination and a strong sense of dramatic

Krzysztof Penderecki.

effect, he has developed an eclectic style in which elements derived from folk-song and Gregorian chant, Bartók and Stravinsky mingle with avant-garde procedures. His popularity stems from his ability to use contemporary techniques in order to project music that makes a strong emotional impact.

A case in point is his *Threnody for the Victims of Hiroshima* (1960), for fifty-two stringed instruments. The piece exploits a remarkable range of string sonorities. As in so much of the new music, pitch here is made subsidiary to timbre and rhythm, dynamics, textures, and densities; indeed the score of the work uses an elaborate notation to indicate the many unusual effects of bowing, vibrato, mass glissandos, quarter tones, percussive effects (such as those obtained by striking the sounding board of the violin with the wooden part of the bow or with the fingertips), and very rapid tremolos not in precise rhythm. The player is asked to obtain the highest possible tones on his instrument by placing his finger on the string very close to the bowing point, producing sounds that do not have an exact pitch but that contribute a distinctive color to the sonority. Also employed are tone clusters, containing all the pitches within a specified interval; these unfold in bands of sound that expand or contract, divide or merge, almost in the manner of chord progressions.

The piece opens with high, glassy sonorities that are sustained like a cry of anguish. These are presently heard against percussive noises in the bass and plangent outcries that can hardly be described as dissonant, so far removed is this music from traditional notions of dissonance and consonance. From this torrent of sound emerges an occasional point where the instruments play in a normal manner; these moments stand out in powerful contrast to the cataclysm that surrounds them. Resemblances to electronic sound permeate the changing densities, colors, and continual contrasts of register. In such a context even silence becomes charged with feeling. The somber noise at the end has a density and thrust that are remarkable when one remembers it is produced only by strings. It brings this agonized music to a close as though seen "through a glass darkly."

Babbitt: *Ensembles for Synthesizer*

"Anyone who hears well can be educated to appreciate my music. The more you listen to serial music, the better able you are to recognize its grammar, its configurations, its modes of procedure."

Just as composers of the nineteenth century related their music to romantic poetry and painting, several among the avant-garde composers of our time tend to relate their work to the exact sciences, thereby exalting the intellectual-rational element in art over the intuitive-emotional one. A leading proponent of this ultrarational attitude is Milton Babbitt (Philadelphia, 1916–). "Some people say my music is 'too cerebral,' " he states. "Actually, I believe in cerebral music—in the application of intellect to relevant matters. I never choose a note unless I know precisely why I want it there and can give several reasons why it and not another."

Babbitt studied with Roger Sessions. When Sessions was asked to form a graduate department of music at Princeton University he invited his brilliant pupil, then twenty-two, to join its faculty. Babbitt has taught at Princeton ever since, and as professor of composition has had a strong influence on musicians of the younger generation. Given his kind of mind, he was inevitably attracted to the almost scientific logic of the twelve-tone method, which for him represented a revolution in musical thought "whose nature and consequences can be

Milton Babbitt.

compared only with those of the mid-nineteenth-century revolution in mathematics or the twentieth-century revolution in theoretical physics." He soon realized the possibilities for further development inherent in Schoenberg's system. It became his conviction that "the twelve-tone set must dominate *every* aspect of the piece."

As a result, he led the way toward an ultrarational music in which the composer would control every dimension of the musical fabric. His *Three Compositions for Piano* (1947) and *Composition for Four Instruments* (1948) were the first examples of total serialization. He applied the principle of the series not only to pitch but also to rhythm, dynamics (including not only the soft-loud element but also the attack and decay of the sound), and timbre. Therewith he developed the premises of Schoenberg's method into an all-inclusive system in which the basic row—or set, as Babbitt calls it—totally controlled the relationships and processes within a particular piece.

By the same token Babbitt was one of the first to evaluate the possibilities of electronic music, not because of the new sonorities it made possible— "Nothing," he holds, "becomes old as quickly as a new sound"—but because it offered the composer complete control over the final result. At the Columbia-Princeton Electronic Music Center in New York City he was able to work out his ideas on the RCA Synthesizer. "When you live through as many bad performances of your music as I have, I must confess that I look forward to walking into the electronic studio with my composition in my head and walking out with the performance on the tape in my hand." Out of this "unique and satisfying experience," as he calls it, came two important works in which he explored the possibilities of the new medium: *Composition for Synthesizer* (1960–61) and *Ensembles for Synthesizer* (1962–64).

All the same, it has never been Babbitt's intention that the Synthesizer should supplant the live musician. "I know of no serious electronic composer who ever asserts that we are supplanting any other form of music or any other form of musical activity. We're interested in increasing the resources of music." The next step, Babbitt saw, was to combine electronic music with live performers. This new area he explored in *Vision and Prayer* (1961), for soprano and synthesized accompaniment; *Philomel* (1964), for soprano, recorded soprano, and synthesized accompaniment; and *Correspondences* (1966–68), for string orchestra and synthesized accompaniment. Nor did he forsake the field of live music; two connected works, *Relata I* (1965) and *Relata II* (1968) are for orchestra.

Ensembles for Synthesizer offers the listener an excellent introduction to the world of electronic sound. The piece is based on a series (B♭-A-C-B-G♭-A♭-D-E♭-C-F-D♭-E), which Babbitt uses not only in the Schoenbergian fashion; he also uses the internal symmetries of the series to derive new series and combinations, in a manner inspired by the techniques of Webern. In addition, the rhythm of the work is serially controlled.

At the same time *Ensembles for Synthesizer* achieves great variety of effect through its imaginative exploitation of electronic resources. The introduction, which presents the basic material both in its pitch and rhythmic relationships, is paralleled by the concluding section of the work. In between, the main body of the composition, as the composer describes it, "consists of 126 short sections, no two of which are alike from a standpoint of timbral, rhythmic, or pitch 'ensembles,' but all of which derive from the material set out in the introduction. The number 126 is itself, of course, of no importance, but it does indicate that each of the sections is of but a few seconds' duration, and that the uniquely electronic aspect of the composition rests upon this speed and flexibility of pitch, registral, durational, timbral, and dynamic succession."

The piece unfolds as a series of vivid contrasts. High bell-like sounds are pitted against dark rumblings in the low register; musical sounds are pitted against what may strike the listener as organized noise; handfuls of rapid notes are splattered in between long, sustained ones; areas of greater tension alternate with those of lesser. The piece builds up as a kind of action-music propelled by powerful rhythmic impulses. Needless to say, this is not music preoccupied with either personal feelings or picturesque atmosphere. It has rather a certain coolness, a quality of detachment that suggests the classical stamp of Babbitt's mind. Yet the piece is very accessible, and certain passages have an almost popular flavor.

The significant artist is one who incarnates the significant impulses of his time. Milton Babbitt is such a one. His music embodies important intellectual currents in the contemporary scene.

Berio: *Circles*

"Nationalism only divides people. It produced Hitler. There is a more global type of thinking today, a concern with musical processes that has nothing to do with geography."

Luciano Berio (Oneglia, 1925–) is a leading figure among the radicals of the post-Webern generation in Italy. He was one of the founders of the Milan electronic studio that became a center for the Italian avant-garde. Since 1965 he has taught composition at the Julliard School in New York City.

In his earlier works Berio used a very strict serial technique, but into these procedures he injected the lyricism that is his birthright as an Italian. In addition, a strong sense of theater pervades his music, especially such works as *Passaggio* (1965), an opera for solo soprano, two choruses, and orchestra; and the *Sinfonia* (1968) for vocal ensemble and orchestra.

Circles (1960), for soprano, harp, and two percussionists, is based on poems of e. e. cummings. It shows Berio's brilliant sense of sound and his imaginative exploitation of new performance techniques. Indeed, the piece is a study in the new vocal virtuosity, embodied in the extraordinary talents of Cathy Berberian, who has been Berio's ideal interpreter. No less striking is the mastery embodied in the writing—and performance—of the instrumental parts. In this work voice and instruments are no longer thought of as two separate entities, to be welded into an artistic whole. They form a single entity in which the instruments may

Luciano Berio.

continue what the voice has just finished doing, as when a hissing sound in the voice part is prolonged by a cymbal stroke, or the voice introduces percussive-sibilant sounds which the instruments presently take over. Because of this unity, Berio explains, the instrumental parts "are occasionally not completely defined in conventional musical notation, but the general nature of the action is indicated. The specific result thus depends somewhat on the personal characteristics of each performer."

I. *Stinging.* "stinging gold swarms upon the spires/silver chants the litanies/ the great bells are ringing with rose/the lewd fat bells/and a tall wind is dragging the sea with dreams . . ." Having passed beyond the strict serialism of his earlier years, Berio has modified the serial principle in the formal organization of his later works. In *Circles* he first analyzed the sounds of the text, dividing them into phonetic categories (for example, in his opening word "stinging," the *s* is an unvoiced dental sibilant, the *t* an unvoiced plosive, the *i* a high front vowel, and so on). He then divided his instruments into groups, assigning one to each of his phonetic categories; thus, the high front vowel *i* is associated with chimes, vibraphone, harp, marimbaphone, celesta, and triangles. As a result, the shift from one phonetic category to another in the text is accompanied by a corresponding change from one instrumental combination to another. Tempos, exchanges of harmonic complexity, and the movement from definite pitch to more or less undetermined instrumental action are organized along similar lines. Thus the periodic recurrence of phonetic elements causes a corresponding periodicity in the other elements. This circular movement in all the elements gives the piece its title. Notice that the first song is rounded off by a brief instrumental postlude.

II. *Riverly is a flower.* "riverly is a flower gone softly by tomb/rosily gods whiten befall saith rain/anguish of dream-send is hushed in moan-loll where night gathers morte carved smiles/cloud-gloss is at moon-cease/soon verbial mist-flowers close ghosts on prowl gorge sly slim gods stare . . ." Several features of the music remind us that Berio belongs to a generation whose starting point was the heritage of Webern: the discontinuous setting, the fragmenting of words and syllables, the rarefaction of texture with maximum emphasis on individual sounds, subtle dynamic nuances, jagged melody line with wide leaps, "prose" rhythms, and the intense expressivity that informs the whole. The "circular" principle of organization causes certain intervals and motives to recur, giving the music its homogeneous texture. The second song ends with a brief instrumental interlude, after which the last four words of text are repeated.

III. *Now.* "now the how disappeared cleverly word is slapped with lightning/ at which shall pounce up crack will jumps of thunder blossom/invisibly among banged fragments sky/what meaninglessness unrollingly strolls whole over domains collide high . . ." Berio uses not only song and speech but all the subtle gradations in between, relying occasionally on an expressive *Sprechstimme* that links this work to the esthetics of the Viennese school. He does not try to make sense of the words or to interpret them in music. Rather he treats them as pure phonetic material, wrenching syllables apart or slapping them together, or causing certain consonants to stand out with violent emphasis, with the result that the voice at times becomes another percussion instrument of his ensemble. Of course, cummings's use of words as sound, independent of their meaning, lends itself ideally to such an approach.

A coda based on explosive sounds in the vocal part is followed by an instrumental interlude that leads into the fourth song. This repeats the text of the second, and presents vivid contrasts between sung and spoken words. The fifth song repeats the text of the first in a new and highly poetic setting, and the piece ends *ppp*.

Berio's sense of the theatrical pervades the work, so that we respond to its dramatic quality even without knowing what the drama is about. He is without question one of the most inventive musicians among the avant-garde.

Carter: *Variations for Orchestra*

"I like music to be beautiful, ordered, and expressive of the more important aspects of life."

Of the composers who have come into prominence in recent years, none is more widely admired by musicians than Elliott Carter (New York City, 1908–). His works are not of the kind that achieve easy popularity; but their profundity of thought and maturity of workmanship bespeak a musical intellect of the first order.

Carter started out with a musical idiom rooted in diatonic-modal harmony, but gradually assimilated a dissonant chromaticism that places him (if one must attach a label) among the abstract expressionists. He employs fluctuating tempo as a form-building element, through the use of a novel technique that he calls "metrical modulation," whereby the speed of the rhythmic pulse is subtly modified. When several instruments are playing together, each with its

Elliott Carter.

own pulse and each changing that pulse independently in a different direction, there results an original and powerful kind of texture.

The works of Carter's maturity explore the possibilities of this technique in a variety of ways. The two string quartets (1951, 1959) are bold, uncompromising works that constitute the most significant contribution to this medium since Bartók; the Second brought the composer a Pulitzer Prize. Beginning with this work, Carter's music has also sought to throw into relief the characteristics of different instruments and instrumental masses. In the Double Concerto (1961), two contrasting keyboard instruments—piano and harpsichord—are place at opposite sides of the stage, each partnered by its own chamber orchestra, and carry on a sort of musical argument. A similar confrontation pervades the dramatic Piano Concerto (1965), the soloist asserting his individuality against the mass. More recently, the *Concerto for Orchestra* (1969) exploits the opposition of particular groups and soloists within the orchestra.

The *Variations for Orchestra* (1955) utilizes the resources of the orchestra in virtuoso fashion. The conception is thoroughly symphonic; at the same time the orchestral texture is of an almost chamber-music delicacy and refinement. Carter applies the variation procedure continuously instead of in self-contained units, as was done in the variation forms of the eighteenth and nineteenth centuries. The piece is based on a theme that undergoes many transformations, and on two ritornels (refrains) which are repeated literally except for transpositions of pitch and speed. The first of these is stated rapidly near the outset and becomes progressively slower with each restatement. The second, contrariwise, is played in slow notes by the solo violin as a counterpoint to the theme and accelerates with each reappearance. The ritornels emphasize the unity of the conception even as the variations themselves—each with its own method of development—nourish the diversity of the work.

The introduction, marked Allegro, takes on urgency from a leaping figure in the strings and a repeated-note motive in the brass. It serves as a kind of summary of the melodic and harmonic configurations to be heard throughout the piece. The theme, an Andante, is a serene idea that unfolds in a series of

lyric phrases interpersed with flickering figures on instruments of contrasting color. Variation 1, Vivace leggero, is a rapid dialogue of motives drawn from

various parts of the theme, presented in contrasting rhythms, Variation 2, Pesante (heavy), unfolds a more dramatic aspect of the basic idea. The theme is introduced by the brass in an almost literal quotation, and is pitted against other versions of itself that are derived by expanding and diminishing its intervals. This results in striking contrasts of character and mood. Variation 3, Moderato, opens with a singing melodic line in the violins and builds up tension to a climax that surges through the whole orchestra.

The fourth, fifth, and sixth variations are more uniform in character. Variation 4 is a study in controlled ritardando based on changing units. Variation 5, Allegro misterioso, has an almost Webernian immobility and transparency of texture, in which the changing orchestral combinations stand out with remarkable clarity. The sixth variation balances the fourth, being a study in controlled accelerando. Thenceforth the process of development moves beyond the single variation: the seventh, eighth, and ninth variations are interlocked in a continuous process on a single plane of rhythm established mostly by the woodwinds. Variation 7 is an Andante. One of its ideas is carried over into Variation 8 within the changed emotional context of an Allegro giocoso. Variation 9, also an Andante, develops the ideas of Variation 7 in a contrapuntal texture, thereby exemplifying the twentieth-century fondness for presenting simultaneously elements that were first heard in succession.

The finale, Allegro molto, juxtaposes a variety of elements in animated interplay, thus intensifying the contrasts between them. The rapid motion is interrupted, first, by an expressive section for strings that leads to a quotation of the two ritornels; then by a recitative for trombones, based on the notes of the first half of the theme, while muted strings play those of the other half.

625

The work ends as the first ritornel slowly ascends through a quiet string background while the winds rush downward with the second. The *Variations for Orchestra*, the composer points out, is not a twelve-tone work. "Its quality of harmony is derived from the theme and is arrived at by ear and not by a system." At the same time, the piece shows Carter's involvement with the issues that have concerned advanced musicians since the mid-century, and confirms his position as one of the most important composers in America

Cage: *Fontana Mix*

"I am more like a hunter or inventor than a lawmaker."

John Cage (Los Angeles, (1912–) is one of the daring experimenters of his generation. He studied, among others, with Henry Cowell and Schoenberg, each of whom exercised a strong influence upon his thinking. From the beginning of his career he was interested in Oriental philosophy and music, in non-Western scales, and in percussive rhythm as a form-building element. His music for percussion ensembles grew out of this interest. Characteristic are the *Third Construction* of 1940 and the *Construction in Metal* (1944) for seven percussionists who play bowls, pots, bells, metal bars, tin sheets, and an assortment of gongs. Cage attracted much attention with his music for "prepared piano." The preparation consisted of muffling and altering the piano tone by inserting sundry objects of rubber, felt, or wood, as well as screws, nuts, bolts, and coins between the strings. This transformed the instrument into an ensemble of gentle percussive timbres that conjured up the gongs and drums of the Balinese orchestra known as *gamelan*. His Sixteen Sonatas and Four Interludes for prepared piano (1946–48) explored the possibilities of this limited medium. He evolved a vocabulary evocative of Eastern idioms in the subtlety and luminosity of its timbres; he developed rhythm, as Virgil Thomson wrote, "to a point of sophistication unmatched in the technique of any other living composer."

Cage has rejected the development of themes, the arousal of emotion, and the buildup of architectural forms that constitute the great tradition in Western music. The phrases in his music unfold in fragments, punctuated by dramatic points of silence; this he derived from the twelve-tone composers, especially Webern. He was one of the first to deny the supremacy of pitch as an organizing principle. By freeing himself from the problems of melodic line and harmonic progression, Cage was able to concentrate his attention on rhythm and timbre. This, we have seen, developed into one of the main trends in the new music. He became an eloquent spokesman for the attempt to achieve total freedom in music through dependence on chance and randomness. To quote one of the cardinal tenets of his philosophy, "My purpose is to eliminate purpose." To the ultra-rationality of the total serialists Cage opposed the anti-rationality of total freedom, using dice and kindred procedures to produce

John Cage.

an aleatory music that freed the performer—and the musical events—from the composer's control. For example, in his famous (according to some, notorious) *Imaginary Landscape* (1951), twelve radios were set going simultaneously, tuned to different stations. The material, consequently, was completely random. The only predetermined element was the time span within which this assemblage of sounds and noises takes place.

To set up a framework within which unpredictable events will take place is relatively simple to do in the realm of live performance; but to transfer this indeterminacy to tape—by its nature a fixed medium—requires considerable ingenuity. Cage solved the problem in *Fontana Mix* (1958), the first work on tape to establish conditions whose outcome could not be foreseen. The material consists of a set of drawings and transparent sheets, plus a graph, which can be combined in innumerable ways to produce patterns that suggest specific activities of the performer (or performers). Such a program allows change to operate, so that *Fontana Mix* sounds different with each performance.

The three recordings that have been made of *Fontana Mix* represent three totally different realizations of the material. The version for magnetic tape alone is most animated, consisting of a montage of disassociated events—hissings, whisperings, groanings, gurglings, twitterings, and rumblings woven into a tapestry of sounds as varied as the free association of ideas when the mind is permitted to wander. These ever-shifting images at times give the same sense of randomness as when one turns the knob of the radio and hears successive fragments of music or speech from various stations. Here then is a perfect realization of Cage's desire to create "indeterminate music" through discontinuous works that unfold random events within a fixed span of time.

The second, and liveliest, of the three recordings combines *Fontana Mix* with an *Aria* that is sung by Cathy Berberian. This version focuses interest on

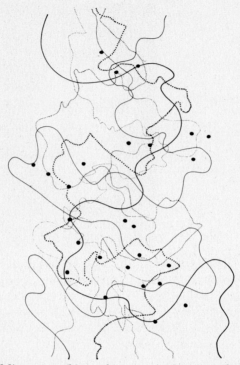

Cage, *Fontana Mix*: one possible combination of a drawing and a transparent sheet.

Miss Berberian's remarkable performance. The *Aria* is notated in such a manner as to allow the performer to share with the composer in creating the work. "The notation," Cage explains, "represents time horizontally, pitch vertically, roughly suggested rather than accurately described." The vocal line is drawn in black or in one or more of eight colors, each representing another style of singing; jazz, contralto and contralto lyric, sprechstimme, dramatic, Marlene Dietrich, coloratura and coloratura lyric, folk, oriental, baby, and nasal. The text employs vowels and consonants and words from five languages: Armenian, Russian, Italian, French, and English. The composer concludes his instructions by pointing out that all aspects of the performance not notated (such as dynamics, type of attack, and the like) may be freely determined by the singer. Miss Berberian makes the most of this program, the result veering from nonsense singing to satire and parody of a rather delicious kind.

The third recording, by the percussionist Max Neuhaus, represents "the interaction and mixture of feedback channels set up by resting contact microphones on various percussion instruments that stand in front of loudspeakers." (*Feedback* is the acoustical phenomenon that occurs when a microphone

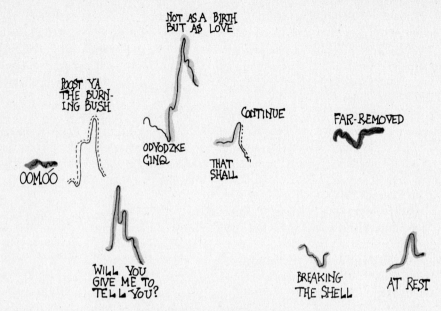

A page from John Cage's *Aria.*

picks up the sound from a loudspeaker and "feeds it back" into the same loudspeaker: the result is a howling noise.) This realization consists of a series of signals each of which is sustained for so long a time as to approach—at least for sensitive ears—the threshold of physical pain. The impression of absolute immobility is akin to that in certain yoga exercises which tend to empty the mind of all thought. Towards the middle of the record the sustained noises take on the relentless quality of an electric drill, ending as abruptly as they began.

"I like to think that I'm outside the circle of a known universe, and dealing with things that I don't know anything about." John Cage belongs to the category of eternally questing artist whose innovations may have greater value because of the new domains they open up than as finished works of art. In any case he has exerted a vital influence in the music of our time.

Other Contemporaries (American)

The proponents of the new music in America include composers of several generations, representing a variety of personal styles and esthetic viewpoints.

Stefan Wolpe (Berlin, 1902–) came to the United States in 1939, and his most important work has been done in this country. Such pieces as his Trio

(1963) for flute, cello, and piano, and the *Chamber Piece No. 1* (1964) are examples of what has aptly been called "cumulative form." They are based on tiny motivic cells that generate increasing energy and tension as the music unfolds, yet retain their character despite the many coloristic, registral, rhythmic, and dynamic changes they undergo. Wolpe's is a single-minded and highly distinctive idiom.

Arthur Berger (New York City, 1912–), whose earlier music shows the influence of Stravinskyan neoclassicism, has in recent years developed a more complex, rhythmically abrupt, and melodically disjunct style that adheres to a post-Weberian esthetic. Among his works are *Polyphony for Orchestra* (1956), a String Quartet (1958), and the elegant, witty Three Pieces for Two Pianos (1961).

Hugo Weisgall (Ivančice, Czechoslovakia, 1912–) came to the United States when he was eight; he has specialized primarily in opera, writing in an arresting idiom he describes as "pretty much the place where Schoenberg was before his final decisive leap into serialism, and where Berg was in *Wozzeck*." *The Tenor* (1950) is derived from a play by Wedekind. Other European dramas have formed the basis for his expressionist-oriented works: *The Stronger* (after Strindberg, 1952), *Six Characters in Search of an Author* (after Pirandello, 1956), and *Purgatory* (after Yeats, 1958). *Nine Rivers to Jordan* (1968) is on a libretto by Denis Johnston.

George Perle (Bayonne, New Jersey, 1915–) has won a reputation as a theorist as well as a composer; his book *Serial Composition and Atonality* is one of the best studies of the twelve-tone method. He has sought to combine serial technique with the possibilities for harmonic direction and tension inherent in the major-minor system, and has evolved a technique of "harmonic modes." This line of thought is fully explored in the eloquent String Quartet No. 5 (1966). Among Perle's works available on records are Six Preludes for Piano (1947) and the String Quintet (1958).

Leon Kirchner (Brooklyn, 1919–) was a student of Schoenberg and Roger Sessions, and has assimilated many of the important traditions of the century into his expressive style. As Aaron Copland has put it, Kirchner's best pages "are charged with an emotional impact and explosive power that is almost frightening in intensity." Two string quartets—No. 1 (1949), with its Bartókian ancestry, and No. 3 (1966), which uses electronic sounds—exemplify the range of Kirchner's resources and the development of his personal language.

Among John Cage's important colleagues in the development of indeterminate music have been Morton Feldman (New York City, 1926–) and Earle Brown (Lunenberg, Massachusetts, 1926–), who led in the development of, respectively, aleatory techniques and open form. A more recent adherent of indeterminancy is Lukas Foss (Berlin, 1922–), who came to America in 1937 and composed first in a Hindemithian neoclassic style. Later Foss developed an interest in group improvisation, and formed an ensemble that developed great facility in a contemporary idiom. More recently, he has become fascinated with aleatory procedures and with the use of pre-existing music as a basis for composition: in his *Baroque Variations* (1967), pieces by Handel, Scarlatti, and Bach are modified and distorted as if by a fun-house mirror. A more substantial work is *Time Cycle,* which exists in two versions: the first (1960) for soprano and orchestra, with improvised interludes by Foss's ensemble; the second (1963) for soprano and chamber group. Foss has been one of the most active performers and propagandists of new musical styles.

Among the many other composers who deserve mention here are: Salvatore Martirano (1927–), whose vivid theater pieces make extensive use of jazz materials and improvisation; Mario Davidovsky (1934–), who has written a number of striking pieces combining live instruments and electronic tapes; Ben Johnston (1926–), whose String Quartet No. 2 makes subtle and convincing use of microtonal materials; Charles Wuorinen (1938–), the brilliant and prolific co-director of the Group for Contemporary Music at Columbia University; and George Crumb (1929–), whose delicate and imaginative use of vocal and percussion sonorities creates a breathless tension. These are just a few members of the immensely varied and talented community of composers who comprise the younger generation of American music.

Other Contemporaries (European)

Luigi Dallapiccola (Pisino, 1904–), like his pupil Berio, unites the age-old tradition of Italian vocal lyricism with the twelve-tone techniques of the Viennese school. Within the serial framework he unfolds his virtuoso handling of contrapuntal and canonic procedures, yet always retains the essentially melodic, vocal character of his lines. A notable choral work is his *Canti di prigionia* (Songs of Captivity, 1938–41), recording a sensitive artist's reaction to the ominous events that led up to the Second World War. Also important are several operas: *Volo di notte* (Night Flight, after Saint-Exupéry, 1940), *Il prigioniero* (The Prisoner, 1944–48), and *Ulisse* (Ulysses, 1968).

Olivier Messiaen (Avignon, 1908–) was the most important teacher in France during the years after the war, when many of the younger Europeans soon to become prominent flocked to Paris to study with him. In particular, Messiaen's theories about rhythm, based on the study of Stravinsky and of the asymmetrical patterns of Hindu music, aroused great interest and proved suggestive for the serial treatment of rhythm. A strong strain of Catholic mysticism runs through such works as the *Trois petites liturgies de la présence divine* (Three Little Liturgies of the Divine Presence, 1944), for female chorus, percussion, Ondes Martenot, and strings. The songs of birds also play an important role in Messiaen's music, as can be heard in *Oiseaux exotiques* (1956), for piano, winds, and percussion. Messiaen's incisive personality, distinctive musical style, and strongly held views have made him a major influence in European music.

631

Messiaen's most important pupil is Pierre Boulez (Montbrison, 1925–), who became a leading advocate of total serialism, believing that the classical twelve-tone works of the Viennese school suffered from an imbalance between their revolutionary methods of pitch organization and their traditional approach to rhythm. Boulez's music is marked by great concentration of thought and a brilliant ear for sonorities. The best-known of his works is *Le Marteau sans maître* (The Hammer Without a Master, 1953–54), for voice and chamber ensemble; its delicate bell-and-percussion sonorities doubtless reflect Messiaen's interest in Eastern music, but the tautness of its organization is Boulez's own. In recent years the demands of a conducting career seem to have limited his compositional output; Boulez is a brilliant interpreter of twentieth-century music, and succeeded Leonard Bernstein as musical director of the New York Philharmonic.

The German counterpart of Pierre Boulez is Karlheinz Stockhausen (Modrath, near Cologne, 1928–), another Messiaen pupil. Beginning from the same Webern-derived point of departure, Stockhausen has nevertheless developed in different directions. He early became interested in the possibilities of electronic music, and has also explored the use of spatial dimensions, as in *Gruppen* (Groups, 1955–57), in which three orchestras, placed on different sides of the audience, play independently, occasionally merging in common rhythm or echoing each other. Both Boulez and Stockhausen have also been influenced by the thought of John Cage, and the German composer has recently developed a number of elaborate, partially aleatory works using both singers and traditional instruments, plus electronic devices for modifying the sounds they produce.

Another approach to contemporary composition is exemplified by the Greek composer Iannis Xenakis (Barila, Rumania, 1922–), who was trained as an engineer, studied music with Messiaen, and bases his musical theories on the laws of mathematics and physics. Whether these theories are valid or not, Xenakis has developed a distinctive musical idiom, as can be heard in such works as *Pithoprakta* (1955–56)—the title means "action by probabilities"— for forty-six strings, two tenor trombones, xylophone, and wood block. In fact, this work is the source of many of the unusual sound effects we hear in Penderecki's *Threnody* and other works of the Polish school.

Other important European figures include the German Hans Werner Henze (1926–), who began as an experimentalist of the Stockhausen stamp but has turned toward a more conventionally eclectic idiom; the English Peter Maxwell Davies (1934–), who has developed an arresting and highly expressive personal style using the techniques and materials of medieval and Renaissance English music; and the Hungarian György Ligeti (1923–), whose choral music achieved wide attention through its use on the soundtrack of the film *2001*. There are many others, whose works prove that our time is as rich in gifted composers as was any era of the past.

Postscript

We have included in these pages a variety of facts, historical, biographical, and technical, that have entered into the making of music and that must enter into an intelligent listening to music. For those who desire to explore the subject further we include a list of books that will guide the music lover in his reading. But books belong to the domain of words, and words have no power over the domain of sound. They are helpful only insofar as they lead us to the music.

The enjoyment of music depends upon perceptive listening. And perceptive listening (like perceptive anything) is something that we achieve gradually, with practice and some effort. By acquiring a knowledge of the circumstances out of which a musical work issued, we prepare ourselves for its multiple meanings; we lay ourselves open to that exercise of mind and heart, sensibility and imagination that makes listening to music so unique an experience. But in the building up of our musical perceptions—that is, of our listening enjoyment—let us always remember that the ultimate wisdom resides neither in dates nor in facts. It is to be found in one place only—the sounds themselves.

APPENDICES

APPENDIX I

Suggested Reading

The following list is merely a starting point, with emphasis on recent and easily available books. Those desiring to pursue the subject further will find specialized bibliographies in many of the works listed below. An asterisk (*) denotes a book available in a paperback edition.

ON THE NATURE OF ART

* Dewey, John. *Art as Experience.* New York: Putnam, 1959.
Fleming, William. *Art and Ideas.* New York: Holt, Rinehart & Winston, 1968.
Lesure, François. *Music and Art in Society.* University Park, Pa.: Penn. State, 1968.
*Meyer, Leonard B. *Music, the Arts and Ideas: Patterns and Predictions in 20th Century Culture.* Chicago: Univ. of Chicago, 1969.
*———— *Emotion and Meaning in Music.* Chicago: Univ. of Chicago, 1961.
* Read, Herbert. *Art and Society.* 2nd ed. New York: Schocken, 1945.
Sachs, Curt. *The Commonwealth of Art.* New York: Norton, 1946.

DICTIONARIES

Apel, Willi. *Harvard Dictionary of Music,* 2nd rev. ed. Cambridge: Harvard, 1969.
*————, and R. T. Daniel. *The Harvard Brief Dictionary of Music.* Cambridge: Harvard, 1970.
Baker's Biographical Dictionary of Musicians, 5th ed. (ed. Nicolas Slonimsky). New York: Schirmer, 1958; with 1965 supplement.
Grove's Dictionary of Music and Musicians, 5th ed. (ed. Eric Blom). New York: St. Martin's, 1954, supplement 1961.
Scholes, Percy A. *Concise Oxford Dictionary of Music.* 2nd ed. (ed. J. O. Ward). New York: Oxford, 1964.
Thompson, Oscar. *The International Cyclopedia of Music and Musicians,* 9th ed. (ed. Robert Sabin). New York: Dodd, Mead, 1964.
*Westrup, J. A., and F. Ll. Harrison. *The New College Encyclopedia of Music.* New York: Norton, 1960.

THE MATERIALS OF MUSIC

*Bekker, Paul. *The Orchestra.* New York: Norton, 1963.
*Bernstein, Leonard. *The Joy of Music.* New York: New American Library, 1967.
Castellini, John. *The Rudiments of Music.* New York: Norton, 1962.
Clough, John. *Scales, Intervals, Keys and Triads.* New York: Norton, 1964.
*Cooper, Grosvenor W., and Leonard Meyer. *The Rhythmic Structure of Music.* Chicago: Univ. of Chicago, 1963.
*Copland, Aaron. *What to Listen for in Music.* New York: Mentor, 1964.
Grove's Dictionary of Music and *Harvard Dictionary of Music:* articles on melody, harmony, rhythm, meter, tempo, timbre, etc.
Ratner, Leonard G. *Music: The Listener's Art,* 2nd ed. New York: McGraw-Hill, 1966.
Sachs, Curt. *Rhythm and Tempo.* New York: Norton, 1953.
*Tovey, Donald F. *The Forms of Music.* New York: Meridian, 1956.

MUSIC HISTORY (ONE-VOLUME WORKS)

Crocker, Richard L. *A History of Musical Style.* New York: McGraw-Hill, 1966.
*Dorian, Frederick. *The History of Music in Performance.* New York: Norton, 1966.

637

*Einstein, Alfred. *A Short History of Music*. New York: Vintage, 1954.
*Gerboth, Walter, *et al.* (eds.). *An Introduction to Music: Selected Readings*. New York: Norton, 1964, 1969.
Grout, Donald. *A History of Western Music*. New York: Norton, 1960.
*Janson, H. W., and Joseph Kerman. *A History of Art and Music*. New York: Abrams, 1968.
Lang, Paul Henry. *Music in Western Civilization*. New York: Norton, 1941.
Sachs, Curt. *Our Musical Heritage: A Short History of Music*, 2nd ed. Englewood Cliffs, N. J.: Prentice-Hall, 1955.
*Wiora, Walter. *The Four Ages of Music* (tr. M. D. Herter Norton). New York: Norton, 1967.

MUSICAL INSTRUMENTS

Baines, Anthony (ed.). *Musical Instruments Through the Ages*. New York: Walker, 1966.
Harrison, Frank Ll., and Joan Rimmer. *European Musical Instruments*. New York: Norton, 1964.
Marcuse, Sybil. *Musical Instruments: A Comprehensive Dictionary*. New York: Doubleday, 1964.
Sachs, Curt. *History of Musical Instruments*. New York: Norton, 1940.
Winternitz, Emanuel. *Musical Instruments of the Western World*. New York: McGraw-Hill, 1967.
——— *Musical Instruments and Their Symbolism in Western Art*. New York: Norton, 1967.

STYLES AND PERIODS

ANTIQUITY

Sachs, Curt. *The Rise of Music in the Ancient World*. New York: Norton, 1943.
*Strunk, Oliver (ed.). *Source Readings in Music History: Antiquity and the Middle Ages*. New York: Norton, 1965.

MEDIEVAL

Reese, Gustave. *Music in the Middle Ages*. New York: Norton, 1940.
*Seay, Albert. *Music in the Medieval World*. Englewood Cliffs, N.J.: Prentice-Hall, 1965.

RENAISSANCE AND BAROQUE

* Blume, Friedrich. *Renaissance and Baroque Music*. (tr. M. D. Herter Norton). New York: Norton, 1967.
Bukofzer, Manfred F. *Music in the Baroque Era*. New York: Norton, 1947.
*Palisca, Claude V. *Baroque Music*. Englewood Cliffs, N.J.: Prentice-Hall, 1968.
Reese, Gustave. *Music in the Renaissance*, rev. ed. New York: Norton, 1959.
*Strunk, Oliver (ed.). *Source Readings in Music History: The Baroque Era*. New York: Norton, 1965.
*——— *Source Readings in Music History: The Renaissance*. New York: Norton, 1965.

CLASSIC AND ROMANTIC

Abraham, Gerald. *A Hundred Years of Music*, 3rd ed. Chicago: Aldine, 1964.
*Blume, Friedrich. *Classic and Romantic Music* (tr. M. D. Herter Norton). New York: Norton, 1970.
Einstein, Alfred. *Music in the Romantic Era*. New York: Norton, 1947.
*Longyear, Rey M. *Nineteenth-Century Romanticism in Music*. Englewood Cliffs, N.J.: Prentice-Hall, 1969.
*Praz, Mario. *The Romantic Agony*. New York: Meridian, 1951.
*Strunk, Oliver (ed.). *Source Readings in Music History: The Classic Era*. New York: Norton, 1965.
*——— *Source Readings in Music History: The Romantic Era*. New York: Norton, 1965.

CONTEMPORARY

Austin, William. *Music in the Twentieth Century*. New York: Norton, 1966.
*Copland, Aaron. *The New Music, 1900–1960*. New York: Norton, 1968.
*Cowell, Henry. *American Composers on American Music*. New York: Ungar, 1962.
*Lang, Paul Henry, and Nathan Broder (eds.). *Contemporary Music in Europe*: A *Comprehensive Survey*. New York: Norton, 1965.
Machlis, Joseph. *Introduction to Contemporary Music*. New York: Norton, 1961.
Reis, Claire. *Composers in America*. New York: Macmillan, 1947.
*Salzman, Eric. *Twentieth-Century Music. An Introduction*. Englewood Cliffs, N.J.: Prentice-Hall, 1967.

JAZZ

*Blesh, Rudi, and Harriet Janis. *They All Played Ragtime*, rev. ed. New York: Oak, 1966.
*Ellison, Ralph. "Sound and the Mainstream," in *Shadow and Act*. New York: Random House, 1964.
Feather, Leonard. *The Encyclopedia of Jazz*, rev. ed. New York: Horizon, 1960.
*Hodeir, André. *Jazz: Its Evolution and Essence*. New York: Grove, 1961.
*———— *Toward Jazz*. New York: Evergreen, 1962.
Murray, Albert. *The Omni-Americans*. New York: Outerbridge and Dienstfrey, 1970.
Schuller, Gunther. *Early Jazz: Its Roots and Musical Development*. New York: Oxford, 1968.
*Shapiro, Nat, and Nat Hentoff (eds.). *Hear Me Talkin' to Ya: The Story of Jazz by the Men Who Made It*. New York: Dover, 1966.
Spellman, A. B. *Four Lives in the Bebop Business*. New York: Pantheon, 1966.
*Stearns, Marshall. *The Story of Jazz*. New York: Mentor, 1958.
*Williams, Martin. *Where's the Melody? A Listener's Introduction to Jazz*, rev. ed. New York: Pantheon, 1969.
*———— (ed.). *Jazz Panorama*. New York: Crowell-Collier, 1962.
————*The Jazz Tradition*. New York: Oxford, 1970.

GENRES

Grout, Donald. *A Short History of Opera*. 2nd ed. New York: Columbia, 1965.
Hamm, Charles. *Opera*. Boston: Allyn & Bacon, 1966.
*Kerman, Joseph. *Opera as Drama*. New York: Vintage, 1956.
Stevens, Denis (ed.). *A History of Song*. New York: Norton, 1961.
Ulrich, Homer. *Chamber Music*. 2nd ed. New York: Columbia, 1966.
———— *Symphonic Music*. New York: Columbia, 1962.
*Weisstein, Ulrich (ed.). *The Essence of Opera*. New York: Norton, 1969.

COMPOSERS (ON AND BY)

BACH

*David, Hans T., and Arthur Mendel (eds.). *The Bach Reader*, rev. ed. New York: Norton, 1966.
Geiringer, Karl, with Irene Geiringer. *Johann Sebastian Bach: The Culmination of an Era*. New York: Oxford, 1966.

BARTÓK

*Stevens, Halsey. *The Life and Music of Béla Bartók*, rev. ed. New York: Oxford, 1967.

BEETHOVEN

Anderson, Emily (ed. & tr.). *The Letters of Beethoven*, rev. ed. New York: St. Martin's, 1964.

Burk, John N. *Life and Works of Beethoven.* New York: Modern Library, n.d.
*Grove, George. *Beethoven and His Nine Symphonies,* 3rd ed., 1898. New York: Dover, 1962.
Kerman, Joseph. *The Beethoven Quartets.* New York: Knopf, 1967.
*Sonneck, O. G. (ed.). *Beethoven: Impressions by His Contemporaries,* 1926. New York: Dover, 1967.
Thayer, Alexander W. *Life of Beethoven,* rev. ed. (ed. Elliot Forbes). Princeton: Princeton Univ., 1964.

ALBAN BERG

Reich, Willi. *Alban Berg* (tr. C. Cardew). New York: Harcourt, Brace & World, 1965.

BERLIOZ

*Barzun, J. *Berlioz and the Romantic Century,* 2 vols., 3rd ed. New York: Columbia, 1969.
Berlioz, Hector. *Memoirs* (ed. and tr. David Cairns). New York: Knopf, 1969.
———— *Evenings with the Orchestra* (tr. J. Barzun). New York: Knopf, 1956.

BIZET

Curtiss, Mina. *Bizet and His World.* New York: Knopf, 1958.
Dean, Winton. *Bizet.* London: Dent, 1948.

BRAHMS

Geiringer, Karl. *Brahms: His Life and Works,* 2nd ed. New York: Oxford, 1947.

BRUCKNER

*Doernberg, Erwin. *Life and Symphonies of Anton Bruckner.* New York: Dover, 1968.
Redlich, H. F. *Bruckner and Mahler.* New York: Farrar, Strauss & Cudahy, 1955.
Simpson, Robert. *The Essence of Bruckner: An Essay Toward the Understanding of His Music.* New York: Chilton, 1968.

BYRD

Fellowes, Edmund H. *William Byrd,* 2nd ed. London: Oxford, 1948.

COPLAND

*Copland, Aaron. *Copland on Music.* New York: Norton, 1963.
Smith, Julia. *Aaron Copland.* New York: Dutton, 1955.

CORELLI

*Pincherle, Marc. *Corelli: His Life, His Work.* New York: Norton, 1956.

CHOPIN

Huneker, James G. *Chopin: Man and His Music* (ed. H. Weinstock). New York: Dover, 1966.
Walker, Alan. *Frédéric Chopin: Profiles of the Man and the Musician.* New York: Taplinger, 1967.

COUPERIN

Mellers, Wilfrid. *François Couperin and the French Classical Tradition,* London: Dobson, 1950.

CAGE

*Cage, John. *A Year from Monday; New Lectures and Writings.* Middletown, Conn.: Wesleyan, 1969.
*———— *Silence: Lectures and Writings.* Cambridge: MIT, 1961.

DEBUSSY

*Debussy, Claude. "Monsieur Croche," in *Three Classics in the Esthetics of Music.* New York: Dover, 1962.

Lockspeiser, Edward. *Debussy: His Life and Mind*, 2 vols. New York: MacMillan, 1962.
*———— *Debussy: His Life and Times*. New York: Collier-Macmillan, 1962.
* Vallas, Léon. *Theories of Claude Debussy, Musicien Française* (tr. Maire O'Brian).
   New York: Dover, 1967.

DVOŘÁK

*Burghauser, Jarmil. *Antonín Dvořák* (tr. J. Layton-Eislewood). Prague: Artia, 1967.
Clapham, John. *Antonín Dvořák, Musician and Craftsman*. New York: St. Martin's,
   1966.
Dvořák, Antonín. *Letters and Reminiscences* (ed. Otokar Šourek). Prague: Artia, 1954.

FRANCK

*Demuth, Norman, *César Franck*. London: Dobson, 1949.

GERSHWIN

*Goldberg, Isaac. *George Gershwin*. New York: Ungar, 1958.

GLUCK

* Einstein, Alfred. *Gluck*. New York: Collier-Macmillan, 1955.
Gluck, C. W. *The Collected Correspondence* (ed. H. Asow, tr. S. Thomson). London:
   Barrie & Rockcliff, 1962.

HANDEL

Abraham, Gerald (ed.). *Handel, A Symposium*. London: Oxford, 1954.
Dean, Winton. *Handel's Dramatic Oratorios and Masques*. London: Oxford, 1959.
Deutsch, Otto Erich. *Handel: A Documentary Biography*. New York: Norton, 1955.
Lang, Paul Henry. *George Frideric Handel*. New York: Norton, 1966.

HAYDN

*Geiringer, Karl. *Haydn, a Creative Life in Music*, rev. ed. Los Angeles, Cal.: Univ. of
   Cal., 1963.
Haydn, Joseph. *Collected Correspondence and London Notebooks* (ed. H. C. Robbins
   Landon). New York: Oxford, 1959.
Landon, H. C. Robbins. *The Symphonies of Joseph Haydn*. London: Rockcliff and
   Universal Edition, 1955; supplement, 1961.

HINDEMITH

* Hindemith, Paul. *A Composer's World*. New York: Doubleday Anchor, 1961.

IVES

*Cowell, Henry, and Sidney Cowell. *Charles Ives and His Music*, rev. ed. New York:
   Oxford, 1969.
* Ives, Charles. *Essays Before a Sonata and Other Writings* (ed. Howard Boatwright).
   New York: Norton, 1962.

LISZT

*Searle, Humphrey. *The Music of Liszt*. New York: Dover, 1966.

MACDOWELL

Gilman, Lawrence. *Edward MacDowell, a Study*. New York: DaCapo, 1969.
MacDowell, Edward. *Critical and Historical Essays*. New York: DaCapo, 1969.

MAHLER

Cardus, Neville. *Gustav Mahler: His Mind and His Music*. New York: St. Martin's,
   1965.
Mahler, Alma Schindler. *Gustav Mahler: Memories and Letters* (ed. Donald Mitchell).
   New York: Viking, 1969.

641

MENDELSSOHN

Werner, Eric. *Felix Mendelssohn*. New York: Free Press, 1963.

MONTEVERDI

Arnold, Denis. *Monteverdi*. New York: Farrar, Strauss & Giroux, 1963.
Arnold, Denis, and Nigel Fortune (eds.). *The Monteverdi Companion*. New York: Norton, 1968.
*Schrade, Leo. *Monteverdi, Creator of Modern Music*. New York: Norton, 1950, 1969.

MOZART

Anderson, Emily (ed.). *Letters of Mozart and his Family*, 2 vols., 2nd ed. (eds. A. Hyatt King and Monica Carolan). New York: St. Martin's, 1966.
*Blom, Eric. *Mozart*. New York: Collier, 1966.
Deutsch, Otto Erich. *Mozart: A Documentary Biography*, 2nd ed. Stanford, Cal.: Stanford Univ. Press, 1966.
*Landon, H. C. Robbins, and Donald Mitchell (eds.). *The Mozart Companion*. New York: Norton, 1956, 1969.
*Lang, Paul Henry (ed.). *The Creative World of Mozart*. New York: Norton, 1963.

MUSORGSKY

*Calvocoressi, M. D. *Mussorgsky*. New York: Collier, 1962.
Leyda, J., and S. Bertensson (eds.). *The Mussorgsky Reader*. New York: Norton, 1947.

PROKOFIEV

Nestyev, Israel V. *Prokofiev* (tr. Florence Jonas). Stanford, Cal.: Stanford Univ. Press, 1960.

PUCCINI

Ashbrook, William. *The Operas of Puccini*. New York: Oxford, 1968.
Carner, Mosco. *Puccini*. New York: Knopf, 1959.

PURCELL

Zimmerman, Franklin B. *Henry Purcell, His Life and Times*. New York: St. Martin's, 1967.

RACHMANINOV

Bertensson, S., and J. Leyda. *Sergei Rachmaninoff: A Lifetime in Music*. New York: New York Univ. Pr., 1956.

RAMEAU

*Girdlestone, C. M. *Jean-Philippe Rameau: His Life and Work*. New York: Dover, 1969.

RAVEL

Stuckenschmidt, Hans Heinz. *Maurice Ravel* (tr. S. R. Rosenbaum). Philadelphia: Chilton, 1968.

SCARLATTI, D.

*Kirkpatrick, Ralph. *Domenico Scarlatti*. New York: Apollo, 1968.

SCHOENBERG

Schoenberg, Arnold. *Letters* (eds. E. Stein and E. Kaiser). New York: St. Martin's, 1965.
———— *Style and Idea*. New York: Philosophical, 1950.
Stuckenschmidt, Hans Heinz. *Arnold Schoenberg* (trs. E. T. Roberts and H. Searle). New York: Grove, 1961.

SCHUBERT

Brown, Maurice J. E. *Schubert: A Biography with Critical Digressions*. New York: St. Martin's, 1958.

Deutsch, Otto Erich. *Schubert: A Documentary Biography* (tr. Eric Blom). London: Dent, 1947.
—— *Schubert: Memoirs by His Friends.* New York: Hillary, 1958.
Einstein, Alfred. *Schubert: A Musical Portrait.* New York: Oxford, 1951.

SCHUMANN

* Chissell, Joan. *Schumann.* New York: Collier-Macmillan, 1962.
Plantinga, Leon B. *Schumann as Critic.* New Haven, Conn.: Yale, 1968.
*Schumann, Robert. *On Music and Musicians.* New York: Norton, 1969.

SESSIONS

*Sessions, Roger. *The Musical Experience of Composer, Performer, Listener.* New York: Atheneum, 1962.
—— *Questions About Music.* Cambridge: Harvard, 1970.

SIBELIUS

Johnson, Harold E. *Jean Sibelius.* New York: Knopf, 1959.

STRAUSS

Mann, William S. *Richard Strauss: A Critical Study of the Operas.* New York: Oxford, 1966.
Marek, George. *Richard Strauss: The Life of a Non-Hero.* New York: Simon & Schuster, 1967.
Strauss, Richard, and Hugo von Hofmannsthal. *A Working Friendship.* New York: Random House, 1962.

STRAVINSKY

*Lang, Paul Henry (ed.). *Stravinsky: A New Appraisal of His Work.* New York: Norton, 1963.
*Stravinsky, Igor. *Autobiography.* New York: Norton, 1962.
*—— *Poetics of Music.* New York: Vintage, 1956.
—— with Robert Craft. *Conversations with Igor Stravinsky.* New York: Doubleday, 1959.
—————— *Retrospectives and Conclusions.* New York: Knopf, 1969.
—————— *Themes and Episodes.* New York: Knopf, 1969.
Vlad, Roman. *Stravinsky.* London: Oxford, 1967.
White, Eric Walter. *Stravinsky, the Composer and His Works.* Berkeley & Los Angeles, Cal.: Univ. of Cal., 1966.

TCHAIKOVSKY

*Abraham, Gerald. *Tchaikovsky.* Chester Springs, Pa.: Dufour, 1968.
Weinstock, Herbert. *Tchaikovsky.* New York: Knopf, 1943.

THOMSON

*Thomson, Virgil. *Music Observed: 1940–1954.* New York: Vintage, 1967.
—— *The Art of Judging Music.* New York: Greenwood, 1969.
—— *Virgil Thomson.* New York: Knopf, 1966.

VIVALDI

*Pincherle, Marc. *Vivaldi: Genius of the Baroque.* New York: Norton, 1962.

VERDI

*Toye, Francis. *Giuseppe Verdi, His Life and Works.* New York: Vintage, 1959.

WAGNER

Gutman, Robert. *Richard Wagner: The Man, His Mind, and His Music.* New York: Harcourt, Brace & World, 1968.
Newman, Ernest. *The Life of Richard Wagner,* 4 vols. New York: Knopf, 1933–46.

*———— *Wagner as Man and Artist.* New York: Vintage, 1924.

Wagner, Richard. *Wagner on Music and Drama* (eds. Goldman and Sprincharn). New York: Dutton, 1964.

White, Chappell. *An Introduction to the Life and Works of Richard Wagner.* Englewood Cliffs, N.J.: Prentice-Hall, 1967.

WEBERN

Kolneder, Walter. *Anton Webern: An Introduction to His Works* (tr. Humphrey Searle). Berkeley & Los Angeles, Cal.: Univ. of Cal., 1968.

Moldenauer, Hans, and Demar Irvine (eds.). *Anton von Webern: Perspectives.* Seattle, Washington: Univ. of Washington, 1966.

APPENDIX II

Comparative Range of Voices and Instuments

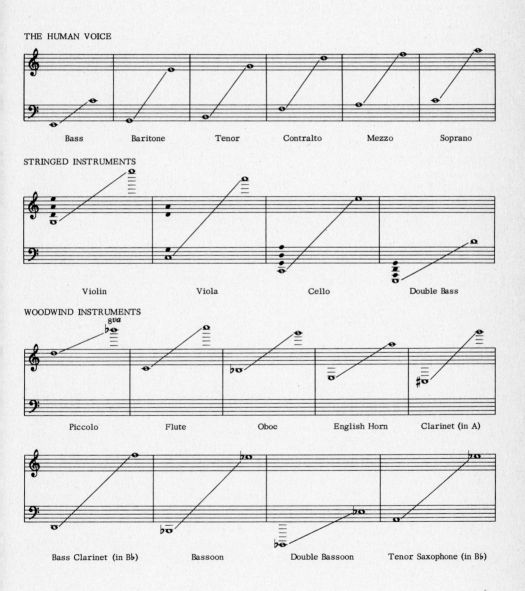

THE HUMAN VOICE

Bass Baritone Tenor Contralto Mezzo Soprano

STRINGED INSTRUMENTS

Violin Viola Cello Double Bass

WOODWIND INSTRUMENTS

Piccolo Flute Oboe English Horn Clarinet (in A)

Bass Clarinet (in Bb) Bassoon Double Bassoon Tenor Saxophone (in Bb)

BRASS INSTRUMENTS

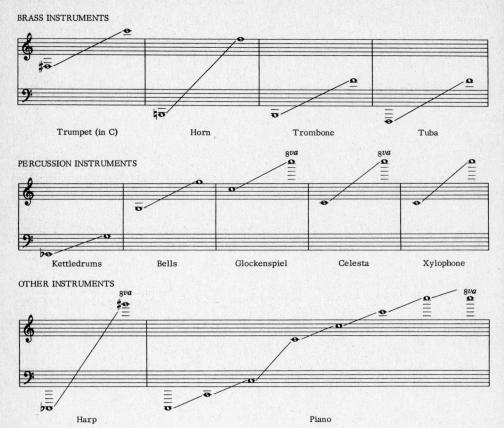

Trumpet (in C)   Horn   Trombone   Tuba

PERCUSSION INSTRUMENTS

Kettledrums   Bells   Glockenspiel   Celesta   Xylophone

OTHER INSTRUMENTS

Harp   Piano

APPENDIX III

Complete List of Major and Minor Scales

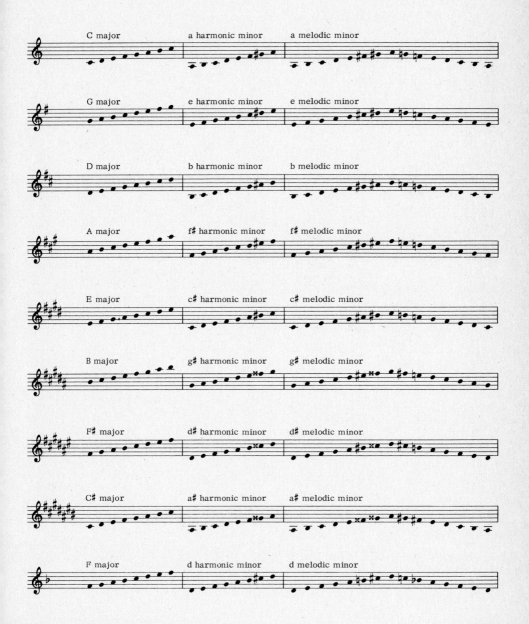

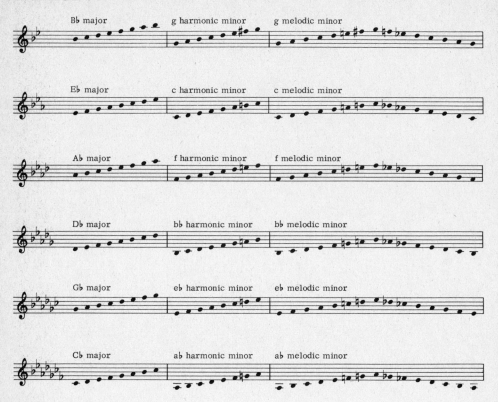

APPENDIX IV

A Chronological List of Composers, World Events, and Principal Figures in Literature and the Arts, 1400–1969

Guillaume Dufay
(c. 1400–74)

1415 John Huss burned for heresy. Henry V defeats French at Agincourt.

1453 Constantinople captured by Turks.

1456 Gutenberg Bible.

Josquin des Prez
(c. 1450–1521)

1492 Columbus discovers New World.

1506 St. Peter's begun by Pope Julius II: Bramante, Raphael, Michelangelo, *et al.*

1509 Henry VIII becomes King of England.

1513 Ponce de Leon discovers Florida. Balboa reaches Pacific.

1517 Luther posts 95 theses on Wittenberg church door.

1519 Cortez begins conquest of Mexico.

1520 Magellan reaches Philippines.

1534 Henry VIII head of Church of England.

1536 Anne Boleyn beheaded.

1541 De Soto discovers the Mississippi.

Giovanni da Palestrina
(c. 1525–94)
Roland de Lassus
(c. 1532–94)
William Byrd
(1543–1623)
Tomás Luis de Victoria
(c. 1549–1611)
Luca Marenzio
(c. 1553–99)
Giovanni Gabrieli
(c. 1557–1612)
Thomas Morley
(1557–c. 1603)
Carlo Gesualdo
(1560–1613)

1558 Elizabeth I becomes Queen of England.

1572 St. Bartholomew's Eve Massacre.

1587 Mary Queen of Scots executed. Virginia Dare, first English child born in New World.

1588 Drake defeats Spanish Armada.

1590 First three books of Spenser's *Faerie Queene* published.

Luca della Robbia
(1400–82)
Giovanni Bellini
(1430–1516)
François Villon
(1431–c. 1465)
Sandro Botticelli
(1447–1510)
Leonardo da Vinci
(1452–1519)
Erasmus (1466–1536)
Niccolò Machiavelli
(1469–1527)
Albrecht Dürer
(1471–1528)
Michelangelo
(1475–1564)
Titian (1477–1576)
Raphael (1483–1520)
François Rabelais
(1490–1553)
Hans Holbein
(1497–1543)
Benvenuto Cellini
(1500–71)
Pierre de Ronsard
(1524–85)
Pieter Brueghel
(1525-69)
Michel de Montaigne
(1533–92)
El Greco (1542–1614)
Miguel de Cervantes
(1547–1616)

Edmund Spenser
(1552–99)

William Shakespeare
(1564–1616)

649

Claudio Monteverdi
(1567–1643)
John Wilbye
(1573–1638)

Thomas Weelkes
(c. 1575–1623)
Orlando Gibbons
(1583–1625)
Heinrich Schütz
(1585–1672)

1601–09   Shakespeare's best tragedies (*Hamlet, Othello, Macbeth, Lear, Antony and Cleopatra*) and comedies (*As You Like It, Twelfth Night, Much Ado About Nothing*).

1607   Jamestown settled.

1609   Henry Hudson explores Hudson River.

1618–48   Thirty Years' War.

1620   Mayflower Compact. Plymouth settled. Francis Bacon's *Novum Organum*.

1626   Manhattan Island purchased from Indians.

1628   Harvey discovers circulation of blood.

1637   Descartes's *Discourse on Method*.

1642–49   Puritan Revolution in England.

1649–60   Commonwealth and Protectorate in England.

1651   Hobbes's *Leviathan*.

Jean-Baptiste Lully
(1632–87)

1661–1715   Reign of Louis XIV. Absolutism.

1664   New Amsterdam becomes New York.

Dietrich Buxtehude
(1637–1707)
Arcangelo Corelli
(1653–1713)
Henry Purcell
(1659–95)
François Couperin
(1668–1733)
Antonio Vivaldi
(1678–1741)
Georg Telemann
(1681–1767)
Jean-Philippe Rameau
(1683–1764)
Johann Sebastian Bach
(1685–1750)
Domenico Scarlatti
(1685–1757)
George Frideric Handel (1685–1759)

1666   Newton discovers Law of Gravity.

1667   Spinoza's *Ethics*.

1669   Academy of Music (Paris Opera) founded.

1682–1725   Reign of Peter the Great.

1685   Locke's *Two Treatises on Civil Government*.

1702–14   War of the Spanish Succession.

1712   Queen Anne succeeded by George I, Handel's patron.
1715   First Opéra Comique founded.
1715–74   Reign of Louis XV.
1719   Herculaneum and Pompeii rediscovered. Classical Revival.
1732   Linnaeus's *System of Nature*.

John Donne
(1573–1631)
Ben Jonson
(1573–1637)
Peter Paul Rubens
(1577–1640)
Frans Hals
(1580?–1666)
Giovanni Lorenzo Bernini (1598–1680)
Anthony Van Dyck
(1599–1641)
Diego Velázquez
(1599–1660)
Rembrandt
(1606–69)
Pierre Corneille
(1606–84)
John Milton
(1608–74)
Molière (1622–73)
John Bunyan
(1628–88)
John Dryden
(1631–1700)
Jan Vermeer
(1632–75)
Sir Christopher Wren
(1632–1723)
Jean Baptiste Racine
(1639–99)
Daniel Defoe
(1659?–1731)

Jonathan Swift
(1667–1745)
Joseph Addison
(1672–1719)
Richard Steele
(1672–1729)
Jean Antoine Watteau
(1684–1721)

Alexander Pope
(1688–1744)
Voltaire (1694–1778)
Giovanni Battista Tiepolo (1696–1770)
William Hogarth
(1697–1764)
François Boucher
(1703–70)

Giovanni Battista Pergolesi (1710–36)

1732–99 George Washington.

Henry Fielding (1707–54)

1737 San Carlo Opera, Naples, opened.

Samuel Johnson (1709–84)

1740–96 Age of Enlightened Despots.

Jean Jacques Rousseau (1712–78)

1743–1826 Thomas Jefferson.

Laurence Sterne (1713–68)

Christoph Willibald Gluck (1714–87)
Carl Philipp Emanuel Bach (1714–88)
Johann Stamitz (1717–57)

1751–72 Great Encyclopedia. Age of Enlightenment.

1752 Franklin's discoveries in electricity.

Thomas Gray (1716–71)
Sir Joshua Reynolds (1723–92)
Thomas Gainsborough (1727–88)
Oliver Goldsmith (1728–74)

Joseph Haydn (1732–1809)

1756–63 Seven Years' War (in America, the French and Indian War).
1759 Wolfe captures Quebec.

Pierre Augustín Caron de Beaumarchais (1732–99)
Jean Honoré Fragonard (1732–1809)

Johann Christian Bach (1735–82)
Domenico Cimarosa (1749–1801)

1763 Canada ceded to England.

1765 Watt's steam engine.

Edward Gibbon (1737–94)
Jean Antoine Houdon (1741–1828)
Francisco José de Goya (1746–1828)

1767 Hargreaves's spinning jenny.

Jacques Louis David (1748–1825)

c. 1770 Beginning of the factory system.

Johann Wolfgang von Goethe (1749–1832)

Wolfgang Amadeus Mozart (1756–91)
Maria Luigi Cherubini (1760–1842)

1771 First edition, *Encyclopedia Britannica*.

William Blake (1757–1827)
Robert Burns (1759–96)

1774 Priestley discovers oxygen.

Johann Christoph Friedrich von Schiller (1759–1805)

Ludwig van Beethoven (1770–1827)

1775–83 American Revolution.

William Wordsworth (1770–1850)

1776 Declaration of Independence.

Sir Walter Scott (1771–1832)
Samuel Taylor Coleridge (1772–1834)

Gasparo Spontini (1774–1851)

1776 Adam Smith's *The Wealth of Nations*.

J. M. W. Turner (1775–1851)
John Constable (1776–1837)

1778 La Scala Opera opened in Milan.
1781 Kant's *Critique of Pure Reason*.
1787 Constitutional Convention.
1789–94 French Revolution.
1791 Bill of Rights.
1793 Eli Whitney's cotton gin.

Jean Dominique Ingres (1780–1867)

George Gordon Byron (1788–1824)

Niccolo Paganini
(1782–1840)
Carl Maria von Weber
(1786–1826)
Giacomo Meyerbeer
(1791–1864)
Gioacchino Rossini
(1792–1868)

Gaetano Donizetti
(1797–1848)
Franz Schubert
(1797–1828)

Vincenzo Bellini
(1801–35)

Hector Berlioz
(1803–69)
Johann Strauss (the
father: 1804–49)
Michael Glinka
(1804–57)

Felix Mendelssohn
(1809–47)

Frédéric François
Chopin (1810–49)
Robert Schumann
(1810–56)
Franz Liszt (1811–86)

Richard Wagner
(1813–83)
Giuseppe Verdi
(1813–1901)

Charles Gounod
(1818–93)

1796   Jenner introduces vaccination.

1798   Malthus's *Essay on Population*.

1800   Laplace's mechanistic view of universe.
        Volta invents voltaic pile.

1803   Louisiana Purchase.

1807   Hegel's *Phenomenology of Mind*.

1807   Fulton's steamboat.

1812   Napoleon invades Russia.

1815   Battle of Waterloo. Congress of
        Vienna.

1817   Ricardo's *Political Economy and Tax-
        ation*.

1819   First steamship to cross Atlantic.

1823   Monroe Doctrine.

1824   Bolivar liberates South America.

1829   Independence of Greece.

1830   First railroad, Liverpool–Manchester.
        July Revolution in France.

1832   Morse invents telegraph.

1833   Slavery outlawed in British Empire.

1834   McCormick patents mechanical reaper.

1837–1901   Reign of Victoria.

Alphonse Lamartine
(1790–1869)
Jean Louis Géricault
(1791–1824)
Percy Bysshe Shelley
(1792–1822)
John Keats
(1795–1821)
Thomas Carlyle
(1795–1881)
John Baptiste Camille
Corot (1796–1875)
Alexander Pushkin
(1799–1837)
Honoré de Balzac
(1799–1850)
Eugène Delacroix
(1799–1863)
Alexander Dumas
(1802–70)
Victor Hugo
(1802–85)
Ralph Waldo Emerson
(1803–82)
Nathaniel Hawthorne
(1804–64)
George Sand
(1804–76)
Honoré Daumier
(1808–79)
Edgar Allan Poe
(1809–49)
Nikolai Gogol
(1809–52)
Alfred Tennyson
(1809–92)

William Makepeace
Thackeray
(1811–63)
Charles Dickens
(1812–70)
Robert Browning
(1812–89)
Charlotte Brontë
(1816–55)
Henry David Thoreau
(1817–62)
Emily Brontë
(1818–48)
Ivan Sergeyevich Tur-
genev (1818–83)
Herman Melville
(1818–91)

Jacques Offenbach
(1819–80)

1839   Daguerrotype invented, beginnings of photography. N.Y. Philharmonic Society and Vienna Philharmonic founded.

George Eliot
(1819–80)
Walt Whitman
(1819–92)

John Ruskin
(1819–1900)
Pierre Charles Baudelaire (1821–67)
Gustave Flaubert
(1821–80)

1846   Repeal of Corn Laws. Famine in Ireland.

César Franck
(1822–90)
Édouard Lalo
(1823–92)
Bedřich Smetana
(1824–84)
Anton Bruckner
(1824–96)
Johann Strauss (the son: 1825–99)
Stephen Collins Foster
(1826–64)

1848   Revolutions throughout Europe.

Feodor Mikhailovich Dostoievsky
(1821–81)

1848   Gold Rush in California. Mill's *Political Economy*. Marx's *Communist Manifesto*.

1852   Second Empire under Napoleon III. *Uncle Tom's Cabin*.

1853   Commodore Perry opens Japan to West. Crimean War.

Dante Gabriel Rossetti
(1828–82)
Henrik Ibsen
(1828–1906)
George Meredith
(1828–1909)
Leo Nikolaevich Tolstoi (1828–1910)
Emily Dickinson
(1830–86)
Camille Pissarro
(1830–1903)
Édouard Manet
(1832–83)
James McNeill Whistler (1834–1903)
Hilaire Germain Edgar Degas (1834–1917)
Mark Twain
(1835–1910)
Winslow Homer
(1836–1910)
Algernon Charles Swinburne
(1837–1909)
William Dean Howells
(1837–1920)
H. H. Richardson
(1838–86)
Henry Adams
(1838–1918)
Paul Cézanne
(1839–1906)
Alphonse Daudet
(1840–97)

1855   Charge of the Light Brigade.

1857   Dred Scott decision.

1858   Covent Garden opened as opera house.

1859   Darwin's *Origin of Species*. John Brown raids Harper's Ferry.

Johannes Brahms
(1833–97)
Alexander Borodin
(1834–87)

1861   Serfs emancipated in Russia.
1861–65   Civil War in America.
1863   Emancipation Proclamation.
1865   Lincoln assassinated.
1866   Transatlantic cable completed.
1867   Marx's *Das Kapital* (first vol.). Alaska purchased.
1870   Franco-Prussian War.
1871   William I of Hohenzollern becomes German Emperor. Vatican Council proclaims papal infallibility. Paris Commune. Unification of Italy complete; Rome becomes capital. Stanley and Livingston in Africa.

Camille Saint-Saëns
(1835–1921)
Léo Delibes
(1836–91)
Mily Balakirev
(1837–1910)

Georges Bizet
(1838–75)

1873   Dynamo developed.

1875   New Paris Opera House opened.

Modest Musorgsky
(1839–81)

1876   Telephone invented. Internal-combustion engine. Bayreuth theater opened.

1877   Phonograph invented.

Peter Ilyich Tchaikovsky (1840–93)

1880 Irish Insurrection.

1881 Tsar Alexander II assassinated. President Garfield shot.

1881–1914 Panama Canal built. Boston Symphony founded.

Auguste Rodin
(1840–1917)
Claude Monet
(1840–1926)
Thomas Hardy
(1840–1928)
Émile Zola
(1840–1902)
Pierre Auguste Renoir
(1841–1919)

Emmanuel Chabrier
(1841–94)
Antonín Dvořák
(1841–1904)
Jules Massenet
(1842–1912)
Edvard Grieg
(1843–1907)
Nicholas Rimsky-Korsakov (1844–1908)

1882 Koch discovers tuberculosis germ. Berlin Philharmonic founded.

1883 Brooklyn Bridge opened. Nietzsche's *Thus Spake Zarathustra*. Metropolitan Opera opened. Amsterdam Concertgebouw founded.

1884 Pasteur discovers inoculation against rabies.

1886 Statue of Liberty unveiled in New York Harbor.

1887 Daimler patents high-speed internal-combustion engine.

Stéphane Mallarmé
(1842–98)
Henry James
(1843–1916)
Paul Verlaine
(1844–96)
Friedrich Wilhelm
Nietzsche
(1844–1900)
Anatole France
(1844–1924)

Gabriel Fauré
(1845–1924)
Henri Duparc
(1848–1933)

1889 Eiffel Tower, Paris World's Fair opened. Brazil becomes republic.

1890 Journey around world completed in 72 days.

1892 Duryea makes first American gas buggy.

Paul Gauguin
(1848–1903)
Augustus St. Gaudens
(1848–1907)
Joris Karl Huysmans
(1848–1907)
Guy de Maupassant
(1850–93)
Robert Louis Stevenson (1850–94)
Vincent Van Gogh
(1853–90)
Arthur Rimbaud
(1854–91)
Oscar Wilde
(1856–1900)
Louis H. Sullivan
(1856–1924)
John Singer Sargent
(1856–1925)
George Bernard Shaw
(1856–1950)
Joseph Conrad
(1857–1924)

Vincent d'Indy
(1851–1931)

Leoš Janáček
(1854–1928)
Ernest Chausson
(1855–99)

1893 World's Columbian Exposition, Chicago.

1894 Nicholas II, last Tsar, ascends throne.

1894–1905 Dreyfus affair.

1895 Roentgen discovers X-rays. Marconi's wireless telegraphy.

1896 Becquerel finds radioactivity in uranium. Olympic games revived. Gold rush in Alaska.

Sir Edward Elgar
(1857–1934)
Ruggiero Leoncavallo
(1858–1919)
Giacomo Puccini
(1858–1924)

1897 Queen Victoria's Diamond Jubilee.

1898 Pierre and Marie Curie discover radium. Empress Elizabeth of Austria-Hungary assassinated. Spanish-American War.

Georges Seurat
(1859–91)
A. E. Housman
(1859–1936)
Anton Chekov
(1860–1904)

Hugo Wolf
(1860–1903)

1899 Boer War. First International Peace Conference at the Hague.

654

Isaac Albéniz
(1860–1909)
Gustav Mahler
(1860–1911)
Edward MacDowell
(1861–1908)
Charles Martin Loef-
fler (1861–1935)
Claude Debussy
(1862–1918)
Frederick Delius
(1862–1934)
Pietro Mascagni
(1863–1945)
Richard Strauss
(1864–1949)
Alexander Grechaninov
(1864–1956)
Paul Dukas
(1865–1935)
Alexander Glazunov
(1865–1936)
Jean Sibelius
(1865–1957)
Ferruccio Busoni
(1866–1924)
Erik Satie
(1866–1925)

Enrique Granados
(1867–1916)

Albert Roussel
(1869–1937)

1900   Boxer Insurrection in China. Count
Zeppelin tests dirigible balloon. Philadelphia
Symphony founded.

1901   Queen Victoria dies, Edward VII succeeds. De Vries's mutation theory.

1903   Wrights' first successful airplane flight.
Ford organizes motor company.

1904–05   Russo-Japanese War. London
Symphony founded.

1905   Sigmund Freud founds psychoanalysis.
Norway separates from Sweden. First Russian Revolution.

1905   Einstein's theory of relativity first published.

1906   San Francisco earthquake and fire.

1907   Second Hague Conference. Triple
Entente. William James's *Pragmatism*.

1908   Model T Ford produced.

1909   Peary reaches North Pole.

1910   Discovery of protons and electrons.
Edward VII dies, George V succeeds.

James M. Barrie
(1860–1937)
Aristide Maillol
(1861–1945)

Gerhart Hauptmann
(1862–1946)
Maurice Maeterlinck
(1862–1949)
Gabriele D'Annunzio
(1863–1938)
Henri de Toulouse-
Lautrec
(1864–1901)

Rudyard Kipling
(1865–1936)
William Butler Yeats
(1865–1939)

Romain Rolland
(1866–1943)
Wassily Kandinsky
(1866–1944)
H. G. Wells
(1866–1946)
Arnold Bennett
(1867–1931)
John Galsworthy
(1867–1933)
Luigi Pirandello
(1867–1936)
Edmond Rostand
(1868–1918)
Maxim Gorky
(1868–1936)
Edward Arlington
Robinson
(1869–1935)
Henri Matisse
(1869–1954)
Frank Lloyd Wright
(1869–1959)
André Gide
(1870–1951)
John Marin
(1870–1953)
John M. Synge
(1871–1909)
Marcel Proust
(1871–1922)
Theodore Dreiser
(1871–1945)

Alexander Scriabin
(1871–1915)
Ralph Vaughan Williams (1872–1958)

Max Reger
(1873–1916)
Sergei Rachmaninov
(1873–1943)
Arnold Schoenberg
(1874–1951)
Charles Ives
(1874–1954)

Maurice Ravel
(1875–1937)
Manuel de Falla
(1876–1946)
John Alden Carpenter
(1876–1951)
Carl Ruggles
(1876–   )

Ottorino Respighi
(1879–1936)

Ernest Bloch
(1880–1959)
Ildebrando Pizzetti
(1880–1968)
Béla Bartók
(1881–1945)
Georges Enesco
(1881–1955)
Igor Stravinsky
(1882-1971)
Zoltán Kodály
(1882–1967)
Gian Francesco Malipiero (1882–   )

1911   Amundsen reaches South Pole.

1912   China becomes republic. *Titanic* sinks.

1912–13   Balkan Wars.

1914–18   World War I.

1915   *Lusitania* sunk.

1917   U.S. enters World War I. Russian Revolution. Prohibition Amendment.

1918   Kaiser abdicates.

1919   Treaty of Versailles. League of Nations formed.

1920   Nineteenth Amendment (women's suffrage).

1922   Discovery of insulin. Fascist revolution in Italy. John Dewey's *Human Nature and Conduct.*

1924   Lenin dies.

1927   Lindbergh's solo flight across Atlantic.

1928   *Graf Zeppelin* crosses Atlantic. First radio broadcast N.Y. Philharmonic Orchestra.

Georges Rouault
(1871–1958)
Sergei Diaghilev
(1872–1929)
Piet Mondrian
(1872–1946)
Willa Cather
(1873–1947)

Robert Frost
(1874–1963)
Hugo Von Hofmannsthal (1874–1929)
Gertrude Stein
(1874–1946)
W. Somerset
Maugham
(1874–1965)
Rainer Maria Rilke
(1875–1926)
Thomas Mann
(1875–1955)
Constantine Brancusi
(1876–1958)
Isadora Duncan
(1877–1927)
Marsden Hartley
(1877–1943)
John Masefield
(1878–1967)
Vachel Lindsay
(1879–1931)
Paul Klee
(1879–1940)
E. M. Forster
(1879–1969)
Raoul Dufy
(1879–1953)
Guillaume Apollinaire
(1880–1918)
Jacob Epstein
(1880–1959)
Fernand Léger
(1881–1955)
Pablo Picasso
(1881–   )
Georges Braque
(1882–1963)
James Joyce
(1882–1941)
Jean Giraudoux
(1882–1944)
Virginia Woolf
(1882–1945)
Franz Kafka
(1883–1924)

Edgard Varèse
(1883–1965)
Anton von Webern
(1883–1945)

Charles T. Griffes
(1884–1920)
Alban Berg
(1885–1935)
Wallingford Riegger
(1885–1961)

Heitor Villa-Lobos
(1887–1959)

Bohuslav Martinu
(1890–1959)
Jacques Ibert
(1890–1963)
Serge Prokofiev
(1891–1952)
Arthur Honegger
(1892–1955)
Darius Milhaud
(1892–   )
Douglas Moore
(1893–1969)

1930   Penicillin discovered.

1931   Japan invades Manchuria. Empire
State Building completed.

1933   Franklin D. Roosevelt inaugurated.
Hitler takes over German government.

1935   Italy invades Ethiopia.

1936   First sit-down strike. Sulfa drugs introduced in U.S.

1937   Japan invades China. Spanish Civil
War.

1938   Munich appeasement.

1939   World War II starts: Germany invades Poland, Britain and France declare
war on Germany, Russia invades Finland.
U.S. revises neutrality stand.

1940   Roosevelt elected to third term.

1941   U.S. attacked by Japan, declares war
on Japan, Germany, Italy.

1942   British stop Rommel at El Alamein.
U.S. forces land in North Africa; U.S. army
lands in Sicily. Bataan Death March. Cor-
regidor surrendered. Six million Jews die in
Nazi extermination camps. First nuclear
chain reaction.

1943   Germans defeated at Stalingrad and in
North Africa. Italy surrenders.

José Clemente Orozco
(1883–1949)
Maurice Utrillo
(1883–1955)
José Ortega y Gasset
(1883–1955)
Amadeo Modigliani
(1884–1920)
D. H. Lawrence
(1885–1930)
Sinclair Lewis
(1885–1951)
François Mauriac
(1885–   )
André Maurois
(1885–1967)
Diego Riviera
(1886–1957)
Juan Gris
(1887–1927)
William Zorach
(1887–   )
Georgia O'Keefe
(1887–   )
Hans Arp
(1887–1966)
Marc Chagall
(1887–   )
Marcel Duchamp
(1887–   )
Kurt Schwitters
(1887–1948)
Giorgio de Chirico
(1888–   )
T. S. Eliot
(1888–1965)
T. E. Lawrence
(1888–1935)
Thomas Hart Benton
(1889–   )
Karel Čapek
(1890–1938)

Max Ernst
(1891–   )
Grant Wood
(1892–1944)

John P. Marquand
(1893–1960)
Joan Miro
(1893–   )
Ernst Toller
(1893–1939)

Walter Piston
(1894–)
Karol Rathaus
(1895–1954)
Paul Hindemith
(1895–1963)
William Grant Still
(1895–)
Carl Orff (1895–)
Howard Hanson
(1896–)
Roger Sessions
(1896–)
Virgil Thomson
(1896–)
Henry Cowell
(1897–1965)
Quincy Porter
(1897–1966)
George Gershwin
(1898–1937)
Roy Harris (1898–)

Carlos Chávez
(1899–)
Randall Thompson
(1899–)
Francis Poulenc
(1899–1963)
Aaron Copland
(1900–)
Ernst Krenek
(1900–)
Kurt Weill
(1900–50)

Sir William Walton
(1902–)
Stefan Wolpe
(1902–)

Luigi Dallapiccola
(1904–)

1944   D–Day. Invasion of France.

1945   United Nations Conference at San
Francisco. Germany surrenders. Atom
bomb dropped on Hiroshima. Japan
surrenders.

1946   First meeting of U.N. General
Assembly.

1947   Truman Doctrine. Marshall Plan.
India wins independence. Communists take
power in Hungary and Romania.

1948   Gandhi assassinated. Communists take
over Czechoslovakia. Israel proclaimed a
nation. Soviet blockade of Berlin; airlift
begun. Organization of American States
(OAS) founded.

1949   Communists defeat Chiang Kai-shek
in China. USSR explodes atomic bomb.
North Atlantic Treaty Organization.

e. e. cummings
(1894–1962)
Aldous Huxley
(1894–1963)

F. Scott Fitzgerald
(1896–1940)
Robert Sherwood
(1896–1955)
John Dos Passos
(1896–)
William Faulkner
(1897–1962)
Louis Aragon
(1897–)
Sergei Eisenstein
(1898–1948)
Bertolt Brecht
(1898–1956)
Ernest Hemingway
(1898–1961)
Alexander Calder
(1898–)
Henry Moore
(1898–)
Hart Crane
(1899–1932)
Federico García Lorca
(1899–1936)

Thomas Wolfe
(1900–38)
Ignazio Silone
(1900–)

André Malraux
(1901–)
John Steinbeck
(1902–68)
Langston Hughes
(1902–67)
George Orwell
(1903–50)
Mark Rothko
(1903–70)
Salvador Dali
(1904–)
George Balanchine
(1904–)
Christopher Isherwood
(1904–)

Marc Blitzstein
(1905–64)

1950 North Koreans invade South Korea. U.S. Marines land at Inchon. U.S. plans hydrogen bomb.

Willem de Kooning
(1904–)
Arthur Koestler
(1905–)
Jean-Paul Sartre
(1905–)
David Smith
(1906–62)

Dmitri Shostakovich
(1906–)

1951 Schuman Plan pools coal and steel markets of six European nations.

Samuel Beckett
(1906–)
W. H. Auden
(1907–)

Elliott Carter
(1908–)
Olivier Messiaen
(1908–)

1952 George VI dies; succeeded by Elizabeth II. Eisenhower elected President.

Theodore Roethke
(1908–63)
Richard Wright
(1908–60)
Stephen Spender
(1909–)

Samuel Barber
(1910–)
William Schuman
(1910–)
Gian Carlo Menotti
(1911–)
Vladimir Ussachevsky
(1911–)
Arthur Berger
(1912–)
John Cage (1912–)
Hugo Weisgall
(1912–)
Benjamin Britten
(1913–)

1953 Stalin dies. Armistice in Korea.

1954 First atomic-powered submarine, *Nautilus,* launched. War in Indo-China.
1955 Warsaw Pact signed. Salk serum for infantile paralysis.

1956 Soviet leaders disavow Stalinism and "cult of personality." Egypt seizes Suez Canal. Uprising in Hungary.

Franz Kline
(1910–62)

Philip Guston
(1912–)
Eugene Ionesco
(1912–)
Jackson Pollock
(1912–56)
Albert Camus
(1913–60)
Ralph Ellison
(1914–)
Dylan Thomas
(1914–53)
Tennessee Williams
(1914–)
Arthur Miller
(1915–)
Robert Motherwell
(1915–)

David Diamond
(1915–)
George Perle
(1915–)
Milton Babbitt
(1916–)
Alberto Ginastera
(1916–)
Ulysses Kay
(1917–)
Leonard Bernstein
(1918–)
George Rochberg
(1918–)
Leon Kirchner
(1919–)

1957 First underground atomic explosion. USSR announces successful intercontinental missile, and launches Sputnik, first man-made satellite.

1958 Alaska becomes 49th state. Fifth Republic in France under De Gaulle.

1959 Castro victorious over Batista. Hawaii becomes 50th state.

Ingmar Bergman
(1918–)

J. D. Salinger
(1919–)
Federico Fellini
(1920–)

Lukas Foss
(1922–   )
Iannis Xenakis
(1922–   )
György Ligeti
(1923–   )
Peter Mennin
(1923–   )
Mel Powell
(1923–   )
Luigi Nono
(1924–   )
Luciano Berio
(1925–   )
Pierre Boulez
(1925–   )
Gunther Schuller
(1925–   )
Morton Feldman
(1926–   )
Ben Johnston
(1926–   )
Hans Werner Henze
(1926–   )
Salvatore Martirano
(1927–   )
Karlheinz Stockhausen
(1928–   )
George Crumb
(1929–   )

Krzysztof Penderecki
(1933–   )
Mario Davidovsky
(1934–   )
Peter Maxwell Davies
(1934–   )

1960   Kennedy elected President. Eichmann tried and executed in Israel. U–2 overflight incident.

1961   First manned space flights. Wall erected dividing East and West Berlin. Dag Hammarskjold killed.

1962   Cuban missile crisis. Algeria declared independent of France. Opening of Lincoln Center for the Performing Arts in New York.

1963   President Kennedy assassinated. Lyndon Johnson becomes 36th President.

1964   Tonkin Gulf resolution; escalation of Vietnam War. Khrushchev replaced by Kosygin as premier of USSR. Communist China successfully tests its first atomic bomb.

1965   First walk in space. White minority in Rhodesia proclaims itself independent of Britain. Alabama Civil Rights March.

1966   France withdraws from NATO alliance. Establishment of Medicare.

1967   Israeli-Arab "6-Day War." First successful heart transplant in South Africa.

1968   Richard M. Nixon elected President. Soviet occupation of Czechoslovakia. Martin Luther King and Robert F. Kennedy assassinated.

1969   Apollo 11: first manned landing on the moon. De Gaulle resigns as French president. Eisenhower dies.

Richard Wilbur
(1921–   )

James Baldwin
(1924–   )
Robert Rauschenberg
(1925–   )

Allen Ginsberg
(1926–   )

Claes Oldenburg
(1929–   )
John Barth
(1930–   )
Jean-Luc Godard
(1930–   )
Jasper Johns
(1930–   )
Harold Pinter
(1930–   )
Andy Warhol
(1931–   )
Yevgeny Yevtushenko
(1933–   )
LeRoi Jones
(1934–   )

APPENDIX V

The Harmonic Series

When a string or a column of air vibrates, it does so not only as a whole but also in segments—halves, thirds, fourths, fifths, sixths, sevenths, and so on. These segments produce the *overtones*, which are also known as *partials* or *harmonics*. What we hear as the single tone is really the combination of the fundamental tone and its overtones, just as what we see as white light is the combination of all the colors of the spectrum. Although we may not be conscious of the partials, they play a decisive part in our listening; for the presence or absence of overtones in the sound wave determines the timbre, the color of the tone. Following is the table of the Chord of Nature: the fundamental and its overtones or harmonics. Those marked with an asterisk are not in tune with our tempered scale.

Half the string gives the second member of the series, the octave above the fundamental. This interval is represented by the ratio 1:2; that is to say, the two tones of this interval are produced when one string is half as long as the other and is vibrating twice as fast. The one-third segment of the string produces the third member of the harmonic series, the fifth above the octave. This interval is represented by the ratio 2:3. We hear it when one string is two-thirds as long as the other and is vibrating one and a half times (3/2) as fast. The one-fourth segment of the string produces the fourth member of the series, the fourth above. This interval is represented by the ratio 3:4, for its two tones are produced when one string is three-fourths as long as the other and vibrates one and a third times (4/3) as fast. One fifth of the string produces the fifth member of the harmonic series, the major third, an interval represented by the ratio 4:5. One sixth of the string produces the sixth member of the series, the minor third, represented by the ratio 5:6; and so on. From the seventh to the eleventh partials we find approximate whole tones. Between the eleventh harmonic and its octave, 22, the semitone appears. After partial 22 we enter the realm of microtones (smaller than semitones)—third tones, quarter tones, sixth and eighth tones, and so on.

On the brass instruments, the player goes from one pitch to another not only by lengthening or shortening the column of air within the tube, which he does by means of valves, but also by splitting the column of air into its segments or partials, going from one harmonic to another by varying the pressure of his lips and breath. The bugle does not vary the length of the air column, for it has no valves. The familiar bugle calls consist simply of the different harmonics of the same fundamental.

INDEX

a cappella, 329, 337
a tempo, 25
A-B form, 52, 357-358, 380
A-B-A form, 50-52, 322, 367, 610
   in symphony, 138, 230-231
Absence (Berlioz), 89-90
absolute music, 137-168, 243
   compared to program music, 101
   twentieth-century use, 485
abstract expressionism, 602
Academic Festival Overture (Brahms), 153
accelerando (ah-cheh-leh-rón-doh), 25
accent, 20-23
accidentals, 55
accompagnato (ah-com-pah-nyáh-toh),
   262
active chords, 17-18
adagio (ah-dáh-joh), 24, 25
Adagio for Strings (Barber), 573
Addison, Joseph, 411
Adieu m'amour et ma maistresse
   (Binchois), 326
affections, doctrine of, 355-356
Agee, James, 573
agitato (ah-jee-táh-toh), 66
Agnus Dei, musical setting of, 322
Agoult, Countess Marie d', 115
agréments, 430
Agrippina (Handel), 409-410
Aïda (Verdi), 132, 174, 175, 179-182
   Triumphal March, 4, 15, 23
air (lyric movement), 390-391
Air for the G String (Bach), 390
Aix-la-Chapelle, Peace of, 418
Albéniz (Oll-báy-nith), Isaac, 472
album leaf, 70
Alcott family, 556
aleatory, 606
Alembert, Jean le Rond d', 237, 434
Alexander VI, Pope, 329
Alfano, Franco, 208
alla breve (ah-la bréh-veh), 57
allegretto (ah-leh-gréh-toh), 24, 25
allegro (ah-léh-groh), 24, 25
allegro assai (ah-sígh), 269, 392
Allegro barbaro (bár-bar-oh) (Bartók),
   473, 508
allegro con brio, 154, 279
allegro giusto (joó-stoh), 123
allegro moderato, 161, 163
allegro non troppo, 112, 156, 160
Allegro vivace (vee-váh-cheh), 139

allemande (dance), 380
Amati family, 31
America (Carey), 12, 13, 22, 218, 224
American music, 547-595
   colonial, 547-548
   jazz, 577-595
   nationalism, 549
   nineteenth-century 548-550
   postromantic 550-551
   twentieth-century 551-595
American Revolution, 62, 237
American Society of Composers,
   Authors, and Publishers (ASCAP),
   506
ancient music, 311-314
andante (ahn-dáhn-tay), 24-25
andante con moto, 141, 304
andantino (ahn-dahn-tée-noh), 24, 25
andantino grazioso, 168
Anhalt-Cöthen, Prince of, 384
Anne, Queen, 410
Annie Laurie, 22
answer, fugue, 388
Antheil (Ann-tile), George, 474
antiphonal style, 337
antique cymbals, 464
Antonioni, Michelangelo, 605
Apaches (society), 467
Apollinaire, Guillaume, 600
appassionato (ah-posh-oh-náh-toh), 300
aria, 170, 254, 402
aria da capo, 395-396
arioso, 402
Arlésienne, L' (Bizet), 102, 195
Armide, Overture (Lully), 368-369
Armstrong, Louis, 582-585, 589, 592, 593
   West End Blues, 584-585
Arp, Hans, 599
arpeggio (ar-péh-djoh), 41, 229-230
ars antiqua, 323
ars nova, 323
Art and Revolution (Wagner), 185
art song, 8-9, 69, 344-345
Artusi, Giovanni Maria, 355
Ashbery, John, 605
atonality, 488-489, 552
Auden, W. H., 495, 576
Aufschwung (Schumann), 82-84
augmentation, 226
   in counterpoint, 310
augmented fourth, 535
Augustan Age, 238

663

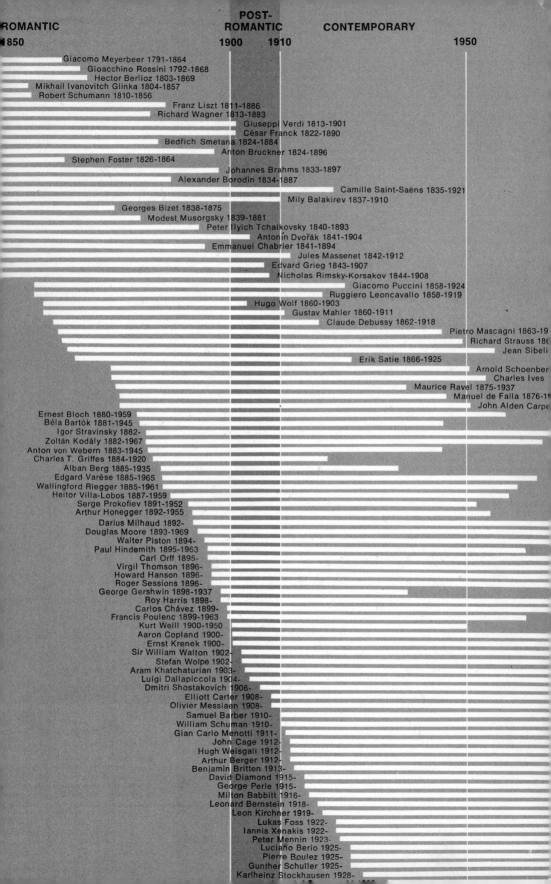

ROMANTIC | POST-ROMANTIC | CONTEMPORARY

850 | 1900 1910 | 1950

Giacomo Meyerbeer 1791-1864
Gioacchino Rossini 1792-1868
Hector Berlioz 1803-1869
Mikhail Ivanovitch Glinka 1804-1857
Robert Schumann 1810-1856
Franz Liszt 1811-1886
Richard Wagner 1813-1883
Giuseppi Verdi 1813-1901
César Franck 1822-1890
Bedřich Smetana 1824-1884
Anton Bruckner 1824-1896
Stephen Foster 1826-1864
Johannes Brahms 1833-1897
Alexander Borodin 1834-1887
Camille Saint-Saëns 1835-1921
Mily Balakirev 1837-1910
Georges Bizet 1838-1875
Modest Musorgsky 1839-1881
Peter Ilyich Tchaikovsky 1840-1893
Antonín Dvořák 1841-1904
Emmanuel Chabrier 1841-1894
Jules Massenet 1842-1912
Edvard Grieg 1843-1907
Nicholas Rimsky-Korsakov 1844-1908
Giacomo Puccini 1858-1924
Ruggiero Leoncavallo 1858-1919
Hugo Wolf 1860-1903
Gustav Mahler 1860-1911
Claude Debussy 1862-1918
Pietro Mascagni 1863-19
Richard Strauss 186
Jean Sibeli
Erik Satie 1866-1925
Arnold Schoenber
Charles Ives
Maurice Ravel 1875-1937
Manuel de Falla 1876-1
John Alden Carpe
Ernest Bloch 1880-1959
Béla Bartók 1881-1945
Igor Stravinsky 1882-
Zoltán Kodály 1882-1967
Anton von Webern 1883-1945
Charles T. Griffes 1884-1920
Alban Berg 1885-1935
Edgard Varèse 1885-1965
Wallingford Riegger 1885-1961
Heitor Villa-Lobos 1887-1959
Serge Prokofiev 1891-1952
Arthur Honegger 1892-1955
Darius Milhaud 1892-
Douglas Moore 1893-1969
Walter Piston 1894-
Paul Hindemith 1895-1963
Carl Orff 1895-
Virgil Thomson 1896-
Howard Hanson 1896-
Roger Sessions 1896-
George Gershwin 1898-1937
Roy Harris 1898-
Carlos Chávez 1899-
Francis Poulenc 1899-1963
Kurt Weill 1900-1950
Aaron Copland 1900-
Ernst Krenek 1900-
Sir William Walton 1902-
Stefan Wolpe 1902-
Aram Khatchaturian 1903-
Luigi Dallapiccola 1904-
Dmitri Shostakovich 1906-
Elliott Carter 1908-
Olivier Messiaen 1908-
Samuel Barber 1910-
William Schuman 1910-
Gian Carlo Menotti 1911-
John Cage 1912-
Hugh Weisgall 1912-
Arthur Berger 1912-
Benjamin Britten 1913-
David Diamond 1915-
George Perle 1915-
Milton Babbitt 1916-
Leonard Bernstein 1918-
Leon Kirchner 1919-
Lukas Foss 1922-
Iannis Xenakis 1922-
Peter Mennin 1923-
Luciano Berio 1925-
Pierre Boulez 1925-
Gunther Schuller 1925-
Karlheinz Stockhausen 1928-